Foundations of Economics

Foundations of Economics

Structures of Inquiry and Economic Theory

edited by

MAURO BARANZINI

and

ROBERTO SCAZZIERI

Basil Blackwell

First published 1986

Basil Blackwell Ltd
108 Cowley Road, Oxford OX4 1JF, UK

Basil Blackwell Inc.
432 Park Avenue South, Suite 1505,
New York, NY10016, USA

British Library Cataloguing in Publication Data

Foundations of economics.
1. Economics
I. Baranzini, Mauro II. Scazzieri, Roberto
330.1 HB171

ISBN 0–631–14253–3

Library of Congress Cataloging in Publication Data

Main entry under title:

Foundations of economics.
Bibliography: p.
Includes index.
1. Economics—Addresses, essays, lectures.
I. Baranzini, Mauro. II. Scazzieri, Roberto.
HB171.F62 1985 330 85–11102
ISBN 0–631–14253–3

Typeset by Photo·Graphics, Honiton, Devon

Printed in Great Britain by TJ Press, Padstow, Cornwall

Contents

List of Contributors

Maurice Allais Professor of Economics, Ecole Nationale Supérieure des Mines de Paris, Director of the Centre d'Analyse Economique (Centre National de la Recherche Scientifique, Ecole Nationale Supérieure des Mines de Paris et Université de Paris–X)

Michael O. L. Bacharach University lecturer in economics and fellow of Christ Church College, University of Oxford

Mauro Baranzini Professor of Economics, Faculty of Law, Catholic University of Milan; formerly lecturer and tutor in economics, The Queen's College, University of Oxford

Krishna Bharadwaj Professor of Economics, Centre for Economic Studies and Planning, Jawaharlal Nehru University, New Dehli; currently visiting professor, Stanford University, California; formerly fellow of Clare College, University of Cambridge

Christopher Bliss Reader in international economics and professorial fellow of Nuffield College, University of Oxford

Nicholas Georgescu-Roegen Professor of Economics, Vanderbilt University, Nashville, Tennessee

Dieter Helm University lecturer in economics, and fellow of Lady Margaret Hall, University of Oxford

Klaus H. Hennings Professor of Economics, University of Hanover; formerly lecturer in economics, University of Reading, and tutor and lecturer in economics, St Edmund's Hall, University of Oxford

John R. Hicks Fellow of All Souls' College, University of Oxford; formerly Drummond Professor of Economics, University of Oxford

Michael A. Landesmann Fellow of Girton College, University of Cambridge, and research officer, Department of Applied Economics, University of Cambridge

Luigi L. Pasinetti Professor of Economic Analysis, and Chairman of the Department of Economics, Catholic University of Milan; formerly reader in economics, University of Cambridge and fellow of King's College, Cambridge

Alberto Quadrio-Curzio Professor of Economics, Faculty of Political Sciences, and Director of the Centre for Research in Economic Analysis, Catholic University of Milan; formerly Chairman of the Faculty of Political Sciences, University of Bologna

Roberto Scazzieri Professor of Economics, Faculty of Political Sciences, University of Bologna

Bernard Schmitt Professor of Economics, University of Dijon (France) and University of Fribourg (Switzerland), Director of the Centre d'Etudes Monétaires et Financières of Dijon (Centre National de la Recherche Scientifique)

Preface

This volume is about the conceptual foundations of theory building in economics. This topic took shape after several years of work in economic theory. In particular, Mauro Baranzini has organized, over a number of years, the economic theory seminar at The Queen's College, University of Oxford, in which special attention was given to the assessment of comparative theories. He has also edited a selection of the papers presented at that seminar (*Advances in Economic Theory*, Basil Blackwell, 1982). On his side, Roberto Scazzieri has been involved, since 1977, in a research project on comparative theories in the history of economic thought, the results of which are in course of publication (*Protagonisti del pensiero economico*, edited jointly with A. Quadrio-Curzio, Il Mulino, 1977–83, five volumes). The apparent persistence of conflicting views in our subject convinced us of the need of a thorough examination of the structures of inquiry in economic theory, seen as the unfolding of a plurality of research lines. To this purpose we have gathered a number of closely connected contributions specifically written by economists working from different points of view on the foundations of our subject.

The conception and planning of the volume and the editing of the papers are the product of long hours of common work and discussion. Chapter 1 ('Knowledge in Economics: A Framework') is also the product of common thinking. However, each of us has been principally responsible for individual sections: sections I, II and III are due to Roberto Scazzieri, sections IV and V are due to Mauro Baranzini, whereas the work for sections VI and VII is common. It goes without saying that the final text is the outcome of thorough discussion and mutual criticism.

Mauro Baranzini and
Roberto Scazzieri

Acknowledgements

We want to express our gratitude to all those institutions and persons who contributed to the realization of this volume. Thanks are first due to the University of Bologna, the Catholic University of Milan (in particular the Centre for Research in Economic Analysis, CRANEC) and to the University of Oxford (in particular to The Queen's College) for providing research facilities and a stimulating intellectual environment. We would like to thank the Italian Consiglio Nazionale delle Ricerche (CNR) and the Swiss Science Foundation for providing research help. We are also indebted for editorial and bibliographical assistance to Maria Cristina Bacchi and Adrian Pollock. Finally, our gratitude to our wives for their encouragement and support knows no bounds.

M.B. & R.S.

1

Knowledge in Economics: A Framework

MAURO BARANZINI AND ROBERTO SCAZZIERI

I CONFLICTING VIEWS AND THE GROWTH OF KNOWLEDGE IN ECONOMICS

Economists often attribute the existence of disagreement within their own profession to error and incompetence, if not to fraud. Maffeo Pantaleoni, the friend of Walras and Pareto, once wrote that, in economics, there are two 'schools' continually at war with each other: one whose followers know economics, and another whose followers do not (Pantaleoni, 1897, p. 502). Such extreme positions reflect a misconception about the role of unanimity in the growth of knowledge, and should not deter economists from recognizing that their subject, like most other disciplines, is in fact open to a variety of points of view, many of which may lead to distinct lines of research.[1]

[1] A *line of research* is here defined as a sequence of theories sharing certain thematic concepts and hypotheses, such that each theory can be located as a step on a given trajectory (this condition requires that the theory under consideration depends on theories previously formulated along the same line, and/or that this theory is essential in the formulation of the subsequent theories in that line). Distinct lines of research may have a number of points in common, for a given theory can be influenced by theories belonging to line of research A, while being, at the same time, essential to the formulation of another theory, which belongs to line of research B. A different conception of 'line of research' has been used by Papineau, with the aim of stressing continuities in scientific change (Papineau, 1979, pp. 107–9). Our formulation of this concept aims at covering both the continuities and the cases in which, even at the most basic level of research, the scholars of a given discipline seem to accept different thematic concepts and hypotheses (this latter case seems to be excluded by Papineau). A line of research is distinct both from a Kuhnian paradigm and from a Lakatosian research programme. The reason for this is that many different paradigms could be located on the same line of research (a given research line could be compatible with different problem-solving strategies and with different standards and methods of research). On the other hand, any given line of research may connect different scientific research programmes with each other (a certain theory might depend for its formulation on a theory developed within an alternative programme, without implying that the two programmes are the same).

The work of philosophers and historians of science has indeed dispelled the conventional view of scientific progress as a sequence of periods, each dominated by a single ruling theory. As Sir Karl Popper has pointed out, this latter interpretation 'does not fit, for example, the evolution of the theory of matter; or of the biological sciences since, say, Darwin and Pasteur. In connection with the problem of matter, more especially, we have had at least three dominating theories competing since antiquity, the continuity theories, the atomic theories, and those theories which tried to combine the two' (Popper, 1970, pp. 54–5). Indeed, according to Popper, 'there was, ever since antiquity, constant and fruitful discussion between the competing dominant theories of matter' (Popper, 1970, p. 55). This point of view of Popper has been reinforced by Imre Lakatos's contention that in the evolution of sciences 'research programmes have achieved complete monopoly only rarely and then only for relatively short periods, in spite of the efforts of some Cartesians, Newtonians and Bohrians. *The history of science has been and should be a history of competing research programmes (or, if you wish, "paradigms"), but it has not been and must not become a succession of periods of normal science: the sooner competition starts, the better for progress*' (Lakatos, 1970, p. 155; author's italics).

It would be a pity for economics, if our subject could not provide at least as fertile ground as the analysis of matter or biology for that special kind of critical discussion that is associated with competition between alternative lines of research. Indeed, it would be remarkable to find a body of knowledge so immediately relevant to social and political issues, and yet based on a single research programme common to all the scholars of the field – something that is far from the case even in the natural sciences.

If the dynamics of scientific knowledge are reconstructed as the outcome of the competition and mutual influence between distinct lines of research, there is no reason why economics should be an exception. Indeed, if it is accepted that an essential ingredient in the progress of knowledge is provided by 'a critical discussion and a comparison of the various frameworks' (Popper, 1970, p. 56), it appears that the times in which economics provides least scope for such a discussion are also periods in which economic knowledge is most prone to fall under the influence of particular interests and ideologies.

The above considerations suggest that economists should not give up the habits of critical thinking and rational discussion about frameworks, if economics is to maintain certain features that characterize the pursuit of 'objective knowledge' in general.[2] In particular, a more positive attitude

---

[2] One possible way of defining 'objective knowledge' is suggested by Popper:

> There is knowledge in the subjective sense, which consists of dispositions and expectations. . . . But there is also knowledge in the objective sense, human

towards disagreement between economists is required, together with the explicit acknowledgement that the evolution of economics has often consisted of the almost simultaneous development of separate lines of research.

Such an approach to the past and present of our discipline might appear to be vitiated by epistemological relativism, and to be incompatible with the identification of what economic knowledge is. This would certainly be the case if it is believed that 'science grows by repeated overthrow of theories with the help of hard facts' (Lakatos, 1970, p. 97).[3] It would also be true if it is assumed that 'simplicity' is the standard by which alternative theories can be compared, so that scientific progress ought to be identified with the replacement of complex theories by increasingly simpler ones.[4] But the above criticism would not apply if the dynamics of (objective) knowledge are reconstructed as a network of lines of research, in which new problems might emerge from work conducted within different scientific traditions, and in which a new theory is 'progressive' when 'our discussion shows that it has really made a difference to the problems we wanted to solve; that is, if the newly emerging problems are different from the old ones' (Popper, 1981, p. 288).[5]

As this latter position is taken, the coexistence of distinct lines of research appears not as an anomaly, but as the normal pattern of 'scientific progress'. And the standard by which to measure the growth of objective knowledge would be given not by a simple criterion for theory choice (as the inductivist or the conventionalist one), but by an evaluation of how worthwhile it is to work within any particular line of research. It is thus possible to have disciplines, or periods in the evolution of any given discipline, in which 'The rivalry of two research programmes is . . . a protracted process during which it is rational to work in either (or, if one can, in both)' (Lakatos, 1978, p. 112n). Under such conditions, as Lakatos pointed out, 'It is very difficult to decide, especially since one must not demand progress at each single step,

---

> knowledge, which consists of linguistically formulated expectations submitted to critical discussion. . . . Subjective knowledge is not subject to criticism. . . . As opposed to this, objective knowledge can change and grow by the elimination . . . of the linguistically formulated conjecture: the 'carrier' of the knowledge can survive – he can, if he is a self-critical person, even eliminate his own conjecture. (Popper, 1981, p. 66)

[3] This position characterizes the inductivist reconstructions of the history of science.

[4] This position is characteristic of the conventionalist reconstructions of the history of science.

[5] The progressive character of a theory meeting this requisite is ascribed by Popper to the fact that, 'If the newly emerging problems are different then we can hope to learn a great many new things when we proceed to solve them in their turn' (Popper, 1981, p. 288).

when a research programme has degenerated hopelessly or when one of two rival programmes has achieved a decisive advantage over the other' (Lakatos, 1978, p. 113). Indeed, 'One must realise that one's opponent, even if lagging badly behind, may still stage a comeback' (Lakatos, 1978, p. 113). If this is so, the growth of 'objective knowledge' is a process in which the coexistence of 'rival' lines of research is the dominant feature, and where any given line may be superseded by the same 'rival' line over which it once exerted a temporary dominance, at some earlier period of intellectual history.

If the above point of view is adopted, the dynamics of (objective) economic knowledge may be reconstructed as a sequence of changes in the dominant focus of attention, where the shift from one focus to another can be reconstructed as a shift from an (at least temporarily) stagnating line of research to an (at least temporarily) progressing one.[6]

If this is so, it would be possible to trace (at least in principle) the growth of 'objective' economic knowledge, and to allow at the same time for the coexistence in our discipline of distinct lines of research. For the growth of objective knowledge is possible, even in the case of a discipline characterized by repeated defeats and comebacks of the same fundamental lines of research, as long as the switch-points between lines of research coincide with situations in which the line that comes to be more widely followed appears to be more promising (i.e. leading to discoveries at a faster rate) than the line that is temporarily 'shelved'. (Of course, this may not be the whole story, since 'external' history often has to supplement the 'internal' history of the discipline in order to explain both the changing speed of progress within any given line of research and the relative importance of each line within the discipline.)

It is the purpose of this volume to contribute to the appraisal of the view that economic knowledge is to be associated with the concurrent development of two distinct lines of research, one dealing primarily with allocation and choice (the 'exchange' research line), the other dealing primarily with social organization, production and structural change (the 'production' research line).

This chapter provides a general framework for the papers in parts I–IV. The plan of the remaining sections of this chapter is as follows. Section II discusses the recent literature, in which the dynamics of economic knowledge are reconstructed in terms of the mutual influence and 'competition'

---

[6] A line of research is stagnating or progressing, depending on how frequently connected discoveries are made by the scholars working within its boundaries. A progressing line of research would thus be characterized by the clustering of discoveries around certain central themes. A stagnating line of research, on the contrary, would be characterized by a low frequency of connected discoveries and by a great dispersion of themes.

between the 'exchange' and 'production' lines of research. Section III examines whether the distinction between the above research lines could be explained by a deeper gulf between different views about the 'scope and method' of economics. Section IV presents in detail the 'ideal' models behind the exchange and production research lines. Section V examines various methodological issues arising from the 'exchange' versus 'production' duality. Section VI tackles the issue of the possibility of 'general' and 'objective' laws in economics. Finally, section VII presents brief introductions to the papers of parts I–IV and discusses a number of topics of further research that this volume brings to light.

II THE 'EXCHANGE'–'PRODUCTION' DUALITY

At first sight, it might appear to be difficult to identify the distinctive features of the exchange and production research lines in economics, particularly because the empirical domains of these two lines tend to overlap, if such lines are compared at some late stage of development.

To identify alternative (and possibly 'competing') lines of research requires special consideration of the fact that what we are after are rival scientific traditions, whose 'hard cores' may be concerned with different sets of phenomena, but that tend to stretch themselves so as to cover the whole field of economic inquiry. Two rival lines of research, when considered at a relatively mature stage of development, would normally offer alternative explanations of a common set of phenomena, even if the respective empirical domains do not need to coincide. In addition, neither research line should be too shortlived, and the comeback of certain themes and hypotheses that had been previously 'shelved' should count as an important element for identifying such themes and hypotheses as essential to any given line of research.

In the case of economics, an initial concentration of attention on certain aspects of exchange or production, respectively, often led to the formulation of 'ideal' models of the economy in which what is essential in one model appears to be of secondary importance, or altogether irrelevant, in the other model. This may be clearly seen by comparing Ricardo's and Jevons's approaches to the theory of value.

According to Ricardo:

> Utility ... is not the measure of exchangeable value, although it is absolutely essential to it. If a commodity were in no way useful, – in other words, if it could in no way contribute to our gratification, – it would be destitute of exchangeable value, however scarce it might be, or whatever quantity of labour might be necessary to procure it. Possessing utility, commodities

> derive their exchangeable value from two sources: from their scarcity, and from the quantity of labour required to obtain them.
>
> There are some commodities, the value of which is determined by their scarcity alone. No labour can increase the quantity of such goods, and therefore their value cannot be lowered by an increasing supply. . . . Their value is wholly independent of the quantity of labour originally necessary to produce them, and varies with the varying wealth and inclinations of those who are desirous to possess them. These commodities, however, form a very small part of the mass of commodities daily exchanged in the market. By far the greatest part of those goods which are the objects of desire, are procured by labour; and they may be multiplied, not in one country alone, but in many, almost without any assignable limit, if we are disposed to bestow the labour necessary to obtain them.
>
> In speaking then of commodities, of their exchangeable value, and of the laws which regulate their relative prices, we mean always such commodities only as can be increased in quantity by the exertion of human industry, and on the production of which competition operates without restraint. (Ricardo, 1951, pp. 11–12; 1st edn 1817)

This passage shows that Ricardo's view of what is important in determining the value of commodities (their relative conditions of production) depends on the assumption that producibility rather than scarcity is the dominant feature of a modern economy. Utility and scarcity are excluded from Ricardo's ideal model of the economy, as well as from his theory of value, even if Ricardo is ready to admit the operation of scarcity as a value-determining factor outside his model economy. (See Ricardo, 1951, ch. XXX.)

Let us now turn to Jevons's view of exchangeable value:

> Pleasure and pain are undoubtedly the ultimate objects of the Calculus of Economics. To satisfy our wants to the utmost with the least effort – to procure the greatest amount of what is desirable at the expense of the least that is undesirable – in other words, *to maximise pleasure*, is the problem of Economics. . . .
>
> It is desirable to introduce at once, and to define, some terms which facilitate the expression of the Principles of Economics. By a *commodity* we shall understand any object, substance, action or service, which can afford pleasure or ward off pain. The name was originally abstract, and denoted the quality of anything by which it was capable of serving man. Having acquired, by a common process of confusion, a concrete signification, it will be well to retain the word entirely for that signification, and employ the term *utility* to denote the abstract quality whereby an object serves our purposes, and becomes entitled to rank as a commodity. (Jevons, 1879, pp. 40–1)

> The keystone of the whole Theory of Exchange, and of the principal problems of Economics, lies in this proposition – *The ratio of exchange of any two commodities will be the reciprocal of the ratio of the final degrees of utility of*

> *the quantities of commodity available for consumption after the exchange is completed.* (Jevons, 1879, p. 103; author's italics)

> *Value depends solely on the final degree of utility. How can we vary this degree of utility? – By having more or less of the commodity to consume. And how shall we get more or less of it? – By spending more or less labour in obtaining a supply.* (Jevons, 1879, pp. 178–9; author's italics)

A general theory of the ratio of exchange between any pair of commodities may be formulated, in Jevons's view, by simply focusing on utility and scarcity. The cost of production regulates the degree of scarcity of produced commodities, but relative costs of production are not sufficient to determine the relative scarcities of any two commodities.[7] Jevons's 'ideal' model is a pure allocation economy in which both scarcity and utility play a crucial role (this is a result of the fact that no meaningful problem of allocation can be formulated if resources are unlimited and no choice criterion is available). Production itself is considered by Jevons to be an aspect of 'painful exertion of mind or body . . . with a view to future good' (Jevons, 1879, p. 183). Labour activity becomes economically relevant as far as it can be considered a special case of allocative choice.[8]

The exchange and production lines of research are competing in the sense that, starting from two mutually exclusive 'ideal' models of an economic system (a pure allocation model and a pure production model, respectively), they have been gradually extended so as to cover empirical

---

[7] This is explained by Jevons, noting that:

> *labour once spent has no influence on the future value of any article*: it is gone and lost for ever. In commerce, by-gones are for ever by-gones; and we are always starting clear at each moment, judging the values of things with a view to future utility. Industry is essentially prospective, not retrospective; and seldom does the result of any undertaking exactly coincide with the first intentions of its promoters. (Jevons, 1879, p. 178; author's italics)

[8] This particular view of labour is shown by the following remarks:

> It is true that labour may be both agreeable at the time and conducive to future good; but it is only agreeable in a limited amount, and most men are compelled by their wants to exert themselves longer and more severely than they would otherwise do. When a labourer is inclined to stop, he clearly feels something that is irksome, and our theory will only involve the point where the exertion has become so painful as to nearly balance all other considerations. Whatever there is that is wholesome or agreeable about labour before it reaches this point may be taken as a net profit of good to the labourer; but it does not enter into the problem. *It is only when labour becomes effort that we take account of it.* (Jevons, 1879, pp. 183–4; our italics)

domains that are partially overlapping. Economists starting with a pure allocation model of an exchange economy have studied, on the premisses of that model, production and income distribution. On the other hand, economists starting with a pure production model have also dealt with domestic and international trade.

The dynamic of economic thought is characterized by repeated defeats and revivals of each of the two lines of research, whose resilience through time provides a basic framework against which to appraise the changes in economic theory.

The fact that the areas of direct confrontation between the two lines of research are, in a certain sense, external to the respective ideal models (for example, prices and income distribution, a typical field of economic controversy, are to be explained as special cases either of the pure production model or of the pure allocation model) might be an important reason why economists took a long time before realizing that the 'scope' of economics can be defined in two distinct ways, and that each definition can be the basis of an independent line of research. Indeed it may well be that a number of studies have been carried out within the exchange or the production research line, without realizing that each line derives from an 'ideal' model in which certain aspects of economic life are 'shelved' or completely overlooked.

The idea that the opposition between research lines in economics can be traced back to a difference between their respective 'ideal' models was sometimes expressed by linking the formation of each 'ideal' model to a particular phase of economic history. In particular, Luigi Pasinetti has maintained that we ought to distinguish between economic theories that deal primarily with trade, and economic theories that deal primarily with industry. He has also argued that trade and industry, by marking two different stages in the formation of the modern economic world, have shaped in a different way the theories that had their origin in either stage:

> The phase of trade is the first to break through. It can be perceived even as early as at the turn of the first millennium, but more clearly later on, after the Renaissance 'opening of the minds' towards the outside world. ... Much slower to manifest itself is the phase of industry, which requires already, and thus presupposes, trade. Industry is a process of augmenting wealth through a material increase in the quantity and number of products, to be reached by the practical application of the advances of science, division and specialization of labour, better organization, invention and utilization of new sources of energy and new materials. Unlike trade, industry requires changes in the organizational structure of society. Therefore, it comes about slowly; but progressively. (Pasinetti, 1965, p. 573)

Each phase brings to the fore a different set of conceptual issues, and calls economists' attention to one or other of the two lines of research described above:

> The concept of trade is, so to speak, a static concept. It is associated with a situation in which a plurality of economic systems (or of individuals) are endowed with particular resources or products and try to gain advantages by exchange. The interest that such a situation arouses in an economist concerns the problem of how to reach the best allocation of given resources, namely of how to make the best use of what one has already. . . . The problem involved is a problem of rationality, which may be expressed by a mathematical function to be maximised under certain constraints. The concept of, and the problems entailed by, industry are quite different. Industry is, so to speak, a dynamic concept. It means production, i.e. the engagement and the application of man's ingenuity to make and shape the products he wants. But since by doing and experiencing man learns, it is implied in the very nature of carrying on a production activity that new and better methods of production will be discovered. Of course, to find new methods takes time, and takes time in a persistent way. The economist is faced here no longer with a problem of rationality, but with a process of learning. (Pasinetti, 1965, pp. 574–5)

The impact of the first industrial revolution might explain, in Pasinetti's view, the interest shown by the English and Scottish classical economists in the conceptual issues entailing modern industry, thus marking a fundamental break from the previous intellectual tradition, that was dominated by mercantilism and by its concern with allocation problems (Pasinetti, 1981, p. 4).[9] The subsequent evolution of economic theory is reconstructed by Pasinetti as a gradual shift back to the consideration of a pure allocation model. This basic model was first refined and made rigorous, then extended from the consideration of exchange to the study of problems that had never before been examined within the framework of scarcity and rational choice:

> We may say that the typical marginalist scheme of general equilibrium, as it has been called, is a model of what has become known as a *pure exchange* economy. The model presupposes the existence of given natural resources in fixed quantities and of a given number of individuals, who are endowed with them. These individuals own the resources in a way which is accepted as given and they have well-defined utility preferences. The economic problem that is investigated is that of finding those prices (equilibrium prices) which bring about, through exchange, an optimum allocation of the given resources; this optimum allocation being defined as that situation at which the individuals maximise their utilities, relative to the original distribution of resources among them. This model is worked out, in its basic features, with no reference whatever to the process of production. . . . From this point on, a

[9] This is also shown by the fact that mercantilist writers, when dealing with production, were mainly concerned with 'preserving and strengthening the productive powers of the nation' (Suviranta, 1923, p. 155) by ensuring an adequate supply of productive factors. The problem of how to increase the annual product obtained from the existing resources was not in the foreground.

> vast theoretical movement started, the task of which has turned out to be that of *extending* the same elegant tools of marginal utility analysis to all branches of economic analysis. This tendency has become clearer and clearer especially in the twentieth century, and is in fact being continued nowadays by the great majority of economists. (Pasinetti, 1981, p. 9)

Sir John Hicks, in a number of recent papers (Hicks, 1975, 1976, 1983a, 1983b), has also analysed the characteristics of research lines in economic theory, maintaining that each line of research involves a selective concentration of attention (this seems, for Hicks, to be the distinctive characteristic of any given research line in economic theory, rather than the consideration of a particular 'ideal' model of the economic system):

> Our theories, regarded as tools of analysis, are blinkers in this sense. Or it may be politer to say that they are rays of light, which illuminate a part of the target, leaving the rest in darkness. As we use them, we avert our eyes from things which may be relevant, in order that we should see more clearly what we do see. It is entirely proper that we should do this, since otherwise we should see very little. But it is obvious that a theory which is to perform this function satisfactorily must be well chosen; otherwise it will illumine the wrong things. (Hicks, 1975, p. 320)

This particular point of view leads Hicks to reconstruct the dynamics of economic theory as a sequence of changes of attention, in which the switch from research line A to research line B at a certain time, as well as the switch back from B to A at a different time, may both be essential to the 'progress' of economic knowledge:

> since it is a changing world that we are studying, a theory which illumines the right things at one time may illumine the wrong things at another. This may happen because of changes in the world (the things neglected may have gained in importance relatively to the things considered) or because of changes in ourselves (the things in which we are interested may have changed). There is, there can be, no economic theory which will do for us everything we want all the time. (Hicks, 1975, p. 320)

This characteristic of economic knowledge gives a special feature to the history of economics:

> The history of economics ... throws much light upon its philosophy. But when we look at the history of economics, we find that it does not fit into the scientific pattern. In the sciences, when one system of thought – call it A – gives way to another (B) it is required: (1) that some facts have been discovered with which A could not cope, (2) that B should be able to cope with those new facts, *and* (3) that B should be able to cope with all those facts which were already coped with by A. ... Economics, also, is prone to revolutions; but they are mostly, I believe, of a different character. They do

> not fit into the pattern which has just been described. They are not clear *advances* in the scientific sense. (Hicks, 1975, pp. 319–20)

Consideration of the history of economic thought permits Hicks to identify two fundamental lines of research or intellectual traditions, each of which acquired a definite shape in the course of a particular 'revolution' in theory. Such research lines are the classical and the catallactic (or marginalist), respectively.

The classical line of research had its origin in the work of the French Physiocrats and of Adam Smith. Its basic theme is the identification of national wealth with the flow of production, and the assumption that this latter 'is so far homogeneous that it can be greater or less' (Hicks, 1976, p. 210). This particular point of view made it necessary 'to distinguish between market values (which might not be significant as a means of valuation) and "natural" or normal values which should be' (Hicks, 1976, p. 211). In addition, the classical economists found it necessary 'to find a "standard of value" so as to be able to correct for changes in the value of money' (Hicks, 1976, p. 211). This is shown by the fact that 'already in Smith, *political economy* is based upon a theory of value' whose primary purpose 'is not to explain prices, that is to say, to explain the working of markets', but rather 'to identify the values which are needed for the *weighing* of the social product, the reduction of the heterogeneous commodities which compose it to a common measure' (Hicks, 1976, p. 211).

Production of wealth, rather than exchange of existing goods and resources, is the distinctive feature of the classical line of research and keeps it separate from the catallactic (or marginalist) line. This latter line took a definite shape with the work of economists such as Jevons and Menger, who used the 'marginal' method in order to study the equilibrium conditions of exchange. The catallactic or marginalist revolution is thus described by Hicks:

> The economists who led [such a revolution] are commonly called 'marginalists'; but that is a bad term, for it misses the essence of what was involved. The 'margin' is no more than an expression of the mathematical rule for a maximum (or minimum); any sort of economics is marginalist when it is concerned with maximising. ... The essential novelty in the work of these economists was that instead of basing their economics on production and distribution, they based it on exchange. I therefore propose to make use of a term which was sometimes used, at the time in question, to mean the theory of exchange; it was called catallactics. So I shall re-name the so-called marginalists as catallactists.
>
> There is, of course, no doubt that exchange is a basic feature of economic life, at least in a 'free', or what Marx would have called a 'capitalist' economy. By none of the classical economists would that have been denied. But while the classics looked at the economic system primarily from the production angle, the catallactists looked at it primarily from the side of

exchange. It was possible, they found, to construct a 'vision' of economic life out of the theory of exchange, as the classics had done out of the social product. It was quite a different vision. (Hicks, 1976, p. 212)

The classical and catallactic revolutions appear, in Hicks's account, much more than two isolated, albeit important, episodes in the history of economic theory. For Hicks thinks that catallactics and political economy have remained the two fundamental ways of looking at economic life throughout the subsequent evolution of theory. This is shown by the fact that, even after the catallactic revolution, 'there were occasions when it was necessary to think about the whole economy. . . . Partly as a result of the Keynesian revolution, but more (perhaps) because of statistical labours that were initially quite independent of it, the Social Product has now come right back into its old place. Modern economics . . . is centred upon the Social Product, the Wealth of Nations, as it was in the days of Smith and Ricardo, but as it was not in the time that came between' (Hicks, 1975, p. 324). At the same time, 'catallactics has grown up into a rival system of thought' (Hicks, 1975, p. 324). Catallactics and political economy are based on different concentrations of attention and 'they do not fit together' (Hicks, 1975, p. 325).[10]

Political economy and catallactics are therefore much more than two 'schools' of economic thought that were competing at some stage in the history of our discipline. They are, rather, two different lines of research (each one based on a selective concentration of attention), whose persistence may be traced throughout the history of economic theory, in spite of the recurring attempts to reconstruct this latter in terms of progress within either research line to the exclusion of the other.[11]

Hicks's and Pasinetti's viewpoints complement each other, in the sense that Pasinetti stresses the influence of external events on the internal dynamics of economic theory (see his associations between the phase of trade and mercantilism, the phase of industry and classical political

[10] In Hicks's view, this is shown, among other things, by the different position of the concept of income in the two intellectual traditions. Classical political economy considers wealth in a 'flow' sense, as the power of producing a certain annual income. On the other hand, catallactics thinks of wealth as capital wealth, thus making the concept of income unnecessary (see Hicks, 1974, pp. 171–81; 1975, p. 325).

[11] Schumpeter's *History of Economic Analysis* (1954), is '[a] superb example of the way in which commitment to a catallactic outlook can blind one to the importance of the alternative' (Hicks, 1976, p. 214). On the other hand, Marx's *Theories of Surplus Value* is a characteristic attempt to reconstruct the progress of economic knowledge by identifying this latter with the research line of production (Marx, 1969; 1st edn 1905–10).

economy); whereas Hicks stresses how changes in economists' concentration of attention might also be independent of changes in the basic characteristics of economic life (see his explanation of the 'triumph of catallactics' which runs in terms of the intellectual superiority of the exchange over the production research line at the time when the overtaking took place) (Hicks, 1976, pp. 214–15). More recently, Alberto Quadrio-Curzio and Roberto Scazzieri (1982a, 1982b, 1984) have attempted a reconstruction of the history of economic theory in which the relative strength or weakness of the exchange and production research lines depends on a special interplay of 'internal' and 'external' history. Changes in the organization of economic life are considered to be influential, particularly when they determine a change in the relative importance of two distinct aspects of productive activity: (1) production of commodities by means of commodities; (2) the transformation of primary resources into final consumption goods. In this interpretation, economists tend to be more interested in (1) or in (2), depending whether their description of the productive system is framed in terms of inter-industry relationships or in terms of vertically integrated sectors, respectively. The structural dynamics of the economic system may thus influence the evolution of economic thought, but cannot determine uniquely its course. In particular, phases in which the 'transformation' aspect of production is more clearly in view might focus the economists' attention on to the exchange research line, on the condition that the productive system is described as a set of vertically integrated sectors. On the other hand, phases in which the 'production of commodities by means of commodities' is prominent might focus economists' attention on to the production research line, provided the productive system is described as a network of inter-industry relationships. According to Quadrio-Curzio and Scazzieri, external history is an important influence on the evolution of the exchange and production research lines, and on the relationships between these two lines of research. For external history brings to the fore certain aspects of economic life and favours a particular concentration of attention. On the other hand, internal history is often a decisive factor in determining the actual choice between competing lines of research. (See, in particular, Quadrio-Curzio and Scazzieri, 1982a, pp. 24–8 and 37–8; 1982b, pp. 24–8 and 46–8; 1984, pp. 71–3. See also chapter 13 below.)

The endurance of the 'exchange' and 'production' research lines makes it worth while to examine more closely the reasons for this special kind of 'disagreement' among economists and the characteristics of economic knowledge in either line of research. The analysis of the next section suggests that the endurance of different 'truths' in the economic discourse depends on the variety of purposes for which economic knowledge might be sought. It also shows that the distinction between the 'exchange' and 'production' research lines can be traced back to the classical philosophical distinction between practical knowledge and theoretical knowledge.[12]

III ECONOMIC KNOWLEDGE AND ECONOMIC THEORY

Meaning Variance in Economics

Recent work in philosophy of science has led a number of authors to interpret scientific change in terms of the 'meaning variance thesis', according to which 'with every change of theory there will be a change of meaning' (Papineau, 1979, p. 41). The dynamics of economic knowledge suggest a combination of meaning variance with the endurance of certain thematic concepts and hypotheses.

A useful introduction to the study of meaning variance in economics is given by Richard Whately's considerations in the appendix on 'ambiguous terms' of his *Logic*, originally published in 1826.[13] There Whately maintains that disagreements between economists are partly a result of the special character of economic knowledge, and that conflicting views might ultimately be reduced to different meanings of primitive terms:

> The foundation of Political Economy being a few general propositions deduced from observation or from consciousness, and generally admitted as soon as stated, it might have been expected that there would be as little difference of opinion among Political-Economists as among Mathematicians; that, being agreed in their premises, they could not differ in their conclusions, but through some error in reasoning. . . . And if they had possessed a vocabulary of general terms as precisely defined as the mathematical, this would probably have been the case. But as the terms of this science are drawn from common discourse, and seldom carefully defined by the writers who employ them, hardly one of them has any settled and invariable meaning, and their ambiguities are perpetually overlooked. (Whately, 1853, pp. 230–1; 1st edn 1826)

These considerations are followed by a review of ambiguities in the language of economic theory, in which Whately discusses a number of

---

[12] This distinction goes back to Plato's argument that we ought to treat differently practical science, 'that is presupposed for its own nature in human actions', from theoretical knowledge, which has no relation to actions (Plato, *Politicus*, 258 d–e). Aristotle distinguished between theoretical knowledge (σοφία) and practical knowledge, arguing that the former uses demonstrative reason, the latter dialectical reason (see, amongst others, *Metaphysics*, VI, 1, 1025 b 22, and *Ethica Nicomachea*, I, 2, 1094 b). Locke's application of this distinction when discussing the type of knowledge provided by the 'moral sciences' will be recalled in section III below.

[13] Richard Whately, philosopher and economist, succeeded Senior in 1829 as Drummond Professor of Political Economy in Oxford.

economic terms, reporting explanations 'furnished by the kindness of the Professor of Political Economy' (Whately, 1853, p. 230; 1st edn 1826).[14]

In Whately's account, economic knowledge is subject to two main sources of confusion, which he illustrates by considering the terms 'value' and 'wealth'. In the case of 'value', Whately writes:

> There is no subject as to which [the economists] are less agreed. The popular, and far the most convenient use of the word, is to signify the capacity of being given and received in exchange. So defined, it expresses a relation. The value of any one thing must consist in the several quantities of all other things which can be obtained in exchange for it. ... Adam Smith defines Value to mean either the *utility* of a particular object, or the power of *purchasing other* goods which the possession of that object conveys. The first he calls 'value in use', the second 'value in exchange'. Mr Ricardo appears to set out by admitting Adam Smith's definition of value in exchange. But in the greater part of his 'Principles of Political Economy', he uses the word as synonymous with *Cost* ... Mr McCulloch [*Principles of Political Economy*, part II, section 1] distinguishes between real and exchangeable, or relative value. And in his nomenclature, the exchangeable, or relative, value of a commodity, consists in its capacity of purchasing; its real value in the quantity of labour required for its production or appropriation. All these differences appear to arise from a confusion of cause and effect. Having decided that commodities are valuable in proportion to the labour they have respectively cost, it was natural to call that labour their value. (Whately, 1853, p. 231; 1st edn 1826)

In the above case, confusion is created by the fact that the meaning of a term denoting x is made to coincide with the cause of x (this we may call the *displaced-meaning fallacy*).

In other cases, confusion might be created by the fact that some structural characteristics of economic theory derive from the ordinary-language meaning of certain keywords. This possibility was noted by Whately in his discussion of the term 'wealth':

> It were well if the ambiguities of this word had done no more than puzzle philosophers. One of them gave birth to the mercantile system. In common language, to grow rich is to get *money*; to diminish in fortune is to lose money: a rich man is said to have a great deal of *money*; a poor man, very little: and the terms Wealth and Money are in short employed as synonymous. In consequence of these popular notions ... all the different nations of Europe have studied every means of accumulating gold and silver in their respective countries. This they have attempted by prohibiting the exportation of money, and by giving bounties on the exportation, and imposing restrictions on the importation, of other commodities, in the hope of producing

[14] The Professor of Political Economy in Oxford was then Nassau William Senior.

> what has been called a 'favourable balance of trade'; that is, a trade in which, the imports being always of less value than the exports, the difference is paid in money. (Whately, 1853, p. 232; 1st edn 1826)

In this latter case, the ordinary-language meaning of a term that is also used in theory suggests a wrong causal relationship (this we may call the *misplaced-causality fallacy*). In both cases, a fallacy arises from the special relationship between (ordinary) economic language and economic theory. The former gives an informal description of economic activities and is used to express popular beliefs about such activities. The latter uses the same vocabulary in order to express causal relationships.

Not only is economic theory often about ordinary language and beliefs, but it also often reflects ordinary language and these ordinary beliefs. This characteristic of economic theorizing has two important consequences. On the one hand, economists are often confronted with ordinary practical problems formulated independently of theoretical considerations. On the other hand, the formulation of economic theories generally requires considerable polishing of ordinary economic concepts. Economic theory has thus a special position in the field of knowledge about society. For only political theory has a similar concern with social activities that, requiring almost daily adaptation, lead men to formulate a set of specialized beliefs and problem-solving strategies.

The special relationship between the practical and the theoretical branches of economic knowledge brings to the fore the problem of the meaning of economic concepts. In the present volume, Sir John Hicks deals with this important issue, arguing that

> many of the terms that are used by economists are derived from business practice; businessmen knew what they meant, or thought that they knew what they meant, by capital and income, long before economists began to think in those terms. But when we seek to lay down general principles, even very weak principles, which use terms like that, we have to face the question, often a very difficult question, of whether the way in which those terms are used in business is appropriate for us. It is my own belief that a good part of what is called economic theory is best regarded as a criticism of those concepts, finding out what adjustments have to be made to the business concepts in order that we may use them as instruments of more general thought. (Hicks, p. 99 below)

Whately called attention to certain instances of ambiguity and vagueness in the use of economic terms by the classical economists, due to an imperfect distinction between the meaning of a term in ordinary language and its meaning in economic theory. He also stressed that wrong theorizing may sometimes derive from the causal associations generated by the meaning of economic terms in ordinary language (see above). More recently, L. M. Fraser considered various cases of ambiguity *both* in ordinary language and in economic theory, pointing out that:

> we need not be surprised at the terminological difficulties with which the advance of economic theory has been so continually beset, or at the frequency with which economists have not merely misunderstood each other's arguments but have even failed to grasp the implications of their own contentions. (Fraser, 1937, p. 20)[15]

It is our view that the formation and survival of competing economic theories derives in part from the existence of a common vocabulary in economics as a discipline and in ordinary economic language. In ordinary language, more than one meaning is often associated with the same word. This ambiguity is transferred into the discipline of economics, both through the persistence of different meanings for the same word in a given theory (see Smith's use of 'value' in order to mean either utility or purchasing power), *and* through the formation of theories using a common vocabulary, but assigning different meanings to their respective primitive terms. The language of each 'competing' theory is partly derived from ordinary language through a process of semantic specialization. As a result, term x, having meanings (m_1, m_2, . . ., m_n) in ordinary language, might end up having meaning m_1 in theory A and meaning m_2 in theory B. (In Ricardo 'value' means essentially production cost, whereas in Jevons 'value' means essentially utility.)

The competing theories appear to be dealing with the same 'object' because of the common vocabulary. But in fact each theory picks up from common discourse a particular use of this vocabulary and deals (at least initially) with a particular set of issues (the issues that are suggested to economic theory by the use it makes of its own vocabulary). In this case, alternative economic theories derive from abstract models of economic reality that address different questions, rather than competing with each other, for each model is associated with a specialized use of ordinary economic language. This might suggest to somebody that alternative economic theories are incommensurable and that there are no grounds for a comparison of theories based on some rational or 'objective' criterion.

Our view is different, since we believe that, in the case of economics, each theory is characterized by a specialized use of ordinary language that derives, in its turn, from one of the many specialized uses of economic

---

[15] The ambiguity of important economic terms, such as 'value' and 'capital', is described by Fraser as follows: 'We talk in everyday life of getting value for our money, of selling goods below (or above) their true value, of particular things being valuable in particular ways, of valuing one thing more (or less) than another' (Fraser, 1937, p. 56). '[The word "capital"] may stand for productive equipment, for the use of purchasing power and the control over resources, and for claims to, or expectations of, that kind of income which goes by the name of "interest"' (Fraser, 1937, pp. 237–8). Fraser's book contains detailed analyses of many more ambiguities in ordinary economic language, and of the way in which such ambiguities are transferred into economic theory.

vocabulary in common discourse. This implies that alternative theories, though seemingly mutually exclusive when their respective 'ideal models' are compared, are in fact related to each other through the relationships between the different uses of the same word in ordinary language.

Any given word may have different meanings, and the switch from one meaning to another derives in general from a change in the purpose for which that word is used. (The same person may attach different meanings to the same word and yet be considered to be perfectly rational, as long as the speech contexts are clearly differentiated.) In a similar way, the survival of mutually exclusive economic theories (as well as the switch from one theory to another) should be seen as a result of the complex nature of economic theorizing, in which the economist derives his (her) primitive terms by assigning a specialized meaning to unspecialized terms of ordinary language. This operation is done by considering the remaining meanings of the same word as 'pre-scientific' or irrelevant for the purposes of the theory under consideration. But a meaning that is excluded from one theory can be accepted in a different theory (this would normally be a theory constructed for different purposes).

Alternative economic theories derive their identity from this 'one-sided' use of ordinary economic language. This suggests that the relationship of one theory to another could be explained in the same way as we explain the relationship of one meaning to another in ordinary language, that is, as a result of the plurality of purposes for which economic knowledge is needed. This also suggests that, in the case of two competing theories, the substitution of one theory for another is associated with a change in the way in which economists think that economic knowledge ought to be used.

The 'scope and method' of economics: a historical reconstruction

The foremost instance of meaning variance in economic theory is given by the definition of 'economics' itself. The *Oxford English Dictionary* (1933) gives, as the early meaning of 'economics', that of 'science or art of managing a household'. A similar meaning is associated with the early use of the German equivalent *'Wirtschaft'* (cf. Brunner, 1968, ch. VI) and of the Italian equivalents *'Economica'* and *'Economia'* (cf. Vocabolario degli Accademici della Crusca, 1741). In all these three cases, economics is initially considered as a 'practical science', that is, as a type of knowledge whose purpose is the 'Right applying our own Powers and Actions for the Attainment of Things good and useful' (Locke, 1979, p. 720; 1st edn. 1690).[16]

[16] Ethics, law, politics and economics were traditionally considered under one head as practical sciences whose end 'is not bare Speculation and the Knowledge of Truth; but Right, and a Conduct suitable to it' (Locke, 1979, p. 720; 1st edn 1690).

The French use of the term *'économie'* has a different character since the end of the seventeenth century: the 1694 edition of the French Academy Dictionary gives, in addition to the traditional meanings of the word, also the following one: '[economics] is, in a metaphorical sense, the order on which a political body is principally founded'. (See also Richelet, 1785, vol. I, s.v. 'Economie'.) This latter conception of economics is associated with an alternative type of economic knowledge, whose purpose is speculative truth, rather than the discovery of 'suitable' rules of action.[17] The French Physiocrats were among the first economic writers who conceived economic knowledge as a type of purely speculative activity, independent of the practical purposes to which it might serve.

The idea that economic prescriptions also ought to be based on a speculative science of society was clearly expressed by Pierre-Samuel Dupont de Nemours, the pupil of Quesnay:

> Men . . . did not come to live together in a civil society as a result of chance. It is not without reason that they have extended the natural chain of reciprocal duties, that they have submitted themselves to a sovereign authority. They had, they have a goal that is *essentially* marked by their nature, so that they behave in a certain determined way. Now, their own physical constitution, that of the other beings around them, do not allow the use of arbitrary means to achieve that goal, since nothing arbitrary is possible in physical acts aiming at a determined end. . . . There is thus a *necessary* route that takes us nearest to the goal of civil society and of political bodies. There is thus a natural *order*, essential and general, that comprises the essential laws of all civil societies; *an order* from which any society cannot detach itself without becoming less of a society . . . *an order* that cannot be completely abandoned without bringing about the disintegration of society. (Dupont de Nemours, 1846, pp. 337–8; 1st edn 1768)

The subsequent evolution of economics shows the survival of both conceptions of economic knowledge.

Economics as a practical science concerned with the management of private resources generated political economy as a science dealing with the management of national resources.[18] Economics as a branch of 'natural philosophy' led to political economy as the science studying 'how wealth is

---

[17] Economic knowledge in this latter sense is no longer a 'practical science'. It is rather a branch of 'natural philosophy' whose end is to know 'the Nature of Things, as they are in themselves, their Relations, and their manner of Operation' (Locke, 1979, p. 720; 1st edn 1690).

[18] The relationship between 'private' economics and political economy is clearly stated by Sir James Steuart:

> Economy, in general, is the art of providing for all the wants of a family, with prudence and frugality. *If any thing necessary or useful be found wanting, if*

produced, distributed and consumed' (Say, 1817, p. i; 1st edn 1803). Classical political economy, in spite of its many practical applications, was speculative rather than practical in character. Its central concern was to explain the working of a *given* system for the production and allocation of material resources. This system works through the investment of saving and the productive utilization of labour (in surplus-producing activities), and can be studied as a 'natural' mechanism independently of the allocative procedures that it presupposes. As a result, the focus of attention of classical economists shifted

> from the problem of allocating *given* resources among different industries to maximise the consumers' satisfaction to the problem of increasing the physical productivity of labour and the total volume of economic activity. The subjective level of analysis was pushed to the background by the broad assumption that quantities of consumers' satisfaction are roughly proportional to the quantity of physical product. (Myint, 1946, p. 123)

Production of commodities by the utilization of augmentable resources (labour and capital goods) moved to the foreground, and the problem of

---

> *any thing provided be lost or misapplied*, if any servant, any animal, be supernumerary or useless, if any one sick or infirm be neglected, we immediately perceive a want of economy. . . . *What economy is in a family, political economy is in a state.* . . . The *statesman* . . . is neither master to establish what economy he pleases, or, in the exercise of his sublime authority, to overturn at will the established laws of it, let him be the most despotic monarch upon earth. The great art therefore of political economy is, first to adapt the different operations of it to the spirit, manners, habits, and customs of, people; and afterwards to model these circumstances so, as to be able to introduce a set of new and more useful institutions. The principal object of this science is to secure a certain fund of subsistence for all the inhabitants, to obviate every circumstance which may render it precarious; to provide every thing necessary for supplying the wants of the society, and to employ the inhabitants (supposing them to be free-men) in such a manner as naturally to create reciprocal relations and dependencies between them, so as to make their several interests lead them to supply one another with their reciprocal wants. (Steuart, 1966, pp. 15–17; our italics; 1st edn 1767)

In Steuart's view, economics is a practical science (an 'art') concerned with the allocation of given resources. The allocation problems of private economics have the same nature as the allocation problems faced by a statesman, except for the fact that the statesman has a narrower range of options. The action of a statesman may either provide directly what is necessary to the population or it may bring about a system of 'reciprocal relations and dependencies' that make direct state intervention redundant. The 'practical' conception of political economy had a lasting influence, even after the publication of Smith's *Inquiry* (1776). (See, for example, the criticism of Smith in Bentham's *Manual of Political Economy*, written about 1793–5.)

how to manage an existing stock of given resources disappeared from mainstream economics for almost one century. During this period, economics established itself as the science dealing with the production of (a growing amount of) wealth, and many traditional economic concepts received a new definition compatible with this conceptual framework.[19]

Production of wealth was based on the assumption that men are related to each other 'so as to make their several interests lead them to supply one another with their reciprocal wants' (Steuart, 1966, p. 17; 1st edn 1767). Specialization of productive activities was taken for granted, and the circulation of the social product was associated with the existence of market transactions between individuals. However, as Quesnay pointed out at an early stage, these transactions ought not to be confused with ordinary market exchanges:

> It seems necessary to me to point out that the new science of economics does not confuse *Trade* with the profession of the Merchant, who buys in order to sell; by *Trade* it means the transaction between the original seller and the consumer; this type of transaction can be direct or indirect: in the former case, Trade or exchange is effected without any intermediary Agent, i.e. without the service of any Merchant. (Quesnay, 1767, pp. 167–8)

> Trade consists of Production and Consumption, whereas Traffic consists only of purchase, transport and sale. (Quesnay, 1767, pp. 176–7)

Classical political economy was developed on the assumption that the relationships between producers are in fact *market* transactions. However, the consistency between production and consumption decisions was generally taken for granted, so that the problems of allocation were seldom explicitly considered.

In the following years, the classical conception of economics was criticized by various authors on the ground of its alleged 'materiality'. Against the classical view, a number of critics maintained that economics should study the production and circulation of wealth as it is affected by the organization of economic functions in any given society. An early formulation of this point of view can be found in Giandomenico Romagnosi, who

---

[19] The change affected first of all the concept of wealth, which was identified with the annual product of a country, rather than with its stock of material resources or with monetary wealth (Quesnay, 1758; Smith, 1776, Introduction and Plan of the Work). The scarcity of commodities was defined in terms of their producibility (rather than availability), so that any commodity appeared to be more or less 'scarce' depending on its 'difficulty of production'. Demand itself became an aspect of the production of wealth. For, in the classical view, '[demand] is increasing when the over-all capital accumulation increases, it is diminishing when capital accumulation declines. . . . Demand is thus ultimately regulated by the extent and pressure of socially productive labour' (Pietranera, 1963, pp. 120–1).

maintained that political economy ought to study 'the social order of riches' (Romagnosi, 1827, p. 24) and that it should not 'assume an abstract and unconstrained individual, driven by an unlimited quest of profit' (Romagnosi, 1827, p. 26). The purpose of economic studies should rather be 'to consider the economic functions in their driving motives and in their complex outcomes' (Romagnosi, 1827, p. 26). In particular, Romagnosi argued that:

> the logical and moral nature of economics is to establish the quality and the arrangement of [economic] functions. The study of *how* each function is performed belongs to technology. (Romagnosi, 1835, p. 23)

Other writers drew attention to the role of market relationships *per se*, and to the allocative procedures implicit in classical political economy. Clear signs of this attitude can already be seen in Destutt de Tracy's *Traité d'économie politique*, in which the economic society is defined as 'purely and only a continuous series of exchanges' (Destutt de Tracy, 1823, p. 68). To this definition, Destutt de Tracy adds that 'this is the greatest praise one could express of society, for exchange is an admirable transaction, in which the two contractors are both always obtaining an advantage: as a result, society is an uninterrupted series of advantages that are continuously renovated for all its members' (Destutt de Tracy, 1823, p. 68).

This new attitude led a number of authors to question the classical definition of economics and to substitute for it the conception of economics as the 'science of exchanges'.[20] Whately, in particular, maintained that:

> The name ... of *Political Economy* is most unfortunately chosen. ... The name I should have preferred as the most descriptive, and on the whole least objectionable, is that of *Catallactics*, or the 'Science of Exchanges'. Man might be defined, 'An animal that makes *Exchanges*' ... And it is in this point of view alone that Man is contemplated by Political Economy. (Whately, 1847, pp. 3–6)

Renewed interest in the mechanism of exchange (the allocation system that was presupposed by the classical economists) led a number of authors to study the behavioural principles on which exchange is founded.

[20] Condillac is credited for an early formulation of this view. But his definition of 'commerce' is similar to Quesnay's (see above). In his view, 'commerce' is a concept derived from 'production' and 'consumption' rather than a primitive one: '[t]rade presupposes two things: surplus production on the one hand, consumption to be made on the other hand. *Surplus production* since I can only give in exchange something in excess of what I need; *Consumption to be made*, since I can only exchange it with somebody who needs it for his own consumption' (Condillac, 1776, p. 32).

Research of this type led certain economists to consider their subject as a science studying a special category of human actions. This approach was clearly formulated by Francesco Ferrara:

> the economic phenomenon is only one, in the individual man as in the whole human race . . . We must persuade ourselves that it is impossible to formulate sound and reliable theories of the social or national economy unless we start by recognizing them in a state that may be undeveloped but is complete in all its parts in the elements constituting an individual economy. In the field of the social economy, I have seen a great number of theories to rise, fall, and come back once again, under the same or a different shape; but the only theories that survived and prevailed were those that considered the attitudes and senses of the individual in order to explain the social evolution of mankind. (Ferrara, 1854, p. 38)

This approach led Ferrara to argue that 'value in its most complex form, as *exchange value*, has all its constituent elements . . . in the individual man, independently of any exchange relation with other men' (Ferrara, 1854, p. 49). As a result, the classical conception of economics was challenged, on the ground that it would be 'a capital error' to see the object of economics 'in material things rather than in actions' (Ferrara, 1859, p. 81). In particular, Ferrara maintained that economic science ought to study 'voluntary acts, and this is not all: they have to be acts by which Man is seeking means of improving his own existence' (Ferrara, 1859, p. 82). Hermann-Heinrich Gossen chose a similar approach by pointing out that economics should be conceived as a 'practical' science, whose purpose is 'to help man obtain the greatest sum of pleasure during his life' (Gossen, 1983, p. 39; 1st edn 1854).

The view that economics ought to set out rules of behaviour called Gossen's attention to the study of exchange as an allocation mechanism capable of augmenting the quantity of 'pleasure' that men can derive from a given amount of existing resources:

> An individual attempting to put to practical use the various specific conditions for fulfilling his life purpose to the fullest must realize immediately that they suggest contradictory requirements. On the one hand, the necessity to satisfy partially the greatest variety of pleasures requires the splintering of strength among all these different pleasures; on the other hand, the requirement to develop his skills to their highest level in order to reduce his work as much as possible requires that he limit his activity to producing the smallest possible variety of commodities, but in far greater quantities than he can use directly for his own satisfaction. Moreover, natural resources, whose use in conjunction with labor is essential for achieving the desired results, are distributed very unevenly over the surface of the earth. . . . The fact that, according to the laws of enjoyment, the value of a given thing passes through all gradations for different people has aided in discovering the way by which the contradictory requirements mentioned may be simultaneously satisfied:

> *Simple barter, in most instances, results in an extraordinary augmentation in value of the goods traded, even though they undergo no change at all in the process of the barter.* (Gossen, 1983, pp. 95–6; 1st edn 1854)

Both Ferrara and Gossen brought to the fore certain implications of catallactics. In so doing, they formulated a conception of economics that was effectively opposed to the classical view of this subject.

An early critic of the reduction of political economy to catallactics was John Stuart Mill, who defended the classical approach by maintaining that exchange is essential in some, but not all the possible arrangements of society:

> One eminent writer has proposed as a name for Political Economy, 'Catallactics', or the science of exchanges: by others it has been called the Science of Values. . . . This view of the nature of Political Economy is too confined. . . . It is nevertheless evident that of the two great departments of Political Economy, the production of wealth and its distribution, the consideration of Value has to do with the latter alone; and with that, only so far as competition, and not usage or custom, is the distributing agency. (Mill, 1965, p. 455; 1st edn 1848)

The subsequent evolution of economics is characterized by the survival, in economists' pronouncements and practice, of the two distinct conceptions considered so far.

The 'classical' conception continued to be held by a number of authors, though their definitions often stressed different aspects of the classical view. In this field, a broad distinction can be made between the authors who considered economics as the science of wealth, and the authors who focused on the organizational aspects presupposed by the social production and distribution of wealth. In the former category, we have authors such as Henry Sidgwick and John Neville Keynes. Keynes defined economic activity as 'human activity which directs itself towards the production and appropriation of such means of satisfying human needs as are capable of being made the subject of exchange' (J. N. Keynes, 1890, pp. 99–100). In the latter category, we might recall Michel Chevalier's definition of economics: 'political economy is the science of material interests. It is its duty to teach how such interests may arise, how they develop, how they get organized: I stress this latter word' (Chevalier, 1851, p. 22).

Another 'political' definition of economics was recently proposed by James Buchanan: 'Economics, the science of markets or of exchange institutions, commences with a well-defined structure or set of individual rights and offers explanatory, predictive propositions concerning the characteristics of outcomes along with conditional predictions about the effects of imposed structural changes on such outcomes' (Buchanan, 1975, p. 19).

A 'materialist' conception of economics may be found behind the practice of most contemporary economists, even if the classical attributes of the 'science of wealth' are no longer in the foreground. For the actual practice of most contemporary economists can probably be described as 'having to do with the more material side of human happiness' or as 'having to do with material welfare' (Cannan, 1923, p. 17). On the other hand, the alternative idea that economics ought to be defined as a discipline dealing not with particular objects, but with a particular category of human actions found increasing acceptance after the marginalist revolution, even if economics continued for some time to be considered as a science dealing with particular human *goals* (Edgeworth, Pantaleoni).[21]

The philosopher Croce, in his exchanges with Pareto in the *Giornale degli Economisti* (July 1900, August 1900, February 1901), was among the first to maintain that 'the economic fact is the practical activity *per se*, when it is spoiled of any particular meaning, be it a moral or an immoral one' (Croce, 1900, p. 25).

Philip Henry Wicksteed recognized that, by reducing economics to the study of individual 'planning' activities, economic science ought to be considered as a branch of the 'general science of administration of resources' (Wicksteed, 1933, p. 16):

> 'Economics' . . . may be taken to include the study of the general principles of administration of resources, whether of an individual, a household, a business, or a State. . . . It is the author's firm conviction that [the comprehension of the mechanism and spontaneous organisation of industrial and commercial life] can be best achieved by a thorough preliminary study of 'Economics' in their widest scope; that is to say, a study of the principles of administration of resources and selection between alternatives, conceived without any formal or conventional limitations. (Wicksteed, 1933, p. 17; 1st edn 1910)

Wicksteed's conception, in Lionel Robbins's words, threw 'the whole corpus of economic science into an entirely new light – a light in which Economics is seen to be a discussion not of the nature of certain *kinds* of behaviour arbitrarily separated off from all others, but of a certain *aspect* of behaviour viewed as a whole' (Robbins, 1933a, p. xxii).

Some of the implications of Wicksteed's methodology were discussed by Robbins himself, in his *Essay on the Nature and Significance of Economic Science*:

---

[21] This belief is clearly expressed by Edgeworth: '[there are] two fields into which the Calculus of Pleasure may be subdivided, namely Economics and Utilitarian Ethics. The Economical Calculus investigates the equilibrium of a system of hedonic forces each tending to maximum individual utility: the Utilitarian Calculus, the equilibrium of a system in which each and all tend to maximum universal utility' (Edgeworth, 1881, pp. 15–16).

> when time and the means for achieving ends are limited *and* capable of alternative application, *and* the ends are capable of being distinguished in order of importance, then behaviour necessarily assumes the form of choice. It has an economic aspect. . . . There are things in the external world which are present in such comparative abundance that the use of particular units for one thing does not involve going without other units for others. . . . But, in general, human activity with its multiplicity of objectives has not this independence of time or specific resources. . . . Scarcity of means to satisfy ends of varying importance is an almost ubiquitous condition of human behaviour. Here, then, is the unity of subject of Economic Science, the forms assumed by human behaviour in disposing of scarce means. . . . Economics is the science which studies human behaviour as a relationship between ends and scarce means which have alternative uses. (Robbins, 1935, pp. 14–16)

This point of view, which derived from the substitution of the subjective for the classical theory of value, had the effect of extending the range of the possible applications of economic theory far beyond the horizon that characterized economic knowledge in the classical authors. The reason of this is that, once we accept a *formal* definition of economics *à la* Robbins, economics becomes 'the science of every kind of human action. . . . Out of the political economy of the classical school emerges the general theory of human action, *praxeology*. The economic or catallactic problems are embedded in a more general science, and can no longer be severed from this connection . . . economics becomes a part, although the hitherto best elaborated part, of a more universal science, praxeology' (Mises, 1949, p. 3).

Mises's research is the final stage of a process that started in the aftermath of classical political economy, and that led economists to pay increasing attention to the allocation mechanism. The focus on allocation through exchange brought about the conception of economics as catallactics (Whately, Ferrara, Gossen) and led to the theories of the early marginalists. The subsequent reflections on the nature of exchange brought to the fore the formal characteristics of economics as a general theory of the administration of resources (Wicksteed, Robbins). Finally, certain authors developed the view that catallactics is nothing but a special branch of the 'practical' knowledge about men's purposeful behaviour.[22] In this way,

---

[22] The close relationship between the study of exchange and the theory of human action was stressed by Mises as follows:

> Action always is essentially the exchange of one state of affairs for another state of affairs. If the action is performed by an individual without any reference to cooperation with other individuals, we may call it autistic exchange. An instance: the isolated hunter who kills an animal for his own consumption; he exchanges leisure and a cartridge for food. Within society cooperation substitutes interpersonal or social exchange for autistic ex-

economics appeared once again as 'Art' rather than 'Science', thus going back to a situation that had characterized economic knowledge before the intellectual revolution associated with Quesnay and Smith.

Exchange, Production and the Foundations of Economics

The historical dynamics of economic knowledge show the interplay of two distinct conceptions of our discipline. We might call them the *practical* and the *speculative* conception respectively. The practical conception was developed first. This conception later became the basis of the early marginalist theories and of their development into a formal system of practical rules. In this latter case, economic theory focused on the allocative dimension of purposeful behaviour (that is, on how to use given resources in order to achieve competing ends). Exchange was a privileged field of analysis for authors who adopted this point of view, possibly because the study of exchange offered a simple framework within which to develop formal rules for the allocation of resources. Production was studied as a special case of the allocation of *given* resources, rather than as a process whereby *additional* resources are made available.[23]

The speculative conception of economics took a long time to develop, and did not take complete shape before the work of the Physiocrats and of the classical political economists. Its distinctive feature is the search for laws, rather than the formulation of rules (when rules were formulated, like the free trade principle, they were derived from 'objective' laws, rather than from the explicit solution of an allocation problem).

This conception of economics was associated with a concentration of attention on productive activities as processes whereby income is created, and on distribution through exchange as the means whereby the reproduc-

---

> changes. Man gives to other men in order to receive from them. ... The exchange relation is the fundamental social relation. (Mises, 1949, p. 195)

Earlier approaches to economics as a branch of a more general science of human action are to be found in Bentham (1952–4).

[23] Robbins's definition of production is a case in point. For he considers production to be 'the use of scarce resources to increase opportunities of consumption' (Robbins, 1933b, p. 463). A similar position is that of Koopmans: 'Managers choose between, or employ efficient combinations of, several processes to obtain in some sense best results. Speaking still in terms of one product of given quality, an efficient manager chooses that combination of productive activities which maximizes the amount produced for given available quantities of factors' (Koopmans, 1951, p. 34). Indeed 'The choice of the best modes of operation and of the best combination of such processes is ... one particular manifestation of the general problem which forms the recurrent theme of economics: the best utilization of scarce means for given ends' (Koopmans, 1957, p. 70).

tion of income through time is made possible. In this latter case, the economists' attention focuses on *producing* and *exchanging*, considered as actual processes, rather than on *production* and *exchange*, considered as abstract cases of purposeful behaviour. Economic theory is thus constructed as a positive, rather than 'practical' (normative) body of knowledge, and the ends–means relationship recedes into the background.

Both exchange and production can be studied in either framework. However, the 'allocation' aspect is often more prominent in exchange than in production phenomena, whereas the 'ongoing' aspect is more prominent in production than in exchange. This might explain the relative importance of exchange and production in the economic theories that have been formulated by adopting the 'practical' or the 'speculative' definition of economics, respectively. For the 'practical' conception of economics is primarily concerned with the allocation problems of exchange, and the 'planning' aspect of production is mainly considered by economists as an extension of the allocation model of an exchange economy.[24] On the other hand, the 'speculative' conception of economics is primarily concerned with the objective outcomes of economic actions and with their interaction in a given system of existing relationships (such relationships might be considered the result of institutional arrangements or technical constraints). In this case, both exchange and production are studied as 'objective' phenomena, but production is generally given a prominent position, owing to the greater stringency of social and technical constraints in production with respect to exchange activities. Exchange itself is mainly considered as an aspect of the existing institutional arrangements, rather than as an instance of purposeful behaviour.[25]

---

[24] This is clearly stated by Koopmans: 'The insights into this general problem [the best utilization of scarce means for given ends] that economics has gained primarily by the study of allocation through a price system and a market mechanism are relevant also to allocation problems arising within the productive establishment. Where exchange and pricing do not exist as market phenomena, they may still be useful as constructed conceptual aids to decision making' (Koopmans, 1957, p. 70).

[25] A complete formulation of this approach may be found in Marx's *Capital*. There, a commodity is seen as 'an object outside us, a thing that by its properties satisfies human wants of some sort or another' (Marx, 1983, p. 43; 1st edn 1867). The link between commodities and exchange phenomena is described by stressing 'objective' relationships rather than free human actions:

> It is plain that commodities cannot go to market and make exchanges of their own account. We must, therefore, have recourse to their guardians, who are also their owners. . . . In order that these objects may enter into relation with each other as commodities, their guardians must place themselves in relation to one another, as persons whose will resides in those objects, and must behave in such a way that each does not appropriate the commodity of the

IV CONCEPTUAL FRAMEWORKS VERSUS OBJECTS OF ANALYSIS

Introduction

The basic idea of this section is that, in order to examine a given line of research, emphasis must be placed on the *conceptual tools* rather than exclusively on the *objects of analysis*. There might be a possible confusion as to the alleged generality of the two research lines of 'exchange' and 'production', since one might argue that a genuinely general theory ought to embrace both the 'exchange' and 'production' cores; indeed this may well be the case, since the development of each line of research has come to cover most of the domain of the competing line. But differences between conceptual frameworks remain, even after extending each approach to the whole area of economic reality. This leads us to give particular emphasis to the conceptual tools used by the two competing lines of research. We shall hence attempt to analyse briefly the more relevant differences between the exchange and production research lines, once such lines have reached a stage of 'maturity' or sufficient generality to be able to deal with most of the domain of economics.

We might spend a few words on the nature of tools and objects of economic analysis. A tool, generally speaking, is an instrument of analysis, whereas an object relates to the questions that one is set to answer. This distinction between these two concepts is sometimes blurred, due to the relationship that exists between them (this will be explored in the next subsection). For Hicks (1976, p. 208), the tools of analysis can be compared to 'rays of light, which illuminate a part of the target'. But again according to Hicks, since economic reality changes continuously, a theory that focuses on 'the right things now may illumine the wrong things another time'. Moreover objects of analysis which were left aside for many years may reappear and suddenly become the central point of focus.[26]

> other, and part with his own, except by means of an act done by mutual consent. They must therefore, mutually recognise in each other the rights of private proprietors. ... The persons exist for one another merely as representatives of, and, therefore, as owners of, commodities. In the course of our investigation we shall find, in general, that the characters who appear on the economic stage are but the personifications of the economic relations that exist between them. (Marx, 1983, pp. 88–9; 1st edn 1867)

[26] This position is markedly different from the one maintained by John Neville Keynes in his book on economic methodology. That author suggests a clear separation between 'scope' and 'method' of economics, arguing that method can only be chosen after scope has been defined:

> In seeking to define the *scope* of any department of study, the object in view

The choice of the object of analysis may of course have an ideological content, at least as far as the 'core' of the research line is concerned. Modifications of ideology are hence bound to lead to modifications in objects of analysis. Most research lines, if not all, are characterized by a particular *Leitmotiv* or 'vision' (the latter being a term of Schumpeter); it is through this 'vision' that economists proceed, in connection with the major issues that, according to them, society is confronted with. In this way, the 'rays of light', that is, the tools of analysis, will be used to throw light on the objects of analysis.

A given set of tools of analysis (related to a specific set of objects of analysis) may originate a research line. The relationship between the 'tool–object' characteristic of any research line and the particular theories formulated along this line may be clarified by considering that any economic theory generally consists of three elements: (1) a taxonomy, that is, a system of classification, more or less restricted, which defines certain categories or data then employed in constructing the theory; (2) a set of assumptions relative to what is felt to be important to the construction of the theory; and (3) a set of hypotheses about economic behaviour, that is, a set of propositions logically derivable from the set of assumptions that are used (see also Lichtenstein, 1983, pp. 8–10).

After this short introduction on the methodological aspects of theory-building, we shall try to study the way in which the two research lines of 'exchange' and 'production' differ.

Conceptual Frameworks of the Exchange and Production Research Lines

Each scientific research line is made possible by the use of a certain number of conceptual tools, in order to focus on certain objects of analysis. In order to avoid possible confusion, it may be useful to stress that: (1) any given tool may be applied, in general, to a variety of objects, even to objects quite different from the ones originally envisaged; (2) any given object of analysis may in general be studied with different tools; (3) any given tool cannot be applied to all conceivable objects, and any given object cannot be studied with all existing tools.

---

is primarily to determine the distinguishing features of the phenomena with which it deals, and the kind of knowledge that it seeks concerning these phenomena. The enquiry also involves an examination of the relations between the study in question and cognate branches of study. In passing to the consideration of *method*, we are dealing with a branch of applied logic, the object being to determine the nature of the logical processes specially appropriate to the study – that is, the methods of investigation and proof of which it can avail itself – and the logical character of its conclusions as affected thereby. (J. N. Keynes, 1890, pp. 2–3)

Hence it follows that there is a certain degree of interdependence between the choice of tools and the considered objects, in the sense that the choice of given tools may well prevent us from the consideration of particular aspects of reality and, probably to a minor degree, the choice of certain objects may well exclude certain tools. This makes it more convenient to take into consideration research lines that have reached a considerable degree of generality in terms of the domains covered, instead of focusing on the first 'ideal' models at the origin of each line. For this purpose, we shall find it useful to compare the respective conceptual frameworks of each line, that is, the fundamental visions of economic reality offered by any given line at a late stage of development. In a sense, a conceptual framework is the combination of compatible tools and objects, allowing us to assess the full scope of a research line well beyond the limitations of the first 'ideal' models.

The appraisal of the 'exchange' and 'production' research lines will be based on the consideration of conceptual frameworks to be found at a late stage of development, when each line has already been stretched to include most of the domain of economics. This explains why our comparison of the two approaches can be conducted by examining the two alternative points of view with respect to the same 'objects'. We shall compare the two research lines by taking into consideration the following aspects in turn: the nature of the commodities considered; the 'vision' of the production process; the criteria of distribution; the role of social classes; the time-framework and economic growth; the role of accumulation; the types of causal relationships.

The Conceptual Frameworks of 'Exchange' and 'Production'

The Nature of the Commodities Considered

Commodities are connected with the principle of *scarcity* within 'exchange-oriented' theories, and that of *producibility* within 'production-oriented' theories. Within this framework, the two approaches are bound to consider different aspects of the system of production. As a matter of fact, the marginalist world of exchange and allocation is dominated by the scarcity of the factors of production, whereas classical theories tend to give more emphasis to the state of technology and to the structure of social classes, by assuming in certain cases an unlimited amount of resources or, in any case, by giving less emphasis to their scarcity. This distinction between scarce and producible commodities has been emphasized by Pasinetti (1965, p. 576; 1981, pp. 9–11). In particular, Pasinetti maintains that the marginalist model:

> is worked out, in its basic features, with no reference whatever to a process of production. The only type of commodities that exist are given by nature and,

> in equilibrium, their prices will be either zero (and they will be called *free goods*) or positive, and they will be called *scarce goods*, the only ones to be economically relevant. In such a context, the economic problem is only one of *rational choice*. (Pasinetti, 1981, p. 9)

On the other hand, classical economists did not rule out the existence of 'scarce' commodities (for instance art objects). But these commodities were considered of secondary importance since, as Ricardo (*Works*, vol. I, p. 12) states:

> By far the greatest part of those goods, which are the object of desire, are procured by labour, and they may be multiplied, not in one country alone, but in many, almost without assignable limit, if we are disposed to bestow the labour necessary to obtain them. (Ricardo, 1951–73, vol. I, p. 12)

Commenting upon this passage, Pasinetti (1981, p. 7) writes that these goods may be defined as of the 'production type'; and it is uniquely to these commodities that Ricardo makes reference in his analytical system.

Hence we can talk of *scarcity-type* commodities, on the one hand, and of *production-type* commodities, on the other. For both of these concepts it is possible to give an interpretation in 'factual terms', referring, on the one hand, to natural resources and, on the other, to all those goods whose availability might be assumed as (theoretically) unlimited, the latter being uniquely determined by technical conditions. We are confronted with two alternative ways of considering the same economic reality. The full implication of this difference will appear more clearly as we progress towards the end of this section.

What we might stress for the moment is that the concept of 'scarce commodity' seems to imply a static vision of economics, since all commodities that are used for the production of other commodities, including those produced during the preceding periods, are exogenously given and hence treated, in analytical terms, as natural resources. In this perspective, the fundamental economic problem becomes that of the most efficient utilization of the given resources. The latter is a classical problem of maximization for individuals who behave according to a criterion of choice.

On the other hand, the concept of 'producible commodity', which is associated with the classical model in particular, is related to the possibility of producing certain commodities, as quoted above, 'almost without any assignable limit, if we are disposed to bestow the labour necessary to obtain them'. It is hence not surprising that in this case attention is focused on the dynamic aspect of the production process and on its historical evolution, with particular emphasis on the expansion of the productive capacity of the economic system as it is brought about by technical progress.

This difference of approach as to the nature of the commodities considered is of course reflected in the scheme of price determination.

Generally speaking, the price of 'scarce commodities' will be determined by the availability of resources on one side (the supply side), and the structure of tastes on the other side (the demand side), quite independently of the production process.[27] Within the production-oriented framework, prices are instead determined by historical considerations, since the concept of 'required labour' is strictly associated with the productivity of labour in a particular phase of economic history.

The 'Vision' of the Production Process

The classical and post-Keynesian theories exhibit a 'circular' vision of the productive process, whereas the neoclassical theories have a 'unidirectional' view of it. The circular vision of the classical and post-Keynesian economists can be related to a 'closed' system, within which a vital role is played by the 'objective' relationship among the various sectors, as determined by the particular technology of production of the system. Within this framework the commodities are, to a certain extent, primarily means of production (for other commodities) and only secondarily consumption goods for the fulfilment of both individual and public needs. Clearly, within this framework 'final' consumption fulfils a secondary function in the economic system, although more recent works (see, for instance, Spaventa, 1962; Pasinetti, 1965 and 1981; Leon, 1967; Cozzi, 1969) have attempted to introduce the composition of demand as a crucial variable for the explanation of the long-term dynamic of the system.[28]

---

[27] This aspect of the 'exchange-oriented' model has been recently stressed as follows:

> In the pure-exchange model prices have nothing to do with production. Also, the mere fact that a commodity may be useful in some sense does not mean that it has value – that its price is positive. Certain goods and services may be in such plentiful supply relative to the demand for them that no unit commands a positive price. For commodities that have value, equilibrium prices measure a balance between supply and demand, where demand itself depends on prices and the given endowments and preferences of consumers. The balance of supply and demand for all commodities is therefore interdependent and thus requires the simultaneous solution of a whole set of relationships between quantities and prices. (Walsh and Gram, 1980, p. 404)

[28] A common feature of the above-quoted works is to link the structural dynamics and the disposable income of the average consumer unit. It is at this point that technical progress comes into the picture, for it generates increases in the per-capita income and henceforth is bound to modify the composition of effective demand, which in its turn might end up by modifying the composition of production. In this way the circularity of the production–consumption process emerges neatly.

The vision of the process, which is associated with a 'scarcity' of the available resources, is quite different; the model is essentially static, and at the beginning of each period the resources available are exogenously given, so that the analysis ends up by concentrating on the formulation of the criteria for the best utilization of these resources. For this reason, the aspect of circularity must forcibly be replaced with that of unidirectionality.[29] In particular, the marginalist framework does not consider the 'objective requirements' of the economic system (these are the necessary conditions that have to be satisfied, if the economic system is to reproduce itself through time). It follows that, for the marginalist scheme, the set of consumers' preferences becomes crucial for the determination of the equilibrium levels of the economic variables of the system. In this way, as Sraffa (1960, p. 93) points out, it becomes possible to explain the abandonment by the marginalist theory of a circular vision of the production and consumption system and its replacement with a 'one-way avenue that leads from "Factors of production" to "Consumption goods"'.

The 'circular' and 'one-way' views of the production process are respectively associated with the consideration either of the 'viability' or the 'feasibility' of production. As Walsh and Gram point out:

> The reproduction of commodities by means of commodities is central to all modern treatments of classical theory: an economy exists through time only if it continually replaces the material basis for production. This is the starting point for classical theory and the associated conditions of viability, its initial concept. ... Here, the most important and historically significant insight is the distinction between systems that are just viable and those that yield a surplus over the inputs needed to maintain the flow of production. (Walsh and Gram, 1980, p. 397)

This interpretation is based on the belief that classical theory focuses on the long-term tendencies of economic systems, that is, on the capacity of such systems to reproduce and expand themselves. Moreover, it is relevant to note that the question of reproduction and expansion of the system is not simply a matter of technology in an engineering sense, since a share of

---

[29] This aspect has recently been underlined by Lichtenstein (1983, p. 16), who notes that nothing systematic can be said about the origin of the resources in the marginalist model, since the model takes them as given. This fact is the direct outcome of the one-way direction in which given factors of production are assumed to materialize in outputs which end up in consumption. On this point, Walsh and Gram observe that marginalist theories, in general, do not focus on the distinction of inputs on the basis of the process (or mechanisms) by which they were produced: 'Indeed, the *only* historical fact that has any bearing on the analysis is that a given quantity of resources has come into existence and is now available at a point in time to be used in ways that may or may not have been anticipated when these resources were produced' (Walsh and Gram, 1980, p. 182).

total output is made up of the commodities for workers' maintenance and reproduction.

A different approach is adopted by theories within the 'exchange' tradition. In that case, the feasibility of certain transformations of primary resources into consumption goods becomes central, and the issue of whether any given economic system is viable or not recedes into the background.

> Viability is not a concept of the [neoclassical] theory since its resources are parametric. In this way the theory incorporates production simply by changing the given quantities of goods and services of the pure-exchange model into variables and then adding sufficient structure to determine these variables from other data: given factors and their distribution among resource owners *via* consumers, and the technology that specifies how inputs are transformed into outputs. Feasibility is again central to the analysis, the starting point being the production possibilities set defined by the intersection of resource constraints. (Walsh and Gram, 1980, pp. 404–5)

To sum up, we may say that the 'exchange-oriented' framework depends on a short-term concept of unidirectionality or feasibility, where the main focus of analysis remains the best allocation of given resources. On the other hand, the 'production-oriented' framework is primarily concerned with long-term structural issues, as they are determined by changes in the productive capacity, and by income and wealth distribution and accumulation. This latter framework is thus directly concerned with the conditions necessary for reproduction and growth. In this way it becomes possible to locate 'specific points at which inconsistency may arise in the course of reproduction in the capitalist economy' (Harris, 1978, p. 250).

The Criteria of Distribution

Generally speaking, income distribution in the exchange model is determined by (1) the level of demand for the factors of production; (2) the willingness of factors' owners to lend the services of these factors to firms; (3) technology, which determines factor productivity; and (4) the initial endowment of factors of production. With (3) and (4) being exogenously determined, income distribution is entirely determined within the resource market, in which individual owners of resources meet buyers.

For the theories formulated within the research line of production, economic as well as social and demographic factors come into play to determine income distribution. For instance, in the case of the Ricardian model, demographic and social factors are to be taken into account, besides technical factors. The 'natural' wage-rate, for Ricardo, will be 'at that level which in a given country and in a given state of society, besides allowing workers to live, induces them to perpetuate themselves "without either increase or diminution"' (Pasinetti, 1960, p. 80). In the case of post-

Keynesian models, we find historical factors (which determine the distribution and accumulation of wealth in the long run) and demographic, technical and economical factors as well. (The rate of technical progress, the capital/output ratio, the rate of population growth, and the propensities to consume and to save determine, in equilibrium, the rate of profits and hence the distribution of income.)

Another important difference between the two main lines of research concerns the existence of a residual income. Within the marginalist framework, all payments to the factors of production exhaust the total production, that is, the sum of the payments to the factors is, by definition, equal to national income. Conversely, in the case of the Ricardian theory, profits are a residual (once wages and rent have been determined by demographic and technical factors); in the case of the post-Keynesian model, the order is reversed, and once the equilibrium share of profits is determined, wages are considered a residual.

We may add that for the marginalists the differences between ownership patterns do not affect income distribution at all; which is surely not the case of the classical and post-Keynesian theories. In fact these latter theories consider the income share of any given group or class as not uniquely connected with the marginal productivity of any single factor, but rather to be associated with the social position of the group or class to which it belongs. Within this framework there exists a definite 'causal chain' in the determination of income shares, the first shares to be determined being those relative to the productive factors fulfilling given requirements for reproduction and growth (labour and capital for the classical models; capital for the post-Keynesian models).

Within the marginalist scheme there is no 'causal chain' in determining income shares, and all factors of production are placed on the same footing, quite independently of their ownership pattern. The distributive shares will thus be simultaneously determined by the marginal productivity and the intensity of each factor.

The Role of Social Classes

Another important feature of the exchange and production research lines is closely connected with the treatment of income and wealth distribution, for a 'social-class' vision and an 'individualistic' vision are associated, respectively, with the former and the latter research lines. Sir John Hicks, who uses the term 'political economy' for production-oriented theories and that of 'catallactics' for exchange-oriented theories, claims that:

> political economy is always in some sense socialist, catallactics individualist; though one cannot make that fit the history unless one distinguishes between means and ends. The Old Political Economists were socialists (or at least 'social') in the ends they set up; but they were individualist in practice, because they held that individualism was the way to the achievement of their social ends. (Hicks, 1976, p. 213)

The above point of view stresses the relevance of social classes in the productive process, whether they be the physiocratic 'sterile' and 'productive' classes, the Ricardian workers, capitalists and landlords, or the post-Keynesian capitalists and workers. Individualism as a means for the functioning of a market economy, however, is accompanied, in 'political economy', by the stress on ownership relationships as the major determinant of the distribution of income and wealth among the different individuals in society. In Quesnay and Smith, and then even more clearly in Ricardo and Marx, political economy considers 'laws' by which the social product is distributed among classes, and these latter are defined according to the ownership relationships between individuals and productive factors:

> The produce of the earth ... is divided among three classes of the community; namely, the proprietor of the land, the owner of the stock or capital necessary for its cultivation, and the labourers by whose industry it is cultivated. But in different stages of society the proportions of the whole produce of the earth which will be allotted to each of these classes, under the names of rent, profit, and wages, will be essentially different. ... To determine the laws which regulate this distribution is the principal problem in Political Economy. (Ricardo, 1951, p. 5; 1st edn 1821)

Ownership relationships had already lost some of their importance in J. S. Mill's *Principles of Political Economy*, where we read that:

> The laws and conditions of the production of wealth partake of the character of physical truths. There is nothing optional or arbitrary in them. (J. S. Mill, 1965, p. 199; 1st edn 1848)

On the other hand,

> It is not so with the Distribution of Wealth. That is a matter of human institution solely. ... The distribution of wealth ... depends on the laws and customs of society. The rules by which it is determined, are what the opinions and feelings of the ruling portion of the community make them, and are very different in different ages and countries; and might be still more different, if mankind so chose. (J. S. Mill, 1965, pp. 199–200; 3rd edn 1852)

But after having limited in this way the generality of the economic laws that consider the distribution of the social product, Mill proceeds to the study of distribution by assuming 'private property ... as a fact' and by enumerating 'the different classes of persons to whom it gives rise; whose concurrence, or at least whose permission, is necessary to production, and who are therefore able to stipulate for a share of the produce' (J. S. Mill, 1965, p. 235; 1st edn 1848). Property rights are fundamental determinants of distribution, if the production process requires some form of 'cooperation' from individuals who have the power of 'withdrawing' certain essential inputs.

Distribution of the social product may be explained by considering the property rights of 'classes' of individuals, on condition that the claim of any individual to a certain share of the product is determined by the input category, within which that individual may exert his own 'withdrawal capacity'. The idea that land, capital and labour are 'separately appropriated' (Mill, 1965, p. 235), and that each input category is associated with a 'withdrawal capacity' of a different kind, characterizes the classical theories of income distribution.

Social classes remain fundamental in post-Keynesian theories (Kaldor, 1955/6, 1957; Pasinetti, 1962; Joan Robinson, 1962), even if, in the case of Pasinetti, the distinctive feature of each class is given by its saving and consumption behaviour. In Pasinetti's theory, the assumption of 'separate appropriation' of each productive factor is no longer in the foreground, and workers' incomes are made up of wages and interests on accumulated savings.[30] In this type of theory, it is postulated that there are different rates of saving associated with different classes. The overall rate of saving, then, depends on the distribution of income among such categories of individuals.

In post-Keynesian models, those who own means of production and whose income is mainly derived from this ownership make up the capitalist class, which in general exhibits a high propensity to save and reinvest. Those who do not own means of production and whose income is derived mainly from work have a much lower propensity to save; they are called the workers.

The assumptions that permit the use of the concept of social class in classical and post-Keynesian economic theories are dropped in theories of the 'catallactic' type. For these latter share, to a greater or lesser degree, the following three assumptions: (1) different inputs may be appropriated by the same individual, or by the same group of individuals; (2) property right to any input gives the owner an abstract 'withdrawal capacity', which

---

[30] We might say that the post-Keynesian theories reject the strong version of the 'social-class' theory of income distribution (in which each income share meets a 'claim' associated with the property of an essential input), while maintaining a 'weak' concept of social class, in which the distinctive features of each class are found in its consumption and saving behaviour, rather than in its rights and entitlements. In this way the post-Keynesian theories 'contrast with all models of competitive economics where individuals react only to the direct stimulus of the markets in which they operate and have no appreciable effects on those markets' (Craven, 1979, p. 79). Indeed the post-Keynesian approach simplifies the model to such an extent 'that the interests of each group can be clearly seen and the outcome is fairly easy to work out' (Craven, 1979, p. 79).

is identical for all categories of inputs;[31] (3) individuals' decisions are likely to be affected in a more significant way by market signals than by the 'traditional' choices made in the past (such choices depend on custom, social status, etc., rather than on preferences and prices).

Assumptions (1)–(3) make the concept of social class redundant in economic theory. This implies that income distribution and capital accumulation is no longer tied to the behavioural characteristics associated with ownership of productive inputs. Income distribution and capital accumulation (the latter associated with saving behaviour) thus become entirely consistent with the theory of an individualistic market economy, in the sense that they can be explained by exchange relationships between individuals (or even *within* individuals, as is the case of the time-preference theory of saving). Institutional constraints such as the differential 'powers' associated with ownership of different inputs are removed from the picture, as they cannot easily be explained by considering exchange relationships only.[32] In particular, saving behaviour becomes part of the range of phenomena on which a theory of choice and allocation throws light: 'household saving and dissaving emerge from a treatment of intertemporal

---

[31] This attitude is shown, for example, by Pareto's classification of 'capitals' into three main categories: '*capitali fondiari*' (such as agricultural and building land, mines, etc.), '*capitali mobiliari*' (machinery, factories, commodity stocks, etc.), and '*capitali personali*' (human beings as capable of work) (Pareto, 1906, pp. 416–18).

[32] We might say that the 'catallactic' theories of distribution and accumulation appear to be more in line with the ideal model of a 'possessive market society' than the classical theories could be. For in this type of society (like in 'catallactic' theories of the economy):

> the market, responding to countless individual decisions, puts a price on everything, and it is with reference to prices that the individual decisions are made. The market is the mechanism through which prices are made by, and are a determining factor in making, individual decisions about the disposal of energies and the choice of utilities. Exchange of commodities through the price-making mechanism of the market permeates the relations between individuals, for in this market all possessions, including men's energies, are commodities. In the fundamental matter of getting a living, all individuals are essentially related to each other as possessors of marketable commodities, including their own powers. All must continually offer commodities (in the broadest sense) in the market, in competition with others. (Macpherson, 1962, p. 55)

consumption planning that is formally closely analogous to . . . static consumption theory' (Bliss, 1975, p. 133).[33]

The Time-Framework and Economic Growth

We want to assess here whether dynamic issues are treated in a distinct way by 'exchange' and 'production'-oriented theories. The vision of these issues is influenced by the way in which commodities are defined in each economic theory. This brings us back to the distinction between the 'scarcity' and 'producibility' points of view discussed above (see pp. 31–3). For when 'scarcity' is focused upon, all produced means of production are considered to be limited in the same way as natural resources (here, again, the most relevant problem remains that of maximising a given function, subject to given constraints). On the other hand, the consideration of producibility is associated with the idea that goods 'may be multiplied, not in one country alone, but in many, almost without any assignable limit, if we are disposed to bestow the labour necessary to obtain them' (Ricardo, 1951, p. 12; 1st edn 1821).

The feasibility versus viability distinction mentioned above (pp. 33–5) gives further insight into the difference between 'trade-oriented' and 'production-oriented' theories, linked with dynamic issues. It may be useful to recall the scientific issues associated with the different way in which commodities are defined. A pure exchange model does not require any explanation of the fact that certain commodities exist in the economy, nor does it explicitly consider whether the exchanges taking place today may be repeated tomorrow; the reconstitution of factor supplies is also not explicitly discussed. Indeed, there is no reason to suppose that the allocations which now yield a certain commodity-output will be repeated tomorrow.

---

[33] This position may be traced back to Fisher's theory, according to which the rate of interest influences the saving decisions through the action of the preference for present goods with respect to future goods (see Fisher, 1907, 1930). An early criticism of the time-preference theory of saving was formulated by G. Del Vecchio:

> The accumulation of wealth is taking place for a number of reasons of a social character: the relative position of social strata, general variations of technique, and so on. The economic calculus governs the allocation of the available resources between the various branches of the productive system, it also governs the allocation of the available resources between the various forms of consumption, but it does not determine the distribution of available resources between production and consumption, not even between forms of consumption that take place at different time periods. The rate of interest, that is the expression of economic calculus through time, is not therefore a determining element of accumulation and is, in turn, determined independently of this latter. (Del Vecchio, 1956, pp. 43–4; 1st edn 1915)

As Walsh and Gram (1980, pp. 404–5) point out, 'feasibility in neoclassical theory . . . lacks the dynamic character of viability in classical theory'. On the other hand, a pure production model gives priority to the way in which the economic system gets organized in order to deliver a given set of commodities alternatively to other possible sets. This brings to the fore the issue of 'viability' and makes it relevant to assess whether any given form of productive organization may repeat itself through time.

Within this context, it is important to stress the different role that economic growth plays in the two research lines of production and exchange. With the transition from classical to neoclassical theory, slowly but steadily, long-term dynamics ceases to be one of the main focuses of economic theory. This does not mean, of course, that the fundamental ideas of the classical economists are abruptly brushed aside; this is particularly true for some of the works of Walras, Marshall and Clark. For instance, Walras, in the 36th lecture of his *Eléments d'économie politique pure* (1874), expounds a theory of economic development which draws heavily on Ricardo, since it stresses the role of capital accumulation and population increase for economic growth. Something similar might be said for Marshall and his analysis on the growth of population and wealth, as carried out in book IV of his *Principles of Economics*. But more insight, within this context, might be gained from John Bates Clark's *Distribution of Wealth* (1899). Clark is convinced that in a modern industrial economy two kinds of forces are continuously at work: the first is of a dynamic nature, which contributes to the transformation of economic structures; the second is of a static nature, which, in the absence of the dynamic forces, would bring the economy to a state of equilibrium. A characteristic idea of Clark's is that economic laws might be formulated by focusing upon a static economy: 'fluid, perfectly competitive, free to seek the ultimate equilibrium levels dictated by the controlling factors in force at any given time' (J. M. Clark, 1952, p. 603).

However, as Clark repeatedly points out, the reaching of the equilibrium is continuously prevented by the operating of the dynamic forces of the system; he identified such forces with population growth, capital accumulation, technical progress, changes in economic organization and consumers' preferences. In Clark's opinion, a simple extension of static analysis could provide the basis for the theory of economic dynamics, provided that all dynamic factors (such as those mentioned above) operate instantaneously. For in this case only can dynamic equilibrium be determined as a sequence of momentary equilibria.

In spite of these attempts to speculate on general aspects of long-term dynamics,[34] it must be said that post-classical economists seldom made an

[34] Cf., for instance, Robertson (1961, pp. 5–6), who considers in great detail the approach to economic growth by several authors writing around the turn of the century.

effort to identify, within a theoretical framework, the fundamental dynamic forces which shape the growth of industrial nations. And when they did, they rarely added anything new to the insights provided by the classical authors. The problems of long-run dynamics became again the main concern of the work of theoretical economists only after the analyses of von Neumann (1935–7) and Harrod (1939).

Generally speaking, one might say that the long-run perspective of most economic theories is closely connected with the rate of capital accumulation of any given system. However, the variables on which the two lines of research tend to focus are different. Neoclassical theories stress the role of factors such as inter-temporal discount rates, rate of interest on accumulated savings, and individual utility functions, thus bringing in the life-cycle allocation of income between consumption and saving. Theories of the classical type also focus on the allocation of income between consumption and saving, but have it determined by (1) technology that yields a given surplus and (2) institutional factors determining saving propensities.

The above distinction may be traced back to the different logical structure of the research lines of 'exchange' and 'production'. In the former case, economic dynamics are the outcome of individual allocating behaviour. It has for instance been argued that:

> the Walrasian analysis aims at interpreting the structures that are potentially stable and that the system tends to acquire at a certain date in correspondence to some values of a set of exogenous parameters. The Walras model, therefore, does not deal with a temporal process; that does not mean that it cannot take account of the time dimensions of the various choices. It is, in fact, enough to pass from a . . . space with n dimensions (where n is the number of goods) to a temporal one of nT dimensions (where T is the number of periods considered). (Lombardini and Nicola, 1974, p. 309)

Theories of the 'production' type focus instead on the system of productive activities (cf. von Neumann and Leontief), rather than on patterns of allocation of given resources. In particular, these models can do without assumptions on initial conditions, and tend to see the economy as an open system, by relying upon a continuous inflow of external resources, instead of upon the stock of existing resources at any given time (see Lombardini, 1983, p. 186).

The Role of Accumulation

Accumulation, defined as the process by which men store stocks of commodities, independently of whether such commodities will or will not be consumed in the future, is not always associated with productive capital. For men may store consumable and not perishable commodities, as well as accumulate means of production that cannot be consumed. In the former case, accumulation is independent of production (non-produced commodities can also be stored) and is directly connected with the possibility of future consumption. In the latter case, accumulation is a necessary step in order to reproduce the economic system on a larger scale.

The accumulation that is carried out in order to expand the scale of the economy may concern both means of production that cannot be consumed and consumable commodities that may be used as means of production (such as the commodities entering the 'normal' real wage of productive workers). But in this latter case, consumption is not the 'end' of the accumulation process: it is simply an intermediate stage, having little or no autonomy with respect to the expansion of the productive capacity.

These two different ways of dealing with accumulation appear to be followed in the theories formulated within the exchange and the production research line, respectively. In 'catallactic' theories, accumulation is defined as the postponement of present consumption with a view to having more to consume in the future. This case of substitution over time is explained in terms of time-preference, and the accumulation process comes to be closely connected with the determination of the rate of interest (the rate at which future satisfactions ought to be discounted in order to make them comparable with present satisfactions) (Böhm-Bawerk, 1884–9; Fisher, 1907, 1930).

The 'catallactic' approach to accumulation derives its basic assumptions from the ideal model of a pure 'exchange–consumption' economy, in which 'capital' appears to be a store of wealth from which a stream of consumption can be derived, rather than a stock of accumulated products to be used in the production of wealth (Solow, 1963, 1967; see also Bliss, 1975, pp. 215–50).

On the other hand, the 'political economy' approach derives its assumptions from the ideal model of a pure production economy in which the accumulation process concerns produced means of production (independently of whether they are or are not currently produced in the economy, and also independently of whether they can or cannot be consumed by individuals). This approach focuses on the concept of 'surplus' (the excess of the social product over aggregate means of production) and connects accumulation with the distribution of the surplus between social classes. (Ricardo, for example, assumes that the surplus of an economic system coincides with the share of the social product accruing to capitalists and rentiers, and establishes a direct association between capitalists' profits and the accumulated share of that surplus (Ricardo, 1951; 1st edn 1817).)

The Ricardian approach to accumulation is shared, in many respects, by Marx (1867–94) and by various economists concerned with economic fluctuations and crises (Tugan-Baranovsky, 1894; Spiethoff, 1903; Bouniatian, 1908; Aftalion, 1913).

In modern economic literature, Keynes's and von Neumann's contributions brought again to the fore the 'objective' concept of accumulation; the former by stressing that individual savings are linked to the level of income, rather than to the rate of interest;[35] the latter by drawing attention to the formation of aggregate surplus and to its connection with the maximum sustainable growth of the economic system (von Neumann, 1935–7).

The relationship between capital accumulation and long-run dynamics is also focused upon by the post-Keynesian (as well as 'neoclassical') literature on the type of income distribution consistent with equilibrium, full employment growth. This literature shows that there is a close relationship between the growth rate of the economy and the distribution of income between social classes. It is at this point that capital accumulation comes into play, since the total saving of each class is the product of the exogenously determined saving propensity times the capital stock. In equilibrium, full employment growth, the parameters of the model (saving propensities included) determine the capital share of each class (see, for example, Pasinetti, 1962; Meade, 1963; Baranzini, 1981, 1982).

'Catallactic' theories tend to consider accumulation as a special case of exchange (less consumption in the current period is 'traded' against greater consumption in a future period). On the other hand, the theories of the 'political economy' tradition consider accumulation as the process by which the capital stock of the economy is determined. They tend to focus on the process of capital expansion, considered as an essential mechanism for the reproduction of the economic system on an extended scale.

The Types of Causal Relationships

According to a number of economists, the 'truth criterion' for 'catallactic' theories is mainly aprioristic, whereas it is *a posteriori* or inductive for theories of the 'political economy' type. Åkerman, for instance, has pointed out that:

> Economic theory rests on only two mental operations: one aiming at rationalizing the planning of economic agents and at assessing the relevance of the means which he uses to attain his goal; the other trying to reframe economic fact as a whole through significant combinations of quantitative time-series and qualitative descriptive elements. ... The relationships between deduction and induction represent the fundamental problem of economics. (Åkerman, 1955, p. 1; 1st edn 1944)

The former approach has found a rigorous formulation in the theories of the 'catallactic' type; the latter is associated by Åkerman with the 'causal' analysis of economic phenomena, which (in his opinion) in general cannot be satisfactorily carried out within the models of rational behaviour and

[35] This link is given by Keynes's 'fundamental psychological law', according to which 'men are disposed, as a rule and on the average, to increase their consumption as their income increases, but not by as much as the increase in their income' (Keynes, 1936, p. 96).

choice. This particular issue is discussed by considering the way in which inflationary processes ought to be treated by economists:

> A cumulative movement like the inflationary process ... may only be explained within a causal framework: it is not the outcome of a rational speculation nor of a plan which may be translated under the form of an alternative analysis in equilibrium economic theory; nor is it the outcome of a set of means put into practice in order to reach a given goal; it cannot be tied to a unique economic agent, since it [the inflationary process] appears due to a non-orchestrated action among the majority of social groups. The development path which causal analysis tries to reconstruct is the outcome of different plans of different groups. Henceforth the impossibility of rationalizing it under the form of a unique plan, nor under the form of an aggregate plan, since the object of analysis is the development itself, a real and temporal process. (Åkerman, 1955, p. 3; 1st edn 1944)

This point was also taken up by Joan Robinson, who writes that:

> To build up a causal model, we must start not from equilibrium relations but from the rules and motives governing human behaviour. We therefore have to specify to what kind of economy the model applies, for various kinds of economies have different sets of rules. ... The independent elements in the model must correspond with the features of reality which are given independently of each other, either by the brute facts of nature or by the freedom of individuals within the economy to decide how they will behave. (Joan Robinson, 1962, p. 34)

Phyllis Deane has written recently that:

> Probably the most distinctive general characteristics of the Cambridge school's approach to growth theory are that its models tend to be explanatory rather than predictive, involving behaviouristic rather than mechanistic assumptions, and strongly concerned with directions of causation through time rather than with mutually determining sets of variables. They focus (as Keynes did) on the causes and mechanisms of change rather than the conditions of equilibrium and they stress the need to develop theories which are designed to apply to specific types of economy and to particular periods of historical time i.e. to construct 'historical' or causal models. (Phyllis Deane, 1978, p. 203)

Pasinetti has put forward a view concerning the logical structure of marginalist and classical theories which might reinforce the previous statements:

> the marginalist theory of general equilibrium ... is essentially based upon a system of simultaneous equations. Suffice it to think of the elegant formulation of Vilfredo Pareto. For Pareto the entire economic system is represented by a number of demand functions and a number of supply functions. When

> these functions apply simultaneously it is possible to derive the equilibrium conditions, i.e. market prices and physical quantities to be exchanged. Necessarily the logical scheme is that of a system of simultaneous equations. Nothing of the sort was the determination of the various economic magnitudes in the theoretical schemes of classical economists; here there is no necessity for the variables to be always determined in a simultaneous way. As a matter of fact most of the explanations are of a uni-directional nature. (Pasinetti, 1964/5, pp. 243–4)

In order to differentiate between the two schemes, Pasinetti (1964/5) introduces the concepts of 'symmetry' and 'asymmetry', maintaining that the marginalist model can be represented by a system of interdependent equations, where 'interdependence' means 'simultaneous and symmetric relationships among variables' (that is, where the variable x_n depends on x_m, and simultaneously x_m depends on x_n). Classical and modern classical models are characterized by the absence of such a symmetry: here the relationships among variables are unidirectional, and not bi-directional. The variable x_m may be a function of x_n, but not the other way round. This asymmetry determines a 'causal relationship' (or 'causal chain') or 'recursivity'.[36]

It might appear that the *a posteriori* explanations, which the authors mentioned above associate with the classical approach, could be related to the recursivity of the logical structure of the underlying theories. Conversely, the difficulty that has been associated with causal analysis in the neoclassical approach might be related to the symmetry of the relationship between variables characterizing this approach, according to the view expounded above. This might explain why authors like Åkerman, Robinson and Deane suggest that the study of the historical evolution can be more easily carried out within a recursive framework. A reason for this could be that it is much easier to put forward explanations of a straight kind (A determines B, but not vice versa) when dealing with models of a recursive type. Explanations of this kind would be much more difficult in the case of models of the simultaneous type.

The use of asymmetric relationships in the explanation of economic history has been stressed by Sir John Hicks in his *Causality in Economics*. Here Hicks calls attention to the fact that chains of events often have to be interpreted in terms of 'sequential causality' (A causes B on condition that A happens before B and also on condition that there are sufficient reasons for maintaining that all intermediate events are causally related to one another so as to produce the final effect B during the given time interval (see Hicks, 1979, pp. 87–8)). In his treatment of this issue, Hicks does not make any explicit reference to the existence of a causal ordering of the

---

[36] This does not mean, as Pasinetti (1964/5, pp. 245–6) points out repeatedly, that one cannot find a certain number of simultaneous relationships, for instance, in the Keynesian macroeconomic model; but in these cases we are confronted with subsystems of simultaneous equations, which are incorporated in an explicitly predetermined causal chain.

recursive type. In fact, recursivity and sequentiality might appear to be quite independent from each other. The reason for this is that sequentiality is a property of the actual process by which A produces B, whereas recursivity might be considered as a logical property of theory independent of the actual process of causation. However, the recursive ordering could be linked with the process of causation through time, if one adopts the realist view that the causal structure of any given theory reflects the way in which causation takes place in the real world. (See Harré and Madden, 1975; Zamagni, 1983.)

V ECONOMICS AND THE METHODS OF SCIENCE

Introduction

The nature of the exchange and production research lines has been considered in the preceding sections, whereas here we shall focus on the main differences to be found between economics and the other sciences, in particular the natural ones.

The task of drawing an exhaustive list of the main differences between branches of scientific knowledge is not an easy one, since this issue may be considered from different perspectives. In this section, we shall confine our analysis to the following aspects: the nature of the variables involved, the methods of enquiry employed, the issue relative to the type of knowledge provided by economics (positive *versus* normative) and, finally, the patterns of advancement in economics and other disciplines.

The Nature of Economic Variables

From this point of view the gap between economics and the natural sciences is remarkable. This has led a number of scholars to maintain that economic theories are not always as rigorous and compelling as the theories of natural sciences are considered to be, even if it seems that economists have succeeded in building up more comprehensive and rigorous models than most other social scientists. This latter impression may be due to the fact that quantitative aspects are in certain cases easier to handle in economics than other social sciences.[37]

---

[37] Blaug has recently stressed the methodological peculiarity of economics by arguing that:

> economics is [also] a peculiar science, set apart from, say, physics because it studies human actions and therefore invokes the reasons and motives of human agents as the 'causes of things' and from, say, sociology and political science because it manages somehow to provide rigorous, deductive theories of human action that are almost wholly lacking in these other behavioural sciences. (Blaug, 1980, p. xi)

In this subsection we shall examine the nature of economic variables by considering the following aspects: the number of variables involved; the historical dimension of economic variables; the identification of the variables; the human component of the variables.

The Number of Variables Involved

It has often been pointed out that the larger the number of variables involved, the more difficult the setting up of a model, especially when most of them are interrelated. This is even harder in the case in which some of them remain unknown or are particularly difficult to measure. This seems to be the case of economics, for which, according to Caldwell (1982, pp. 238–9), consideration of 'numerous initial conditions' is essential, since 'in general not all exogenous variables are known, and a number of them vary simultaneously'. This, of course, may easily lead to gross simplifications and distortions of reality in the attempt to construct a comprehensive model. Economists have usually reacted to this situation in three different, but partially unsatisfactory ways.

1 *By introducing the 'ceteris paribus' condition* in order to isolate a particular causal mechanism. But the *ceteris paribus* clause, though appealing at times, raises doubts as to its validity within an 'open' model. Hicks (1983b, pp. 367–72) maintains that the *ceteris paribus* clause may lead to a loss of generality, since all economic laws depend for their validity (or applicability) on the assumption that the variables on which they are based are the only ones to matter. This leads, again according to Hicks, to an important corollary – that predictions in economics are of a 'weak' nature, as opposed to 'strong' predictions of certain natural sciences – thus requiring a 'judgement about their reliability'. Hicks concludes that:[38]

> Once it is accepted that economic theories (those which are not mere tautologies) can offer no more than weak explanations – that they are always subject to a *ceteris paribus* clause – it becomes clear that they cannot be verified (or 'falsified') by confrontation with fact. (Hicks, 1983b, p. 371)

2 *By limiting the number of variables included in the model.* Although this may well have certain advantages, it is beyond doubt that the deletion of even a limited number of variables will affect the estimated value of

---

[38] On this point, see also Schoeffler (1955), Wilber and Harrison (1978), and Blaug (1980, p. 68). By referring to a specific example, Blaug concludes that 'In short, unless we somehow manage to restrict the meaning of a *ceteris paribus* clause, placing definite limits on the operation of "disturbing" or "counterbalancing causes", the entire argument fails to produce a refutable prediction even in terms of the direction of the total change, much less in terms of the magnitude of that change' (Blaug, 1980, p. 68).

most variables included in the model. This is likely to have serious consequences in the case of 'exchange-oriented' models characterized by complete interdependence of all variables, but it may be more justified for those models characterized by recursivity or asymmetric causal relationships (cf. pp. 44–7 above), provided that no key variables are left aside. Recursivity seems to dominate in a number of natural sciences, thus making it easier to formulate explanatory models.

3 *By making a certain number of variables endogenous.* This procedure is often used, especially in complex econometric models; but as Grunberg (1978) points out, it may lead to infinite regress, due to the fact that a variable originally considered exogenous is often itself determined by other exogenous variables.

The actual procedure adopted may well reflect a combination of the above points. In fact most econometric models include a limited number of endogenous variables and a limited number of exogenous variables (not requiring an explanation within the model), while a large number of the remaining variables (individually of little relevance, but of significance in their aggregate) are taken into account by adding a stochastic term.

This procedure has been analysed, from a methodological point of view, in two distinct ways. A number of authors have traditionally maintained that the use of stochastic methods of testing is consistent with theories of the deterministic type (see, in particular, Simon, 1955). More recently, however, philosophical developments such as Suppes' theory of probabilistic causality (Suppes, 1970) have induced other writers to recognize the 'stochastic nature of theories and to accept that a causal ordering can be established on condition that all variables of the model, including those called "exogenous", ought to be treated as random variables' (Gambetta and Sartore, 1983, p. 96).

The Historical Dimension of the Variables

As Knight (1956) has pointed out, the material of economics differs substantially from that of other sciences, since it has the tendency of changing over time ('in the course of history') in a way in which, for instance, the material of physics does not change. This gives to economics, as well as to other social sciences like politics and sociology, a historical dimension which natural sciences rarely exhibit (on this point see also Collini, Winch and Burrow, 1983, pp. 33–4). This issue is also raised by Hicks, who maintains that: 'The facts which we study are not permanent, or repeatable, like the facts of natural sciences; they change incessantly, and change without repetition. Considered as individual events, they are often events of great interest. Every business has a history of its own, every consumer a history of his own' (Hicks, 1976, p. 207). Later on, Hicks (1979, p. xi) writes that economics is 'on the edge of science and on the edge of history', and that, when considered in a dynamic context, 'it becomes less like a science, and more like history'. Popper has also stressed that the historical character of economic variables introduces a definite gap between economics and most natural sciences:

> In physics, for example, the parameters of our equation can, in principle, be reduced to a small number of natural constants – a reduction which has been successfully carried out in many important cases. This is not so in economics; here the parameters are themselves in the most important cases quickly changing variables. This clearly reduces the significance, interpretability, *and testability* of our measurements. (Popper, 1961, p. 143)

The relevance of history to economics is strengthened by the role of learning processes in human activity. This aspect has been underlined in a number of recent writings on economic evolution and technical progress. For instance, Pasinetti writes that:

> human beings are able to learn from past experience and to communicate among themselves the results of their learning activity. Then, if men, on the average, are born with the same degree of intelligence in time, each generation is bound to go further than the previous one; not because it is more intelligent, but because it starts from a better position, by taking advantage of longer experience. (Pasinetti, 1981, p. 22)

Therefore it should not be surprising that major changes and new points of interest in our science have been brought about by historical changes in social and political institutions. This is well illustrated by Phyllis Deane (1978, p. xiii) who, by analysing the patterns of progress of economic ideas, maintains that 'Theories and concepts may drift away from objective truth because the nature of economic reality is changing'.

Hence an appraisal of any given economic theory ought not to be isolated from the historical context in which that theory has been formulated. This does not necessarily mean that, due to the fact that economic phenomena change continuously, economic theory should change at the same pace, since in so doing one might confuse causal relationships with different degrees of stability over time. Economists, for example, should be careful not to revise a theory aiming at explaining long-term structural change as a result of short-term variations in economic reality.

The Identification of the Variables

A further characteristic of economics is that a number of variables cannot be independently checked. Caldwell (1982, p. 239) lists, among the most important, the state and role of information, as well as tastes and preferences. This, of course, is bound to further increase the complexity of the modelling. J.N. Keynes states that:

> In the first place, economic science deals with phenomena that are more complex and less uniform than those with which the natural sciences are

> concerned; and its conclusions, except in their most abstract form, lack both the certainty and the universality that pertain to physical laws. . . . Different methods are appropriate, according to the materials available, the stage of investigation reached, and the object in view; and hence arises the special task of assigning to each its legitimate place and relative importance. (J.N. Keynes, 1890, p. 6)

The complexity and heterogeneity of variables has often been connected with the unpredictability of human behaviour (which we shall consider next). Marshall (1961, p. 772; 1st edn 1890) points out this aspect forcefully, stating that the variables and forces with which economics deals are 'more numerous, less definite, less well known, and more diverse in character than those of mechanics; while the material on which they act is more uncertain and less homogeneous'. Marshall also stresses the high degree of unpredictability of the variables as well, by drawing attention to the 'arbitrariness' of many economic phenomena, as opposed to the 'simple regularity' of pure mechanics. An example is to be found in the increase of a 'man's income': if this increase is small, this may well end up by increasing his expenditure 'a little in every direction'. But for Marshall a large increase may drastically alter his habits, perhaps by modifying his social conscience and making him 'cease to care for some things altogether' (Marshall, 1961, p. 772; 1st edn 1890).

The Human Component of the Variables

The 'complexity' of modelling in social sciences, and economics in particular, has often been associated with certain fundamental characteristics of human behaviour. Hayek maintains that:[39]

> When we consider the question from the angle of the minimum number of distinct variables a formula or model must possess in order to reproduce the characteristic patterns of structures of different fields (or so exhibit the general laws which these structures obey), the increasing complexity as we proceed from the inanimate to the (more highly organized) animate and social phenomena becomes fairly obvious. (Hayek, 1967, p. 26)

This distinction between social and natural sciences was also present in J.M. Keynes's mind, as the following remark shows:

> In chemistry and physics and other natural sciences the object of the experiment is to fill the actual values of the various quantities and factors appearing in an equation or a formula; and the work when done is once and for all. In economics this is not the case and to convert a model into a quantitative formula is to destroy its usefulness as an instrument of thought. (John M. Keynes, *Collected Writings*, vol. XIV, p. 299)

---

[39] On this issue see also, for instance, Lombardini (1983, pp. 225–31).

On this issue Phyllis Deane points out that Keynes's departure from the neoclassical paradigm was deeper than usually thought, since:

> he [Keynes] was in revolt against the tendency, implicit in the mechanistic analytical techniques of marginal economics, towards visualising economic science as capable of providing a vehicle for scientific prediction by analogy with the natural sciences. 'Economics' he maintained, in a letter to Harrod in 1938, 'is essentially a moral science and not a natural science'. (Phyllis Deane, 1978, p. 181)

Phyllis Deane then quotes another statement of Keynes (cf. *Collected Writings*, vol. XIV, pp. 297–300) in which he maintains that in economics one should never consider the material as immutable and homogeneous, since 'it deals with motives, expectations, psychological uncertainties'. This leads Deane (1978, p. 181) to conclude that Keynes's concept of economic modelling is a 'vehicle for analysis rather than for prediction'.

The fact that the material of economics has to do with human nature, and hence is subject to change, depending on man's relative freedom of action, makes the study of the growth of economic knowledge more demanding than that of most natural sciences. This point is considered, among many others, by Lakatos (1971, p. 91) and Hutchison (1978, pp. 298–301); we shall return to this point below (pp. 61–5). This issue is also taken up in the two papers by Hicks and Schmitt published in this volume.

The Methods of Analysis: Some Basic Issues

Introduction

The relevance of the 'tools' and 'objects' of economics for the two lines of research of exchange and production has been considered in the previous section. In this context we briefly discuss a number of methods of analysis in order to point out some distinguishing features of the way in which economists work. Of course our sample of methods is clearly incomplete, but we hope to draw a representative picture of the main differences between 'natural' and 'social' sciences. We shall first consider the role of economic history in economics, then the relevance of mathematical techniques, and finally the issue of testing procedures in economics.

The Uses of Economic History

The historical character of the material of economics was recognized long ago, as the structure of Adam Smith's *Wealth of Nations* clearly shows. In Adam Smith's book, pure theory is not yet sharply distinguished from descriptive and historical accounts.

The subsequent development of economic thought is towards a progressive distinction between the field of economic theory (the discovery of 'economic laws' derived from assumed postulates) and the field of economic historiography (the description and explanation of past economic events). This distinction has been carried into modern and contemporary economics up to the point that many economists today would probably agree with the following statement by John Neville Keynes:

> Neither [economic history nor economic theory] can take the place of the other. For, on the one hand, mere historical research cannot by itself suffice for the solution of theoretical problems; and, on the other hand, the actual evolution of economic habits and conditions cannot be constructed *a priori*. (J.N. Keynes, 1890, p. 268)

However, most contemporary economists would probably disagree with this other statement by the same author:

> The more specific functions of economic history in connection with the theoretical problems of political economy may be roughly classified as follows: first, to illustrate and test conclusions not themselves resting on historical evidence; secondly, to teach the limits of the actual applicability of economic doctrines; thirdly, to afford a basis for the direct attainment of economic truths of a theoretical character. (J.N. Keynes, 1890, p. 270)

The task of providing illustrations and confirming evidence for theory is nowadays more often ascribed to statistical techniques (see pp. 56–8 below). The function of economic history for the critical appraisal of economic theories is almost entirely overlooked. The conception of economics as a special field of historical research has been almost generally rejected (this was the distinctive position of the German historical school).

In spite of these considerations, the history (actual evolution) of economic facts continues to influence the formation of economic theory, providing the latter with topics for research, if not tools of analysis. The more difficult issue of whether economic history also influences the formation of the basic economic concepts is not considered here, but will be examined in various contributions to this volume (see, for instance, Hennings, Bharadwaj, Quadrio-Curzio and Scazzieri, and Pasinetti).

Mathematics in Economics

It is not an uncommon conviction that economics does not fully meet the qualifications for being classified as a full science. To this conviction many economists have reacted by progressively borrowing mathematical tools of analysis from certain natural sciences (especially physics), in the belief that in this way economics may gain 'respectability' and hence reach the stage of maturity of the most progressive natural sciences (cf. Phyllis Deane, 1983, p. 2).

It may be useful to retrace the genesis and early motivations of the adoption of mathematical tools in our discipline. The use of mathematical notation and concepts in economics may be traced back to John Briscoe's

Discourse (Briscoe, 1694) and to Giovanni Ceva's *De re numaria* (Ceva, 1711). Briscoe limited himself to set an equation depicting the relation between the stock of money and the product of real income and the price level (cf. Schumpeter, 1954, p. 314), whereas Ceva presents us with a theoretical model containing explicit functional relationships (cf. Jevons, 1879, p. xlv; Bianchini, 1982, p. 17).

Mathematical arguments remained quite common in the economic writings of continental authors well into the first quarter of the nineteenth century.[40] But it is with Cournot's *Recherches sur les principes mathématiques de la théorie des richesses* (1838) that the mathematical method is fully exploited to show its high logical power. As Jevons pointed out, Cournot's treatise,

> apart from its economic importance ... presents a beautiful example of mathematical reasoning, in which knowledge is apparently evolved out of ignorance. In reality the method consists in assuming certain simple conditions of the functions as conformable to experience, and then disclosing by symbolic inference the implicit results of these conditions. (Jevons, 1879, p. xxxiii)

Jevons's appraisal of the 'mathematical character' of economics may be considered as a *locus classicus* for the argument that economics is in some essential way connected with 'the methods and language of mathematics':

> It is clear that Economics, if it is to be a science at all, must be a mathematical science. . . . My theory of Economics . . . is purely mathematical in character. Nay, believing that the quantities with which we deal must be subject to continuous variation, I do not hesitate to use the appropriate branch of mathematical science, involving though it does the fearless consideration of infinitely small quantities. The theory consists in applying the differential calculus to the familiar notions of wealth, utility, value, demand, supply, capital, interest, labour, and all the other quantitative notions belonging to the daily operations of industry. As the complete theory of almost every other science involves the use of that calculus, so we cannot have a true theory of Economics without its aid. (Jevons, 1879, pp. 3–4)

Jevons's views, although apparently outdated because of the stress on calculus, have in common with more recent appraisals the idea that the use of mathematical arguments gives higher logical power to economic reasoning.

---

[40] Cf. Theocharis (1983). One of the latest cases is given by the exchange between Gioja and Valeriani on the form of the functional relationship between price and the number of sellers (Gioja, 1815–17; Valeriani, 1816, 1817). This exchange is an offspring of a mathematical school that included a number of followers throughout the eighteenth century (see Bernouilli, 1738; Beccaria, 1764; Isnard, 1781).

Koopmans, for instance, when discussing the economic applications of the mathematical theory of linear spaces, stressed that such mathematical tools permit us 'to perceive with *greater clarity* and express in *simpler terms* the logical structure of important parts of economic theory' (Koopmans, 1957, p. 5; our italics). According to Koopmans, important results have been obtained by using powerful mathematical tools. For instance, remarkable intellectual achievements have been obtained by substituting 'a few elementary concepts and theorems borrowed from the mathematical theory of *linear spaces*' (Koopmans, 1957, p. 6) for models studying competitive equilibria 'through unique, or at least locally determinate, solutions of equations systems' (Koopmans, 1957, p. 5). The new mathematical tools led to the discovery of necessary and sufficient conditions for the optimal allocation of resources. This discovery was made possible because the theory of linear spaces considers issues that the previous mathematical tools (theory of equation systems, calculus, theory of implicit functions) could not deal with:

> In the first place [the old mathematical tools] did not permit recognition of restraints on choice that require expression by inequalities rather than by equations. Owing to this limitation of the tools in use, the literature of an entire period almost completely ignored such simple facts as the impossibility of consuming negative quantities of goods or of rendering negative quantities of labour, or the impossibility of running production processes in reverse. Secondly, the calculus, used in this way it was used to scan the (restricted) domain of the target function for a maximum position, is a myopic instrument. It served only to compare the would-be-maximum position with alternative positions in its immediate neighborhood. For this reason, the problem of formulating conditions under which a position could stand comparison with more distant rivals was not faced. (Koopmans, 1957, p. 6)

'Intellectual economy' (that is, simplicity) and greater intelligibility of the structure of economic theory are commonly considered to be advantages of mathematical economics. (See also Debreu, 1984.)

However, it is worth recalling that the use of mathematics in economics is subject to a particular condition originally expounded by Pareto:

> Given the mathematical laws according to which certain beings do behave on average, [mathematical economics] has to assess the consequences of these laws. (Pareto, 1911, p. 591)

In Pareto's view, mathematical economics is thus based on two assumptions: (1) it is possible to formulate mathematical laws, according to which individuals behave (at least 'on average'); (2) the consequences of such laws are relevant to economics (see Zawadzki, 1914, p. 16).

The mathematical modelling of human behaviour has remained a characteristic feature of most 'catallactic' economic theories since the marginalist revolution. In recent times, mathematical economics has found remarkable applications also in theories of the 'production' type (consider the mathematical contributions associated with the work of von Neumann, Leontief and Sraffa). In the former case, usefulness of mathematical methods depends crucially on the degree of reliability of the mathematical description of human behaviour. In the latter case, the usefulness of mathematics depends on how well mathematical laws may describe the technical process of production on given behavioural and institutional assumptions.

In both cases, the advantages of mathematical methods are likely to become disadvantages, if economists lose sight of three important facts: (1) the mathematical *descriptions* ought to express 'some general relations and some short processes of economic reasoning' (Marshall, 1961, p. 781; 1st edn 1907) that could also be formulated in ordinary language; (2) greater simplicity and intelligibility is sometimes due to the removal of economically significant factors (Brand, 1961, p. 26); (3) the use of mathematical techniques that are not fully suitable for the problem under investigation might introduce into economic theory a dangerous source of inexactness (Brand, 1961, p. 37; see also chapter 3 below by Schmitt).

The Testing Procedures

In chapter 2 of this volume, Sir John Hicks maintains that the difficulties relative to observation and experimentation in economics are not to be underestimated. 'Economics, obviously, is not an experimental science' he maintains (p. 97); and this means that economic predictions must be of a weak nature, because the propositions on which they are based rely heavily on the *ceteris paribus* clause. He adds:

> The rigorous testing under precaution, which is practicable in the experimental sciences, is for the most part not possible for us. What we get, at best, remains subject to exogenous disturbances, as we call them. So our predictions, though somewhat strengthened by this method, still remain weak. (Hicks, p. 98 below)

This point is taken up by Hicks elsewhere (1983b, p. 372), when he stresses that in the natural sciences it is usually possible to test theories by repeated *ad hoc* experiments.

The experimentation issue has been widely treated in recent economic literature (for instance, Lakatos, 1970; Blaug, 1976; Hutchison, 1976, 1981; Boland, 1982; Caldwell, 1982, part II; Lombardini, 1983, pp. 215–39). We shall not enter into the details considered in this literature, but will just touch upon the main differences between economics and the natural sciences. Eichner (1983, p. 10) agrees with Hicks's opinion quoted above, and adds that economics does not lack mathematical rigour or formulation skills, but confirming empirical evidence. Without empirical support, economics will not meet the requirements necessary for it to be considered a science.

The almost general impossibility of carrying out planned experiments has sometimes been considered a major difficulty for the empirical testing of economic theories (see Tintner, 1968). Clearly, important reasons for which planned experiments in economics are so difficult must be found in the particular nature of the variables involved (that is, in their large number, their human component and their historical nature). An important outcome of this situation, recently pointed out by Hicks, is that in the case of economics we cannot apply the criterion according to which 'when theory and fact come into conflict it is theory, and not fact, that must give way' (Hicks, 1983b, p. 348). In fact we should never forget Hume's claim that 'all that it is shown by such a conflict is that *either* the theory *or* the fact is wrong' (Hicks, 1983b, p. 348). As a result, no economic theory should be rejected out of hand simply because certain facts appear to be in conflict with it, since that theory may well have been tested against the 'wrong' facts. This is commonly due to a lack of correspondence between the terms of the theory which is being tested and the terms in which the facts are described (Hicks, 1983b, p. 372). (On this point, see also Pasinetti, chapter 14, section VI below.)

The difficulty of carrying out planned experiments is associated with a characteristic feature of economic arguments: they always seem to lead to weak predictions (that is, predictions depending on the *ceteris paribus* assumption). The fact that the *ceteris paribus* condition is seldom satisfied makes it very difficult to produce reliable empirical tests of any given theory.[41]

---

[41] Shackle has recently pointed out that: 'Choice of a course of action, of an enterprise, an ambition, is not an experiment which can be repeated indefinitely under broadly unchanged conditions. The very making of this experiment will alter the conditions irreversibly; such an "experiment" is by its essential nature inherently self-destructive, it is once-for-all' (Shackle, 1979, pp. 53–4). It may be interesting to recall that Cairnes also recognized this impossibility of controlled experiments, but did not think that it represented a major drawback for economic enquiry:

> In the case of the physical premises ... of Political Economy, equally with the mental, we are entirely independent of those refined inductive processes by which the ultimate truths of physical science are established. The economist may thus be considered at the outset of his researches as already in possession of those ultimate principles governing the phenomena which form the subject of his study, the discovery of which in the case of physical investigation constitutes for the enquirer his most arduous task; but, on the other hand, he is excluded from the use of experiment. There is, however, an inferior substitute for this powerful instrument at his disposal, on which it may be worth while here to say a few words. I refer to the employment of

The statistical techniques used for testing economic theories have to take into account the special problems associated with data collection, so that certain methods that may be used for designed experiments (such as the analysis of variance) are seldom available to econometricians (Tintner, 1968, pp. 66–7). Econometric tests generally depend on sampling methods and estimation of certain characteristics of a given unknown 'population'. This makes it difficult to reach conclusive tests. The danger of accepting false hypotheses ought to induce economists to 'raise the level of significance at which [they] screen hypotheses' (Blaug, 1980, p. 704). But of course setting a high level of significance implies that we might have to reject some true hypotheses, whereas the setting of a low level of significance is associated with the opposite danger.[42]

The special circumstances under which economic observations are made make it very difficult to test economic theories by taking full account of the particular conditions of space and time in which the relevant observations were collected. This characteristic might explain why economists have often shown little interest in the use of statistical techniques for reaching conclusive tests of their general theories. In this respect, the economists' practice seems to follow quite often the criterion that was described by Cairnes more than a century ago: 'In connection with the processes . . . of verification and the discovery of disturbing causes, or (to express the same idea differently) the discovery of the minor influences affecting economic phenomena, we find the proper place of statistics in economic reasoning' (Cairnes, 1875, p. 85).

The current use of statistical techniques shows another important feature worth mentioning in connection with other points of this chapter (see, in particular, the following subsection). This feature concerns the spread of Bayesian statistics, which relies on a subjective notion of probability[43] and may be traced back to a theory of rational actions (see Bayes, 1763; de Finetti, 1931; Ramsey, 1931; Suppes, 1981). Bayesian techniques draw attention to certain issues of decision theory and imply a conception of statistics that is nearer to praxeology than standard techniques used to be (see section III above, and the following subsection).

> hypothetical cases framed with a view to the purpose of economic enquiry. For, although precluded from actually producing the conditions suited to his purpose, there is nothing to prevent the economist from bringing such conditions before his mental vision, and from reasoning as if these only were present, while some agency comes into operation – whether it be a human feeling, a material object, or a political institution – the economic character of which he desires to examine. (Cairnes, 1875, p. 77–8)

[42] The relevance and implications of the choice of a level of significance for econometric tests is considered in detail in Morgenstern (1963, 1971).

[43] Where the probability of any event is defined as the degree of belief held by a particular subject (and which may vary from subject to subject).

Economics as a 'Positive' or 'Normative' Discipline

Empiricist methodology has generally denied that there is any significant divide between the methodological principles of the social and natural sciences (see Carnap, 1938; Hutchison, 1938; Blaug, 1980). An opinion closely associated with this methodological standpoint is that 'the whole conception of a contrast between normative and positive sciences is fundamentally false' (Schlick, 1930, p. 14), and that statements of the form 'such-and-such a measure will have such-and-such effects or fulfil such-and-such ends' should fulfil the criterion of empirical testability (cf. Hutchison, 1938, p. 154).[44]

In the case of economics, the distinction between 'Art' and 'Science', that is between normative and positive, goes back to the origin of our discipline (see section III above).

It is worth recalling how such a distinction is outlined in Sidgwick's *Principles*:

> It was because a monarch or statesman was conceived to have the function of arranging the industry of the country somewhat as the father of a family arranges the industry of his household, that the Art which offered him guidance in the performance of his function was called Political Economy. . . . Adam Smith [had] really not seen the extent to which, in the hands of the Physiocrats as well as his own, the method of Political Economy has changed its fundamental character and become the method of a science rather than an art. . . . As regards the 'plentiful revenue or subsistence of the people', Adam Smith, instead of showing the statesman how to provide it, has to show him how Nature herself would make ample provision if only the statesman would abstain from interfering with her processes. (Sidgwick, 1883, pp. 14–18)

The latter point leads Sidgwick to the following remarkable statement: 'instead of recommending laws (in the jurist's sense) by which the national production and distribution of wealth *ought to be* governed, he [Adam Smith] has to trace the laws (in the naturalist's sense) by which these processes actually *are* governed' (Sidgwick, 1883, p. 18). The separation between 'scientific' and 'normative' arguments is reflected in the structure of Sidgwick's work, where books I and II deal with production, and with distribution and exchange respectively, whereas book III is devoted to the

---

[44] At the beginning of the nineteenth century Valeriani (Professor of Economics in Bologna) criticized the distinction between economics as 'Art' and economics as 'Science', moving from an apparently similar methodological standpoint and arguing that, in the case of economics, there is a logical continuum going from the more general propositions of pure theory to the 'practical' propositions of economic policy (these latter being distinguished from the former only on account of the greater number of particular conditions that have to be satisfied for such propositions to be true). (See Valeriani, 1804.)

'Art of Political Economy', considered as a 'department of the general Theory of Practice' (Sidgwick, 1883, p. 401).

In the subsequent evolution of economics, the distinction between positive and normative aspects of the discipline again becomes rather blurred (see, for instance, Hutchison's position, quoted above). More recently, the distinction has become crucially important for the theories of the 'catallactic' type, particularly as the result of two separate intellectual developments: (1) the discovery that general equilibrium theory can at best provide 'very weak' causal propositions;[45] (2) the explicit formulation of the view that economics is a special field of praxeology.[46]

The former result reflects a more general view, according to which 'positive' economic theory, in its present state, can at best provide benchmark constructions from which economic reality would normally differ. The latter view has drawn attention to the normative side of economics, which has acquired growing autonomy up to the point of leading to the development of specialized 'praxeological' disciplines such as operations research, cybernetics, programming, and so on.

The ambitions of economics as a 'Science' are drastically underpinned when, at the same time, many functions of economics as 'Art' are taken up by the specialized techniques of efficient action mentioned above. This sequence of events is to be associated with important changes relative to the value judgements and goals of a number of contemporary economists. As a matter of fact, economics is often considered to be part of the 'advising profession', as Lucas (1980, p. 207) has pointed out, so that economists are often tempted (or constrained) to go beyond the stages of description and explanation, and to set standards and schemes of behaviour.

The fact that a number of economists are convinced of the 'causal weakness' of economic theory (see above), combined with the growing influence of praxeological techniques, has changed the character of economics. Economists are often more interested in putting forward persuasive arguments than in formulating 'objective' laws and causal explanations. Economic 'laws' are frequently seen as setting standards of behaviour,

---

[45] Hahn describes the type of causality permitted by general equilibrium theory with the following proposition: 'no plausible sequence of economic states will terminate, if it does so at all, in a state which is not in equilibrium' (Hahn, 1973, p. 7). The argument for this proposition is that 'agents will not continue in actions in states in which preferred or more profitable ones are available to them nor will mutually inconsistent actions allow given prices to persist' (Hahn, 1973, p. 7).

[46] Praxeology has been defined as a science whose goal is 'to investigate the essence of the process of action, and to clarify all those concepts which are indispensable for the description, appraisal, and planning of action, and for the general theory of efficient action' (Kotarbiński, 1960, p. 215). See also Kotarbiński (1965) for a general presentation of the sciences of efficient action.

thereby committing the error, already censured by Sidgwick, 'of thinking and speaking of economic "laws" as liable to "violation", and as needing to be realised by voluntary conformity or even enforced by public opinion' (Sidgwick, 1883, p. 13).

The praxeological drift of many contemporary economists certainly needs some rethinking. This would probably require a closer study of the causal relationships among the events considered in the framework of efficient action (see Kotarbiński, 1960). This study might also provide some common ground between the 'catallactic' and the 'political economy' approaches to economic theory.

On the 'Progress of Knowledge' in Economics and other Sciences

In order to carry out an analysis on the patterns of progress, that is of 'successive creative work' in scientific activity, in economics (and other sciences as well), one should, *inter alia*, focus on the following points:

1 Has economics been characterized at each moment by a unique approach or by the coexistence of two or more lines of research during long periods of its history?
2 Has economics been characterized by a 'step-by-step building brick' approach or by 'scientific revolutions' *à la* Kuhn?

Question (1) has already been explored in sections I–III above: economics, since its initial steps, seems to have been characterized by the coexistence of the two research lines of exchange and production, each of them looking at our science from different angles and having a different core, and each of them competing with each other by building a protective belt around the core in order to incorporate some of the material of the competing line.

Question (2) will be the focus of this subsection which may be introduced by a statement of Sir John Hicks, according to whom the economist finds it difficult to escape from his past:

> When the natural scientist has come to the frontier of knowledge, and is ready for new exploration, he is unlikely to have much to gain from a contemplation of the path by which his predecessors have come to the place where he now stands. Old ideas are worked out; old controversies are dead and buried. The Ptolemaic system may live on in literature, or it may form the framework of a mathematical exercise; it has no direct interest to the modern astronomer.
>
> Our position in economics is different; we cannot escape in the same way from our own past. We may pretend to escape; but the past crowds in on us all the same. To 'neoclassical' succeeds 'neomercantilist'; Keynes and his contemporaries echo Ricardo and Malthus; Marx and Marshall are still alive. Some of us are inclined to be ashamed of this traditionalism, but when it is properly understood it is no cause for embarrassment. (Hicks, 1976, p. 207)

The behaviour of the scientist at the frontiers of the science is surely symptomatic of the patterns of advancement of his own science, and will help us to clarify the way in which it develops and progresses. We shall consider below the issue of 'maturity' or 'immaturity' of a science, in order to assess the nature of a research line better. First, however, we shall consider the way in which any research line is brought forward and extended.

'Cumulative' and 'Non-Cumulative' Evolution of Knowledge

The issue as to whether the evolution of scientific knowledge follows a cumulative or non-cumulative pattern is widely debated. Hicks (1976, p. 207) and Hutchison (1978, pp. xi–xii), for instance, maintain that economists, much more than natural scientists, are likely to gain from the study of the analyses traced by their predecessors. Although many scholars would not agree with this view (see, for instance, Say, 1817, 'Discours préliminaire'), Hutchison is convinced that the historical dimension of economic knowledge is particularly important, if compared with the case of natural sciences:

> [The] readiness to disregard the history of economics is partly based on the confidently held assumption that, as is assumed for the natural sciences, their history has, since their origins, been one of smooth, more-or-less unbroken progress, recognisable as such by the professionally qualified, or by those with sufficient knowledge to form a judgement. (Hutchison, 1978, pp. x–xi)

The question of how 'progress' has come about in economics and other sciences seems to be the focal point of a number of recent works. (See, for instance, those of Blaug, 1976, 1980; Hicks, 1976; Hutchison, 1978 Quadrio-Curzio and Scazzieri, 1977, 1982a, 1982b, 1984.) We shall not recall here the main issues at stake, but just set the argument against the main theme of our volume.

Among economists, the 'fits-and-start' vision of scientific progress is not uncommon. As Peter Oppenheimer points out:

> [Economics] is only to a limited extent cumulative or progressive. Partly because of this, it is only to a very limited extent self-propelled. These terms are a shorthand way of saying that economics does not show to anything like the same extent as the natural sciences a continuous, step-by-step build-up of systematic knowledge about the way things work. Progress comes in fits and starts. (Oppenheimer, 1983, pp. 128–9)

This statement depicts clearly the perception that many economists have of progress in their discipline, since they usually focus on that body of research which emerges in the foreground at any given time and comes under close scrutiny. But such an interpretation is bound to change, if one takes into account the progress of the distinct lines of research which we have identified in those of 'exchange' and 'production'. Within each line of research, progress is likely to be cumulative, first by deepening the core of the 'programme' and then by extending the analysis to embody most aspects of economics. But the alternative emergence and recurrence of the two distinct lines[47] is bound to leave the impression of the 'fits-and-starts' advancement mentioned above. This interpretation is, partially at least, shared by Hutchison, who, by considering the nature of 'revolutions' in economics, states that:

> 'Revolutions' in economics are not total and final in the way, or to the same extent, that they tend to be in some or most of the natural sciences. Acceptance of the new 'revolutionary' doctrines does not spread as rapidly, or to as high a degree of consensus, as in physics or chemistry. Moreover, theories once apparently eclipsed by a successful 'revolution' may sooner or later revive. (Hutchison, 1978, p. 287)

On the 'Maturity' and 'Immaturity' of Economics

Some philosophers of science, notably Popper, Kuhn, Lakatos and Ravetz, have made a clear distinction between 'mature' sciences (such as physics and chemistry) and 'immature' ones (such as social sciences in general).[48] The implications of this view are far reaching, since it does not simply refer to the way in which a given science develops, but it is strictly connected with the way in which we consider the 'object' of a science and the method appropriate to it.

The above distinction may be traced back to a unity-of-science approach, and leads to the view that social sciences should progress in the same way as natural sciences do, with a similarity of methods and objectives. Only in this way might a science acquire 'maturity'.

A number of economists are highly critical of this vision. Among the critics we find Hutchison and Hicks. Hutchison, for example, stresses that Popper, Kuhn and Lakatos have derived their theory about 'maturity' and 'immaturity' mainly from the history and philosophy of physics. This implies, again according to Hutchison, 'a kind of epistemological parity between economics and physics, which will render the methodological analysis, prescriptions, strategy or tactics, derived from the one science, entirely appropriate, almost without qualifications or reservations, to the other science' (Hutchison, 1976, p. 185). It is this view of science which is

---

[47] Rejection, even for a short period of time, of a given line of research (as Hicks (1976, p. 208) points out) may not necessarily be due to the appearance of more powerful theory, but simply because the former line of research 'has become inappropriate'.

[48] Lakatos bases this distinction on the following considerations: 'Mature science consists of research programmes in which not only novel facts but, in an important sense, also novel auxiliary theories, are anticipated; mature science – unlike pedestrian trial-and-error – has "heuristic" power' (Lakatos, 1970, pp. 175–6).

rejected; for the definition of 'immature' science either implies (1) that in the course of 'maturation' it will become like physics or chemistry ('the supremely "mature" sciences') or (2) that if 'maturation' does not take place, it is to be ascribed to wrong methodological prescriptions. Sciences, according to this interpretation, must pass through certain 'stages of development' in order to acquire maturity.[49] Hutchison rejects this opinion and emphasizes that:

> Suggestions of . . . 'laws', or stages, of development, fail to take account of fundamental differences in material: notably, for example, that the material of physics possesses constancies and an absence of significant historical change and development, which the material of economics does *not* possess. If the material which economics deals with was to come to resemble, sufficiently significantly, the material which physics deals with, then the science of economics might come in due course to resemble the science of physics in 'maturity' and 'development'. (Hutchison, 1976, p. 184)

Hicks (1976) adheres to this line, as already mentioned above, by maintaining that while for natural scientists in general 'old controversies are dead and buried', economists cannot easily escape from their past. The special reason for this, again according to Hicks, is that the empirical contents of economics (the 'economic facts') are constantly changing as a result of two related phenomena: (1) the change in economic reality; (2) the change in the economists' 'concentration of attention'. Either phenomenon might reinforce the other (through economic policy also) and exert a combined influence in modifying the 'empirical basis' of economics.

This outcome might explain why the progress of economic knowledge appears to be particularly difficult to assess if attention is focused on the empirical content of theory, rather than on the refinement of concepts and techniques. Both Hutchison's and Hicks's statements draw attention to issues which can be better understood if we stress that economics is a body of knowledge that may be of immediate relevance to business strategy and public policy. Its material may be changing not just because reality is mutable, but also because economists themselves may be induced to consider urgent issues as they come up from the world of economic decisions.

These considerations suggest a linkage between the peculiar 'traditionalism' of economic theory (old themes are seldom buried for ever) and the 'practical' dimension that has been associated with economics since its 'pre-scientific' age. They also suggest that the history of economic knowledge might perform, in this connection, a much more fundamental role than the history of a natural science usually does. For it is through a consideration

---

[49] 'It seems even to be suggested that possibly there are inevitable "stages of development" . . . which must and will be passed through in the development of sciences, as in the development of economics' (Hutchison, 1976, p. 183).

of how their subject evolved through time, that economists become aware of what the 'object' of their discipline is or might become.

VI ON THE RECURRENCE OF PARTICULAR THEMES IN ECONOMIC THOUGHT AND IN ECONOMIC REALITY

The Problem

At this stage, we propose to consider the state of economics by focusing on one important issue in the dynamics of economic knowledge, namely the fact that the same themes seem to resurface from time to time both in economic life and economic thought. We believe that the nature of this recurrence is crucial for assessing the specific character of economics. Indeed, as we shall point out below, this recurrence permits us to avoid two alternative positions that have emerged among economists as to the relationship between theoretical and 'practical' economics. It will also reinforce the fundamental theme of this volume – the coexistence of distinct lines of research since the beginning of our science – for each research line gives prominence to certain features of economic life that are likely to re-emerge from time to time. Finally, we shall be able to put forward certain conclusions as to how economists ought to approach their subject, by stressing the need for considering critically both the past of our discipline in relation with present theoretical needs, and the past evolution of actual economic systems in relation to their present performance.

Two Alternative Positions: the 'Purist' versus 'Anti-theoretical' Views

Controversies about the 'scope and status' of economics have often centred on the distinction between those economists who believe that it is possible to study the relationships between economic variables independently of institutional or historical consideration, and those economists who are convinced that economic evidence may change through time and from one place to another, so that economic facts may not be adequately reduced to any general theory. These two positions can be traced back to the classical economists. In particular, Ricardo may be associated with the former position,[50] and Stuart Mill with the latter.[51]

---

[50] Ricardo's attitude is clearly shown in his letter to Malthus of 24 January 1817 (Ricardo, 1951–73, vol. VII, p. 120): 'It appears to me that one great cause of our difference in opinion on the subjects which we have so often discussed is that you have always in your mind the immediate and temporary effects of particular changes, whereas I put these immediate and temporary effects quite aside, and fix

A similar distinction may be found between the position of early marginalists (Jevons, Menger, Walras) and the German historical school (Schmoller, Spiethoff, Sombart). 'Pure economics', as it developed from early marginalism through the work of Wicksteed and Pareto, was uninterested in the historical processes by which its data ('ends' and 'means') came about. As Adolph Löwe put it, the research programme of pure economics 'does not include a critical investigation into the substance of ends, into the causes of nature's stinginess, into the scope or the constitution of the community in question. Pure theory only tries to handle a *given* body of ends and means in a particular, the "economic" way of co-ordination' (Löwe, 1935, p. 43).

On the other hand, the critics of pure economics would draw attention to the fact that market laws presuppose special assumptions about the 'substance of ends' as well as about the 'constitution' of society. The reason for this is that market laws presuppose both the existence of 'rational' economic men and perfect factor mobility. But these two conditions are in turn related to a particular organization of society, in which individuals are free to decide how to bargain their own properties, and in which the structure of productive capital does not prevent the shifting of investment from one business to another.

The 'historical' critics of pure economics would thus point out how this latter, far from being generally true, is in fact built upon 'a concrete idea of

---

my whole attention on the permanent state of things which will result from them. Perhaps you estimate these temporary effects too highly, whilst I am too much disposed to undervalue them.'

[51] Mill thought that a characteristic feature of his *Principles of Political Economy* was 'the ... distinction between the laws of the Production of Wealth, which are real laws of nature, dependent on the properties of objects, and the modes of its Distribution, which, subject to certain conditions, depend on human will' (Mill, 1924, pp. 174–5). Mill criticized 'The common run of political economists' for confusing these laws together, and for 'ascribing the same necessity to things dependent on the unchangeable conditions of our earthly existence, and to those which, being but the necessary consequences of particular social arrangements, are merely co-extensive with these: given certain institutions and customs, wages, profits, and rent will be determined by certain causes: but this class of political economists drop the indispensable presupposition, and argue that these causes must, by an inherent necessity, against which no human means can avail, determine the shares which fall, in the division of the produce, to labourers, capitalists, and landlords' (Mill, 1924, p. 175). On the other hand, Mill maintained that his own *Principles* 'yielded to none of its predecessors in aiming at the scientific appreciation of the action of these causes, under the conditions which they presuppose; but it set the example of not treating those conditions as final. The economic generalizations which depend, not on the necessities of nature but on those combined with the existing arrangements of society, it deals with only as provisional, and as liable to be much altered by the progress of social improvement' (Mill, 1924, p. 175).

social psychology, of the political and legal constitution', combined with 'a definite conception of technique: small-scale organization of many independent producers' (Löwe, 1935, pp. 58–9). The central criticism of the historical school was thus formulated by Löwe: 'Far from presenting a pure theory appropriate to any social conditions, so simple a law as the law of supply and demand . . . depicts the essential features of a very concrete society: the liberal society of early capitalism' (Löwe, 1935, p. 59). (See also Hollis and Nell, 1975.)

A Comprehensive View: Permanent Relationships and Recurrence of Economic Issues

Moving away from the two positions examined in the previous subsection, one may well accept that economic life is not free from institutional and historical influences, while maintaining at the same time that it is possible to discover behind such influences a relatively permanent structure of economic relationships. The latter are not subject to variance to the same degree as everyday economic events, thus permitting the formulation of economic theories. In the absence of such relatively permanent relationships, economic theorizing would be confined to purely abstract argument, and economic facts could only lead to descriptive treatments.[52]

It is the existence of relatively permanent economic relationships that may explain the recurrence of certain economic issues (even if this recurrence may take place at irregular time intervals). To take a few examples, from time to time economic growth is stopped by slackening effective demand or slow capital accumulation; a low wage share in national income is associated either with a high profit share or with a high share of scarcity rents; bottlenecks in the supply of certain essential inputs bring about a wave of technical innovations.

The relative constancy over long time periods of certain relationships permits us not to consider recurrence in random terms, but as the outcome

[52] This view of the relationship between theorizing and economic reality goes back at least to the physiocratic distinction between the 'natural' and the historical or institutional features of an economic system (Quesnay's *Tableau économique* is a device for studying the 'natural order' of the economy rather than the actual economic life of society). Marx went back to Quesnay's *Tableau*, and built upon its basis his own reproduction schemes. However, his analysis of the dynamics of a capitalist economy is based on the idea that the reproductive conditions of such an economy, which must be satisfied in the schemes, are seldom automatically met in any real economy expanding through time. The uneven dynamics which characterize this type of economy are then explained through a comparison between the historical dynamics of the economy and the natural dynamics of the reproduction schemes.

of the working of the economic system's basic structure. Recurrence may thus be considered as the result of certain initial impulses operating within the given structure. The nature of this recurrence is of a causal type, since it is the expression of objective properties of the system, quite independently of how often any event is repeated through time.

The recurrence of economic issues might help us in interpreting the dynamics of economic theory, characterized by the clustering of discoveries on certain points of distinct research lines (each line shows recurring periods of vitality and lethargy, which could be related with recurrence of certain phenomena in actual economic dynamics). Recurrence of facts may thus be connected with recurrence of themes in economic theory. It follows that the study of economics should make allowance for a careful consideration of economic history and of past economic theorizing. Recurrence of facts is also associated with the recurrence of certain policy problems. Knowledge of past policy experiences should therefore be another important point in the economist's agenda.[53]

VII THE STRUCTURE OF THE VOLUME

The Core and Extensions of the 'Exchange' and 'Production' Research Lines

It is the purpose of this volume to evaluate the past evolution and perspectives of economic knowledge by considering the 'concurrent' development of two distinct lines of research, one dealing primarily with allocation and 'rational' decisions of individuals (the 'exchange' framework), and the other dealing primarily with the 'objective' laws of production of wealth and income distribution (the 'production' framework). According to this view, economic theory appears to be characterized by a phenomenon that is not uncommon in the development of scientific knowledge: the coexistence of distinct lines of research, originating from mutually exclusive

[53] It is even more so if we consider economic policy to be itself affected by theory in any significant way. For in this latter case policies would be influenced not only by the recurrence of facts, but also by the recurrence of theoretical clusters on the different lines of economic research. The abstract and 'speculative' aspect of economic policy was stressed long ago by Luigi Valeriani in his inaugural lecture at the University of Bologna. There Valeriani pointed out that economic policy 'can be reduced to an increasingly accurate theory, that is to the knowledge of more specific data, none of which can be overlooked if we want the practical result to coincide with the theoretical one, even if all other conditions are as required' (Valeriani, 1804, p. XXV). The reason for this is that economic policy requires the application of general economic theory to 'transversal data of place, time, circumstances' (Valeriani, 1804, p. XLIII).

conceptual cores (in the case of economics, a pure 'exchange' and a pure 'production' core respectively). As already mentioned, each line of research has been extended, in a sequence of steps, to include much of the entire domain of economics (that is, production and social distribution in the case of exchange-oriented theories, and exchange and prices in the case of production-oriented theories).

This view of the evolution of economic knowledge brings to the fore the problem of how economics has taken shape as a distinct discipline since its early steps, and the issue of how it is related to the development of other disciplines. In particular, we shall look into the reasons for which our subject seems from the beginning to show the endurance of certain thematic concepts and hypotheses, as well as the distinction between lines of research. This may suggest that economics is the outcome of the welding together of two distinct areas of interest, partially overlapping and thus allowing for the existence of some common ground. (It is the existence of this common ground which may well induce many scholars to consider economics as a single and homogeneous science.) It is an aim of this volume to suggest that both the historical reconstruction and the current appraisal of economics would greatly benefit from the explicit recognition that economists' work has developed around distinct thematic concepts and that at the same time there have been continuous and not always apparent exchanges with other disciplines.[54] We believe that the same plurality of approaches and openness to other disciplines should be kept in mind by present-day economists when studying the functioning of actual economic systems.

The structure of the volume reflects our concern with the nature and implications of: (1) the endurance of diverging thematic beliefs in economics, and (2) the connection of such thematic beliefs with frameworks of knowledge provided by other disciplines. In particular, the relationships between economics and other types of knowledge are assessed in part I of the volume ('Perspectives on economics and the dynamics of knowledge'). The contributions in part II ('The core and extensions of exchange-oriented theories') and in part III ('The core and extensions of production-oriented theories') consider the logical structure of the lines of research expounded above; they also focus on the historical processes through which each line of research generates themes of enquiry belonging to the whole domain of economics. Part IV ('From the ancients to the moderns: a reappraisal of the dynamics of change in economic theory') fulfils a double aim: on the one hand, to reconsider critically the exchange–production duality as a suitable analytical framework; on the other hand, to revisit the

[54] In particular, for the early stages in the evolution of economic knowledge it is not easy to draw clear-cut boundaries between economics, on the one hand, and politics, administration, science and law, on the other hand. (Suffice it to mention the cases of French physiocracy and Adam Smith.)

historical dynamics of economic knowledge in the light of such a distinction.

The Contributions

Part I of this volume, in particular, is meant to assess the types of knowledge characteristic of economics and social sciences in general with respect to other sciences. One important result of this enquiry is that it is relevant to distinguish between objects and methods of economics, and analytical tools developed by other disciplines. This can be inferred from the main conclusions drawn in this part. The first concerns the use in economics of testing procedures common in natural sciences, which are shown to be often inadequate; the second points to a number of apparent analogies to be found in the logical structure and evolution of economics and of a 'developed' natural science such as physics.

In his paper 'Is economics a science?' *Sir John Hicks* considers the distinguishing characters that a 'body of propositions' must meet in order to be defined as a science. The propositions must (1) be about real and observable phenomena, (2) be general about a whole class of phenomena, and (3) lead to predictions commanding a certain degree of belief. According to Hicks, 'all of these three [conditions] appear to be necessary, if the body of propositions is to be a science'. After considering the case of natural sciences, and mathematics in particular, he turns his attention to the nature of predictions in general. Hicks then points out that while economics might in certain cases pass test (1), it fails on the other two. Economics lacks generality and is not an experimental science because the facts analysed are, in general, non-repetitive. Even more importantly, economic predictions are of a 'weak' nature, so tied to the *ceteris paribus* clause as they are; but he adds that 'even though our propositions are weak it does not mean that they are useless'. Hicks concludes by stressing that economics 'is on the edge of science', because it uses quasi-scientific methods, 'and on the edge of history', because it is very much connected with the institutions and overriding concerns of the period considered.

Bernard Schmitt, in his paper on 'The process of formation of economics in relation to other sciences', first considers the exchange–production duality within different traditions of economic thought. He maintains that, whereas for classical theorists production is determined before exchange, for the marginalists production is analysed in the same way as exchange. He also maintains that, for John Maynard Keynes, all exchanges imply productions and there is full integration between the two phenomena. Schmitt then considers the analogies to be found between economics and natural sciences (physics in particular) by outlining three specific cases. First, the structures of Newton's classical mechanics and classical economic theories are compared; then Einstein's theory of relativity is related to marginalist general equilibrium. Finally, Keynesian economics finds its 'physical correspondence' in the theory of quanta. The 'quantum theory of production', whose origins are to be found in Keynes's work, allows for a concept of production and income that is radically different from that of the previous economists, and overcomes the difficulties associated with the dichotomy between real and monetary phenomena. This would allow economics to reach a 'golden age' status.

Part II has been conceived with two specific aims: first, to assess the foundations of the pure 'exchange' model, independently of its many applications; and second, to evaluate its present state and to open up new lines of enquiry.

The first chapter of this part is by *Maurice Allais* on 'The concepts of surplus and loss and the reformulation of the theories of stable general economic equilibrium and maximum efficiency'. It is to be situated within that framework of allocation where, given a flow of fixed resources, economic agents try to maximize their welfare. His analysis retraces the major steps of the progressive elaboration of the concepts of surplus and loss (starting from Ricardo, Cournot, Dupuit, Gossen, Jevons, Walras and Pareto), and leads him to reformulate the general theory of equilibrium and maximum efficiency. According to Allais, the concept of surplus represents 'the most powerful instrument of analysis in the entire theory of economics', both in the context of economic equilibrium and maximum efficiency, as well as for the study of the dynamic evolution of society. (In a situation of maximum efficiency, according to Pareto, it is impossible to improve the situation of one person without undermining that of others.) The analysis of the surplus also allows for the integration of money into theories of general equilibrium and maximum efficiency. Stable general economic equilibrium exists, if, and only if, there is no realizable surplus for any good. Allais gives the conditions which any indicator of efficiency must satisfy and formulates a new theory of the economy of markets which essentially bases economic dynamics on the search for the realization and distribution of surpluses, whereas the previous literature focused on the search for a system of equilibrium prices.

In the following chapter ('The problem of agents' beliefs in economic theory'), *Michael Bacharach* addresses himself to another fundamental issue in the 'exchange' research line. This is the fact that economic theories formulated within this scientific tradition refer to a 'model economy', in which individuals react to each other's signals by following certain basic assumptions ('beliefs') about the way in which other agents behave. Bacharach finds that the 'standard belief theory' consists of the following special theories: uncertainty is represented by assuming that the economic agent has a subjective probability distribution over states of the world that he regards as possible; 'learning by reasoning' requires that the agent believes all logical consequences of what he believes; learning by experience is associated with Bayesian revision; information gathering is based on expected utility maximization; the agents involved in a non-cooperative game (such as perfect competition) are assumed to choose actions that are optimal against each other; the agents hold the 'correct' theory and revise it according to the econometrician's standards; the agent knows all possibilities relevant to his decision. Bacharach shows that standard belief theory has its provenance in methodological rationalism (a view associated with Robbins, Mises, Machlup), and that 'rationality in belief' cannot be assessed unless the assumed 'good reasons' for holding a belief imply a condition that is practically feasible for the agent. The latter result shows that a true theory of rational beliefs involves elements of *a posteriori* knowledge and makes methodological rationalism incompatible with methodological apriorism. Standard belief theory is thus shown to be wanting on the basis of its own methodological criteria. It is also suggested that a better theory of beliefs might be developed by following an '*a posteriori*, deductive, rationalistic' approach.

In his paper on 'Price formation and the costs of exchange', *Dieter Helm* argues that exchanging goods and money involves time, information, effort and payments: it thus has associated costs and can be partially integrated with production theory. The Hicks–Pasinetti duality then comes under close scrutiny, and Helm maintains that 'taking a cost approach to price formation suggests that exchange is a special case of production'. According to a quite general definition, production costs are the costs of change, including both physical and psychological costs. Helm stresses the extent to which transactions are not only exchanges taking place in markets, but are themselves produced decisions incurring costs associated with their administration. Prices do not appear, nor are they just costlessly given, as in Walras. For firms facing transactions costs and imperfect competition, prices, rather than being exogenous data, can be considered as the outcome of a production activity. Helm then extends his analysis to the consumers' side, and argues that production also enters consumption decisions, based on two 'production activities' of the consumers – the investment in time in order to increase the utility associated with consumption; and search activity over goods to discover which will yield greatest utility. Thus the spheres of exchange and production appear to be closely knit together as the result of introducing a 'subjectivist' definition of production.

The historical process by which the original 'catallactic' framework was extended to include production and income distribution is reconstructed by *Klaus Hennings* in his chapter, 'The exchange paradigm and the theory of production and distribution'. The analytical core of early 'catallactics' took the quantities of the commodities available for exchange as given from outside the theory. However, as Hennings points out, it is conceptually possible to formulate models of the 'exchange' type, in which varying and endogenously determined stocks of commodities are allocated and traded. A first step in the extension was made with Jevons's consideration of exchange and production as a means for the satisfaction of wants. Menger conceived production as a process by which goods of 'higher order' are converted into goods of 'lower order' so as to increase final utility. Pareto introduced the idea of the formal equivalence between exchange and production through the concept of 'transformation'. (The latter can alternatively be interpreted as describing production or exchange.) This process of generalization also permitted economists to consider income distribution (interpreted as the reward for productive services) as a special case of the standard allocative model. Hennings points out that the extensions of the original 'exchange' paradigm were initially carried out within quite separate intellectual traditions (such as Marshall's theory of the 'industry', the Austrian theory of the time structure of production, the general equilibrium approach of Walras–Pareto). The acceptance gained by the general equilibrium approach since the 1930s with an increasing number of economists had, in Hennings's view, the effect of shifting the main emphasis within the 'exchange' paradigm towards theories more explicitly formulated within an equilibrium, static and 'perfectly competitive' framework.

Part III focuses upon the domain of the pure 'production' model, starting from the existing theories and with the aim of identifying a number of general issues. This will allow us to assess the existing contributions and to identify new directions of development.

The chapter by *Nicholas Georgescu-Roegen* ('Man and production') examines the general framework of productive activity, considered as man's most distinctive feature. After stressing that production, which makes use of 'exosomatic' organs, establishes the relative autonomy of mankind with respect to the availability of natural resources, Georgescu-Roegen maintains that non-renewable inputs remain a permanent constraint behind men's productive efforts. Coming to the consideration of production processes, it is argued that the determination of the 'analytical boundary' of each process is a necessary condition for describing input and output quantities. It is also argued that knowledge of what goes on inside any given process involves the division of that process by additional boundaries. Both inputs and outputs may consist of two distinct elements: the flows that enter the production process, but do not come out of it (or the flows coming out without having gone in), and the funds that enter and leave the process remaining unchanged. Georgescu-Roegen points out that the concepts of fund and flow bring to light new aspects of production activity, and that only in the special case of 'steady-state' factory production does the use of production functions *à la* Wicksteed not lead to a substantial loss of descriptive and analytical power. The flow–fund framework also allows new insights into the substitutability versus limitationality issue. Finally, it is maintained that the feasibility of single 'recipes' for production does not imply that the overall technology is viable,and that a necessary condition for viability is the existence of a given material (environmental) support. This latter requisite makes energy analysis an essential component of the theory of production. In particular, Georgescu-Roegen argues that dissipation of matter undermines the long-term survival of any technology, thus making productive activity depend either on conservation of resources or on revolutionary innovations affecting energy production.

The appraisal of the economists' approaches to production is continued in the paper by *Michael Landesmann* ('Conceptions of technology and the production process'). Landesmann draws a broad distinction between two ways of dealing with production: the 'descriptive-analytical' approach and the 'optimization' approach. The 'optimization' approach concentrates not on the production sphere itself, but on the rules which govern purchases and sales in input markets. The 'descriptive-analytical' approach concentrates on studying production activity in the first instance in the sphere where these activities actually take place. Landesmann expounds a number of behavioural principles that have been discovered by the followers of the 'descriptive-analytical' approach (these include the classical economists, students of industrial organization and modern economists such as Georgescu-Roegen). The chapter considers in detail how the two approaches confront each other in examining productive efficiency. The 'optimization' view considers efficiency problems to be mainly external to the individual productive unit. This presumption is not held by the other approach, for which efficiency problems, both technical and economic, usually arise in individual production units and are a crucial subject for research. In particular, the paper considers in detail the problems of input utilization, by adopting a 'time-structure' representation of the production process. This point of view permits Landesmann to reconsider the 'classical' theories of division of labour and productive organization (Smith, Babbage, Marx and Taylor). The 'time-structure' approach is then used in order to formulate an analytical framework for the study of factory production.

The 'descriptive-analytical' approach to technical change is shown at work in the paper by *Alberto Quadrio-Curzio* ('Technological scarcity: an essay on production and structural change'). This paper covers a field ('scarcity') that has traditionally been associated with the 'catallactic' or 'praxeological' approaches to economics. Quadrio-Curzio defines 'scarcity' in a non-praxeological way, following the theories of Ricardo and Sraffa. Instead of considering how scarcity influences the actions of individuals who allocate limited means amongst competing ends, Quadrio-Curzio sets himself the task of examining how non-produced, essential resources might constrain technical choice if the expansion path of the economy is subject to the full-employment condition. This approach leads to the discovery of a number of new results in the theory of linear production models. In particular, Quadrio-Curzio shows that the techniques would normally outnumber the produced commodities, and that two different methods of describing the production system ought to be used, depending on whether we focus on the 'single-period' or on the dynamic properties of the economy. In the former case, production is best described by the 'combined techniques' method. (This method allows a careful description of the 'linkages' between techniques at any given time.) In the latter case, production is best described by the 'disjointed techniques' method, in which the production system is split into a number of different subsystems, each one associated with a particular 'own' rate of maximal growth. On these premises, Quadrio-Curzio shows that the economy's 'physical' efficiency is continuously changing, that technical choice is influenced by the relative compatibility of the different techniques, and that technical progress 'embedded' into individual techniques is not necessarily the source of higher efficiency for the 'overall' technology. It is also shown that the 'optimal' sequence in which techniques might be operated depends on whether techniques are ranked according to relative profitability or according to their respective 'growth potential'.

Krishna Bharadwaj, in her paper 'Production and exchange in theories of price formation and economic transition', outlines an interpretation for 'primacy of production' in classical political economy, and for the 'shift to circulation' in the marginalist theories. In particular, Bharadwaj argues that, in the classical theories, the extent and form of the exchange relationships are intimately connected with the social organization of production. In such theories, exchange is mainly related to produced commodities, and commodity markets are conceived as an outcome of the way in which the corresponding production processes are carried out. 'Primacy of production' was suggested by certain authors of the medieval period, such as Aquinas, as a result of their concern for the needs of social reproduction. After the mercantilist period, it is with Petty and Cantillon that we again find a consideration of the material conditions of production and of the way in which exchanges are an essential element in the 'reproduction' of the economy. Their approach was taken up by Quesnay, Smith and Ricardo, thereby laying the foundations of classical political economy, which had a final development with Marx's surplus-value approach. A common feature of these latter contributions is the view that the nature of markets and the form that price takes depends on the existing organization of society. The marginalist writings marked a shift back to the primacy of exchange, and this is considered by Bharadwaj as a paradoxical outcome of the higher stage of development reached by European society in the marginalist period. (The large extension of division of labour in this period makes price appear to be generated by autonomous market forces, on which the marginalist writers concentrated their attention.) In the final section of her paper, Bharadwaj suggests that recent developments both in advanced industrial economies and in 'developing' economies have again brought to the fore the primacy of production.

Part IV offers a number of critical views on (1) the identification of the relationships between possible lines of research in economics; (2) the connections between changes in economic knowledge and the dynamics of economic reality; and (3) the character of scientific progress within economic theory.

The first chapter in this part is by *Christopher Bliss* on 'Progress and anti-progress in economic science'. His aim is to assess critically whether our science is characterized by the existence of alternative paradigms and, if so, whether this division follows the lines of the 'production' versus 'exchange' duality. In order to do this, Bliss defines three basic features required for a method to become a science: (1) the line of the discourse should respect the tenets of open and rational argument; (2) the discipline must embody some evidence (not necessarily experimentation); and (3) a comprehensive record of the results obtained should be kept and passed on to the next generations. According to Bliss, economics ought to pass fairly easily these three tests; he then concludes that in this sense economics may be considered as a science. Bliss is also convinced that economics has an inherent progress tendency, which comes from the accumulation of knowledge and from the fact that it deals with an 'objective reality which can be comprehended more or less effectively', without of course including consensus among scholars. Bliss is firmly convinced that disagreements have in many cases not resulted in schism, for the coexistence within a science of more than one paradigm indicates a fundamental division. And such a fundamental division is not to be found today in economics (leading him to reject the exchange–production dichotomy); although he accepts that it may have played a role in the history of the discipline.

The issue of alternative 'paradigms' in economic theorizing is also considered in the chapter by *Alberto Quadrio-Curzio* and *Roberto Scazzieri* ('The exchange–production duality and the dynamics of economic knowledge'). This paper maintains that it would not be entirely appropriate to consider the relationship between 'exchange'-oriented and 'production'-oriented theories as a dichotomy between mutually exclusive paradigms. Indeed it is stressed that in a variety of cases the development of economic knowledge has shown the mutual influence between the 'exchange' and the 'production' lines of research. The special interplay between these two research lines leads Quadrio-Curzio and Scazzieri to consider whether the general development of economic knowledge might not be interpreted as the outcome of two joint influences: a 'filter-up' effect from economic life to economic theories, and a 'filter-down' effect from economic theories to economic life. Quadrio-Curzio and Scazzieri argue that both effects work their way through a special correspondence between economic life and theories. When producibility prevails over scarcity in economic life and economists privilege a circular 'vision' of the economic system, the 'filter-up' and 'filter-down' effects tend to reinforce each other and the 'production' research line comes to the foreground. The same coincidence and mutual reinforcement occurs when scarcity prevails over producibility in economic life and economists favour a 'one-way' vision of the economic system. When the latter coincidence takes place, the 'exchange' research line dominates the economic profession. The authors stress that this mutual reinforcement of the two effects is not the rule; in this case the extensions of either research line to cover aspects of economic life that were originally excluded from it may often be interpreted as a reaction of accepted theory to the 'filter-up' effect from economic reality.

The final chapter of the volume is by *Luigi Pasinetti* on the 'Theory of value – a source of alternative paradigms in economic analysis'. In this paper, Pasinetti argues that the exchange–production duality can be traced back to a deeper dichotomy in the theories of value. Many precious insights are to be gained from the pre-theoretical stages of the discussions on value, where diverging principles become acceptable being considered within a normative framework. Pasinetti then identifies in Adam Smith and William Stanley Jevons, respectively, the reference points for discussing two alternative paradigms: (1) the *pure-preference model* (or pure-exchange model), which looks at all economic problems as if they were problems of optimum allocation of resources, and where prices are determined by individuals' preferences and resource endowment; (2) a *pure-labour economy model*, where production and exchange are inherently linked by labour specialization and where prices emerge from the necessity of an extensive division of labour. In particular, Pasinetti stresses the importance for each paradigm of developing its basic structure ('first skeleton') by concentrating on one single principle. This basic structure may be unfolded, in spite of successive generalizations of each paradigm, by identifying what is essential and cannot be left out from the theory under consideration. The exposition of the distinct ways in which prices are determined, and of the way in which the two lines of research are successful in integrating exchange and production leads Pasinetti to maintain that alternative visions of economic life may be associated with different aims of analysis. This ought to ensure a degree of autonomy for alternative frameworks.

Epilogue

Taken in their unity, the essays of this volume suggest that alternative lines of research in economics can be conceived as 'short cuts' which economists have been tracing in order to obtain 'task-specific' theories. (This feature of economic theories is prominent in the original formulations of each research line, even if it becomes somehow blurred by subsequent extensions of each line.) Such 'short cuts' have sometimes crossed each other, leading to cases of mutual fertilization. In the main, however, they have remained quite separate, in spite of the branching out of new research programmes from the original, 'task-specific' theories.

This situation ought to encourage economists to go deeper into the foundations of their subject, and to consider whether the material of economics might suggest new perspectives for the development of our discipline. After all, economic actions require aims, means and objective conditions involving the 'system of events' to which the actions belong. It may be that careful distinction between 'exchange'-oriented and 'production'-oriented theories highlights something that is missing from both types of theory and helps to bridge the gap between them.

REFERENCE BIBLIOGRAPHY

Accademici della Crusca (1741) *Vocabolario*, Francesco Pitteri, Venice.

Aftalion, A. (1913) *Les crises périodiques de surproduction*, M. Rivière, Paris.

Åkerman, J. (1940) 'The Meaning of Induction in Social Sciences', *Theoria*, 6, pp. 171–90.

— (1955) *Structures et cycles économiques* (1st edn 1944), 3 vols, Presses Universitaires de France, Paris.

Arrow, K.J. (1974) 'Limited Knowledge and Economic Analysis', *American Economic Review*, 64, pp. 1–10.

Baranzini, M. (1981) 'Taux d'intérêt, distribution du revenu, théorie des cycles vitaux et choix du portefeuille', *Kyklos*, 34, pp. 593–610.

— (1982) 'Introduction', and 'Can the Life-Cycle Theory Help in Explaining Income Distribution and Capital Accumulation?', in *Advances in Economic Theory*, ed. M. Baranzini, Basil Blackwell, Oxford, pp. 1–16, 243–61.

Battaglia, S. (1968) *Grande Dizionario della lingua italiana*, UTET, Turin, vol. V.

Bayes, T. (1763) 'An Essay toward Solving a Problem in the Doctrine of Chances', *Philosophical Transactions of the Royal Society*, 53, pp. 370–418.

Beccaria, C. (1764) 'Tentativo analitico sui contrabbandi', *Il Caffè*, 1, pp. 118–19. (English translation in *Precursors in Mathematical Economics: An Anthology*, ed. W.J. Baumol and S.M. Goldfeld, 1968, London School of Economics, London, pp. 149–50.)

Bentham, J. (1952–4) *Economic Writings* (critical edition, based on his printed works and unprinted manuscripts), ed. W. Stark, George Allen and Unwin, London.

Bernouilli, D. (1738) 'Specimen theoriae novae de mensura sortis', *Commentarii Academiae Scientiarum Imperialis Petropolitanae*, V, pp. 175–92. (English translation: *Econometrica*, 22 (1954), pp. 23–36.)

Bhaskar, R. (1979) *The Possibility of Naturalism* (*A Philosophical Critique of the Contemporary Human Sciences*), Harvester Press, Brighton.

Bianchini, M. (1982) *Alle origini della scienza economica*, Editrice Studium Parmense, Parma.

Blaug, M. (1976) 'Kuhn versus Lakatos *or* Paradigms versus Research Programmes in the History of Economics', in *Method and Appraisal in Economics*, ed. S. Latsis, Cambridge University Press, Cambridge, pp. 149–80.

— (1980) *The Methodology of Economics*, Cambridge University Press, Cambridge.

Bliss, C.J. (1975) *Capital Theory and the Distribution of Income*, North-Holland, Amsterdam/Oxford.

— (1983) 'Two Views of Macroeconomics', *Oxford Economic Papers*, 35, pp. 1–12.
Böhm-Bawerk, von, E. (1884–9) *Kapital und Kapitalzins*, Wagner, Innsbruck.
Boland, L.A. (1982) *The Foundations of Economic Method*, George Allen and Unwin, London.
Bortis, H. (1984) 'Employment in a Capitalist Economy', *Journal of Post Keynesian Economics*, 6, pp. 590–604.
Bouniatian, M. (1908) *Wirtschaftskrisen under Ueberkapitalisation*, E. Reinhard, Munich.
Brand, H.W. (1961) *The Fecundity of Mathematical Methods in Economic Theory*, D. Reidel, Dordrecht.
Briscoe, J. (1694) *A Discourse on the Late Funds of the Million-Act, Lottery-Act, and Bank of England*, 2nd edn, printed by J.D. and sold by R. Baldwin, London.
Brunner, O. (1968) *Neue Wege der Verfassungs- und Sozialgeschichte*, Vandenhoek & Ruprecht, Göttingen.
Buchanan, J.M. (1975) *The Limits of Liberty. Between Anarchy and Leviathan*, University of Chicago Press, Chicago/London.
Cairnes, J.E. (1875) *The Character and Logical Method of Political Economy*, Macmillan, London.
Caldwell, B.J. (1982) *Beyond Positivism: Economic Methodology in the Twentieth Century*, George Allen and Unwin, London.
— (1984) 'Praxeology and its Critics: an Appraisal', *History of Political Economy*, 16, pp. 363–79.
Cannan, E. (1923) *Wealth. A Brief Explanation of the Causes of Economic Welfare*, 2nd edn, P.S. King, London.
Capra, F. (1982) *The Turning Point: Science, Society and Rising Culture*, Fontana, London.
Carnap, R. (1938) *Logical Foundations of the Unity of Science*, in *International Encyclopaedia of Unified Science*, vol. 1, n. 1, Chicago University Press, Chicago.
Ceva, G. (1711) *De re numaria quoad fieri potuit geometrice tractata*, apud Albertum Pazzonum, Mantuae.
Chevalier, M. (1851) *Cours d'économie politique*, Meline, Cans, Brussels.
Clark, J.B. (1899) *The Distribution of Wealth*, Macmillan, New York/London.
Clark, J.M. (1952) 'J.M. Clark on J.B. Clark', in *The Development of Economic Thought, Great Economists in Perspective*, ed. H.W. Spiegel, John Wiley, New York; Chapman and Hall, London, pp. 592–612.
Coats, A.W. (1964) 'Value Judgements in Economics', *Yorkshire Bulletin of Economic and Social Research*, 16, pp. 53–67.
— (1969) 'Is there a "Structure of Scientific Revolutions" in Economics?', *Kyklos*, 22, pp. 289–96.
Collini, S., Winch, D. and Burrow, J. (1983) *That Noble Science of Politics. A Study in Nineteenth-Century Intellectual History*, Cambridge University Press, Cambridge.
Condillac (Bonnot, abbé de) E. (1776) *Le Commerce et le Gouvernement considérés relativement l'un à l'autre*, Amsterdam; Jobert et Cellot, Paris.
Cournot, A.A. (1838) *Recherches sur les principes mathématiques de la théorie des richesses*, Hachette, Paris.
Cozzi, T. (1969) *Sviluppo e stabilità dell'economia*, Fondazione Luigi Einaudi, Turin.

Craven, J. (1979) *The Distribution of the Product*, George Allen and Unwin, London.
Croce, B. (1900) 'Sul principio economico. Lettera al Professore Vilfredo Pareto', *Giornale degli Economisti*, ser. II, 21, pp. 15–26.
Daire, E. (ed.) (1846) *Physiocrates*, Guillaumin, Paris.
Deane, P. (1978) *The Evolution of Economic Ideas*, Cambridge University Press, Cambridge.
— (1983) 'The Scope and Method of Economic Science', *Economic Journal*, 93, pp. 1–12.
Debreu, G. (1959) *The Theory of Value*, John Wiley, New York.
— (1984) 'Economic Theory in the Mathematical Mode', *American Economic Review*, 74, pp. 267–78.
De Finetti, B. (1931) 'Sul significato della probabilità', *Fundamenta Mathematicae*, 17, pp. 298–329.
Del Vecchio, G. (1956) *Capitale e interesse* (1st edn 1915, under the title *Lineamenti generali della teoria dell'interesse*), Edizioni Scientifiche Einaudi, Turin.
Destutt de Tracy, A.L.C. (1823) *Traité d'économie politique*, Bougnet et Lévi, Paris.
Dupont de Nemours, P.S. (1846) 'De l'origine et des progrès d'une science nouvelle', in *Physiocrates*, vol. 1, ed. E. Daire, Guillaumin, Paris, pp. 335–66.
Edgeworth, F.Y. (1881) *Mathematical Psychics. An Essay on the Application of Mathematics to the Moral Sciences*, C. Kegan Paul, London.
Eichner, A.S. (1976) *The Megacorp and Oligopoly: Micro Foundations of Macro Dynamics*, Cambridge University Press, Cambridge.
— (ed.) (1983) *Why Economics is not yet a Science*, Macmillan, London.
Engle, R.F., Hendry, D.F. and Richard, J.F. (1982) 'Exogeneity', *Econometrica*, 51, pp. 277–304.
Ferrara, F. (1854) 'Introduzione', in *Biblioteca dell'Economista*, ser. I, vol. V, UTET, Turin, pp. V–LXIV.
— (1859) 'Introduzione', in *Biblioteca dell'Economista*, ser. II, vol. VII, UTET, Turin, pp. V–CXXV.
Fisher, I. (1907) *The Rate of Interest*, Macmillan, New York.
— (1930) *The Theory of Interest*, Macmillan, New York.
Fraser, L.M. (1937) *Economic Thought and Language. A Critique of Some Fundamental Economic Concepts*, A. and C. Black, London.
Friedman, M. (1953) 'The Methodology of Positive Economics', in *Essays in Positive Economics*, ed. M. Friedman, University of Chicago Press, Chicago, pp. 3–43.
Gambetta, G. and Sartore, O. (1983) 'Il concetto di causalità in econometria', in *Causalità e modelli probabilistici*, ed. M.C. Galavotti and G. Gambetta, CLUEB, Bologna, pp. 89–110.
Garegnani, P. (1984) 'Value and Distribution in the Classical Economists and Marx', *Oxford Economic Papers*, 36, pp. 291–325.
Georgescu-Roegen, N. (1971) *The Entropy Law and the Economic Process*, Harvard University Press, Cambridge, Mass.
Gioja, M. (1815–17) *Nuovo Prospetto delle Scienze Economiche*, Pirotta, Milan.
Gossen, H.H. (1983) *The Laws of Human Relations* (German original, published in 1854), MIT Press, Cambridge, Mass./London.

Grunberg, E. (1978) '"Complexity" and "Open Systems" in Economic Discourse', *Journal of Economic Issues*, 12, pp. 541–60.
Hahn, F.H. (1973) *On the Notion of Equilibrium in Economics. An Inaugural Lecture*, Cambridge University Press, Cambridge.
Hahn, F.H. and Matthews, R.C.O. (1964) 'The Theory of Economic Growth: A Survey', *Economic Journal*, 74, pp. 779–902.
— (1971) 'Postscript to the Theory of Economic Growth: A Survey', mimeo (English version of the postscript contained in the French translation published by Editions Economica, Paris, 1971).
Hanson, N. (1965) *Patterns of Discovery*, Cambridge University Press, Cambridge.
Harré, R. and Madden, E.H. (1975) *Causal Powers*, Basil Blackwell, Oxford.
Harris, D.J. (1978) *Capital Accumulation and Income Distribution*, Stanford University Press, Stanford, Calif.; Routledge and Kegan Paul, London.
Harrod, R.F. (1939) 'An Essay in Dynamic Theory', *Economic Journal*, 49, pp. 14–33.
Hayek, F.A. (1967) *Studies in Philosophy, Politics and Economics*, University of Chicago Press, Chicago.
Hempel, C. (1966) *Foundations of Natural Science*, Prentice-Hall, Englewood Cliffs, NJ.
Hicks, J. (1974) *Value and Capital. An Inquiry into Some Fundamental Principles of Economic Theory* (1st edn 1939), Clarendon Press, Oxford.
— (1975) 'The Scope and Status of Welfare Economics', *Oxford Economic Papers*, 27, pp. 307–26.
— (1976) '"Revolutions" in Economics', in *Method and Appraisal in Economics*, ed. S.J. Latsis, Cambridge University Press, Cambridge, pp. 207–18.
— (1977) *Economic Perspectives*, Clarendon Press, Oxford.
— (1979) *Causality in Economics*, Basil Blackwell, Oxford.
— (1983a) 'Preface', in *Classics and Moderns*, vol. III of *Collected Essays on Economic Theory*, Basil Blackwell, Oxford, pp. xiii–xvi.
— (1983b) 'A Discipline not a Science', in *Classics and Moderns*, vol. III of *Collected Essays on Economic Theory*, Basil Blackwell, Oxford, pp. 365–75.
Hollis, M. and Nell, E.J. (1975) *Rational Economic Man*, Cambridge University Press, Cambridge.
Hume, D. (1955) *An Inquiry Concerning Human Understanding* (1st edn 1748), ed. C.W. Hendel, Bobbs & Merrill, Indianapolis, Ind.
Hutchison, T.W. (1938) *The Significance and Basic Postulates of Economic Theory*, Macmillan, London.
— (1964) *'Positive' Economics and Policy Objectives*, Allen and Unwin, London.
— (1976) 'On the History and Philosophy of Science and Economics', in *Method and Appraisal in Economics*, ed. S.J. Latsis, Cambridge University Press, Cambridge, pp. 181–205.
— (1978) *On Revolutions and Progress in Economic Knowledge*, Cambridge University Press, Cambridge.
— (1981) *The Politics and Philosophy of Economics (Marxians, Keynesians and Austrians)*, Basil Blackwell, Oxford.
Isnard, A.N. (1781) *Traité des richesses*, F. Grasset, London and Lausanne.
Jeffrey, R. (1984) 'De Finetti's Probabilism', *Synthèse. An International Journal of Epistemology, Methodology and Philosophy of Science*, 60, pp. 73–90.
Jevons, W.S. (1879) *The Theory of Political Economy* (1st edn 1871), 2nd edn, revised and enlarged, Macmillan, London.

Kaldor, N. (1955/6) 'Alternative Theories of Distribution', *Review of Economic Studies*, 23, pp. 83–100.
— (1957) 'A Model of Economic Growth', *Economic Journal*, 67, pp. 591–624.
— (1972) 'The Irrelevance of Equilibrium Economics', *Economic Journal*, 82, pp. 1237–55.
Keynes, J.M. (1936) *The General Theory of Employment, Interest and Money*, Macmillan, London.
— (1973–) *The Collected Writings of John Maynard Keynes*, ed. A. Robinson and D. Moggridge, Macmillan, London; Cambridge University Press, Cambridge.
Keynes, J.N. (1890) *The Scope and Method of Political Economy*, Macmillan, London.
Klappholz, K. (1964) 'Value Judgements and Economics', *British Journal for the Philosophy of Science*, 15, pp. 97–114.
Knight, F.H. (1956) *On the History and Method in Economics, Selected Essays*, Chicago University Press, Chicago.
Koopmans, T.C. (1951) 'Analysis of Production as an Efficient Combination of Activities', in *Activity Analysis of Production and Allocation*, ed. T.C. Koopmans, Yale University Press, New Haven/London, pp. 33–97.
— (1957) *Three Essays on the State of Economic Science*, McGraw-Hill, New York/Toronto/London.
— (1979) 'Economics among the Sciences', *American Economic Review*, 69, pp. 1–13.
Kornai, J. (1971) *Anti-Equilibrium*, North-Holland, Amsterdam/Oxford.
Kotarbiński, T. (1960) 'Concept of Action', *Journal of Philosophy*, 57, pp. 215–22.
— (1965) *Praxiology. An Introduction to the Sciences of Efficient Action*, Pergamon Press, Oxford; PWN-Polish Scientific Publishers, Warsaw.
Kregel, J.A. (1976) 'Economic Methodology in the face of Uncertainty', *Economic Journal*, 86, pp. 209–25.
Kuhn, T.S. (1962) *The Structure of Scientific Revolutions*, University of Chicago Press, Chicago.
— (1977) *The Essential Tension: Selected Studies in Scientific Tradition and Change*, University of Chicago Press, Chicago.
Lakatos, I. (1970) 'Falsification and the Methodology of Scientific Research Programmes', in *Criticism and the Growth of Knowledge*, ed. I. Lakatos and A. Musgrave, Cambridge University Press, Cambridge, pp. 91–195.
— (1978) 'History of Science and its Rational Reconstructions', (1st edn, 1971), in *Philosophical Papers*, vol. I: *The Methodology of Scientific Research Programmes*, ed. J. Worrall and G. Currie, Cambridge University Press, Cambridge, pp. 102–38.
Lakatos, I. and Musgrave, A. (ed.) (1970) *Criticism and the Growth of Knowledge*, Cambridge University Press, Cambridge.
Latsis, S.J. (ed.) (1976) *Method and Appraisal in Economics*, Cambridge University Press, Cambridge.
Leon, P. (1967) *Structural Change and Growth in Capitalism*, Johns Hopkins University Press, Baltimore, Md.
Leontief, W.W. (1953) 'Static and Dynamic Theory', Part 1 of *Studies in the Structure of the American Economy*, ed. W.W. Leontief, Oxford University Press, Oxford/New York, pp. 1–90.
— (1971) 'Theoretical Assumptions and Nonobserved Facts', *American Economic Review*, 61, pp. 74–81.

— (1983) 'Foreword', in *Why Economics is not yet a Science*, ed. A.S. Eichner, Macmillan, London, pp. vii–xi.

Leroy-Beaulieu, P. (1896) *Traité théorique et pratique d'économie politique*, Guillaumin, Paris.

Lichtenstein, P.M. (1983) *An Introduction to Post-Keynesian and Marxian Theories of Value and Price*, Macmillan, London.

Locke, J. (1979) *An Essay Concerning Human Understanding* (1st edn 1690), Clarendon Press, London.

Lombardini, S. (1983) *Il metodo della scienza economica: passato e futuro*, UTET, Turin.

Lombardini, S. and Nicola, P. C. (1974) 'Income Distribution and Economic Development in Ricardian and Walrasian Models', in *Proceedings of the 11th Polish–Italian Conference on Applications of Systems Theory to Economy Management and Technology*, Pugnochiuso, Italy, pp. 294–320.

Löwe, A. (1935) *Economics and Sociology. A Plea for Co-operation in the Social Sciences*, George Allen and Unwin, London.

— (1965) *On Economic Knowledge. Toward a Science of Political Economics*, Harper and Row, New York/Evanston.

Lucas, R.E. (1980) 'Rules, Discretion, and the Role of the Economic Adviser', in *Rational Expectations and Economic Policy*, ed. S. Fischer, University of Chicago Press, Chicago, pp. 199–210.

McCloskey, D.N. (1983) 'The Rhethoric of Economics', *Journal of Economic Literature*, 21, pp. 481–517.

Macpherson, C.B. (1962) *The Political Theory of Possessive Individualism. Hobbes to Locke*, Oxford University Press, Oxford.

Malinvaud, E. (1966) *Statistical Methods of Econometrics*, Rand-McNally, Chicago.

Marshall, A. (1961) *Principles of Economics* (1st edn 1890; 5th edn 1907), ed. C.W. Guillebaud, Macmillan, London.

Marx, K. (1969) *Theories of Surplus Value* (1st edn 1905–10), Lawrence and Wishart, London.

— (1983) *Capital. A Critique of Political Economy* (German original, published in 1867), vol. 1, book 1, Lawrence and Wishart, London.

Meade, J.E. (1963) 'The Rate of Profits in a Growing Economy', *Economic Journal*, 73, pp. 161–5.

Menger, C. (1871) *Grundsätze der Volkswirtschaftslehre*, W. Braumüller, Vienna.

— (1883) *Untersuchungen über die Methode der Sozialwissenschaften und der politischen Oekonomie insbesondere*, Duncker and Humblot, Leipzig.

— (1963) *Problems of Economics and Sociology* (1st edn 1883), ed. L. Schneider, University of Illinois Press, Urbana, Ill.

Mill, J.S. (1924) *Autobiography*, published from the original manuscript in the Columbia University Library, Columbia University Press, New York.

— (1965) *Principles of Political Economy with Some of Their Applications to Social Philosophy* (1st edn 1848), ed. J.M. Robson, with an Introduction by R.F. McRae, University of Toronto Press, Toronto; Routledge and Kegan Paul, London.

Mises, L. von (1949) *Human Action. A Treatise on Economics* (German original, published in 1940), William Hodge, London/Edinburgh/Glasgow.

Morgenstern, O. (1963) 'The Limits of the Use of Mathematics in Economics', in *Mathematics and the Social Sciences Monographs*, American Academy of Politi-

cal and Social Science, Philadelphia, Penn.
— (1971) 'L'économie est-elle une science exacte?', *La Recherche*, Paris, 18, pp. 1023–8.
Myint, H. (1946) 'The Classical View of the Economic Problem', *Economica*, 13, pp. 119–30.
Neumann, J. von (1935–7) 'Ueber ein Oekonomisches Gleichungs-System und eine Verallgemeinerung des Brouwerschen Fixpunktsatzes', in *Ergebnisse eines Mathematischen Kolloquiums*, Vienna, vol. VIII, pp. 73–83; English translation: 'A Model of General Equilibrium', *Review of Economic Studies*, 1945/6, pp. 1–9.
Neurath, O. (1911) 'Nationalökonomie und Weltlehre [eine systematische Untersuchung]', *Zeitschrift für Volkswirtschaft, Sozialpolitik und Verwaltung*, 20, pp. 52 ff.
Nozick, R. (1977) 'On Austrian Methodology', *Synthèse. An International Journal for Epistemology, Methodology and Philosophy of Science*, 36, pp. 353–92.
Oppenheimer, P.M. (1983) 'A Little Clear Thinking. A Centenary Appraisal of J.M. Keynes', *New Society*, 70, pp. 128–9.
Oxford English Dictionary (1933), vol. III, Clarendon Press, Oxford.
Pantaleoni, M. (1897) 'Del carattere delle divergenze d'opinione esistenti tra economisti', *Giornale degli economisti*, 2nd ser., 15, pp. 501–30.
Papandreou, A. (1958) *Economics as a Science*, J.B. Lippencott, Chicago.
Papineau, D. (1979) *Theory and Meaning*, Clarendon Press, Oxford.
Pareto, V. (1906) *Manuale di economia politica, con una introduzione alla scienza sociale*, Società Editrice Libraria, Milan.
— (1911) *Economie mathématique,* in *Encyclopédie des sciences mathématiques*, tom. I, vol. IV, Gauthier-Villars, Paris.
Pasinetti, L.L. (1960) 'A Mathematical Formulation of the Ricardian System', *Review of Economic Studies*, 27, pp. 78–98.
— (1962) 'The Rate of Profit and Income Distribution in Relation to the Rate of Economic Growth', *Review of Economic Studies*, 29, pp. 267–79.
— (1964/5) 'Causalità e interdipendenza nell'analisi econometrica e nella teoria economica', *Annuario dell'Università Cattolica del S. Cuore*, Milan, pp. 233–50.
— (1965) 'A New Theoretical Approach to the Problems of Economic Growth', in *Econometric Approach to Development Planning*, North-Holland, Amsterdam, pp. 571–696.
— (1974) *Growth and Income Distribution, Essays in Economic Theory*, Cambridge University Press, Cambridge.
— (1981) *Structural Change and Economic Growth, A Theoretical Essay on the Dynamics of the Wealth of Nations*, Cambridge University Press, Cambridge.
— (1983) 'The Accumulation of Capital', *Cambridge Journal of Economics*, 7, pp. 405–11.
Pietranera, G. (1963) *Teoria del valore e dello sviluppo capitalistico in Adamo Smith*, Feltrinelli, Milan.
Popper, K. (1961) *Poverty of Historicism* (1st edn 1944), Harper and Row, New York.
— (1970) 'Normal Science and its Dangers', in *Criticism and the Growth of Knowledge*, ed. I. Lakatos and A. Musgrave, Cambridge University Press, Cambridge, pp. 51–8.
— (1981) *Objective Knowledge: An Evolutionary Approach* (1st edn 1972), Clarendon Press, Oxford.

Quadrio-Curzio, A. and Scazzieri, R. (ed.) (1977) *Protagonisti del pensiero economico*, vol. I: *Nascita e affermazione del marginalismo (1871–90)*; vol. II: *Tradizione e rivoluzione in economia politica (1890–1936)*, Il Mulino, Bologna.
Quadrio-Curzio, A. and Scazzieri, R. (1982a) 'La formazione delle "idee cardine": rivoluzione industriale e economia politica', in *Protagonisti del pensiero economico. Rivoluzione industriale e economia politica (1817–1848)*, ed. A. Quadrio-Curzio and R. Scazzieri, Il Mulino, Bologna, pp. 11–42.
— (1982b) 'La formazione delle "idee cardine": struttura produttiva, scambio e mercati', in *Protagonisti del pensiero economico. Struttura produttiva, scambio e mercati (1848–1872)*, ed. A. Quadrio-Curzio and R. Scazzieri, Il Mulino, Bologna, pp. 11–48.
— (1984) 'Sui momenti costitutivi dell'economia politica', *Giornale degli Economisti e Annali di Economia*, 43 (new ser.), pp. 37–76.
Quesnay, F. (1758) *Tableau économique*, Versailles.
— (1767) 'Lettre de M. Alpha, Maître ès-Arts, à l'Auteur des Ephémérides, sur le langage de la Science économique', in *Ephémérides du citoyen*, vol. 10, pt 2, pp. 163–217.
Ramsey, F.P. (1931) 'Truth and Probability', in *The Foundations of Mathematics and other Logical Essays*, ed. F.P. Ramsey, Harcourt Brace, New York, pp. 156–98.
Ravetz, J. (1971) *Scientific Knowledge and its Social Problems*, Clarendon Press, Oxford.
Ricardo, D. (1951) *On the Principles of Political Economy and Taxation* (1st edn 1817; 2nd edn 1819; 3rd edn 1821), vol. I of *Works and Correspondence of David Ricardo*, ed. P. Sraffa, Cambridge University Press, Cambridge.
— (1951–73) *The Works and Correspondence of David Ricardo*, 11 vols, ed. P. Sraffa with the collaboration of M. Dobb, Cambridge University Press, Cambridge.
Richelet, P. (1785) *Dictionnaire de la langue française ancienne et moderne*, Brandmüller, Basle.
Robbins, L. (1933a) 'Introduction', in P.H. Wicksteed, *The Common Sense of Political Economy and Selected Papers and Reviews on Economic Theory*, Routledge, London.
— (1933b) 'Production (Theory. Definition of the Term)', in *Encyclopaedia of the Social Sciences*, ed. E.R.A. Seligman, vol. XI, Macmillan, New York, pp. 462–7.
— (1935) *An Essay on the Nature and Significance of Economic Science*, 2nd edn, Macmillan, London.
— (1981) 'Economics and Political Economy', *American Economic Review, Papers and Proceedings*, 71, pp. 1–10.
Robertson, D.H. (1961) *Growth, Wages, Money*, Cambridge University Press, Cambridge.
Robinson, J. (1956) *The Accumulation of Capital*, Macmillan, London.
— (1962) *Essays in the Theory of Economic Growth*, Macmillan, London.
Romagnosi, G. (1827) 'Quesito. Il modo usato da alcuni scrittori di oggidì nel trattare le Dottrine economiche è forse plausibile?', *Annali Universali di Statistica*, 13, pp. 23–30.
— (1835) 'Ordinamento della economica dottrina', in *Opere*, vol. X, Piatti, Florence, pp. 21–40.

Samuelson, P.A. (1947) *Foundations of Economic Analysis*, Harvard University Press, Cambridge, Mass.
Say, J.B. (1817) *Traité d'économie politique* (1st edn 1803), 3rd edn, Déterville, Paris.
Schlick, M. (1930) *Fragen der Ethik*, Julius Springer, Vienna.
Schmitt, B. (1984) *Inflation, Chômage et Malformations du Capital,* preface by H. Guitton, Economica, Paris; Castella, Albeuve.
Schmoller, G. (1883) 'Zur Methodologie der Staats- und Sozialwissenschaften', *Jahrbuch für Gesetzgebung, Verwaltung, und Volkswirtschaft*, 7, pp. 965–94.
Schoeffler, S. (1955) *The Failure of Economics: A Diagnostic Study*, Harvard University Press, Cambridge, Mass.
Schumpeter, J.A. (1954) *History of Economic Analysis*, edited from manuscript by E. Boody Schumpeter, Allen and Unwin, London.
Sen, A.K. (1971) 'Choice Functions and Revealed Preference', *Review of Economic Studies*, 38, pp. 307–17.
— (1978) 'On the Labour Theory of Value: Some Methodological Issues', *Cambridge Journal of Economics*, 2, pp. 175–90.
Shackle, G.L.S. (1972) *Epistemics and Economics: A Critique of Economic Doctrines*, Cambridge University Press, Cambridge.
— (1979) 'On Hicks's Causality in Economics: A Review Article', *Greek Economic Review*, 1, pp. 43–55.
Sidgwick, H. (1883) *The Principles of Political Economy*, Macmillan, London.
Simon, H.A. (1955) 'Causality and Econometrics: Comment', *Econometrica*, 23, pp. 193–5.
Smith, A. (1776) *An Inquiry into the Nature and Causes of the Wealth of Nations*, W. Strahan and T. Cadell, London.
Solow, R.M. (1963) *Capital Theory and the Rate of Return*, North-Holland, Amsterdam/Oxford.
— (1967) 'The Interest Rate and Transition between Techniques', in *Socialism, Capitalism and Economic Growth: Essays Presented to Maurice Dobb*, ed. C.H. Feinstein, Cambridge University Press, Cambridge, pp. 30–9.
— (1970) *Growth Theory: An Exposition*, Clarendon Press, Oxford.
Sombart, W. (1929) 'Economic Theory and Economic History', *Economic History Review*, 2, pp. 1–19.
Spaventa, L. (1962) 'Effetti di variazioni strutturali nella composizione della domanda sulla produttività del lavoro e sulla occupazione', in *Nuovi problemi di sviluppo economico*, ed. L. Spaventa, Boringhieri, Turin, pp. 256–81.
Spiethoff, A. (1903) 'Die Krisentheorien von Tugan-Baranovsky u. Pohle', *Jahrbuch für Gesetzgebung, Verwaltung und Volkswirtschaft*, 27, pp. 679–708.
— (1952) 'The "Historical" Character of Economic Theories', *Journal of Economic History*, 12, pp. 131–9.
— (1953) 'Pure Theory and Economic Gestalt Theory: Ideal Types and Real Types', in *Enterprise and Secular Change*, ed. F.C. Lane and J.C. Riemersma, Irwin, Homewood, Ill., pp. 444–63.
Sraffa, P. (1960) *Production of Commodities by Means of Commodities*, Cambridge University Press, Cambridge.
Stegmüller, W., Balzer, W. and Spohn, W. (ed.) (1982) *Philosophy of Economics. Proceedings, Münich, July 1981*, Springer-Verlag, Berlin/New York.
Steuart, Sir J. (1966) *An Inquiry into the Principles of Political Oeconomy* (1st edn 1767), Oliver and Boyd for the Scottish Economic Society, Edinburgh/London.

Stigler, G.J. (1984) 'Economics – The Imperial Science?', *Scandinavian Journal of Economics*, 86, pp. 301–13.

Suppe, F. (1977) *The Structure of Scientific Theories*, University of Illinois Press, Urbana, Ill.

Suppes, P. (1970) *A Probabilistic Theory of Causality*, North-Holland, Amsterdam.

— (1981) *Logique du probable*, Flammarion, Paris.

Suviranta, B.R. (1923) *The Theory of the Balance of Trade in England. A Study in Mercantilism*, Helsinki, Suomal. Kirjall. Seuran Kirjap. O.Y.

Theocharis, R.D. (1983) *Early Developments in Mathematical Economics*, 2nd edn, Macmillan, London.

Tintner, G. (1968) *Methodology of Mathematical Economics and Econometrics*, Chicago University Press, Chicago.

Tribe, K. (1978) *Land, Labour and Economic Discourse*, Routledge and Kegan Paul, London.

Tugan-Baranovsky, M.I. (1894) *Promyshlennye krizisy v sovremennoi Anglii* (*Industrial Crises in England*), I.N. Skorochodova, St Petersburg.

Valeriani, L. (1804) *Lezione inaugurale di pubblica economia,* a S. Tommaso D'Aquino, Bologna.

— (1816) *Apologia della formola p=i/o*, Marsigli, Bologna.

— (1817) *Discorso apologetico (. . .)*, Marsigli, Bologna.

Walras, L. (1874) *Eléments d'économie politique pure*, Corbaz, Lausanne.

Walsh, V. and Gram, H. (1980) *Classical and Neoclassical Theories of General Equilibrium*, Oxford University Press, Oxford.

Whately, R. (1847) *Introductory Lectures on Political Economy*, delivered at Oxford in Easter Term, 1831, 3rd edn, revised and enlarged, John W. Parker, London.

— (1853) *Elements of Logic* (1st edn 1826), reprinted from the ninth (octavo) edition, John W. Parker, London.

Wicksteed, P.H. (1933) *The Common Sense of Political Economy* (1st edn 1910), J. Routledge, London.

Wilber, C. and Harrison, R. (1978) 'The Methodological Basis of Institutional Economics: Pattern Model, Story Telling, and Holism', *Journal of Economic Issues*, 12, pp. 61–89.

Winch, D. (1983) 'Science and the Legislator: Adam Smith and After', *Economic Journal*, 93, pp. 501–20.

Zamagni, S. (1983) 'Strumentalismo causale *versus* realismo causale in economia', in *Causalità e modelli probabilistici*, ed. M.C. Galavotti and G. Gambetta, CLUEB, Bologna, pp. 111–46.

Zawadzki, W. (1914) *Les mathématiques appliquées à l'économie politique*, Rivière, Paris.

Part I
Perspectives on Economics and the Dynamics of Knowledge

2

Is Economics a Science?

JOHN HICKS

I INTRODUCTION

The first thing to decide, when one attempts to answer my question, is what one is to mean by science. The English, and French, word *science* – it is substantially the same word in many other languages – is derived from the Latin verb *scire*, to know; the German *Wissenschaft*, derived from *wissen*, has the same origin. So one may take it that etymologically science just means knowledge. Now if science just means knowledge, a science is just a body of knowledge; but I think that all would agree that that is too wide a definition to be of use. A good biography, say of Napoleon or of Beethoven, contains a body of knowledge; but no one would want to say that it is a science. If my discussion is to be at all interesting, I must start from a narrower definition.

II DEFINITION OF SCIENCE

I need something which fits the natural sciences, which all would agree to be sciences, but it must not be a mere list of the natural sciences. It must be something which can be used as a test, to settle what is a science and what is not. The best definition I can think of, which would meet this demand, is the following.

A science, I would say, consists of a body of propositions, which have three distinguishing characters. (1) They are about real things, things we observe, about phenomena. (2) They are general propositions, about classes of phenomena, about relations between the properties of classes of phenomena. (3) They are propositions on which it is possible to base predictions, predictions which command some degree of belief. All of these three appear to be necessary, if the body of propositions is to be a science.

It is clear at once from this definition why biography, or indeed any piece of narrative history, is not a science. It passes my first test, since it is concerned with real events, which actually happened; but it fails on the second. It is not concerned with classes of phenomena; for each of the events which it records is unique. Only when they are not treated as unique, but they are in some way classified, can they be analysed by something analogous to scientific method.

That, I think, will be non-controversial; but there is another consequence of my definition which may be found more surprising. Mathematics is not a science. It is about concepts, and the relations between concepts, not about phenomena. Its propositions are logically true; no observation is needed to confirm them. It did indeed take many centuries of mathematical development before mathematicians themselves became clear on the matter. (There are propositions in Euclid that look as if they were being 'proved' by cutting up bits of paper, or papyrus, and moving them about.)[1] One may, however, now take it to be established that mathematics is purely formal, that it is a branch of logic. The sciences, though they make use, enormous use, of mathematics, are themselves not branches of logic.

This holds, it is important to notice, not only for pure mathematics, but also for some branches of mathematics which we commonly describe as applied. The problems that are studied in applied mathematics have often been suggested by the scientist; but the mathematics is independent of the relation to science. It may be that Newtonian mechanics would never have been invented if there had not existed important phenomena that could be explained with its assistance; nevertheless its central propositions do not depend on those observations. It would still be true that a particle which moved with an acceleration directed toward a fixed point would exhibit the property known as constancy of angular momentum (Kepler's second law, equal areas in equal times), even though no body, the motion of which could even approximately be explained by this theorem, had ever been discovered. In spite of the intimate connection between science and applied mathematics, it makes for clarity to distinguish between them.

This, we shall find, is a matter of importance in relation to economics. There is a branch of economics, mathematical economics, which has an unquestionable status as a branch of applied mathematics; it is indeed a much more unquestionable status nowadays than it was when I first came to it myself fifty years ago.[2] But this does not mean that it is to be included in science, nor even that it necessarily counts, like Newtonian mechanics, as auxiliary to science. The relation to observable phenomena of those

[1] Thus it was that Hume could say, in 1739, that 'algebra and arithmetic are the only sciences, in which we can carry on a chain of reasoning to any degree of intricacy, and yet preserve a perfect exactness and certainty. . . . Geometry can scarce be esteemed a perfect and infallible science' (*Treatise* III.1.). Though the arithmetization of geometry had been begun by Descartes, it had not, in Hume's day, made much progress. He naturally took his idea of geometry from Euclid.

[2] The turning-point was von Neumann's 'Model of General Economic Equilibrium', first published, in German, in Vienna in 1937.

parts of mathematical economics that are mathematically most interesting remains very much an open question.

III THEORY AND PREDICTIONS

I now turn to my third test, by prediction, on which I have much more to say. There are several kinds of prediction, which it is most important to distinguish. Extraordinary confusions, in philosophy and, as we shall see, in economics also, have resulted from failure to distinguish them.

The first line to be drawn is between the conditional and the unconditional. A conditional prediction says that something will happen, if some condition is satisfied – a condition that we know how to describe. An unconditional prediction makes no such qualifications.

The unconditional prediction, that something will happen – just like that – is the plain man's idea of prediction. It is what the kings of old expected from their prophets, their astrologers and their soothsayers; and it is what the modern forecaster, in economics or in other fields, will be taken by the public to be doing, unless he takes great pains to protect himself. The scientist, however, does not claim to foresee the future; although, as we shall see, there are some sciences which, for special reasons, are able to make some sorts of unconditional predictions, the normal type of scientific prediction is the conditional. With experimental sciences that is very obvious. Every prediction of the result of an experiment is a conditional prediction; the steps which have to be taken to set up the experiment are the condition from which it is claimed that the results will follow. It may indeed be said that the propositions, or laws, which, on the view I have been advancing, themselves constitute the science, are also predictions that the law will hold when its condition is realized.

It is no derogation from the status of a science that its predictions are conditional predictions; for it is indeed by its conditional predictions that science has been able to transform the world. It has helped us to foresee the consequences of human actions, of many kinds and in many fields. The action is the condition, or one of the conditions, for the event to follow.

Once we recognize that the normal scientific prediction is a conditional prediction, the special case of the scientific unconditional prediction fits into place. It is one that has grown out of a conditional prediction; but the conditions are such that their fulfilment is taken for granted. (Compare what happens in everyday life, in fields that have little directly to do with science. It has been arranged that an event will occur at some date in the future; that there will be a presidential election in the United States in November 1988 is a good example. Something might come along that would upset that arrangement; but we regard it as so unlikely that we leave it out of account.)

The chief examples of unconditional prediction that are scientific are in astronomy. The astronomer can tell us, with remarkable precision, just when there will be an eclipse of the moon; he can do this quite unconditionally. He bases his prediction upon scientific laws, which are conditional; but he has similarly been able to satisfy himself that in the particular case the conditions must be met. One reason he can do this is that the phenomena he studies are beyond the range of being influenced by human action; but there is another, that he has been able so to circumscribe his description of the phenomena that he can feel sure that there are no conditions which he has not taken into account.

I now turn to a second distinction, within the field of conditional predictions. A conditional prediction itself may be strong or it may be weak. If it is strong, it states that, given the stated conditions, the event will follow; if it is weak, it says no more than that the event will follow, if there is no disturbance. That is to say, no more is claimed in the case of a weak prediction than that some of the conditions for the event to follow have been identified. There may be others, which we cannot specify, or cannot specify as yet.

Much of what is written about scientific method takes it for granted that scientific, conditional, predictions are strong predictions. Thus when it is claimed by Popper (1959) that the test of a prediction being scientific is that it can be falsified by experience, it must be of strong predictions that he is thinking. A strong prediction, that the predicted event will occur, under stated conditions, must be either confirmed or refuted by the event. Either what is predicted does occur, or it does not. A weak prediction, that the event will occur, if there are no disturbances, cannot be confirmed, nor can it be refuted, by what is found to happen. If the event does occur, all we can say is that if the prediction was correct, there appear to have been no disturbances, or no sufficient disturbances. If the event does not occur, we can say no more than that if the prediction was correct, then there were disturbances. In neither case is it shown, at all directly, by the experience that the prediction was right or wrong.

Now it is undoubtedly true that there are many scientific predictions which we treat as being strong predictions (just as – we saw – there are many predictions which we treat as unconditional, like the case of the apparently unconditional prediction about the American election). But even in case of such assured predictions, it is doubtful if it is wise to make a rule of regarding them as perfectly strong. To claim that a scientific law is perfectly strong would seem to imply that knowledge in that direction has reached its limits; that in that direction there can be no further progress. That is a large claim to make. In the great days of Newtonian mechanics it was natural to make it:

> Nature and Nature's laws lay hid in night;
> God said, Let Newton be! and all was light.
>
> (Pope)

but even physics, in this century, does not look quite like that.

Once it is recognized that the perfectly strong prediction is a limiting case, the structure of science becomes easier to understand. All scientific laws are based on observations; they are generalizations from observations; that is to say, they are inductions. Now it is well known that however many instances have been found where a relation holds, that in itself gives no guarantee that exceptions will not be discovered. No induction can provide a proof, a complete proof. Nevertheless, when there are several propositions that have been (provisionally) established by induction, they can have logical, or particularly mathematical, consequences; and the consequences may be such that they can be tested empirically. The test, again, is an induction; it provides no proof. But when several (inductive) propositions have been provisionally established, and it has also been shown that there is a logical connection between them, each of them fortifies the others. The evidence in favour of each becomes evidence in favour of others. The inductions, having been shown to be logically related, have more evidence in their favour than each would have if it were taken separately. So it may be possible to build it up, until the evidence for the whole interconnected group, or theory, becomes such that we can draw what we are prepared to regard as strong predictions from it.

That, I believe, is the proper use of the term *theory* in science. The word has other meanings in other branches of knowledge. A mathematical theory (theory of numbers, theory of functions and so on) is just a branch of mathematics. A scientific theory is a body of reasoning with an empirical basis. When Newton said *'hypotheses non fingo'* (I am not just making hypotheses), what he meant by hypothesis was a piece of reasoning without empirical basis, something which had just been thought up – as we might say, a pure hypothesis. Scientific theories are not pure hypotheses; that is what Newton meant. In spite of the Romantics, who attach such importance to the scientist's flashes of inspiration (as if the scientist were a poet!), I maintain that Newton was right.[3]

It is of course not only previously established empirical relationships which the scientist joins together by his reasoning. The reasoning often suggests new empirical relations, which, if the previous inductions are accepted, we should expect to hold; these in their turn can be tested, by observation or experiment. If the experiment is successful, it adds to our confidence, not only in the theory, but also in the previous inductions on which it had been based.

But what is to happen when a theory, which has seemed to have a good

---

[3] The outstanding Romantic was Imre Lakatos, for whom the story of science was like the story of literature – a series of styles which had their temporary successes, but then 'degenerated'. It does not seem to me at all necessary to read the story in this peculiar manner.

empirical basis, is on further testing not confirmed? The Popperian view would be that it shows that the theory must be rejected. But that is much too simple. A well-established theory, based on many observations, cannot be falsified by a single experiment. The scientist, when confronted with this situation, will quite properly begin by examining the conditions in which the new experiment has been performed, expecting to find that some of the conditions that were present in the previous cases have not in the new case been present. This will sometimes enable him to dismiss the new result, concluding that, after all, it is not relevant. Sometimes, however, he cannot so dismiss it; he must then conclude that there were some unnoticed conditions, which in the previous case were present, but in the new case are not. To have his attention directed to such conditions takes him a step forward.

It is, for instance, nowadays well accepted that the famous experiments which were popularly supposed to confute the Newtonian theory of gravitation are better regarded as setting restrictions on the range of phenomena to which that theory applies. Its applicability to a very wide range of phenomena, which had been established by countless experiments and observations, extending over centuries, was not at all upset. What was shown was that there exist phenomena, for interpretation of which it is necessary to introduce qualifications. Within the Newtonian field they are negligible, but outside it they have to be taken very seriously indeed.[4]

I have one more thing to say before I pass to economics. The establishment, by chains of reasoning, of connections between different kinds of observation is not the only means which is available to science for strengthening its inductions; there is another, which in the experimental sciences is of outstanding importance. This is done by concentrating attention, not on the single experiment, but on a sequence of experiments, a sequence which we are prepared to accept to be repetitious of the same test.

The prediction then takes the form of asserting that in the long run, over a long series of trials, the results will average out in the way predicted. A classic example is Mendel's theory of inheritance. What is asserted is not that the proportions in which characteristics will appear in a single family, or cross, can be predicted by theory, but that in a long series of similar crosses, when their results are taken together, the proportions will approximate to those predicted. If we had an indefinitely long sequence, that prediction would be tested directly; it would indeed have been made into a strong prediction about the sequence. But we do not have indefinitely long sequences; we have to make do with sequences of finite length.

---

[4] This was read in an excellent modern textbook (N.G. Barford, 1973, Preface): 'In this book emphasis is put on recognising that physical theory is "true" only for certain ranges of the quantities described for certain classes of observer.' Unless we are sure (and how can we be sure?) that we can define these classes without exceptions, it is impossible for such a theory to be falsified in Popper's sense.

Much reliance, then, must be placed on the theory of probability, a theory which is a branch of mathematics, so it is a theory in the mathematical sense. The shorter series, which is all that is at our disposal, is then regarded as a sample from the longer series, which is not at our disposal. It will then be fair to ask what proportion of the samples which we might think of as being drawn from the longer series will show the result which is actually shown by the shorter series. If this proportion is high, we say that the likelihood of the prediction, about the longer series, being correct is high; and we regard that as evidence for the validity of the theory being tested. In this way we can test, even though the prediction in question, about the individual experiment, is quite weak.

The same thing can be put in another way. If the disturbances, which admittedly affect the particular experiment, can be expected to be without effect on the average outcome of a long series of experiments, we say that the disturbances are random disturbances. It is the same thing to say that in a sufficiently long run the effect of the disturbance will be negligible, as to say that they are random disturbances. If it is probable, on the evidence, that the disturbances which affect the outcome of a particular experiment are random disturbances, we accept that the stochastic prediction, and the theory on which it is based are probably valid.

So what is shown when a stochastic prediction appears on the evidence to have a low probability can often be interpreted as indicating that the disturbances are not random, but in some way systematic. If they are systematic, it may be possible for them to be identified; one may then be able to proceed to reformulate the theory, modifying it in such a way that what were disturbances cease to be disturbances. This is parallel to what we have seen may happen even in the case of a strong prediction which fails: it is replaced by something wider. So stochastic predictions can be used, up to a point, as if they were strong predictions.

I am now in a position to come, at last, to economics. Economics, obviously, is not an experimental science. I have, however, found it necessary to set out these elementary principles, which most closely apply to experimental sciences, because their applicability, or non-applicability, to economics is the main question to which I am leading.

It seems to me to be clear that most, if not all, economic predictions are essentially weak predictions. 'This is what will happen, if something does not come up to prevent it.' They must take that form, because the propositions on which the predictions are based are characteristically weak propositions; they are always subject to a *ceteris paribus* (other things being equal) clause. And though we can give examples, we are usually unable to give a list of all the things those other things might be.

But even though our propositions are weak, it does not follow that they are useless. Far from it. It is better to have some knowledge of what to expect than no knowledge at all. Prognostications of the future have to be made, as a basis for current action, and it is very desirable that they should be as good as possible. But we should see them for what they are. It is not desirable that more should be claimed for them than they deserve.

Science, I have tried to show, has found two ways of strengthening the weak propositions, which it has derived from observation. One is to tie them together by chains of reasoning; the other is the stochastic method. The former can be used, and is widely used, in economics; a good part of our economic theory is trying to do just that. This is the traditional way of applying economic theory. It is useful as far as it goes. But the tying together of weak propositions, derived, as we say, from experience – often no more than introspection or casual empiricism – is rarely sufficient to give the resulting structure anything like the strength that is often attained by scientific theories. The rigorous testing under precaution, which is practicable in the experimental sciences, is for the most part not possible for us. What we get, at best, remains subject to exogenous disturbances, as we call them. So our predictions, though somewhat strengthened by this method, still remain weak.

It should, however, be noticed that the word prediction, as used in economics, commonly has a rather different meaning from what it has in experimental sciences. This is because our predictions are in time, in historical time, in a way that most scientific predictions are not. They are predictions about the future, the future from now, the moment of time in which we are living: predictions which, if we are wise, we make as conditional predictions – so that, for instance, they are changeable by changes in policy – but predictions about the future all the same. Yet though the predictions relate to the future, the evidence on which we base them comes from the past.

Though our practical object is to give guidance about the future, our information relates to the past; it may be the recent past, but it is the past none the less. So the part of our work that corresponds most nearly to the work of the natural scientist, or at least of the pure scientist, is not that which is directed towards the future, but that in which our immediate object is the explanation of the past, the understanding of what has happened. The records of the past are our phenomena; we seek to find, as best we can, some general principles to tie them, or some of them, together. That is what the scientist does. But though there is this parallel with the work of the scientist, there is perhaps a closer parallel with the work of the historian. Not, here, the purely narrative historian, who does not seek for explanations, but the higher, or more ambitious, kind of historian, who does attempt to explain.

Our difficulty, in economics, is rather special, however. Our supply of data (which correspond to the observations of the scientist) is rather abundant; and further – what makes it look as if our problem is similar to that of the scientist – is very largely of a quantitative character. It may indeed be said that men could not begin to act in an economic manner before they could add and subtract. But this has a consequence which is not so fortunate. The data, with which we are presented, have already been processed, by those directly concerned with them; they have already been classified, for particular purposes, which may not be at all the purposes for which we economists want to use them. It is obvious that many of the terms that are used by economists are derived from business practice; businessmen knew what they meant, or thought that they knew what they meant, by capital and income, long before economists began to think in those terms. But when we seek to lay down general principles, even very weak principles, which use terms like that, we have to face the question, often a very difficult question, of whether the way in which those terms are used in business is appropriate for us. It is my own belief that a good part of what is called economic theory is best regarded as a criticism of those concepts, finding out what adjustments have to be made to the business concepts in order that we may use them as instruments of more general thought. That is a different meaning of *theory* from either of those which I have previously identified; but it is nearer to the mathematical usage of *theory* than to the scientific. (Think of the way the mathematician has had to refine the common-sense notion of continuity.)

I return, in conclusion, to the relation between economics and history. It is becoming understood, by historians, that causal explanation of general changes that have occurred in the past requires the use of a model. To say that A was a cause of B is to say that if A had not happened, B would not have happened. But how can we say that? We know that A did happen; we do not know, in the same way, what would have happened, if A had not happened. We can only guess it or, better, deduce it from general principles; but for that limited purpose quite weak principles may suffice. A model is a structure that is based on such principles. I think that this is what historians mean when they describe their method as counterfactual.

This is not the only kind of historical explanation. When the historian finds himself unable to use it, because of the character of the particular problem in which he is interested, he will fall back on more traditional methods, in terms of the personalities of the actors in his story, and so on. But it remains a powerful method. It can be used, at least to some extent, in any field of history. In any such field we may look for patterns in the past, which may give us some guidance on what may happen in the future. That is just as true of the comparative study of government as it is of economics. But in economics it looks more scientific, less conventionally historical, because our material, what we have to explain, is so largely quantitative. It may indeed be said that men could not begin to act in an economic manner before they could add and subtract. And so our economic theory, regarded as the link which ties our inductions together, is bound to be quantitative, and thus to some degree mathematical.

Why, then, should we not use the stochastic method, which (as I have shown) has been established as one of the main mathematical methods in the natural sciences? That was a question that was bound to be asked; the attempt to use that method was bound to be made. We now have thousands of econometrists who make it their business to use it; that they have some achievements to their credit is not to be denied. One may nevertheless ask: how far is it justifiable to treat our data, consisting of a series of observations over a period of history, as being repetitions of an experiment in the scientific sense? How far can we be justified in claiming that a model has been successfully fitted, when the deviations of experience, from what has been predicted by the model, satisfy tests of randomness? That must presumably mean that in a sufficiently long series they would average out. But how can one apply that notion to a period of history? It is almost inevitable that there will have been things which occurred in that period, and which cannot be tracked down by any general model applied to that period, or it may be that there were things which were peculiar to that period, so that they cannot repeat. The years that are being studied are particular years, 1960–80 (say), not 1860–80; but that is a distinction which in the econometric method is liable to slip through.

Let me just take one example, which at the time of writing is a major example. We are seeking for the causes of the Great Inflation of the 1970s. That was an event for which there was no precedent. So large an inflation, common to many countries, had never occurred in peacetime before. There were many aspects of it for which there were precedents; some of them, undoubtedly, can usefully be traced by econometric methods. But if we confine ourselves to the econometric approach, it is hard not to come to the conclusion that explanation is to be found in the movement of some single variable, such as the quantity of money – that being the most popular. But why did the quantity of money behave like that? When one asks such further questions, one is bound to look for explanations in terms of things that had no precendent – the breakdown of the Bretton Woods system, the oil squeeze and so on; one is bound, that is, to turn to history. Econometrics can help, but it does not finish the job.

Economics, I have said elsewhere (Hicks, 1979) is 'on the edge of science and on the edge of history'. It is on the edge of science, because it can make use of scientific, or quasi-scientific, methods; but it is no more than on the edge, because the experiences that it analyses have so much that is non-repetitive about them. If a scientific theory is good, it is good now, and it would have been good a thousand years ago, if it had been available; but the aspects of economic life which we need to select in order to make useful theories can be different at different times (see Hicks, 1976, 1983). Economics is in time, and therefore in history, in a way that science is not.

REFERENCES

Barford, N.G. (1973) *Mechanics*, John Wiley, London and New York.
Hicks, J. (1976) 'Revolutions in Economics', in *Method and Appraisal in Economics*, ed. S.J. Latsis, Cambridge University Press, Cambridge, pp. 207–18.
— (1979) *Causality in Economics*, Basil Blackwell, Oxford.
— (1983) 'Revolutions in Economics', in *Classics and Moderns*, vol. III of *Collected Essays on Economic Theory*, Basil Blackwell, Oxford, pp. 3–16.
Neumann, J. von (1937) 'Ueber ein Oekonomisches Gleichungs-System und eine Verallgemeinerung des Brouwerschen Fixpunktsatzes', in *Ergebnisse eines Mathematischen Kolloquiums*, Vienna, vol. VIII, pp. 73–83; English translation: 'A Model of General Equilibrium', *Review of Economic Studies,* 1945/6, pp. 1–9.
Popper, K. (1959) *Logic of Scientific Discovery*, Hutchison, London.

3

The Process of Formation of Economics in Relation to other Sciences

BERNARD SCHMITT

I INTRODUCTION

Economics can be said to have evolved in three stages. In the first, political economy considered that production was prior to exchange and not determined in exchange. In the second stage, economics is founded on the general equilibrium of supply and demand; exchange thus encompasses production. In the third stage, production is again pre-eminent: all exchange pertains to production.

It is convenient to distinguish the three periods as classical, neoclassical and Keynesian. Although economists are clear about the first two, which are historical, the third stage is contemporary and consequently the new definition of exchange is more problematic. To exchange products for each other actually means to exchange productions, that is, actions which have products as their result.

II CLASSICAL ECONOMICS

In classical economics the object of every exchange is produced goods; exchange thus follows production. According to Adam Smith:

> The annual labour of every nation is the fund which originally supplies it with all the necessaries and conveniences of life which it annually consumes, and which consists always either in the immediate produce of that labour or in what is purchased with that produce from other nations. (Smith, 1976, p. 11; 1st edn 1776)

Human labour is seen as the origin and principle of all goods available in society. Now, it is existing goods, that is, the products of previous labour, which are extra to the requirements of their original holders, that are brought to the market to be exchanged with other goods.

I am grateful to Elisabeth Castellani-Kyrke for her translation of the French manuscript and to Monique Bersier and Sergio Destefanis for their assistance.

> It is this same trucking disposition which originally gives occasion to the division of labour. (Smith, 1976, p. 27; 1st edn 1776)

In a society where the division of labour were unknown, each worker would consume what he produced; but in a less 'primitive' society, a portion of what each worker produces is exchanged on the market against goods produced by others. In a perfectly developed society, a situation would exist where the entirety of the product of each worker is exchanged for the product of others. What, then, of the product which feeds non-wage incomes, rents, profits and interest? Classical theory makes no distinction. Landlords, entrepreneurs and lenders receive their share of the product of land, of physical and monetary capital. Just as with wage goods, these products are exchanged against others on the market, enabling income-receivers to acquire the greatest possible 'value in use'.

In modern terms, the act of producing is a 'flow' and for classical economists the terms of trade are produced goods and not 'productive flows'. It follows that exchange in no way determines the measure of the commodities exchanged on the market. According to classical political economy, this measure is already fully determined before commodities reach the market; exchange merely ensures the circulation of commodities of given value. It is true that theorists, Smith among them, question that all exchange must be equivalent thus. They maintain, however, that if an exchange is 'unequal', this simply means that the purchaser or the seller makes an undue profit. Since the loss incurred by one party is necessarily equal to the gain made by the other, exchange still preserves the exact value of the commodities as defined at the production stage, prior to exchange.

Today, it is clear why the classical doctrine was not the definitive formulation of economic theory. A science cannot remain stable as long as it is internally incoherent. Classical political economy has a basic logical flaw, which lies in the conception of production. Not being integrated into the process of exchange, production cannot be, as the classical economists claim it is, the operation which determines the value of goods. Let us demonstrate this in stages.

1 For the classical economists, production is not an object of exchange.
2 It follows that workers cannot sell their activity, nor can the services of monetary capital, physical capital or land be sold.
3 In the 'primitive state of society', workers do not sell their production, but produce directly for their own consumption.
4 With the appearance of the division of labour, workers produce for factories. According to classical theory, they receive their own product as in the 'primitive state of society'. Indeed, if they were to receive the 'value' of their product or its 'counterpart' wholly or in part, for example as money, it would imply that they sell their production and this is not admitted by the 'paradigm'.

5 Even in nations in a developed state, exchange merely moves existing products around. Hence workers do not effect exchanges at the level of productive activity; they exchange that part of their product which is surplus to their needs for surpluses of others. 'Every man thus lives by exchanging, or becomes in some measure a merchant, and the society itself grows to be what is properly a commercial society' (Smith, 1976, p. 37; 1st edn 1776). At the stage of commodity production, society is not yet commercial; it becomes so only at the later stage, when surpluses are exchanged between producers.

6 Given these terms, however, it is impossible to explain income formation. How can workers receive incomes, if they are not at least the partial countervalue of products? It is logically unacceptable to consider wages as the countervalue of a product without accepting that a worker sells his productive activity. As the national economy consists in the sale of products and not of production, it follows that wages, rents, profits and interest are not explained, at least not in economic terms.

This latter difficulty is of major importance and not just a question of semantics. If wages do not define the paid worker's product, then they must be its whole or partial countervalue. If this is the case, then wages are received in exchange for something else, which can only be production. Classical theory excludes the possibility of exchange at the level of production, so each worker's wage must define his own product, which can only be received in *kind*. At this point there are only two possible solutions *a priori*. One is that incomes do not take the form of money, unless we take to be money the 'basket' in which each worker's product is placed when he is paid. The second term of the alternative is of a metaphysical nature within the terms of reference of classical theory and it implies, as will become apparent, that production is indeed an object of exchange, even the sole object of all exchange. It is plain therefore that income formation receives no satisfactory explanation in classical theory.

Why did classical economists exclude production from the class of exchangeable commodities? It seems that Adam Smith did at first include the act of production amongst the objects of exchange:

> Labour was the first price, the original purchase-money that was paid for all things. It was not by gold or silver, but by labour, that all the wealth of the world was originally purchased; and its value, to those who possess it, and who want to exchange it for some new productions, is precisely equal to the quantity of labour which it can enable them to purchase or command. (Smith, 1976, p. 48; 1st edn 1776)

However, the exchange of labour for its product is an operation that classical economists could not retain as a 'principle,' because it offered no 'measure' of the wealth of society. Value is a 'value in exchange' and comes into existence only on the market, in the actual exchange of commodities amongst themselves.

The exclusion of production from exchangeable goods is the more surprising because, according to Adam Smith, value is equal to 'commanded labour':

> [A man] must be rich or poor according to the quantity of labour which he can command . . . the value of any commodity, therefore, to the person who possesses it, and who means not to use or consume it himself, but to exchange it for other commodities, is equal to the quantity of labour which it enables him to purchase or command. (Smith, 1976, p. 47; 1st edn 1776)

However, a simple argument leads from labour commanded, the origin of the purchased commodity, to the labour *contained* in commodities exchanged. It runs as follows: the value of product A is equal to the labour required to produce B, which can be purchased by the sale of A. The converse is also true. It follows that the value of A and B, and by generalization of all commodities, is equal to the labour they 'contain'. Exchange is the operation which reveals the labour embodied in commodities. 'They contain the value of a certain quantity of labour which we exchange for what is supposed at the time to contain the value of an equal quantity' (Smith, 1976, pp. 47–8; 1st edn 1776).

But how can commodities measure commodities? The question is not adequately dealt with by referring to the principle of labour embodied. Society still needs a specific commodity, the property of which is to act as a 'practical' unit of measurement, and this is money.

> Gold and silver, however, like every other commodity, vary in their value, are sometimes cheaper and sometimes dearer, sometimes of easier and sometimes of more difficult purchase. The quantity of labour which any quantity of them can purchase or command, or the quantity of other goods which it will exchange for, depends always upon the fertility of the mines which happen to be known about the time when such exchanges are made. (Smith, 1976, p. 49; 1st edn 1776)

Money, then, is an objectively imperfect instrument of measurement. This, however, is not the point. It is the theory which is flawed and seriously so. It claims to measure commodities in reciprocal exchange. Exchange of products for money can only 'reveal' a pre-existing value: only the exchange of real *production* and its *transformation* into the production of money could explain the appearance or formation of values which are confronted on the commodities' markets.

The conclusion is thus confirmed: being incapable to locate exchange at the level of production, the classical theory cannot explain, in economic terms only, the formation of national income and its distribution among profits, wages and rents.

Karl Marx, at the close of the period, clearly perceived the logical flaw in the classical paradigm: labour is not a commodity; nevertheless it must be one, if wages are to be determined. Marx solves the problem with a *tour de force* of metaphysical argumentation: labour power is a commodity and is sold like any other. Even if his solution were acceptable, it would be ineffective, except to explain incomes in a society in a primitive state. Once incomes include profits (or surplus value), productive activity is sold to the amount of labour power expended. All other production is excluded from the system of exchange. One is led to the conclusion either that the national product is absorbed by wages, or else that non-wage incomes are arrived at by reference to principles outside the framework of the theory.

III NEOCLASSICAL ECONOMICS

In neoclassical economics, exchange is first defined as in the classical paradigm, being already formed in an 'exchange economy'. However, productive services are now assimilated to products. The exchange of productive services for their products is therefore assumed to be consistent with the exchange of goods.

Since Léon Walras, economics has included productive services in the class of exchangeable goods. This is a revolution in economic thinking, for classical economics had excluded production from the commodities market. Walras and all the theorists of the neoclassical school do not isolate production in order to make it an action prior to exchange; instead they make the interaction of supply and demand determine simultaneously the price of productive services and that of products in the strict sense.

The term 'productive services' as used by Walras has two meanings: one, the services offered by any existing commodity, which are the services producing utility. The second meaning is that of services which produce goods. The two meanings correspond to two steps: in the first place, productive services are constant flows of satisfaction which commodities afford human beings; secondly, productive services create the commodities which will give rise to these flows.

The determination of productive services of the first type is essential for the analysis. Commodities themselves are *stocks*, whereas the services they offer are flows. Since the theory deals with incomes, it must limit itself to productive services of the first type. Commodities are only 'bearers' of incomes which benefit agents, households and firms, and which disappear as soon as they are consumed. 'It cannot be too strongly impressed upon the reader that it is not correct to contrast income or macroanalysis of, say, the Keynesian type with Walrasian microanalysis as if the latter were a theory that neglects, and stands in need of being supplemented by, income and macroanalysis' (Schumpeter, 1954, p. 999).

The heuristic value of the second type of productive services is plain: if it were not for the production of consumption and investment goods, the economy would not enjoy the productive services of the first type. If neoclassical economics were unable to assimilate productive services of the second type in the category of objects of generalized exchange, its field of investigation would be limited to the exchange economy. As early as Léon Walras's *Elements* (1874), however, the theory has much wider ambitions: it also covers the production economy, which is considered as a particular instance of the exchange economy.

For the sake of clarity, we shall call productive services I incomes deriving from goods, and productive services II the 'factors of production' of consumption and investment goods. Production services I are not in fact commodities, but flows of utility and satisfaction which commodities afford their agents. Productive services II, however, *are* commodities, otherwise they would not be objects of exchange. The general equilibrium system applies to production economies precisely because productive services II are counted amongst the exchangeable commodities.

It is worth emphasizing that productive services I are unlimited in number and undetermined; human beings can derive benefit from any object whatsoever. Productive services II, on the other hand, correspond to the triad of classical economics: labour, land, and physical and monetary capital, these three 'factors' alone being able to supply economies with all kinds of commodities. From now on in this chapter, productive services II will be meant wherever the term 'productive services' is used.

The central problem facing the neoclassical paradigm can now be examined: in general equilibrium are productive services goods distinct from their products? At first glance they are quite distinct. On the one hand, there are the services offered by the three factors and, on the other, the result or product of the services expended. How, then, is the price of productive services determined? Since the price of products defines that of their productive services or of their factors of production, if products have no price, neither have their productive services. Considered as objects measured by economics, productive services and their products are identical.

Let us determine the price of a productive service, PS, in relation to its product, P. If PS and P are the only commodities to be exchanged in relation to the *numéraire*, the solution should bear out the equation:

price of PS in the *numéraire* = price of P in the *numéraire* (1)

If PS were a commodity, the prices of PS and P, expressed in the *numéraire*, would be independent of each other; they could then be determined in the general equilibrium and the equation (1) could be written. But PS is the productive service of P, and by definition has the same price. The price of P in the *numéraire* and equally the price of PS are thus completely undetermined: they cannot be the solution to any equation. Equation (1) is therefore meaningless.

Of course, if PS were a flow of utility in its own right, its price would be independent of the price attached to the flow of services offered by P. It would then be possible to compare and try to equalize the two flows with each other. But in the general equilibrium system, PS cannot be a flow, other than the flow actualized at the moment of exchange of utilities deriving from the product, P. As soon as PS is treated as a stock, its price is by definition the price of its product. Thus if the price of P is equal to x units of the *numéraire*, the price of PS must simultaneously be equal to x units of the *numéraire*. The price of PS is not determined in the exchange of PS and P, but in the *production* of P by PS.

Let us examine the first interpretation: *Productive services produce a flow which is none other than the flow deriving from the products*. In an economy consisting of two commodities, prices can be determined by Walras's law, since it means that the price of commodity A in terms of B is the inverse of the price of B in terms of A. Only one 'independent' price has then to be determined, that of A in terms of B or of B in terms of A. But as soon as one of the commodities present on the market is the productive service of the other, it becomes impossible to determine the price. This can be expressed in a particularly striking manner: the price of the productive service must simultaneously be the price of the product and the inverse of this price. In other words, the price of the productive service expressed in terms of its own product can only be the *number* 1.

The equations of the general equilibrium system cannot be extended to cover the independent determination of the price of productive services in relation to products. It follows that neither can they cover the exchange of productive services for their own products.

It is not even possible to determine the price of productive services among themselves, because this price is necessarily the passive translation of the price of their products with each other. Schumpeter maintains that:

> Since the equilibria in the two basic markets, the consumers' goods and the service markets, and the way in which they interlock – simultaneously determining each other – are of decisive importance for the strength of the Walrasian structure we shall consider these two markets separately. (Schumpeter, 1954, p. 1003)

In fact, the two equilibria and their simultaneous determination are reduced to one and the logical structure of Walras's system falls apart.

Indeed, in the instantaneous exchange of flows in the general equilibrium system, the productive flows of commodities and the flows of satisfaction deriving from them measure each other. The measure, moreover, goes from the flow derived from commodities in the direction of the flow which produces them. To produce a flow of commodities means at one remove to produce a flow of utility which they afford. The general equilibrium of flows, then, does not extend to productive services, the utility of which is merely the mirror image of the utility of commodities.

Now let us examine the other interpretation, according to which the terms of exchange are stocks. The flow of utility which each productive service is calculated to bring in the future is actualized in an instantaneous magnitude. Similarly, the flow of utility expected of commodities in all future time is completely realized at the moment of generalized exchange. It is to be noted that any rate of interest affects both sides in equal measure. The same conclusion is reached, namely that the measure of the two stocks, productive services and commodities, is given simultaneously in one and the same operation. This does not yield the solutions to the equations of exchange: the price of the productive services is simply the mirror image of the price of their products. 'Walras first developed brilliantly the theory of (competitive) exchange of two commodities' (Schumpeter, 1954, p. 1004). If the two terms of exchange are a commodity and its productive service, then Walras's theory is quite unable to determine their price for reasons which should now be obvious. Competition between the holder of the commodity and the holder of the service is impossible, because the two agents possess exactly the same commodity. No game of trial and error can account for the equilibrium price of productive services in terms of their own products. In general equilibrium, all the equations relating productive services and their products are empty. This means that Walrasian theory does not provide even the scantiest information about the allocation of productive resources.

> We perceive immediately that Walras strove for a solution of this problem that was to be entirely symmetrical with the solution he had previously worked out in his general theory of barter in a multi-commodity consumers' goods market. In fact, his theory of production may be described as an attempt to resolve, in the spirit of J.B. Say, the case of production into the more general case of exchange between services and goods and, in the last analysis, simply between services. (Schumpeter, 1954, p. 1011)

The difficulty encountered by Walras lies at the heart of the neoclassical paradigm: how can production be integrated into the generalized exchange of commodities? One might speak of *external* exchanges in the case of products which exchange among themselves, and of *internal* exchanges when productive services are transformed into products. External exchanges presuppose the existence of commodities. Internal exchanges give rise to products. How can both exchanges, internal and external, be covered by a single coherent explanation within the logical structure of general equilibrium theory? It proves to be impossible, because internal exchanges must take place *first* for there to be products to exchange. The first sixteen lessons of Walras's *Elements* (1954, 1st edn 1874) are devoted to developing the theory of external exchange; lessons 17–22 seek to reduce internal to external exchange. This method is characteristic of the entire neoclassical school; using the exchange economy as their starting point, they endeavour to integrate the production economy into it. But it is a procedure which is bound to fail, for reasons of which Walras himself was aware:

> But the process of groping ['*tatônnement*'] in production entails a complication which was not present in the case of exchange. In exchange, [the total existing quantities of] commodities do not undergo any change. When a price is cried, and the effective demand and offer corresponding to this price are not equal, another price is cried for which there is another corresponding effective demand and offer. In production, productive services are transformed into products. After certain prices for services have been cried and certain quantities of products have been manufactured, if these prices and quantities are not the equilibrium prices and quantities, it will be necessary not only to cry new prices but also to manufacture revised quantities of products. (Walras, 1954, p. 242; 1st edn 1874)

Supply and demand equations cannot be required to determine simultaneously the unit price of exchanged goods and their physical quantities and, *in addition*, the quantities of commodities available on the market. Walras believes he has avoided the difficulty when he writes:

> In order to work out as rigorous a description of the process of groping [towards equilibrium] in production as we did in exchange and yet take this additional circumstance into account, we have only to imagine, on the one hand, that entrepreneurs use tickets ['bons'] to represent the successive quantities of products which are first determined at random and then increased or decreased according as there is an excess of selling price over cost of production or vice versa, until selling price and cost are equal. (Walras, 1954, p. 242; 1st edn 1874)

However, the problem noted by Walras remains unsolved. The determination of general equilibrium on the commodities market is not dependent on the quantities of goods available. It follows that any quantity of goods randomly specified on the tickets allows prices to be determined in the general equilibrium system. If there is a problem of existence of the solution, this is not related to the inclusion of productive services in the class of objects of exchange. So another criterion is needed which will allow for choice between the different quantities produced. Walras finds this in the treatment of business profits and losses. The quantity of goods retained confirms the equality of cost and selling prices. The validity of the argument depends on a hypothesis: is the occurrence of business profits and losses a function of quantities produced? It is a hypothesis that is nowhere tested. At every level of physical production, randomly selected, the payment of productive services is determined univocally by the price of products. Any difference which may arise is to be attributed to social economics and not to pure economics, because it originates in differences between classes of people, business firms and owners of labour, land and capital services.

There is a second complication, likewise noticed by Walras, which is quite as serious as the first:

> Once the equilibrium has been established in principle, exchange can take place immediately. Production, however, requires a certain lapse of time. We shall resolve the second difficulty purely and simply by ignoring the time element at this point. And later on, in Part VI, we shall bring in circulating capital and money and thereby make it possible for productive services to be transformed into products instantaneously, provided that the consumers pay the interest charges on the capital required for this sort of transformation. (Walras, 1954, p. 242; 1st edn 1874)

We see that if the productive flow is construed so as to derive from a pre-existent capital, production (the act of producing) no longer takes up length of time. But the suppression of production time means the suppression of production itself. Indeed, the pre-existent capital can only reproduce the incomes which originally formed it.

It is only with the 'Keynesian revolution' that economics succeeds in integrating production into exchange. Consequently, by a curious reversal, it will appear that all exchanges are acts of production so that exchanges between physical goods are reduced to mere abstractions.

IV MODERN ECONOMICS

Both the classical and neoclassical paradigms logically exclude the integration of production into the class of objects of exchange. Nevertheless, Léon Walras's analysis is a clear advance on Adam Smith's. General equilibrium theory sets out to encompass productive services and accomplishes the first important steps towards the realization of this initial purpose in distinguishing two main markets:

> The first is the *services market*. Here land-owners, workers and capitalists appear as sellers, and entrepreneurs as buyers of the various productive services. (Walras, 1954, pp. 242–3; 1st edn 1874)

> The second market is the *products market*. Here the entrepreneurs appear as sellers, and the land-owners, labourers and capitalists as buyers of products. (Walras, 1954, p. 243; 1st edn 1874)

Only the commodity market was known to classical theorists, because they did not hold production to be an exchange. Walras, however, notes the existence of two markets, which are related in that incomes arising on the market of productive services are expended on the commodity market.

This theoretical insight, one which corresponds to observable facts, is decisive; it is central to the Keynesian revolution, which marks the beginning of the last stage of the development of economics.

Once the two markets, productive services and commodity markets, are put in relation to each other, only two possibilities are available *a priori*: (1) either every purchase on one market is a sale on the other, (2) or every positive purchase on one market is a 'negative purchase' on the other (and every positive sale a negative sale on the other market).

Walras adopted the first as his working hypothesis. Entrepreneurs buy and factors of production sell productive services. Income holders buy and firms sell the product. But this is not all: exchanges between the two markets occur between *real* terms. In the process of exchange between the two markets, firms demand productive services and supply products, whilst income holders supply productive services and demand products. We note that every purchase or sale on the productive services market is a sale or purchase on the commodity market. The first hypothesis, then, does not allow, logically, for any degree of freedom to be introduced between the two markets. On the contrary, each purchase on one market is identically a sale on the other, and each sale a purchase. Only the presence of money can create the illusion of freedom, but as soon as we argue in terms of the *numéraire*, then 'Walras's law' necessarily applies to transactions taking place between the two markets just as it does to purchases and sales of commodities in an exchange economy. Hence the non-existence of profits and losses in business is a law and not a condition of equilibrium, being a formal consequence of hypothesis (1). It is only with hypothesis (2) that we have a theoretical model which accommodates the real world, allowing for profits, positive or negative. Hypothesis (2), however, was unknown to Walras.

The second hypothesis is the only one that constitutes a satisfactory answer to the neoclassical paradigm. Here, operations on the two markets are distinguished *objectively* and no longer with reference to the parties to the contract. Each transaction on one of the markets is identically an operation on the other, of opposite algebraic sign. Thus, all transactions on the two markets are defined as taking place, positively and negatively, on the commodity market alone. 'Direct' purchases and sales observed on the commodity market are positive, whereas 'indirect' purchases and sales on the same market (by which are to be understood purchases and sales on the market of productive services) are negative. This second hypothesis is in fact the covert or overt thesis of all modern macroeconomics. Our next task, then, will be to present it in broad outline and in contrast with hypothesis (1).

According to the neoclassical paradigm, purchases and sales are operations of the same algebraic sign, whether they take place on the commodity market or on the market of productive services. To purchase means to change or convert a sum of money into goods; conversely, to sell is to exchange goods for a sum of money. We can say that simple exchanges between money and goods are 'Walrasian' operations. The opposition of purchases and sales is personal, as each purchase (sale) is someone else's sale (purchase). The distinction, which is subjective rather than objective, does not imply negative numbers. If we use the terms negative sale or negative purchase to indicate purchases or sales, we simply mean that these are personal transactions in which the partners face each other. The two poles of every transaction are persons. Once one disregards the parties to the contract and adopts the point of view of society as a whole, then the operation is revealed as *purely positive*: a sum of money is changed into a commodity or a commodity into a sum of money.

Now, if the argument is taken one step further, it leads to the conclusion that the sum of Walrasian operations is necessarily zero in society as a whole, for the statement that the purchase of a product defines its sale and the sale its purchase is tautological. It follows that there is no transaction on the commodity market that is simultaneously positive for both subsets of society, buyers and sellers, as each purchase is a sale and each sale a purchase for each of these two subsets. Transactions, then, are purely neutral when considered on the commodity market alone. Pre-existent goods and money are 'circulated' and pass through transactions without undergoing any increase or decrease in value. In this sense, it is correct to state that the Walrasian analysis cannot account for the formation of any new product, and, therefore, that social income lies beyond its reach.

If there were only objectively positive purchases and sales on the commodity market, then society would be deprived of incomes. The discovery that negative purchases and sales exist on the commodity market belongs to post-Walrasian economics. Schumpeter's claim, quoted earlier, must thus be refuted; in fact only the modern (Keynesian) theory is able to account for national income. Walras's distinction between the market of productive services and the market of commodities was undoubtedly the premiss for modern theoretical development. However, there are two ways of conceiving this interrelation between the markets: productive services can either be considered as commodities like others, or as '*anti-commodities*'. Walras was obviously only acquainted with positive commodities and counted productive services amongst them. The neoclassical paradigm, based as it is on a hypothetical order in which there are only positive commodities, must exclude all exchanges which are not between pre-existent objects, whether these be 'products', the *numéraire* or money. In such conditions, exchange can increase the utility of goods, but it cannot encompass their production. Social income, defined in terms of the numerical value of goods, must emerge from the process of exchange as constantly nil.

According to the line of thought which goes back to Keynes, in the modern paradigm purchases and sales are objectively operations of opposite agebraic sign, according to whether they take place on the commodity market or on the market of productive services. Let us begin by stating the new definitions. Once economic theory includes *negative* purchases and sales, the terms *positive* purchases and sales undergo a notable shift in meaning. We need to return a moment to the traditional definitions: purchase and sale set in motion money and real goods; the objects exist prior to exchange of which they are the terms. Purchases and sales are displacements of pre-existent goods between the parties to a contract. The new definitions are radically different:

> *Positive purchase* is the exchange between an existing sum of money and a commodity which does not yet exist. Conversely, positive sale is the exchange between a product which does not yet exist and an already existing sum of money.
>
> *Negative purchase* is the exchange between an existing commodity and a sum of money which does not yet exist. Conversely, negative sale is the exchange between an as yet non-existent sum of money and a pre-existing commodity.

Let us look more closely at these definitions.

Negative purchase defines the payment of productive services. At the moment they are 'paid' for their services, 'factors of production' create the physical goods, firms which employ them instantaneously acquire the real product and exchange it for a sum of money which is created in the operation. True, it is conceivable that the money exists prior to the payment of factors, but in fact the money received by the factors is the new product's 'numerical form', and this it could not be before the new real product was exchanged for or changed into money. Even if the money exists before the payment of factors, it is still 'pure money', a purely nominal magnitude and not a sum of 'money linked to the product'. This money integrated with the product is the definition of monetary income. Negative purchase creates the link between money and the product, it is the formation of this link which defines the creation of monetary income. Income is a macroeconomic magnitude precisely because the payment of factors creates *real* money. Before it is paid as wages, money is not yet linked with the (new) product; in other words, real money or monetary income is wholly created by the payment of the factors of production. Income earned by factors is not lost by anyone; it follows that it is net in society as a whole.

Positive purchase derives its meaning from negative purchase, with which it is identified, but for the algebraic sign. Here money – that is, monetary income – exists prior to exchange, but in this case it is the product which does not yet exist. This might seem surprising, but it follows logically from the existence of negative purchases. In the time-gap before positive purchases match negative purchases, real goods are replaced by real money created in wage payments. As a consequence, social income is at first net in a monetary form, and it is then still nil in purely physical terms. Positive purchases literally *summon up* commodities in households and businesses. Commodities had no real existence until then, *not even firms possessed them*. True, firms 'acquired' the product in paying the factors of production, but they still did not own it, as it was wholly paid in wages. Businesses can take possession of the product only in so far as they manage to derive profits from the incomes they have issued. In other words, firms, like households, gain possession of the product only in *positive* purchases which they are able to finance. The product is not acquired by negative purchase; the product which is still to be sold will only emerge from purchases. We can see, then, that final purchases in national accounting are net in society as a whole. They are macroeconomic magnitudes, because the monetary income expended by income holders is destroyed. Positive purchases destroy the objective link between money and goods that negative purchases created. Analysis thus arrives at an unexpected conception of exchange.

According to the classical and neoclassical paradigms, exchange takes place between commodities, or in the case of a production economy between the results of the nation's productive activity. For modern economics, exchange (which is an action) concerns not the results of production, but production itself, to exchange means *to change*.

In negative purchase, goods are changed into money and this is an objective transformation. Negative purchases literally define income production or income formation: national income. Considered from the point of view of society as a whole, the actual physical product is changed or converted into a monetary product. In the same way, positive purchases do not move pre-existent goods. The money held by buyers (income holders) is real and so the physical product is already defined by real money before positive purchases take place. These are merely the transformation of the monetary product into a purely physical product. Again, we note that to purchase means to produce:

negative purchases are the positive production of national income;
positive purchases are the negative production, or destruction, of national income;
purchases which are both positive and negative define the transfer of national income on the financial market, between lenders and borrowers.

Before turning to a comparison of the development of economics with the development of physics, it is of interest to show how the new conception of purchase is already formulated either explicitly or by implication in the writings of John Maynard Keynes, the originality of whose thinking still awaits full recognition.

Effective demand is the concept which best shows Keynes as the creator of a new paradigm, central to which is an original analysis of the algebraic opposition between the two markets. On the market of productive services, purchases are objectively negative, whereas they are objectively positive on the commodity market. The algebraic sign of the operations, positive or negative, is independent of the observers and is manifest to society as a whole. When dealing with the concept of effective demand, however, we must be aware of the fact that the world over it is presented and taught as a demand in the neoclassical sense (Walras–Marshall), whereas, in fact, effective demand is a revolutionary concept: 'the *effective demand* is simply the aggregate income (or proceeds) which the entrepreneurs expect to receive, inclusive of the incomes which they will hand on to the other factors of production, from the amount of current employment which they decide to give' (Keynes, 1930, p. 55). We see that effective demand is defined as a two-way flux, firms 'giving' and 'receiving' the same product. If the market for factors of production on which employment is determined carried operations of the same algebraic sign as the commodity market, then entrepreneurs would have one concern only, that of making marginal payments to factors according to the value they added to the product. Now, effective demand does not entail the comparison between what factors receive in money and what they bring in kind, but that between the national product received by factors in monetary form and the national product they demand subsequently in kind. What is at issue is the formation and expenditure of the income of society as it is created by the combined activity of all individual firms. We must understand, then, that the national product is paid out in wages, consumer and investment goods being included as deposited in the wage units paid. This is the stage of *negative purchases* which create incomes. Later, holders convert their incomes which cease to be monetary and become purely physical, this is the stage of *positive purchases* which destroy incomes. The deep logic of the principle of effective demand is now clear: if, in business forecasts, positive purchases do not perfectly coincide with negative purchases, either because they are partly lacking or because they are directed elsewhere (for example, towards investment, rather than consumer goods), then the firms, to which the real money they issued does not flow back in its entirety, register a positive loss and as a result cut back on the employment they offer.

Another proof of Keynes's intuition is given by his definition of the unit of measurement of economic magnitudes. Before Walras, economic measurement was considered to be dimensional; theory presupposed the existence of an axiological dimension to economic goods which was construed as the result of labour. It was in fact presumed that goods contained labour, their measure being thus the numerical value of the labour dimension of objects. Walras introduced the quite new conception of the numerical value of the objects themselves, denying their economic dimension. Accordingly, products are matter or energy and their value is the direct association of numbers (without dimension) to commodities, which have purely physical dimensions.

Walras's intuition was brilliant, but the argument needed taking one step further. It is true that the value of goods is no more than their numerical expression as it is registered in national accounting. The attribution of an economic dimension to goods is metaphysical. However, the association of numbers with commodities is not a convention, it must be established and proved. Walras relied on the *numéraire*, which he had every right to do, but he decided that the price of the *numéraire* in terms of the *numéraire* is the number 1. This is faulty logic, for in fact the price of the unit of *numéraire* in terms of the *numéraire* is not the number 1, but the unit of *numéraire*. We are therefore bound to conclude that Walrasian economics – indeed all neoclassical theory – lacks a unit of measurement.

It was Keynes who discovered that the true unit of economic measurement is not just a number without dimension, but a number which becomes a unit of measurement in the actual operation of wage emission, for it is in the payment of monetary wages that the physical product receives its monetary form. 'It is my belief that much unnecessary perplexity can be avoided if we limit ourselves strictly to the two units, money and labour, when we are dealing with the behaviour of the economic system as a whole' (Keynes, 1936, p. 43). The unit of measurement is the wage unit, because monetary wages define the equivalence of form and substance, that is, of the product and the number of units of money paid out in wages.

V THE FORMATION OF ECONOMICS AND OTHER SCIENCES: A COMPARISON

In this examination of the formation of other sciences, our attention will be limited almost exclusively to physics. A comparative study of the development of all sciences would be a major undertaking, far beyond the space available here. Nevertheless, even a rapid enquiry into the evolution of physics and economics will help us to answer the following questions: Is economics an exact science? Is economics a purely positive science or is it also normative? Will economics evolve indefinitely or will it reach a final stage?

Before we study these points more closely, we shall need to look in broad outline at the comparative development of economics and physics. Comparison with physics can be made at each of the three stages of the formation of economic theory: between classical political economy and classical mechanics; between neoclassical economics and the physics of relativity; and between modern economics and quantum physics.

Classical Political Economy and Mechanics

Classical physics is the science of mechanics. As early as the seventeenth century Christian Huygens wrote: 'In true philosophy, one conceives the cause of all natural effects in terms of mechanical motions. This, in my opinion, we must necessarily do, or else renounce all hopes of our comprehending anything in physics' (Huygens, as quoted in Nagel, 1961, p. 154). Some 250 years later, Heinrich Herz maintained: 'All physicists are unanimous in holding that the task of physics is to reduce the phenomena of nature to the simple laws of mechanics' (Hertz, as quoted in Nagel, 1961, p. 154).

Mechanics is the study of the motion of 'bodies'; at first sight, classical political economy would seem to have little in common with classical mechanics, for economic theorists from Adam Smith to Karl Marx paid scant attention to the 'dynamics' of the economy. However, at a deeper level, a parallel does exist between the two sciences, in that both assume space and time to be predetermined. Newton's first two laws of motion state:

> Law I. Every body perseveres in its state of rest, or of uniform motion in a right line, unless it is compelled to change that state by forces impressed thereon.
>
> Law II. The alteration of motion is ever proportional to the motive force impressed; and is made in the direction of the right line in which that force is impressed. (Newton, as quoted in Nagel, 1961, p. 158)

Newton assumes space, even Euclidean space, in which bodies are at rest or move on a straight line. He similarly assumes time (that is, absolute time), in relation to which the instantaneous velocity of a moving body can be calculated, whatever the state, at rest or in motion, of the other bodies in the universe.

The question, then, arises as to what logical status is to be ascribed to the laws of Newtonian mechanics. Are they experimental facts, truths established *a priori*, definitions or conventions? Although Newton's laws have an empirical content, it would be anachronistic to require that they should be tested, for classical physics is constructed like mathematics, by abstract thought alone. It is true that Newton took experimental data into account; in framing his third law of motion, he quotes decisive experiments which he and other scientists had conducted.

> Law III. To every action there is always opposed an equal reaction: or the mutual actions of two bodies upon each other are always equal, and directed to contrary parts. (Newton, as quoted in Nagel, 1961, pp. 158–9)

The collision of two bodies does indeed obey the law of action–reaction. This is observable evidence; however, observation is not necessarily valid proof. It could only be so, if the mass of the bodies (Newton speaks of 'quantities of matter') were measurable. Now, Newton merely states that the measure of the mass of a body is equal to the product of its density and its volume.

In the last analysis, classical mechanics is an aprioristic intellectual construct, which claims to be able to 'reinvent' the world as it is.

On the three fundamental points that have been mentioned (that is, the predetermination of space and of time, and the abstract nature of science), classical political economy and classical mechanics are at one. The product in classical political economy, like the bodies of classical mechanics, exists in a predetermined space.

Active labour is the application of a force, identified with a motion, 'cause' of the product. The product, then, is comparable to a distance travelled. Production is the motion existing in 'economic space'. Now, motion can only be measured in its result, and for this reason production is not an object of exchange; in classical economics it is freely *given*.

Similarly, classical mechanics explains the motion of bodies, but not the actions which move them. 'Absolute motion is the translation of a body from one absolute place into another; and relative motion, the translation from one relative place into another' (Newton, 1964, p. 82). But why does a body move from one place to another? It moves only because it is moved. Why do men work? The *final* cause is known: men work to survive and even to enrich themselves, but the *efficient* cause of labour is not defined. Men work of their own free will; not even in the 'primitive state of society' are they in bondage. Men at work, then, are the source of a motion to which they are not themselves subjected. Determinism exists in classical theory, but in the space occupied by products, where production plays no part. Consider the gravitational force of the earth; how is it to be measured? It is proportional to the acceleration of a falling body relative to the earth. Similarly, the measurement of labour is proportional to the 'value in exchange' of its product. In neither case is the force itself accounted for. Gravitation exists in science, because it can be observed and measured. Labour, too, is quantifiable, because its product is. But neither gravitation nor labour are forces which are to be defined in themselves, independently of their results.

As soon as science (in our case physics and economics) assumes space to be predetermined, it falls into the contradiction which Bradley pointed out:

> Space is not a mere relation. For any space must consist of extended parts, and these parts clearly are spaces. So that, even if we could take our space as a collection, it would be a collection of solids. The relation would join spaces which would not be mere relations. And hence the collection, if taken as a *mere* inter-relation, would not be space. We should be brought to the proposition that space is nothing but a relation of spaces. And this proposition contradicts itself. (Bradley, 1964, p. 133)

This contradiction can be observed in classical political economy. If goods appear in a predetermined space, it is because production is defined by the product 'travelled in the unit of time'; this is to say that goods exist before production has taken place, for production is defined as a flow per unit time. The inconsistency can only be avoided if the product is conceived as a space created by production. For this to be possible, the product must define a space, whereas classical science conceives it as an object set out in a pre-existent 'space'.

The product in classical political economy, like bodies in classical mechanics, pertains to predetermined time. Production time is a positive duration, since no instantaneous production can be positive. For classical economics, a worker has to work ten hours for society to obtain the product of ten hours' labour. Like space, time is given and economic activity can in no way influence it. Thus economic time is identical to time in physics, in that any positive duration can be divided indefinitely. Labour which is expended over a certain period can be said to be deposited in the object produced, which then contains it. More exactly, the object is a product, because it contains labour time. A given object contains ten hours' labour because it is the result of a ten-hour stretch of labour which 'socially' could not have lasted less. We observe that not only labour, but also time, is introduced into the object, so that the product could be termed a 'coagulation' of labour time.

In classical physics, too, the movement of an object between two points in space is said to take up or consume time, and the distance travelled is also the product of the time spent travelling the distance. The terms of the comparison between physics and economics are now complete; in both sciences, the space travelled is measured by the time spent to that end.

In dealing with time, we again come up against the naïvety of the conception of space. On this score it is worth returning to Bradley, for his critique is equally pertinent to both concepts in classical science:

> It is usual to consider time under a spatial form. It is taken as a stream, and past and future are regarded as parts of it, which presumably do not coexist, but are often talked of as if they did. Time, apprehended in this way, is open to the objection we have just urged against space. It is a relation – and, on the other side, it is not a relation. (Bradley, 1964, p. 135)

Classical political economy, like classical mechanics, is a science of abstract thought. The two quotations which follow are taken from the writings of Adam Smith and of Newton. The comparison underlines how both classical writers conceived their science as the result of abstract thought.

> But it is not easy to find any accurate measure either of hardship or ingenuity. In exchanging, indeed, the different production of different sorts of labour for one another, some allowance is commonly made for both. It is adjusted, however, not by any accurate measure but by the higgling and bargaining of

the market, according to that sort of rough equality which, though not exact, is sufficient for carrying on the business of common life. (Smith, 1976, pp. 48–9; 1st edn 1776)

But because the parts of space cannot be seen, or distinguished from one another by our senses, therefore in their stead we use sensible measures of them. . . . And so, instead of absolute places and motions, we use relative ones; and that without any inconvenience in common affairs; but in philosophical disquisitions, we ought to abstract from our senses, and consider things themselves, distinct from what are only sensible measures of them. (Newton, 1964, pp. 83–4)

'Common life' and 'common affairs' are where the life of the senses is played out. The intellect should rise above the immediacy of sense perceptions and seek its proper object, the divine or natural laws in the mind itself. The reality to which we have access through senses in commonplace. The classical scientist knows in advance where experiments will lead, as long as they do not stray from the narrow path of truth into the deceptive byways of appearance; in practice, however, this rigour is not always possible.

I do not define time, space, place and motion, as being well known to all. Only I must observe, that the common people conceive those quantities under no other notions but from the relation they bear to sensible objects. And thence arise certain prejudices, for the removing of which it will be convenient to distinguish them into absolute and relative, true and apparent, mathematical and common. (Newton, 1964, p. 81)

Absolute truth is not experimental, but aprioristic and beyond contradiction. So the laws of motion and production do not derive from the observation of facts; on the contrary, they are imposed on facts and govern them.

In classical science, laws are framed not through the operation of men's free will, but by virtue of the scientist's faculty of discovering, spontaneously, through the exercise of abstract thought, the hidden laws of the physical and economic worlds.

Classical science is neither inductive nor deductive; it is not experimental and it is not built on hypotheses; it is neither a 'reading' of facts, nor a 'model'. It is nothing less than man's re-creation of the world in which he lives. Scientific enquiry leads to the statement of laws which have, so to speak, reached self-awareness. In this process of cognitive revelation, the scientist has the role of neutral instrument, neutral because unburdened by prejudice.

To the modern mind, classical science lacks modesty. When it seeks to grasp reality in its perfect simplicity, it is often left empty-handed. Unchecked abstract thought frequently leads the scientist to beg fundamental questions. Two striking examples of this are Newton's definition of the density of bodies and that of complex labour (or the density of labour) in classical political economy. Both cases give substance to Ernst Mach's judgement:

> No one is competent to predicate things about absolute space and absolute motion; they are pure things of thought, pure mental constructs, that cannot be produced in experience. ... No one is warranted in extending these principles [of mechanics] beyond the boundaries of experience. In fact, such an extension is meaningless, as no one possesses the requisite knowledge to make use of it. (Mach, 1964, p. 127)

According to Nagel, Newton:

> defines the 'mass' of a body (or its 'quantity of matter') as the product of its density and volume; but since he nowhere indicates how density is to be measured, and since the density of a body is commonly defined and measured in terms of the body's mass and volume, his account of mass is quite useless. (Nagel, 1961, pp. 192–3)

Newton's definition of density is circular; any usefulness it has is limited to allowing the distinction between the mass and weight of a body.

Neoclassical Economics and the Physics of Relativity

It is not uncommon to find economists denying the developments which have taken place in their discipline and making projections into the past to find confirmation of their own concerns. In 1965, for example, Gordon writes:

> Smith's postulate of the maximizing individual in a relatively free market ... is our basic paradigm; economics has never had a major revolution; its basic maximizing model has never been replaced ... it is, I think, remarkable when compared to the physical sciences that an economist's fundamental way of viewing the world has remained unchanged since the eighteenth century. (Gordon as quoted in Blaug, 1978, p. 160)

It could just as well be claimed that some other modern notion is present in the writings of the founding fathers. Thus, in 1969, Coats writes that economics has been 'dominated throughout its history by a single paradigm – the theory of economic equilibrium via the market mechanism' (Coats as quoted in Blaug, 1978, p. 160).

Whether or not we refer back every new development of our science to the founding fathers, we should still define the nature of the upheaval which dethroned classical thought in favour of neoclassicism. Quite simply, economists ceased to believe in the existence of *absolute* values and substituted them by the notion of *relative* prices. In the presence of two products, A and B, classical economists saw *two independent values*, the labour value of A and of B. Neoclassical authors, on the contrary, saw a single value: the price of A in terms of B or, conversely, the price of B in terms of A. The conclusion is unchanged if one of the two commodities is the *numéraire*; if it is money, Walras and his school maintain that the price of money and the price of the other commodity are subject to the general law:

> Prices, or ratios of values in exchange, are equal to the inverse ratios of the quantities exchanged. The price of any one commodity in terms of another is the reciprocal of the price of the second commodity in terms of the first. (Walras, 1954, p. 87; 1st edn 1874)

Even if detached from metal, money is a pure number – 'The word *franc* is the name of a thing which does not exist' (Walras, 1954, p. 188; 1st edn 1874) – yet, given two goods, A and B, one and only one exchange value can be defined, both empirically and theoretically, since the monetary price of A is not independent from the monetary price of B. As soon as value is objective, it is necessarily relative. The *raretés*, being absolute, are subjective or personal; 'they are in us and not in things' (Walras, 1954, p. 188; 1st edn 1874).

For classical economists, the relation between money and each commodity was determined by the labour contained in both. Now, since labour was not an object of exchange, the monetary values of commodities were independant of each other. Walras denies the existence of absolute numerical values, holding that the determination of the monetary price of one commodity was always implied in the determination of the prices of all other commodities.

If, for classical economics, value was considered a property of objects, in neoclassical theory it becomes a mere relation. The classical notion of value is that of a space occupied by commodities, in other words an 'absolute' space. Neoclassical economists conceive it as a space defined 'between' commodities, that is, a relative space.

This transformation of the concept of value in neoclassical theory has its analogy in physics. If we take as the terms of comparison the notion of value in economics and of space–time in physics, then *mutatis mutandis* the two sciences can be seen to have undergone a similar 'quantum leap' from Smith to Walras and from Newton to Einstein. Within the limits of the space available here, we can no more than touch on the essentials of the theory of relativity in physics. It is, however, enough to show the deep similarities which exist between Einstein's theory and the neoclassical paradigm in economics. In Newton's physics, each particle of matter occupies a 'point' in space, the unchanging dimensions of which would be known, even if it were empty. Matter does not define space, that is the medium in which matter exists. For this reason, one particle can be at rest in space whilst another is in motion. Thus the velocity of the movement of a particle on which no other external force is exerted is constant in unvaried direction in the 'aether' (to use Maxwell's term). Michelson and Morley's (1887) experiments proved, however, that the velocity of light in relation to the earth is the same in all directions. Now, according to classical physics, the motion of the earth in relation to the 'aether' should result in a slight, but measurable variation in the speed of light in relation to the earth. FitzGerald and Lorentz advanced the hypothesis that became a cornerstone of Einstein's theory, namely, that bodies contract in the direction of their motion (see Lorentz, 1937; 1st edn 1886). Einstein's theory of relativity is based on the experimental fact that information cannot be propagated at a velocity greater than that of light. The notion of the absolute simultaneity of two discrete events in space has then to be abandoned. It is apparent that if the universe were made up of two particles, one could not conceivably be in motion whilst the other was at rest, for the displacement of particle A defines exactly the displacement of particle B, the two displacements being *relative* one to the other.

Although 'relative value' in economics may be a less mysterious concept than 'curved space' in physics, it would be mistaken to infer from this that neoclassical economic theory is easily mastered. The conceptual foundations of the discipline make constant demands on the powers of abstraction of the mind. As is the case with Einstein's paper of 1905, we are obliged to consider the philosophical implications of the issues raised. If two products, A and B, admit a single value 'between them', then the space of goods must be defined in production itself, just as matter creates its own space, which is in expansion as the debris of the Big Bang moves away.

The question then arises as to how production creates the space of exchange values. As we have seen, neoclassical theory has no explanation, because productive services are logically excluded from general equilibrium equations. It was troublesome issues like these which paved the way for the Keynesian revolution.

Modern Economics and Quantum Physics

Keynes's theory is revolutionary because it lays the foundations for a quantum interpretation of the economy. For Keynes, production is the paramount macroeconomic phenomenon, which can be explained only in terms of creation and destruction. Neoclassical economics corresponds to Lavoisier's adage: nothing is created, nothing is destroyed. Alfred Marshall (1961; 1st edn 1890) chose '*Natura non facit saltum*' as the epigraph for his *Principles*: everything that exists at a given moment has always existed and will always exist in one form or another in the continuum and the continuum does not admit positive production, because to produce means to create. If the income of economic agents is determined by the expenditure of the incomes of others, then there can be no net income in society. For the national income to be positive, household and business incomes must necessarily be formed without their being subtracted from their incomes or (financial) capital. In other words, income is macroeconomic because it is created without being destroyed in the same process.

In the tradition of Walras and Fisher, not only does income disappear the moment it is consumed, it is consumed as soon as it appears. If this were true, income would have no temporal existence and could not be discerned either in the economic system or by science.

In fact, income is not destroyed at the moment of its formation, but later; income destruction and income formation do not coincide in chronological time. How, then, can we explain the interposition of positive duration between income formation and expenditure? The theory offers only one answer, which is that the existence of positive time between the formation and expenditure of incomes is identical to the existence of money between production and consumption: *time is money*.

Money is not then something trivial, which pure theory can afford to ignore. Without money, production would be instantaneous consumption and economics would have no object, objects simultaneously 'created and destroyed' being necessarily nil. Money is not matter, but the form which goods take in non-nil duration and is the only conceivable mode of existence for products in time, 'for the importance of money essentially flows from its being a link between the present and the future' (Keynes, 1936, p. 293).

Physical production must first be money creation, otherwise it would be immediate consumption and so zero production, simultaneously positive and negative. Thus, money and the product are comprehended in a unitary theory, according to which to produce means to create money, and to create money means to produce *physically*. In this way the classical and neoclassical dichotomy between money and product gives way to a distinction between form and substance. Money is the numerical form, in a constant process of re-creation, into which the products of a given period are integrated.

The striking parallels between this new paradigm and quantum physics will become apparent once we recall the three theories that support the structure of quantum physics.

Heisenberg's Matrixes

These are not commutative, for there is a difference in the result according to whether we measure first the position of a particle and then its velocity, or first its velocity and then its position. In economics, we find the principle of non-commutativity in the case of the integration of the real product into money. We can conceive of the product as divided into elementary parts; if the 'position' of each part (that is, its attribution to an economic agent) is determined first, then that part belongs to its producer, who received it in the form of the money which defined his payment. But if we determine first the velocity of disposal of the part of the product, its position now differs, for it belongs to the agent, who brought it into existence when he withdrew it from its monetary form.

Heisenberg's Principle of Indeterminacy

The position of the product and its velocity of disposal cannot be determined simultaneously, since the position is dictated by production and the disposal by consumption. The product is *undifferentiated* in money, which is to say that in this state, any one of its parts is interchangeable with any other. Each part of the product is consequently distributed at every moment in the total mass of available monetary incomes. The final attribution to an agent of a part of the product produced by another agent could only be decided stochastically. The part of the physical product has literally no existence until the 'observer-consumer' withdraws it from the mass of similar parts undifferentially distributed in monetary incomes.

Bohr's Complementary Principle: Wave–Particle Duality

Production is net in society as a whole, because to purchase labour is to purchase an economic anti-matter. If labour (or its power) were matter, then the issue of wages would already be the expenditure of positive 'purchasing power', business firms would lose the income earned by the factors of production and society's net gain could not be defined by income.

We have a quantum theory of production because the act of producing is a *wave*, which quantizes production time. Although production is an action extended through time, it is linked to the product by a relation of equivalence, which is *independent of time*. It follows that the mathematical product of production and time is a '*quantum integral*', production time being the integer 1, or a whole multiple of this number. In economics, unlike in Newtonian mechanics, production, a velocity, is equal to the distance travelled (the product), the equivalence being verified only because production time is the *time quantum*, an indivisible unit. Production is the wave which travels the integral time of production, instantaneously and in both opposite directions.

Production is also a *particle* phenomenon, because the product is real and production means the integration of the real product into its monetary or numerical form. Income is defined both as a time quantum and as the real output, which is invested in money. Thus the identity of monetary income and product, which Keynes expounded in his *Treatise on Money*, is a quantum-theoretical proposition – and not at all tautological. Income is a monetary magnitude and the product a physical magnitude, but together they form a whole, or an identity, since the *physical* product is integrated into money, which is its purely *numerical* form.

There is a similar quantum identity between savings and investment: savings are a fraction of income, whereas investment is a fraction of the product. They are identical magnitudes, because income which is created is necessarily destroyed (in economics there are equal quantities of matter and anti-matter), and the distinction between the formation and the expenditure of income is purely temporal. On the other hand, income saved is spent on the financial market (bank money is a deposit), and through this market comes to be spent on the commodity market on behalf of the final borrower. We can see now the injustice of Samuelson's criticism:

> Moreover, there is reason to believe that Keynes' thinking remained fuzzy on one important analytical matter throughout all his days: the relationship between 'identity' and functional (or equilibrium-schedule) equality; between 'virtual' and observable movements; between causality and concomitance; between tautology and hypothesis. Somewhere, I believe in his early writings, he already falls into the same analytic confusion with respect to the identity of supply and demand for foreign exchange which was later to become his stumbling-block with respect to the identity of saving and investment. (Samuelson, 1947, p. 157).

It was not Keynes but Samuelson who was unclear about the fundamental distinction between tautological and macroeconomic identities. Bohr's principle of complementarity cannot be avoided by referring to virtual magnitudes ('hidden variables'), and wave–particle association is neither concomitance nor tautology. It is not surprising that Samuelson, having seen in the concept of the identity of money and product no more than a truism, should have dismissed Keynes's contribution to economic theory as insignificant: 'It is remarkable that so active a brain would have failed to make any contribution to economic theory; and yet except for his discussion of index numbers in Volume I of the *Treatise* and for a few remarks concerning 'user cost', which are novel at best only in terminology, he seems to have left no mark on pure theory' (Samuelson, 1947, p. 155).

Finally let us try, with all due caution, to reply to the questions about the nature of economics which were formulated earlier.

VI IS ECONOMICS AN EXACT SCIENCE?

This question is always asked in relation to physics, and one would be justified in replying that not even physics is an exact science.

> In quantum mechanics, which applied to microscopic objects (elementary particles, atoms, molecules), one has to work ... entirely in terms of the ideas of observation and probability. The set of abstract mathematical rules of which quantum mechanics consists allows only statistical prediction, and the appearance of the so called *interference terms* in the expression of the

> transition probabilities prevents one from ascribing to a certain quantity a value independent of an actual observation of it. (Prosperi, 1971, p. 55).

In fact it might modestly be claimed that economics is an exact science, whereas the natural sciences are not. For, despite Planck's celebrated judgement (1920), economics is a considerably simpler field than physics, chemistry, biology or medicine.

Its precise limits must, however, be defined. If one expects economics to explain human behaviour – such as the famous consumption function – then clearly its results can never be more than econometric and conjectural. Moreover, we should not require economics to predict the future in given sectors of the national economy, for it would then resemble meteorological 'science'. The proper field of economics was defined by classical political economy: it lies in discovering the laws of production and the distribution of 'exchange values' in nations and their relations. In this respect it can be considered an exact science, though it is true that it is only teleologically so. The theory of labour value is much further from the truth than classical mechanics is from quantum physics. The general equilibrium model, because it is unable to encompass production, cannot be considered an 'approximation' to Keynesian theory. If, during its development, economics appears less exact than physics, this derives from the nature of the objects compared in the two fields of study. From the outset, economics concerned itself with production, whereas in physics the concept of creation appeared only in the modern study of microscopic phenomena. But matter – and its existence is the subject of debate amongst physicists – can also be approached macroscopically even today. Provided the velocity of displacement of a magnitude is not very large (approaching the speed of light), then it can be calculated according to the laws of classical mechanics, which retain their validity in certain areas, for example, in aerospatial physics.

Economic magnitudes, on the other hand, can only be conceived correctly in macroeconomic terms; in this particular case macro-theory is the counterpart of microphysics. Economics was 'pre-scientific' until it discovered that the product was a macroeconomic phenomenon. As soon as analysis transcends the search for the 'micro-foundations' of the macroeconomy, it achieves an exact definition of macroeconomic magnitudes. These are not obtained by aggregation; they are *sets* in the mathematical sense. Each product, however 'small', is a set; the product of every individual is macroeconomic, the sum of products gives a macroeconomic result quite simply because each product is already a macroeconomic magnitude. This means that the product is the result of a *net* creation, the corresponding destruction can occur only later, the product having temporarily taken refuge in money. Each product thus increases the wealth of *society as a whole*, even if it appears in the possession of a single individual.

The product is a set because it appears as an undivided and indivisible whole. The emission of wages in the national economy defines all products together; each wage-unit is already an elementary set in which the product takes form.

The whole of macroeconomics can be constructed 'exactly' on the emission of wages, which are positive (on the market of the factors of production), negative (on the commodity market), and both positive and negative (on the financial market). On the basis of emissions, the theory builds the concepts of time-capital and fixed capital, magnitudes which are 'nominal-real', financial and material, since both aspects belong to the same phenomena.

Finally, we should note that there are two types of *inductive* science. In the natural sciences, induction is grounded in and proceeds by experimentation, at least to test hypothesis (this is what distinguishes quantum theory from classical mechanics). But in economics, the inductive method begins with an account of the facts, then immediately ceases to be 'Humean' and becomes purely *logical*, the criterion of internal coherence being of primary importance. Thus, the day when economists recognize the illogicality of equating the Walrasian *numéraire* with a number without dimension, whatever it may be, they will be ready to take the Keynesian revolution seriously.

VII IS ECONOMICS A 'POSITIVE-NORMATIVE' SCIENCE?

Here we can be brief. Once macroeconomic laws are known, the origins of disequilibria in the national economy, manifest in inflation and unemployment, can be studied, the remedy being implicit in the theory itself. Economics is thus both positive and normative; the norm is given in the logical development of the analysis.

Biology, for example, and particularly microbiology, is not normative, since at a certain point it must refer to ethics, politics and even religion. Economics, on the other hand, is 'self-contained', for once the economist has discovered the nature of such phenomena as unemployment and inflation, he has thereby found the solution and politicians are no longer burdened with problems of conscience, they have only to comply.

VIII WILL ECONOMICS EVOLVE INDEFINITELY?

On this last point the greatest caution is called for. However, if one accepts that the economy is governed by a number of 'principles', it is quite conceivable that the true principles, which classical and neoclassical economists came close to defining, will one day be perfectly known. At such a time, economics will be complete in its essentials. It is impossible to predict a similar 'golden age' for any of the natural sciences or for mathematics.

A 'pure and perfect' understanding of the economy will enable humans to master capitalism and the imbalances which afflict it today. As Keynes foresaw, men and women then will be able to devote themselves to their proper concerns, and the economic order, national and international, will continue to function with the logic of a faultless mechanism which economics will have helped to perfect.

Clearly, operations research and economic programming will continue to develop. The future of 'mathematical economics' and of econometrics is assured, provided they are not asked to decide on fundamental principles. The founders of economics, who worked in a period when mathematics was already solidly established, knew perfectly well that these principles are not of a mathematical nature.

REFERENCES

Blaug, M. (1978) 'Kuhn versus Lakatos or Paradigms versus Research Programmes in the History of Economics', in *Method and Appraisal in Economics*, ed. S.J. Latsis, Cambridge University Press, Cambridge.

Bohr, N. (1913a) 'On the Theory of the Decrease of Velocity of Moving Electrified Particles on passing through Matter', in *London, Edinburgh, and Dublin Philosophical Magazine and Journal of Science*, vol. XXV (6th series), January, pp. 10–31.

— (1913b) 'On the Constitution of Atoms and Molecules', in *London, Edinburgh, and Dublin Philosophical Magazine and Journal of Science*, vol. XXVI (6th series), July, pp. 1–25; September, pp. 476–502; November, pp. 857–75.

Bradley, F.H. (1964) 'The Unreality of Space and Time', in *Problems of Space and Time*, ed. J.J.C. Smart, Macmillan, London.

Coats, A.W. (1978) 'Is there a Structure of Scientific Revolutions in Economics?', in *Method and Appraisal in Economics*, ed. S.J. Latsis, Cambridge University Press, Cambridge.

Einstein, A. (1905) 'Zur Elektrodynamik bewegter Körper', in *Annalen der Physik*, Vierte Folge, vol. 17, pp. 891–921.

Heisenberg, W. (1931) *Physics and Beyond*, Allen and Unwin, London.

Keynes, J.M. (1930) *A Treatise on Money*, Macmillan, London.

— (1936) *The General Theory of Employment, Interest and Money*, Macmillan, London.

Lorentz, H.A. (1937) *Collected Papers* (1st edn 1886), Martins Nijhoff, The Hague.

Mach, E. (1964) 'Newton's Views of Time, Space and Motion', in *Problems of Space and Time*, ed. J.J.C. Smart, Macmillan, London.

Marshall, A. (1961) *Principles of Economics* (1st edn 1890), ed. C.W. Guillebaud, Macmillan, London.

Michelson, A.A. and Morley, E.W. (1887) 'On the Relative Motion of the Earth and the Luminiferous Aether', in *London, Edinburgh, and Dublin Philosophical Magazine and Journal of Science*, vol. XXIV (5th series), December, pp. 449–63.

Nagel, E. (1961) *The Structure of Science. Problems in the Logic of Scientific Explanation*, Harcourt, Brace and World, New York.

Newton, I. (1964) 'Absolute Space and Time', in *Problems of Space and Time*, ed. J.J.C. Smart, Macmillan, London.
Planck, M. (1920) *Das Wesen der Lichts*, Vortrag, Berlin.
Prosperi, G.M. (1971) 'Macroscopic Physics, Quantum Mechanics and Quantum Theory of Measurement, in *Quantum Theory and Beyond*, Cambridge University Press, Cambridge.
Samuelson, P.A. (1947) 'The General Theory' in *The New Economics. Keynes's Influence on Theory and Public Policy*, ed. F.H. Deymour, Derris Dobon, London.
Schmitt, B. (1971) *L'Analyse macro-économique des revenus*, Dalloz, Paris.
— (1972) *Macroeconomic Theory: A Fundamental Revision*, Castella, Albeuve (Switzerland).
— (1984) *Inflation, Chômage et malformations du Capital*, Economica, Paris; Castella, Albeuve (Switzerland).
Schumpeter, J.A. (1954) *History of Economic Analysis*, Allen and Unwin, London.
Smith, A. (1976) *An Inquiry into the Nature and Causes of the Wealth of Nations* (1st edn 1776), ed. R.H. Campbell, A.S. Skinner, W.B. Todd, Clarendon Press, Oxford.
Walras, L. (1874) *Eléments d'économie politique pure*, Corbaz, Lausanne; English translation: *Elements of Pure Economics*, ed. W. Jaffé, Allen and Unwin, London, 1954.

Part II
The Core and Extensions of Exchange-Oriented Theories

4

The Concepts of Surplus and Loss and the Reformulation of the Theories of Stable General Economic Equilibrium and Maximum Efficiency

MAURICE ALLAIS

> Economics is a science of thinking in terms of models joined to the art of choosing models which are relevant to the contemporary world.
> ... Good economists are scarce because the gift for using 'vigilant observation' to choose good models, although it does not require a highly specialized intellectual technique, appears to be a very rare one.
>
> J.M. Keynes

> The ideas and theories of our predecessors can only be preserved to the extent that they represent the present state of science, but they are clearly doomed to change unless we accept that science should no longer make any progress, which is impossible.
>
> Claude Bernard

> The concrete phenomenon always decides whether a theory should be accepted or refused. There is, and there can be no other criterion of truth of a theory than its full or partial agreement with concrete phenomena.
>
> Vilfredo Pareto

I am grateful to Andrew Garfield for his contribution to the translation of the French manuscript.

The extracts are taken from: J.M. Keynes, Letter to R.F. Harrod, 4 July 1938, *Collected Writings*, vol. XIV, pp. 296–7 (I owe this very apt citation to Henry K.H. Woo, *The Crisis in Economics and the Hong Kong Response*, Hong Kong Institute of Economic Science, p. 7); Claude Bernard, *Introduction à l'étude de la médecine expérimentale*, 1865, pp. 74–5; Vilfredo Pareto, *Manuel d'Economie Politique*, 1909, p. 16.

I FUNDAMENTAL CONCEPTS

The Concept of Surplus

If economic agents engage in acts of exchange and production, it is because they thereby obtain certain benefits. For units of production these benefits in fact take the form of monetary gains. But for units of consumption the question is more complex. If I purchase a loaf of bread, this loaf has greater subjective value for me than the value which corresponds to the sum I give in payment. Similarly, and for the economy as a whole, transactions (and the concomitant productive operations) enable it, in the absence of *external costs*, to be placed in a preferable situation. In both cases, we are merely talking about propositions of a qualitative order. To give them a more precise form, the notion of *surplus*, under various names and with different expressions, was introduced into economic analysis, but only gradually has this concept emerged from the field of intuition and entered that of rigorous definition.

A long approach going back over a century has made possible an increasingly precise grasp of the vague and blurred concept of the 'advantages' drawn from the functioning of the economy. The concept of surplus, properly worked out, provides us with an operational definition of these advantages which in no way implies resort to the concept of cardinal utility, and is free of all consideration of prices, and any hypothesis of continuity, derivability or convexity.

For the study of situations of economic equilibrium and maximum efficiency, and especially for the study of the dynamic evolution of the economy, the concept of surplus, appropriately defined, probably constitutes the most powerful instrument of analysis in the entire theory of economics. It makes possible both the dynamic study of the evolution of the economy out of equilibrium and the study of equilibrium situations, and the analysis of conditions of maximum efficiency for the economy as a whole or for a particular sector of the economy, to be integrated in the same coherent whole. It also enables the foundations to be laid for the integration of money into theories of general economic equilibrium and of maximum efficiency.[1]

Situations of Maximum Efficiency

A situation of maximum efficiency can be defined, following Pareto, as a situation in which it is impossible to improve the situation of some people without undermining that of others (that is, to increase certain preference indices without decreasing others).

When hypotheses of continuity and derivability can be assumed, the conditions of maximum efficiency include conditions of the first and second order. The former can be reduced to easily analysable equalities or inequalities. The study of the latter, however, is relatively complex and even authors of the greatest repute have stumbled in attempting to come to grips with them.[2]

The Concept of Economic Loss

Since the beginning of the nineteenth century, the history of the analysis of the concept of surplus has been studded with contributions of very unequal value, but they include some very remarkable contributions from Ricardo (1817), Cournot (1838), Dupuit (1844, 1849, 1853), Gossen (1854), Jevons (1871), Walras (1873–7), Edgeworth (1881), Auspitz and Lieben (1889), Marshall (1890), Irving Fisher (1892), Pareto (1896–7, 1901a, 1901b, 1906), 1911, 1916), Wicksell (1901–6), Barone (1908), Hotelling (1938–9), Hicks (1939, 1941, 1942, 1943, 1946, 1956), Allais (1943, 1967, 1971, 1973a, 1973b, 1974a, 1981), Boiteux (1951), and Debreu (1951, 1954). Taking these contributions as a whole, they all have in common, to a greater or lesser extent, the explicit search for an indicator to represent greater or lesser economic efficiency, and they have all played their part, whether by positive contributions or errors, in uncovering little by little the conditions which such an indicator must satisfy.

The greater the level of efficiency, the more inefficiency is reduced. The search for a representative indicator for the efficiency of an economy thus boils down to a search for an indicator to represent its inefficiency. The main conditions which such an indicator must fulfil are that it be nil for any situation of maximum efficiency, that it be positive for any situation which is not of maximum efficiency, and that it decreases when one passes from a given situation to one where certain preference indexes are found to be raised without any corresponding decrease in the other preference indexes. Such an indicator, when associated with a given situation, can be considered as representative of the loss, expressed in a convenient unit, which the economy is undergoing in that situation.

Distributable Surplus and Economic Loss

The distributable surplus relative to a good (U) and to a realizable modification of the economy that leaves all preference indexes unchanged is defined as the quantity of this good that can be released, following this shift.

I defined in 1943 the loss for a good (U) which is associated with a given situation as the greatest quantity of this good which can be released in a transformation of the economy for which all the preference indexes remain unchanged. It is a well-determined function of the preference indexes and of the disposable resources in the situation considered.

The reformulation of the general theory of equilibrium and maximum efficiency which is presented here rests essentially on two basic propositions:[3]

1 the necessary and sufficient condition for maximum efficiency is that the distributable surplus be negative or nil for any feasible modification of the economy;
2 the maximum value of distributable surplus in a given situation can be regarded as representing the loss associated with the situation considered, and this quantity fulfils all the conditions which it is necessary to allot to such an indicator.

In fact, all the other concepts of surplus and loss that have hitherto been proposed in the literature run into major objections. Only the concepts of distributable surplus and loss that I have just defined and are analysed below entirely avoid these objections.

Situations of Stable Economic Equilibrium

In essence, all economic operations of whatever type may be considered as being reduced to the search for, the achievement of and the distribution of surpluses. Thus stable general economic equilibrium exists if, and only if, in the situation under consideration, there is no realizable surplus for any good.

Equivalence Theorems

From the definitions of the situations of maximum efficiency and stable general economic equilibrium, it follows, with the greatest generality and without any restrictive hypothesis of continuity, differentiability or convexity that:

1 any state of stable general economic equilibrium is one of maximum efficiency (*first theorem of equivalence*);
2 any state of maximum efficiency is one of stable general economic equilibrium (*second theorem of equivalence*).

Object of this Chapter

To illustrate the concepts of surplus and loss, the present chapter is limited to a brief examination of the cases of an economy in which no particular good is used as money, and of one where a particular good is used as money. The following exposition will be free of any restrictive hypothesis, except, in the second case, that of continuity relative to the good which is being used as money.

Finally, some general considerations will be presented regarding the gradual elaboration of the concepts of surplus and loss in the literature, and regarding the reformulation of the general theory of equilibrium and maximum efficiency.

II THE GENERAL THEORY OF DISTRIBUTABLE SURPLUS AND LOSS WHEN NO PARTICULAR GOOD IS USED AS MONEY

Production Functions

In the most general case, the set of feasible techniques for a unit of production *j* can be represented by a condition of the form

$$f_j(U_j, V_j, \ldots, W_j) \geqslant 0 \qquad (1)$$

where every quantity V_j is considered as representing a consumption or an output, depending on whether it is positive or negative.

The extreme points corresponding to the boundary between possible and impossible situations represent states of maximum efficiency for the production unit considered. They may be represented by the condition

$$f_j(U_j, V_j, \ldots, W_j) = 0 \qquad (2)$$

The function f_j may be called the *production function*. No hypotheses of continuity or derivability are made.

Ordinal Preference Indexes

Human needs are either individual or collective. The decision-taking centres corresponding to these different needs may be called *units of consumption*.

Given the assumption that every unit of consumption can classify its different possible consumptions U_i, $V_i, \ldots,$ W_i of different goods in order of preference, as far as consumption is concerned, their needs can be entirely defined by considering a preference index

$$I_i = f_i(U_i, V_i, \ldots, W_i) \qquad (3)$$

Equation (3) is its consumption function, increasing as it passes from a given situation to one it finds preferable. Every quantity V_i is counted positively if it refers to a consumption, and negatively if it refers to a service supplied. No hypothesis of continuity or derivability is made.

Distributable Surplus and Maximum Distributable Surplus of a Given Good for a Set of Operators, and Economic Loss

In a given situation, the distributable surplus σ_v of any good (V) for any set of operators (units of consumption and units of production) disposing of given resources, which corresponds to a given modification of the economy, can be defined as the quantity of the good which can be made available by this modification under three conditions:

1 for this modification, all the preference indexes of the units of consumption belonging to this group maintain values at least equal to those which they have in the initial situation;
2 the resources utilized remain at the most at levels equal to those which correspond to the initial situation;
3 the outputs placed by this group at the disposal of the rest of the economy remain at levels at least equal to those which they have in the initial situation.

The maximum distributable surplus σ_v^* for any group of operators is defined as being equal to the maximum of the distributable surplus σ_v for this group, when one considers all the modifications of the economy which are compatible with the constraints. This maximum is necessarily finite, since it is impossible to produce an infinite quantity of good (V) from finite resources. It is a well-determined function of the preference indexes I_i of the group under consideration and the resources it has at its disposal.

As the definition of the maximum distributable surplus σ_v^* only depends on ordinal fields of choice, the maximum distributable surplus is invariant under any transformation $I_i' = h(I_i)$ of the preference indexes. If the set of operators under consideration includes all the units of consumption and production, the maximum distributable surplus is naturally defined with reference to the economy as a whole.

If the distributable surplus of a good (V) corresponding to a given modification of the economy is positive, it corresponds to a pure loss for the economy, since, with better management of the economy and with the same resources, it would be possible to release it without damage to anyone. The loss for a good (V) which the economy suffers in a given situation can thus be defined as equal to the maximum distributable surplus corresponding to that situation.

States of Maximum Efficiency

For the economy as a whole, a state of maximum efficiency relative to the satisfaction of needs can be defined as one in which every preference index is maximum for given values of the other preference indices. It immediately follows that the necessary and sufficient condition for the economy to be in a state of maximum efficiency is that the maximum distributable surplus of every good be nil. This is a necessary condition, since if it were not fulfilled, a distributable surplus could be released and distributed, which might enable at least one preference index to increase, which is impossible if there is maximum efficiency. By the same token it is sufficient, for, if it is realized, no surplus could be released and consequently it would be impossible to increase one at least of the preference indexes while keeping the others the same.

For a set of operators, one could define similarly a state of maximum efficiency by the condition that for this group the maximum distributable surplus is nil. It can straightaway be seen that if there is maximum efficiency for a set of operators, there is also maximum efficiency for every subset of that set. It can be deduced from this that if for the economy as a whole maximum efficiency obtains relative to the satisfaction of needs, then there is necessarily maximum efficiency for the set of the units of production. This is a necessary condition, but it obviously could not be sufficient.

In the hyperspace of preference indexes, a field corresponding to a set of feasible situations and a field corresponding to unrealizable situations can both be defined. The set of states of maximum efficiency represents the boundary between the possible and the impossible. An immediate consequence of this property is that for any state of maximum efficiency, the distributable surplus of any good is zero. It also follows that in such a situation the distributable surplus of any good is zero or negative for all possible modifications of the economy compatible with its structural relations.

Foundations of the Economic Dynamics

In their essence, all economic operations, whatever they may be, can be thought of as essentially the pursuit, realization and allotment of distributable surpluses. It follows that the surplus approach enables us to replace the unrealistic model of the market economy, in which the fundamental assumption is that a unique price system obtains at all times, by the model of the economy of markets in which all transactions are carried out at prices which are specific to them.

Equivalence of States of Stable General Equilibrium and States of Maximum Efficiency

Since the essence of the economy is the pursuit, realization and allotment of distributable surpluses, there can be no stable general economic equilibrium, if there is any distributable surplus. Every state of stable general economic equilibrium is therefore a state of maximum efficiency.

Conversely, if there is maximum efficiency, there is no realizable surplus, and consequently every state of maximum efficiency is a state of stable general economic equilibrium. (See Allais, 1981, pp. 28–34.)

III THE THEORY OF DISTRIBUTABLE SURPLUS AND LOSS WHEN A PARTICULAR GOOD IS USED AS MONEY

Assumptions

In this section, the case is considered in which a good exists which serves for all processes of exchange, is used by all operators, and whose quantities can be considered as continuous variables.

The above definitions are extremely general and do not ascribe any special role to any good. However, in a complex economy, a particular good is used by all operators in their transactions. We will designate this good by the letter U. It is in fact money, and it appears in all the preference functions I_i and in all production functions f_j. For this very reason, the following theory integrates money into the analysis of economic equilibrium and maximum efficiency.

Walras, Auspitz and Lieben, and others following their examples, quite rightly integrated money into their general theory of economic equilibrium. However, with the demonetization of metallic coinage and the spread of payments by pure and simple book-keeping operations, it has become common, in developing models, to exclude money from preference indexes, production functions and theories of maximum efficiency. I am now convinced that this is an error.

The quantities U_i and U_j of the good (U), which correspond to the units of consumption i and to units of production j, can be considered as continuous variables and can appear with negative values when the operators are in debt. It can be supposed that all the f_i and f_j functions are continuous functions of the quantities U_i and U_j.

Once there exists a good (U) whose quantities are continuous variables appearing in all preference functions and all production functions, the condition of maximum efficiency for a determinate set of operators becomes simpler. Whereas in the general case the necessary and sufficient condition of maximum efficiency is that the maximum distributable surplus is nil for every good, it is now sufficient that this condition be fulfilled only for the good (U) used by all the operators.

Distributable Surplus Corresponding to a Given Modification of the Economy

Let us consider an initial state (ξ_1) characterized by consumption values U_i, $V_i, \ldots,$ W_i and U_j, $V_j, \ldots,$ W_j (positive or negative) of the different units of consumption and production. We have

$$\begin{cases} \sum_i U_i + \sum_j U_j = U_0 \\ \sum_i V_i + \sum_j V_j = V_0 \\ \dots \\ \sum_i W_i + \sum_j W_j = W_0 \end{cases} \tag{4}$$

where $U_0, V_0, \dots, W_0$ designate available resources.

Let $(\delta\xi_1)$ be a feasible modification of (ξ_1) characterized by finite variations $\delta U_i, \delta V_i, \dots, \delta W_i, \delta U_j, \delta V_j, \dots, \delta W_j$ and let

$$(\xi_2) = (\xi_1) + \delta(\xi_1) \tag{5}$$

represent the new state. According to equation (4), we naturally have

$$\sum_i \delta V_i + \sum_j \delta V_j = 0 \tag{6}$$

for every good (V). We also have, for every unit of production j,

$$f_j(U_j + \delta U_j, V_j + \delta V_j, \dots, W_j + \delta W_j) = 0 \tag{7}$$

The preference indexes become

$$I_i + \delta I_i = f_i(U_i + \delta U_i, V_i + \delta V_i, \dots, W_i + \delta W_i) \tag{8}$$

Let us now define a third state (ξ_3) by the condition that by the modifications $-\delta\sigma_{ui}$ of just the quantities $U_i + \delta U_i$ all the preference indexes return to their initial values. We then have the conditions

$$f_i(U_i + \delta U_i - \delta\sigma_{ui}, V_i + \delta V_i, \dots, W_i + \delta W_i) = f_i(U_i, V_i, \dots, W_i) \tag{9}$$

The state (ξ_3) can be termed *isohedonous* with the state (ξ_1). In passing from (ξ_1) to (ξ_3), the quantity

$$\delta\sigma_u = \sum_i \delta\sigma_{ui} \tag{10}$$

of the good (U) is released, as all the units of consumption find themselves again in situations which they consider equivalent, since their preference indexes return to the same values.

The surplus $\delta\sigma_u$ has been released during the passage from (ξ_1) to (ξ_3). It may then be considered that in the situation (ξ_1) this surplus was both realizable and distributable. It may further be considered that in passing from (ξ_1) to (ξ_2), it has in effect been distributed (see Table 4.1).

It is essential to emphasize that because of the hypotheses made for the good (U), it is always possible to define $\delta\sigma_{ui}$ by the condition (9). Figures 4.1a and b illustrate the generation of the surplus $\delta\sigma_{ui}$ in the case of a consumption unit in a situation of convexity (but in fact no hypothesis of convexity is necessary). In the case in which the common good (U) is money, necessarily $U_{i3} > 0$.

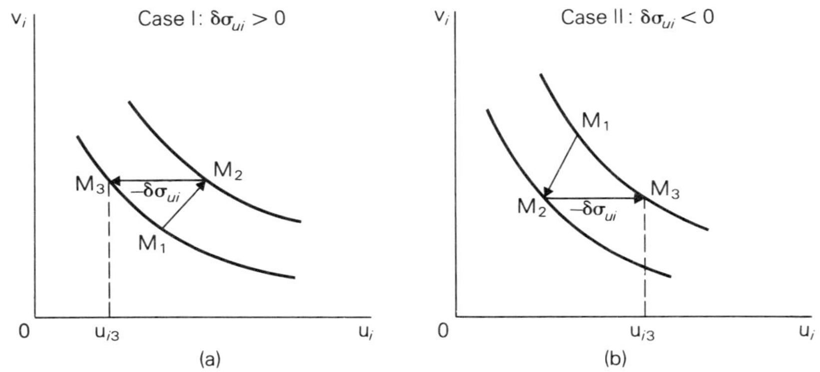

FIGURE 4.1 Situation of a consumption unit in the states (ξ_1), (ξ_2) and (ξ_3)

It should be emphasized that, by the same token, the definition of the distributable surplus corresponding to the modification $(\delta\xi_1)$ of the initial economic state involves no assumptions as regards the states (ξ_1) and $(\xi_1) + \delta(\xi_1)$, which may be or may not be states of maximum efficiency. As regards the state (ξ_3), its definition results entirely from that of the states (ξ_1) and (ξ_2). In fact, the state (ξ_3) may be or may not be a state of maximum efficiency.

Finally, the quantity $\delta\sigma_u$ only constitutes an actually distributable surplus, if it is positive. If it is negative, the positive quantity $-\delta\sigma_u$ stands for the additional quantity of good (U) which must be supplied for the economy to pass from the state (ξ_2) to the state (ξ_3).

Condition for Maximum Efficiency of the Economy

From the foregoing, it follows that the necessary and sufficient condition for the situation (ξ_1) to be of maximum efficiency for the set of operators under consideration is that the distributable surplus $\delta\sigma_u$ be negative or zero, i.e.

$$\delta\sigma_u \leqslant 0 \tag{11}$$

for every feasible modification $(\delta\xi_1)$, that is, every modification that is compatible with the structural relations of the economy. This condition is

TABLE 4.1 PROCESS OF RELEASE OF DISTRIBUTABLE SURPLUS $\delta\sigma_u$ CORRESPONDING TO A MODIFICATION $(\delta\xi_1)$ OF THE ECONOMIC STATE (ξ_1) WITH NO RESTRICTIONS ON (ξ_1) AND $(\delta\xi_1)$

First state: (ξ_1)	Linear structural relations
Operator i: $U_i, V_i, \ldots, W_i$ Operator j: $U_j, V_j, , \ldots, W_j$	$(1)\ \begin{cases} \sum_i U_i + \sum_j U_j = \sum_i (U_i + \delta U_i) + \sum_j (U_j + \delta U_j) = U_0 \\ \sum_i V_i + \sum_j V_j = \sum_i (V_i + \delta V_i) + \sum_j (V_j + \delta V_j) = V_0 \\ \ldots \\ \sum_i W_i + \sum_j W_j = \sum_i (W_i + \delta W_i) + \sum_j (W_j + \delta W_j) = W_0 \end{cases}$
Second state: $(\xi_2) = (\xi_1) + \delta(\xi_1)$	
Operator i: $U_i + \delta U_i, V_i + \delta V_i, \ldots, W_i + \delta W_i$ Operator j: $U_j + \delta U_j, V_j + \delta V_j, \ldots, W_j + \delta W_j$	
Third state: $(\xi_3) = (\xi_2) + (\delta\xi_2)$ isohedonous with $(\xi_1)^a$	Resources: $U_0, V_0, \ldots, W_0$
Operator i: $U_i + \delta U_i - \delta\sigma_{ui}, V_i + \delta V_i, \ldots, W_i + \delta W_i$	Index i: unit of consumption
Operator j: $U_j + \delta U_j, V_j + \delta V_j, \ldots, W_j + \delta W_j$	Index j: unit of production

[a] In the state (ξ_3) all the preference indexes have the same value as in the state (ξ_1).

necessary, since were it not to be satisfied, there would be at least one feasible modification ($\delta\xi_1$) which would release a surplus, and maximum efficiency could not obtain. It is also sufficient since, if it is satisfied, no surplus can be realized and there would be maximum efficiency.

Condition (11) is also the condition for the existence of stable general equilibrium in the economy.

Maximum Distributable Surplus and Economic Loss

If the state (ξ_3) is one of maximum efficiency, the distributable surplus $\delta\sigma_u$ is equal to the maximum $\delta\sigma_u^*$ of the releasable surplus corresponding to the initial situation (ξ_1) defined above and vice versa. If in fact, the state (ξ_3) is one of maximum efficiency, no distributable surplus exists in that state and therefore necessarily $\delta\sigma_u = \delta\sigma_u^*$. Conversely, if $\delta\sigma_u = \delta\sigma_u^*$, the state ($\xi_3$) is necessarily a state of maximum efficiency.

Naturally, if $\delta\sigma_u = \delta\sigma_u^*$ the modification ($\delta\xi_1$) of the economy is no longer free of any restriction. It must correspond to the condition that the releasable surplus $\delta\sigma_u = \delta\sigma_u^*$ is a maximum.

In a given situation (ξ_1), the maximum releasable surplus $\delta\sigma_u^*$ is a well-determined function

$$\delta\sigma_u^* = F[\mathrm{I}_1, \mathrm{I}_2, \ldots, \mathrm{I}_n, \mathrm{U}_0, \mathrm{V}_0, \ldots, \mathrm{W}_0] \tag{12}$$

of the preference indexes I_i and of the resources V_0 which characterize this situation. The maximum releasable surplus $\delta\sigma_u^*$ represents the loss suffered by the economy in the situation considered (ξ_1).

The function F is naturally a decreasing function of the preference indexes I_i. If a preference index goes up while the others remain constant, the loss $\delta\sigma_u^*$ must necessarily diminish.

Releasable Surplus, Distributable Surplus, and Distributed Surplus—Maximum Distributable Surplus and Economic Loss

It is important to distinguish clearly between the concepts of realizable surplus, of distributable surplus, of released surplus, and of distributed surplus. In the case studied above, the quantity $\delta\sigma_u$ of the good (U) represents a surplus actually realizable by moving from state (ξ_1) to state (ξ_2). If it is *released*, it becomes *distributable*, and in the passage from state (ξ_1) to state (ξ_2) it is actually *distributed*.

Considering the set of all feasible states (ξ_2) and the corresponding states (ξ_3), the distributable surplus $\delta\sigma_u$ necessarily has a maximum $\delta\sigma_u^*$, for it is impossible to release an infinite quantity of the good (U) with limited resources. The quantity $\delta\sigma_u^*$ represents the *maximum distributable surplus* which corresponds to the situation (ξ_1). The generally well-determined states (ξ_2^*) and (ξ_3^*) correspond to this maximum. The maximum distributable surplus $\delta\sigma_u^*$ represents the *pure loss* expressed in good (U) which the economy suffers in the situation (ξ_1).

If a positive distributable surplus $\delta\sigma_u$ corresponds to a given modification of the economy, one can be certain that by suitably distributing this surplus, it will always be possible to act in such a way that in the new state of the economy which emerges from this modification and the distribution of the surplus $\delta\sigma_u$, all the units of consumption will be in a preferable situation.

Representation of the States of Maximum Efficiency in the Hyperspace of the Preference Indexes

As the preference indices I_i are continuous functions of the quantities U_i of the common good (U), the boundary between the possible and the impossible situations in the hyperspace of preference indexes is constituted by a continuous surface which can be represented by an equation

$$H[I_1, I_2, \ldots, I_n, U_0, V_0, \ldots, W_0] = 0 \tag{13}$$

where $I_1, I_2, \ldots, I_n$ are the preference indexes of the different units of consumption, whilst the resources $U_0, V_0, \ldots, W_0$ are taken as given.

This surface coincides with the surface corresponding to the condition

$$\delta\sigma_u^* = 0 \tag{13*}$$

where $\delta\sigma_u^*$ is defined by the relation (12).

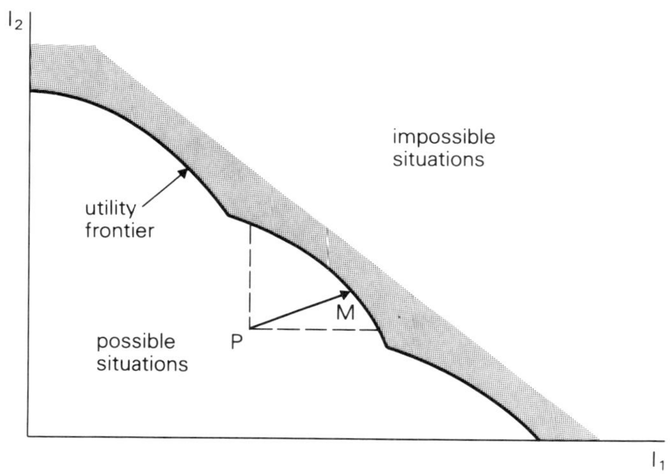

FIGURE 4.2 Situations of maximum efficiency in the space of preference indexes

In the general case, the surface of maximum psychological possibilities has a complex form which cannot be specified *a priori*. The only condition to which it is subject is that, for every displacement on this surface, it is impossible for all the indifference indexes to increase simultaneously.

To illustrate, Figure 4.2 represents, in the case of a particular model and of two preference indexes, the maximum efficiency curve, that is, the boundary between the possible and the impossible.[4] Such a representation enables very complex situations to be represented and discussed in a great number of cases. Thus it can be seen straightaway that for every feasible situation which is not a state of maximum efficiency, represented by a point such as P, there are an infinity of realizable displacements PM enabling a situation of maximum efficiency M to be approached, and such that all the preference indexes have greater values than in the initial situation P. It may be inferred from this that a set of dispositions can always be found such that the displacement PM can actually be achieved.[5]

Surfaces of Equal Loss

For each situation (ξ_1) of the economy, the corresponding loss is

$$\pi_u = \delta\sigma_u^* \tag{14}$$

where $\delta\sigma_u^*$ is the maximum distributable surplus.

In the space of the preference indexes, to every realizable point corresponds a well-determined loss π_u and the set of the points corresponding to a given value of π_u represents a surface of equal loss (Figure 4.3)

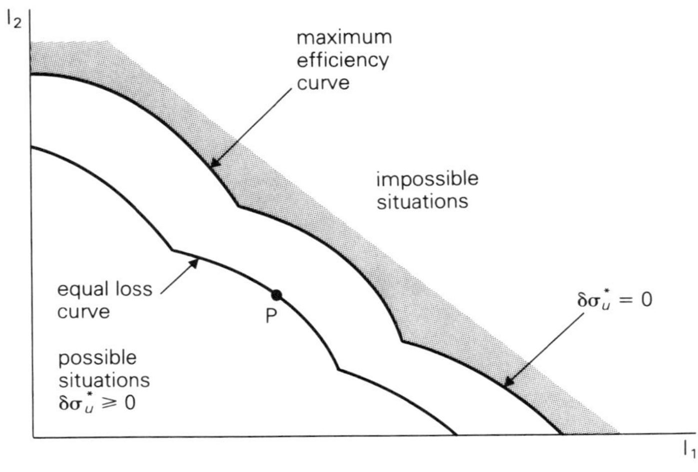

FIGURE 4.3 Equal loss curves

In fact, the different economic situations corresponding to given amounts of resources can be ranked in order of increasing efficiency by ranking them according to the decreasing value of loss. A given situation can be said to be the more efficient as the loss π_u which corresponds to it becomes smaller. (See Allais, 1981, pp. 35–48.)

General Principle of Economic Calculation

In fact, a decision can only be economically correct, if it is likely to release a surplus. Such is the basis of all economic calculations.

Let us suppose, for example, that we have to decide whether a motorway ought to be built or not. The problem is obviously extremely complex, for what should be taken into account in the calculation is not only the present and future cost of building and maintaining the motorway, but also external effects, for example the nuisance for people living on the roadside caused by traffic noise, the gains made by those living near the exits and entrances, the consequent losses of traffic undergone by the existing railways and waterways, the losses of clientele suffered by businesses situated near the former thoroughfares, the decrease in nuisance corresponding to the lower traffic on other thoroughfares, etc. In so complex a case, only the theory of distributable surplus and of loss, suitably applied, can bring about a correct economic calculation.[6]

IV PROGRESSIVE ELABORATION OF THE CONCEPTS OF SURPLUS AND LOSS

Approaches in the Literature

Six paths of research can be distinguished in the literature.[7]

Approach I

The first approach considers not a surplus defined with a common unit, but surpluses defined as either 'gains' in physical quantities, or as 'utility gains', corresponding to increases in the cardinal preference indexes. 'Gains' are possible, according to either definition, when the marginal coefficients of equivalence of the different goods are not equal for the different operators. No 'gain' is possible when they are equal.

The principal approaches of this type are those of David Ricardo (1817), Herman Heinrich Gossen (1854), Stanley Jevons (1871), Léon Walras (1873–1900) and Knut Wicksell (1901–6).

Approach II

The second approach defines surplus as the supplement of value produced in a given modification of the economy, market prices being considered as given. Two characteristic contributions can be retained here, Augustin Cournot's (1838) and Barone's (1908).[8]

Approach III

The third approach defines surplus as the sum of 'consumer's surpluses', themselves defined from the consideration of the supply and demand curves and the system of existing prices. The work of Jules Dupuit in 1844 was the starting point for this research, which has continued to this day, the most notable contributions being those of Alfred Marshall (1890, 8th edn 1920),[9] and of John Hicks (1939, 1941, 1942, 1943, 1946, 1956)[10] (see also the comments of Blaug (1970, pp. 377–83)).

Approach IV

The fourth approach defines surplus as equal to the variation in the global value of the cardinal utilities, weighted or not, the most outstanding contributions being without doubt those of Francis Ysidro Edgeworth (1881),[11] of Wilhelm Launhardt (1885)[12] and of Irving Fisher (1892).[13]

Approach V

The fifth approach rests on the consideration of the fields of choice of consumption units, the most notable contributions being those of Jules Dupuit (1844–54),[14] Auspitz and Lieben (1889),[15] and Harold Hotelling (1938–9).[16] But this approach does not really take the interdependences within the economy into account.

Approach VI

The sixth approach rests on the consideration of a global surplus for the whole economy, defined on the basis of the fields of choice of the consumption units, without any recourse to the concept of cardinal utility, and actually taking into account all the interdependences in the economy. The most notable contributions are those of Vilfredo Pareto (1896–7, 1901a, 1901b, 1906, 1911),[17] Maurice Allais (1943, 1967, 1971, 1973a, 1973b, 1974a, 1981),[18] Marcel Boiteux (1951) and Gérard Debreu (1951 and 1954).[19]

The Concept of Surplus

For a long time, authors merely spoke of 'utility gains', 'exchange advantages' or 'surplus', without going any further. But little by little there emerged the need to measure all surpluses in a common unit. Basically, if one looks for a common guiding principle in the research into the theory of surpluses, one is led to consider each approach as essentially a more or less explicit search for an indicator to represent the global surplus realized by the economy, corresponding to the 'gains' accruing from production and exchange, whether this means 'utility gains' or gains expressed in physical quantities. This indicator would increase when 'mutually advantageous' acts of exchange or production are carried out. It should be both maximum and nil in a situation of maximal efficiency, and it ought to enable the different possible economic situations to be ranked in order of increasing efficiency.

This search has given rise to debates which have often been confused, mainly because of the fact that the same words have been used in very different senses. Thus the concept of utility employed by Dupuit, and Auspitz and Lieben, is utterly different from the concept of utility employed by Jevons and Walras. So also, consumer's surplus as Marshall used the term is completely different from Barone's concept of surplus. For some authors, the gains made in transactions and operations of production are monetary gains, for others, they are physical quantities of certain goods; for still others, they are gains in 'utility'.

Unfortunately, the same word 'gain', or 'advantage' or 'surplus', covers very different interpretations; yet authors, more often than not, have felt no need to be more precise about what they mean. In addition, some authors only know of works in foreign languages through translations, which are sometimes not very accurate.

If we limit ourselves to synthetic formulations of surplus, two main conceptions have been put forward: the first is linked with the concept of equivalent surplus (Pareto and Boiteux); the second with the concept of distributable surplus (Allais and Debreu). Pareto and Allais refer to a particular good; Debreu and Boiteux to complex goods.

Having defined surplus (distributable or equivalent), two questions need naturally to be answered, when the hypothesis of continuity and differentiability can be admitted: the calculation of the first differential of the surplus in a situation removed from the set of states of maximum efficiency, and the calculation of the second differential of surplus when the first differential is nil.[20] The consideration of the second differential is obviously indispensable for the study of states of maximum efficiency.[21]

A long process of groping for answers has been necessary in order to tackle and solve these different questions.

The Loss Associated with an Economic State

Linked with the concept of surplus is the concept of loss, introduced by Cournot (1838), but first properly analysed in 1844 by Dupuit. Rather curiously, the concept of loss is not considered by Pareto. Hotelling in 1938 gave a quite extensive commentary of pure loss following Dupuit, but his analysis is in fact flawed.

The definition of loss as equal to the maximum value of distributable surplus that can be realized in the different feasible modifications of the economy under the condition that the preference indexes remain constant was first given by Allais in 1943. Thus defined, loss depends solely on the state considered (see pp. 137, 140–1 above). This definition enabled considerable progress to be made beyond the point reached by previous analyses.

The Synthetic Nature of the Theory of Surpluses

The calculation of the surplus corresponding to the movement from one situation to another, and of the loss associated with a given situation, can only be made when *all* the conditions that characterize the whole of the economy are taken into account.

This explains why the graphic analyses, which many authors have indulged in following Marshall, have remained and can only remain absolutely unfruitful. They have only given rise to confusion, diverting economists from the surplus approach, which indeed is certainly fundamental. I maintain that the concepts of surplus and loss, when appropriately defined, are the most important concepts of all economic analysis in real terms.

The Dynamics of Economic Evolution

Although the analysis of the concept of surplus near a situation of maximum efficiency is of importance, the analysis of the dynamic processes that enable surpluses to be generated from a given situation is much more important. From this point of view, the discussion by Ricardo, Dupuit, Jevons, Edgeworth, Pareto, and the marginalist school in general, appears much more realistic than the contributions that rest upon the consideration of Walras's general model of equilibrium. In fact, what is really important is not so much the knowledge of the properties of a state of maximum efficiency as the rules of the game which have to be applied for the economy effectively to move nearer to a state of maximum efficiency. (See Allais, 1967, pp. 49–58; 1974a, p. 192, n. 193).

The Conditions which any Indicator of Inefficiency must Satisfy

For an inefficiency indicator to be worth while, it must fulfil a certain number of conditions, the necessity of which appears clearly from the analysis of the literature since the beginning of the nineteenth century. These conditions are essentially as follows.

1 An inefficiency indicator must only depend on the situation considered and be a well-determined function of the values of the preference indexes of the consumption units and of the available resources in that situation.

2 It must take into account *all* the structural conditions of the economy and *only* those conditions, and in particular without the consideration of any system of prices or of a particular system of organization.
3 It must include in a symmetrical way all the goods other than the reference good, all the preference indexes, and all the production functions.
4 It must be nil in every state of maximum efficiency.
5 It must be positive in every feasible situation which is not a state of maximum efficiency.
6 It must decrease in any modification of the economy whereby some preference indexes increase, others remaining unchanged, or whereby some surpluses are released with no decline in some preference indexes.
7 Variations in it must be easily calculable for any specific group of operators and in any situation.
8 It must be invariant under any transformation $I'_i = h_i(I_i)$ of ordinal preference indexes.
9 It must refer to a common good actually used by all operators. This good can only be money.
10 It must also lend itself as easily to the analysis of the dynamic evolution of the economy in whatever system of organization, as it does to the analysis of states of stable general equilibrium and maximum efficiency.
11 It must be independent of any consideration relating to the distribution of income.
12 It must be independent of any needlessly restrictive condition of continuity, derivability or convexity, while the condition of continuity must only be required for the reference good.

From these conditions, it follows that any appropriate indicator of economic inefficiency must be minimum and nil in any state of maximum efficiency, and only in such a situation.

When the hypotheses of continuity and derivability can be considered admissible, it follows from these conditions that the first differential of an appropriate indicator must be identically nil for any feasible and reversible displacement and that its second differential must be a positive semi-defined quadratic form.

None of the concepts presented in the literature from Ricardo to Debreu fulfils all these conditions. Only the loss σ_u^* *defined as the maximum value of the distributable surplus* σ_u (that is, as the maximum value of the surplus in goods (U) realizable in any feasible isohedonous transformation according to the definition given by Allais in 1943) entirely fulfils all these conditions.

The Concepts of Loss and Distributable Surplus, Indispensable Instruments of Economic Analysis

In the light of the preceding discussion, the concept of loss and the associated concept of the distributable surplus appear to be indispensable instruments for economic analysis, as they permit the study both of the economic dynamics in real terms and of states of stable general equilibrium and maximum efficiency.

From the analysis above, not only do both concepts fulfil entirely the conditions that have been just specified, but they are also free of all the objections levied against the formulations that have previously been put forward.

The Profound Underlying Unity of all the Literature on Surplus

Although of very unequal value, the different contributions to the theory of surplus enable the different aspects of a very complex question to be made comprehensible, and point out the path which must be taken if the errors committed by even the best economists, or the reefs on which they foundered, are to be avoided.

In the light of the general theory outlined above, the profound underlying unity between these diverse contributions, at first sight so different, cannot but become obvious. It rests essentially on the search for a measure of efficiency, or, which amounts to the same thing, for a measure of inefficiency in a given economic situation.

With very few exceptions (such as Ricardo, for example), every major step forward in the analysis of surplus has passed unnoticed or encountered the incomprehension, opposition or even the hostility of contemporaries. This happened to Dupuit, Gossen, Jevons, Walras, Edgeworth and Pareto, to name but a few. The reason is that at every stage, economic thought was dominated by a certain system of ideas, and that the scientific 'establishment' of a particular age is always resistant to any new way of thinking. This lesson, of which the history of thought never ceases to remind us, ought to put us on our guard against all kinds of dogmatism. (See Allais, 1981, pp. 296–332.)[22]

V THE DECENTRALIZED SEARCH FOR SURPLUSES: THE MODEL OF AN ECONOMY OF MARKETS VERSUS THE MODEL OF THE MARKET ECONOMY

The Decentralized Search for Surpluses and the Model of an Economy of Markets

The logical inconsistencies and the unrealistic character of the model of the market economy (Allais, 1971, pp. 338–42, 365–8; 1974a, pp. 135–9, 157–

60; 1981, pp. 336–55) led me in 1967 to replace it by a new model, that of the economy of markets.

In the *model of the economy of markets*, the rules of behaviour of the economic agents are as follows. Every operator tries to find one or several other operators ready to accept a bilateral or multilateral exchange (accompanied by corresponding production decisions), which will release a surplus that can be shared out. In general, no exchange leads to general equilibrium of the economy, but every exchange brings it nearer. In contrast to the rules of behaviour of a market economy, the rules of behaviour of an economy of markets can never be at fault from the point of view of the theory of efficiency, for they always create an actually distributed surplus.

Since the fundamental driving force of the economy of markets is the search for and realization of surpluses, a state of stable general equilibrium must be defined, in which there is no possibility of generating any surplus whatsoever. A state of maximum efficiency remains defined as a situation in which any preference index can be considered as maximum for given values of all the other indexes.

Since in the evolution of an economy of markets surpluses are constantly being realized and allotted, the preference indexes of some of the consumption units are never decreasing at the same time as others are increasing. This means that, for a given structure (that is to say, for given psychology, resources and technical know-how), the working of an economy of markets tends to bring it nearer and nearer to a state of stable general economic equilibrium, and this state is a state of maximum efficiency. Figure 4.4 presents an illustration of such a process. (See Allais, 1967, pp. 54–5; 1968, p. 191; 1981, p. 121.)

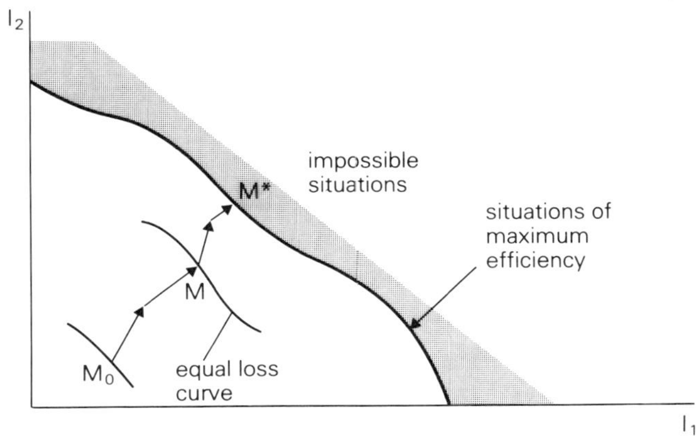

FIGURE 4.4 Process of dynamic evolution by releasing and sharing out surpluses

The theory of the economy of markets enables one to understand how the achievement of a situation of maximum efficiency is made much easier by the decentralized search for all realizable surpluses and by the incentive resulting from their partial or total appropriation by the operators involved, and how this search cannot be effective without sufficient information about the opportunities for realizing surpluses.[23]

This theory highlights the conflict between the two points of view of ethics and efficiency, since the private appropriation of surpluses appears as a very useful, if not indispensable, driving force from the point of view of efficiency, whereas it may seem questionable from an ethical point of view, at least to some people. In fact the whole question is dominated by a very simple fact: one can share only what is produced. At all events, history contains no example of egalitarian societies that were efficient.

The Economy of Markets and the Market Economy

The essential difference between the model of the market economy and the model of the economy of markets is that in the latter the transactions that lead to equilibrium are realized successively at different prices, and that at a given instant the systems of prices used by different operators are not necessarily the same.

In actual fact, the model of the economy of markets fundamentally corresponds to the economic reality as it works in practice, whereas the model of the market economy is totally unrealistic. Economically, the model of the former is more complex, so that its theory may appear at first sight to be more difficult. But the theory of such a model is in fact much simpler, for it makes it possible to demonstrate easily, without any restrictive hypothesis and in all cases, on the one hand, the tendency of the economy to approach a state of stable general equilibrium, and, on the other, the equivalence of states of stable general equilibrium and of maximum efficiency.[24]

Not only is the model of an economy of markets much more realistic than the model of a market economy, not only does it lend itself to much simpler and easier proofs, but these proofs can be made without being subject to any restrictive hypothesis of continuity, derivability or general convexity. In particular, they hold whether or not fields of choice and production are convex at all points, and there is no need to introduce any restrictive condition to demonstrate the stability of the general economic equilibrium. They do not even imply that in a situation of stable general equilibrium there is necessarily local convexity for each operator. Finally, the simplicity of these proofs enables the basic reasons for a stable equilibrium to be seen easily, as well as the equivalence of states of stable general equilibrium and maximum efficiency.

Whereas in the market economy model the search for situations of general economic equilibrium is essentially focused on the determination of a particular system of prices, the model of the economy of markets centres all its analysis on the search for surpluses and their realization, and on the corresponding operations of exchange and arbitration (and on the production operations they imply). The specific prices used for each system of operations only appear as auxiliary parameters, of relatively minor economic importance; only the realized surpluses have real importance.

The evolutionary process of an economy of markets consists of a series of successive equilibria on partial markets. If the structure of the economy is assumed to remain the same over time, and if its dynamic principles are observed, it will necessarily result in a state of stable general equilibrium, which is also one of maximum efficiency, or at the very least very near to the set of the states of maximum efficiency.

By its very nature, by emphasizing the realization of surpluses, the model of the economy of markets is essentially dynamic, whereas by stressing only the equilibrium price system, the model of the market economy is purely static. The model of the market economy only really takes into consideration the interdependence of economic phenomena in a situation of general economic equilibrium, whereas the model of an economy of markets focuses all its analysis on causal links, with the search for realizable surpluses and their realization constituting the fundamental and synthetic principle of the working of the whole economy. Interdependence in the neighbourhood of an equilibrium situation only appears as a consequence of a much more general process.

Whereas the model of the market economy rests on the hypotheses of perfect competition and the existence of a very large number of operators, the model of the economy of markets is completely free of such hypotheses.[25]

This model lends itself as readily to the analysis of the international economy as it does to that of national economies, and just as well to the analysis of Eastern and Third World economies as to that of Western economies.

Once one realizes how utterly inadmissible, and indeed absolutely aberrant, is Walras's and his followers' model of the market economy, one conclusion is unavoidable: the theories of general economic equilibrium and maximum efficiency, as they are still generally accepted and taught by the scientific 'establishment', must be radically overhauled, if not abandoned altogether.[26] Another approach must be substituted for Walras's, and in fact the decentralized search for surpluses is really the only dynamic principle from which a realistic conception, both elaborate and fundamentally very simple, of the working of the economy can be derived. (See appendix I.)

As I wrote more than twenty years ago, but apparently without any success:

No system of assumptions can be maintained that is directly or indirectly invalidated by observed data. ... The basic rule should be subordination to the data of observation and experience. ... Assumptions should not be chosen as a function of a theory; it is the theory that should be chosen so that its assumptions are in line with observed data. A theory should be selected not because of the aesthetic qualities of its mathematics and of its theorems, but as a function of a single criterion, analysis of the facts and conformity to the facts. ... Paradoxically from the scientific point of view, infinitely more care has been lavished on the mathematical elaboration of models than on the discussion of their structure and assumptions as they relate to the analysis of facts. An immense flood of mathematics has relegated the discussion of essential assumptions to the background, and too many authors seem to be more preoccupied with the enunciation of theorems in pure mathematics than with analyzing real facts. ... The exaltation of formal rigor has generally only one consequence: failure to understand reality. ... As Pareto said: 'If the premises are false, mathematically drawn deductions will be just as erroneous as those provided by ordinary logic.'

It is paradoxical that most contemporary theoretical research uses an unrealistic model, the market economy model, and relies on assumptions that are contradicted by observation, such as the assumptions of general convexity, rather than a model that is closer to reality, simpler to analyze, and free of restrictive assumptions. The arbitrary simplification of reality, which generates erroneous ideas, only complicates the mathematical discussion of the model. For these reasons, the current theories of equilibrium and maximum efficiency need to be reformulated. (Allais, 1971, pp. 375–81; 1974a, pp. 335–65)

Overview

The new theory of the economy of markets, completely breaking with the previous literature, essentially bases economic dynamics as a whole on the search for the realization and distribution of surpluses, whereas the previous literature based it on the search for a system of equilibrium prices. The hypothesis of Walras's model of the existence at any one moment of a unique system of prices for all operators is rejected altogether.

Whereas within the framework of the model of the market economy the search for efficiency is essentially focused on the determination of a certain system of prices, the analysis of the model of an economy of markets bases its approach on the search for realizable surpluses and on their realization. It is in fact the three concepts of distributable surplus, of loss, and of the surface of maximum possibilities in the space of the preference indexes, which I worked out in 1943, that constitute the basis of this new theory.

This analysis, entirely free of any unrealistic hypotheses of continuity, derivability or convexity, includes among other particular cases the approaches of Walras and Pareto, Edgeworth's 'recontract' approach, the marginalist approach, the Marshallian approach of external economies and costs, the coalition theory, and all the contemporary approaches as far as they are valid. It enables all the fundamental propositions to be demonstrated easily and thoroughly.

As regards the search for maximum efficiency situations, it replaces the search for a certain system of prices, the same for all operators, by the search for a situation in which no surplus is realizable. The concept of prices is relegated to the background of the analysis and only plays a subsidiary role. It is the concept of surplus which plays the major role in the new formulation.

Not only does this theory make possible a realistic representation of economic dynamics, disencumbered of all useless and arbitrary hypotheses, but it enables the real meaning of the workings of the economy to be better understood, as regards double aspect of management and distribution of income, which it enables to be presented in an entirely different perspective. (See Allais, 1971; 1974a; 1981, pp. 335–65.)

APPENDIX I

Market Economy and Markets Economy: Fundamental Principles Underlying the Two Models and their Implications

	Market economy model	*Economy of markets model*
Assumptions	Transactions envisaged by operators are made in an undefined environment in which partners are not specified.	Transactions are made between specific partners.
	The prices used by all operators are the same, whether general equilibrium obtains or not.	The prices used are specific to the transactions.
	Supply and demand are virtual and do not result in actual exchanges as long as the condition that supply and demand be equal for all goods is not satisfied. The price of any good whose demand exceeds supply is assumed to rise, and conversely.	Supply and demand result in actual exchanges, if a surplus is realized.
	The transition from the initial situation to the final one is made in one single movement, when the set of prices implementing the overall equality of supply and demand for all goods has been found.	Exchange transactions occur even though general equilibrium is not a consequence.

	Market economy model	*Economy of markets model*
Definition of states of equilibrium	Equilibrium exists if, under the set of prices considered, overall demand and supply are equal for each good.	Equilibrium exists if there is no realizable surplus for any good.
Definition of states of maximum efficiency	Maximum efficiency exists if every preference index is maximal for given values of the other indexes.	
Fundamental theorems of equivalence	1 Every state of stable general economic equilibrium is a state of maximum efficiency. 2 Every state of maximum efficiency is a state of stable general economic equilibrium.	
Approaches used	Set theory Assumptions of continuity and convexity for every consumption and production unit.	Set theory No assumption at all.
	Differential calculus Assumptions of continuity and differentiability.	Differential calculus Assumptions of continuity and differentiability.
Criteria for achieving a state of maximum efficiency	The two principles of: maximization of the preference index of a consumption unit at given prices maximization of income of a production unit at given prices have no general validity and can be shown to lead to wrong decisions.	The dynamic principle of realizing surpluses is of absolutely general validity.
	The principle of equalization of demand and supply by the price mechanism (non-discrimination principle) is in no way a necessary condition for maximum efficiency.	
	The iterative price process which is considered as leading to a general equilibrium situation may not be convergent and may never bring about a state of maximum efficiency.	The process of the gradual realization of possible surpluses leads to a state of maximum efficiency in all cases.

	Market economy model	*Economy of markets model*
Demonstration of the fundamental theorems of equivalence	Requires very restrictive and unrealistic conditions, whatever the approach.	Does not require any restrictive condition.
Nature of the model	The model applies only to an economy with perfect competition.	The model is general. It covers all cases from perfect competition to cartels and monopoly, whatever the economic system considered.
	By stressing only the equilibrium price system, the model is purely static; only interdependences at equilibrium are considered.	By stressing the realization of surpluses, the model is essentially dynamic; it considers both causal sequences and the interdependence in the neighbourhood of the resulting general equilibrium.

See also Allais (1968a, pp. 230–2; 1971, pp. 372–3; 1974a, pp. 164–5).

APPENDIX II

The General Theory of Surplus, When Continuity and Differentiability Can Be Assumed[27]

Generation of distributable surplus

When continuity and differentiability can be assumed, the general expression of the distributable surplus which can be generated by a marginal modification of the economy, expressed in units of a good (U), can be written as

$$d\sigma_u = \sum_{v} \sum_{i,j}^{i<j} \frac{v^i - v^j}{u} \, dV_{ij} \tag{17}$$

with

$$\sum_i dV_i = 0 \ldots \sum_i dW_i = 0 \tag{18}$$

Each quantity V_i represents the consumption of a consumption or a production unit, when it is positive. The parameter dV_{ij} is the quantity of (V) received by unit *i* from unit *j*. The parameter v^i represents the marginal value of V to unit *i*, when the unit of good (U) is taken as the unit of value for all operators. (See Allais, 1943, Introduction to 2nd edn 1952, p. 31; 1968a, vol. II, pp. 173–5; 1973b, p. 132; 1974a, p. 174, n. 15; 1981, p. 89.)

Equation (17) above summarizes *all* the developments of the marginalist theory in a single formula.

First differential of the distributable surplus

The first differential $d\sigma_u$ of the distributable surplus can also be written

$$d\sigma_u = \sum_i \frac{dI_i}{I'_{iu}} \tag{19}$$

(See Allais, 1943, n. 263, p. 614, eqn 17; 1968, vol. II, p. 193, eqns 11, 13; 1974a, p. 174.)

Second differential of the distributable surplus

If

$$d\sigma_u = 0 \tag{20}$$

for any potential modification of the economy, the second differential $d^2\sigma_u$ of the distributable surplus becomes [28]

$$d^2\sigma_u = \sum_i \frac{\overline{d^2 I_{iu}}}{I'_{iu}} + \sum_j \frac{\overline{d^2 f_{ju}}}{f'_{ju}} \tag{21}$$

The symbol $\overline{d^2 g}$ represents the second differential of the function *g* when all parameters in that function are considered as independent, while the symbol $\overline{d^2 g_u}$ represents what this second differential becomes after *du* has been replaced by its expression derived from $dg = 0$. (See Allais, 1968, vol. II, pp. 77–8; 1973b, pp. 151–5; 1981, app. I, pp. 437–42.)

Equation (21) lends itself without difficulty to extremely interesting economic interpretation, especially in the local convexity conditions implied by a state of maximum efficiency. It indicates that, if maximum efficiency obtains, at most one operator has increasing marginal returns in a given direction. (See Allais, 1968, vol. II, p. 197; 1973b, pp. 129–30; 1974a, p. 175; 1981, p. 84.)

Conditions of stable general economic equilibrium and maximum efficiency

The necessary and sufficient conditions for stable general economic equilibrium and maximum efficiency are

$$d\sigma_u = 0 \tag{22}$$

$$d^2\sigma_u \leqslant 0 \tag{23}$$

for any realizable and reversible modification ($\delta\xi_1$), where the expressions of $d\sigma_u$ and $d^2\sigma_u$ are given by equations (19) and (21). (See Allais, 1943, n. 263, pp. 610–12; 1968, vol. II, p. 193; 1981, pp. 62, 81, 403–5.)

Differentials of the economic loss in a situation of maximum efficiency

Economic loss is defined by

$$\sigma_u^* = F[\mathrm{I}_1, \mathrm{I}_2, \ldots, \mathrm{I}_n, \mathrm{U}_0, \mathrm{V}_0, \ldots, \mathrm{W}_0] \tag{24}$$

In a situation of maximum efficiency we have

$$\sigma_u^* = 0 \quad \text{and} \quad d\sigma_u^* \geqslant 0 \tag{25}$$

with

$$d\sigma_u^* = -d\sigma_u = -\sum_i \frac{d\mathrm{I}_i}{\mathrm{I}'_{iu}} \tag{26}$$

We always have

$$\delta\sigma_u \leqslant \delta\sigma_u^* \tag{27}$$

since the loss is the maximum value of σ_u (Allais, 1981, pp. 135, 113). Thus we have necessarily:

$$\delta\sigma_u^* \geqslant 0 \quad \text{if} \quad \delta\sigma_u \leqslant 0 \tag{28}$$

$$\delta\sigma_u \leqslant 0 \quad \text{if} \quad \delta\sigma_u^* = 0 \tag{29}$$

$$d^2\sigma_u^* - d^2\sigma_u \geqslant 0 \quad \text{if} \quad d\sigma_u^* - d\sigma_u = 0 \tag{30}$$

(see Allais, 1981, pp. 113–15).

Approximate value of the economic loss in the neighbourhood of a situation of maximum efficiency

The loss evaluated in terms of good (U) characterizing the economic state (ξ_1) is equal to the *largest distributable surplus realizable* from the state (ξ_1). It is the maximum distributable surplus (Allais, 1943, n. 260, pp. 638–9).

Equation (17) can be integrated along a path leading to a state of maximum efficiency and leads to the following expression of the loss involved in the initial situation

$$\sigma_u^* \sim \frac{1}{2u} \sum_{v} \sum_{k,l} (v_k - v_l)\, \delta V_{kl}^* \qquad k < l \tag{31}$$

as a first approximation, i.e. to within third-order accuracy, since the quantities $v_k - v_l$ and δV_{kl}^* are all of the first order. (See Allais, 1943,

Introduction to 2nd edn, 1952, p. 32; 1968, p. 207; 1973b, p. 134; 1983, pp. 107 and 411.)

In expression (31) the quantities $v_k - v_l$ represent the differences of marginal values in the initial state considered, and the δV^*_{kl} are the quantities of the good (V) received by operator k from operator l in the transition from the initial to the final state.

Expression (31) is of the broadest generality, and holds whatever the initial state.[29]

APPENDIX III

On the General Theory of Surplus and Maximum Efficiency and on the Theory of General Economic Equilibrium and their Extensions

The preceding exposition is merely a very brief presentation of the general principles of the general theory of surplus as I have developed it progressively over the past fifty years. The reader will find any necessary further information in my papers and books listed below. For a general analysis of these works, see especially Allais (1981, pp. 366–98; 1978).

1 *General theory of surplus*

See Allais (1943, N. 263, pp. 610–27; N. 270–1, pp. 637–55; and Introduction to 2nd edn, 1952; 1945, pp. 63–8; 1967; 1968a; 1968b; 1968c; 1971; 1973b; 1974a; 1974d, pp. 30–41; 1975; 1978, pp. 10–26, 27–42; 1981).

2 *Theories of general economic equilibrium and of maximum efficiency in the case where the hypotheses of continuity and differentiability can be admitted*

See Allais (1943; 1945; 1974b).

3 *Extensions of the theories of general economic equilibrium and of maximum efficiency*

(a) Theory of demographic optimum: demographic structure corresponding to maximum productivity. See Allais (1943, n. 322–7, pp. 749–55).

(b) Case in which the future generations are taken into account. See Allais (1947, pp. 153–78).

(c) Theory of maximum capitalistic efficiency. See Allais (1947, pp. 179–228, 634–771; 1962; 1963a; 1963b; 1968d; 1978, pp. 44–60).

(d) Theory of general economic equilibrium and of maximum efficiency in the case of risk. See Allais (1952a; 1952b; 1979).

(e) Integration of money into the theory of general economic equilibrium and of maximum efficiency. See Allais (1965b; 1966; 1968d; 1972; 1973c; 1974c).

4 *Applications of the general theory of surplus*

(a) Applications to the management of basic industries. See Allais (1953; 1961; 1964; 1965a) and Allais *et al.* (1965).

(b) Applications to the economic policy – efficiency and income distribution. See Allais (1964a; 1964b; 1977; 1981, pp. 426–30).

NOTES

1. The present chapter only discusses the essence of what is essential.
   For a more thorough and detailed analysis of the general theory of surplus, the reader is referred mainly to the following works (Allais, 1967, 1968b, 1971, 1973b, 1974, 1981). See also appendix III.
2. Such, in particular, is the case of the analyses of Pareto, Hotelling and Boiteux, and of the critical analysis by Samuelson of Pareto's concept of surplus. On Pareto's analysis of the second differential, see Allais (1973b, pp. 144–6); on Hotelling's analysis, see Allais (1981, pp. 258–94, 639–44); on the analysis of Boiteux, see Allais (1981, pp. 301–2); on the critical analysis of Pareto by Samuelson, see Allais (1973b, pp. 146–51, 155–9). On the analysis of the case where the hypotheses of continuity and derivability can be admitted, see some very brief indications in appendix II below. See also Allais (1981, pp. 49–156; 1973b).
3. Allais (1943) gives two proofs of the theorems of equivalence of states of maximum efficiency and states of stable general equilibrium of a market economy. The first very intuitive proof is based on the consideration of the marginal coefficients of equivalence (Allais, 1943, vol. 1, n. 266, pp. 617–27), and the second is based on the Lagrange theory of multipliers (ibid., n. 267, pp. 628–35).
   For the first time in the literature, with a very high degree of generality, the proofs presented of the two theorems of equivalence in the case in which continuity and differentiability hypotheses can be admitted take account of the decomposition of the production system into distinct industrial activities and each activity into different firms; of the consideration of time and of the rate of interest; of second-order conditions and stability; of income distribution. These proofs are free of any hypothesis of general convexity. See Allais (1981, pp. 368–81) on these proofs.
4. This illustrative model is examined in detail by Allais (1974b, p. 644). It illustrates very general conditions.
5. I think I was the first in the literature to present the concept of the maximum efficiency surface in the space of the preference indexes, as well as the representation of figure 3 in my book (Allais, 1943, vol. 1, pp. 641–3). In this work I defined and studied this boundary, which is economically very suggestive and certainly of fundamental importance, in the case in which the

hypotheses of continuity and differentiability can be admitted. At that time, I called it the *surface de rendement social maximum* (surface of maximum social efficiency) and made a thorough analysis of its properties with many graphical illustrations. I used this concept and this representation again in my works (Allais, 1945; 1947, ch. VI). Thus it was with great astonishment that I found the paternity of this concept (the 'utility possibility curve') attributed to Paul Samuelson (see for example Mishan, 1960, p. 228; 1968, p. 509). In view of the considerable importance of this concept and this representation in economic analysis, I think I should emphasize the great antecedence of my work (seven years as regards Samuelson). For more detailed comments on this question, see Allais (1971, p. 385; 1974a, pp. 176–7; 1981, n. 127,3, pp. 45–7).

6. For an illustration see, for example, Allais (1964, 1965a). On the applications of the general theory of surpluses, see appendix III below.
7. To a large extent, this classification is arbitrary, for certain authors could validly be classified under two different headings. In fact, I have attempted to classify contributions according to their most important characteristics. In all the questions examined in the following comments, the economic literature is immense. Thus I can only limit myself to essential contributions and for lack of space I have deliberately forgone a large number of comments, however interesting, on these six approaches.
8. For a critical analysis of Barone's contribution, see Allais (1981, pp. 238–57).
9. Marshall (1842–1924) had the very great merit of creating the term 'consumer surplus', a very suggestive and appropriate expression, but he basically took over Dupuit's analysis without referring to it, and in fact he introduced some errors of his own. His whole analysis is based on graphical considerations. On Marshall's attitude towards Dupuit, which can indeed be criticized from an ethical standpoint, see Schumpeter (1954, p. 839) and Allais (1981, pp. 161–3).
10. All works of Hicks from 1939 to 1956 are based essentially, following Dupuit and Marshall, on graphic considerations. However, his articles of 1942 and 1946 resort to differential calculus. Hicks's approach to surplus concerns only the consumer's surplus. Thus it remains partial and does not take into account the economy as a whole. The question of the link between the theory of surplus and the theory of maximum efficiency and of economic loss is not tackled. Those are very essential lacunae.

As regards the effects of price changes analysed by Marshall and his concept of 'consumer's surplus', Hicks has elaborated four different concepts of this surplus: 'the compensating and equivalent variations in income, C and E; the compensating and equivalent surpluses c and e' in relation with 'the Marshall measure of the surplus M'. According to Hicks, M should be equal to $(C+E)/2 = (c+e)/2$ (1956, pp. 101–2). Hicks's four consumer's surpluses are of first order, when the corresponding price variations are themselves of the first order.

It follows on from the above that the analysis of consumer's surplus cannot usefully be disassociated from the analysis of the whole economy, and an absolutely essential circumstance ought to be fully taken into account: that in the vicinity of a situation of maximum efficiency, the effects of monopoly, tariffs and taxes policy bring about first-order variations of consumer's surpluses which cancel out overall, the residual effect being of the second order. It is this major circumstance which Hicks's approach does not take into account.

Hicks's exposition is often not very clear; furthermore, like his terminology and notation, it has been modified over time. There is no room to discuss these aspects here. I will merely state that they give rise to major objections.

In his *Foundations of Economic Analysis* Samuelson makes the following comment on Hicks's consumer's surplus (1947, p. 208); see also his analysis (pp. 195–7): 'Careful perusal of his argument simply confirms my belief that the economist – mathematical, literary, beginner, expert – had best dispense with consumer's surplus. It is a tool which can be used only by one who can get along without its use, and not by all such'. It is absolutely true that Hicks's concept of consumer's surplus aroused major and decisive criticism, but if the criticism of the Hicks concept of surplus seems justified, that does not prove in any way that, suitably defined, the concept of surplus cannot be powerfully useful. Samuelson here makes a hasty and superficial generalization, which in reality is totally unfounded. On the Hicks analysis, see Allais (1975).

11. F.Y. Edgeworth (1845–1926) wrote *Mathematical Psychics* in 1881, a work of genius in many respects. Edgeworth defines surplus as gains in cardinal utility. On the Edgeworth theory, see Allais (1981, pp. 355–9) and also p. 169, n. 25 below. The well known Scarf–Debreu theorem was enunciated for the first time by Edgeworth (1881), to whom the paternity of this theorem should therefore be attributed.
12. W. Launhardt (1832–1918) wrote *Mathematische Begründung der Volkswirtshaftslehre* in 1885. He defines surpluses as gains in cardinal utility and considers the maximization of the sum of cardinal utilities.
13. I. Fisher (1867–1947) wrote *Mathematical Investigations in the Theory of Value and Price* in (1892). He considers the gains in 'cardinal utilities' and the maximization of the weighted sum of cardinal utilities, the weighting coefficients being inversely proportional to marginal utilities.
14. In his two papers of 1844 and 1849, works of a rare intelligence, Jules Dupuit must be regarded as having paved the way to fundamental progress for economic theory. In fact Jules Dupuit made two great strides. First, by introducing the concept of *relative utility*, which it seems preferable to call *distributable surplus*, he freed the analysis of value from any consideration of cardinal utility. Secondly, for the first time in the literature, he made a very penetrating analysis of the concept of economic loss. The works of Jules Dupuit have long been ignored, and they still remain badly interpreted and wholly underestimated. For a thorough analysis of Dupuit's work, see Allais (1981, pp. 157–97).
15. R. Auspitz (1837–1906) and R. Lieben (1842–1919), in most of their book (1889), base their analysis on a wholly analogous concept to that of Dupuit's and Allais's distributable surplus, and they take into account the production sector. Unfortunately their almost entirely graphic analysis lacks rigour, although it is very suggestive. I should note, however, that the French translation of their work (the only version I was able to consult) is often very bad.
16. Hotelling's theory, whose worth has been wholly exaggerated in the literature, is only too significant as to the kinds of errors which too many authors are too inclined to make. For a thorough analysis of the Hotelling work, see Allais (1981, pp. 260–95).

17. In four exceptionally penetrating works (1896–7, 1906, 1911, 1916), Pareto made a fundamental contribution to the surplus theory. Of all Pareto's contributions to economics, the most important, and yet the most unrecognized, is that of the concept of equivalent surplus, as it can be designated, although Pareto did not coin any specific term for it.

    The Pareto equivalent surplus δs_u for the whole economy is defined by the relations

$$\delta s_u = \sum_i \delta s_{ui} \tag{15}$$

$$I_i(U_i+\delta U_i, V_i + \delta V_i, \ldots, W_i + \delta W_i) = I_i(U_i + \delta s_{ui}, V_i, \ldots, W_i) \tag{16}$$

    which are similar to the relations (9) and (10) above, but whose meaning and implications are wholly different.

    Pareto showed that in the case of situations characterized by non-zero values of parameters, the first-order conditions of maximum efficiency are identical to the conditions under which the first differential of the equivalent surplus is nil.

    However, when not only the first-order conditions, but also the second-order conditions of maximum efficiency are considered, the concept of equivalent surplus is no longer appropriate for economic analysis. The basic reason for this is that the second-order differential of the equivalent surplus is not necessarily negative or nil in any situation of maximum efficiency (see Allais, 1973b, p. 145; 1981, pp. 218–23, 628–33).

    This is why Allais was led in 1943 to replace Pareto's equivalent surplus concept by the concept of distributable surplus, which precisely is such that it is negative or nil for any situation of maximum efficiency (see pp. 139–40 above and appendix II below).

    For a thorough analysis of Pareto's contributions to the theories of general economic equilibrium and maximum efficiency, see Allais (1973a; 1973b; 1981, pp. 198–235). The true value of Pareto work was not fully appreciated for many years.
18. Allais (1943) based all his analysis of the theories of stable general equilibrium and of maximum efficiency on the concepts of distributable surplus and loss. The starting point of his analysis was inspired by Pareto's theory of equivalent surplus, but in fact by its definition and development it differs completely from Pareto's theory. On the progressive development of the Allais general theory of surplus see Allais (1981, pp. 366–98).
19. From the point of view of this chapter and, in particular, on account of their synthetic character, in the line of approach of Allais (whose former students they were), the works of Boiteux and Debreu warrant specific mention here. Boiteux's concept of distributable surplus is subject to the same objection as Pareto's concept of equivalent surplus (see p. 157 n. 16 above). As regards Debreu's work, it is based on the unrealistic and totally unacceptable assumption of general convexity. For a critical analysis of the theories of Boiteux and Debreu, see Allais (1981, pp. 301–4; n. 545,4, p. 326).
20. Despite its very great interest, this calculation cannot be presented here for lack of space. Appendix II below only presents a few basic results. It should be

underlined that most authors have not even taken up this calculation. Those, like Hotelling, who did, made errors (see p. 165 n. 2 above).

21. As I wrote in 1981 (Allais, 1981, pp. 325–6):

> Although the theory of general economic equilibrium was developed without difficulty, once the first order conditions alone were examined, major problems arose in the study of the conditions of stability and in the attempt to secure rigorous analysis for the second order conditions of the theorems of equivalence, the conditions of general equilibrium of a market economy, and the conditions of maximum efficiency.
>
> To do away with these mathematical difficulties, and not because of any analysis of the data derived from our introspection or from observation, many authors, such as Debreu, have assumed general convexity of the consumption units fields of choice and of the production units fields.

(See also Allais, 1971, § 43, pp. 359–64; 1974a, § 43, pp. 153–7; 1981, pp. 342–5).

What can indeed represent the claim to rigour of these authours, when the premisses of their theories are totally contradicted from the outset by observed data? (See p. 169, n. 26 below.)

22. May I finally say that when one makes a careful study of all the literature on surplus, one can only be deeply upset by the attempts by some authors, running from cynicism to dishonesty, to push their own contributions or those of their linguistic community, at the expense of others, or to try to appropriate to themselves anteriority which they do not have. Thus one appreciates still more the acknowledgement given by Jevons to the earlier work of Dupuit and Gossen; by Walras, bowing to the earlier work of Gossen and Jevons; or by Pareto, paying admirable hommage to Walras, and this, despite the differences between them, which had somewhat clouded their relations. At a certain level of genius, antecedence and intellectual debt are willingly acknowledged.

23. Concretely, this information comes largely from advertising.

24. Perhaps the only drawback of this theory is its simplicity. For as I wrote in 1971: 'For many the beauty of a theory lies in its complexity rather than in the ease with which it can be used to analyse the facts' (Allais, 1971, p. 403, n. 7; see also Allais, 1974a, pp. 194, 211).

25. In fact what characterizes reality are coalitions of all sorts; and as Edgeworth has shown, the model of perfect competition is only a particular asymptotic case of a much more general model, that of the search by every group for the largest surplus it can secure in the situation of the economy considered.

    However, although Edgeworth's 're-contract' model is a remarkable step forward from the Walrasian model, it nevertheless remains unrealistic. Once a contract has been settled, the fact is that it is impossible to re-contract.

    See Allais (1981, pp. 355–9); see also Allais (1971, p. 400, n. 14; 1974a, p. 179, n. 36).

26. All these theories are based on totally unrealistic and unacceptable hypotheses, especially the double postulate of general convexity of the fields of choice and production. Gérard Debreu's theory of value is a good illustration of these theories. For a critical analysis of this theory, see Allais (1971, pp. 342–64, 375–81; 1974a, pp. 145–57, 167–71; 1981, pp. 341–5).

As I have written previously (Allais, 1971, p. 364; 1974a, p. 157): 'In fact, from an economic viewpoint, all the work based, for the past twenty years, on the postulate of general convexity has been built on sand. It is devoid of any economic interest and is merely a fascinating intellectual plaything for mathematicians.' See also p. 169, n. 21 above.

27. See pp. 139–40 above, especially for the definitions and notations. On this theory, see Allais (1943, and Introduction to 2nd edn 1952; 1967; 1968a, vol. II; 1968b; 1971; 1973b; 1974a; 1981).
28. Equation (21) holds whether the dI_i are zero or not, subject only to the constraint in equation (20). See Allais (1968, vol. II, p. 196; 1973b, p. 129; 1974a, p. 175; 1981, pp. 65, 82, 376, 405).
29. On the generalization of the preceding relations, see Allais (1983, pp. 49–146, esp. pp. 147–56).

REFERENCES

Allais, M. (1943) *A la Recherche d'une Discipline Economique, Première Partie, L'Economie Pure,* Ateliers Industria, Paris, 2 vols; 2nd edn, *Traité d'Economie Pure*, Imprimerie Nationale, Paris, 1952 (2nd edn identical to 1st edn, except for new Introduction).
— (1945) *Economie Pure et Rendement Social*, Sirey, Paris.
— (1946a) 'Organisation Concurrentielle ou Planisme Autoritaire', *Mémoires des Ingénieurs Civils de France*, fasc. 12, 99è année, pp. 399– 414.
— (1946b) *Abondance ou Misère*, Librairie de Médicis, Paris.
— (1947) *Economie et Intérêt*, Imprimerie Nationale and Librairie des Publications Officielles, Paris.
— (1952a) 'L'Extension des Théories de l'Equilibre Economique Général et du Rendement Social au cas du Risque', Colloques Internationaux du Centre National de la Recherche Scientifique, *Econométrie*, vol. XL, pp. 81–120. Summarized version published in *Econometrica*, 1953, pp. 269–90.
— (1952b) 'Fondements d'une Théorie Positive des Choix comportant un Risque et Critique des Postulats et Axiomes de l'Ecole Américaine', Colloques Internationaux du Centre National de la Recherche Scientifique, *Econométrie*, vol. XL, Paris, 1953, pp. 257–332. Republished in *Annales des Mines*, 1955 and by Imprimerie Nationale, Paris, 1955. English translation in Allais (1979).
— (1953) *La Gestion des Houillères Nationalisées et la Théorie Economique*, Imprimerie Nationale, Paris.
— (1961) 'Les Aspects Essentiels de la Politique de l'Energie', *Annales des Mines*, pp. 201–88.
— (1962) 'The Influence of the Capital Output Ratio on Real National Income', *Econometrica*, vol. 30, pp. 700–28. Republished in *Readings in Welfare Economics*, American Economic Association, vol. XII, 1969, pp. 682–714.
— (1963a) 'Some Analytical and Practical Aspects of the Theory of Capital', Cambridge Conference of the International Economic Association; published in *Activity Analysis in the Theory of Growth and Planning*, ed. E. Malinvaud and M. Bacharach, St Martin's Press, New York; Macmillan, London, 1967, pp. 64–107.
— (1963b) 'The Role of Capital in Economic Development', in *Study Work on the*

Econometric Approach to Development Planning (7–13 October 1963), Pontificiae Academiae Scientiarum Scripta Varia, 28, Pontificia Academia Scientiarum; North-Holland, Amsterdam; and Rand McNally, New York, 1965.
— (1964) 'La Théorie Economique et la Tarification Optimum de l'Usage des Infrastructures de Transport', *La Jaune et la Rouge*, special issue *Les Transports*, pp. 108–14.
— (1965a) 'Programme d'Investissement et d'Exploitation Optimum d'une Infrastructure de Transport', in *Bedrijfseconomische Verkenningen, Opgedragen aan Professor Doctor Jacob Louis Meij*, N.V. Uitgeversmaatschappij v/h, G. Delwel, The Hague, pp. 199–238; and *Automobilismo e Automobilismo Industriale*, Revue de la Fédération Internationale de l'Automobile, juillet-août, no. 4, pp. 447–93.
— (1965b) *Reformulation de la Théorie Quantitative de la Monnaie*, Editions Sedeis, Paris.
— (1966) 'A Restatement of the Quantity Theory of Money', *American Economic Review*, 56, p. 1123–57.
— (1967) 'Les Conditions de l'Efficacité dans l'Economie', Fourth International Seminar, Centro Studi e Ricerche su Problemi Economico-Sociali, Milan. Italian translation: 'Le Condizioni Dell' Efficienza Nell' Economia', in *Programmazione E Progresso Economico*, ed. Franco Angeli, Milan, 1969, pp. 13–303. Original French text: in M. Allais, *Les Fondements du Calcul Economique*, Ecole Nationale Supérieure des Mines de Paris, Paris, vol. I, 1967.
— (1968a) *Les Fondements du Calcul Economique*, Ecole Nationale Supérieure des Mines, Paris, 3 vols.
— (1968b) 'The Conditions of Efficiency in the Economy', *Economia Internazionale*, 21, pp. 399–420.
— (1968c) 'Pareto, Vilfredo: Contributions to Economics', *International Encyclopedia of the Social Sciences*, Free Press, New York, vol. 11, pp. 399–411.
— (1968d) 'Growth and Inflation', American Bankers Association, Conference of University Monetary Economists, Ditchley Park, 10–13 September 1968; published in *Journal of Money, Credit and Banking*, 1, 1969, pp. 355–462.
— (1971) 'Les Théories de l'Equilibre Economique Général et de l'Efficacité Maximale – Impasses Récentes et Nouvelles Perspectives', Congrès des Economistes de Langue Française, 2–6 June; published in *Revue d'Economie Politique*, mai–juin 1971, no. 3, pp. 331–409. English translation in Allais (1974a).
— (1972) 'Forgetfulness and Interest', *Journal of Money, Credit and Banking*, 4, pp. 40–71.
— (1973a) 'La Théorie Générale des Surplus et l'Apport Fondamental de Vilfredo Pareto', *Revue d'Economie Politique*, Nov.–Dec. 1973, no. 6, pp. 1044–97.
— (1973b) 'The General Theory of Surplus and Pareto's Fundamental Contribution', *Convegno Internazionale Vilfredo Pareto*, Rome, 25–27 October 1973; Rome, Accademia Nazionale dei Lincei, 1975, pp. 109– 63.
— (1973c) 'Le Concept de Monnaie, la Création de Monnaie et de Pouvoir d'Achat par le Mécanisme du Crédit, et ses Implications', in *Essais en l'Honneur de Jean Marchal*, ed. Paul Coulbois, Editions Cujas, Paris, 1975, vol. 2, pp. 106–45.
— (1973d) 'The Concept of Money, the Creation of Money and Purchasing Power through the Credit Mechanism, and its Implications for Growth and the Income Distribution', revised and expanded version of 1973c, forthcoming in a volume in honour of Kenneth Arrow edited by George R. Feiwel.

— (1974a) 'Theories of General Economic Equilibrium and Maximum Efficiency', Institute for Advanced Studies, Vienna, 1974; published in *Equilibrium and Desequilibrium in Economic Theory*, ed. G. Schwödiauer, Reidel, Dordrecht, 1977, pp. 129–201.

— (1974b) 'Les Implications de Rendements Croissants et Décroissants sur les Conditions de l'Equilibre Economique Général et d'une Efficacité Maximale', in *Hommage à François Perroux*, Presses Universitaires de Grenoble, Grenoble, 1978, pp. 605–74.

— (1974c) 'The Psychological Rate of Interest', *Journal of Money, Credit and Banking*, 6, pp. 285–331.

— (1974d) *Contributions Originales à la Science Economique 1943–1974*, Centre d'Analyse Economique. Centre National de la Recherche Scientifique, Paris.

— (1975) *De Quelques Contributions Significatives à la Théorie des Surplus de David Ricardo à John Hicks*, Centre d'Analyse Economique, Paris.

— (1977) *L'Impôt sur le Capital et la Réforme Monétaire*, Hermann, Paris.

— (1978) *Contributions à la Science Economique. Vue d'ensemble 1943– 1978*, Centre d'Analyse Economique. Centre National de la Recherche Scientifique, Paris.

— (1979) 'The So-Called Allais Paradox and Rational Decisions under Uncertainty', in *Expected Utility Hypotheses and the Allais Paradox, Contemporary Discussions under Uncertainty with Allais Rejoinder*, ed. M. Allais and O. Hagen, Reidel, Dordrecht, pp. 437–699.

— (1981) *La Théorie Générale des Surplus,* Institut de Sciences mathématiques et économiques appliquées, Paris.

Allais, del Viscovo, Duquesne de la Vinelle, Oort, and Seidenfus, (1965) *Options de la Politique Tarifaire dans les Transports*, Etudes, Séries Transports, no. 1, Communauté Economique Européenne, Brussels. English translation: *Options in Transport Tariff Policy*, European Economic Community, Brussels.

Auspitz, R. and Lieben, R. (1889) *Untersuchungen über die Theorie des Preises.* French translation: *Recherches sur la Théorie des Prix*, Giard, Paris, 1914.

Barone, E. (1908) 'Il Ministro della Produzione nello Stato Collettivista', *Giornale degli Economisti*, pp. 267–93; published in French as 'Le Ministre de la Production dans un Etat Collectiviste', in *l'Economie Dirigée en Régime Collectiviste*, ed. F.A. Hayek, Paris, 1939, pp. 245–99; published in English as 'The Ministry of Production in the Collectivist State', in *Collectivist Economic Planning*, ed. F.A. Hayek, George Routledge, London, 1935, pp. 245–90.

Bernard, C. (1865) *Introduction à l'Etude de la Médecine Expérimentale*, rev. edn 1966, Garnier-Flammarion, Paris.

Blaug, M. (1970) *Economic Theory in Retrospect*, 2nd edn 1970, Heinemann Educational Books, London.

Boiteux, M. (1951) 'Le Revenu Distribuable et les Pertes Economiques', *Econometrica*, vol. 19, no. 2, pp. 112–33.

Coase, R.H. (1968) 'Consumer's Surplus', *International Encyclopedia of the Social Sciences*, vol. 3, pp. 354–8.

Cournot, A. (1838) *Recherches sur les Principes Mathématiques de la Théorie des Richesses*, Rivière, Paris; published in English as *Researches into the Mathematical Principles of the Theory of Wealth*, New York, 1929.

Debreu, G. (1951) 'The Coefficient of Resource Utilization', *Econometrica*, 19, pp. 273–92.

— (1954) 'A Classical Tax-Subsidy Problem', *Econometrica*, 22, pp. 14–22.
— (1959) *Theory of Value*, Wiley, New York.
Dupuit, J. (1844) 'De la Mesure de l'Utilité des Travaux Publics', *Annales des Ponts et Chaussées*, 2è série, Mémoires et Documents, no. 116, vol. VIII, pp. 332–75.
— (1844–54) *De l'Utilité et de sa Mesure; Ecrits choisis et republiés par Mario de Bernardi*, Turin, 1933.
— (1849) 'De l'Influence des Péages sur l'Utilité des Voies de Communication', *Annales des Ponts et Chaussées*, 2è série, pp. 170–248.
— (1853) 'De l'Utilité et de sa Mesure', *Journal des Economistes*, XXXVI, no. 147, pp. 1–28.
— (1854) 'Péage', *Dictionnaire de l'Economie Politique*, vol. II, pp. 372–7, Méline, Brussels.
Edgeworth, F.Y. (1881) *Mathematical Psychics: An Essay on the Application of Mathematics to the Moral Sciences*, London, 1881; Kelley, New York, 1953.
Fisher, I. (1892) *Mathematical Investigations in the Theory of Value and Price*, Yale University Press, New Haven, Conn., 1965.
Gossen, H.H. von (1854) *Entwickelung der Gesetze des menschlichen Verkehrs und der daraus fliessender Regeln für menschliches Handeln*, 3rd edn 1927, introduction by Friedrich Hayek, Präger, Berlin.
Hicks, J.R. (1939) 'The Foundations of Welfare Economics', *Economic Journal*, 49, pp. 696–712.
— (1941) 'The Rehabilitation of Consumer's Surplus', *Review of Economic Studies*, VIII, no. 2, pp. 108–16.
— (1942) 'Consumers' Surplus and Index-Numbers', *Review of Economic Studies*, IX, 2, pp. 126–37.
— (1943) 'The Four Consumer's Surpluses', *Review of Economic Studies*, XI, 1, pp. 31–41.
— (1946) 'The Generalised Theory of Consumer's Surplus', *Review of Economic Studies*, XIII (2), no. 34, pp. 68–74.
— (1956) *A Revision of Demand Theory*, Clarendon Press, Oxford.
Hotelling, H. (1938) 'The General Welfare in Relation to Problems of Taxation and of Railway and Utility Rates', *Econometrica*, pp. 242–69.
Hotelling, H. and Frisch, R. (1939) 'Papers on the Dupuit Taxation Theorem', *Econometrica*, 7, pp. 145–60.
Jevons, W.S. (1871) *The Theory of Political Economy*, 5th edn 1957, Kelly, New York; French translation: *La Théorie de l'Economie Politique*, Giard, Paris, 1909.
Keynes, J.M. (1938) Letter to R.F. Harrod, 4 July 1938, *The Collected Writings of J.M. Keynes*, vol. XIV, *The General Theory and After*, part II, Macmillan, London, 1973.
Launhardt, W. (1885) *Mathematische Begründung der Volkswirtschaftslehre*, Engelmann, Leipzig.
Marshall, A. (1890) *Principles of Economics*, 8th edn 1920, Macmillan, London.
Mishan, E.J. (1960) 'A Survey of Welfare Economics, 1939–1959', *Economic Journal*, 70, pp. 197–265.
— (1968) 'Welfare Economics', *International Encyclopedia of the Social Sciences*, New York, vol. 16, pp. 504–12.
Pareto, V. (1896–7) *Cours d'Economie Politique*, Rougé, Lausanne; Droz,

Geneva, 1964.
— (1901a) 'L'Economie Pure', *Metroeconomica*, 7, April 1955, pp. 1–15.
— (1901b) 'Anwendungen der Mathematik auf Nationalökonomie', *Encyklopädie der Mathematichen Wissenschaften*, Leipzig, vol. I, sect. 2, pp. 1094–120.
— (1906) *Manuale d'Economia Politica*, Milan; published in French as *Manuel d'Economie Politique*, Giard et Brière, Paris, 1909; Droz, Geneva, 1966; published in English as *Manual of Political Economy*, Kelley, New York, 1971.
— (1911) 'Economie Mathématique', *Encyclopedie des Sciences Mathématiques*, Gauthier-Villars, Paris, pp. 591–641; also in *Statistique et Economie Mathématique*, Droz, Geneva, 1966, pp. 319–376; published in English as 'Mathematical Economica', *International Economic Papers*, no. 5, New York, 1955, pp. 58–102.
— (1916) *Trattato di Sociologia Generale*, Barbera, Florence; French translation: *Traité de Sociologie Générale*, Payot, Paris, 1919; English translation: *A Treatise on General Sociology – The Mind and Society*, Dover, New York, 1935.
Ricardo, D. (1817) *On the Principles of Political Economy and Taxation*, vol. I, in *Works and Correspondence*, ed. P. Sraffa, Cambridge University Press, Cambridge, 1951–5; French translation: *Principes de l'Economie Politique et de l'Impôt*, Alfred Costes, Paris, 1933–4.
Samuelson, P.A. (1947) *Foundations of Economic Analysis*, 2nd edn 1948, Harvard University Press, Cambridge, Mass.
Schumpeter, J. (1954) *History of Economic Analysis*, Oxford University Press, New York.
Walras, L. (1874–7) *Eléments d'Economie Politique Pure – Théorie de la Richesse Sociale*, Guillaumin, Paris; 6th edn 1952, Pichon et Durand-Auzias, Paris. English translation of 6th edn: *Elements of Pure Economics*, ed. W. Jaffé, Allen & Unwin, London, 1954.
Wicksell, K. (1901–6) *Vorlesungen über National Ökonomie*. English translation: *Lectures on Political Economy*, 1934, 2 vols, Routledge, London.

5

The Problem of Agents' Beliefs in Economic Theory

MICHAEL O. L. BACHARACH

THE PROBLEM

There is, I shall argue, a serious gap in our theoretical understanding of how economies work. What is missing is a satisfactory Theory of Belief for individual economic agents. By a Theory of Belief for economic agents, I mean a theory that encompasses many disparate sorts of phenomena. A Theory of Belief deals not just with the beliefs that an agent has at a moment of time, but also the way he comes by them, and the way he comes to abandon them; the weight he gives to the testimony of authorities, the strength of his beliefs; the different categories of his beliefs – his expectations about the future values of variables, certainly, but also the theories of the economy and the proverbs about the economy that he believes, his beliefs about the motives of other economic agents, his beliefs about what he himself believes; the very possibilities that his stock of concepts allows him to conceive.

There are two reasons, I shall be arguing, why there is a gap in our knowledge about all this. We have not got enough theory of beliefs; and the little we have does not look as if it is the right kind of thing. The problem of beliefs is, as I have said, many-faceted, and the first reason for the gap is that some of the facets have suffered from *neglect* in economic theory. To others modern economic theory does offer answers, various 'special theories' of belief, as I shall call them, for different aspects of the problem. These special theories are typically thought of by the theoreticians who use them as being justified in virtue of certain methodological principles. This supposed justification is implicit and indistinct, and it is necessary to do some 'rational reconstruction' to bring it into clear view. But when one has done so, it can be seen, I think, to fail. This is the second reason for saying that there is a gap.

There are several connections between the beliefs of individual economic agents and the general development of economic knowledge, the subject of this volume. For one thing, if the beliefs of individual agents are important economic variables – and who doubts this? – then lack of a satisfactory theory about them means that *ipso facto* our economic knowledge is deficient. That much would be true of any economic phenomenon; but there are other connections that are peculiar to the case of beliefs. These connections have to do especially with economic agents' *theoretical* economic beliefs, with 'common-sense economics'. Among the beliefs that are significant in economic theory are some that are moulded by that same economic theory – one needs think only of beliefs about next year's price level, or the effects of a decrease in income tax: there is a filter-down effect from how economists think things work to how the man in the street thinks they do. Perhaps too, there is, as Schumpeter thought, a filter-up effect from common-sense ideas about economic life to the contents of high theory. Little is known about the network of these pathways or what traffic it carries, although Moscovici's work on the 'social representation' of the concepts and theories of other sciences is highly suggestive (see, for example, Moscovici and Hewstone, 1981). But agents' beliefs about theories, important as they are, are only one aspect among many of the problem of agents' beliefs. My subject is the whole gamut of these beliefs – and the activities and attitudes which accompany them – and what I take to be the unsatisfactory state of economic theory about these matters in general.

My discussion is in four parts. In section II, I explain why agents' beliefs matter at all in economics, and give a partial list of the varied sorts of belief-phenomena that are critical for our subject. In section III, I describe 'standard practice' in economics today in dealing with beliefs. If my description is accurate, the special theories which make up this standard practice address themselves only to a fraction of my critical belief phenomena: standard practice is incomplete. The second half of the paper addresses the question of whether the special theories we *do* have are satisfactory. In section IV, I describe a plausible defence of the orthodox special theories, which is intended to be true to orthodoxy's own view of the matter, the 'Standard Apologetic'. It hinges on the methodological thesis (methodological rationalism) that one should do economic theory by assuming that people are rational. In the present case, this means assuming that they are rational in matters pertaining to beliefs. But it is far from clear what is meant by 'rational' in such matters, so if the orthodox defence is to be judged, this notion must first be clarified. To this end, I propose some necessary conditions for rationality in belief. In the last section, drawing on these, I show that there are powerful reasons to think that, quite contrary to the conventional wisdom, the epistemic behaviour that is described in the standard special theories of belief is not *rational* behaviour at all! And so in theorizing about beliefs in economics, today's theoretical orthodoxy fails by the canons of methodological rationalism, the very principle which is often assumed to give it its strongest support.

II THE ROLE IN ECONOMICS OF INDIVIDUALS' BELIEFS

The Ineliminability of Beliefs

Phenomena of belief are, in economics, ineliminable, critical and endogenous. They are of very varied kinds. Studying them – modelling them and investigating the properties of the models – constitutes not one topic for economic theory, but rather a programme consisting of many topics. The goal of this programme would be a general theory of belief for economics, an assemblage of special theories, each dealing with a particular sort of belief phenomenon, just as macroeconomic theory is an assemblage of special theories, each dealing with a particular sort of macroeconomic phenomenon.

Beliefs are here to stay: there cannot be a belief-less economics. It is the business of economics – of both microeconomics and macroeconomics – to account for economic events at least in part in terms of individual actions.[1] The usual form of explanation of an individual action in everyday discourse is psychological; it runs in terms of the desires and the beliefs of the agent. This is just as true of theoretical economic discourse, although we may not always put the matter in such words: we speak of the preferences of the agent, rather than his desires, and of the probabilities he attaches to the states of the world, rather than of his beliefs. Often, when something is assumed to be known by an agent, we omit any explicit assumption to this effect. But in all cases there is, at least implicitly, an interaction of what the agent is assumed to desire with what he is assumed to believe, to yield the explanandum or the predictand, the thing the agent does. When we use expected utility theory, this interaction is precise and explicit; at other times it may be hidden from view.

But granted that our explanations of economic events are explanations in terms of desires and beliefs, the question remains whether they ought to be, or whether there is some preferable alternative. It was at one time thought, when the influence of logical positivism was at its height in economics, that economics should rid itself of the term 'utility', because what it purported to refer to was not observable.[2] Just as in those days talk of desires was condemned, so too, no doubt, would talk of beliefs have been, if people had only noticed how much of it was going on! Nowadays, no one campaigns for the abolition of mental terms in economics. One reason for this new tolerance is, perhaps, some sideways filter from the philosophy of science: it

---

[1] This by no means implies the much stronger thesis of methodological individualism, the claim that all truths of economics are derivable from truths about individual action together with boundary conditions.

[2] Nor logically reducible to observables.

is now widely agreed that there is no hope in general of reducing individual non-observational terms (such as 'utility') to observational expressions (such as 'takes three loaves and hands over 54 pence'). There are also arguments, of which economists are less aware, against the specific possibility of defining mental states behaviourally – in terms of dispositions to produce observable bits of behaviour in response to external stimuli, in the way urged by Ryle. According to the doctrine of 'functionalism' in the philosophy of mind – the sophisticated descendant of Ryle's analytical behaviourism – beliefs and desires may be defined in terms of stimuli, behaviour and *each other*, but it is impossible to 'solve for' beliefs and desires in terms of the other two classes of variables alone. There is another direction in which one may consider going in order to eliminate the use of mental terms – to the neurophysiological and thence to the physical – but this could not be regarded as a practical proposal for a social science, even if it were – as now seems doubtful – a possibility in principle. A third way of not having mental states is, rather than eliminating them, doing without them from the start: thus Skinner's 'psychological behaviourism' proposed constructing an experimental science of behaviour by observing direct relationships between stimuli and behavioural responses. But it has long been clear that this cannot be done: the desired simple relationships between stimulus and response do not exist, and a science of behaviour cannot be built up without bringing in internal-state variables.[3]

Beliefs are part of the fabric of economic life, woven into it in such a way that they cannot be taken out without disintegration of the cloth. But this by itself does not create a need for a Theory of Belief in economics. The need for this depends on belief variables being *critical* variables in determining economic outcomes. We shall see that they are. But even granting this, it might be objected that there is no need for economists themselves to provide a theory of a class of belief variables, however critical. Economic epistemics might be a shared undertaking: after all, the weather, the wars, are critical determinants of economic outcomes, and economists reasonably leave them to others. But I think there is a reason why we cannot always farm out the study of economic agents' beliefs in this way. It lies in the *endogeneity* of belief variables. Some belief variables are endogenous to the economic system in the ordinary sense that there are economic variables that are critical influences on *them*. There are also certain categories of belief phenomena that are endogenous to economics in a slightly different sense. These are belief phenomena that are more or less specific to economic life. Among the belief variables that are critical and endogenous in the usual

[3] A decisive contribution to the refutation of behaviourism was Chomsky's argument for the impossibility of predicting speech behaviour from observable stimuli alone. Many of the developments in philosophy of mind mentioned in this paragraph are illuminatingly discussed in Dennett (1979).

sense are expectations of economic variables: their criticality has been obvious since Fisher and Keynes, and their endogeneity since the adaptive expectations hypothesis. Among those that are critical and endogenous in the second way are the beliefs about each other's strategy choices held by the players in economic games. Here there are no meteorologists and students of international relations to help: if economists do not address themselves to these variables, no one may. They, too, like expectations of economic variables, are not only an epistemological worry, but also an epistemological responsibility for economic theory.

I have suggested already that there are a number of distinct categories of belief phenomena critical in economics. Just as there is, today, a high degree of awareness among economists about the problem of expectations, so there is a low degree of awareness of the problem posed by, and indeed the very existence of, some of the other categories. Let me now identify some of these critical belief phenomena. It will not be an exhaustive list, but it is, I think, representative, and at any rate it is inclusive enough for my subsequent discussion.

Eight Critical Belief Phenomena

(1) Representing Uncertainty

Man faces an uncertain world. He is aware of this, that is, he is aware that different states of the world are possible. How does he represent this multiplicity of possibilities? How is his belief *distributed* over them? Many different ways are conceivable. It may be spread over a great number or concentrated on a few, or even a single one. The question arises ubiquitously in economics: a simple case is the investment decision in the face of an uncertain demand for the product. Different answers give rise to theories of investment of quite different forms.

(2) Learning by Reasoning

Man may acquire beliefs by reasoning from beliefs that he already has. (Indeed he may also shed beliefs in this way.) Many different sorts of transformations are conceivable, which map a set of existing beliefs into a next set: the transformation may produce many or few new beliefs, and it may match more or less well with the rules of formal deductive logic. What do people do? An important economic context, in which the answer that is given to this question is crucial, is optimization under certainty, by which I mean the class of situations in which an agent is faced with finding the optimum of a function. Describing the agent's problem in these terms, saying it is that of optimizing a function, presupposes that he knows the data of the optimization problem and – less obviously – that he has the opportunity to learn, by the use of his reason, its solution from its data. That is, he is in a position to transform certain initial beliefs (those about the data of the problem) into a certain terminal belief (its solution). What do people do? Does the answer depend on the complexity of the problem, on the nature of the mathematical techniques that may be involved? (I remark that this question is not disposed of by saying that the agent is only an 'as-if' optimizer. If he behaves as if he tried to optimize, then he also behaves as if he undertook the transformation of initial into terminal beliefs.)

(3) Learning by Experience

Man also alters his beliefs by observing the world through his senses. Observation changes his belief set in two ways, by adding observational beliefs and by forcing the revision of existing beliefs. The latter adjustment may conform more or less well to the canons of formal inductive logic. What account should we give of these processes? How do the beliefs of an insurance company about the possible number of claims of a certain type develop, as it accumulates experience of such claims? How do a seller's beliefs about how much he will sell at his present price change, as he observes how much he has sold thus far?

(4) Information Gathering

Observation is partly a matter of choice. To explain and predict the economic man, we need not only a theory about how he reacts to his observations, but also a theory about which ones he chooses to make. Of course we may combine these theories in considering economic problems. Search behaviour and market-research behaviour are economic problems in which information-gathering is central, side by side with learning experience.

These four categories of epistemic phenomena, vital as they may be in the workings of the economy, are not at all peculiar to economics, or even to social life, but are quite universal. The next three, on the other hand, are characteristic of the economic domain.

(5) Attribution

It is not only economists who are interested in the actions of economic agents; so are other economic agents. The essential reason why they are is that each agent has an epistemic interest in happenings (in particular, the values assumed by economic variables) that depend on, *inter alia*, the actions of other agents. And because explanation or prediction of someone's actions means taking a view about his desires and beliefs, so an indispensable sort of belief for the economic agent are beliefs about other economic agents' desires and beliefs. How such beliefs are formed, and which ones, is the subject of the theory of 'attribution' in social psychology (see, for example, Hewstone, 1983). It will be noticed that attribution theory is about second-order beliefs, beliefs about beliefs (and other second-order 'propositional attitudes', such as beliefs about desires). One problem of economics in which the attribution component is – or should be – clearly visible is the so-called revelation of private information by market prices. Each agent believes the price to be the effect of others' actions, and these to be the effects of the others' desires and beliefs; but the latter beliefs depend on their holders' private information or 'signals', together with their background beliefs. Thus observing the price enables the agent to arrive at beliefs about the private signals of others. Which beliefs it leads him to hinges on his attribution of desires and background beliefs to the other agents.

(6) Games

A 'game' between two persons is usually described in something like the following way: there is a matrix of payoffs, that is to say a function from possible pairs of actions by the players to pairs of utilities for the players; both players are rational; and these facts are known by both players (and known by them to be). The question is: what actions will the players choose? It is supposed that they arrive at their choices by the exercise of pure reason, given only the above information. Now the problem 'what should I do?' would be solved by solving the problem 'what should I believe you will do?' – the link being the uncontentious 'best-reply principle', that I should do the action that gives me the best outcome I can get, if you do what I believe you will. Thus games are essentially epistemic situations in which each player makes inferences from what he knows (payoff matrix, etc.), to something else (what the other player will do). Indeed they are a subclass of 'learning by reasoning' situations. But they are a special kind of such situations, in which the subject of the reasoning is the mental processes of another person, himself known to be engaged in pure reasoning.

The assumptions about what the players know at the start make games implausible as descriptions of most economic encounters. Effectively, a player is assumed to have no attribution problem, to know, when his reasoning begins, everything he needs to know about the beliefs of the other player (as to what the available actions are, what outcomes they would produce) and about his desires (which outcomes have high utility for him, which low). This assumption rarely corresponds to the facts. However, a combination of an attribution exercise and a game exercise may describe a rich variety of two-person – or several-person – belief phenomena in economics. Oligopoly is a well-known example. Less obviously, there are embedded games in the interaction between the (representative) citizen and a government choosing a macroeconomic policy, and in the question people face when they deliberate whether to accept money in settling transactions.

(7) Theory Acceptance

Men's belief systems are not vast assemblages of unsorted bric-à-bric, but structured wholes in which generalizations and other sorts of ordering devices play key roles in processing information – in particular, in generating beliefs about individual questions. Among these devices there may be topic-specific theories, including economic theories. What determines which theories people accept in this domain? Is their provenance demotic or scientific? Do they come from low or high intellectual life? How many are entertained at a time? Is theory change conservative or precipitate? Is it imitative? Is it catastrophic? The answers are critical for understanding the formation of popular expectations of economic variables.

The last aspect of beliefs that I shall mention comes logically at the very beginning of a general Theory of Beliefs, and its implications for economics may be very far-reaching.

(8) Possibility Spaces

To believe is to believe something. Thus beliefs may be described as attitudes with propositions as their objects. One consequence of this is that the beliefs that are possible for an agent depend on the set of propositions that are, so to speak, at his command. St Augustine expressed this by saying 'No one, indeed, believes anything unless he previously knows it to be believable'. Another way of saying it is that the objects of someone's belief are (partial) descriptions of possible states of affairs, and that each person has a more or less rich 'possibility space' consisting of such descriptions. His possibility space is the set of possible states of the world that he entertains. What sorts of possibility spaces do economic agents have? Do the concepts of economic theory appear in them? Do they allow for all the possibilities that our theories do? The importance of all this may be seen by considering shocks to expectations. These may be of two sorts: shocks of degree, as when an expectation that someone holds is more or less badly falsified; and shocks of kind, as when something happens that was not even on his list of possibilities, when the Augustinian condition was not fulfilled. Of which of these two sorts was the shock at the oil price rise of 1973–4? Was the price rise a possibility that had been contemplated and dismissed as negligible? Or was it a turn of events that had not even been dreamed of? To decide this is to decide whether the price rise was an element of economic agents' possibility spaces.

A second consequence of the fact that beliefs are attitudes to propositions, to *descriptions* of states of affairs, is the so-called 'non-extensionality' of beliefs. If two propositions, p and p', differ only in the way they truly describe some given object or event, let me call them 'objectively equivalent'. For example, p might be the proposition that the 1 kg packet of rice on the shelf costs 2000 lire, whereas p' is the proposition that the white packet of rice on the shelf costs 2000 lire, where the 1 kg packet *is* the white packet. Now p and p', though objectively equivalent, are not the same proposition, and an agent may clearly believe one without believing the other (for example, if he does not know how much the white packet weighs). Let us say that there is a 'non-extensionality' in the agent's belief system, if this happens. Non-extensionalitites are 'distinctions without differences'. Roughly speaking, we could exclude non-extensionalities, only if we could assume that the agent always knew about the objective equivalences in question. And it seems that there is no general reason why he should.

All this can be put in terms of possibility spaces. An agent's belief system is free of non-extensionalities only if, for all p and p' in his possibility space, he takes the same belief attitude to p and p' if they are objectively equivalent. If this were so, then his possibility space would consist, in effect, of 'indifference sets' of propositions, each indifference set being a collection of propositions objectively equivalent to each other.

Arrow (1982) has recently discussed the closely related phenomenon of non-extensionality of preferences. It has exactly the same source – the fact that preferences are attitudes to objects 'under descriptions' and that people may fail to appreciate that two descriptions describe one and the same thing. Arrow points out that the possibility of non-extensionalities needs to be taken into account in giving a rigorous theory of money illusion, and argues that it is a critical empirical question in the theory of risk assessment. The implications of non-extensionality phenomena by no means stop there: the fact that beliefs and preferences pertain to descriptions of the world may create a case for the radical reconstruction of the whole of choice theory. Kahneman and Tversky's (1979) 'prospect theory' is a step in that direction.

These are my critical epistemic phenomena – the representation of uncertainty, learning by reasoning, learning by experience, information gathering, attributing beliefs and desires to others, predicting opponents' choices in games, adopting theories, and describing possibilities. They vary along several different dimensions. Some regard the future, some the past, some both future and past. Some concern the content of beliefs, others concern how beliefs are arrived at. In some deduction plays a role, in others induction. Some have much to do with other people, some nothing in particular. In some the agent chooses, in others the value of his belief variable is dictated to him by the evidence and the laws of inference.

What sort of thing would an adequate 'Theory of Belief' for economics be? It would, I contend, provide answers to all the different questions I have described – and some more besides. It would say how individuals' possibility spaces are related to the space of all logical possibilities, it would say how people distribute their beliefs over the possibilities they entertain, it would say what new beliefs they arrive at by deductive operations, it would describe their attribution of beliefs and desires to each other, it would say what they expect their opponents to do in game situations, and so on. Thus a Theory of Belief would contain numerous special belief theories of particular epistemic phenomena. Each of these may be thought of as something like a 'behaviour relation': each would deal with a certain type of personal epistemic variable as the dependent variable, and specify how this varies with certain other attributes of the agent or his situation (the independent variables). A theory of expectations of the usual kind is such a special belief theory: here, the dependent epistemic variable is some variable that represents an individual's belief about the future value of an economic variable, and the attributes of the individual in terms of which this is explained are such things as the values of past values of economic variables known to the agent.

In the next section I want to take stock. I want to see what there is in 'standard' economic theory today by way of a Theory of Belief – that is, what answers standard theory is offering to my list of questions, what special theories of belief it contains. We should not necessarily expect to find clear answers – or even any answers – to all these questions, because there is no presumption that economic theorists have all of these questions on their agenda. Nor should we be surprised if it turns out, on inspection, that sometimes a problem of economics whose analysis depends on a prior analysis of an epistemic problem is a victim of neglect in standard economic theory, or that, in other cases, a theory of an epistemic phenomenon is residing silently in the precincts of economic thought, without anyone's meaning to lodge it there, or perhaps having the least idea of its presence.

III THEORIES OF BELIEF IN STANDARD ECONOMIC THEORY

'Standard economic theory' is a theoretical concept, an *abstractum* of meta-economics, but I do not think that it is a fiction. The term is no doubt ambiguous: it may denote different things to different people. I am thinking of the whole of trends that have emanated from the United States, broadly neoclassical, and of hypotheses that today have become rather well entrenched, so that they are not very much the objects of either defence or attack, but tend to be taken for granted by those who employ them. Beyond this, what I intend the term to cover will, I hope, largely explain itself as I use it.

I suggest the following as the special belief theories corresponding to my eight headings that may be found in standard economic theory. Some are explicit, for example, (1), (2), (4), (6) and (7) – others are not – (2), (8).

(1) Representing Uncertainty

The agent has a *subjective probability distribution* over the states of the world that he regards as possible.

(2) Learning by Reasoning

The agent's set of beliefs is *logically closed*, that is to say he believes all logical consequences of what he believes.[4] 'Logical consequence' here means consequence in the logic underlying ordinary mathematics, that is, first-order predicate calculus. This description of the standard theory about this aspect of beliefs probably needs a qualification: 'all' means only all relevant consequences (that is, if the agent is assumed in a model of standard theory to have the set B of beliefs, the model also takes him to believe that p if p is a logical consequence of B, and the outcome of the economic–theoretical argument (the solution of the model) depends on whether or not he believes that p). In short, in attributing beliefs to the agent, the theory 'helps itself' to logical consequences of the agent's assumed beliefs. It is to be noted that this part of standard belief theory is never – at least to my knowledge – explicitly stated.

(3) Learning by Experience

The agent learns from experience by *Bayesian revision*.[5] There are various ways of expressing this theory, but perhaps the simplest is this: the agent has a 'prior' probability distribution P over his possibility space and if, at time t, his total evidence is E_t, then his subjective probability distribution at time t is P conditioned on E_t. If he forgets no evidence, this implies that he keeps revising his current distribution according to Bayes's theorem for his latest evidence. The 'evidence' is usually taken to be what the agent learns by observation; the theory implies that he always attaches probability one to his evidence,[6] and there is no dependence of current evidence on current beliefs, so the theory appears to make a sharp observation–

[4] Logical closure is one of the central features of *epistemic logics* such as Hintikka's (1962), formal systems which purport to axiomatize the relations among the beliefs of ideally rational persons. Such systems (and standard economic theory) also have the feature that persons' belief sets contain no inconsistencies. Further axioms and inference rules in these systems concern iterated knowledge and belief. It would appear that in work in standard economic theory in which iterated knowledge and belief appear, for example, in models involving 'common knowledge', agents are taken to satisfy strong conditions of these further sorts. See, for example, Bacharach (1983).

[5] The Bayesian account of learning by experience is not the only one to be found in standard economics. Agents are sometimes depicted as following classical methods of statistical inference. It appears, however, to be the 'top' account, and fast achieving dominance.

[6] Jeffrey's proposal (1968) for accommodating uncertain evidence in a Bayesian account has not been taken up in economics.

theory distinction, characteristic of positivism and now widely rejected in the philosophy of science.

Notice that in this theory the agent is depicted as always revising his beliefs about everything as the evidence comes in. This feature of the theory ascribes to the agent unlimited computational powers – a matter to which I shall return. Less often noticed, it is incompatible with a model in which the agent's belief system, like the scientist's, is a hierarchically organized structure, and the highest-level beliefs in the structure are altered only discontinuously and only after a prolonged build-up of tension (see, for example, Kuhn, 1962; Nisbett and Ross, 1980). Nor is it easy to accommodate within the Bayesian model the acquisition of new concepts by the agent and the enlargement of his possibility space that this brings with it.

(4) Information Gathering

The agent decides what information to gather (that is, what observations to make) by *maximizing* his *expected utility*, the expectation being with respect to his subjective probability distribution for the variables on which he takes utility to depend. Thus this theory draws on the concept of the agent's utility. The latter is always taken to depend on economic objectives such as his income or consumption: the general principle determining his information gathering is comparing the economic costs of doing so with the likely economic gains from what he discovers. Thus the agent is not supposed to have any non-economic motive for his enquiry, such as curiosity or a desire for understanding as an end in itself.

(5) Attribution

There is no theory of attribution in standard economic theory. That is, there is no non-trivial theory, no epistemic behaviour relation or set of such relations which determines the values of the agent's attributional variables (his beliefs about other people's desires and beliefs) as a function of other variables, paying due attention to the distinctive features of attributional beliefs. When I speak of the 'distinctive features', I have in mind such things as these: the way in which people understand and predict each other by consulting a socially inculcated catalogue of 'roles' (businessman, Northerner, etc.) or the fact that the beliefs I attribute to you must depend on the degree of rationality that I attribute to you – for example, on whether I believe you capable of revising your beliefs in the wake of new evidence in accordance with Bayes's theorem. Wherever attributional beliefs matter for the analysis in hand, they are handled in standard theory by means of exogenous assumptions: standardly, the assumption is simply that the agent *knows* the relevant beliefs and desires of the other agents. In more sophisticated work, or when – as in studying moral hazard – assuming knowledge would throw away an essential feature of the problem, it may be assumed that the agent has a probability distribution for some mental property of others. Such work may even describe, as a Bayesian revision process, the evolution of the agent's attributions as he makes a series of observations of the other people's behaviour. But such an application of a general learning theory fails to be an attribution theory, because it fails to take attribution seriously as a problem *sui generis*.

(6) Games

The players of a (non-cooperative) game believe that the other players will choose *Nash equilibrium* actions.[7] (Nash equilibrium actions are actions that are optimal against each other.)

(7) Theory Acceptance

The *rational-expectations hypothesis* is less well entrenched than, say, the theory that people learn in the Bayesian way, or have Nash expectations in games. All the same, I think it is reasonable to say that this hypothesis provides the standard response to my question: what economic theories govern agents' expectations of economic variables? This response is vulgarly expressed by saying that agents' expectations are (on average) in accordance with the 'true' theory, or the 'objective', or the 'relevant' theory. But these clumsy catch-phrases are poor descriptions; they give little idea of the peculiar parasitic character of this special theory of agents' beliefs. The rational-expectations hypothesis does, indeed, attribute to the agent expectations that are in accordance with a correct theory, but it does this in quite special senses of both 'theory' and 'correct'. A 'theory' turns out to be a set of (usually stochastic) numerically specified simultaneous equations in economic variables, of the kind estimated in econometrics. To be 'correct' is to be correct *relative to* the set of available statistical data on these variables, and *by the standards of* certain statistical norms for the acceptance and rejection of forecasting hypotheses.

In this way, the rational-expectations hypothesis seems to liken the ordinary economic agent to the econometrician – his representations of experience are numerical, his cognitions are cool, his tools mathematical–statistical. In the measure that it does so portray him, this special theory is typical of a general tendency in the standard theories to liken the ordinary agent to the professional scientist. This is an important theme in standard theory to which I shall return in due course. But in the present context – the phenomenon of theory acceptance – it would be easy to overstate the point. Muth (1961) himself in 1961 was careful to dissociate the rational-

[7] A recent tendency in standard economic theory refines this account; it assumes that in games with several Nash equilibria, the agents choose (and expect the others to choose) actions which form a special type of Nash equilibrium called a *perfect equilibrium*.

expectations hypothesis from the hypothesis that agents *employ* the models with which their expectations accord; he preferred to see agents only as coming to know the predictions of these models, through the medium of some indirect market process. There is, I think, as yet no 'standard' view about this matter of the provenance of agents' 'rational' expectations (see, for example, Bacharach, 1984b). Rather, the standard theory contains a family of rational-expectations hypotheses, which assimilate the agent's cognitive practices to those of professional econometricians in varying degrees. The identification of the two types is relaxed in various concessions to the agent's human frailty. Perhaps he only uses weak statistical criteria (for example, unbiasedness); or, he only uses some of the publicly available information; or, he only employs the *output* of the scientist's exercises (the model's predictions); or, only the *average* agent satisfies some given version of hypothesis. Nevertheless, the agent is always to some degree made in the econometrician's image. In even the weakest versions of the special theory, his beliefs are governed by statistical norms (so that his data are essentially statistical in character); and the terms in which his problem is formulated are ours.

(8) Possibility Spaces

At least implicitly, the agent's possibility space is always assumed to be the space of *all* possibilities relevant to the matter in hand – more exactly, the space of all the relevant possibilities considered by the economic theorist himself. There is no allowance for conceptual limitations (and no place, therefore, for conceptual learning). We might call this the 'large-world hypothesis', in allusion to Savage's distinction between the 'large world' of all logically possible states of affairs, and the 'small worlds' of everyday thought (Savage, 1954).

To summarize, I am proposing that standard economic theory contains the following special theories of the belief phenomena (1)–(8): (1) subjective probability; (2) logical closure; (3) Bayesian revision; (4) economic utility maximization; (5) none; (6) Nash equilibrium; (7) rational expectations; (8) large world. By Standard Belief Theory (SBT) I shall mean the collection of these seven.

It will not have escaped the reader's notice that there are some close links among these eight special theories of belief of standard economic theory. The large-world hypothesis feeds into the subjective-probability theory and the rational-expectations theory. Bayesian revision entails both subjective probability distributions and, less obviously, logical closure (it does so in the sense that if p is totally believed – that is, has subjective probability one – then so is every logical consequence of p in the possibility space): thus the Bayesian theory is extremely strong. And the classical games to which the standard theory addresses itself are, as I have already noted, a special class of joint agency problems obtained by exogenously assuming that the participants have solved their attribution problems and so are in the position before they begin of knowing each other's desires and beliefs.

I think that my survey, if it is a fair description of the contents of the received Theory of Belief in economics, establishes that that theory is seriously deficient. It is not just a matter of outright lacunae – the absence of any theory at all of attribution or of certain other belief phenomena not on my list.[8] Absence is here a matter of degree. One may have more or less of a theory, in terms of how much work and thought has gone into it: at one extreme, there will have been careful consideration of alternative proposals, including ones made in related disciplines; at the other extreme, no more than a facilitating assumption casually adopted or even an implicit one of which the theorist is more or less unconscious. In this sense it must be said that neither the large-world hypothesis nor logical closure is much of a theory.

If the standard Theory of Belief in contemporary economics is unsatisfactory in extent, how satisfactory are the portions of a general theory that it *does* offer? This is the question to which I now come.

IV THE DEFENCE OF STANDARD BELIEF THEORY

What do the seven subtheories of the Standard Belief Theory (SBT) which I have listed have in common? All, of course, are individualistic – but that is merely a part of what we have agreed to mean by a theory of beliefs. Beyond this there are four striking properties they share. They are all deductive theories; they are all aprioristic; they are all rationalistic; and they are all contradicted by empirical evidence.[9] We should not be surprised, therefore, if a defence of SBT as a whole, a body of fundamental principles and arguments that is held to justify it, is one that praises theories that are deduced from *a priori* principles, puts rational economic man on a methodological pedestal, and has not much time for empirical psychology.

I shall not undertake in this paper the ambitious task of assessing the absolute defensibility of SBT – of asking whether there exists *any* adequate

[8] For example, the vast area of the social inculcation of beliefs, including ideological beliefs; agents' beliefs about their own beliefs and other phenomena of epistemic self-consciousness; and still others.

[9] Much of the relevant empirical evidence may be found collected in Nisbett and Ross's survey (1980) of the empirical psychological literature on human cognitive performance.

case that could be made for it. Instead, I shall jack up my exploration of 'standard' thought by one level, and ask: what do standard economists themselves take to justify their theory? Then I shall consider the adequacy of this in-house defence, which I am going to call the Standard Apologetic (for Standard Belief Theory). If I find it wanting, then, I shall not, strictly speaking, have shown SBT indefensible – only indefensible on one flank. All the same, if the Standard Apologetic does not work, there is not, I think, much hope of justifying the theory. It is hard to conceive a brief of any promise that does not look a good deal like the Standard Apologetic.

There are high-level principles that inform the thought of the theorists who subscribe to SBT and that, because they rationalize the theory, sustain standard theorists in their attachment to it. They constitute a kind of immanent folk-philosophy of economics in the minds of standard economists. But they are expressed only occasionally, unsystematically and informally: they are more attitudes than conscious doctrines. They do not appear in appendices to the articles that put forward, or apply, the theories, for economists do not regard it as part of their job to produce, themselves, ultimate justifications of their theoretical postulates. Therefore, to discover these rationalizing principles one must perform a 'rational reconstruction'. One must climb through the clouds to the high domain of the ultimate principles; or perhaps root them out like truffles from the substratum of thought on which the theory rests. In the present case, the quarry in this interpretative quest is what I have called the Standard Apologetic for Standard Belief Theory. I suggest that it goes something like this.

The Standard Apologetic

'There is, it is true, empirical evidence from psychology and elsewhere that people often do not behave as SBT says they do. But this does not mean that SBT should be rejected. And there are particular reasons why it does not mean that SBT should be rejected in favour of some Empirical Belief Theory (EBT). (By an Empirical Belief Theory, I mean one that incorporates the results of empirical investigations in psychology and elsewhere.)

'There are powerful arguments, well-known to economists, that economic theory should be an account of the behaviour, in the economic arena, of *rational* agents. Perhaps the most important of these is provided by the fact that, at least in economic life, most agents are in fact pretty rational on the whole. (There are others. For instance, it is not a valid objection to assuming rationality that rationality postulates are difficult to test empirically – indirect testing of the postulates, through their logical consequences, is enough. In fact, it probably does not really matter whether the postulates are true or not anyway: they should not be taken literally, as statements about people; they are mainly a way of generating useful predictions.

There is reason to think that they will do just this, because there are mechanisms which promote as-if-rational behaviour – economic natural selection processes are the clearest case.)

'Standard Belief Theory is precisely what this principle – the principle that we should model economic agents as rational agents – calls for in the present context. It is an account of the behaviour of rational economic agents in matters of belief. I do not say that all the special theories within SBT have already got it absolutely right. However, I am quite confident that the better-established special theories, especially the Bayesian theory, are correct descriptions of rationality. And if one of these days there are improvements or extensions in other parts, these will have the same general characteristics; in particular there will no doubt be just as much counter-evidence from empirical psychology and so forth.

'I come now to arguments for SBT based on the advantages of *a priori* theories over empirically-based theories. The first is that the results of empirical investigations, chiefly because they lack the necessary formal simplicity, do not lend themselves to deductive development; they are not deductively tractable. But economic theory is an essentially deductive discipline; and properly so, because of the immense power of deductive methods to generate new results.

'Secondly, as everyone agrees, I think, the only sort of empirical findings that could serve as a postulational basis for a worthwhile theory are ones of at least a certain degree of generality (across individuals, and over time). But there is almost no hope of finding such empirical generalizations in psychology. (Incidentally, psychology is a discipline beset by so many difficulties – such as the inevitable unreliability of what people say about themselves – that one must always treat its findings with some scepticism; this means that there may be much less solid empirical counterevidence to SBT than might appear.)

'In any case, even if there are some features of SBT which may not be to everyone's liking (and there certainly are gifted and thoughtful economists who take a different view from the one I have been putting, people who wish to give more weight to purely empirical considerations, for instance), objections based on them are academic – for the simple reason that there is, currently, no alternative theory. Since we clearly cannot, nowadays, do economic theory at all without modelling expectations and other beliefs, this is enough by itself to justify the use of SBT.'

If I am right that the Standard Apologetic runs something like this, if this – or something like it – is what the practitioner of Standard Belief Theory would say (under appropriate experimental conditions) in defence of that theory, then the Standard Apologetic greatly resembles (and very likely has its provenance in) the view of certain writers on economic methodology of the interwar period. These writers and their successors – Robbins (1932), von Mises (1960), Machlup (1978) – may be loosely grouped together as rationalists, who believed that economic knowledge can be acquired by logical reasoning from postulates arrived at *a priori*. They can be contrasted with a group of empiricists of whom Hutchison (1938) was representative, with whom they engaged in a fierce debate. The first group all held the position of the Apologist, that 'economic theory should be an account of the behaviour, in the economic arena, of *rational* agents'. I shall call this position methodological rationalism (MR) – for it advocated a general method of doing economic theory, and that method is to describe possible economies inhabited by purely rational beings.[10] (The rationalist writers defended MR in differing ways – Robbins held that describing behaviour as rational is a good first approximation, von Mises that it is a conceptual truth that actions are rational, Machlup that rational economic man is a description of real economic man which abstracts from irrelevant detail; this, he held, fitted it for deductive theorizing. Of these versions, I take it that it is for Robbins's and Machlup's that the standard economist would have most sympathy.) Secondly, the old rationalists maintained, like the apologist, that 'economic theory is properly a deductive discipline'. I shall call this view methodological deductivism. Thirdly, all held some form of what, for want of a better term, I shall call methodological apriorism. By this I mean the methodological principle that the postulates of economic theory should be *a priori* truths. Methodological apriorism is a consequence of methodological deductivism, together with the belief that empirical investigations are a poor source of economic postulates. Like the apologist, the members of the rationalist school took this pessimistic view about empirical postulates, both on the ground that 'the results of empirical investigations are not deductively tractable' and on the ground that 'there is almost no hope of finding empirical generalizations in psychology': the facts which we may find by looking, are either too baroque or too parochial – or, like certain seventeenth-century village churches, both.[11]

A Dilemma for the Apologist

There is much in the views of my imaginary apologist – just as there is in those of their interwar progenitors – against which old protests spring

[10] It should not be confused with the epistemological doctrine of rationalism, to which I have also described Robbins, von Mises and Machlup as adhering.

[11] Hutchison's position was, roughly, to accept Robbins's pessimism about empirical postulates, but to reject methodological deductivism, and with it methodological apriorism. Instead, Hutchison recommended that we do economics by compiling the results of as many independent empirical investigations as might be necessary.

readily to mind. But I want to avoid reopening old debates. For the most part, my own critique of the Standard Apologetic will not depend on objections to the general methodological principles it espouses.

The point of departure for my scrutiny of the Standard Apologetic is the question of what is meant by *rationality in beliefs*. The (partial) answer I shall offer to this question has the effect of placing the apologist for Standard Belief Theory in an acute dilemma. There are two distinct elements in the Standard Apologetic. First, it is held that a Belief Theory should be an *a priori* theory (in the sense that its postulates are not the output of empirical investigations), and secondly, that it should be 'an account of the behaviour of rational agents in matters of belief'. In other words, a Belief Theory should satisfy both methodological apriorism and methodological rationalism. The apologist thinks that Standard Belief Theory satisfies both requirements. He believes (what is obvious) that SBT is an *a priori* theory. And he believes that 'SBT is an account of the behaviour of rational agents in matters of belief'. I shall label this last belief the Description Thesis.

Suppose, however, that our enquiry into the notion of rationality in belief were to lead to the conclusion that whatever describes rationality cannot be known *a priori*. Then, there would no longer be harmony, but a painful conflict, between the calls of the methodological precepts – methodological apriorism and methodological rationalism would pull in opposite directions. And if identifying a true theory of rational beliefs involves elements of *a posteriori* knowledge, we cannot certify *a priori* that SBT, which contains none such, indeed describes rational behaviour in belief – we cannot be sure that the Description Thesis is true. I shall argue this and that, moreover, it is false – that the theories of subjective probability, Bayesian revision, Nash equilibrium, and the rest, are not theories of *rational* belief.

Rationality in Belief

An imposing literature is devoted to the attempt to clarify the complex notion of rationality, yet much remains undecided and unclear. Now the concept of rationality plays a crucial role in the Standard Apologetic, so some clarification is needed if this apologetic is to be assessed. Fortunately, what is required for this assessment falls short of a full explication of the notion of rationality in belief. I shall offer in this section a set of *necessary* conditions for a belief, or a belief activity, to be a rational one. These turn out to be sufficient for my purpose.

It will be recalled that what I mean by a special theory of belief, or a theory of a particular belief phenomenon, is something like a behaviour relation, in which a belief variable of some kind or other is the dependent variable and one or more other properties of the agent or the situation in which he finds himself are independent variables. For example, the adaptive expectations hypothesis is a theory of the belief phenomenon of forming expectations of an economic variable on the basis of known past values of that variable. The situation can be described semi-formally without losing too much, as follows: write b for the belief variable and x for the (ordered) set of independent variables. Then a theory of the belief phenomenon in question is a mapping T from x to b.

My suggestion[12] as to what is entailed by saying that a value of a belief variable is rational is relative to a particular belief phenomenon. It can be expressed in the following three propositions.

1 If b^* is a rational value of the belief variable, then there exist good reasons for b^*.
2 A 'reason for' b^* is given by its satisfying some axiom, rule, or other general condition C, which jointly restricts the values of belief variable b and the independent variables x.
3 The axiom or rule C provides a 'good' reason, only if following C
  (a) further high-level goals of the agent,
  (b) is feasible for the agent.

What it is for a theory T to describe, or be a theory of, rationality in belief behaviour is simply stated. T is such a theory if, and only if, it maps each x in its domain into rational values of its belief variable b.

What I mean by all this can be brought out by considering the idea of a *logically justified* inference. An inference may be logically justified whether or not there is anyone around to *believe* its premisses or conclusions, so logically justified inference is clearly not a belief phenomenon. (Of course, it plays a central part in the belief phenomenon of learning by reasoning.) Given a set P of premisses, we say that a conclusion $\mathbf{q}$ is logically justified if, and only if, first, the move from $\mathbf{P}$ to the conclusion q satisfies inference rules; and second, these inference rules are good ones. The most important criterion for appraising an inference rule in logic is that it be truth-preserving, for, if it is, using it will tend to promote the goal of having many true beliefs. The analogy between this picture of logically justified deductive inference and my conditions for rationality in an arbitrary belief phenomenon is clear enough: the inference rules play the role of my Cs, giving reasons for the conclusion q, but having themselves to be assessed by reference to high-level goals. (There is also a disanalogy: in assessing the logical justifiability of a deductive inference, one does not have to bother about whether it is feasible for an individual to behave in accord-

[12] Much in the following analysis is inspired by Fetzer's (1981) account of inductive inference.

ance with the inference rules, the counterparts of the *C*s. I shall return to this difference in a moment.)

There is room for some brief remarks about my three propositions. First, it must be emphasized that (1) only gives a *necessary* condition. It would be implausible as a sufficient one, because it says nothing about any of the relations which must obtain between the agent and the reasons for the belief (or other belief variable). At the very least, one might want to insist that there also exist a causal mechanism in the agent which makes the variable have the value for which there are the reasons. Second, there is some deliberate ambiguity in the idea implied by (1) and (2) taken together that, to be rational, b^* should 'satisfy conditions' C. It is left open how defeasible the individual conditions can be, how many of them there can be, and whether, to be rational, b^* must be the unique value which satisfies the conditions. Third, something needs saying about the 'high-level goals' of (3) (a). They must be in some sense appropriate to the belief enterprise that is being considered. It would be absurd to propose counting as rational only, say, beliefs that could be expressed in English without using the letter z: z-lessness has altogether too little to do with what forming beliefs is 'all about'. So here, too, it looks as if there are further necessary conditions for the rationality of b^* – but once again, this does not prejudice the *necessity* of condition (1).

Fourth, I am suggesting, in my condition (3) (b), that 'ought to' implies 'can'. If, on a walk in the hills, my companion has a heart attack, I do not have a good reason to run for a doctor at 100 m.p.h.; but I may well have a good reason to run as fast as I can. Equally, accepting the axioms of group theory does not give me good reasons to believe all its theorems; and I should not be condemned as epistemically irrational because I fail to possess all those beliefs. (If someone showed me why they followed, it might be another story; but then the independent variables of the belief phenomenon would be different ones.) Herein, as I noted, lies a disanalogy with deductive logic; the rational conclusions of an agent engaged in learning by reasoning are a proper subset of the logically justified inferences. Logic is concerned with what conclusions could *ever* be reached by justifiable steps. A theory of rational belief, on the other hand, is about the belief variables of agents; it must proceed, therefore, by setting down agent-relative norms. To be rational is to be rational for a person.

With the possible exception of part (b) of condition (3) – the feasibility clause – I suspect there is little in my discussion of the general conditions for rationality in belief with which a proponent of standard theory would wish to quarrel. His attitude to (3) (b) is likely to be ambivalent. The idea that the rational must be construed as subject to constraints is at the heart of the 'theory of rational choice', which itself is the rock on which the whole edifice of standard economics stands, and this may commend (3) (b) to the standard economist. But he may resist the conception in its application here, to rationality in belief – perhaps because he sees the trouble it may hold for him, perhaps because it smacks of Herbert Simon and warning lights are set flashing. But can the standard economist, without inconsistency, build feasibility constraints into rational action and banish them from rational belief? This is a complex question, which I cannot discuss fully here. He might defend his consistency by pointing out that in defining rational choice he makes no concession, either, to facts about the agent's limited capacity to compute optima – the only constraints that are built in are 'situational'. This is true, and it suggests that one who accepts (3) (b) must be prepared, also, to urge a revision of the standard account of rational *choice* in the direction of Simon (1976). There is, however, room for accepting an 'unbounded' model of rationality in one domain, while rejecting it in others. It should be noted that most of the careful thought that has gone into the defence of the neoclassical account of rational choice has been concerned with a special and relatively undemanding sort of choice problem – that facing the competitive agent choosing under certainty. There, the organic limitations of the agent may not handicap him much. The challenges of epistemic life are of a different order.

If my rationality conditions are accepted, someone who wishes to defend the Description Thesis, the claim that standard theories of belief are rational theories of belief, is obliged to do two things. For each theory, he must, first, display axioms or other conditions and show that they imply the behaviour relation asserted in the theory; secondly, he must establish the *efficiency* of the axioms, that is, he must display some high-level goals and show that obeying the axioms is a feasible-for-the-agent way of approaching those goals. Let me call these two obligatory tasks *validation* and *vindication*.[13]

I turn, lastly, to the question of whether these two tasks have been, or ever could be, carried out. Can the standard theories of belief – subjective probability, Bayes, Nash, and the rest – be validated and vindicated, and thereby shown to be rational?

V THE FAILURE OF THE DEFENCE

The Falsity of the Description Thesis

People who use standard theories of belief to help in solving economic problems certainly think that these theories describe rational behaviour in matters of belief. Indeed it is usually taken for granted that they do. If the name of Bayes, Nash or Muth appears on a printed page, the conditional

[13] 'Validation' and 'vindication' are Fetzer's terms. These are not the only things he must do; he must also show that the goals are worthy ones.

probability that the word 'rational' is also printed on it cannot be low! What is the source of this confident association of these theories with the notion of rationality? I think there is no single answer, but that part of the explanation is that many of these theories are thought to bear the ultimate guarantee of rationality, the Appellation Contrôlée of 'Science'. It is supposed that the belief practices described by these standard theories are the practices that are followed in science, and that their rationality is thereby demonstrated. To be sure, this varies with the case: there could be no scientific backing invoked for claiming the rationality of Nash equilibrium, since scientists, *qua* scientists, play games against nature and not against each other; and none is claimed in this case. But Bayesian revision is (rightly) seen as a recognized tool of scientific statistics, scientific arguments are seen as being subjected to unconstrained standards of deductive logic, the rational expectation-hypothesis is seen as describing the practices of the scientific discipline of econometrics.

Even if it is true that science fits the standard belief theories, this in itself does nothing to prove that those theories describe rational epistemic behaviour in the economic agent, nothing to show that the Description Thesis is true. For that, three further things would also have to be shown: that scientific belief is itself rational, that the high-level goals of science are those of the individual economic agent, and that what is epistemically feasible for science is also epistemically feasible for the individual. The first of these may be true, the second is doubtful, and the third is certainly false. Its falsity derives from the vast disparity between the scientific community and the economic individual in information-processing facilities and professional epistemic training.

The tendency among economists to identify individual rationality with the methods of science is an echo of a movement in cognitive and social psychology which reached its height some years ago and now seems to be dying away (see, for example, Hewstone, 1983). Like the story of the influence of logical positivism on economics, this one seems to illustrate the rule that economists are not impervious to neighbouring disciplines, but just slow on the uptake. Round the 1960s, attribution theorists like Heider and Kelley believed not merely that ordinary people should arrive at their explanations (of other people's behaviour) as scientists do – looking at all the evidence, weighting it properly, testing for significant partial correlations – but that they do arrive at them in this way. In the following period (very roughly, the 1970s), there was a massive accumulation of evidence, much of it in the United States, against the Heider–Kelley thesis, evidence of systematic errors, by scientific standards, in ordinary people's inferential practices: the work of Kahneman and Tversky in this area is the best-known to economists. The reaction to the evidence of unscientific practices was on the whole to deplore it: the departures from scientific norms were described as 'errors' and 'biases', and psychologists speculated piously on their corrigibility. Today, however, the scientific ego-ideal seems to have passed its peak: it is recognized that individuals do not have the same ultimate epistemic goals (that there are, for example, purely social motives for the accumulation of beliefs); and the great influence of the information-processing view of human cognition developed by Simon and others has thrown doubt on the sense of norms that have no regard to the shape and size of the processing device.

To my question 'why is the Description Thesis believed?' I have suggested that one answer may be that the standard theories seem to describe science. Now I want to say what the belief is *not* due to – the successful outcomes of exercises in what I have called 'validation' and 'vindication'. For these exercises, the first obligatory task of someone who wishes to defend the Description Thesis, have, for the most part, simply not been undertaken. Now axiomatization is validation, so this seems a surprising thing to say. Is it not the case, after all, that standard economics believes in the axiomatic method? I am not sure: it may subscribe to it, but that is not the same thing. Savage's book (1954), building on Ramsey's ideas to axiomatize the subjective-probability theory, is a distinguished example of the validation of a special theory. But apart from this, there is very little. Bayesian revision is not implied by the Savage axioms, and though there is a small literature in decision theory on the problem of its validation, this is at a formative and inconclusive stage (see, for example, Eells, 1982) (and it is very doubtful that it is known to standard economic theorists). The rational-expectations theory of theory acceptance is hardly in a fit state for axiomatization, and I know of no example of one. And the Nash equilibrium theory of anticipations in games has not been successfully axiomatized, although several attempts have been made. There is a peculiarity in this case. A number of axioms, closely related to ideas appearing in Luce and Raiffa's discussion of the Nash equilibrium as a 'solution concept', have been repeatedly cited, often together with assertions, or sketches of arguments to the effect that they entail Nash equilibrium. Yet, on close examination, they appear not to do so. The validation does not work (see, for example, Bacharach, 1984a; Cubitt, 1984). The failure of this to be known, while the Nash equilibrium concept is pressed into service at an ever-increasing rate in the name of rationality, is disturbing; it must even raise doubts as to the sincerity of those who proclaim their own devotion to this deity.

So much for the validation of the standard theories. If validation has been patchy, of vindication there is virtually nothing. Sometimes axioms are taken to be self-evidently true, or obvious to intuition, and no attempt is made to assess them, as I have suggested they should be assessed, by asking whether they help in the accomplishment of well-defined ends. At other times, there is some informal discussion of this sort. It has been argued, for example, that Bayesian revision leads, on certain assumptions, towards belief in the true data-generating hypothesis as observational evidence accumulates; or again, that theory-acceptance of the kind implied by rational-expectations theory conduces to financial success on securities markets. (I pause to remark that at the highest level of justification, at which the pursuit of truth and the pursuit of profit are weighed against each other as proper aims of the epistemic subject, we find no discussion. By now this will hardly seem surprising.)

In short, the Description Thesis has not been shown to be true, because much of what would be required to show it true has not been undertaken. And so that half of the Standard Apologetic that adduces methodological rationalism and the Description Thesis has not been shown either. But that is not all. It is easy to see what the outcome of thorough attempts at vindication *would* be. The standard theories would be seen to involve wholesale violations of the feasibility clause (3) (b); it would be seen that they hopelessly overburden man's cognitive resources. It would be easy to misunderstand my point. It is not that the descriptions given in the theories are contradicted by weighty empirical evidence – the evidence of departures from the scientific norms to which I have alluded (though it is true that they are). For that evidence might only be evidence of 'do not', but 'could'. I am saying that people *cannot possibly* do the things they are credited with in the standard theories. Man's cognitive abilities are limited by his biological design. He is unable to count objects at a glance, if there are many more than seven of them. He is unable to grasp the sentence 'A knows that B knows that A knows that B knows that A knows that B knows that A knows that the price of copper will rise'. He is unable, however hard he may try, to know all the theorems of group theory, by knowing the axioms. All of this means that, if to be rational in belief is what I have claimed it is, the Description Thesis is not merely unproven, but also false. It means that, whatever else may be the merits of the standard theories of belief, it is not their merit that they are accounts of rationality in matters of belief.

The Prospects for the Theory of Belief

I argued in the first part of my paper that standard economic theory does poor service to the need of economics for a general Theory of Belief. An adequate Theory of Belief in economics would deal with a wide variety of problems. I gave a rough and partial taxonomy of these; I listed eight. Standard economics, I suggested, offers well-articulated theories of some, has little to say about others, and next to nothing about yet others. In the second part of the paper, I have been suggesting that the special theories that it does offer are implicitly defended in standard economics on the ground (the first half of the Standard Apologetic) that it is good to model agents as rational, and that that is just what these theories do. I have argued that, on the contrary, these theories do not do this, that the Description Thesis is unproven and very probably false.

If the Description Thesis is rejected, and with it the first argument in the Standard Apologetic, how serious are the implications for Standard Belief Theory – for Bayes, Nash and the other special theories so widely accepted today? Must these be discarded? If they were to be, what options would be left, what could economics do about beliefs? The first implication is straightforward: if methodological rationalism is upheld, then Standard Belief Theory must be replaced by an alternative Belief Theory of which the Description Thesis is true. In effect, an economist who accepts my partial account of rationality is obliged to choose between renouncing the established theories of belief and giving up the claim that his economics is the economics of rational man. He must choose between practice and principle, between his concrete and abstract affiliations. I imagine that if it came to such a choice, it is the methodological rationalism that would be sacrificed.[14]

The second implication is that a new Theory of Belief, which satisfied methodological rationalism by truly describing rationality in belief, would employ empirically discovered facts about agents' cognitive capacities. And so such a new Theory of Belief would violate methodological apriorism. Again, there is a painful choice for the standard economist to make. This time it is between two high-level principles that he must choose: he can be true to methodological rationalism or to methodological apriorism, but not, where beliefs are concerned, to both.

But now I want to point to another flaw in the Standard Apologetic, which I have not yet mentioned and which, by a lucky irony, largely makes up for the collapse of the Description Thesis and rescues the apologist from his dilemma. The flaw lies in the apologist's reasons for espousing methodological apriorism, namely, his pessimism about the chances of discovering viable empirical postulates, empirical facts which are at once general and deductively tractable. What makes empirical findings deductively intractable? Essentially, the lack of simplicity of facts, their impurity, the pocks and warts and wrinkles of the factual surface of the world, the unmanageable, tropical abundance of the dimensions of experience: all this is reflected in the rigmarole of applied econometrics – the endless proliferation of explanatory variables, the confidence intervals and Durbin–Watson statistics, the plurality of measures of a given economic concept. Not even the high-powered deductive methods of advanced

---

[14] As Spohn (1983) notes: 'Scientists are the more inclined to accept an idea, the more concretely it can be put to work and the more successful its concrete applications are, whereas philosophers are the more inclined to accept an idea, the better it stands in their procedure of exposing it to more and more sophisticated arguments and counterarguments.'

mathematics can deal with raw material like this. (It is true, however, that although analytical solutions cannot be had, numerical ones often can be, by the use of modern computers. But resorting to numerical methods of deduction militates against our *understanding* of the results and thus against the *explanatory* function of theory. And the idea that explanation is an ultimate goal of economic science and that explanation entails understanding is one of the fundamental reasons for favouring the use of deductive methods.)

But these drawbacks of empirical findings are drawbacks only of the direct output of statistical or econometric studies, and these are not the only form that *a posteriori* knowledge takes in economics. There are also 'stylized facts',[15] simplified versions of the output of such studies or, sometimes, simple expressions of the impressions left by exercises in 'casual empiricism'. And is it not precisely with these that much of economic theory – and most of macroeconomic theory – *does* work, deductively and without difficulty? There is nothing intractable, and nothing local, about the entirely *a posteriori* claim that the marginal propensity to consume is less than one, or about the celebrated stylized facts of Kaldor themselves. Or, to take examples from psychology, consider the stylized facts that people try to reduce cognitive dissonance, or that they switch to search activity if and when an aspiration level is not reached.[16] Economists have worked successfully, in deductive mode, with these (see, for example, Radner, 1975; Akerlof and Dickens, 1982); nor do they lack generality. And it cannot be (with consistency) objected by the apologist that stylized facts should be ruled out because they involve some departure from the truth. The apologist freely admits that people are only *approximately* rational, and claims that it is none the less right, on other grounds, to model them as wholly so, as ideally rational agents. If ideal types, why not stylized facts?

These considerations provide, then, a way in which the apologist may resolve his dilemma. He can sacrifice a principle (methodological apriorism) without sacrifice of the underlying principles which it was intended to serve. By drawing on stylized empirical facts about the cognitive capacities of economic agents, it may prove possible to build a deductive Theory of Beliefs for economics, with all the fruitfulness of results and all the explanatory power of such theories; a theory which is, moreover, a true (enough) description of the epistemic behaviour of agents who are rational (but only as rational as their natures allow). There is nothing impossible about an *a posteriori*, deductive, rationalistic Theory of Beliefs in economics.

---

[15] I shall not use this term in a sense that implies the truth of what is claimed.

[16] On my account of belief rationality, the first of these behaviour patterns is probably *ir*rational, and the second probably rational.

I do not say that the answer to the straight question 'what sort of a Theory of Beliefs should we try to build?' is that it should be of *this* sort, one that is *a posteriori*, deductive and rationalistic. I have not been concerned, in the second half of this paper, to make *ab initio* methodological prescriptions of my own, but to investigate the coherence of a received implicit methodological position which purports to justify the received Theory of Beliefs. Perhaps the most critical issue that would be faced by one who asked the 'straight question' is the case for building a rationalistic theory at all. Is the hypothesis that economic agents are rational in belief – in however an attenuated sense may be given to the notion of 'rational' – the place we should start from? That is a distinct question.

REFERENCES

Akerlof, G.A. and Dickens, W.T. (1982) 'The Economic Consequences of Cognitive Dissonance', *American Economic Review*, 72, June, pp. 307–21.
Arrow, K.J. (1982) 'Risk Perception in Psychology and Economics', *Economic Inquiry*, 20, January, pp. 1–9.
Bacharach, M.O.L. (1983) 'Properties of Two-person Information Structures in a Formal Theory of Knowledge', Christ Church, University of Oxford.
— (1984a) 'Against Nash', Istituto di Economia, University of Siena.
— (1984b) 'Scenarios of Fulfilled Expectations', Christ Church, University of Oxford.
Cubitt, R. (1984) 'Rational Expectations and the Economic Policy Game', M.Phil. Dissertation, University of Oxford.
Dennett, D.C. (1979) *Brainstorms*, Harvester Press, Hassocks.
Eells, E. (1982) *Rational Decision and Causality*, Cambridge University Press, Cambridge.
Fetzer, J.H. (1981) *Scientific Knowledge*, Reidel, Dordrecht.
Hewstone, M. (ed.) (1983) *Attribution Theory*, Basil Blackwell, Oxford.
Hintikka, J. (1962) *Knowledge and Belief*, Cornell University Press, Ithaca, NY.
Hutchison, T.W. (1938) *The Significance and Basic Postulates of Economic Theory*, Macmillan, London.
Jeffrey, R.C. (1968) 'Probable Knowledge', in *Inductive Logic*, ed. I. Lakatos, North-Holland, Amsterdam.
Kahneman, D. and Tversky, A. (1979) 'Prospect Theory: an Analysis of Decision Under Risk', *Econometrica*, 47, March, pp. 263–91.
Kuhn, T. (1962) *The Structure of Scientific Revolutions*, University of Chicago Press, Chicago.
Machlup, F. (1978) 'The Problem of Verification in Economics' (1st edn 1955), in *Methodology of Economics and Other Social Sciences*, ed. F. Machlup, Academic Press, New York.
von Mises, L. (1960) *The Epistemological Problems of Economics* (1st edn 1933), Van Nostrand, Princeton.

Moscovici, S. and Hewstone, M. (1981) 'Social Representations and Social Explanations: from the "Naive" to the "Amateur" Scientist', in *Attribution Theory*, ed. M. Hewstone, Basil Blackwell, Oxford.
Muth, J. (1961) 'Rational Expectations and the Theory of Price Movements', *Econometrica*, 29, July, pp. 315–35.
Nisbett, R. and Ross, L. (1980) *Human Inference*, Prentice-Hall, Englewood Cliffs, NJ.
Radner, R. (1975) 'Satisficing', *Journal of Mathematical Economics*, 2, June–September, pp. 253–62.
Robbins, L. (1932) *An Essay on the Nature and Significance of Economic Science*, Macmillan, London.
Savage, L.J. (1954) *The Foundations of Statistics*, John Wiley, New York.
Simon, H.A. (1976) 'From Substantive to Procedural Rationality', in *Method and Appraisal in Economics*, ed. S. Latsis, Cambridge University Press, Cambridge.
Spohn, W. (1983) 'Probabilistic Causality', in *Causalità e Modelli Probabilistici*, ed. M.C. Galavotti and G. Gambetta, CLUEB, Bologna.

6

Price Formation and the Costs of Exchange

DIETER HELM

I INTRODUCTION

John Hicks's classificatory distinction (1976) between theories focusing on production and distribution, on the one hand, and exchange, on the other, is a powerful tool in examining the history of economic thought. Production, cost-based theories associated with Smith, Ricardo and Marx can be compared and contrasted with exchange or 'catallactic' theories associated with Walras, Menger and Jevons. The marginal revolution of the 1870s becomes, then, a turning point in the evolution of economics, not because of the method of the margin itself,[1] but because of the shift of emphasis. Cost and supply gave way to utility and demand as the primary source of value.

Like many good simplifications, the usefulness of it depends on the problem at hand. And the shift of emphasis has not been wholly beneficial. Focusing on exchange is frequently (though, of course, not necessarily) identified with 'market' economics[2] and, in particular, with flexibility in prices acting to allocate resources efficiently. Catallactics typically assume flexibility, unless otherwise clearly stated. In this paper, I am going to stress the extent to which exchange itself involves production, and thus that the Hicksian contrast is not as complete as some of his followers have taken it to be. Exchanging goods and money involves time, information, effort and payments: it thus has associated costs, and can be examined at least in part by production theory. Importantly, this occurs on *both* sides of the market. Producers make decisions, fix prices and employ people to transact. Consumers engage in search, travel and research when making purchases, as well as make investments in order to improve the quality of their consumption.

---

[1] Hicks (1983, p. 9) notes that any economics can be 'marginalist' – the margin itself is nothing more or less than a mathematical expression.

[2] Pareto optimality is itself utility-based, and it is this concept which has added to the market's theoretical appeal. See Becker (1976) and Reder (1982).

The significance of choosing one view rather than another is not in seeing problems as ultimately either matters of 'supply' or 'demand'. Classical and catallactic economists had both in their models. Rather, it effects the determination of prices. Taking a cost approach to price formation suggests that exchange is a special case of production. Prices are produced by consumers' search, by market makers, and by firms. However, such a strong claim itself rests on a deeper methodological assumption – a quite general definition of production. Production on this view is the changing of economic arrangements, and production costs are the costs of change, and may include any type of cost, physical or psychological. Production includes anything which produces utility, not merely the translation of inputs into outputs in a physicalist sense. Much of this paper will be devoted to exploring this claim, and the limits to its validity.

In this paper, I consider first two different definitions of production, and then I tackle the role of the firm in producing prices. I consider the literature on transactions costs in the modern theory of the firm and the relative costs of market allocation versus planning by firms. On the other side of the market, I examine the role of the consumer, modern household production theory, and the consumer side of the exchange transaction. Having tackled the production of prices by firms, and individuals' costs of transactions, these are then integrated to form the framework for a general theory of price formation in administered markets.

II DEFINITION OF PRODUCTION

The basis of the claim that price formation can be partially explained in terms of production – that prices are produced, rather than given – is a particular definition of production. I want therefore to start by distinguishing between two views of production, which I shall call 'objective' and 'subjective', for want of better terms.

The objective view of production is the most familiar one. It is physicalist, relating production to the making of 'things'. Inputs are translated into outputs. It is the Ricardian view, carried on by Marshall and Sraffa. Costs of production are the inputs of capital and labour required to produce output, plus perhaps interest, where production takes time.

The subjectivist, on the other hand, views production as essentially the alteration of economic arrangements to meet human preferences. Scarce factors of production are combined to yield the highest levels of utility. This is ultimately an opportunity-cost notion, where the value of the next best alternative relates to consumer demands. The ultimate objective of subjectivist production is final utility. Production is directed at human needs. Anything that is directed towards that end is production.

The differences between the two definitions are in terms of their domains and in measurement. The test case for inclusion between these views is whether making something which is not demanded by anyone is to be called production or not. Utility measures of production value depend on indirect price observations, and these may well be distorted by market imperfections such as monopoly and externality.

III FIRMS AND THE PRODUCTION OF PRICES

The Context of Pricing: the Growth of Firms and Concentration

One further characteristic of Hicksian methodology is that theories should be appropriate to the problem at hand, and hence limited in applicability to particular historical periods. Hicks argued that the classical theory was replaced by the catallactic alternative, in part, in response to the growth of the market. I want therefore to begin the examination of prices by noting a few 'stylized facts' about the modern economy to which such a theory is to apply.

The growth of concentration in production and the rise of the modern corporation are two major trends in capitalist economies.[3] Accounts of their causes are diverse, relating to economies of scale, growth rather than profit-maximizing objectives of managers, the growth of the state, the rise of unions, and the concentration of wealth. If the modern economy is a concentrated one, then the pricing decision takes place in the context of the large corporations competing as price-making oligopolists.

The second characteristic of the context of price formation is that it occurs in an uncertain world, where information is costly. These two factors – the form of competition and uncertainty – combine to give transactions costs a central role in the theory of price formation. In this part, I want to suggest why, increasingly, market allocation has been replaced by internal firm allocation or, in Chandler's terms (1977), the 'visible hand' has increasingly replaced the 'invisible' one. This involves a review of some of the reasons for the growth of concentration.

My concern with the replacement of market allocation by administered decisions arises because I wish to explain some of the motives for firms' internalizing transactions that would otherwise have occurred via the market and market prices. I want to explain pricing as a theory of the production of this decision; prices are produced in firms just as output is produced. They are one of the decisions of the firm. The division between exchange and production is of less use, to the extent that almost all exchanges incur costs. Whether these exchanges take place in markets or in firms depends on the relative costs and benefits. Since these change over

[3] A survey of the evidence can be found in Hannah (1983). See also Hannah and Kay (1975).

time, there is a tendency towards fixity rather than flexibility, as concentration increases in response to altered transactions costs.

The Market versus Planning

Amongst the numerous perspectives from which the modern economic organization can be viewed, two broad and conflicting approaches can be identified.[4] The first concentrates on the apparent competitive nature of the non-government sector, and stresses the flexibility of the price mechanism, in bringing about near-optimal solutions. Pareto-efficient, informationally undemanding solutions are arrived at under the 'invisible hand's' guidance. This view of the economic system takes its cue from the Smithian individualistic concept of the market,[5] and is reinforced by Walrasian models of market clearing and general equilibrium. This is what I shall call the *decentralized market view*, describing an economic system that takes no proper account of large-scale concentrated production.

The other sees firms not as atoms in a sea of efficient market competition, with flexible prices determining equilibria, but rather firms visibly co-ordinating productions, with managers taking the place of markets, internally fixing prices. The main dichotomy in this second vision is not a choice between state-planned and private-firm allocation of resources, but rather planned firm allocation versus markets. Firms in the latter view arise and grow because of market failure,[6] and the growth of firms, especially by merger and take-over, represents the replacement of markets. This latter version I shall call the *planned managerial view*.

Typically, the theory of production centres on the theory of costs and supply, in the face of given prices. However, recent theoretical work has stressed the extent to which transactions are not only exchanges taking place in markets, but have themselves produced decisions, which have incurred costs associated with their administration. Prices do not appear, nor are they just costlessly given, as in the Walrasian model: they are produced. Fixing prices and arranging transactions incurs managerial costs. Rather than being exogenous *data* to the firm, choosing and altering prices has become increasingly a specialist managerial function. The extent to which a decision is an administered, rather than a market exchange decision, depends, in part, on the relative costs of these two alternative (but related) means of allocation.

[4] Broad classifications such as the two I am employing are discussed in Schumpeter (1954). See also Dobb (1973) and Hicks (1976).

[5] See Viner (1929), Sowell (1974) and Hahn for different views of Smith. See also Wilson and Skinner (1977).

[6] Coase (1937) was the first to point out that the firm's very existence depended on market failure.

In order to present a tentative outline of a theory of price formation as produced decisions, three questions need to be tackled: how are the prices arrived at, how are they revised, and what are the constraints. Prices are directly the product of firms rather than individuals, in as far as firms set them. Individuals' choice indirectly constrains pricing. One component of a theory of price formation is therefore the role of firms.

A fully flex-price market is a logical construction with no direct empirical counterpart (see Hahn, 1973; Helm, 1983). The absence of product differentiation, the existence of many small buyers and sellers, the absence of uncertainty, the existence of a costless auctioneer; these are all simplifications which are both required for the model and have little resemblence to the widespread oligopoly and quasi-monopoly of developed economies. Such a theory is at best a theoretical abstraction.

There are a series of consequences that flow from planned prices. First, administered decision-making is a method involving at least temporary *fixing* of prices. Types of price-fixing regimes may vary considerably, according to the nature of the firm and its competitive environment. What, however, remains constant is the fact of rigidity. A second consequence is that adjustment under fix-price regimes is necessarily more irregular; hence one of the disadvantages of administered fix-price decision-making is the costs associated with having the 'wrong' relative prices, at least for some time-periods and some products.[7] The advantages accrue to the firm in the form of fixity, because of a degree of certainty to themselves, and the avoided costs of more frequent revisions. But there is also an important certainty-effect externality to other firms and consumers; they now know for the period other firms' prices, whereas under a flex-price regime they would not (unless of course perfect information is assumed). Fix-price regimes produce a collective good – increased certainty – but at a price, the misallocation as a result of the 'wrong', non-optimal prices prevailing. So the answer to the first question that confronts us, as to why prices should be fixed at all, is in terms of a balance between these costs and benefits. Using the traditional approach, the optimal decision will depend on the relevant marginal costs and benefits of the rigidity.

A third consequence of planned prices, where prices diverge from what would be the 'correct' flex-price set of relative prices, is that the appropriate concept of efficiency alters. Typically, economists discuss efficiency or inefficiency of practices according to the bench-mark of a perfectly competitive flex-price economy. However, prices do not and cannot adhere to this standard; it is not attainable.[8] Thus a concept of efficiency as the optimal fix-

[7] It also means that the structure of the economy is different from what it would be under flex-price, hence the 'right' relative prices are also different. Correct second-best prices are not those that would rule in a first-best world.

[8] Elsewhere I have called this the 'feasibility' problem; see Helm (1984b).

price system is required, the optimally (necessarily) imperfect fix-price economy in the face of oligopolistic competition and uncertainty.

What, then, is the optimal method of fixing prices? The crucial issue is whether this is a maximizing or satisficing procedure. Actual economies display a plurality of institutional arrangements for decision-making. These lie between two extremes: democratic or consultative, on the one hand, and dictatorial, on the other. The committee and the hierarchy, which form the norm in large firms, lie between the two. Forms of decision-making evolve to mediate between conflicts of managerial preferences, differing expectations of future events, and methods of implementation. Resolving these difficulties is a major concern of organizational theories of the firm, and the need for compromise and 'managerial slack' has been argued to generate 'satisficing' rather than optimizing outcomes (see Simon, 1955; Winter, 1964; Cyert and March, 1963). If the outcome is indeed a satisficing one, involving a degree of cross-inefficiency (see Leibenstein, 1976), then the concept of optimality will therefore also be a satisficing one. This result stems from considerations of organization and also from the uncertainty surrounding decision-making. Rather than addressing the typical economists' question of – given the costs of information itself, and the labour and capital needed to extract it – 'what is the optimal method of decision-making?' We need to consider how managers decide these costs, and how the content of information is first arrived at. Information is also not exogenously given, and neither are the costs of discovering it *ex ante*.

Where markets are administered and prices are fixed, the third question, of the optimal time for price revision, arises. Revision may take two forms: it either occurs at a regular time (for example, annual wage-fixing), or it occurs when certain trigger mechanisms suggest the need to alter prices. The former case produces the increasing certainty-effect externality that I have already mentioned, whereas, the latter case may or may not, depending on the degree of public knowledge concerning the triggers. These might be the responses to a variety of variables, including changes in input prices, changes in the inventory levels as a response to demand changes, or because of failure to achieve financial targets. It is unlikely that the same regime will be appropriate to 'trigger mechanisms' as will be applicable to annual revisions.

The consequences of an examination of fix-price markets along the lines of the above suggestions are threefold. First, the focus moves away from the narrow neoclassical concern with prices as the key variable in the system, partially or totally exogenous to the firms in the economy, towards the prior question of the way in which they are formed and administered. Analysis moves from the question of *what* are existing prices, to *why* prices are what they are. Analysis shifts from the competitive structure as the determinant of price, towards the consequences of that structure on decision-making methods in order to explain prices. Traditional 'black-box' theories of the firm disregard the internal decisions of the firm, typically because the purpose of these theories is to predict outcomes, rather than explain how they are reached. Following Friedman (1953), assumptions concerning the internal procedures of the firm need not be realist, since the sole test of the validity on this methodology is predictive success. Challenges to this position are at two levels: that the methodology is incorrect, and that empirically internal procedures do in fact affect predicted outcomes.[9] Managerial disputes must be resolved, if consistent objective functions are to be produced. Such consistency requires a viable aggregation procedure, and, in common with more general aggregation problems, it must not fall foul of the Arrow result.[10]

The second consequence of examining the fix-price markets is the need to examine the constraints facing price selection. Competitive selection, take-overs and bankruptcy are amongst the most important of these. Third, administration of prices leaves more room for discretion and policy. Prices may yield successful (in the sense of profitable) outcomes over a range, rather than there being a unique profit-maximizing price and output decision. This is because the alternative to a fix-price regime is yet another fix-price regime, and not a flex-price regime in administered markets. Discretion exists under administered systems, whereas it is absent under flex-price ones. Policy can operate directly on the decision (for example, forms of wage and price control), it can alter the constraints, or it can alter the selection mechanism.

The policy implications are thus considerable. Pricing under a fix-price regime is at best an optimizing, rather than a maximizing activity. Since relative prices under a fix-price regime are rarely, if ever, the 'correct', full-information ones, inefficiency in the traditional sense of comparison with the *perfectly decentralized* economy always exists. Firms fix prices in order to achieve optimal levels of inefficiency, given the transactions and information costs. Any policy must therefore expect to face lags in response, lags which vary in length according to the time interval of price-fixing. If it is a 'trigger mechanism' which activates decisions, then policy may need to be directed towards the appropriate variable. If it is a regular time-interval revision, policy should be timed so as to precede or coincide.[11]

The way in which fix-price decisions are implemented and the functioning of administration is not a specific concern for theories which focus on

---

[9] Cyert and March (1963) discuss the managerial conflict over objectives. Empirical work dating from Hall and Hitch (1939) questions the extent of marginal-cost pricing. Helm (1984b) questions the validity of the Friedman methodology.

[10] The application of Arrow's problem to managerial decision-making has been noted by Winter (1964) and Scherer (1971).

[11] An example of the latter is the coincidence of labour-market policies with the timing of the annual round of labour pay increases.

exchange. To the extent that the choice of market versus non-market pricing depends on cost structures, institutional arrangements, and uncertainty, analysis should focus on production theory, and in particular the production of economic knowledge, information and transactions. As the costs of the administration of prices fall relative to the benefits, the degree of fixity tends to rise. The implication of this is a longer-run move towards fix-price regimes, as analysed by Hicks (1969, 1977). As he put it (1977, p. xi), 'the unorganised flexprice market, the old type, is on the way out . . . modern markets are predominantly of the fixprice type'.

IV THE ORIGIN OF PRICE-FIXING: THE TRANSACTIONS-COST APPROACH

An account of price-fixing, and its growing dominance, is naturally an account of the growth of the firm. I have suggested that one of the reasons why prices are fixed by firms is associated with the costs of transactions and information. I shall begin to explain this in a somewhat unconventional way by asking the question of why firms exist at all. A purely decentralized economy of the first view or vision described above, with full information, constant costs and flexible prices, has no firms in the sense that we see them in the modern economy. Prices are given, there are no scale economies, and hence no reason for co-operation.

In the literature on the theory of the firm, the transactions-cost approach associated with Coase (1937), Chandler (1977) and Williamson (1981) has stressed an important source of co-operative benefit excluded from the conventional discussion of scale economies. Coase was the first to point out that the entrepreneurial coordinator inside the firm directs production, whereas prices fulfil that function in markets, and that the two methods of coordinating production are alternatives. He proposed a marginalist (profit-maximizing) principle for deciding between the two alternatives, according to which the extent or boundary of the firm is limited at the point where 'the costs of organising an extra transaction within the firm become equal to the costs of carrying out the same transaction by means of an exchange in the open market or the costs of organising in another firm'. Firms exist, for Coase, where markets deviate from perfect competition; that is, when information is imperfect and there are scale economies of administration. But the extent of the failure must be great enough to offset the expected transactions costs, *ex ante*.

The transactions-cost approach to explaining the internal and external organization of firms is only one approach. There may be other reasons for firms' growth and the replacement of markets – because of other sources of scale economies, principal-agent problems, or for non-economic reasons. Nevertheless, transactions costs have important effects on organizational design. Williamson (1981, p. 1547) puts forward three principles, which are supportable on transactions-costs reasoning.

1 *Asset specificity principle*: the normal presumption that recurring transactions for technologically separable goods and services will be efficiently mediated by autonomous market contracting is progressively weakened as asset specificity increases.
2 *Externality principle*: the normal presumption that exchange between producers of differentiated goods and distribution stages will be efficiently mediated by autonomous contracting is progressively weakened as demand externalities increase.
3 *Hierarchical decomposition principle*: internal organization should be designed in such a way as to effect quasi-independence between the parts, the high-frequency dynamics (operating activities) and the low-frequency dynamics (strategic planning) should be clearly distinguished, and incentives should be aligned within and between components so as to promote both local and global effectiveness.

Each of these principles is affected by the three influences cited by Williamson on transaction costs – the frequency, uncertainty and asset specificity of exchanges.

The question which arises from this approach concerns the nature of the scale economies. If organizations exist because of such scale economies in both transactions and production, then the nature and extent of modern firms depends on an analysis of these scale economies. It should therefore be pointed out that in the literature there is both theoretical and empirical dispute about the concept. Theoretically, the meaning of scale economies in a multi-divisional, multi-product firm has been questioned, as has their empirical size.[12] The emerging consensus from this literature is negative: that both the concept and the evidence are at best ambiguous.

The importance of scale economies relates to defining the efficient output and price which a firm should choose in order to maximize profits. Yet, as noted above, the production of decisions within firms is at best an optimizing one, based on imperfect information. Firms search for information up to the point where the marginal benefits just exceed the marginal costs. The presence of scale economies in search affects how the costs are made up; in particular, if transactions can be combined so that the firm becomes a multi-transactional centre, unit costs of each transaction may fall where there is a fixed-cost component of transactions considered generally.[13] These include items of communication with fixed rentals (like telephones) at one end, and specialist managers at the other (like foreign exchange experts). But the marginal cost/benefit approach in the literature is not itself unambiguous. The efficient choice of prices is not the *ex post*

[12] See, on the theory, Gold (1981), and on empirical evidence, Silberston (1972).
[13] See Caves (1983) for a discussion with relation to multinationals.

maximal values, but rather the *ex ante* (imperfect) optimizing ones. There may well therefore be a gap between these two sets of decisions.

Now it is typically assumed that this gap represents the costs in terms of efficiency to the firm and the economy of administered, produced prices rather than market allocation. The offsetting benefits are the transactions-cost gains to the firm. Critics of planning, most notably Hayek and Popper, have focused on these claimed efficiency costs. However, their argument includes a fallacy, which is best seen by considering the Walrasian price system as a method of coordination. It is well known that the clearance of the market in such a system requires an auctioneer. Prices do not spontaneously arise; they are given to the firms and customers (who treat them as exogenous) as the outcome of the independent bids of consumers. Yet the coordination problem and the initial price-setting activities of the auctioneer parallel those of the managers in the administered case already considered. The difference in the two (perfectly decentralized and managed allocation) is not, as Hayek argued, an economy of information, but rather the difference in cost assumptions. The Walrasian auctioneer is assumed to act perfectly: he or she chooses the 'right' price without having any incentive to do so (because information is perfect) (see Grossman and Stiglitz, 1980), without costs and without mistakes. These are clearly heroic assumptions.

Since information is imperfect, and since in practice price-fixing is a costly business, the auctioneer (or, better, the merchant) is an imperfect price-maker. His activities are expensive – he requires a rent to give him an incentive to act. Information is not normally free; traders and consumers have to provide it physically, which takes time and possibly inputs. Both have opportunity costs (see Becker, 1965). The Walrasian market system rests essentially on exogenously given prices with *perfect information*. To compare this method of allocation with one with *assumed* administrative costs is a false comparison. What should be compared is two sets of alternative allocative mechanisms, each with their associated imperfections and costs imputed. The choice is a pragmatic one, rather than determined *a priori* by assumption.

V CONSUMERS, PRODUCTION AND PRICES

I have so far presented pricing as the decision of firms, facing transactions costs and imperfect information, and considered them as the outcome of a production activity. But if prices are fixed by firms, it remains the case that there are important constraints which bind that produced decision, and of course one of the most important is that of consumers' choice. The 'visible hand' is put forward in terms of the theory of the firm. I want to strengthen the argument by giving it generality, considering how production also enters into consumption decisions. Consumer choice is not the simple revelation of preferences as is frequently assumed. Consumers engage in much production activity, including the production of choices themselves. The modern household production theory has highlighted this.

There are two particular consumer production activities which directly or indirectly influence prices. These are the investment in time in order to increase the utility associated with consumption, and search activity over goods to discover which will yield greatest utility. In this section, I want to emphasize the production character of these two, and integrate them. In the final section, these will be brought together with firms' fix-price decisions.

The modern household production theory[14] essentially integrates the cost of time into production, and contrasts returns from the allocation of time in market and non-market activities. Instead of the typical utility function:

$$U = U(x_1, \ldots, x_n)$$

which the consumer is assumed to maximize, we can write:

$$U = U(x_1, \ldots, x_n; t_1, \ldots, t_r)$$

where t represents the time spent on each activity. The constraints now include the condition that the sum of time spent on work (t_w) and on non-market production (t_h) sum to t, the total amount of time devoted to the deriving of utility from the various goods available.

If the time and goods are combined, we get a composite bundle, Z, of time and goods jointly yielding utility:

$$U = U(Z_1, \ldots, Z_n)$$

Each Z_i is produced by combining time with goods, so that we can write a production function for each:

$$Z_i = f(\mathrm{x_i}; t_i; E_i)$$

where $i = 1, \ldots, m$ and E_i is the 'ability' characteristics of the individual,

[14] I am here closely following the exposition of Becker (1981), to which the reader is referred.

including human and non-human capital, affecting the productivity over time. E is thus itself partially produced, giving a further production function, discussed in the familiar human capital literature (for a survey of which, see Blaug, 1976). Final utility, then, combines all these production activities, and thus actual choice is quite complex.

To these, further considerations may be added. Household production theory, as a theory of produced utility, is quite general. We can thus make a further step, not one commonly made in the literature, and integrate search theory for consumers with the production of choice. If information is imperfect about the goods actually available, and their utility-yielding characteristics, then again the consumer must decide how to allocate time to search, and possibly transport and other resources as well. The way in which this is done has been analysed by Okun (1981, ch. 4) as 'customer market' behaviour. The consumer is said to set, like the labourer, a reservation price for a good. This analysis then looks at how this will alter in different circumstances. Okun argues, for example, that search will differ according to continuity, experience, and so on. The reservation price is the outcome of a number of expenditures, including time, effort and knowledge.

The Okun analysis, however, assumes that goods are similar, known in utility outcome, and that the consumer is just trying to find the best price. But the consumer's problem is typically one of differentiated products, and of discovering not only the lowest price, but also the utility-yielding characteristics. This involves further investment, and the costs of mistakes where the (*ex ante*) returns are not known may be considerable. The case of 'new' goods is particularly difficult to analyse.

Consumer preferences, typically assumed to be ultimately exogenous, may be endogenously altered, and in two senses. The first is where the consumer decides to improve the quality of consumption, by investing time in an activity. For example, it may take time to 'acquire' a taste for music, wine and so on (see Marshall, 1920; Weiszäcker, 1971; Stigler and Becker, 1977). The second is where information of a persuasive kind (for example, advertising) alters an existing preference, or the method of satisfying a preference. For example, an individual may have a preference to dress fashionably, but since what is regarded as fashionable alters over time, he or she will have to alter their bundle of purchases correspondingly, in order to satisfy an unchanged preference.

We have, then, a series of production activities: time and transactions (search) costs, human capital production, preference production and so on. These are the production activities which, in part, form the consumer-demand side of pricing decisions taken by firms. Exchange yielding final utility to consumers is an expensive business; preferences are not directly revealed on the market. They are revealed in modified form, having due regard to costs and production.

VI ADMINISTERED MARKETS

Utility and Cost Approaches to the Theory of Value

In the traditional presentation of the theory of value and price, the cost and utility approach are typically separated. To answer the question of what something is worth, we either ask how much it costs to produce, or what consumers are willing to pay, dependent on the resulting utility. The cost approach to value is associated with classical economists. The variant one finds in Smith, Ricardo and Mill is the labour theory, where capital is treated in one way or another as embodied labour. The catallactics stressed demand factors; the value of a commodity depended not on how much labour was used to produce it, but on its relative scarcity, dependent on preferences.

Part of the difficulty brought out by this comparison relates to the different answers that the two questions produce. As Hicks (1981) has stressed, only under ideal conditions will the two measures of real income, and hence value, produce the same answer. The ideal conditions are those of perfect competition and consumer sovereignty. It is the primary position given to these two concepts in the history of economic thought – perfect competition and consumer sovereignty – which leads to a neglect of the costs of exchange and of the endogeneity of preferences. Transactions costs and variability in preferences are matters of concern where information is imperfect and costly.

Classification in economics matters. There are alternative sets of 'blinkers' (as Hicks (1976) has termed them), which we can wear when considering a particular question. These are alternative directions, which in themselves are neither right nor wrong. Value can be classified in a utility or a cost way (see Hicks, 1981). Which one is chosen influences the results. What I have argued here is that instead of looking at price as the outcome of production and supply, on the one hand, and exchange and demand, on the other, there are important ways in which production enters into prices directly, and into consumer purchases and preferences.

Unifying Production and Exchange

The consequences of this differing perspective are considerable. One which I have stressed here is price-fixity. Considering the existence of transactions costs, and the context of large corporations in oligopolist competition, suggests that fix-price regimes are typical. Flex-price is at best a rare exception, occurring perhaps in agricultural markets. The second consequence concerns the method of investigating pricing. Internal organizational considerations directly affect the outcome, and should be investigated under this perspective. Third, the theory of production can be applied directly to the theory of consumer choice over goods. The theory of the allocation of time stresses its opportunity costs. Search is expensive, and will be conducted to the point at which the consumer thinks that gains outweigh losses. The ability to maximize satisfaction from consumption activity depends in part on the amount of consumption capital – skills, human capital, durables, etc. – available. There is a prior optimization problem to be solved. Fourth, preferences themselves may be at least partly produced. These can be acquired by the investment of time in certain activities, and they can be altered, for example, by some types of advertising.

Bringing production theory into exchange decisions and into consumption effectively makes demand and supply curves interdependent. The traditional method is to solve the optimization problem for producers first, then solve that for consumers separately, and only then bring them together to determine price. The notion of exogenous indifference curves, transitive and complete preference orderings, and given and known budget constraints are quite contrary to the perspective I have suggested here. These are in part produced, and should be analysed as such. Costs attach to each of these, and it should be borne in mind that consistency itself, the key ordinal theory preference assumption, can be very costly (see Helm, 1984a, ch. 4). Similarly in the theory of the firm, prices of both outputs and inputs are not necessarily given and exogenous. Even if the firm cannot alter the prices of other firms, it can engage in limited search for the best price amongst competitors, up to the point where it thinks that benefits just exceed costs. In internalizing pricing and planning of resources, instead of using market allocative mechanisms, the firm responds to transactions costs.

VII CONCLUSION

Exchange-based theories of economic behaviour place great emphasis on consumer preferences as the ultimate arbitrators in deciding the value of goods and services. The transactions-costs approach to producing prices and consumer purchases stresses market imperfection and provides an endogenous explanation of consumer preferences and the determination of prices. In doing so, it not only gives a different perspective on the determination of value, but also stresses a different market form. Fixed planned prices predominate flexible market ones. Between the two views of the market – the decentralized market and the planned firm – this perspective supports the latter. The Hayekian argument in defence of the market (because it economizes on information) and the libertarian argument (stressing the sovereignty of consumer choice) are both compromised by these imperfections. Not only does policy have a differing and more explicit role in a fixed-price world in affecting those pricing decisions, but it also has another role with respect to preferences. It can affect the costs and supply of information, thereby influencing search. It can also, perhaps most powerfully, alter the supply and costs of human capital.

REFERENCES

Becker, G.S. (1965) 'A Theory of the Allocation of Time', *Economic Journal*, 75, pp. 493–517.

— (1976) *The Economic Approach to Human Behaviour*, University of Chicago Press, Chicago.

— (1981) *A Treatise on the Family*, Harvard University Press, Cambridge, Mass.

Blaug, M. (1976) 'Human Capital Theory: a Slightly Jaundiced Survey', *Journal of Economic Literature*, 14, pp. 827–55.

Caves, R. (1983) *Multinational Enterprise and Economic Analysis*, Cambridge University Press, Cambridge.

Chandler, A. (1977) *The Visible Hand: the Managerial Revolution in American Business*, Harvard University Press, Cambridge, Mass.

Coase, R.H. (1937) 'The Nature of the Firm', *Economica*, 4, pp. 386–405.

Collard, D., Helm, D., Scott, M. and Sen, A. (1984) *Economic Theory and Hicksian Themes*, Oxford University Press, Oxford.

Cyert, R.M. and March, J.G. (1963) *A Behavioural Theory of the Firm*, Prentice-Hall, Englewood Cliffs, New Jersey.

Dobb, M. (1973) *Theories of Value and Distribution since Adam Smith*, Cambridge University Press, Cambridge.

Fama, E. (1980) 'Agency Problems and the Theory of the Firm', *Journal of Political Economy*, 88, pp. 288–307.

Friedman,M. (1953) 'The Methodology of Positive Economics', in *Essays in Positive Economics*, ed. M. Friedman, University of Chicago Press, Chicago.

Gold, B. (1981) 'Changing Perspectives on Size, Scale and Returns: an Interpretative Survey', *Journal of Economic Literature*, 19, pp. 5–53.

Grossman, S.J. and Stiglitz, J.E. (1980) 'On the Impossibility of Informationally Efficient Markets', *American Economic Review*, 70, pp. 393–407.

Hahn, F. (1973) *On the Notion of Equilibrium in Economics*, Cambridge University Press, Cambridge.

Hall, R.L. and Hitch, C.J. (1939) 'Price Theory and Business Behaviour', *Oxford Economic Papers*, new series 2, pp. 14–45.

Hannah, L. (1983) *The Rise of the Corporate Economy*, 2nd ed., Macmillan, London.

Hannah, L. and Kay, J. (1975) *Concentration of Modern British Industry: Theory, Measurement and UK Experience*, Macmillan, London.

Hayek, F. von (1937) 'Economics and Knowledge', *Economica*, new series 4, pp. 33–54. Reprinted in F. von Hayek (1948) *Individualism and Economic Order*, University of Chicago Press, Chicago.

Helm, D.R. (1983) 'Three Views of Methodology', *Greek Economic Review*, 5, pp. 278–85.

— (1984a) 'Enforced Maximisation: Competition, Evolution and Selection', D.Phil. thesis, University of Oxford.
— (1984b) 'Predictions and Causes', *Oxford Economic Papers*, supplement; and also in *Economic Theory and Hicksian Themes*, ed. D. Collard, D. Helm, M. Scott and A. Sen, Oxford University Press, Oxford, 36, pp. 118–34.
Hicks, J.R. (1969) *A Theory of Economic History*, Oxford University Press, Oxford.
— (1976) '"Revolutions" in Economics', in *Method and Appraisal in Economics*, ed. S.J. Latsis, Cambridge University Press, Cambridge; also in J. Hicks, *Collected Essays on Economic Thought*, vol. 3, *Classics and Moderns*, Basil Blackwell, Oxford, 1983.
— (1977) *Economic Perspectives*, Oxford University Press, Oxford.
— (1981) *Wealth and Welfare*, Basil Blackwell, Oxford.
— (1983) *Classics and Moderns*, Basil Blackwell, Oxford.
Leibenstein, H. (1976) *Beyond Economic Man*, Harvard University Press, Cambridge, Mass.
Marshall, A. (1920) *Principles of Economics*, 8th ed., Macmillan, London.
Nyman, S. and Silberston, A. (1978) 'The Ownership and Control of Industry', *Oxford Economic Papers*, new series 30, pp. 74–101.
Okun, A.M. (1981) *Prices and Quantities: a Macroeconomic Analysis*, Basil Blackwell, Oxford.
Reder, M.W. (1982) 'Chicago Economics: Permanence and Change', *Journal of Economic Literature*, 20, pp. 1–38.
Scherer, F.M. (1971) *Industrial Market Structure and Economic Performance*, Rand McNally, Chicago.
Schumpeter, J.A. (1954) *History of Economic Analysis*, Allen and Unwin, London.
Silberston, A. (1972) 'Economies of Scale in Theory and Practice', *Economic Journal*, supplement, 82, pp. 369–91.
Simon, H.A. (1955) *Models of Man*, John Wiley, New York.
Smith, A. (1776) *An Enquiry into the Nature and Causes of the Wealth of Nations*. Republished in ed. R.H. Campbell, A.S. Skinner and W.B. Todd (1976), 2 vols, Clarendon Press, Oxford.
Sowell, T. (1974) *Classical Economics Reconsidered*, Princeton University Press, Princeton.
Stigler, G.J. and Becker, G.S. (1977) 'Das Gustibus Non Est Disputandum', *American Economic Review*, 67, pp. 76–90.
Vickers, J. (1985) 'Delegation and the Theory of the Firm', *Economic Journal*, supplement, 95.
Viner, J. (1929) 'Adam Smith and Laissez Faire', *Journal of Political Economy*, pp. 198–232.
Weiszäcker, C. von (1971) 'Notes on Endogenous Change in Tastes', *Journal of Economic Theory*, 3, pp. 345–72.
Williamson, O.E. (1981) 'The Modern Corporation: Origins, Evolution and Attributes', *Journal of Economic Literature*, 19, pp. 1537–68.
Wilson, T. and Skinner, A. (1977) *Essays on Adam Smith*, Oxford University Press, Oxford.
Winter, S.G. (1964) 'Economic "Natural Selection" and the Theory of the Firm', *Yale Economic Essays*, 4, pp. 225–72.

7

The Exchange Paradigm and the Theory of Production and Distribution

KLAUS H. HENNINGS

I INTRODUCTION: TRADE AND PRODUCTION IN ECONOMIC THEORY

Economic activity can take two distinct forms: trade and production, or, to use older terms, commerce and industry. The gist of trade is to establish, by means of exchange, another allocation of available commodities; the gist of production is to increase the availability of commodities. Both these activities coexist in all known economic societies, except perhaps the most primitive and stagnant ones. Industrial societies, in particular, are characterized by an increasing importance of production, and an increasing sophistication of trade. Economic theory, therefore, has to deal with both. But the point of view from which economic theories have dealt with them has changed. Pre-classical authors have typically been more interested in trade than in production.[1] The Physiocrats and the classical economists have by and large been more interested in production than in trade, and typically looked at trade from the vantage point of production. The neoclassical economists, by contrast, looked at production from the vantage point of trade; theirs was a theory of exchange in which production did not play much of a role. Later generations have attempted to give production a place in economic theory more commensurate with its place in modern industrial society, while retaining the vantage point adopted by the first neoclassicals. In essence, this involved the extension of the exchange model, or exchange paradigm, as it was developed by Jevons, Menger and Walras in the 1870s to include production by a succession of economists, culminating in the reconstruction of economic theory in the 1930s by Sir John Hicks and others.

This reconstruction also involved the theory of distribution. This was no accident. Whenever production is organized on the basis of a division of

[1] Like all generalizations, this statement, and the following ones, are subject to qualifications which cannot be spelled out here.

labour, the joint product has to be divided in one way or another. While different forms or modes of distribution have been common at different times and places (Polanyi, 1957, pp. 250–6), distribution by exchange has been the dominant form in industrial societies. It was discussed as such by pre-classical, classical and neoclassical economists. The extension of the exchange paradigm to distribution followed naturally, therefore, from its extension to production. Yet the particular way in which this was done by the neoclassical economists wrought changes to the theory of distribution as much as it did to the theory of production.

In this paper, an attempt will be made to reconstruct, in as much detail as is possible in such a short compass, the way in which the exchange paradigm was extended to production and distribution by neoclassical economists, and to trace the changes it brought to the theory of production as well as the theory of distribution.

II THE EXCHANGE PARADIGM

The analytical core of the three seminal works of neoclassical economic theory (Jevons, 1871; Menger, 1871; Walras, 1874) is a theory of exchange in which rational economic agents exchange commodities on markets. Both the commodities that are exchanged and the markets on which they are exchanged are taken as given, as is the fact that economic agents act rationally, are free to do so, and are subject only to economic constraints.[2] These (and other) assumptions result in a model of pure exchange in which the behaviour of individual economic agents is considered as the result of choice at the margin. As various options are open to an individual (to trade or not to trade, to trade more or less of a particular commodity at a particular price, etc.), he has to choose between them, and does so on the basis of weighing advantages and disadvantages, costs and benefits, of the particular courses of action open to him. Individual economic behaviour on markets is the analytical centre-piece of the model: the fact that supply and demand on markets are *derived* from postulates about individual economic behaviour is the theoretical novelty which distinguishes the neoclassicals from earlier traditions in economic theory.[3]

There are various versions of this pure exchange model which differ according to the specific assumptions made. Together they form the basis for an approach which I shall call the exchange paradigm. In this vision, economic phenomena are explained by reference to the market behaviour

---

[2] These assumptions, and the last one in particular, are the reason why Robinson Crusoe (who had already done service for classical economists) was asked so often to serve as model economic agent.

[3] No attention can be paid here to forerunners such as Gossen.

of individual economic agents as it is manifested by demand and supply. Individual economic behaviour is seen as determined primarily by individual preferences for, and availabilities of, commodities. The interaction of subjective preferences and equally subjective perceptions of available commodities results in market prices which are interpreted as the societal expression of these individual preferences and perceptions. There is thus more to the process of price determination than a process in which demand and supply are equated. It is also seen as a process in which individual economic behaviour is coordinated in such a way as is required for mutual compatibility. In this interpretation, market equilibrium is not, as is often argued, a state of harmony. On the contrary, market equilibrium is the result of a equilibration of opposing forces. The basic assumption is that there are conflicting interests: that they are of the same nature as the conflict between traders on a market who have contrary interests, but depend on each other; who are prepared to give and to take, but adhere to shared rules; and who therefore aim to find a solution to, rather than a compromise between, their divergent interests such that all involved are satisfied with the eventual outcome, and are prepared to accept it as final.

The hallmark of exchange paradigm is the economizing behaviour of individual economic agents, which is visualized as making the best under given circumstances, be they immutable, fixed or changing. Although it is correct that the pure exchange model deals with the allocation of fixed quantities of commodities, this is not in my view essential to the exchange paradigm. It is perfectly possible to construct models of pure exchange evolving through time, in which varying and even endogenously determined amounts of commodities are allocated and traded without violating the vision that is embodied in the notion of the exchange paradigm.

III THE FORMAL EQUIVALENCE OF EXCHANGE AND PRODUCTION

Precisely because the exchange paradigm centres attention on individual economic behaviour as manifested on markets, it can be applied to economic activities other than trade, and has been so applied in view of the ubiquity of markets in the organization of economic activities in industrial societies.[4] Indeed, it is a common feature of all neoclassical economists that the exchange paradigm is used to provide a unified account of the 'laws of production, distribution and consumption' that have been the subject matter of economic theory since at least Adam Smith. Their approach has

---

[4] Hicks (1969) provides a fascinating account of the growth of markets as economic institutions, and as a precondition for the establishment of modern industrial societies.

been to view the economic system as a collection of markets, and economic activities as an attempt to satisfy human wants. Trading is conceived as *the* archetypal economic activity, and economics as a science of markets, or (to use Whateley's term) 'catallactics'.[5] This comes out quite clearly in the way neoclassical authors arranged their treatises. Classical economic treatises had begun with production, followed by distribution and exchange, and finally consumption (Cannan, 1924, ch. II). Neoclassical treatises, by contrast, typically begin with a consideration of consumer wants, then proceed to exchange, and discuss production and distribution last.[6] The analysis of exchange was thus transformed from a mode of distribution, to be considered in the context of production, into a cornerstone of the economic system, associated with the satisfaction of wants, which needs to be discussed before production and distribution can be analysed as means to satisfy wants. Thus Jevons observed 'Both by the use of capital [that is, production] and by exchange we are enabled vastly to increase the sum of utility which we enjoy' (1871, p. 225). Note the juxtaposition; Jevons clearly considered exchange and production as alternative means to increase the satisfaction of wants.

Menger (1871) went a step further when he distinguished between direct and indirect ways of satisfying wants in the context of his notion of 'orders' of goods. Consumer goods, which satisfy wants directly, are called goods of the first order. Goods used to produce them, which therefore satisfy wants only indirectly, are called goods of the second order, and goods used to produce the latter, which satisfy wants still more indirectly, are called goods of the third order, and so on. Menger thus conceives of production as a conversion of goods of higher order into goods of lower order in order to satisfy wants. Economic agents, faced with the problem of how to satisfy human wants, allocate goods to different uses, or arrange them in different orders, according to their changing knowledge of production possibilities in the case of goods of higher order, and of exchange (and consumption) possibilities in the case of goods of the first order. Note the emphasis on information requirements: and note that Menger treats exchange and production not only, as Jevons had done, as parallel means for the satisfaction of wants, but also as subject to the same allocational procedures.

[5] The word 'catallactics' was coined, from a Greek term for 'exchange', by Whately as a better term for economic theory than the then current 'political economy' (Whately, 1834, p. 4). It was used, among others, by Edgeworth, and has recently been suggested by Sir John Hicks as an appropriate designation for neoclassical theory (Hicks, 1983, pp. 9–10).

[6] Marshall's arrangement of the *Principles of Economics* (1890) is the exception; but even he put a discussion of wants first.

Similarly, Walras conceived of the utility of goods used in production as derived from the possibility of producing consumer goods (1874, 3rd edn 1954), and described the linkage by means of production coefficients which are said to depict the state of technical knowledge, that is the production possibilities known to entrepreneurs (1877, 3rd edn 1954).

Pareto went a step further in this argument when he declared:

> When an economic agent gives up some amount of a commodity in order to obtain another we say that he *transforms* the first commodity into the second. He can use the exchange for this purpose, and give up an amount of some commodity to someone in return for another; he can also use production, and himself transform the former into the latter. Or again, he can use for that operation another person, or producer, who transforms commodities. (Pareto, 1906, ch. III, s. 70; author's italics; my translation)

By providing a term (transformation) as the common denominator, Pareto indicated that production and exchange could be studied, formally, on the same level, and using the same concepts. Indeed that was precisely what Pareto himself did when he summed up his economic studies (1911, s. 9): he introduced a function representing consumer demand, and opposed to it a function which connected factors of production and outputs in such a general way that it can be interpreted as either a production function, describing production possibilities, or as a statement of available quantities, describing exchange possibilities. In this, however, he was ahead of his time, for most of his contemporaries argued on a somewhat more concrete plane.

In particular, what the neoclassical economists did on the basis of the juxtaposition of exchange and production was to apply to production the newly introduced apparatus for the analysis of exchange. This involved, on the one hand, the conceptualization of production as a problem of choice between different production methods, the application of the 'marginal calculus' to it, and the development of the marginal productivity theory; and on the other hand, the development of a theory of the entrepreneur or of the firm, which could be used to analyse production processes in terms of market behaviour, which tied the determination of incomes to the 'marginal calculus', and which thus defined distribution as that 'species of Exchange by which produce is divided between the parties who have contributed to its production' (Edgeworth, 1904, p. 159).

These developments ran in parallel and at an unequal pace in the various strands of neoclassical economic theorizing that emanated from the work of Jevons, Menger and Walras, and that were far from speaking with one voice. Indeed it will be seen that different aspects of these developments were emphasized in the various strands, or traditions. It will be best, therefore, to discuss first the work of these three economists, and then to take up the way in which the problem of the exchange paradigm was applied to production.[7]

IV JEVONS, MENGER AND WALRAS ON PRODUCTION

Jevons (1871, ch. 5) describes production primarily in terms of expenditure of labour. Because labour involves 'painful exertion', the production of goods which ultimately yield utility involves disutility. At this point the marginal calculus is applied: production is pushed only to the point where the creation of utilities just counterbalances the disutilities incurred. Production is here seen as the individual effort of rational economic agents who can balance costs and benefits to themselves. On the further assumption that there is choice between different production methods, Jevons derives the equality of the ratio of the prices of two commodities to their costs of production at the margin, to their marginal productivities, and the marginal utilities they yield (1871, pp. 203–5, 210). Jevons uses similar arguments, somewhat less explicitly, in his analysis of the role of capital in time-consuming production processes (1871, ch. VII). Yet, although he quotes approvingly a passage from Hearn's *Plutology* (1863), to the effect that the allocation of capital and labour in a firm comes 'within the ordinary condition of exchange' (1871, pp. 259), he does not provide an explicit statement of how various factors of production co-operate, how they are allocated, or how production methods are chosen. Nor is there, despite some brilliant pointers, much about the connection between factor rewards and output prices.

That such a connection exists is one of Menger's central points. His starting point is the question of how economic agents evaluate goods. Since production is seen as the conversion of goods of higher order into goods of lower order, the evaluation of goods of higher order depends on an economic agent's knowledge of production methods. Menger mentions the possibility that the same good can serve as input in different production processes, and also that the same output can be produced from different input combinations; these 'causal relationships', however, are not all particularly clearly spelled out. Menger rather emphasizes the subjective nature, variability and uncertainty of the knowledge economic agents have of production methods. Entrepreneurial activity is mentioned, but not singled out as something special: it is just one species of economic activity, which consists primarily in economic agents evaluating goods on the basis of their imperfect and changing knowledge of production processes, of the

[7] As the analysis here presented cannot go into details, reference should be made to Hutchison (1953), Stigler (1941), and Williams (1978) even though they deal with the material from different points of view.

availabilities of goods of higher order which can serve as inputs, and of the wants (their own and those of others) which they reckon will manifest themselves as market demand for consumer goods. To be more specific, the evaluation which governs consumer goods is imputed backwards, on the basis of that knowledge, to provide evaluations of goods of higher order, that is those used as inputs, or factors of production.[8] As did Jevons, Menger derives in this context (1871, ch. III, s. 3) relationships between marginal productivities, marginal utilities, and the market prices, which are later shown (1871, ch. IV) to be generated out of economic agents' evaluations when goods are exchanged on markets.[9] Thus no distinction is made between markets for consumer goods, for goods used as inputs, or for factors of production. They are all linked by the knowledge economic agents possess, and the evaluations they form on that basis. Because all such evaluations are ultimately derived from the ability of consumption goods to satisfy consumer wants, Menger emphasizes the vertical integration of markets, and thus the dependence of input prices, and factor prices in particular, on output prices. Menger emphasized himself (1871, p. 143; 1981, p. 173) that this view transforms the theory of distribution into a theory of the determination of factor prices, which is part of a more general theory of price determination on markets. Note that the basis for this transformation is not a theory of production, but a very general description of the subjective views economic agents have at any moment of production possibilities and input availabilities. The crucial assumption is the notion of economic agents shaping and reshaping the production processes according to their knowledge by allocating and reallocating available inputs. To Menger, there are no 'laws of production' that are not the result of economic activities based on evaluations, and hence market prices. It is typical, I submit, that Menger speaks of entrepreneurs rather than firms or any other more permanent organization of production processes. Whatever coordination there is seems to spring spontaneously from human action on markets, to be changed when circumstances change. Such a view has the advantage of emphasizing that the coordination of economic activities, and especially of production processes, is not naturally given. But locating, so to speak, all relevant knowledge in the minds of economic agents, and emphasizing its changing nature, has the disadvantage of not attending to what Marshall was to call 'normal' conditions.

Like Menger, Walras was concerned with the linkages between markets and their effects on the formation of market prices. Contrary to Menger,

[8] I follow contemporary practice by using 'factors of production' to designate land, labour and capital, and 'inputs' to factors of production as well as other means of production.

[9] Menger does not mention costs of production, except when he wishes to emphasize that they do *not* determine prices.

he singled out entrepreneurs as those economic agents that buy inputs, or more precisely, the services of factors of production, and combine them to produce outputs. How this combination is achieved he left (at first) open. Walras simply observed that if competition is strong enough to wipe out surplus profit, costs incurred must equal, in equilibrium, receipts, and wrote down a system of equations (1877 and 1954, ss. 203–4) that relate input prices to output prices on the assumption of fixed production coefficients. Of these he said that they may well be variable, but are taken as given. In another context (1877, s. 307; 1954, s. 325), Walras wrote down an implicit function of all production coefficients, relating to the production of a given (unit) output, and then argued that the specific values used in the earlier passage can be obtained from this function by a cost-minimization procedure. He did not justify this implicit function, beyond arguing that substitution between different coefficients may be possible. He did, however, make a distinction between changes of the function, which are said to represent technical progress, and changes of variables within the function, which Walras identified with economic progress, or growth in the availability of factors of production. This attempt to conceptualize the choice of production methods was to provide the framework within which the neoclassical theory of production and distribution was subsequently developed, in a process in which the ideas advanced by Jevons and Menger were also taken up. Singling out the entrepreneur was also an advance, even though Walras gave him even less to do than Menger had done and although his construction of an entrepreneur who made neither profits nor losses was much disputed.[10] Another difference between them is that Menger was much more concerned with the formation of market equilibrium and the conditions required for it, whereas Walras was interested almost exclusively in the properties of equilibrium states.[11]

Thus what little Jevons had to say on production fostered a rather direct, or production-function, approach. That is also what one finds in Walras. Menger, by contrast, presents a much more complicated account: production is not described, as in Jevons and Walras, in objective (that is, observable) terms, but as knowledge in the minds of economic actors, which induces them to act on markets.

---

[10] Edgeworth (1904), in particular, considered Walras's construct misguided. Quoting Mangoldt (1855), he argued that the *raison d'être* for an entrepreneur was to make profits (and risk-making losses). At bottom, the opposition rested on a less pure notion of competition, and a strong emphasis on the role of organization in production, that is, a typically Marshallian stance (see below).

[11] Walras's artificial *tâtonnement* process cannot be compared to the careful analysis in which Menger discussed what information and behaviour is required of economic agents for markets to reach equilibrium (Menger, 1871 or 1981, ch. 4).

V MARSHALL AND THE THEORY OF THE FIRM

There is next to nothing about firms or entrepreneurs in Jevons, and only a little more in Menger. Walras introduced the entrepreneur as a cost-minimizing producer, but did not discuss his activities in any detail. It was Marshall who placed the firm and the entrepreneur firmly into the centre of neoclassical theory. Marshall had slowly worked out his own version of the theory of demand and supply, starting from J.S. Mill, in the late 1860s and 1870s. He was much influenced by the wages-fund controversy, which Thornton's *On Labour* (1869) had started, and which had directed attention to the role of demand and supply and their determinants, especially on labour markets, as well as to the role of entrepreneurs in a market economy.[12] F.A. Walker's *The Wages Question* (1876), in particular, had emphasized the role of entrepreneurs as employers when sounding the death-knell for the wages-fund doctrine, and had forcefully argued that the classical tripartite division of the agents of production into landowners, labourers and capitalists would no longer do in a world dominated by entrepreneurs and large firms. Somewhat earlier Mangoldt had advanced similar ideas (1855), and had drawn the obvious conclusion (1863) that in the theory of distribution the classical sequential determination of income shares should be replaced by a procedure that places all those who participate in production on an equal footing. In consequence, Mangoldt generalized the Ricardian rent concept and applied the notion of diminishing returns to both capital and labour as well as land. Taking up Thünen (1850), Mangoldt formulated verbally the rule that both wage rates and interest rates are equal in the long run to the 'prospective net revenue of the least productive, i.e. the last, unit' employed in production (1863, ss. 105, 115).[13]

In his *Economics of Industry* (1879), Marshall used these ideas (as well as Cournot's (1838) analysis of monopolies) to formulate an underpinning for supply curves as he used utility analysis to provide an underpinning for demand curves. The result was a theory of supply that centred on variations in the costs of production, and a theory of distribution that was based on the notion of marginal products of the three classical factors of production placed on an equal footing, with management (or organization) added as a fourth. In both, the size of the firm, its access to increasing returns to scale, and the ability of entrepreneurs to exploit them played an important role.

---

[12] An earlier attack on the wages fund was that of Longe (1866). It was Thornton, however, whose strictures provoked not only Cairnes and J.S. Mill, but also Jevons and Fleeming Jenkin, besides Marshall, to think afresh about supply and demand.

[13] For a detailed discussion of Mangoldt, see Hennings (1980).

These analyses were elaborated and improved upon in his *Principles of Economics* (Marshall, 1890). One of its analytical centre-pieces is the concept of the supply curve of a representative firm. Marshall was still too interested in the shape of market supply schedules to work out a genuine theory of the firm;[14] instead, he introduced the 'representative' firm, which allowed him to treat an industry and its supply schedule as if it were a firm, even in a situation in which the firms that make up an industry differ because competition is not perfect and there is growth and change. The supply curve of such a representative firm is determined by the way in which it reacts to changes in demand, in its costs of production, and in its production methods.[15] Marshall made much of the 'Principle of Substitution', but did not write down a production function. He did espouse the notion of marginal productivity, but not without qualifications: 'Marginal uses and costs do not govern value, but are governed together with value by the general relations of demand and supply' (1890, bk V, ch. viii, s. 6). Nevertheless Marshall saw clearly the importance of cost minimization for the choice of production methods. But although he used profit maximization as an entrepreneurial maxim in his analysis of monopoly, he did not see that cost minimization does not necessarily imply profit maximization.

Among the determinants of the supply schedule, both diminishing returns to a factor and increasing returns to scale played a role. Indeed, Marshall was most insistent that the scale of output was only one, and perhaps not even the most important, determinant of cost and supply schedules. Nevertheless his prolix and sometimes intricate analyses were soon simplified into an account which involved static conditions and perfect competition, as well as cost and supply schedules that depended only on the scale of output.[16] Marshall's hostility to those who, like Wieser (1884) or Wicksteed (1888), sought to base the cost concept on subjective evaluations with the help of the notion of opportunity costs, his decision to hide the general equilibrium framework of his theory behind partial equilibrium analyses and a rich tapestry of realistic empirical detail, and his penchant to minimize and even obfuscate theoretical differences no doubt invited such simplifications.[17] But this particular instance of Gresham's Law also owes

---

[14]This approach also characterizes, though perhaps to a lesser extent, his *Industry and Trade* (Marshall, 1919).

[15]Note that Marshall's well-known distinctions between temporary and normal equilibrium, and the long and the short run, were his way of dealing with more or less permanent fixities and more or less protracted adjustment processes.

[16]These concepts were at that time not always clearly distinguished: see Edgeworth (1911) for an attempt at clarification.

[17]Johnson (1899) provides a good summary, which retains many of Marshall's features and yet simplifies them considerably. That such simplifications amount to a misrepresentation of Marshall's thought has been argued by Loasby (1978).

something to the way in which the Walrasian tradition had been developed in the meantime.

Apart from Marshall, Pareto (1896–7, ss. 100, 717) was among the first to produce a theory of costs explicitly based on a theory of production. His treatment was much improved by Barone (1908, ss. 7–13). Both differ from Marshall in that they rigorously consider only static equilibrium situations. There is no evidence that their work was much noticed at the time outside Italy, but what might be called the Marshallian tradition moved in the same direction.[18] This process was hastened in the 1920s by two influential critiques. In 1926, Sraffa raised the question of how U-shaped average cost curves (which Marshall had not used) could be justified, and argued that in the case of constant returns to scale the size of individual firms as measured by the output they produce is indeterminate. This set in train the well-known work by Harrod and Joan Robinson which, together with the independent work of Chamberlin, advanced the theory of imperfect competition.[19] In 1928, Robbins attacked the concept of a representative firm as meaningless in a static situation; this may be said to have led to Pigou (1928) transforming the representative firm into an equilibrium firm. The result of these debates, to which many more economists contributed, were summed up from a Marshallian point of view by Viner (1930) and, from a more Walrasian (or perhaps one should say, Baroneian) point of view, by Amoroso (1930).[20] Together, these two summaries set out the taxonomy of possible shapes that supply schedules can take in a stationary situation, if they vary only with the scale of output, and if the form competition takes is measured by the number of firms in an industry. These possibilities have been the gist of microeconomic textbooks ever since.

Thus the Marshallian analysis, which contained a much richer account of entrepreneurial behaviour, of the choice of production methods, and of the determinants of market supply than either Menger or Walras had provided, was subverted from within and turned into a much more Paretian construct than it originally was. The same happened to the notion of the structure of production, which had been elaborated in the Austrian tradition.

---

[18] A good example is the first edition of Taussig's influential textbook (1911). It was only the fourth edition (1939) in which a chapter on the theory of the firm was added under the influence of the imperfect-competition revolution.

[19] On all this, see the excellent account in Shackle (1967, chs 3–6), where it is also maintained that most of it can already be found in Cournot (1838) and Marshall (1890).

[20] See also Stackelberg (1932), written from a more Paretian point of view, and the textbook account of Robinson (1931).

VI THE STRUCTURE OF PRODUCTION

As part of a controversial attempt to construct a theory of interest, Böhm-Bawerk (1889) transformed Menger's 'subjective' concept of orders of goods into an 'objective' theory of the structure of production, by associating them with the various stages through which production has to pass when (as Jevons had suggested) production takes time. The result was a theory in which 'original' factors of production (land and labour) are transformed, in various stages, into consumer goods. Capital goods are seen, in this scheme, as intermediate inputs which permit division of labour, and hence more productive (or 'roundabout') methods of production. An important feature of this construction is that it embodies an interesting combination of substitution *ex ante* and complementarity *ex post* (without these terms being used, of course). At every stage of production, substitution is possible once a choice has been made by entrepreneurs seeking 'optimal use' for the resources at their disposal, and the available inputs for the next stage of production are fixed in supply. A 'fully integrated' structure of production would exhibit only complementarity between inputs: but as Böhm-Bawerk followed Menger in emphasizing the ever-changing nature of circumstances, the structure of production will, in his view, rarely be fully integrated, substitution is common, and adjustment slow. Like Menger, Böhm-Bawerk determined factor prices by way of the concept of derived demand from output prices; he did so on the basis of a discounted marginal productivity theory, which did not include product exhaustion.[21] The major flaw of this theory is that it is a macroeconomic construct that cannot easily be conceived as derived from the behaviour of individual firms or entrepreneurs, about which Böhm-Bawerk in effect had little to say. It therefore made a strange companion for the microeconomic theory of market behaviour, into which Böhm-Bawerk sought to embed it. Wicksell (1893) provided a more static version of the theory, which brought out more clearly its macroeconomic, almost classical nature, and the discounted marginal productivity theory of distribution that was one of its features.

The core of Wieser's work (1884, 1889) was an attempt to analyse the allocation of inputs by economic agents, who maximize the net return from their activities in circumstances which, again, are conceived as ever-changing. In particular, Wieser developed a concept of costs that corresponds to a view of the production process as Böhm-Bawerk had advanced it, though Wieser placed less emphasis on its temporal nature. Costs of

[21] I leave aside Böhm-Bawerk's intertemporal theory of value, and his associated theory of interest, which were major innovations, but which are not relevant here, as is his attempt to define an average period of production.

production are interpreted, in this context, as opportunities forgone: and the suggestion that they should play a role in determining prices is strongly countered. Using, like Böhm-Bawerk, Menger's notion of derived demand, Wieser sought to determine factor prices by their marginal contributions to the production of outputs. He generalized Menger's loss principle by adding the requirement that factor remunerations should sum to the value of the product. As he did not make use of Böhm-Bawerk's temporal structure of production, he had to argue on the basis of fixed production coefficients (that is, complementarity between inputs), and was, in effect, unable to solve the problem of how factor prices are determined in this context.[22]

Wieser's contributions were much debated. His opportunity-cost concept drew the opposition of Marshall and Edgeworth, who defended the classical (and Jevonsian) concept of real costs. It was eventually accepted, however, because it went well with the Paretian production-function approach; in effect, it foreshadowed the notion of transformation rates. His theory of distribution was soon superseded and is remarkable only for its early use of the adding-up requirement. Böhm-Bawerk's theory was even more disputed, but survived into the 1930s because Hayek (1931) and others attempted to use it to construct a theory of short-term dynamics, in which they sought to exploit the temporary fixity of input supplies inherent in Böhm-Bawerk's construction. It proved difficult to handle, though, on account of its intertemporal aspects, which in the end were simply put aside.[23] What remained was a linear (that is, one-way) view of production, and a concept of capital that did not make much sense in the general equilibrium context, which had by then become the dominant form of neoclassical economic theory.

VII MARGINAL PRODUCTIVITY AND THE PRODUCTION FUNCTION

The notion of marginal poductivity of factors of production, or inputs, was already present, as has been seen, in the work of Jevons (1871) and Menger (1871), in Marshall (1879 and 1890), Böhm-Bawerk (1889) and Wieser (1884). In essence, it was a generalization of the Ricardian rent concept, as used by Thünen (1850) and Mangoldt (1863). What was missing was the explicit derivation from a production function that allowed for substitution between factors, or inputs, placed on an equal footing. This

[22] Wieser's textbook (1914) shows that Wieser was moving in the direction of the Marshallian tradition, but it came too late to have much impact.

[23] Two attempts to reconstruct Böhm-Bawerk's scheme should be mentioned in this context: Strigl (1934) and Hayek (1941).

was provided by Wicksteed (1894), who demonstrated that the determination of factor prices by marginal products could be coordinated, that is placed on an equal footing, be deriving them from a production function; and further, that factor remunerations, if determined thus, would just exhaust the product, if the production function was linearly homogeneous.[24] A similar demonstration was given in 1896 by Barone and, on the basis of his and Wicksteed's work, by Walras. Criticism centred on two aspects of the demonstration. Pareto, in particular, objected (1896–7, s. 717), first, that not all factors or inputs can be placed on an equal footing, because the possibility to substitute between them may apply only to some. Secondly, Pareto denied that substitution among factors or inputs, where it was present, was such as to yield production functions exhibiting linear homogeneity. Edgeworth (1904, p. 31) was prepared to grant the first point, but was scathing about the second: 'Justice is a perfect cube, said the ancient sage; and rational conduct is a homogeneous function, adds the modern *savant*.' However, whereas Pareto argued on the basis of technical facts, Edgeworth refered to 'rational conduct'. In this he was wrong: Wicksell (1901, ch. III/1) had already demonstrated that the assumption of perfect competition would assure product exhaustion, even if the production function was not linearly homogeneous.[25] In spite of these objections, and although Wicksteed felt compelled by them to formally withdraw his proof,[26] his argument was generally accepted by the turn of the century. To a considerable extent this was due to Clark's (1899) reformulation of the doctrine, which, however, added two features that were novel. First, Clark came dangerously near to imputing ethical importance to the doctrine, by arguing that factor remuneration according to marginal products was 'natural' and would preserve 'property by right of creation' (1899, ch. 1); and second, he formulated the doctrine, as Böhm-Bawerk and Wicksell had done, in macroeconomic terms. Although the second feature soon came to be accepted, the first was not. It has nevertheless frequently been used by critics of neoclassical economic theory.

An important side-effect of this development was the explicit formulation of a production function. While earlier neoclassical economists had been content to speak of different production methods in general, Pareto

[24] That this was an application of Euler's theorem was first pointed out by Flux (1894), in a review of Wicksteed (1894). Wicksell (1893) had already provided a similar demonstration, but in a somewhat different model which could not easily be generalized.

[25] This argument, however, was available only in Swedish until 1913, when a German translation of Wicksell's book appeared.

[26] See Wicksteed (1910, p. 373) and note that he retracted only the proof: not the statement.

in particular followed the example of Walras and formalized all existing knowledge about production in a production function. Inasmuch as other economists adopted this conceptualization, the role of the entrepreneur was limited to choosing, in a static world, that set of production coefficients which represents the cost-minimizing production method from among a known set of such methods. Such a role corresponds, of course, to the assumption of perfect competition, and leads to the concept of the Walrasian entrepreneur making neither profit nor loss, which is (as Edgeworth (1904) noted) poles apart from the Marshallian entrepreneur, and even the corresponding concept as used in the Austrian tradition. The adoption of a formal production function was a major step towards a static, perfect-competition view of the economic system, and thus away from the Marshallian and the Austrian traditions towards the Walrasian general equilibrium point of view.[27]

VIII THE RISE OF GENERAL EQUILIBRIUM THEORY

Neoclassical economic theory had many facets up to, and to some extent even after, the First World War. The Marshallian tradition had become, so to speak, the ruling orthodoxy in Anglo-Saxon countries even before the turn of the century. The Austrian tradition had some following both on the European and the North American continents. By contrast, the Walrasian tradition had few followers. Among them, however, were such first-rate economists as Edgeworth and Wicksell, so that their work did not fall on barren ground. Nevertheless, general equilibrium theory was not a dominant feature of neoclassical economic theory up to 1914, not least on account of Pareto's contempt for non-mathematical economists (or *économistes littéraires*, as he (1909) called them).

However, the ideas advanced by Walras, Pareto and their followers slowly percolated into both the Marshallian and the Austrian traditions, which after all were both concerned with the interaction of economic behaviour on markets, and hence the mutual dependence of all economic phenomena. Wicksell tried, in his *Föreläsningar* (1901) as much as in his earlier work (1893), to combine Pareto's insistence on equilibrium econ-

[27] In all this work, the production function was typically written in a very general, unspecific form: as output depending on various amounts of factors, or inputs. Pareto insisted that a scale parameter should be added, but did not go further. It was only in the 1930s that the formal properties of production functions began to be worked out, mainly by Schneider (1934) and Carlson (1939), although a concept such as the isoquant had been used without or under a different name by Bowley (1924, p. 30) and Cobb (1929).

omics with the Austrian concern about the temporal structure of production. Walras found an enthusiastic spokesman in the young Schumpeter (1908). Cassel wrote an influential textbook (1918) from a general equilibrium point of view, although one which was shorn of its utility underpinnings, and thus much of its *raison d'être*. There was also some advance in the spirit of the Walrasian tradition, but outside it. Thus one of Marshall's pupils demonstrated, in a much-neglected masterpiece (Johnson, 1913, pt iv), the formal equivalence of utility maximization by consumers and profit maximization by producers or entrepreneurs. But, in true mathematical spirit, he did not comment upon it. So it was left to Edgeworth (1915, p. 466) to draw the conclusion:

> The formulae which have been obtained in relation to consumption may be transferred almost unaltered to production. As the consumer seeks to lay out any assigned sum of money so as to obtain a maximum of satisfaction, so the producer seeks to incur a minimum of cost in producing any assigned quantity of product. The mathematical expression of the conditions is almost identical. . . .

This is not quite the full recognition of the equivalence between utility maximization and profit maximization, nor the explicit recognition that, in both cases, the economic problem is one of maximization under constraints; but it was a major step forward towards that recognition. Morever, to judge from the symbols used, Edgeworth realized the dual relationship between the two problems, although he did not comment upon it.

The formal equivalence between utility maximization and cost minimization in a static model of perfect competition is also set out by Bowley, in his influential *Mathematical Groundwork of Economics* (1924), which introduced English economists especially to Pareto's version of the mutual dependence of economic phenomena in different regimes of competition.

As dissatisfaction with the Marshallian tradition grew, economists in England and in America turned increasingly to both the Walrasian and the Austrian traditions.[28] Particularly successful, from the point of view of disseminating their views, were Robbins's persistent attempts to introduce English economists to 'continental' ideas (not least by persuading Hayek to accept a chair at the University of London). It was in this context that Hicks turned first to Pareto and then to both the Walrasian and the Austrian traditions, in his attempt to reconstruct economic theory. Hicks was not, of course, the only one to do so, but may fairly be taken as the

---

[28] They also turned to a Swedish tradition, which had grown out of the work of Wicksell and Cassel. But as that was concerned more with macroeconomic issues, it is of no interest here.

foremost representative of his generation of economists, on account of his *Value and Capital* (1939) which, together with Samuelson's *Foundations of Economic Analysis* (1947), inaugurated the dominance, in economic theory, of the general equilibrium point of view.[29] Indeed, the difference to what went on before is sufficiently large to justify taking the 1930s as the dividing line between neoclassical and what might be called, even less felicitously, neo-neoclassical economic theory.[30]

This is not the place to discuss in detail the difference between these two conceptions. Some indications of the major changes, as they relate to the topic at hand, are, however, required. They can be summarized thus.

1 Neo-neoclassical economic theory is much more explicitly general equilibrium economics than neoclassical theory was. Although it is true that Walras and Pareto have always been uncompromising adherents of (and, in the case of Walras, missionaries for) a general equilibrium view of the economic system, economists working in either the Marshallian or the Austrian tradition were much less so. Menger and Böhm-Bawerk, and to a lesser extent Wieser, were much more concerned with disequilibrium processes. Marshall and many of his followers were much more interested in processes of economic growth and change than in equilibrium situations.
2 Correspondingly; neo-neoclassical economic theory adheres much more than neoclassical theory did to static models. It is true that Hicks devoted one-half of his seminal work (1939, pt iii–iv) to 'dynamic economics',[31] but it was the other half, which analysed static models, that was taken up by the profession. It is probably fair to surmise that the second half of Hicks's enquiry was the less influential precisely because he attempted in it to transcend the static equilibrium model with ideas that owe a strong allegiance to the Austrian tradition. It is obvious that this emphasis on static models corresponds much more to the Walrasian tradition than to either the Marshallian or the Austrian traditions.

---

[29] This leaves out of account the work done in Vienna in the early 1930s, mainly by Schlesinger and Wald, which properly belongs to the next period. It also neglects Hicks's earlier work.

[30] That the term 'neoclassical' is not really appropriate has already been noticed. Its use can only be defended if one remembers that it was coined to describe Marshall's insistence on prices being determined not only by utility (demand), but also by cost (supply), the latter being considered a feature of classical theory. 'Neo-neoclassical' is simply meant to emphasize the element of continuity that is inherent in the change here discussed.

[31] Samuelson also discussed 'Some fundamentals of dynamical theory' (1947, ch. xi), but that was more of an appendix to his main argument.

3 Finally, neo-neoclassical economic theory is much more strongly wedded to the concept of perfect competition than neoclassical theory was. Again, this is a matter of degree. Walras and Pareto no doubt adhered strongly to the assumption of perfect competition; monopoly was considered rather an exception. Marshall and Menger and their followers had a more rough and ready concept of competition, which did include perfect competition, or something coming close, as an extreme case; but in general they tried to get by with less strong assumptions, which did not rely on the number of firms in an industry as an indicator of the strength of competition. Moreover, it is one of the characteristics of neo-neoclassical economic theory that in a general equilibrium context only perfect competition is considered, whereas in other (partial equilibrium) contexts other forms of competition are studied as well.

4 From a more formal point of view, neoclassical economic theory describes economic behaviour as utility maximization and disutility minimization as far as households are concerned, and cost minimization as far as entrepreneurs are concerned. Profit maximization applied to monopolies, but not to much else. Neo-neoclassical economic theory, by contrast, treats economic behaviour as maximization under constraints, thus putting households and firms, or utility levels and profits, on an equal footing, and placing more emphasis on the economic nature (and implications) of constraints.

What was involved, therefore, in the change from neoclassical to neo-neoclassical economic theory under the aegis of Hicks and Samuelson was a shift away from the once-dominant 'Marshallian tradition with Austrian admixtures' (as a contemporary called it) to the Walrasian or, better still, Paretian tradition of general equilibrium theory.

IX CONCLUSION: GAINS AND LOSSES

Bringing production and distribution under the purview of the exchange paradigm was not an extension of the paradigm to alien territory. It was a natural consequence of the vision of the economic system adopted by the neoclassicals, and enabled them to provide a unified account of exchange, production and distribution appropriate to a market economy. Various approaches were used to apply the exchange paradigm to production and distribution in the traditions that existed side by side in neoclassical economic theory. After considerable debate, the general equilibrium approach rose to dominance in the 1930s, and with it a particular application of the exchange paradigm. Both the extension of the exchange paradigm to production and distribution, and the particular manner in which this was done, involved gains and losses.

Among the gains, prominence should be given to the fact that this particular paradigm extension enabled the neoclassicals to bring out the dependence of input prices and ultimately factor prices on output prices, and thus on demand, and its implications in a competitive economy. Another gain is that the role of market forces in the determination of incomes is emphasized. A related advantage is that the dependence of resource[32] uses on the demand for consumable commodities is stressed. This has two consequences. Neoclassical theory is particularly good at showing that scarcity is a relative concept, depending on the structure of demand, the production method employed, and the structure of resources available; and also that production is a way, indeed the most important way, in which an economy can reduce scarcities, that is, remove constraints to the satisfaction of wants. Also, the directional nature of production is emphasized. Production is, so to speak, a one-way street. By producing goods for the satisfaction of wants, an economy uses up potentially limited resources; one 'exchanges' resources for consumer goods. Although this may underestimate the circular nature of production, it does stress its ultimate dependence on the use of scarce resources. Finally, it should be reckoned a gain that the role of market forces, and in particular factor prices, in the choice of production methods is emphasized: production methods are not just assumed given, but are conceived as determined by economic activities.

Against such gains one has to set the losses. Looking at production from the point of view of the exchange paradigm implies, first and foremost, that most of the 'sociological' aspects of production as a social institution are set aside. What counts are economic factors. Institutional aspects can be dealt with in principle, but in fact rarely are. The exchange paradigm provides professional blinkers rather than eye-patches. Nevertheless, to analyse both production and distribution as 'species of exchange' tends to relegate to the background those aspects of the institutional organization of production and distribution which relate to hierarchies, to access barriers, and other forms of social coercion and social restrictions.

It is possible to regard these losses as gains because they separate 'relevant' economic aspects from others that are 'irrelevant' to economic theory. However, there are other losses which relate to the particular way in which the exchange paradigm was applied, and which cannot be so regarded. Thus the Paretian concept of a production function gives too simple a portrait of the choices involved in selecting production methods, even if one were to endow every firm with its own production function. There is more to decisions about production than the choice of input levels,

[32] By 'resources' I mean inputs other than labour and capital, which are available either as finite stocks (for example, coal) or as limited flows (for example, solar energy).

given input prices and desired output levels. Moreover, from a macroeconomic point of view, the disregard for any kind of structural relationships in production, whether of the kind formulated by Sraffa and Leontief, or the type formulated by Böhm-Bawerk, suggests an economy with almost no adjustment processes as far as the production sector is concerned: and centres attention on steady states and fully integrated, or viable, structures of production, although little attention is paid to how they became, and stay, fully integrated or viable.

Finally, and perhaps most important, the rise to dominance of the general equilibrium tradition implied a concept of competition which is so perfect that there is hardly any role left for either entrepreneurs or firms. Just as the theory of consumer behaviour was thinned out to a minimal set of assumptions required to derive downward-sloping demand schedules, so the theory of producer behaviour was pared down to a minimal set of assumptions that would allow upward-sloping supply schedules to be derived. As Drèze (1984, p. 1) has recently pointed out: 'The firm fits into general equilibrium theory as a balloon fits into an envelope: flattened out.'

A case could be made, of course, that these losses are acceptable in view of the gains. That does not alter the fact, however, that the ascendency of the exchange paradigm in the form of the general equilibrium tradition was a process that also had its casualties. The Austrian emphasis on the structure of production, the Marshallian emphasis on firms, on entrepreneurs and on non-perfect competition, and the emphasis, common to both traditions, on economic dynamics and disequilibrium situations, posed questions which cannot be answered within a general equilibrium framework. The application of the exchange paradigm to production and distribution in this particular form created a theory of impressive and comprehensive generality; but it did so by concentrating on some aspects of economic behaviour to the exclusion of others. Now that we have it, and have learnt the lessons to be learnt from it, it seems that other questions, particularly but not only those posed by the Austrian and the Marshallian traditions of neoclassical economic theory, prove more interesting. The grass may well be greener on the hills beyond those covered by the exchange paradigm applied to production and distribution in the form of a general equilibrium framework.

REFERENCES

Amoroso, L. (1930) 'La curva statica di offerta', *Giornale degli Economisti*. Translated as 'The Static Supply Curve', *International Economic Papers*, 1954, IV, pp. 39–65.

Barone, E. (1896) 'Studi sulla distribuzione', *Giornale degli Economisti*, 2nd series, 62, pp. 107–55, 235–50.

— (1908) *Principî di Economia Politica*, Tip. Nazionale, Rome.
Böhm-Bawerk, E. von (1889) *Positive Theorie des Kapitales* (Kapital und Kapitalzins, Zweite Ableitung), Wagner, Innsbruck. Translated as *The Positive Theory of Capital*, (1891), Macmillan, London.
Bowley, A.L. (1924) *The Mathematical Groundwork of Economics*, Clarendon Press, Oxford.
Cannan, E. (1924) *A History of the Theories of Production and Distribution in English Political Economy from 1776 to 1848*, 3rd edn, King, London.
Carlson, S. (1939) *A Study on the Pure Theory of Production*, King, London.
Cassel, G. (1918) *Theoretische Sozialökonomie*, Deichert, Leipzig. Translated as *Theory of Social Economy*, 1923, Fisher Unwin, London.
Clark, J.B. (1899) *The Distribution of Wealth*, Macmillan, New York.
Cobb, C.W. (1929) 'Contour Lines in Economics', *Journal of Political Economy*, 37, pp. 225–9.
Cournot, A.A. (1838) *Recherches sur les Principes Mathématiques de la Théorie des Richesses*, Hachette, Paris. Translated as *Researches into the Mathematical Principles of the Theory of Wealth*, 1897, Macmillan, London.
Drèze, J.H. (1984) '(Uncertainty and) the Firm in General Equilibrium', *Core Discussion Paper*, no. 8426, Louvain.
Edgeworth, F.Y. (1904) 'The Theory of Distribution'. Reprinted in *Papers Relating to Political Economy*, 1926, Macmillan, London, vol. I, pp. 13–60.
— (1911) 'Laws of Increasing and Diminishing Returns'. Reprinted in *Papers Relating to Political Economy*, 1926, Macmillan, London, vol. I, pp. 61–99.
— (1915) 'On some Theorems due to Pareto, Zawadski, W.E. Johnson, and Others'. Reprinted in *Papers Relating to Political Economy*, 1926, Macmillan, London, vol. II, pp. 450–91.
Flux, A.W. (1894) '[Review of] P.H. Wicksteed, *An Essay on the Co-ordination of the Laws of Distribution*', *Economic Journal*, 4, pp. 308–13.
Hayek, F.A. (1931) *Preise und Produktion*, Springer, Vienna. Translated as *Prices and Production*, 1931, Routledge, London.
— (1941) *The Pure Theory of Capital*, Routledge, London.
Hearn, W.E. (1863) *Plutology, or the Theory of the Efforts to Satisfy Human Wants*, Robertson, Melbourne.
Hennings, K.H. (1980) 'The Transition from Classical to Neoclassical Economic Theory: Hans von Mangoldt', *Kyklos*, 33, pp. 658–708.
Hicks, J.R. (1939) *Value and Capital*, Clarendon Press, Oxford.
— (1969) *A Theory of Economic History*, University Press, Oxford.
— (1983) *Classics and Moderns* vol. III, *Collected Essays on Economic Theory*, Basil Blackwell, Oxford.
Hutchison, T.W. (1953) *A Review of Economic Doctrines 1870–1929*, Clarendon Press, Oxford.
Jevons, W.S. (1871) *The Theory of Political Economy*, Macmillan, London. Quotations from reprint of 4th edn, 1970, ed. R.D.C. Black, Penguin Books, Harmondsworth.
Johnson, W.E. (1899) 'Supply and Demand', in [Palgrave's] *Dictionary of Political Economy*, vol. III, Macmillan, London, pp. 490–6.
— (1913) 'The Pure Theory of Utility Curves', *Economic Journal*, XXIII, pp. 483–513.

Loasby, B.J. (1978) 'Whatever happened to Marshall's Theory of Value?', *Scottish Journal of Political Economy*, 25, pp. 1–12.
Longe, F.D. (1866) *A Refutation of the Wage Fund Theory of Modern Political Economy*, Longman, London.
Mangoldt, H. von (1855) *Die Lehre vom Unternehmergewinn*, Teubner, Leipzig.
— (1863) *Grundriss der Volkswirtschaftslehre*, Engelhorn, Stuttgart.
Marshall, A. (1890) *Principles of Economics*, Macmillan, London. 9th (Variorum) edn, 1961, Macmillan, London.
— (1919) *Industry and Trade*, Macmillan, London.
Marshall, A. and Marshall, M.P. (1879) *The Economics of Industry*, Macmillan, London.
Menger, C. (1871) *Grundsätze der Volkswirthschaftslehre*, Braumüller, Vienna. Translated as *Principles of Economics*, 1981, New York University Press, New York.
Pareto, V. (1896–7) *Cours d'Économie Politique*, 2 vols, Rouge, Lausanne.
— (1906) *Manuale di Economia Politica*, Società Editrice Libraria, Milan.
— (1909) *Manuel d'Économie Politique*, Giard et Brière, Paris. Translated as *Manual of Political Economy*, 1972, Macmillan, London.
— (1911) *Économie Mathématique*. Reprinted in *Statistique et Économie Mathématique* (Oeuvres complètes), 1966, Droz, Geneva, vol. viii, pp. 319–68.
Pigou, A.C. (1928) 'An Analysis of Supply', *Economic Journal*, 38, pp. 238–57.
Polanyi, K., Arensberg, C. and Pearson, H.W. (eds) (1957) *Trade and Market in the Early Empires*, Macmillan, New York.
Robbins, L.C. (1928) 'The Representative Firm', *Economic Journal*, 38, pp. 387–404.
Robinson, E.A.G. (1931) *The Structure of Competitive Industry*, Nisbet, London; Cambridge University Press, Cambridge.
Samuelson, P.A. (1947) *Foundations of Economic Analysis*, Harvard University Press, Cambridge, Mass.
Schneider, E. (1934) *Theorie der Produktion*, Springer, Vienna.
Schumpeter, J.A. (1908) *Das Wesen und der Hauptinhalt der theoretischen Nationalökonomie*, Duncker and Humblot, Leipzig.
Shackle, G.L.S. (1967) *The Years of High Theory*, Cambridge University Press, Cambridge.
Stackelberg, H. von (1932) *Grundlagen einer einen Kostentheorie,* Springer, Vienna.
Stigler, G.J. (1941) *Production and Distribution Theories*, Macmillan, New York.
Strigl, R. von (1934) *Kapital und Produktion*, Springer, Vienna.
Taussig, F.W. (1911) *Principles of Economics*, 2 vols, Macmillan, New York; 4th edn, 1939, Macmillan, New York.
Thornton, W.T. (1869) *On Labour*, Macmillan, London.
Thünen, J.H. von (1850) *Der isolierte Staat*, pt 2: *Erste Abteilung*, Leopold, Rostock.
Viner, J. (1930) 'Cost Curves and Supply Curves', *Zeitschrift für Nationalökonomie*, III, pp. 23–46.
Walker, F.A. (1876) *The Wages Question*, Holt, New York.
Walras, L. (1874 and 1877) *Éléments d'Économie Pure*, Corbaz, Lausanne; 3rd edn, 1896, Rouge, Lausanne. Translated (from édition définitive, 1926) as *Elements of Pure Economics*, 1954, George Allen and Unwin, London.

Whateley, R. (1834) *Introductory Lectures on Political-Economy*, Parker, London.
Wicksell, K. (1893) *Über Wert, Kapital und Rente*, Fischer, Jena. Translated as *Value Capital and Rent*, 1954, Allen and Unwin, London.
— (1901) *Föreläsningar i Nationalekonomi*, Första Delen: Teoretisk Nationalekonomi, Berlingska Boktryckeriet, Lund. German translation: *Vorlesungen über Nationalökonomie auf Grundlage des Marginalprinzips*, 1913, Erster Band: Theoretischer Teil, Fisher, Jena. English translation: *Lectures on Political Economy*, vol. 1, *General Theory*, 1934, Routledge, London.
Wicksteed, P.H. (1888) *The Alphabet of Economic Science*, Macmillan, London.
— (1894) *An Essay on the Co-ordination of the Laws of Distribution*, Macmillan, London.
— (1910) *The Common Sense of Political Economy*, Macmillan, London.
Wieser, F. von (1884) *Ursprung und Hauptgesetze des wirthschaftlichen Werthes*, Hölder, Vienna.
— (1889) *Der natürliche Werth*, Hölder, Vienna. Translated as *Natural Value*, 1893, Macmillan, London.
— (1914) *Theorie der gesellschaftlichen Wirtschaft* (Grundriss der Sozialökonomik, I. Abteilung), Mohr, Tübingen. Translated as *Social Economics*, 1927, Allen and Unwin, London.
Williams, P.L. (1978) *The Emergence of the Theory of the Firm: From Adam Smith to Alfred Marshall*, Macmillan, London.

Part III
The Core and Extensions of Production-Oriented Theories

8

Man and Production

NICHOLAS GEORGESCU-ROEGEN

I PRODUCTION AND LIFE

The clinching characterization of life-bearing structures is that they struggle to feed themselves, to defend themselves and to perpetuate their kinds. All animals from amoebas to humans spend substantial time and effort in obtaining the things they need for food and defence. Whether the animal catches an insect or an antelope, gathers nectar and pollen, builds termitaria, or makes ovens and bakes bread, it is engaged in 'production', if the ordinary term is used in a justified extension. In the case of the human species, however, production has acquired a uniquely distinct form.

Man has been characterized in endless ways: as a political animal, a reasoning animal, a social animal, a tool-using animal, and a tool-making animal,[1] not to mention the quaint and irrelevant ones: a featherless biped, a cooking animal, or a religious animal.[2] They all (even the last ones) fit the human nature to an appreciable degree, but none in a strictly characterizing way with respect to the other animals. To wit, some animals do live in a stratified society controlled by 'elected' leaders. Animals also use raw stones, clubs and twigs as tools in the way the ape-men did and apes still do. Even humans occasionally may use objects as found in the superficial environment. Familiar cases of tool-making animals – that is, of animals that modify raw environmental objects into tools – are the beavers, the bees, and all the nest-making birds. A most remarkable case is the Galapagos woodpecker finch (*Cactospiza pallidus*), which cuts a cactus

---

[1] Aristotle, *Politics*, I.2; Seneca, *Epistles*, 41.8; Spinoza, *Ethics*, IV.35; Carlyle, *Sartor Resartus*, I.5; Benjamin Franklin, as reported by James Boswell (1922, p. 28 n.).

[2] Boswell (1922); Plato, *Statesman*, 266; Quatrefages (1890, ch. 35); and Plato, *Laws*, X, 902.

spine of a length 'calculated' in each case to reach the worm in the bark (Lack, 1947). The bowerbirds of Australia even display what we may call an aesthetic sense, because they decorate their nests with flowers and colourful things (Young, 1981; Audubon Society, 1982). Ethologists maintain (and we must believe them) that reasoning is not a specifically human faculty, since animals, too, learn from experience (McFarland, 1982).

All animals use the organs that belong to their body (their soma). A broad survey of these organs reveals that many work just like ordinary mechanical tools – shears, pincers, saw, aspirator and rasp (Tributsch, 1982). Lotka (1945) was thus well-inspired in calling them *endosomatic* tools. Some animals are even endowed with some exceptional equipment similar to those of our recent technology; for example, some species of swift are aeronautic ideals, cuttlefish move by rocket propulsion, and bats depend at all times on acoustic radar.

To be sure, what Thomas Carlyle (1937) said of man – that 'without tools he is nothing' – is true of beavers as well as of all tool-using creatures. But, as Henri Bergson (1911) first argued, man is not only a tool-maker; man is the only animal that makes 'tools to make tools'. From what I remember, 'machines to make machines to make machines . . .' was the way Joseph A. Schumpeter used to put the same idea.[3]

Although at the origin man seems by comparison to have been very poorly endowed physically, 'helpless and defenceless' as Prometheus is supposed to have found him (Plato, *Statesman*, 274), no other animal has man's versatile hand and in its skull man's inimitable computer.

II *HOMO SAPIENS*: AN EXOSOMATIC SPECIES

All species, our own not excepted, are subject to an endosomatic evolution, that is, to an evolution as conceived by Charles Darwin and Alfred Wallace. It is by endosomatic mutations that a species may become more efficient (at times, less efficient) in its mode of existence. The horse is the most vivid illustration of this phenomenon, to which G. Simpson (1951) devoted a highly instructive volume. During the Eocene period there lived a quadruped, the size of a beagle, now known as *Eohippus*. Mutations accumulating over the next forty million years reduced its toes to one hard and heavy hoof, increased its skeleton and endowed it with strong muscles. That small animal thus became the powerful horse of today.

Other speciations illustrate even better how extremely slow the process of endosomatic evolution is. In addition, that evolution is truly irregular

[3] Boswell also credited Benjamin Franklin with saying that 'no animal but man makes a thing by means of which he can make another thing'. But Boswell thought that 'this applies to very few species' as well.

and it may also lead to extinction, instead of advancement. Also, the possible scope of any mutation is limited: lions could not evolve into winged animals and, K. Atwood (1965) notwithstanding, humans could not grow 'a photosynthetic area on [their] back so that [they] will not have to eat'.

Although Niko Tinbergen (1972) argued that the human species is not unique from any viewpoint, one could list several criteria with respect to which it is so. The weightiest stems from the fact that at one juncture man transgressed the biological evolution by entering into a far faster evolutionary rhythm – the evolution in which organs are manufactured, instead of being inherited somatically. With these *exosomatic* organs, our species has become able to accomplish not only numberless tasks much better than without them, but also many that could not be achieved in any other way: to fly to the moon, to contemplate what happens this very instant at the antipodes, to use the available energy of radioactive elements, for a few examples. By now the exosomatic organs are as vital for us as some of our endosomatic organs; indeed in some situations they are even more vital. Compare, say, a fire extinguisher with putting out a menacing fire by endosomatic organs alone. With such detachable limbs man is a marvellous prosthesis – not only, as Sigmund Freud thought, a good one.

From the feeble beginnings of the australopithecines, the exosomatic production evolved into the economic process as we know it today. The institutions of the market, money, credit and enterprises of all sorts emerged in response to the progressive evolution of the exosomatic nature of *homo sapiens sapiens*. Mankind's mode of existence is dominated neither by biology nor by economics. It is instead a complex bioeconomic web (Georgescu-Roegen, 1975),[4] and in this web the crucial factor is production – the mushrooming production of exosomatic instruments. From the biological evolution, we learn that over aeons birds evolved from some fishes so that they ultimately became dependent on the air. By the same token, the human species (over a few million years only) became completely dependent on the exosomatic organs. Even ignoring Dollo's law, it is hard to think that *Homo sapiens* could revert to some basically endosomatic hominid.

---

[4]The label 'bioeconomics' for the conception of the economic activity as the extension of the biological life (a theme which had its precedents) was suggested to me in a letter of 24 April 1972 by Jiri Zeman, the editor of *Entropy and Information in Science and Philosophy* (1975), to which I contributed a chapter. The term had already been used by a few writers, albeit with an inverted meaning: the economics of some biota. I should also explain that my use of 'bioeconomics' had not been influenced by the prevailing intellectual fashion of reducing everything to a biological basis.

III EXOSOMATISM AND ITS AFTERMATH

We generally are so enchanted with our technological progress that we have failed to see that, miraculous as the achievements induced by the exosomatic evolution have been, evolution has not been an unadulterated blessing for mankind. Three related predicaments deserve special attention.

First, just as a biological species may branch out geographically into subspecies with different endosomatic ways to sustain life, the human species also branched off into different exosomatic communities, that is, into societies that basically use different exosomatic tools. To wit, *Homo Indicus* ordinarily cooks his food in a rudimental stove fired with dry dung and more often than not travels on foot; *Homo Americanus* cooks in microwave ovens and even for short distances travels in cars, otherwise in planes.[5] This is the predicament of the international inequalities, which, although very acute now, will be ultimately eliminated by a diffusion process totally analogous with that of the diffusion of Darwinian advantageous mutations in the biological domain or by the inexorable migration along income and population gradients.

This way of looking at the problem uncovers a common economic error of great import. The error is to believe that income inequalities among nations can be levelled off as rapidly as we have been advertising for sometime now. However, to eliminate substantial exosomatic differences would be tantamount to implanting wings, as it were, in the place of fins. The process of an exosomatic change would not require aeons, but it cannot take place expeditiously. No wonder that the policy of financial aid has ordinarily succeeded only in creating oases of foreign exosomatic structures.[6]

A second predicament is also associated with mankind's exosomatic existence, but this predicament is perdurable. As production of exosomatic organs became increasingly complex, some of it could no longer be carried out by a few people only. Production thus became a social enterprise, which has to be well planned, set in motion at the opportune moment, and directed and closely supervised thereafter. These new tasks created a division not of *labour* in the sense of Adam Smith (which certainly was already at work), but of *roles* in the production process and the social organization. It is the social division into 'governors' and 'governed'. Its origin makes it clear why this division will persist for as long as mankind

[5] This, to be sure, does not imply that the individual *Homo Indicus* is not apt to do whatever *Homo Americanus* can do, for he generally can.

[6] Financial aid did reach its target, but only in those countries whose exosomatic structure was congruent with that of the donor and needed just to be set on their feet again after the Second World War.

survives as an exosomatic species, which, by what I said earlier about the irreversibility of evolution, means for as long as mankind exists. For the indissolubility of this bond we may listen to none other than F. Engels (1913/14): 'To abolish authority [that is, the 'governors'] would abolish industry itself, would do away with the spinning mill to go back to the distaff.'

Production being then no longer performed by and intended for only the members of a single family or, at most, of one clan, the issues of who may use the product and who should work under command converged into a perennial social conflict. For two particular factors have placed the 'governors' in the special position of reserving for themselves a disproportionate share of what their community produces. First, as their services are not measurable in any manner whatever (as those of bricklayers or weavers, for instance, are), their value can easily be exaggerated. Second, the social elites have always been able to justify their privileges by some social mythology, grounded, however, in the undeniable usefulness of their precise function. One needs to think of the long sequence of elites, from the high priests of Egypt to the modern capitalists, whose social functions were all exaggerated in self-interest just because these functions at bottom were cogent (Georgescu-Roegen, 1971). Of course, we all wish that this conflict, though perennial, should never lead to the loss of life and material wealth through social warfare. From all we know, however, that probably is not in our power.

Production, therefore, is the real hotbed of the social conflict, as Marx initially intuited it, only to slip away in the end from this general idea for the sake of communist propaganda.

IV EXOSOMATISM AND NATURAL SCARCITY

A third predicament stems from man's ineradicable addiction to the comfort provided by exosomatic organs. It also is a truly fateful predicament because, as will become increasingly clear in the sequel, in the final analysis it bears upon the survival of our species. All living creatures tap the environment either directly or indirectly by feeding on other living organisms, but this tapping does not amount to much. The same was true for the early hominids, who disturbed the material environment only for digging some roots. However, after learning how to master fire, man's idle curiosity discovered also that the soil contains useful elements other than roots – salt, refashionable rock and, finally, metals. From then on the production of exosomatic instruments grew increasingly dependent on, and at the same time greatly fostered by the things found in the bowels of the earth. Man thus became a geological agent, an activity which nowadays is most strikingly illustrated by the monstrous gash of open-pit mines. And because the Earth is undoubtedly finite, the third predicament of man's exosomatic nature is the scarcity of natural resources.

We may recall that more than 300 years ago Sir William Petty taught that 'Hands [are] the Father, as Lands are the Mother and Womb of Wealth'. A century later, Richard Cantillon also endorsed this indisputable truth in his famous *Essai* of 1755. François Quesnay, too, adopted it (Institut National d'Etudes Démographiques, 1958, vol. II, p. 484). But having before his eyes a France sapped by the incessant wars of Louis XIV and disorganized by the ineptitude of his successor, Quesnay came to realize that 'nature is the only source of wealth' (vol. II, p. 950).

Now, since labour depends upon the availability of natural resources, it is their scarcity that constitutes the main taproot of economic value. We should note, however, that there are two distinct kinds of scarcity, even though both imply finiteness. One kind is represented by the Ricardian land understood as the perennial, indestructible space. And being finite and useful, it is necessarily scarce. But Ricardian land is not altered or destroyed by use; the same piece of Ricardian land can be used over and over again forever. Its scarcity manifests itself only at each moment in time, not over all time.

The situation is entirely different with the mineral resources. Their amounts – known or not, accessible by the present technology or by any future one – are finite, hence scarce. But in contrast to Ricardian land, natural resources degrade continuously and irrevocably, whether we use them or not. Our using them, however, greatly speeds up their degradation into waste, and in the long run their practical exhaustion. This is the consequence of the entropy law extended so as to apply not only to energy (as in traditional thermodynamics), but also to matter. According to a new thermodynamic law – the fourth – no work can proceed at a constant intensity forever, if it is not fed continuously by a flow of available matter. Work thus needs available energy as well as available matter, both of which are ultimately degraded into waste (Georgescu-Roegen, 1977a, 1977b). The upshot is that the scarcity of mineral resources is far more stringent than that of Ricardian land.

V MODERN ECONOMICS AND NATURAL RESOURCES

Classical economists (David Ricardo, in particular) earned the epithet of 'pessimists' precisely because they were aware of the inevitable degradation of our physical environment. But with the spectacular advance of mankind's exosomatic powers, which has enabled man to tap plentiful virgin deposits with increasing ease, the economic problems raised by scarcity of natural resources faded away from the landscape contemplated by modern economists. Modern economists have focused their attention on the confrontation on the market between the utility of buyers and the profit of sellers. Not only has the problem of natural scarcity been as a rule ignored, but its very existence has been bluntly denied. For quite some time the most praised economic contributions proceeded from the conviction that continuous exponential growth is not only possible, it actually is 'the grand design' of the economic science, 'the aim of economic policy as a whole' (Harrod, 1965). From the viewpoint of the sociology of science, it is not difficult to explain the apparent paradox that this attitude has reached a paroxysm just after definite symptoms of the menacing scarcity of oil became unquestionable. As is often strongly protested, Malthus was a fraudulent scholar masquerading his aberrations as science (Blaug, 1968). The general opinion is crystallized in the refrain 'come what may, we shall find a way', made popular years ago by Wilfred Beckerman (1972).

Defenders of the vision of the economic process as a self-sustaining merry-go-round between production and consumption (as is portrayed in almost every introductory textbook) have insisted that the market can take care of any scarcity of natural resources just as of any other goods. Basic theory was called in to lend scientific prestige to that claim. Price increases will keep depletion of natural resources at the optimal level; a resource will be exhausted when 'it has priced itself out of the market' (Solow, 1974, p. 3).

A far stronger defence argues that 'labor and reproducible capital' can be continuously substituted for the increasingly scarce resources (Solow, 1974, p. 10). But if we recall that labour cannot possibly increase without limit, there remains only the substitution of 'reproducible capital'. A mathematical proof dignified the astounding conclusion that 'even in an economy in which natural resources are essential and exhaustible there may be sustained growth of *per capita* income' (Stiglitz, 1974). However, that proof rests on the bizarre fantasy that capital can be produced and used without any irrevocable depletion of natural resources (Georgescu-Roegen, 1979a). And hard to believe though it may be, Solow (1974, p. 11) went as far as to claim that 'The world can, in effect, get along without natural resources, so exhaustion is just an event, not a catastrophe.'

My own view about the problem of natural resources (Georgescu-Roegen, 1976, chs 1 and 3) has been grossly (and expeditiously) misconstrued. I may therefore stress here one point at least: that nothing is further from my thought than to invite the economic science to discontinue the study of the market. The market represents a paramount human activity, which goes back to the time when *Homo* had not yet crossed completely the exosomatic line.

Early in the nineteenth century, Thomas Arnold, the famous historian, denounced Ricardian political economy as a 'one-eyed' endeavour (Stanley, 1846). That characterization fits the modern economic vision even better. So, what I do propose is not that conventional economists should close their one eye and open the other, but to open the other, too.

VI THE DISSYMMETRY OF ECONOMIC THEORY

The passage from classical to neoclassical economics was brought about by two correlated developments. First, there was the Renaissance in economic thought as the subjective element surfaced in opposition to the tenet that only cost, not man, determines value. After a prolonged indifference, economists, too, absorbed the ideas of Jeremy Bentham, the modern architect of utilitarianism. Second, during the same period the economic progress in England and Western Europe allowed for the first time the consumer at large to have his own choice among multiple alternatives. The economic behaviour of the individual thus became the new focus of the economic discipline, utility determining the behaviour of the consumer and profit that of the producer. In both cases, the problem was reduced to a maximization of a simple Dirichlet function. The following increasing inflow of mathematics was thus natural.

But natural, too, was the opposition of many of social thinker, who denounced the representation of man's actions by deterministic mathematical formulae. The famous 'dismal science' was not Carlyle's only fulmination; he also decried the new economics as 'Pig Philosophy' (1899). John Ruskin (1905, vol. XVII) followed suit with 'The Science of Political Economy *is* a Lie . . . the most cretinous, speechless, paralyzing plague that has yet touched the brains of mankind'. But there were many other protestors of the same sort.

The devotees of the mathematical tool naturally concentrated their defence at that gate of the neoclassical citadel where their adversaries directed their fire. To develop the mathematical theory of utility thus became the first item on the economists' agenda. As a result, that theory is by now the most developed (perhaps, overdeveloped) chapter of modern economics. In this atmosphere, no need was felt for analysing the process of production. Such a process was a combination of physical and chemical phenomena, all of which are governed by mathematical laws, and no one challenged the application of mathematics to the analysis of processes of production. Thus, although the economic literature of the last hundred years, and especially that of the mid-twentieth century, overflowed with exorbitant lucubrations about 'utility', most of them devoid of any empirical content, the process of production was submitted to no epistemological analysis.

We still represent the production process by the formula introduced nearly one hundred years ago by Philip Wicksteed (1894), through the slick tautology: 'The product being a function of the factors of production, we have

$$P = f(a, b, c, \ldots).\text{'} \qquad (1)$$

Not only virtually all textbooks, but also the special works on production by such eminent economists as Sune Carlson and Ragnar Frisch have still used Wicksteed's exact phrasing for presenting 'the production function'.[7]

Traditional economic analysis has thus been distorted internally by a deep dissymmetry, which has had several impeding theoretical consequences, to which I now turn.

The most striking flaw is the hidden contradiction of the conventional production function. The prevailing silence about the nature of the production function was interrupted only by a few economists, who thought of providing the purely formal symbols of relation (1) with some epistemological significance. Some have suggested that all symbols represent quantities of the corresponding elements, in which case relation (1) may be written

$$Q = F(X, Y, Z, \ldots) \tag{2}$$

the capital letters being used for representing proper quantums. Others have intimated that the symbols represent instead flow rates with respect to time. With this interpretation, relation (1) takes the form

$$q = \phi(x, y, z, \ldots) \tag{3}$$

Ragnar Frisch (1965, p. 43) even used both definitions on the same page, which is an undeniable proof that no economist envisioned that relations (2) and (3) might not be equivalent. The truth is that the two formulae are not equivalent, unless *all* processes were indifferent to scale, which, of course, is a repugnant supposition (Georgescu-Roegen, 1970).[8] Yet economists have proceeded completely unaware of the incongruent foundation of production theory.

VII FLOWS AND FUNDS

'Process' is the most abused term not only in economics, but also in virtually all other disciplines. The muddle is that it is used indiscriminately in two strongly distinct senses – a dialectical and an analytical one. First of all, an analytical process must be identified by an analytical boundary, including its boundary in time (the duration). That boundary must be conceived as a vacuous entity, for otherwise we would be drawn into an

[7] Other instructive instances are cited in Georgescu-Roegen (1976, p. 61 n.).

[8] To wit, 'a rectangle with equal sides' and a 'rhombus with equal diagonals' are equivalent descriptions of a square. But 'a convex quadrangle with a centre of symmetry' and 'a quadrangle symmetrical about one diagonal' are not equivalent, unless all quadrangles were rhombuses.

endless regress of processes being bounded by processes bounded by processes. ... What a process thus identified does is analytically represented only by the data of 'import' and 'export', as it were; that is, only by what crosses the boundary. Should we wish to know something about what goes on *inside* a process represented analytically, we must divide it into other processes by additional boundaries. Solely from the dialectical viewpoint are we entitled to speak of internal flows, a principle Karl Marx violated without, however, being rigorously indicted for it (Georgescu-Roegen, 1971, ch. ix).

An analysis of a production process akin to that adopted by Adam Smith and, especially, by Karl Marx shows that what we denote generically by 'inputs' or 'outputs' consists of two essentially distinct elements. There are, first, the *flows*, that is, the elements that enter, but do not come out of the process or, vice versa, come out without having gone in. Second, there are the *funds*, as I have called them, that enter and leave the process unchanged. They are the agents that perform the transformation of input into output flows, and consist of labour (understood as labour power), capital and Ricardian land, that is, of what the classical economists understood by factors of production. To be sure, the classical economists also mentioned occasionally the environmental elements – especially 'the power of the soil' – but neoclassical economists eliminated the environment completely from their picture of the economic process. The gist of the neoclassical standpoint has been admirably crystallized by A.C. Pigou (1935): 'In a stationary state factors of production are stocks, unchanging in amount, out of which emerges a continuous flow, also unchanging in amount, of real income.' In substance, this is tantamount to a conjuring trick of getting something out of nothing.

The true origin of the fund concept is in Karl Marx's diagram of simple reproduction. Ever since, 'capital is being maintained constant' has been a very useful theoretical abstraction. However, in contrast to the Ricardian land, which fits the concept of fund perfectly, capital equipment presents some snags. Although in every enterprise and every household a substantial activity is aimed at keeping all capital items in a state as unchanged as possible, no single piece of capital equipment can in fact be maintained truly constant. Over a short time interval, this can undoubtedly be achieved with acceptable approximation. But in the long run, to keep, say, a spade in proper shape, we need a file, which must in turn be maintained by another tool. This is a regress that would end only after we have included possibly the entire production sector in the process at hand. On this count, Marx's scheme of simple reproduction is apposite, because it encompasses the entire economy.

A physiological analysis of the production process in which the concepts of fund and flow are used in their abstract purity brings to light new aspects that sharpen our understanding of the nature of production and its bioeconomic role. The first concept is the elementary process, which consists of the sequence of tasks applied to one and the same unit (or one batch) of the economic product. It is most conspicuously represented by the undertaking of a single craftsman, in which case the elementary processes are arranged *in series* – the production of, say, one cabinet begins only after another has been completed. In agriculture proper, elementary processes are on the whole arranged *in parallel*. The third arrangement is *in line*, when a new elementary process is set in motion just as soon as the first task is completed on the previous unit. An assembly line is an evident illustration of this arrangement which characterizes the factory system.

Several object lessons become now immediate (Georgescu-Roegen, 1969, 1970). First, in every elementary process, manifestly in any craftsman's shop, virtually every piece of capital is inevitably idle while other tasks are being completed. This idleness of capital, a weighty economic waste, can be reduced, if and only if the intensity of demand increases so that an increasing number of units of the product must be produced during the same period, not by one worker, but by several of different skills. The limit of this progression is the factory system, in which no single fund is idle as long as the factory is in operation.[9] It goes without saying that this system, which does away with idleness, played a paramount role in the industrial revolution.

But let us note that idleness of funds cannot always be abolished. Some elementary processes cannot be arranged in line – digging the Suez Canal or cutting the Simplon Tunnel, for example – because of the exceptional nature of the demand for their products. Agriculture is a salient example because, unlike the industrial elementary processes, the agricultural ones are tied to the climate. The claim of socialists and others, too, that the structure of the agricultural sector may be made identical to that of industry ignores the fantastic cosmological transformation necessitated by that plan.

VIII RECIPES AND PRODUCTION FUNCTIONS

In an elementary process it is not only the funds that are idle; the flow factors are 'idle' too, for they are not in motion continuously. An appropriate analytical description of any process whatsoever must therefore show how the process develops during its duration. Such a description consists of a vector, not of numbers, but of functions of time, t, each function showing how much of the corresponding factor has crossed the

[9] For further important results on capital idleness and the economy of time, see Betancourt and Clague (1981) and Winston (1982).

boundary up to the time t. With a felicitous term used by Kenneth Boulding (1955), we may refer to this special vector as a recipe.

Another felicitous idea is Paul Samuelson's (1948). In a more explicit form it says that the analytical catalogue of all recipes for producing a given product is the production function introduced by Wicksteed. But the proper recipes being now vectors of functions, the production function is a relation between the output function and all other functions – a *functional*, as such a relation is called in mathematics.

Along this analytical furrow, the process whose elementary processes are arranged in line emerges as a little expected singular case. It is a steady-state process, which, with the convenient assumption of all-over continuity, remains always identical to itself. This means that all intensities with respect to time are constant for all elements involved. The functions of the recipes may therefore be replaced by the corresponding rates, that is, by numbers. The functional representing that catalogue thus degenerates into a simple point function

$$q = g(H,K,L;\ r,i,w) \tag{4}$$

Here, H, K and L are the intensities of the services performed by the labour power, capital and Ricardian land. They are expressed by timeless quantums: to wit, the intensity of the service of ten workers is just *ten workers*. The other symbols, q, r, i and w, stand for the rates with respect to time of product, natural resources, items produced by other processes, and (we should no longer ignore it) waste of all kinds. They are time-dimensional, yet timeless, just like the other group.

Duration is absent from relation (4), which tells us only what we may do with the recipe, not what we have done or will do in fact. The catalogue of all processes performed uninterruptedly during *the same duration*, t, is

$$Q = G(\textsc{h},\ \textsc{k},\ \textsc{l};\ R,\ I,\ W;\ t) \tag{5}$$

Here $\textsc{h}$, $\textsc{k}$ and $\textsc{l}$ are the quantities of services performed during that duration, and Q, R, I, W, are the *amounts* of the corresponding flow factors:

$$\textsc{h} = tH, \quad \textsc{k} = tK, \quad \textsc{l} = tL;\ \ Q = tq, \quad R = tr, \quad I = ti, \quad W = tw \tag{6}$$

Unlike g, G contains the time argument, a fact which renders G a homogeneous function of the first degree. We thus have

$$G(t{=}1) = g \tag{7}$$

We can now clarify the analytical contradiction mentioned earlier (in section VI): formula (3) is analogous to formula (4), but (2) is not analogous to (5), because F does not contain duration as an explicit variable. And obviously we cannot determine Q without knowing also the duration during which the process operates. More important still, the preceding argument shows that only a steady-state process can be strictly represented by a point function, such as formulae (4) or (5).

IX SUBSTITUTABILITY AND LIMITATIONALITY

An industrial expert in the field at hand will certainly be able to determine the maximum capacity of any corresponding factory process by examining solely the blueprints of its installation consisting of the material funds $K°$, $L°$. This means that one part of the catalogue of all possible recipes is expressed by

$$q^* = h(K°,L°) \tag{8}$$

where q^* represents the output rate of maximum capacity. The same expert will also be able to specify the composition of labour power, H^*, necessary for the maximum output rate. Hence, still another relation

$$H^* = j(K°, L°) \tag{9}$$

is part and parcel of the analytical description of a production unit.

There are many reasons why a unit of production may not want to work at the maximum capacity, which can be done only by using a smaller labour fund $H \leq H^*$. In that case, relation (8) is replaced by

$$q = \phi(K°, L°, H) < q^* \tag{10}$$

which is a form frequently used in production theory.

However, the last relation, which is the generalization of relation (8), does not tell the whole story. First, it does not show the quantum of product produced during some interval of time, say, t. This amount is given by

$$Q = tq = t\phi(K°, L°, H) \tag{11}$$

not by $Q = \phi(tK°,tL°,tH)$, for ϕ is not homogeneous of the first degree.[10]

---

[10] The noted mistake is associated with the confusion between labour power (number of workers) and amount of labour (man x hours) in numerous applications of the production function. Let us also note that relation (11) vindicates Karl Marx's seemingly paradoxical, but splendid tenet that time measures value, but itself has no value.

Second, relation (10) is silent about the input flows necessary to obtain the product and the means of getting rid of the waste. There is therefore an additional relation

$$Q = \chi(R, I, W) \tag{12}$$

which, in contrast to the functions relating funds to output, is homogeneous of the first degree. For if we double the specific input flows, R and I, the output flows, Q and W, must also double; otherwise, the well-known physico-chemical laws of conservation would be contradicted. Therefore, we have further

$$q = \chi(r, i, w) \tag{13}$$

with the obvious restriction

$$\chi = \phi \tag{14}$$

The upshot of the foregoing analysis is, surprisingly, that the analytical representation of a factory process consists not of a single relation, say (4) or (5), but of two, namely, relations (10) and (13).[11] It is a first challenge to the long-standing principle of substitutability. Economists have often remarked that from a given quantity of gold only a definite number of rings of a certain model may be manufactured: using more machines or more workers would not diminish the amount of gold for the same output. Others similarly noted that drivers cannot be substituted for taxi cabs. Ragnar Frisch (1931) even proposed the term 'limitational' for denoting such cases.

Limitationality, we now see, is a feature of all processes, not only of some exceptional ones. It is not possible, for instance, to decrease any input flow and compensate for it by an increase of a fund. On the one hand, χ would decrease and, on the other, ϕ would increase, hence relation (14) would be violated. There can therefore be no substitution between any fund, of relation (10), and any flow input, of relation (13); in particular, capital cannot be substituted for natural resources (a point mentioned in section V above).

Pursuing this analytical excursion, we reach the result that a well-defined product – say, a 1981 four-door black Renault 12 – can be produced by only one definite recipe. Change just one bolt, the product is no longer the same as before. The catalogue of which we have been speaking thus reduces to a single point in the space of the elements involved. The correct analytical

---

[11] Pushing the physiological analysis further, we find still other relations (Georgescu-Roegen, 1970), but they are irrelevant for the present argument.

picture no longer contains the traditional isoquants along which an amount of one factor is supposed to be substituted for an amount of another.

To illustrate the substitution of capital for labour, we often speak of passing from hand-made shoes to machine-made ones. But precisely in the approach that boasts its superiority, because of the mathematical sublimation of brute facts, this illustration is an inexcusable logical indiscretion. Certainly, there is no way whatsoever for determining how much 'capital' is in an awl and how much in a sewing machine, so as to measure both implements on the same scale. The recipes for hand-made and machine-made shoes cannot be *analytically* represented within the same space; the passing from one to the other requires a shift from one space to an entirely different one.

Yet it does make some good sense to speak of capital and labour being greater or smaller and of substituting one for the other, but that sense is not analytical. It is dialectical, in the way Karl Marx spoke of 'general, abstract labour'. Mathematical theorists of production, although they are not aware of it, have been speaking dialectics all the time. Of course, the product changes from one recipe to another, hence we may say that the product is a 'function' of the factors. But we commit a crucial infraction if we take that 'function' to mean a non-degenerate relation in a Euclidean space, as is the tradition set by Wicksteed. Surprising though it may be, the same semantic sin is absent from the theory of consumer behaviour. The individual's identity does not change if some commodity is substituted for another, and to say whether that substitution is a compensation or not is a fundamental human faculty. That is why the ordinal index of utility is a non-degenerate relation in the commodity space. Mathematics thus is more at home in the utility than in production theory.

As we have learned from Jacob Viner (1931) and Edward H. Chamberlin (1948, app. B), the problems raised by production are attacked better by cost functions than by relations in real terms. But, in spite of the importance of distinguishing between various types of cost, standard theory of production expresses total cost by the formula

$$T = p_x x + p_y y + \dots + p_z z \tag{15}$$

which is as vapid as its inseparable companion (1). That formula tramples over the important distinction between fixed and variable cost, implicitly over the length of the working day. The telling formula

$$T = T_F + \tau T_V \tag{16}$$

where T_F is the fixed cost, τ is the working day as a fraction of the solar day, and T_V is the variable cost for a duration of one day. Explicitly,

$$T_F = P_K K^\circ + P_L L^\circ, \quad T_V = P_H H + p_r r + p_i i + p_w w \tag{17}$$

where P_K, P_L and P_H are the prices of the services for a day (not of the funds!) and p_r, p_i and p_w are the unit prices for the flow quantums.

For every constellation of factor prices and every daily output, $Q = \tau q$, a recipe may be chosen by trial and error, in fact or on paper, that would minimize T. In this way, for any price constellation, T becomes a function of Q alone. From relation (16), it is evident that there is a trade-off between the working day and the intensity of operation, a possibility well known in business circles (Georgescu-Roegen, 1976, ch. 2).

The argument of this section pertains to another essential dialectical concept, namely, the unit of production. There is no analytical definition of that unit, whose only characterization is that it is governed by a coordinating organ. But that organ must display a singular elasticity so as to adapt itself to any feasible scale, that is, to highly involved changes of the optimal recipe. The problem is one of the most demanding in economics, as we have learned from the pre-eminent study of E.A.G. Robinson (1958).[12] We may only mention here that it is because of the coordinating organ that, in contrast to χ (which is necessarily homogeneous of the first degree), the issue of homogeneity cannot even be raised for ϕ. Certainly, a unit with two coordinating organs is unthinkable. However, any recipe for a molecular industry, where identical units of production stand next to each other as molecules do, is homogeneous of the first degree in the restricted sense that all its coordinates are some multiples of those of the component unit.

X FEASIBLE RECIPES AND VIABLE TECHNOLOGIES

When we speak of a recipe, we ordinarily assume that it is feasible, that the final product may be obtained if some factors are available. A feasible recipe is a historical product. Today, for example, we can bake bread, we can fly to the moon, and (mark it well) we can heat a house by some solar collectors. However, we do not know yet how to control thermonuclear energy or how to vaccinate against cancer. We may simply say that the recipes for these ends are not feasible; nor was the recipe of transport by air feasible before the current century.

Recipes are never used in isolation, but within a web. Relations among broad sectors of recipes have been considered first by François Quesnay, later by Karl Marx, and recently by W. Leontief. But none of their analytical representations revealed the bioeconomic nature of the economic process; none considered the flows between this process and the physical environment. In table 8.1 the environmental flows are represented side by side with the flows between the usual sectors of the economic process. That matrix involves six broad feasible recipes (processes) as

---

[12] Some additional details in Georgescu-Roegen (1967).

follows: P_0: transforms matter *in situ*, MS, into controlled matter, CM; P_1: transforms energy *in situ*, ES, into controlled energy, CE; P_2: produces maintenance capital, MK; P_3: produces consumer goods, C; P_4: recycles the garbojunk, GJ (a term to be explained presently) into recycled matter, RM; P_5: maintains the population, H.

TABLE 8.1 A SIMPLIFIED TECHNOLOGICAL MATRIX

Elements	(P_0)	(P_1)	(P_2)	(P_3)	(P_4)	(P_5)
Flow coordinates (quantities)						
CM	x_{00}	*	$-x_{02}$	$-x_{03}$	$-x_{04}$	*
CE	$-x_{10}$	x_{11}	$-x_{12}$	$-x_{13}$	$-x_{14}$	$-x_{15}$
MK	$-x_{20}$	$-x_{21}$	x_{22}	$-x_{23}$	$-x_{24}$	$-x_{25}$
C	*	*	*	x_{33}	*	$-x_{35}$
RM	*	*	$-x_{42}$	$-x_{43}$	x_{44}	*
ES	*	$-e_1$	*	*	*	*
MS	$-M_0$	*	*	*	*	*
GJ	w_0	w_1	w_2	w_3	$-w_4$	w_5
DE	d_0	d_1	d_2	d_3	d_4	d_5
DM	s_0	s_1	s_2	s_3	s_4	s_5
R	r_0	r_1	r_2	r_3	r_4	r_5
Fund coordinates (services)						
Capital fund	K_0	K_1	K_2	K_3	K_4	K_5
People	H_0	H_1	H_2	H_3	H_4	H_5
Ricardian land	L_0	L_1	L_2	L_3	L_4	L_5

A few observations are now called for. First, according to a very useful convention, the input flows are entered with a minus sign, the output flows with a positive sign. Second, every recipe has an output flow of dissipated energy, DE, of dissipated matter, DM, and refuse, R (useless or harmful stuff). Third, the matrix reveals at once that the economic process is entropic in all its *material* fibres. It just degrades entropically useful energy, e_1, and useful matter, M_0, into useless or harmful waste. It is the working of the entropy law extended by the fourth law of thermodynamics to matter in bulk as well. All this is not to say that the product of the economic process is waste. The true product is not a material flow, but a psychological flux: the enjoyment of life, which cannot have room in any material matrix. Finally, according to the fourth law, dissipated matter, just like dissipated energy, cannot be recycled into useful matter in bulk. What we can recycle (and usually do) is only matter in bulk that is no longer in a useful form: broken glass, old paper, worn-out motors, in general, things found among garbage or junk – in a word, garbojunk.

If all $x_{ii} > 0$ – that is, if there is a feasible recipe for every produced input – the matrix will be referred to as a technology. However, technologies, like recipes, are also of two kinds, viable and nonviable. A technology is viable, if and only if the system represented by it can go on steadily as long as the environmental flows of matter–energy are forthcoming in the needed amounts. And I can hardly overemphasize the fact that even though all recipes are feasible, the technology is not necessarily viable (as we shall have occasion to see later). The property of viable technologies is analogous to that of a viable biological organism or of a viable species. But we would be mistaken to think that a viable technology can *create* its needed environmental support. No technology can create energy or matter.

A necessary condition for viability is that the necessary support already exists. Another necessary condition is that by the sustained activity of all recipes P_i, $i \leq 4$, the entire population, H, should be maintained at the minimum standard of living, x^0_{15}, x^0_{25}, x^0_{35}, determined historically. This leads to

$$\Sigma_i \, x_{ki} = x_{k5} \geqslant x^0_{k5} \qquad 0 < k < 4 \tag{18}$$

The coordinates are measured in energy or matter units proper for each case; there are the additional balances of inflows and outflows for energy and matter, which cannot be expressed separately, since R is a messy amalgam of energy and matter. If, for the sake of clarification, we assume, as all energy analyses do by implication, that $r_i = 0$ for all i, then the general balances are

$$\sum_{i \neq 4} w_i = w_4 \qquad \Sigma\, d_i = e_1 \qquad \Sigma\, s_i = M_0 \tag{19}$$

The individual balances for energy are

$$d_1 + x_{11} = e_1 \qquad d_i = x_{1i} \qquad 0 < i \leqslant 5 \tag{20}$$

and for matter,

$$\begin{array}{ll} x_{00} + s_0 + w_0 = x_{20} + M_0 & s_1 + w_1 = x_{21} \\ x_{22} + s_2 + w_2 = x_{02} + x_{42} & x_{33} + s_3 + w_3 = x_{13} + x_{23} + x_{43} \\ x_{44} + s_4 - w_4 = x_{04} + x_{24} & s_5 + w_5 = x_{25} + x_{35} \end{array} \tag{21}$$

XI ENERGY ANALYSIS

The oil embargo of 1973/4 caused most of us – not all, though – to open our eyes to the fast-depleting fossil fuels. The depletion of matter has nevertheless remained ignored. We now speak only of the crisis of energy. As one would have expected, it did not take long before a large number of authors began ploughing this formerly no man's land, all trying to evaluate the necessary amount of energy to support a given viable technology. The salient approaches have clustered as net energy and gross energy analyses.

The concept of net energy may seem quite elementary. As Odum (1973) explained at first, if for ten units of shale oil nine units are 'required to mine, process, concentrate, transport, and meet environmental requirements', the net energy is one unit of that oil. Odum's explicit formula (1977, 1978; Odum and Odum, 1981) is

$$\text{Net energy} = \text{Yield} - \text{Feedback} \tag{22}$$

which he illustrates by a traditional flow diagram in which the feedback is represented by a loop around the yield. It thus appears that the feedback is conceived as an internal flow, since we are explicitly told that feedback is 'a flow [that] goes back from a point downstream in the energy path to interact at an upstream point' (Odum and Odum, 1981). The idea that money is a store of energy and hence its flows must be included in the global picture (Odum, 1977; Odum and Odum, 1981) further obscures the issue. What Slesser said in 1977 – that there was as yet no rigorous definition of net energy – is stll true. 'Definitional and computational' difficulties of the concept have been acknowledged even by ERDA (Energy Research and Development Administration), its official user in the USA (Gilliland, 1978, p. 89).

Also, the anfractuous flow diagrams, the only type used by Odum and by virtually all other analysts, make it next to impossible not only to grasp the global structure, but also to verify the graphic correspondences. For this reason, I proposed to use instead the multiprocess matrix of table 8.1 as a basis for both energy analyses.[13]

At first glance, we may think that x_{11} is the net energy, with e_1 being the yield and d_1 the 'feedback'. However, from table 8.1 it springs to the eye that x_{11} must be reduced by the energy equivalent of the maintenance

[13] This analytical representation of a multiprocess has at least two advantages (Georgescu-Roegen, 1971, ch. ix). It avoids the pitfall of internal flow, which mars the standard input–output models and is represented in the flow diagrams by an idle loop. It disposes of the forbidding flow diagrams that ecologists traditionally use. The reader can immediately see how prodigious is the relative advantage of a table by just trying to represent the very simple table 8.1 by a flow diagram.

capital, x_{21}, used in its production. But to determine this equivalent we must know the energy equivalent of RM used in the production of MK.[14] The upshot is that we cannot determine the energy equivalent of any product by itself: absolutely all must be determined by a single stroke.[15]

Let, then, a_i be the energy equivalent of a unit of x_{ii}. (Naturally, a_1 is unity). The a_i and NE (net energy) are related by the system

$$\begin{aligned} &x_{11} - a_2x_{21} = \mathrm{NE} \\ &-x_{12} + a_2x_{22} - a_4x_{42} = 0 \\ &-x_{13} - a_2x_{23} + a_3x_{33} - a_4x_{43} = 0 \\ &-x_{14} - a_2x_{24} + a_4x_{44} = 0 \end{aligned} \tag{23}$$

which is based on the fact that, given the composition of table 8.1, no process besides P_1 can create net energy.[16] By relations (18) and (23), it follows that NE is equal to NPN, the net energy equivalent of the total net product (as we should have expected):

$$\mathrm{NE} = x_{15} + a_2x_{25} + a_3x_{35} = \mathrm{NPN} \tag{24}$$

By theorem 4 (Georgescu-Roegen, 1951) and relation (18), the solutions of the system formed by the last three equations of (23) are all positive, hence so is NE, and all is in order.

Net energy is therefore measured in units of some controlled energy, say, coal in the yard, or fuel oil in a tank. Gross energy, which represents energy *in situ*, is by convention measured in calories of fossil fuels.[17] To proceed as before, let $b = (b_1, b_2, b_3, b_4)$ be the column vector of gross

---

[14] For the time being I shall adopt the characteristic position of all energy analyses, net or gross, that at least in a static technology all matter is completely recycled and hence P_0 is non-existent.

[15] Odum's numerous examples in which net energy is applied to individual processes therefore raise a baffling question. Still more curious, Chapman (1974) argues that energy analysis must apply only to a '*subsystem*', not to the whole economy.

[16] We could, of course, allow each individual process to absorb some energy *in situ* (as is the case in actuality), but the more complex matrix would only complicate the analytical diction unnecessarily.

[17] Few energy analysts are aware of an important snag in this connection: there are no satisfactory calorific values for nuclear energy and only indirect ones for the mechanical energies supported by solar radiation (the waterfalls, the wind and the tides). This situation creates a serious stumbling block in the way of adapting table 8.1 to the realistic case of a technology supported by energies of different origins, actually, in any global analysis.

energy equivalents, let $e = (e_1, 0, 0, 0)$ be also a column vector, and let X be the x_{ik} matrix of the system (23). We then have

$$Xb = e \tag{25}$$

which yields a similar equality to (24)

$$e_1 = b_1x_{15} + b_2x_{25} + b_3x_{35} = \text{NPG} \tag{26}$$

where NPG is the gross energy equivalent of the net product. The simple comparison of equations (23) and (25) yields

$$b_i/b_1 = a_i \quad e_1/b_1 = \text{NE} \tag{27}$$

from which relation and (26), it follows that all b_i and e_i are positive.

Between the two schools of energy analysis, there have been claims and counterclaims about which one is the better approach.[18] Relation (27) reveals what is pertinent and what is not in that controversy. First, it would seem that gross energy has the upper hand, since the a_i can be derived from the b_i, but the other way around is not possible. However, the a_i and NE are functions only of the flow coordinates x_{ik}; they do not depend at all on e_1. The same is not true of the gross energy equivalents, which by equation (25) depend on the given *flow* e_1 of the recipe P_1 as well. To find out the amount of energy *in situ*, say, b_3, necessary to bring a can of beer to the table of a consumer – as Leach (1975) has defined the programme of gross energy analysis – it would help to know how many units of ES (say, coal calories) are necessary to obtain one unit of CE (say, one kWh of electricity). If we know this ratio (which is b_1), the passing from net to gross is immediate; the two supply us with the same basic information.[19]

Second, in net energy analysis as practised by most experts, the energy equivalent of labour is also deducted from the yield. The argument about this point often invokes the equivalence of energy and labour (for example, Gilliland, 1978, p. 98) – a confusion of labour with the *services* of labour, which *are* work. The energy equivalent of this work is just the energy equivalent of the household inputs if, as assumed, the system is a steady state. Slesser (1977) was thus right in insisting that 'to count the energy for life support is to double count'. To elucidate this issue, let $v = (v_1H_1, v_2H_2,$

---

[18] But dissenters came from many directions. Chapman (1974) admitted that 'there are almost as many methods [of analysis] as there are workers in the field'. And Kenward (1975) added that because 'the energy analysts disagree in their basic rules', energy analysis can prove 'whatever case you choose'.

[19] Chapman (1974) proposed $b_1 = 4$, but missed the result mentioned here. See also n. 17 above.

v_3H_3, v_4H_4) be a column vector, where v_i is the energy equivalent of a unit of the labour services H_i. We have

$$Xb = e + v \tag{28}$$

By (18), it follows as before

$$\mathrm{NP} = e_1 + \sum v_i H_i \quad 1 \leqslant i \leqslant 4 \tag{29}$$

And since in a static economy the net product accrues only to labour for its services, this relation yields $e_1 = 0$, which is unequivocally absurd if ES is a mineral energy. A similar argument starting from equation (23) yields NE = 0, an equally absurd result, which, curiously, Odum (1978, p. 77) presents as a proper conclusion of his system.

Third, we would expect that any energy analysis should help us decide which technology is energy optimal among those that are welfare equivalent for the community. But gross energy analysis cannot provide a proper criterion of optimality for technologies based on solar radiation alone; this radiation is superabundant, hence irrelevant. Therefore, if $\mathrm{NE}^1 < \mathrm{NE}^2$, the first technology should be preferred, even though e_1^1 might be greater than e_1^2. On the other hand, the net energy criterion would be dangerously misleading, if applied to a mineral technology, for as NE is completely independent of e_1, we might again have $\mathrm{NE}^1 < \mathrm{NE}^2$, but $e_1^1 > e_1^2$. And since for a long time to come the only pinching scarcity will be the fossil fuels, it was utterly inept to have net energy analysis established by a Bill of the United States as the only criterion to be used by the official agencies responsible for energy policy.[20]

Fourth, both analyses ignore the material contribution of the environment through P_0. As noted earlier, this omission may be due to the fact that for the present period only energy has been menacingly scarce. To be sure, there have also been pronouncements by some pre-eminent physicists that only energy matters. With an abundant amount of energy we shall be able 'to recycle almost any waste . . . to extract, transform and return to nature when necessary all materials in acceptable form, in an acceptable amount, and in an acceptable place so that the natural environment will remain natural and will support the continued growth and evolution of all forms of life', according to G. Seaborg, a Nobelist (1972). However, having mustered all the arguments in my power, I proved that, on the

[20] 'The potential for production of net energy . . . shall be analyzed and considered in evaluating proposals' (*Federal Nonnuclear Energy and Research Act of 1974*, s. 5:a,5).

contrary, 'matter matters too' (Georgescu-Roegen, 1977a, 1980), and I think that that has not yet been disproved.[21]

A global analysis of both energy and matter must include P_0 too. Hence, let us introduce Y, the inverted matrix of the first five columns and five rows of table 8.1. Let also $f = (f_0, f_1, f_2, f_3, f_4)$ and $g = (g_0, g_1, g_2, g_3, g_4)$ be the column vectors of the new energy and matter equivalents, respectively. Now, if $e = (0, e_1, 0, 0, 0)$ is a column vector, the f_i are determined by the system

$$Yf = e \tag{30}$$

and if $m = (M_0, 0, 0, 0, 0)$, the g_i are determined by

$$Yg = m \tag{31}$$

The upshot is that since there is no potential $\psi\ (M_0, e_1)$ = constant, on which to base a technological grid (similar to that of utility preference), the choice between two technologies such that $e_1^1 > e_1^2$ and $M_0^1 < M_0^2$ cannot be decided by physico-chemical considerations alone. The upshot is that the nature of any choice between two technologies is essentially bioeconomic.

Concerning the application to real technologies of any analysis examined in this section, we should not disregard, nor even gloss over, an insuperable difficulty. For real applications, table 8.1 must cover an immense number of recipes, one for at least every aggregate of similar products. Unfortunately, just to obtain the technical data would be a titanic, if not an impossible task. To recall an earlier thought, we can decide which car gets more miles to the gallon, but not which one is *energy optimal*, unless we also know the energy equivalent of the wear out of tyres, plugs, pumps, brakes, etc. To substitute the money value for the real energy equivalents would falsify the results purposed by energy analysis.[22] Such a substitution presupposes the equation of the economic value of an object with the embodied energy in it, a tenet which, as I shall show next, is based on the greatest algebraic swindle of the century.

---

[21] I deem it well to observe here that I did not put the cart before the horse: I first argued out the case for the fourth law of thermodynamics and only thereafter presented it under the summarizing title 'Matter matters too' (Georgescu-Roegen, 1977a, 1977b). As a curio, I may cite the simple declaration that the fourth law 'does not follow from the view that "matter matters", but is a pure assertion' (Costanza, 1981). But perhaps I should not demur for, curiously also, Costanza thinks that the entropy law, too, is an assertion.

[22] However, virtually all practitioners commit this sin, albeit ingenuously, just as Odum and Chapman have done. See below the argument around equation (34).

XII ENERGY THEORY OF ECONOMIC VALUE

Ever since the earliest Greek philosophers, a basic preoccupation of many luminaries has been to reduce economic value to a single cause. After much ebb and flow, the dominant outlook came to reflect a normal human propensity – that the sky is falling, if one needs something badly, but cannot have it at the desirable amount. By this thought, whatever seemed at the time scarce was propounded as the source of value. To recall, for mercantilism the root of value was in the precious metals; for Physiocrats it was in the dowry of Nature, which in a war-devastated France was barely accessible; and in England, then overwhelmed with the feverish activity induced by the industrial revolution, the classical economists saw the source of value in labour power. But with the growing affluence in the lands of plenty, their consumer at large could for the first time in history have his own choice among an increasing spectrum of commodities. As the consumer became 'king', the idea that individual demand – alias utility – is the source of value started the neoclassicists on their new way. But after some time, the old preoccupation faded away as modern economists developed the creed that economic value is an unscientific concept: prices alone matter in the economic world.

Nevertheless, after the shock caused by the oil embargo it was natural that scarcity should again become an important issue, although not for the school that believes that 'the market knows best'. In other circles, however, the idea that economic value is determined by the embodied energy appeared attractive to some.

There have been some old precedents, we should note, of this idea. The fact is evidenced by the 1875 protest of Engels (1954): 'Let someone try to convert any skilled labor [work] into kilogram-meters and then determine wages on this basis.' Ironically, it was a full-fledged Marxist, Sergei Podolinski, who, in a well-documented essay of 1881, set out to transplant the energetic economic theory on Marx's theory of labour.[23]

The devotees to the energetic theory think of providing it with a great prestige by hailing it from two famous Nobelists, Wilhelm Ostwald and Frederick Soddy. What they apparently do not know is that these famous scholars only expounded the indispensable role of energy for mankind and that Ostwald protested just as keenly as Engels: 'we would be mistaken if we measured value only in proportion to the amount of free energy' (1908).

Hard to believe it, but the irrecusable verdicts of Engels and Ostwald have been ignored, or bypassed, by all subsequent advocates of the energy theory of value. Thus the energetic dogma has been set forth in recent

[23] For Podolinski, see the admirable paper by Martinez-Alier and Naredo (1982).

years not only by Odum, but by a few other eminent natural scientists as well. Berry (1972) claimed that economists 'by looking further and further into the future [will discover that their] estimates would come closer and closer to the estimates made by their colleagues, the thermodynamicists'. Slesser (1975) drew the vision tighter: 'after all [money measure] is nothing but a sophisticated value judgment', a correct measure is provided only by a thermodynamic potential.

An informed sociologist of science would perhaps be able to explain why a dogma concerning the essence of economic value found an enthusiastic reception in *Science*, a weekly devoted to the natural sciences, and also why the *American Economic Review* refused to have anything to do with the refutation of that dogma. Gilliland's hearty recommendation of the equivalence of energy and economic value, which would do away with the economist's impossible task of adding 'apples and oranges', was a leading article in *Science* (15 September 1975). It drew a shower of protests. Huettner (1976) also intervened to make the good point that 'the world is full of other scarcities [than energy] and will always be'. But proceeding from a Wicksteed function of flows only, he offered a simple mathematical proof of the proportionality of prices with the embodied energies. Although, as evidenced by several letters in *Science* (15 March 1977), the advocates of the equivalence saw in the proof a boon, the gift was actually poison. The proof rests on a fundamental fallacy, the flow complex of modern economics (Georgescu-Roegen, 1966, 1971). Actually, Huettner's proof brought to light what may happen if the fund services are left out.

My proof of this point (Georgescu-Roegen, 1979b) was intentionally based on a purely energy technology (without P_0) in order to establish it in the strongest form. Thus, let $p = (p_1, p_2, p_3, p_4)$ be the column vector of the prices of the physical products of the P_i, and let P_H, P_K and P_L be the prices of the services of labour, capital and land, respectively. In this connection, we should mark well that p_2 (the price of various maintenance materials) is not equal to P_K (the price of the service of capital). (Of course, the renter must pay $p_2 x_{2i}$ *and* $P_K K_i$.)

Whatever the economic regimen, in a static perspective the following monetary equality must prevail

$$\text{Total cost} = \text{Total receipts} \tag{32}$$

And as even a baker of a small village would tell you, total cost consists of the cost of the input flows (flour, yeast, fuel, refractory cement for repairing the oven, etc.) and the payments for the fund services (wages, interest and rent proper). The cost of services for P_i, therefore, is

$$D_i = P_H H_i + P_K K_i + P_L L_i \tag{33}$$

And if d denotes the column vector (D_1, D_2, D_3, D_4), from equation (32) we obtain

$$Xp = re + d \tag{34}$$

where r stands for the price of energy *in situ* (that is, for the royalty). The claim of the energetic dogma, being that prices are proportional to the embodied energy, we should have $p_i = b_i r$. Then equation (34), together with (25), yields

$$d = 0 \tag{35}$$

which is yet another utterly absurd economic result, even in any of the actual socialist systems.

The foregoing analytical considerations are, I believe, an irrefutable vindication of the intuition of Engels and Ostwald. I should mention, however, the attempt at refutation by Costanza (1980), who claimed even that actual data verify the equation 'embodied energy = economic value'. He simply extended Huettner's flows-only algebra to an input–output system that included the 'primary factors', an incongruous category consisting of 'capital, labour, natural resources and government services'. In addition, the reader is left at a loss about how these factors have been converted into energy. The point that calls for a still greater censure is that Costanza circumvented this issue by using an input–output table with money values instead of real data. From the above proof that this substitution falsifies the aim of the analysis, it further follows that if the fund services are ignored – relation (35) – then equation (34) in conjunction with equation (25) yields

$$p_i = b_i r \tag{36}$$

This reveals the algebraic secret of how Costanza could read in his data that as more of the indirect energy is taken into account, the embodied energy per dollar's worth 'becomes more nearly constant from sector to sector'. Undoubtedly, even with rough data, money value ought to be fairly correlated with the total energy input, just as it normally is with the amount of labour (and even of land) services.

Economic phenomena certainly are not independent of the chemico-physical laws that govern our external and internal environment, but they are not determined by these laws. It is because the economic has its proper laws that one dollar spent on caviar does not buy the same free energy as when spent on potatoes.

XIII THE PROMETHEAN DESTINY OF MAN'S PRODUCTION

The fossil-fuels bonanza of the past century has raised the exosomatic production to a miraculous level in the developed nations, and somewhat indirectly a little in the rest of the world as well. But the fossil-fuels reserves will sooner rather than later be exhausted. What would happen then to the fantastic technology supported by that source of energy is a question on many people's minds. An increasing number of amateurs and even some eminent scientists have claimed to have a ready solution in their pockets.

The centre of general attraction as an 'alternate' technology has been, as expected, the solar energy, which for an obvious selling point has been qualified as 'renewable'. But no energy, not even the solar, can be renewed in the true sense of the word. The solar matter that is continuously converted into energy radiation cannot certainly be renewed. Only because the sun's mass is as great as it is, that conversion will last for some five billion years more. A proper description of the solar energy reaching the Earth would be 'perennial'.

To speak about the rain, the wind and the daylight as renewable may pass in general because these sources are immediate conversions of the perennial solar energy. But we would greatly err to claim (as we usually do) that forests are renewable. Jonathan Swift (1814) struck a truly modern chord when he said that 'whoever could make two ears of corn, or two blades of grass, to grow upon a spot of ground where only one grew before, would deserve better of mankind'. To think that this miracle has been achieved by Norman Borlaug would be to ignore the fact that Swift had in mind only the usual conditions of that spot, without the addition of other kinds of energies. For if a spot is not fertilized and covered with pesticides and fungicides of all sorts, then even to make only *one* blade of grass grow on the same spot year after year would be a miracle. Proofs of this are the Great Migration and several famous empires which disappeared into dust because a blade of grass could no longer grow on the same spot (Georgescu-Roegen, 1971). The reason why plants cannot continue to grow on the same unaltered spot is the working of the fourth law of thermodynamics. The inevitable and irrevocable dissipation of matter constitutes the main stumbling block of the proposal of steady-state – more exactly, perennial – systems.[24]

---

[24] The idea of ecological salvation by a steady state so admirably advocated by Herman Daly (1973) caves in for this very reason. The most optimistic message nowadays, Daly's naturally became very popular in the advanced economies, which would be thrilled just to stay as they are.

The fourth law bears on the conversion of solar radiation by photosynthesis, because that conversion also involves some substantial matter, as a vehicle of energy or as a building element. Modern agriculture, which is based on high-yield varieties, is the most striking illustration. Yet, notwithstanding our praising it as a hallmark of progress, that agriculture is a move against the grain of the economy of resources. By mechanical tools, fertilizers and other artificial chemicals, the soil is nowadays forced to convert more energy and more matter into food. It all comes to a global substitution of the scarcest resources – the mineral ones – for the abundant, sun's free energy. But we must stick to modern agriculture in order to grow barely enough food for a population that keeps increasing. A traditional organic agriculture, essentially based on solar energy (which is often offered as an enticing solution), could support only a very small population, for land would have to be divided between growing food and growing fodder (Georgescu-Roegen, 1971).

We must not be surprised that we have not been able to improve the efficiency of the billions of years old conversion of solar energy into the green plants. Over those aeons, nature would have certainly discovered a better way, if one existed. The indirect use of solar energy – photosynthesis – is by far the most vital for mankind's existence as a species. To cloud the gravity of the problem, some expatiate on the optimal population – a certainly fallacious concept. Estimates are as low as 5 billion, others as high as 45 billion (Clark, 1963). The question is '*how long* can a population of forty-five billion persist?' And if the answer were, say, 'one thousand years', we still must ask 'what will happen thereafter?'

What to do about the increasing pressure of population has turned into a hornet's nest of political and demographic controversies, which many futurists have sought to bypass by insisting that salvation by some 'alternate' technology is around the corner, simply because it is our inherent nature to keep inventing. This is how from the cave we have reached the moon.

History is indeed studded with inventions of all sorts, so numerous that to list them all would be the task of a lifetime. That we are no longer interested in the link with the past is due to our fascination with the extraordinary innovations of recent times. Even a broad historical examination reveals that, surprising though it may be, only two inventions have constituted momentous steps in the bioeconomic evolution. Perhaps, even more surprising might be the fact that the first fateful innovation was the mastery of fire, some 500 000 years ago.

Let me explain why. First, fire consists of a *qualitative* conversion of the chemical energy of some cool combustible materials into blazing caloric power. Second, fire triggers a *chain reaction*: with just a spark we can cause an entire forest, nay, all forests to burn (provided, as Lord Kelvin noted, there is enough oxygen). Fire enabled humans not only to keep warm and to cook their food, but, above all, to smelt and forge metals and to bake bricks, ceramics and lime. No wonder that the ancient Greeks attributed this miraculous gift not to a mortal, but to Prometheus, a divine Titan.[25] The two properties just mentioned characterize a recipe that could constitute the basis of a viable technology (as defined in section X), to which we may refer as Promethean.

To the viable technology begotten by the gift of Prometheus I (as I shall identify him), we may properly refer as the Wood Age. Indeed, for millenniums thereafter wood was the principal source of caloric power. But the fate of any Promethean recipe is to defeat itself with accelerating speed. Its new power induces economic development, that is, an increasing use of the fuel that supports the Promethean recipe.

Because of the increasing industrial activity, by the second half of the seventeenth century forests began to disappear so fast that cutting trees had to be regulated both in England and in many parts on the continent. Coal was already known as a source of caloric power, but, still burning dirty, it could not be completely substituted for wood in most industries. The greatest impediment, however, was that mines become flooded, even at a relatively shallow depth. The power necessary for draining them was not conveniently available from the sources of that time – the muscular power of people and animals, the wind, and running water. Many mines in England kept hundreds of horses for turning the wheelworks that lifted the flooding water to the surface.[26]

The impending crisis was entirely analogous to the present impasse: the technology based on wood was running out of its vital fuel and the coal alternative did not work. The solution came in time, before an eventual catastrophe, as the unpredictable gift of Prometheus II – the two inspired mortals, Thomas Savery and Thomas Newcomen. The new recipe, the heat engine, is indeed Promethean. Like fire, it achieves a qualitative conversion of the caloric power into motor power. Also, like fire, the heat engine could lead to a chain reaction: with a little coal and a heat engine, we can mine much more coal and other minerals with which to make more engines with which to make more engines. . . . The gift of Prometheus II enabled us to derive motor power from a new and more intensive source, the fire fed by mineral fuels. We still live mainly within that technology characterized by obtaining work from heat.

---

[25] 'I gave them fire . . . and from it they shall learn many crafts [and discover] man's hidden blessing, copper, iron, silver, and gold' (Aeschylus, *Prometheus Bound*).

[26] Incidentally, this is the origin of the term 'horse power', which came about as Boulton and Watt praised any of their steam engines as a better power than that of so many horses.

The problem now is whether a new Prometheus will solve the present crisis as Prometheus II solved that of the Wood Age. The breeder reactor, which converts fertile materials into fissionable fuels, would be a third Promethean gift, but its practical implementation is beset by singular risks and, according to some, even by technical snags. The high hopes once surrounding controlled thermonuclear energy have also faded away. It is not at all excluded that, as I once hazarded to say, thermonuclear energy, like gunpowder and dynamite, may serve only as a bomb (Georgescu-Roegen, 1976).

As hinted earlier, the *direct* use of solar energy has been subject to special attention and persistent hopeful claims. A very careful scholar, Denis Hayes (1978), claimed a few years ago that 'solar technology is here, . . . we can use it now'. What is here now are only several feasible recipes – solar cells and various solar collectors, which, no doubt, are extremely useful in several special situations. But a viable technology based on solar energy is not yet here. The proof is that in spite of the substantial funds spent by the US government and many private institutions to search for a solution, no one has tried to build a pilot plant that would use exclusively its harnessed solar energy to reproduce *at least* the collectors with which it was initially endowed. Solar collectors for home use have been in commerce for the past century (Butti and Perlin, 1977). In spite of some failures, there have been some improvements; but the basic principle of the conversion has not progressed at all. At this time, direct solar energy is just a parasite of the current technology, as electricity and, lest we forget, gasohol are.

Before finishing, I cannot overemphasize, first, that the situation might change any day. Yet it is not pessimism – as Philip Abelson claimed in a *Science* editorial – to point out that no one can be sure one way or the other, nor about the nature of the future Promethean gift (if it is ever invented). Neither Galileo nor Huygens was able to think of a solution to the crisis of the Wood Age.

Second, the only reasonable strategy – to say 'rational' would be utter intellectual arrogance – is conservation (in the sense of consuming less terrestrial resources), so as to have a sufficiently great lead time to wait for Prometheus III or, failing that expectation, to slide slowly, without convulsions, from the present high level of industrial activity to one probably analogous, but not identical, to that of the old Wood Age. Contrary to what we may believe or are made to believe, conservation does not have to be an unbearable reduction of basic conveniences, even if we allow for the necessary reduction of the exosomatic inequalities between the overdeveloped and the underdeveloped nations. People have lived for millenniums without golf carts, without two-garage cars,[27] without Concordes, and

[27] No, it is not a misprint for 'two-car garages', as all typists have corrected in my manuscript. I mean a car that needs two garages for storage.

numberless other exosomatic luxuries, reached because we have let the gift of Prometheus II run heedlessly. Let us fervently hope that the human species can also live not only without nuclear warheads, but also without any other means for killing ourselves (Georgescu-Roegen, 1976).

Finally, we should not fail to realize that conservation is not the business of one or some nations only. It is a programme for the entire human species, which can be undertaken only if *Homo sapiens sapiens* is also wise enough. That there is an energy crisis cannot be denied, but our biggest crisis seems to be the crisis of wisdom. And about this crisis one could indeed be pessimistic, if what Sigmund Freud said about the resilience of our instincts and E.O. Wilson about the indestructible genes that determine behaviour were true.

REFERENCES

Atwood, K. (1965) 'Discussion', in *The Control of Human Heredity and Evolution*, ed. T.M. Sonneborn, Macmillan, New York.

Audubon Society (1982) *Encyclopedia of Animal Life*, Clarkson N. Potter, New York.

Beckerman, W. (1972) 'Economists, Scientists, and Environmental Catastrophe', *Oxford Economic Papers*, 12 (November), pp. 327–44.

Bergson, H. (1911) *Creative Evolution*, Henry Holt, New York.

Berry, R. (1972) 'Recycling, Thermodynamics and Environmental Thrift', *Bulletin of the Atomic Scientists*, 28 (May), pp. 8–15.

Betancourt, R. and Clague, C. (1981) *Capital Utilization*, Cambridge University Press, Cambridge.

Blaug, M. (1968) 'Malthus, Thomas Robert', in *International Encyclopedia of the Social Sciences*, 9, Macmillan, New York, pp. 549–52.

Boswell, J. (1922) *The Life of Dr Samuel Johnson*, vol. IX, Doubleday, New York.

Boulding, K. (1955) *Economic Analysis*, 3rd edn, Harper, New York.

Butti, K. and Perlin, J. (1977) 'Solar Water Heater in California: 1891–1930', *Coevolution Quarterly*, 4 (Fall), pp. 4–13.

Carlson, S. (1956) *A Study on the Pure Theory of Production*, Kelly and Millman, New York.

Carlyle, T. (1899) *Latter-Day Pamphlets*, Chapman and Hall, London.

— (1937) *Sartor Resartus*, Odyssey Press, New York.

Chamberlin, E. (1948) *Theory of Monopolistic Competition*, 6th edn, Harvard University Press, Cambridge, Mass.

Chapman, P. (1974) 'Energy Costs: A Review of Methods', *Energy Policy*, 2 (June), pp. 91–103.

Clark, C. (1963) 'Agricultural Productivity in Relation to Population', in *Man and His Future*, ed. G. Walstenholme, Little, Brown, Boston.

Costanza, R. (1980) 'Embodied Energy and Economic Valuation', *Science*, 210, pp. 1219–24.

— (1981) 'Reply: An Embodied Energy Theory of Value', in *Energy, Economics, and the Environment*, ed. H. Daly and A. Umaña, Westview Press, Boulder, Colorado.

Daly, H. (ed.) (1973) *Toward a Steady-State Economy*, W.H. Freeman, San Francisco.
Engels, F. (1913/14) 'Uber das Autoritätsprinzip', *Die Neue Zeit*, 32 (1), pp. 37–9.
— (1954) *Dialectics of Nature*, Foreign Languages Publishing Houses, Moscow.
Frisch, R. (1931) 'Einige Punkte einer Preistheorie mit Boden und Arbeit als Produktionsfaktoren', *Zeitschrift für Nationalökonomie*, 3, p. 64.
— (1965) *Theory of Production*, Reidel, Dordrecht.
Georgescu-Roegen, N. (1951) 'Some Properties of a Generalized Leontief Model', in *Activity Analysis of Production and Allocation*, ed. T. Koopmans *et al.*, John Wiley, New York.
— (1966) *Analytical Economics*, Harvard University Press, Cambridge, Mass.
— (1967) 'Chamberlin's New Economics and the Unit of Production', in *Monopolistic Competition Theory: Studies in Impact*, ed. R.E. Kuenne, John Wiley, New York.
— (1969) 'Process in Farming versus Process in Manufacturing', in *Economic Problems of Agriculture in Industrial Countries*, ed. U. Papi and C. Nunn, Macmillan, London. Reprinted in Georgescu-Roegen, *Energy and Economic Myths*, Pergamon Press, New York, 1976.
— (1970) 'The Economics of Production', Richard T. Ely Lecture, *American Economic Review*, 60 (May), pp. 1–9. Reprinted in GeorgescuRoegen, *Energy and Economic Myths*, Pergamon Press, New York, 1976.
— (1971) *The Entropy Law and the Economic Process*, Harvard University Press, Cambridge, Mass.
— (1975) 'Energy and Economic Myths', *Southern Economic Journal*, 41 (January), pp. 347–81. Reprinted in Georgescu-Roegen, *Energy and Economic Myths*, Pergamon Press, New York, 1976.
— (1976) *Energy and Economic Myths: Institutional and Analytical Economic Essays*, Pergamon Press, New York.
— (1977a) 'Matter matters too', in *Prospects for Growth: Changing Expectations for the Future*, ed. K. Wilson, Praeger, New York.
— (1977b) 'The Steady State and Ecological Salvation: A Thermodynamic Analysis', *BioScience*, 27 (April), pp. 266–70.
— (1979a) 'Myths about Energy and Matter', *Growth and Change*, 10 (January), pp. 16–23.
— (1979b) 'Energy Analysis and Economic Valuation', *Southern Economic Journal*, 45 (April), pp. 1023–58. (An important errata available from the author.)
— (1980) 'Matter: A Resource ignored by Thermodynamics', in *Future Sources of Organic Raw Materials: CHEMRAWN I*, ed. L. St-Pierre, and G. Brown, Pergamon Press, Oxford.
Gilliland, M. (1975) 'Energy Analysis and Public Policy', *Science*, 189, pp. 1051–6.
— (ed.) (1978) *Energy Analysis: A New Public Policy Tool*, Westview Press, Boulder, Colorado.
Harrod, Sir R. (1965) *Reforming the World's Money*, St Martin's Press, New York.
Hayes, D. (1978) 'We can use Solar Energy now', *Washington Post* (26 February).
Huettner, D. (1976) 'Net Energy Analysis: An Economic Assessment', *Science*, 192, pp. 101–4.
Institut National d'Etudes Démographiques (1958) *François Quesnay et la Physiocratie*, 2 vols, Imprimerie Nationale, Paris.

Kenward, M. (1975) 'The Analyst's Precedent', *New Scientist*, 65 (January), p. 51.
Lack, D. (1947) *Darwin's Finches*, Cambridge University Press, Cambridge.
Leach, G (1975)'Energy Analysis', *New Scientist*, 65 (January), p. 160.
Lotka, A. (1945) 'The Law of Evolution as a Maximal Principle', *Human Biology*, 17 (May), pp. 67–194.
McFarland, D. (1982) *The Oxford Companion to Animal Behaviour*, Oxford University Press, Oxford.
Martinez-Alier, J. and Naredo, J. (1982) 'A Marxist Precursor of Energy Economics', *Journal of Peasant Studies*, 9, pp. 207–24.
Odum, H. (1973) 'Energy, Ecology, and Economics', *Ambio*, 2, pp. 220–7.
— (1977) 'Energy Analysis', *Science*, 196 (15 April), p. 260.
— (1978) 'Energy Analysis, Energy Quality, and Environment', in *Energy Analysis: A New Public Policy Tool*, ed. M. Gilliland, Westview Press, Boulder, Colorado, 1978.
Odum, H. and Odum, E. (1981) *Energy Basis for Man and Nature*, 2nd edn, McGraw-Hill, New York.
Ostwald, W. (1908) *Die Energie*, J.A. Barth, Leipzig.
Petty, Sir W. (1899) *The Economic Writings of Sir William Petty*, 2 vols, ed. C.H. Hull, Cambridge University Press, Cambridge.
Pigou, A.C. (1935) *The Economics of Stationary States*, Macmillan, London.
Quatrefages de Bréau, A. de. (1890) *L'Espèce Humaine*, 10 edn, Felix Alcan, Paris.
Quesnay, F. cf. Institut National d'Etudes Démographiques (1958).
Robinson, E.A.G. (1958) *The Structure of Competitive Industry*, rev. edn, University of Chicago Press, Chicago.
Ruskin, J. (1905) *The Works of John Ruskin*, vol. XVII, George Allen, London.
Samuelson, P.A. (1948) *Foundations of Economic Analysis*, Harvard University Press, Cambridge, Mass.
Seaborg, G. (1972) 'The Erewhon Machine: Possibilities for Reconciling Goals by Way of New Technology', in *Energy, Economic Growth and the Environment*, ed. S. Schurr, Johns Hopkins University Press, Baltimore, Md.
Simpson, G. (1951) *Horses: The Story of the Horse Family in the Modern World and Throughout Sixty Millions of History*, Oxford University Press, New York.
Slesser, M. (1975) 'Accounting for Energy', *Nature*, 254, pp. 170–2.
— (1977) 'Energy Analysis', *Science*, 196 (15 April), pp. 259–60.
Solow, R.M. (1974) 'The Economics of Resources and the Resources of Economics', Richard T. Ely Lecture, *American Economic Review*, 64 (May), pp. 1–14.
Stanley, P.A. (1846) *The Life and Correspondence of Thomas Arnold, D.D.*, 2nd edn, Appleton, New York.
Stiglitz, J.E. (1974) 'Growth with Exhaustible Natural Resources: the Competitive Economy', *Review of Economic Studies: Symposium on the Economics of Exhaustible Resources*, pp. 139–52.
Swift, J. (1814) *The Works of Jonathan Swift*, vol. VII, A. Constable, Edinburgh.
Tinbergen, N. (1972) *The Animal in its World*, Harvard University Press, Cambridge, Mass.
Tributsch, H. (1982) *How Life Learned to Live*, MIT Press, Cambridge, Mass.
Viner, J. (1931) 'Cost Curves and Supply Curves', *Zeitschrift für Nationalökonomie*, 3, pp. 23–46.
Wicksteed, P. (1894) *An Essay on the Coordination of the Laws of Distribution*,

Macmillan, London.
Winston, G.C. (1982) *The Timing of Economic Activities*, Cambridge University Press, Cambridge.
Young, J. (1981) *The Life of Vertebrates*, 3rd edn, Clarendon Press, Oxford.
Zeman, J. (1975) *Entropy and Information in Science and Philosophy*, Elsevier, Amsterdam.

9

Conceptions of Technology and the Production Process

MICHAEL A. LANDESMANN

I INTRODUCTION

In the centre of the discussion in this chapter will be an application of certain features of an approach to production analysis which – without any deep-seated methodological discussion of the term – we will call *descriptive-analytical*. The descriptive-analytical approach in production analysis will be seen as distinct from the more dominant *optimization approach*, which takes the *a priori* methodological position that economic reality is constituted through the interactive behaviour of optimizing economic agents. In the case of the group of descriptive-analytical approaches no such claim is made: a more sceptical stance is taken with respect to using a single unifying behavioural principle and a certain richness in the types of behavioural regulatory mechanisms is retained. The approach also does not usually begin analysis with an *a priori* assumption about the behavioural rules that underlie economic reality, but usually starts off in the first stage with developing an analytical framework in which information about actual economic activity can be (selectively) collected and systematized. Only in the second stage are various behavioural principles employed to analyse certain relationships which might underlie the information obtained.

In production analysis proper, the two types of approaches differentiate themselves both in terms of the spheres in which economically relevant behaviour is analysed as well as in terms of principles by which this behaviour is analysed. The optimization approach, as applied to the economic analysis of production activities, concentrates its analysis of production activity principally not on the production sphere itself, but on the interactions on markets to which production is linked on the input and the output side. Production activities themselves are seen as largely determined by the rules which govern purchases and sales on these two types of markets.[1]

[1] In other disciplines, such as operations research, the optimization approach has in fact been applied to the study of problems of production organization proper, but there the claim is not made that the target of the analysis is the study of actual economic activity, but that it provides the analytical tools for achieving certain managerial objectives; hence the object of the analysis is normative.

The group of descriptive-analytical approaches in production analysis, on the other hand, do in fact concentrate on studying production activity in the first instance in the sphere where these activities actually do take place. A variety of behavioural principles are detected when looking at this sphere (such as principles which establish certain definite technological and social relationships in that sphere), and only then is attention focused upon the interaction between these behavioural features and the market environment in which production takes place. Market orientation is hence not the only behavioural rule which governs the way in which production activities are organized.

The explicit consideration of technological (and social) principles that guide production activity allows the followers of this approach to analyse the mutual conditioning of technological (and social) principles of production and of the competitive process in a market system that would be impossible if these principles are simply taken as 'exogenously given', as is traditionally done in the optimization approach to production analysis. Representatives of the descriptive-analytical approach to production analysis have in the past made a number of important contributions to the study of the principles that govern technological relationships in agrarian and industrial production systems; some of these principles will be discussed in the present chapter.

II A TIME-STRUCTURE REPRESENTATION OF A PRODUCTIVE SYSTEM

As is clear from Nicholas Georgescu-Roegen's contributions, the activities undertaken in an industrial system can for purposes of analysis be divided into '*elementary processes*'.[2] This analytical separation of industrial operations into elementary processes allows the introduction of a time dimension into the analysis of production processes. Take the example of the fabrication processes in a car plant (or, for that matter, in what is statistically considered the car industry). We can distinguish in a particular plant a variety of activities taking place which are interrelated in various ways, both in the production and absorption of intermediate inputs as well as in the common utilization of what Georgescu-Roegen calls 'fund' elements (see, for example, Georgescu-Roegen, 1971, p. 225). These

[2]See, for example, N. Georgescu-Roegen (1971, p. 235): 'every production system of any type whatsoever is a system of elementary processes. In the shop of a cabinet maker the elementary process by which a piece of furniture is produced develops unclouded in front of our eyes. But even in a more complex system, it can be isolated if one follows the rules . . . for . . . recording the analytical coordinates of a partial process. The point is that the concept of elementary process is well defined in every system of production.'

activities last varying lengths of time and represent various stages in the fabrication of particular intermediate inputs or components of the final commodity (the body, engine, tyres, etc. of a car). The different activities might take place alongside each other or in some sort of sequence.

The 'time structure' of the productive system considered in this paper will define a certain time interval as an analytical cutting device,[3] which will lead to the distinction of stages of fabrication within each of these activities (see figure 9.1). We will show later on (see section iv) that the choice of particular time intervals, which allows the distinction of fabrication stages of different activities, is not an arbitrary choice, but depends upon the focus of the analysis pursued.[4] For the moment we will restrict ourselves to pointing out that the choice of these time intervals also determines the number of different types of elementary processes that are analytically distinguished.

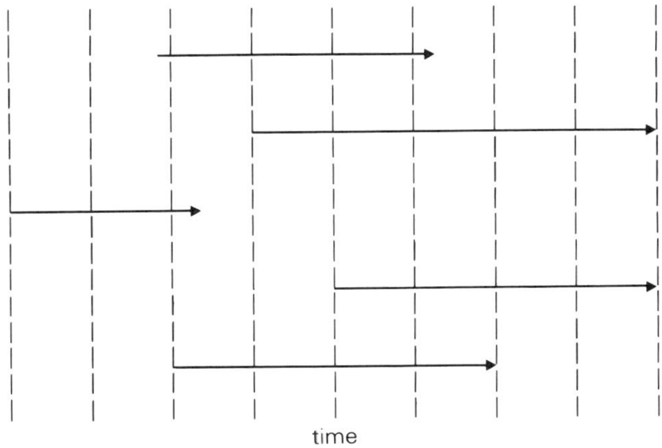

FIGURE 9.1 An example of the time-structure of the productive system

The number of different types of elementary processes thus distinguished and their definition in terms of analytical intervals or 'lengths of duration' allow us to represent a production system in terms of 'production lines', the number of which is equal to the number of different types of elementary processes distinguished (see figure 9.2). In the different periods $t = 1,2,3,$ ... the elementary processes on the different production lines might be

[3]For the importance of drawing 'analytical boundaries' to define 'processes' of any kind, see N. Georgescu-Roegen (1971, pp. 213–15).

[4]See A.K. Sen (1978, p. 177) on the 'choice of focus', when using a descriptive-analytical approach.

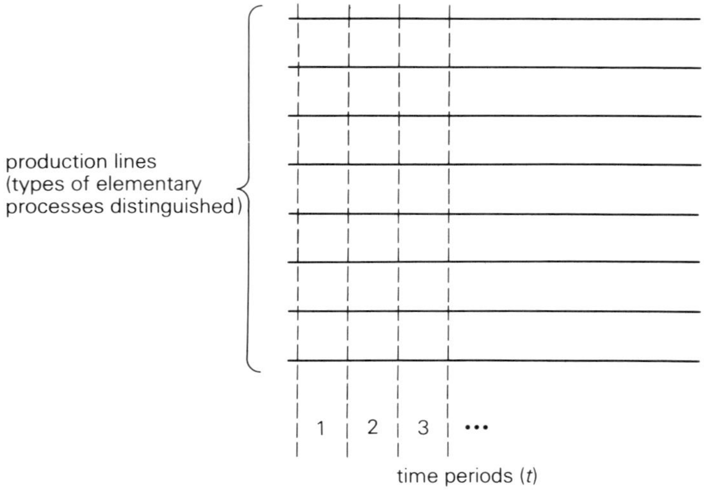

FIGURE 9.2 Representation of a production system in terms of production lines

activated – run at positive intensity levels $y_j(t)$ for elementary process j – or not (that is, run at zero intensity level).

The elementary processes themselves will be characterized by the absorption of flow inputs and by the utilization of the work-capacities of the different types of fund-input elements available to the productive system. These absorptions can be represented by vectors $\mathbf{a}_j(t) \equiv [a_{ij}(t)]$ $(i = 1,\ldots,I)$ for elementary processes $j = 1,\ldots,J$, where $a_{ij}(t)$ is defined as the absorption of flow input of type i by process j in period t, and the utilizations by vectors $\mathbf{b}_j(t) \equiv [b_{kj}(t)]$ $(k = 1,\ldots,K)$, where $b_{kj}(t)$ is defined as the portion of the work-capacity of fund element of type k (for example, two man-hours) utilized in period t by process j.[5]

In this chapter we will not deal with any questions related to multi-commodity production by individual elementary processes. Thus the output of each type of elementary process will only be of one kind, and the number of produced commodities distinguished in the productive system will be equal to the number of types of elementary processes and hence to the number of production lines considered.

III PROCESS INDIVISIBILITIES AND INPUT INDIVISIBILITIES

A prerequisite for our analysis of some of the principles established by the classical writers, such as Adam Smith, Charles Babbage and Karl Marx,

[5] The treatment of the use of durable instruments of production in this analytical framework is thus different from the treatment in joint-production models of the von Neumann type. See J. von Neumann (1937, 1945/6).

governing the productive process in industrial systems, is Georgescu-Roegen's discussion of the notion of 'process indivisibilities'. Georgescu-Roegen describes instances of such process indivisibilities in the following way:

> Examples of processes that are not indifferent to size are so abundant in natural sciences that one can only wonder how their existence may ever be ignored by other disciplines. At the microscale, organic chemistry offers innumerable examples where *new* qualities emerge after polymerization, i.e. after a certain scale is reached. ... At the macroscale, in the theory of structures it is almost impossible to find a linear relation between *homogeneous and perfectly divisible* materials – iron, cement, insulation, etc. – and variables expressing measures of some quality – resistance to strain, elasticity, radiation, and so on.
>
> ... All individual processes whether in biology or technology follow exactly the same pattern: beyond a certain scale some collapse, others explode, or melt, or freeze. In a word, they cease to work at all. Below another scale, they do not even exist. (Georgescu-Roegen, 1976, p. 288; author's italics)

For purposes of analysing the effects of process indivisibilities upon the operation of a productive system, we will characterize processes in terms of their 'scale-specificity', that is, in terms of the ranges of production levels over which a process can be run without changing any of its characteristics.

A process is then characterized by a set of technical coefficients, $\alpha_{ij}(t)$ ($i = 1,\ldots,I$) and $\beta_{kj}(t)$ ($k = 1,\ldots,K$), which indicate the minimum input and utilization requirements when a particular process j is operated at a (chosen) unit-intensity level. In the presence of process indivisibilities, the process will also have to be characterized by the range of intensity levels over which it can be operated without any changes in the sets of technical coefficients. The notion of 'process indivisibility' implies that there might be 'upper' and/or 'lower bounds' on the levels of operation over which a process can be run without changing any of its characteristics as defined above: for example, $\underline{y}_j \leq y_j \leq \bar{y}_j$ or $[\underline{y}_j, \bar{y}_j]$, where $\underline{y}_j$ and $\bar{y}_j$ are the lower and upper bounds of the ranges of intensity levels over which process j can be operated without any changes in its characteristics.

(A special case of 'process indivisibility' is one of '*extreme scale-specificity*', where a particular type of process can only be run at one particular level of operation, so that upper and lower bounds coincide, that is $\underline{y}_j = \bar{y}_j$. The level of intensity y_j then has to take on this unique value, if the process is to operate at all.)

The first thing we want to show in this section is that if a situation with process indivisibilities arises, *two types of lower bounds* will be relevant with respect to employing a particular method of production in a production system:

1 The first of these lower bounds will be the level of operation which will have to be reached before a particular process can be introduced at all,

and that lower bound is synonymous with $\underline{y}_j$ mentioned above.

2 The second type of lower bound on the scale of production will relate to the levels after which *exclusively* processes of a particular type could be operated.

Let us consider an example where a single process of type j could be operated over the following interval $[\underline{y}_j = 0.8; \bar{y}_j = 1.1]$. The first type of lower bound is then represented by $\underline{y}_j = 0.8$. The maximum intensity level at which a single process of type j can be run is 1.1; if production of the output of j is to reach a higher level than the output-equivalent of $y_j = 1.1$, then either other processes of type j will have to be brought into operation (such processes produce the same type of output with exactly the same characteristics in terms of per-unit (minimum) absorption and utilization requirements), or other types of processes with different technical characteristics, but producing the same type of output will have to be brought into operation.

If two and then three, etc. processes of type j are brought into operation, it will be possible to cover the following (combined) activity ranges.

$$\underset{\text{one process in operation}}{\underline{[0.8, 1.1]}} \qquad \underset{\text{two processes in operation}}{\underline{[1.6, 2.2]}}$$

$$\underset{\text{three or more processes in operation}}{\underline{[2.4, \ldots]}}$$

In this particular example, the second type of lower bound, $\underline{\underline{y}}_j$, above which any production levels of the output of processes of type j could be supplied by just employing processes of type j would be $\underline{\underline{y}}_j = 2.4$.[6]

The analysis of 'process indivisibilities' in terms of 'lower bounds' set upon the operation of economic activities before these can be used at all or before they can be used independently of other types of processes, can easily be extended to the case of '*input indivisibilities*'. The classic example of this group of phenomena are blast-furnaces of particular sizes, which require certain (minimum) utilization levels before they can be brought into use at all.[7]

[6] In the case of 'extreme scale-specificity' where $\underline{y}_j = \bar{y}_j$, an argument of a slightly different nature can be employed to define the equivalent of a 'second-type lower bound' $\underline{\underline{y}}_j$. In that case, there will continue to be intervals over which processes of a given type will have to be operated with other types of processes in order to achieve the full range of production targets. However, as the scale of production increases, the fractions of total output produced by these other processes become less and less significant. A certain level of output can be chosen, at which the latter processes produce any fraction ϵ, however small, of total output. This output level could be defined as the 'second-type lower bound'.

[7] In the case of blast-furnaces, the continuity of their utilization leads to another scale requirement. The problem of the utilization of fund elements over time will be dealt with under section V below.

In general, input indivisibilities can refer to units of flow and of fund inputs. Such indivisibilities can be represented in terms of the ranges of absorption and utilization levels over which certain types of inputs do not change their characteristics with respect to the particular processes in which they are being used:

$$\underline{a}_{ij} \leqslant \alpha_{ij} y_j \leqslant \bar{a}_{ij}$$

and

$$\underline{b}_{kj} \leqslant \beta_{kj} y_j \leqslant \bar{b}_{kj}$$

where $\underline{a}_{ij}$, $\bar{a}_{ij}$ and $\underline{b}_{kj}$, $\bar{b}_{kj}$ are respectively the minimum and maximum absorption or utilization requirements of *units* of flow inputs of type i $(i = 1,\ldots,I)$ and fund inputs of type k $(k = 1,\ldots,K)$.

Just as in the case of process indivisibilities,[8] it can easily be shown that there will be two types of *lower bounds*, which are relevant when the use or utilization of 'indivisible' types of input elements is considered:

1 a first type of lower bound in the levels of absorption/use of these input elements, below which they cannot be used at all;
2 a second type of lower bound on the scale of use of these types of inputs, which has to be reached in order to use certain types of input elements for particular types of 'jobs'[9], without having to have recourse to any other types of inputs to perform these jobs.

In between these two types of lower bounds, as the level of production is varied, there will be intervals over which units of the (indivisible) types of inputs will have to be used in combination with other types of inputs for particular types of jobs. This, in turn, will mean that changes in the combinations of methods of production will occur over these intervals (see note 6).

IV TASK SPECIALIZATION AND PROCESS DIFFERENTIATION

In this and the next section, we will focus on the role that process and input indivisibilities have played in some of the classical (in particular, Smithian)

[8] Input indivisibilities can be seen as subcases of the general case of process indivisibilities. This is the case because changes in the types of inputs or in the ways of their use (as represented by per-unit absorption and utilization requirements) will automatically involve changes in the methods of production which have been defined in terms of the full sets of technical coefficients.

[9] The concept of a 'job' will be defined in section IV below.

analyses of the degree of the 'division of labour' that we can find in a productive system. For this purpose, we will choose an alternative representation of a productive process from the one adopted so far. Apart from describing the input elements used up or utilized in a particular process within a particular time span, we can also describe a process from the point of view of the types of '*tasks*' to be accomplished in this process.[10]

If we accept Georgescu-Roegen's advice to subdivide a process into 'elementary processes', then each of these elementary processes can in turn be characterized by the set of 'tasks' to be performed in it. In elementary process j the following set of 'tasks' is to be performed:

$$[\eta_{1j}, \eta_{2j}, \ldots, \eta_{mj}]$$

A subdivision of a productive process into elementary processes will therefore also involve a decomposition of that process into 'sets of tasks' to be performed by the fund elements utilized at the various fabrication stages of the overall productive process.

We obtain thereby a picture of the utilization profiles of the work-capacities of the fund elements available to the productive system. The participation of fund elements in a production activity can be characterized by the *portions* of their available work-capacity, $b_{kj}(k = 1, \ldots, K)$, which are required to perform particular subsets of tasks, or – as we shall call them – '*jobs*' linked to an elementary process $j(j = 1, \ldots, n)$.

A '*job-specification programme*' will then be defined as a mapping from the set of 'jobs' (or subsets of tasks) to the set of available work-capacities of the different types of fund elements. These fund-input elements can, in turn, be identified by the sets of characteristics[11] that distinguish them (see figure 9.3). Different job-specification programmes $(J_\alpha, J_\beta, J_\gamma, \ldots)$ will be identified by different mappings of this sort.

We speak of a 'job-specification programme', in other words, when the work-capacities of the different fund elements available to a productive system have been assigned to the different tasks to be performed in that system.[12] There is no reason why – in principle – fund elements should not be involved in performing tasks (or 'jobs') in a variety of elementary

[10] By a description of 'tasks' we mean the detailed description of the various phases of the actual work processes to be performed (for example, a certain object has to be moved from A to B) of the type done in work and motion studies. See, for example, the classic text by F.B. Gilbreth (1911) on decomposing the work steps in a brick-laying operation.

[11] 'Characteristics' are assumed to be – we thereby follow K.J. Lancaster (1979, p. 18) – objectively quantifiable and objectively identifiable.

[12] For a job-specification programme to be complete, it has to encompass all the tasks to be performed in a productive system. However, not all tasks have to be indispensable for the operation of a productive system.

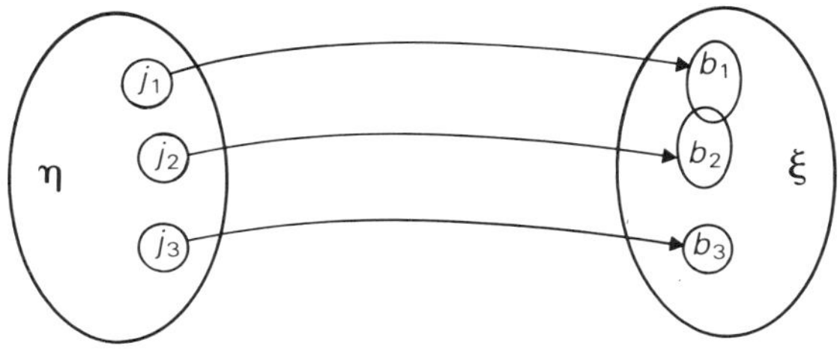

FIGURE 9.3 Job-specification programme; ξ represents the set of characteristics; b_1, b_2, b_3 are the work-capacities of fund elements type 1,2,3; η is the set of tasks; j_1, j_2, j_3 are jobs (subsets of tasks)

processes, as long as their work-capacities allow them to do so. However, since different types of fund elements are distinguished as embodying different sets of characteristics, they will differ in terms of their relative 'task-adequacy'[13] with respect to their performances in particular jobs.

It will here be assumed that an ordering of the different job-specification programmes in terms of some efficiency criterion can be established, which in itself does not yet take account of the infeasibility of certain job-specification programmes at particular scales of production due to process or input indivisibilities. This ordering could be written as[14]

$$J_\alpha \succsim J_\beta \succsim J_\gamma \succsim \dots$$

[13] Relative 'task-adequacy' is a complicated concept to employ, since it involves, usually, an ordering process in a multidimensional space. There are, in general, a variety of performance criteria according to which one might want to judge the performance in a particular job (for example, speed, precision, etc.). These different performance criteria will have to be weighted in order to arrive at an ordering of fund-input elements in terms of their relative performance in particular jobs. The comparison of units of funds engaged in the performance of a particular job involves, furthermore, comparisons of heterogeneous 'bundles of characteristics'; one way of doing that comparison is in terms of comparing the 'effectiveness' of the same amounts of money spent in hiring portions of the work-capacities of different fund elements and measuring the effectiveness in terms of the performance criteria mentioned above. If an ordering of different types of fund elements in terms of their 'relative task-adequacy' in performing particular types of 'jobs' can be achieved in this way, then the different job-specification programmes, which represent different assignments of fund elements to 'jobs' in a productive system, could also be ordered in the form $J_\alpha \succsim J_\beta \succsim J_\gamma \succsim \dots$.

[14] The establishment of such an ordering relationship of job-assignment programmes will of course make use of the information obtained about the relative 'task-adequacy' of the different types of fund elements in performing different types of 'jobs'. See n. 13 and, for a general discussion of 'ordering relationships', G. Debreu (1954).

We are now equipped to establish a link between the scale of industrial production and the *degree of task specialization* in a productive system (or, in Adam Smith's words, between 'the division of labour' and 'the extent of the market'). By a process of *task specialization*, we mean a process whereby input elements become less able to perform a wider range of tasks, but become 'more adequate' to perform more 'specialized' jobs, that is, jobs characterized by a narrower set of tasks. By *process differentiation*, we mean a process whereby the 'jobs' offered by the different elementary processes in a productive system are typically more specialized jobs.

We will now attempt to demonstrate a link between increases in the degree of task specialization and process differentiation, and the scale of activity in a production system. In particular, we will point out the role which process or input indivisibilities play in establishing such a relationship.

Due to the existence of these 'indivisibilities' the following dynamic will emerge. Particular job-specification programmes, which were not feasible at a lower scale, will become feasible as the scale of production activity increases. Furthermore, the job-specification programmes that will be introduced as the scale of production increases will tend to show a higher degree of task specialization and process differentiation than those selected at a lower scale.

Let us examine a case with 'extreme input indivisibility', where only fund elements with very particular work-capacities can be employed in a productive system (for example, workers can only be hired for a complete workday of 8 hours). The utilization coefficients in this case could then be interpreted as the portions of a fixed workday in which a particular type of fund element would be engaged in a particular 'job' associated with his work in an elementary process. For instance, $b_{kj} = 0.5$ means that fund element of type k is engaged for half of its workday (which in our example represents a complete characterization of its work-capacity) in a job performed in elementary process of type j (that is, a particular stage of the overall productive process).

Let us take the example of an elementary process j, which can be characterized by a set of three tasks $[t_1,t_2,t_3]$. We can group these tasks into assigned 'jobs' in a variety of ways. The following 'job specifications' are possible:

$$
\begin{aligned}
J_\alpha &= [(t_1), (t_2), (t_3)] \\
J_\beta &= [(t_1), (t_2, t_3)] \\
J_\gamma &= [(t_1,t_2),(t_3)] \\
J_\delta &= [(t_1, t_3),(t_2)] \\
J_\xi &= [(t_1, t_2, t_3)]
\end{aligned}
$$

where the parentheses ( ) define 'jobs'. J_ξ, represents a job specification that offers only one type of 'job' in which all three tasks are to be performed by the fund element(s) engaged in it; J_α on the other hand, offers 'specialized' jobs in which fund elements would only be engaged in performing one of the tasks each. J_β, J_γ and J_δ offer job specifications of subsets of tasks of different types.

Take first, as an example for the job specification J_ξ, the utilization requirements for an 'unspecialized' type of worker k, who has to perform the job consisting of all three types of tasks (t_1,t_2,t_3), and who would have to spend the following portions of his 'work-capacity' (workday) to perform each of the three tasks:

$$b_{k1} = 0.7 \quad b_{k2} = 0.5 \quad b_{k3} = 0.6$$

With the assumption that workers can only be hired for full workdays (the case of 'extreme' input indivisibility), it will be necessary to hire two workers of type k, if the entire process is to be operated within one workday, since total utilization requirements would then amount to

$$\sum_{i=1}^{3} b_{ki} = 1.8$$

and the unutilized portion of the work-capacity of the two workers would then amount to 0.2 of their combined workday.

Taking job specification J_α next, we can see that the three tasks have been differentiated into different jobs, j_i $(i = 1,2,3)$:

$$j_1^\alpha = (t_1) \quad j_2^\alpha = (t_2) \quad j_3^\alpha = (t_3)$$

If these jobs were to be performed by 'specialized' workers, of types p, q and r, the time requirements (as portions of their workdays) required to perform these jobs would amount to, say[15]

$$b_{p1} = 0.4 \quad b_{q2} = 0.2 \quad b_{r3} = 0.3$$

---

[15] The utilization requirements (per unit level of operation) are here assumed to be lower than in the case of a non-specialized labourer k performing the same tasks. The increased 'dexterity' (Adam Smith) of more specialized workers could either be achieved through learning on the job, as in Adam Smith's description, or could have been achieved already in the training (in the case of workers) or construction phase (in the case of machinery), before such fund elements are actually used in the productive processes. It makes no difference to our analysis which of the alternatives is chosen.

if the process were run, as before, at unit-intensity level. If the same input indivisibility holds for the three types of funds as before, that is, that specialized workers can only be hired for full workdays, and the level of activity cannot be increased above unity (for lack of demand), then one unit of each of the three types of funds ('specialized workers') would have to be installed, and the unutilized portions of their work-capacities would be respectively:

$$1 - b_{p1} = 0.6 \quad 1 - b_{q2} = 0.8 \quad 1 - b_{r3} = 0.7$$

Similarly, other types of structures of underutilization of fund elements (some fully specialized on one type of task, others semi-specialized on a subset of tasks) will emerge when job specifications J_β, J_γ and J_δ are adopted, and the same level of operation of the overall process is aimed at.

We can also easily see that as the level at which process j is being run is varied, different structures of underutilization of the different types of fund elements will emerge for the different job-specification programmes.[16]

We can also see from the example that, given input indivisibilities on the part of more specialized and thus more 'task-adequate' types of fund elements, increasing process differentiation (and thus increased demand for the instalment of more specialized fund-input elements) would lead to large portions of work-capacities remaining unutilized, if production has not reached a certain level.[17]

---

[16] E.A.G. Robinson pointed this out in his study *The Structure of Competitive Industry* (1958, pp. 25–6; 1st edn 1931):

> Mechanical units do not arrange themselves easily into groups such that they give their best results with an output, one of one hundred units a day, another of two hundred, a third of four hundred, so that they can be fitted neatly into the industrial jig-saw. There will be several different mechanical bottlenecks in the firm, each requiring to be used, for greater efficiency, up to its fullest capacity, but each, requiring a different daily output in order that it may be used. The escape from this difficulty may be a compromise, one machine being overdriven, so that it produces slightly more than it can with optimum efficiency, another producing slightly less.

[17] A. Young addressed himself to this problem (1928, p. 530):

> It would be wasteful to furnish a factory with an elaborate equipment of specially constructed jigs, gauges, lathes, drills, presses and conveyors to build a hundred automobiles; it would be better to rely mostly on tools and machines of standard types. ... Mr Ford's methods would be absurdly uneconomical if his output were very small, and would be unprofitable even if his output were what many other manufacturers of automobiles would call large.

On the other hand, any one of the job-specification programmes – representing different degrees and/or types of job differentiation and task specialization – will be associated with a 'second type of lower bound' (see section III above) upon the level of operation of the productive process as well as upon the levels of output associated with it which will lead to the full utilization of all fund elements engaged in it.

This case can be stated analytically in the following way.[18] Take the case with no process indivisibility first, and denote with τ_{kj} the fractions of a fund element's work-capacity utilized in an elementary process j, when the latter is operated at a unit-intensity level. Full utilization of *all* the fund elements engaged in process j will be possible if that process is run at an intensity level at least equal to the smallest common (integer) multiple of the (real) numbers:

$$\frac{1}{\tau_{kj}}, \frac{1}{\tau_{lj}}, \frac{1}{\tau_{mj}}, \ldots$$

for all fund elements, k, l, m, engaged in process j.

Let us now consider the case of process indivisibility (in particular, the case of extreme process indivisibility, where processes of the same kind can only be operated at one particular unit-intensity level). Here, the full utilization requirement of all the fund elements engaged in that process amounts to operate a *number* of such processes at the same points of time, and that number will have to be again at least equal to the smallest common (integer) multiple of the fractions above.

It can easily be seen that as the number of specialized fund elements engaged in a productive system – and hence the degree of task specialization and process differentiation – increases, the scale of production will have to increase, if full or near-full utilization of the different types of fund elements engaged in the productive system is to be guaranteed. It is for this reason that the degree of task specialization and process differentiation will tend to increase as the scale of production is also increased.

It is not by chance that the Taylorist system, which led to an enormous increase in the degree of job differentiation and task specialization,[19] only

---

A hundred years earlier, J. Rae had remarked: 'If any man had all the tools which many different occupations require, at least three-fourths of them would constantly be idle and useless' (1834, p. 165).

[18] See also N. Georgescu-Roegen (1976, p. 91). As we shall see in section V, Charles Babbage established this 'principle' in the early part of the nineteenth century (see Babbage, 1832).

[19] F.W. Taylor (1911, p. 39) claims that: 'Perhaps the most prominent single element in modern scientific management is the task idea', and goes on to say 'a task specifies not only what is to be done but how it is to be done and the exact time allowed for doing it.'

came into full force after the 'second type of lower bound' in the production levels of a number of industries had been reached in the twentieth century, given the potential for the 'division of labour' in industrial systems.

V ARRANGEMENTS OF PRODUCTION PROCESSES: BABBAGE AND MARX ON THE FACTORY SYSTEM

In this section, we shall deepen our understanding about the ways in which fund elements are being utilized in a productive system and about how classical writers, in particular Charles Babbage and Karl Marx, have linked this problem to the arrangement of processes in a productive system.[20] We will review in this context their writings on the specificities of the 'factory system' and the use of machinery in it, and apply the analytical framework developed by Georgescu-Roegen to derive some of their 'principles'.[21]

Karl Marx, in a comparison of 'arrangements' of processes in the old manufacturing system and the modern factory system, states:

> In manufacture, the isolation of each detail process is a condition imposed by the division of labour, but in the fully developed factory the continuity of those processes is, on the contrary, imperative. (Marx, 1970, p. 360; 1st edn 1867)

In a distinction drawn between *heterogeneous manufacture* and *serial manufacture*, Karl Marx characterizes the first as a process organization where each article 'results from the mere mechanised fitting together of partial products made independently' (1970, p. 323). In the second type of manufacturing organization, the article 'owes its completed shape to a series of connected processes and manipulations' (1970, p. 323).

In *heterogeneous manufacture*, there has to be no further coordination of the different partial processes than synchronizing their respective output levels. Partial processes j, k and l have to be run at the relative unit-intensity levels 2 : 3 : 1, if the final product is composed, respectively, of 2 components produced by partial process j, 3 components produced by process k, and 1 component produced by process l.[22]

---

[20] The notion of different 'arrangements' of production processes can again be found in Georgescu-Roegen (1969, pp. 516–18; 1970, pp. 3f; 1971, pp. 236–8; 1972, pp. 289f).

[21] The presentation in this section of the paper links the principles developed by Charles Babbage and Karl Marx on the modern factory system with the analytical work done in this area by Nicholas Georgescu-Roegen.

[22] Karl Marx (1970, p. 327) describes this 'synchronization' problem of partial processes in the following way:

> Different operations take, however, unequal periods, and yield therefore, in equal times unequal quantities of fractional products.

As soon as a temporal sequence of the different stages of a fabrication process is recognized, the question arises whether the different stages of the fabrication process have to be consecutively performed or whether an arrangement of these 'elementary processes' could be imagined which allows such processes to be *continuously operated* alongside each other.

It was an arrangement of the latter kind that Marx had in mind when describing the *serial-manufacture* system:[23]

> If we confine our attention to some particular lot of raw materials, of rags, for instance, in paper manufacture, or of wire in needle manufacture, we perceive that it passes in succession through a series of stages in the hands of the various detail workmen until completion. On the other hand, if we look at the workshop as a whole, we see the raw material in all the stages of its production at the same time. . . . The different detail processes, which were successive in time, have become simultaneous, go on side by side in space. Hence, production of a greater quantum of finished commodities in a given time.

The reason for wanting to find an arrangement of elementary processes that allows these processes to operate *continuously* side by side is partially because it enables production per unit of time to be greatly increased and also because it enables fund elements (labourers, machines) that are specialized on performing particular types of jobs to be *continuously utilized* in the same jobs.

> If, therefore, the same labourer has, day after day, to perform the same operation, there must be a different number of labourers for each operation; for instance, in type manufacture, there are four founders and two breakers to one rubber: the founder casts 2000 type an hour, the breaker breaks up 4000, and the rubber polishes 8000. . . . The division of labour, as carried out in Manufacture, not only simplifies and multiplies the qualitatively different parts of the social collective labourer, but also creates a fixed mathematical relation or ratio which regulates the quantitative extent of those parts – i.e., the relative number of labourers, or the relative size of the group of labourers, for each detail operation. It develops, along with the qualitative sub-division of the special labour-process, a quantitative rule and proportionality for that process.

[23]The features of such a production arrangement had been recognized earlier by Stewart, who saw the side-by-side operation of elementary processes as an extension of the process of the division of labour:

> It [the division of labour] produces also an economy of time, by separating the work into its different branches, all of which may be carried on into execution at the same moment. . . . By carrying on all the different processes at once, which an individual must have executed separately, it becomes possible to produce a multitude of pins for instance completely finished in the same time as a single pin might have been either cut or pointed. (Stewart, 1855/6, p. 319)

The importance of continuous utilization of (specialized) fund elements has been particularly emphasized by Charles Babbage. After having described the optimal subdivision of processes for pin-making (and having therefore assumed as given a certain degree of task specialization and process differentiation in the manufacturing process),[24] Babbage states:

> it is at once apparent, that, to conduct an establishment for pin-making most profitably, the number of persons employed must be a multiple of ten. For if a person with small means has only sufficient capital to enable him to employ half that number of persons, *they cannot each of them constantly adhere to the execution* of the same process; and if a manufacturer employs any number not a multiple of ten, a similar result must ensure with respect to some portion of them. (Babbage, 1832, p. 172; my italics)

Different arrangements of partial processes therefore have to be analysed in terms of how they affect the utilization of fund elements in a productive system.

In the passage quoted above, Babbage also develops an interesting general principle, which can be called Babbage's *Factory Principle* (it appears at the beginning of chapter XXI 'On the causes and consequences of large factories'), in order to distinguish it from what has become known as the Babbage Principle proper.[25]

In the Factory Principle, Babbage describes the way in which increases in the scale of production have to take place such that once a pattern of utilization of funds has been established in a productive system, it can be maintained. This principle is restated by Babbage in the following general form:

---

[24]Babbage furthermore assumes – for reasons of simplification – that each of the partial processes into which it is advantageous to divide manufacturing process is of equal length. As we shall see, we have made a similar assumption – without, however, any loss of generality for a general description of the operation of a productive system – in our definition of elementary processes, which are all of equal length defined by the length of a 'subperiod'.

[25]The Babbage Principle proper addresses itself to what Babbage regarded as the 'most important and influential cause' for the advantages arising from increases in the division of labour:

> the master manufacturer, by dividing the work to be executed into different processes, each requiring different degrees of skill or of force can purchase exactly that precise quantity of both which is necessary for each process, whereas, if the whole work were executed by one workman, that person must possess sufficient skill to perform the most difficult and sufficient strength to execute the most laborious, of the operations into which the art is divided. (Babbage, 1832, pp. 137–8)

> When [from the peculiar nature of the produce of each manufactory] the number of processes into which it is most advantageous to divide it is ascertained, as well as the number of individuals to be employed, then all other manufactories which do not employ a direct multiple of this number, will produce the article at a greater cost. (Babbage, 1832, pp. 172–3)[26]

That Babbage's Factory Principle is linked to some indivisibility property (-ies) of the fund elements involved in such utilization arrangements comes out clearly when Babbage describes the principle's relevance in finding an optimal utilization pattern of (indivisible) maintenance and repair units at different scales/levels of industrial production:

> since the good performance and the duration of machines depend to a very great extent upon correcting, as soon as it appears, every shake or imperfection in their parts, it will soon become apparent that a workman resident on the spot will reduce the expenditure arising from wear and tear of the machinery. But in the case of a single lace-frame, or a single loom, this would be too expensive a plan. Here then arises another circumstance which tends to enlarge the extent of a factory. It ought to consist of such a number of machines as shall occupy the whole time of one workman in keeping them in order, and in making any casual repairs: if it is extended beyond this, the same principle of economy would point out the necessity of doubling or tripling the number of machines, in order to employ the whole time of two or three skilful workmen. (Babbage, 1832, p. 175)

Or, if we think about arrangements of a number of machines of the same type (loom or lace frames) operated by one or more (indivisible) engineers and one indivisible steam engine, the following requirements should be followed:

> it will soon occur to the manufacturer, that if the loom or lace-frame were driven by a steam-engine, the same man might attend to two or more looms at once; and since we already suppose that he has employed one or more operative engineers, he may so *arrange the number of his looms that the charge of keeping them and the steam-engine in order, shall just fully occupy their time*. (Babbage, 1832, pp. 175–6; my italics)

From here it seems a small step to come to a full description of what Marx calls a 'complex system of machinery':

---

[26]Marx reiterates this principle when he writes: 'When once the most fitting proportion has been experimentally established for the numbers of the detail labourers in the various groups when producing on a given scale, that scale can be extended only by employing a multiple of each particular group' (Marx, 1970, p. 327).

> the subject of labour goes through a connected series of detail processes that are carried out by a chain of machines of various kinds, the one supplementing the other. Here we have again the co-operation by division of labour that characterises Manufacture; only now, it is a combination of detail machines. . . . Each detail machine supplies raw material to the machine next in order; and since they are all working at the same time, the product is always going through the various stages of its fabrication, and is also constantly in a state of transition, from one phase to another.
>
> Just as in Manufacture, the direct co-operation of the detail labourers establishes a numerical proportion between the special groups, so in an organised system of machinery, where one detail machine is constantly kept employed by another, a fixed relation is established between their number, their size, and their speed. The collective machine, now an organised system of various kinds of single machines, and of groups of single machines, becomes more and more perfect, the more the process as a whole becomes a continuous one, i.e. the less the raw material is interrupted in its passage from its first phase to its last; in other words, the more its passage from one phase to another is effected, not by the hand of man, but by the machinery itself. In Manufacture the isolation of each detail process is a condition imposed by the nature of division of labour, but in the fully developed factory the continuity of those processes is, on the contrary, imperative. (Marx, 1970, pp. 358, 359–60)

Summing up the interesting analytical points which Marx and Babbage make in their description of the various aspects of a factory system, we are faced with a number of propositions which still need some analytical support.

1 Marx's serial manufacture system (or complex system of machinery) is an arrangement of partial processes that allows all these partial processes to proceed continuously side by side.
2 In such an arrangement, the raw material or the product in its various stages of completion[27] moves uninterruptedly from one stage of fabrication to the next, while the different fund elements engaged in the productive system remain continuously utilized in the same jobs.

---

[27]Georgescu-Roegen (1971, pp. 239–40) has termed 'process-*fund*' what is often called 'work-in-progress'; this, however, is – for our purposes – a misnomer, since a 'fund', as long as it is not completely worn out or scrapped, is identified by 'identity of substance' at different points of time. (See section II.) This is true for a 'process fund' only as long as no changes are introduced in the way in which a productive system operates through time (that is, as long as no changes in the techniques employed, no changes in the composition of the final product, no changes in the overall scale of industrial production, etc. take place). All these are, however, changes which we want to deal with. Georgescu-Roegen's terminology is only appropriate for steady-state analyses, and we therefore have to abandon it.

3 Babbage's Principle proper, which advocates an optimal pattern of division of labour (or, more generally, an optimal pattern of task specialization of all the different types of fund elements), can operate once a particular scale of production has been reached.

4 Given an adequate degree of task specialization, Babbage's Factory Principle prescribes the way in which an industrial (factory) system has to expand, such that the same degree of task specialization and the same pattern of utilization of fund elements can be maintained.

VI ANALYSIS OF THE FACTORY SYSTEM

As a first step, we shall show how the time structure of the production model introduced in section II deals with the features of a 'factory system' analysed by Babbage and Marx. As Marx pointed out, the distinctive characteristics of a factory system are that *the different stages* in the fabrication of each unit (or batch of units) of final output are *consecutively performed*, and that these stages are continuously performed alongside each other.

In the description of an industry's production process as a system of elementary processes (cf. section II), such a '*serial*' arrangement of manufacturing processes has been allowed for at the very outset. Each stage of fabrication that is being distinguished is identified as an 'elementary process', and the same type(s) of elementary processes can be carried out one subperiod after another. At the same time, the fabrication processes as a whole *will have to be arranged in a 'serial' manner* for the continuous operation of the same stages to take place. We can see in figure 9.4 that each of the fabrication processes $P_1, P_2, P_3, \ldots$, which are 'started' at regular intervals of length J, passes through fabrication stages I, II and III. At the same time, each type of stage is activated in every subperiod, since as

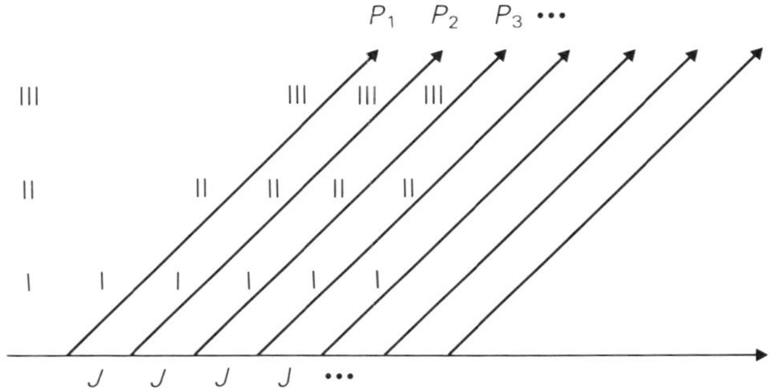

FIGURE 9.4 Serial arrangement of the manufacturing process

soon as fabrication process P_1 has gone through its stage I, another process, P_2, has been started and passes in turn through stage I, etc. (The differentiated stages of fabrication in the model define production lines I, II and III, which allow the same 'stages' or types of elementary processes to be activated in every subperiod; in that sense, they operate 'continuously' and 'side by side'.)

From figure 9.4, it is also possible to observe the conditions that will have to be fulfilled in order to achieve 'continuous utilization' of the work-capacities of the different types of funds engaged in the different stages of these fabrication processes:

1 Processes $P_1, P_2, P_3, \ldots$ will have to be 'started' at the 'right' intervals.
2 $P_1, P_2, P_3, \ldots$ will have to be run at the same activity levels, neglecting any wear and tear or assuming continuous replacement of worn-out capacities.

Neglecting any sort of technical changes, (1) and (2) imply that the elementary processes situated on the different production lines will be run at the same intensity levels in each successive subperiod. As a result, utilization requirements and, indeed, the utilization pattern of the different fund inputs will repeat itself over successive subperiods.

Take any possible utilization pattern of a particular type of fund over the various stages of a fabrication process P (see figure 9.5). Arrange the processes of the same type in a 'serial' pattern, watching the utilization pattern of the same type of fund in the different production lines (see figure 9.6), or turn the diagram a little (as in figure 9.7). We can immediately see that the 'utilization pattern' for the particular type of fund in successive subperiods will be the same. The same portions of this fund's work-capacity (or fund elements of the same capacities) will be utilized in the same types of elementary processes and hence will be engaged in the same types of 'jobs'. No wasteful shifts[28] of fund elements between different

[28]Adam Smith and, later on, Charles Babbage pointed out that the avoidance of this type of 'inefficiency' constitutes one of the three (for Babbage, four) advantages to be gained from the 'division of labour'. Smith calls it 'the advantage which is gained by saving the time commonly lost in passing from one sort of work to another' (Smith, 1976, p. 18; 1st edn 1776), and Babbage emphasizes additionally the savings of instalment costs of tools of various kinds which would have to be shifted between different types of uses (cf. Babbage, 1832, pp. 136–7). Another, more recent, reference to this type of waste is made by a well-known member of the 'scientific management' movement in the early part of this century:

> The setting of machine-shop tasks is today quite different from what it was ten years ago. At that time machine operations took a relatively long time, and the time between operations was of much less importance. Today, when machine operations are, as a rule, three times as fast, the time of changing jobs has become three times as important, and to plan our work so that there will be no time lost in going from one job to another has become a far greater

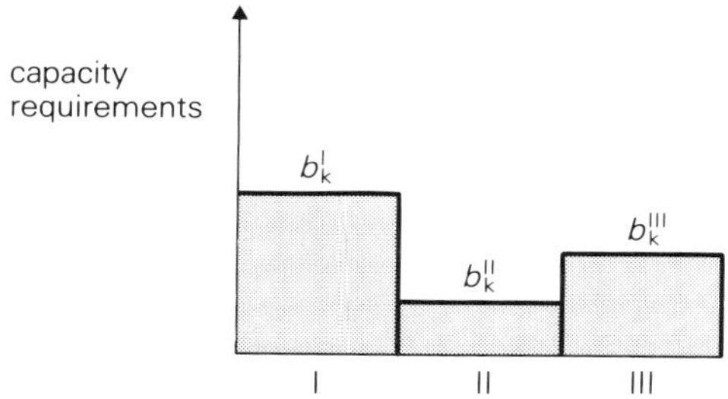

FIGURE 9.5 Utilization pattern of a particular type of fund over various stages of fabrication process

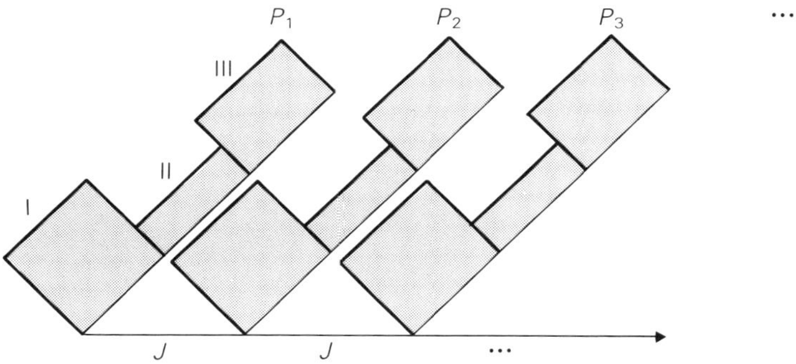

FIGURE 9.6 Serial pattern for different production lines

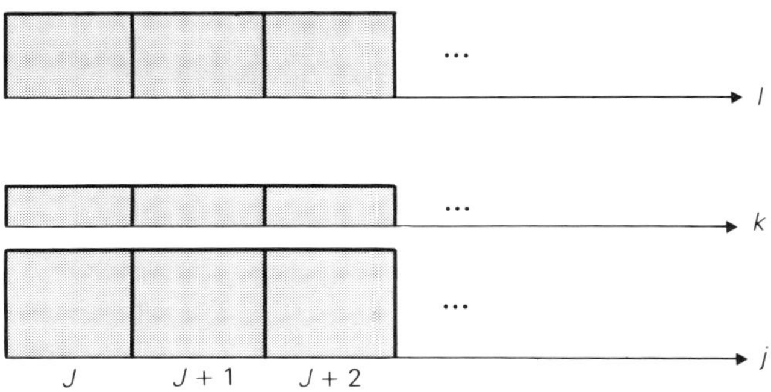

FIGURE 9.7 Capacities installed and utilized in the different production lines

factor. For each machine-tool operative today, there has to be planned nearly three times as much work as formerly, and necessarily the supervising force must be much greater. It is this increase in machine-tool capacity which has induced me to lay emphasis on the general scheduling of work, so that no more time than necessary shall be taken in changing jobs. (Gantt, 1912, p. 72) types of jobs from one time interval to the next will be necessary under these circumstances (that is, if conditions (1) and (2) are satisfied).

Let us now introduce indivisibilities of fund inputs into the picture. Two types of fund-input indivisibilities are of relevance here:

1 an indivisibility at the point of instalment of fund inputs, when only input elements of a particular unit size can be installed in a particular production line;
2 a 'putty-clay'[29] type of indivisibility – units of fund inputs of any size can be installed, but, once a unit of a particular size has been installed, its 'work-capacity' cannot be regulated over the successive periods (we shall assume in this case that the available work-capacity of this fund element will remain constant over the succession of subperiods in question).

Taking the second (weaker) type of indivisibility of fund-input elements first, we can clearly see the advantage of a 'serial arrangement' of processes. This can be seen by comparing the serial arrangement with the *parallel arrangement* of processes (see figure 9.8).[30] In the 'parallel arrangement', where processes P_1,P_2,P_3 are all started at the same points of time and another batch of these processes, P_4,P_5,P_6, are started as soon as the first batch has been completed, there will be serious underutilization of the fund elements installed in the productive system, since the available work-capacity cannot be adjusted to the changing utilization requirements of the different fabrication stages of the processes now moving in parallel.

In the 'serial arrangement', on the other hand, fund elements of the appropriate sizes will be installed in the different production lines, and can consequently be involved in the same fabrication stages (with identical utilization requirements) of a sequence of processes 'staggered' in time. (However, conditions (1) and (2) will have to be upheld, if full utilization is to occur, that is, the processes will have to be 'staggered' in the right intervals and the processes will have to be run on the same intensity levels.)

Now, if the first (stronger) type of fund-input indivisibility is taken into account, that is, fund-input elements of certain types have to be of certain minimum sizes (or the utilization requirements have to reach certain minimum levels) before they can be installed (utilized) at all, then although a

---

[29]The term is used here not in the traditional way, which interprets it in terms of fixity or variability of factor proportions before or after the introduction of a technique/method of production, but it refers to the adjustability of the available work-capacity of a fund element.

[30] The notion of an 'arrangement in parallel' stems from Georgescu-Roegen (1971, p. 239). The 'serial arrangement' is what Marx had in mind when he described the 'serial manufacture' system and which Georgescu-Roegen calls 'arrangement in line'.

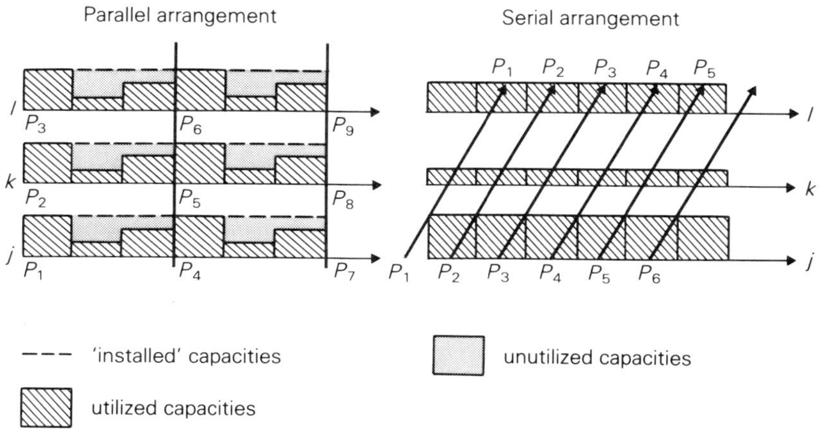

FIGURE 9.8 Comparison of serial and parallel arrangements

more even utilization (over time) of the fund elements installed in a system can be achieved through 'serial arrangement', 'full utilization' of these (indivisible) fund elements cannot be guaranteed. In fact we are led to consider the third of our summary points in the discussion of Marx's and Babbage's analyses of the 'factory system'. There we concluded from Babbage's writings that the use of the most task-adequate types of fund elements in a productive system (which was a generalized formulation of the Babbage Principle proper) was linked to the scale of production reached. If that was not the case, Babbage remarked, these funds could not 'constantly adhere to the same process'.[31] And the reason for that was – as

[31] The link between the scale of production and the possibility of using task-adequate types of funds comes out clearly in another passage of Babbage's:

> *the division of labour* . . . causes large capitals to be embarked in extensive factories. Let us now examine the influence of such accumulation of capital directed to one object. In the first place, it enables the most important principle on which the *division of labour* rests to be carried almost to its extreme limits: not merely the precise amount of skill is purchased which is necessary for the execution of each process, but throughout every stage from that in which the raw material is procured, to that by which the finished produce is conveyed into the hands of the consumer, the same economy of skill prevails.
>
> The quantity of work produced by a given number of people is greatly augmented by such an extended arrangement; and the result is necessarily a great reduction in the cost of the article which is brought to market. (Babbage, 1832, p. 179)

we concluded from our reading of Babbage – that the work-capacities of (indivisible) fund inputs would remain underutilized.

In section IV above, it was shown that without process indivisibility there would be a particular minimum production level such that *in any one period* all the different 'indivisible' types of fund elements installed in the system would be fully employed. With process indivisibility, there will have to be a minimum number of processes to be operated at the same time (and in the terminology of the present section, *run in parallel*) to ensure full utilization of all the different types of (indivisible) fund elements participating in these processes.[32] Once this minimum production level (or the minimum number of processes) has been fixed, it is a matter of 'serial arrangement' to ensure that this full utilization pattern of all the installed units of (indivisible) types of fund-input elements in a productive system is also ensured over time.

---

[32]The way to calculate this minimum process level (or the *minimum number* of (indivisible) unit processes to be operated in parallel) is in the following way. Let us first consider the case without process indivisibility. The proportions of all the (indivisible) fund's work-capacities engaged in a process *j*, when the latter is run at unit level, are:

$$b_{kj}, b_{lj}, b_{mj}, \ldots$$

Now process *j* will have to be run at an activity level at least equal to the minimum integer multiple of the numbers

$$\frac{1}{b_{kj}}, \frac{1}{b_{lj}}, \frac{1}{b_{mj}}, \ldots$$

In this case the work-capacities of all the (indivisible) units of the different types of funds engaged in this process will be fully utilized. As we can see below in the main text it is Babbage's Factory Principle that tells us that any further extensions of the scale of production will then have to proceed in further (integer) multiples of this minimum scale in order to assure full utilization of fund elements thereafter.

For the case of (extreme) process indivisibility (when the scale of production can only be extended by operating further units of the same indivisible process), a number of (indivisible) unit processes will have to be operated *in parallel* equal to at least the minimum integer multiple of the fractions

$$\frac{1}{b_{kj}}, \frac{1}{b_{lj}}, \frac{1}{b_{mj}}, \ldots$$

As before, any other (integer) multiple of this multiple will assure full utilization of all the fund elements installed in the productive system, when the system is expanded in discrete steps thus defined. See also Georgescu-Roegen (1970, p. 91) for a derivation of these full utilization conditions in the presence of input and process indivisibilities.

At appropriate time intervals, processes of the same kind have to be started and run at the same (fixed) process level (these were our conditions (1) and (2) for 'serial arrangement'), or in appropriate intervals the same *bunch* of (indivisible) processes (the number of which is fixed) has to be started. The second variant could be represented graphically, as in figure 9.9.

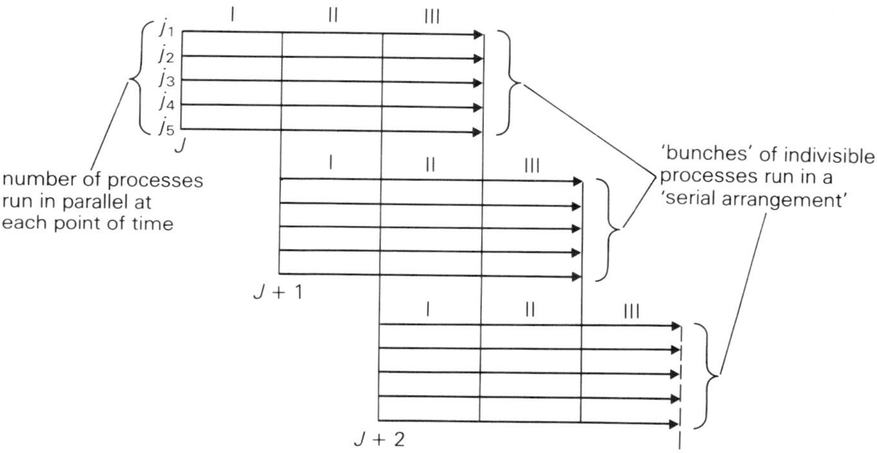

FIGURE 9.9 Bunches of indivisible processes in a serial arrangement

Dealing with the third of our summary points of Babbage's and Marx's discussion of the factory system has led us to determine an important 'data element' of one of the conditions (2), which has to be satisfied in 'serial arrangements'; namely, the determination of the activity level at which the processes (or batches of processes) that are to be 'serially arranged' are to be operated. This determination has occurred on the basis of the requirement for the full utilization of the fund elements engaged in a productive system, after a certain collection of funds of particular types has been chosen to perform jobs in the system; or – as Babbage would call it – after the 'economy of skill' has fully had its way; in other words, after the determination of a certain degree of task specialization.

We come now to investigate the determinants of the other missing 'data element' in our conditions for serial arrangements, namely, the *intervals* with which processes in a serial arrangement will have to be staggered (see condition (1) above). We shall see that if we can determine the length of such an interval (which amounts to the determination of the length of a subperiod in our analytical framework), we will also at the same time be determining the degree of differentiation of processes into stages in the productive system.

Take the case of two types of funds, k and m, which experience the utilization requirements shown in figure 9.10 in the course of a process P of duration T. We can see that the utilization profile of fund of type m is more differentiated than that of fund of type k. If we now continue to differentiate the whole process P into three stages I, II and III (as we did in figure 9.9) and start processes P_1, P_2, P_3, etc., in intervals equal to J (as we did before), not all the fund elements installed in the different production lines will continue to be fully utilized. A reason for this is that where once fund elements of particular sizes have been installed in a particular production line, their work-capacities will remain fixed over successive subperiods.

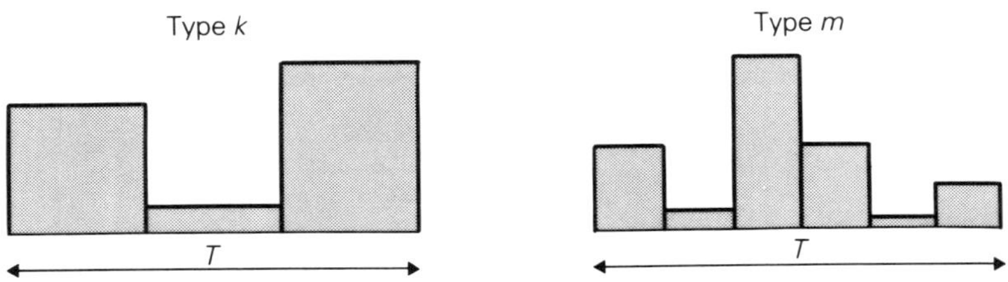

FIGURE 9.10 Utilization patterns of two funds: type k and type m

In order to obtain full employment (in the present case also of fund elements of type m), we would have to make use of the finer detail we have of the utilization profile of fund of type m, and distinguish consequently more stages of fabrication (and hence more production lines in the productive system). As we shall see, the intervals between the 'starts' of the different processes will also have to become shorter (and so will our definition of a 'subperiod'). A serial arrangement of processes $P_1,P_2,P_3,\ldots$ with a new interval $J' = J/2$ should make this possible. Processes will now be 'started' at intervals equal to $J/2$ or J' and the number of stages of fabrication distinguished in the system will be six instead of three as before (hence the number of production lines will also be six).

In our particular example, a 'serial arrangement' made on that basis will lead to full utilization patterns of all the fund elements involved in the productive system (see figure 9.11).[33] Hence, due to the full employment

[33]Of course, where no input elements smaller than a certain minimum size can even be installed in the different production lines, the further conditions related to the scale of industrial production (as discussed above in the main text) will have to

requirement, the number of stages distinguished (equal to the number of production lines specified) will have doubled, because of the finer utilization profile of funds of type m. In general, full utilization will require a definition of the interval by which the different processes will have to be staggered in time, equal to the *largest common denominator* of the fractions

$$\frac{T}{\tau_{ki}}, \frac{T}{\tau_{li}}, \frac{T}{\tau_{mi}}, \ldots$$

where T is the length of process P, and $\tau_{ki}, \tau_{li}, \tau_{mi}$, etc. are the time periods over which distinguishable utilization requirements for funds of types $k, l, m, \ldots$ in the different stages of process P exist. In other words, $\tau_{ki}, \tau_{li}, \tau_{mi}, \ldots$ are the time periods spent by fund elements of type $k, l, m, \ldots$ in different types of jobs i.

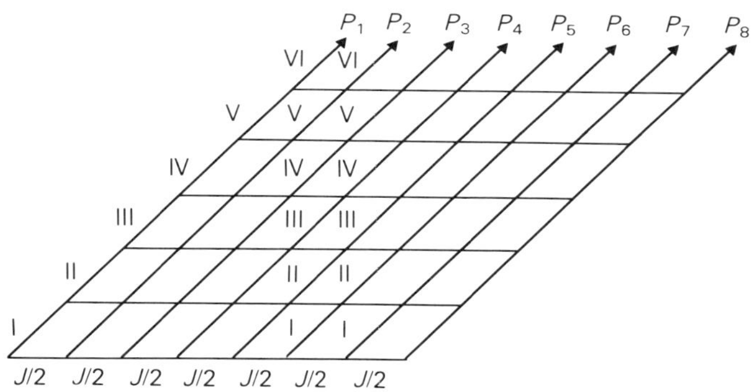

FIGURE 9.11 Full utilization pattern of all fund elements involved in the productive system

---

be satisfied for full utilization. This amounts to specifying the activity levels by which the different processes will have to be run (or the number of unit processes to be 'started' in each interval) in such a way that full utilization would be achieved. Since finer utilization profiles lead to a greater number of starts (over time) in a serial arrangement, but the minimum-utilization requirements have to be satisfied for any units of fund elements installed in the different production lines, the two types of fund-input-indivisibility phenomena can add up to formidable scale requirements, if full utilization of all the fund elements in a productive system were to be achieved.

We may conclude that the higher the degree of job differentiation, then the more detailed the utilization profile of the different types of funds in a productive system will become. In consequence, if the fund elements of different types are to be fully utilized, the number of stages of an industry's productive process will have to be increased and so will the number of production lines. The intervals at which new processes of the same types are 'started' will have to become shorter and, if minimum utilization requirements are furthermore required at each point of time, due to input indivisibilities, the scale of production will have to increase. Even if the number of processes started at each point of time remains the same, the overall scale of industrial production will have to increase, since the intervals at which these 'batches' of processes are being started have become smaller. Again, we have reached the conclusion that a high degree of job differentiation will not pay, if the scale of production is relatively low. (See also the discussion in section IV).

Finally, we will examine the validity of Babbage's Factory Principle, the fourth in our summary account of the classical authors' propositions on the factory system (see above). In this principle, Babbage puts forward the view that, given a particular degree of process differentiation (that is, given the number of stages, elementary processes and production lines into which it was most appropriate to divide an industry's manufacturing process), and given the capacities of the different types of funds installed in these different production lines (and thus 'specialized' on the performance of the particular 'jobs' associated with the elementary processes conducted in these production lines), any expansion in the scale of production of such a system would have to occur in *discrete jumps* of (integer) multiples of the scale achieved. If this rule were not followed, production would be conducted 'less efficiently'.

In a productive system, in which a particular job-specification programme has been chosen (see section IV above); in which, furthermore, the right choice of an interval and of the number of processes to be operated at each 'starting point' has been made for a 'serial arrangement' of processes that assures the continuous full utilization of all the capacities installed in the productive system; then further continuous increases in the scale of production will be possible without the emergence of underutilized capacities, only if either of the following two conditions is satisfied.

1 Indivisibilities of fund elements are of a weak kind, that is, there are only minimum utilization/instalment requirements, but no upper bounds on the unit sizes (or on the utilization ranges).
2 There are upper limits to the range of unit sizes of fund elements available (offering the same degree of 'task-adequacy'), but these ranges are sufficiently large to allow the continuous use of the same types of fund elements in the different production lines.

As soon as we introduce the 'extreme form' of input indivisibility (that is, where fund elements of only particular unit sizes are available for instalment), continuous increases (and, of course, declines) in the scale of production cannot occur without underutilization of capacities appearing as new (indivisible) units of fund elements are being installed.[34] In this case, Babbage's Factory Principle comes into full force: efficiency reversals over certain ranges of increases in production levels can only be avoided if the scale increases take place in 'discrete groups', that is, according to integer multiples of the scale at which full utilization of the work-capacities was achieved.

REFERENCES

Babbage, C. (1832) *On the Economy of Machinery and Manufactures*, Charles Knight, London.

Chamberlin, E.H. (1948) 'Proportionality, Divisibility and Economies of Scale', *Quarterly Journal of Economics*, LXII, pp. 229–62.

— (1949) 'Reply', *Quarterly Journal of Economics*, LXIII, pp. 137–43.

Debreu, G. (1954) 'Representation of a Preference Ordering by a Numerical Function', in *Decision Processes*, ed. R.M. Thrall, C.H. Coombes and R.L. Davies, John Wiley, New York, pp. 159–65.

Gantt, H.L. (1912) 'The Task and the Day's Work', in *Addresses and Discussions at the Conference on Scientific Management held October 12–13–14, 1911*, The Amos Tuck School of Administration and Finance, Dartmouth College, Hanover, New Haven.

Georgescu-Roegen, N. (1964) 'Measure, Quality, and Optimum Scale', in *Essays on Econometrics and Planning Presented to Professor P.C. Mahalanobis*, ed. C.R. Rao, Pergamon Press, Oxford; Statistical Publ. Society, Calcutta, pp. 231–56.

— (1969) *Process in Farming versus Process in Manufacturing: a Problem of Balanced Development*, in *Economic Problems of Agriculture in Industrial Societies* ed. G.U. Papi and C. Nunn, St Martin's Press, New York, pp. 497–528.

— (1970) 'The Economics of Production', *American Economic Review*, vol. LX, May, pp. 1–9.

— (1971) *The Entropy Law and the Economic Process*, Harvard University Press, Cambridge, Mass.

— (1972) 'Process Analysis and the Neoclassical Theory of Production', *American*

[34]As an alternative, it will be possible to change the 'job-specification programme' over these ranges of production levels, that is change the allocation of particular types of fund-input elements to particular types of jobs. However, in this case there will be 'efficiency losses', since the 'most task-adequate' types of fund elements cannot be allocated to the 'jobs' most suitable for them. The degree of 'task specialization' and the pattern of job differentiation will be different from the one that is 'most advantageous (considering) the nature of the produce of (the particular) manufactory (in question)'.

Journal of Agricultural Economics, vol. LIV, May, pp. 279–94.
— (1976) *Energy and Economic Myths, Institutional and Analytical Economic Essays*, Pergamon Press, Oxford.
— (1978) 'Dynamic Models and Economic Growth', in *Equilibrium and Disequilibrium in Economic Theory*, ed. G. Schwödiauer, Reidel, Dordrecht, pp. 413–49.
Gilbreth, F.B. (1911) *Motion Study, A Method for Increasing the Efficiency of the Workman*, Constable, London.
Hahn, F.H. (with F.N. MacLeod) (1949) 'Proportionality, Divisibility and Economies of Scale: Two Comments', *Quarterly Journal of Economics*, LXIII, pp. 131–7.
Kaldor, N. (1934) 'The Equilibrium of the Firm', *Economic Journal*, XLIV, March, pp. 60–76.
Lancaster, K.J. (1966a) 'A New Approach to Consumer Theory', *Journal of Political Economy*, LXXIV, April, pp. 132–57.
— (1966b) 'Change and Innovation in the Technology of Consumption', *American Economic Review*, LVI, Papers and Proceedings, May, pp. 14–23.
— (1979) *Variety, Equity and Efficiency*, Columbia University Press, New York, and Basil Blackwell, Oxford.
Lerner, A.P. (1944) *The Economics of Control*, Macmillan, New York.
Marx, K. (1970) *Capital, A Critical Analysis of Capitalist Production*, vol. 1 (1st edn 1867), Lawrence and Wishart, London.
Mill, J. St (1973) *Principles of Political Economy* (1st edn 1848), ed. Sir William Ashley, A.M. Kelley, Clifton.
Neumann, J. von (1937) 'Über ein ökonomisches Gleichungssystem und eine Verallgemeinerung des Brouwer'schen Fixpunktsatzes', *Ergebnisse eines mathematischen Kolloquiums*, viii (1937), pp. 73–83.
— (1945/6) 'A Model of General Economic Equilibrium', *Review of Economic Studies*, XIII, pp. 1–9.
Rae, John (1834) *New Principles on the Subject of Political Economy*, Hilliard, Gray, Boston.
Robinson, E.A.G. (1958) *The Structure of Competitive Industry*, (1st edn 1931), Cambridge University Press, Cambridge.
Sen, A.K. (1978) 'On the Labour Theory of Value: some methodological issues', *Cambridge Journal of Economics*, 2, June, pp. 175–90.
Slichter, S.H. (1931) 'Efficiency', in *Encyclopedia of the Social Sciences*, ed. E.R.A. Seligman, vol. V, Macmillan, London, pp. 437–9.
Smith, A. (1976) *An Inquiry into the Nature and Causes of the Wealth of Nations* (1st edn 1776), ed. R.H. Campbell, A.S. Skinner and W.B. Todd, Clarendon Press, Oxford.
Stewart, D. (1855/6) *Lectures on Political Economy*, vol. VIII–IX of *Works*, ed. Sir W. Hamilton, T. Constable, Edinburgh.
Taylor, F.W. (1911) *The Principles of Scientific Management*, Harper, New York and London.
Ure, A. (1835, 1861) *The Philosophy of Manufactures: or, An Exposition of the Scientific, Moral, and Commercial Economy of the Factory System of Great Britain* (3rd edn 1861), H.G. Bohn, London.
Young, A. (1928) 'Increasing Returns and Economic Progress', *Economic Journal*, vol. XXXVIII, December, pp. 527–42.

10

Technological Scarcity: an Essay on Production and Structural Change

ALBERTO QUADRIO-CURZIO

I PRODUCTION, PRODUCED AND NON-PRODUCED MEANS OF PRODUCTION: A HISTORICAL AND THEORETICAL INTRODUCTION

The present study takes its point of departure from two ascertainable facts: one from the field of economic history, the other from economic theory. To date, economic history has always shown that production processes are notably influenced by natural resources and raw materials. Economic theory shows that the integration of natural resources and raw materials with the theory of production can still be widened.

I shall return later to these premisses, by which, however, I have already justified this contribution on the role of 'non-produced means of production' (in which natural resources provide the characteristic element) and raw materials in production processes. In more general terms, I shall study the interrelationship between produced and non-produced means of production, between raw materials and those goods on which no direct constraints are imposed by natural resources and, on this basis, some relationships between production, net products, employment, dynamics and technical change.

In this way, I shall link up with themes and analyses dealt with in previous publications, issued over a period of several years (Quadrio-Curzio, 1967, 1975, 1978, 1980, 1983; Quadrio-Curzio and Pellizzari, 1981; Quadrio-Curzio and Scazzieri, 1983), but hitherto available in English only to a very limited extent (Quadrio-Curzio, 1980). For this reason – and, in particular, on the basis of my belief that other studies have not investigated the same lines of research – I have made ample reference to the above-cited earlier publications (essentially, Quadrio-Curzio, 1967, 1975); this has been encouraged by the editors of this volume.

Let us return briefly to examine our premisses, starting from those of a historical type. From the standpoint of the *history of economic thought*, this analysis makes reference to the themes – dear to the heart of the classical economists – of 'land', 'corn' and 'rent'. Such themes immediately recall the work of David Ricardo, and the fact that after him these problems have experienced various ups and downs, passing from the source of inspiration for general theories, to more specific and limited issues, to themes that have been neglected, in so far as they have been considered irrelevant.

In Ricardo, the principle that net products and their accumulation constituted the force for growth were clear. No less clear, however, was the principle that the constraint posed by the limited availability of natural resources would have been able to slow down the rate of growth – even to a standstill – had technical progress not been maintained at a sufficiently high level. Thus, Ricardo introduced the principle of economic dynamics, based on the relative scarcity of natural resources on which, nevertheless, technical progress was able to operate.

This cardinal principle had, as its corollary, other derivative principles relating to price and income distribution themes, as also to themes regarding production. These are as follows.

1 *Rent*. Although salaries and profits are determined as exogenous (or as residual), rent is dependent on the productivity of the lands. It emerges with scarcity, and grows with the latter in accordance with the above-cited dynamics, which thus has a profound influence on the distribution of net products between rent and profit.
2 *The prices* of products generated with the aid of natural resources ('the price of corn produced with land'). These also vary in accordance with the scarcity of resources, in so far as the latter determines recourse to the use of land of gradually diminishing productivity, or the use of gradually more expensive methods of production on the same land. For this reason, the prices of all produced goods are affected by the above-cited dynamics, in that all these goods utilize 'corn' directly or indirectly as a means of production.
3 *Production* and the organization of productive processes is laid out in accordance with the efficiency criterion, by which land is utilized in order of decreasing quality and productivity. From this is deduced the principle of decreasing returns.
4 *The interdependence* between raw materials, primary commodities and produced goods means that the raw materials themselves act as an aspect and, indeed, a constraint on production processes. The latter constraint thus results from an interdependence in which means of production of all kinds assume a combined role with relative substitutability.

This is the framework within which Ricardo built his theory – an essentially dynamic theory – which concerns an economic system with two aspects, themselves interrelated, but not identified: on the one hand, the distribution-price aspects; on the other hand, the aspects relating to production-interdependence. The Ricardian design – indebted also in no small degree to the work of earlier authors – slackened Malthusian pessimism (absolute scarcity), but also the Smithian optimism (absolute productiveness); thus, in terms of the dynamic functioning of economic systems, it would have been able to bring out the generating principle of antagonism-coexistence and synergy between scarcity and producibility. In his lack of full exploitation of this principle and his underevaluation of technical progress, Ricardo ended by predicting the advent of a stationary state. His conclusion, however, in spite of certain well-known shortcomings, does not unduly detract from the design itself, though it is sketchy in many aspects, but not, for this reason, any less grandiose or capable of providing an overall vision.

Later economic theory has taken two very different directions, both of which can nevertheless be traced in some way to the Ricardian theory. The marginalist and neoclassical theory (or theories) was, in origin, the working out of a general plan whose initial nucleus or point of departure lay in the static scarcity of all productive factors (land, labour, capital). Thus, the problems of distribution-prices and of production cease to be distinct, coming together in a general theory of marginal productivity. In this vision, non-produced means of production, raw materials and rent cannot hold a position of relative autonomy, even less one of considerable weight, even if specific contributions on natural resources have not been lacking in the marginalist and neoclassical literature (for a survey see Quadrio-Curzio and Pellizzari, 1981). The general problem, however, in a conceptual framework in which all resources are scarce, concerns the use of all such available resources; on the basis of individual preference, this use must be efficient in such a way as to give the maximum means–ends effect, aided also by the exchange mechanism.

From this initial position, the marginalist and neoclassical theory has subsequently undergone considerable evolution, to such an extent that it is now difficult to crystallize it in terms of the limited conception of scarcity–exchange, since it is oriented rather in the direction of the 'fundamental apparatus of transformation', a specific type of production process discussed elsewhere in the present volume (chapter 13; see also A. Quadrio-Curzio and R. Scazzieri, 1983). In the present context, we are unable to dwell on these aspects. It is, however, important to remember that, explicitly or implicitly, it is also from reflection on the Ricardian theory of the 'marginal land' and of rent that one approach to the theory of marginal productivity is derived. It is sufficient, in this context, to consider the studies of Marshall, Wicksell and Wicksteed, bearing in mind also the warnings offered by Sraffa on the term 'marginal' (Sraffa, 1960, p. vi).

The second great line of thought includes the 'pure post-classical theories' and finds renewed impetus with the 1930s and 1940s. It has maintained its continuity, despite frequent periods of silence, and despite the fact that it has often been propounded by relatively neglected figures (for example, Nazzani, Ziber, Tugan-Baranovski, Dmitriev, von Bortkiewicz). It has also been considered by more famous economists such as Wicksell, whose complex personality makes it very difficult to place him unambiguously into one school of thought.

In the 1930s and 1940s, however, the overall dynamic and macro-economic phenomena, favoured by the classical economists, returned to the forefront of interest. The names of John Maynard Keynes, Roy Harrod, Joseph Schumpeter and Michael Kalecki can all be 'reduced' (though not without certain differentiation) to the pure post-classical theory. This is also true of Piero Sraffa, Wassily Leontief and John von Neumann, whose basic propositions have their roots in the 1930s. The latter authors reconstructed, in uniperiodal or dynamic situations, a Quesnay- or Ricardo-type multi-sector layout, and stressed above all the interdependence of means of production, production processes and produced goods – in other words, the same production system illustrated elsewhere in this volume as a 'structural apparatus' (see chapter 13 below).

All these contributions, with the exception of that of Sraffa, undervalue or actually avoid considerations of non-produced means of production and raw materials. From this standpoint, these theories are more Smithian than Ricardian, even if – above all for multi-sectoral theories – the equipment itself is Ricardian. The implicit or explicit assumption is, then, that scarcity is unable to make itself felt in any important way. This is a judgement of both history and fact that a certain number of future scholars will also share.

Economic history, however, would appear amply to deny this judgement, without even the necessity of recourse to detailed investigation. The actual dynamic of economic systems has, in fact, revealed many cases in which the scarcity of some non-produced means of production has at first slowed down the rate of growth, consequently triggering off technical progress. This, in turn, has removed the above scarcity, which therefore has appeared to be only of a relative type. Among many such cases of 'triggering', it will here be sufficient to mention the relative scarcity of wood and the abundance of mineral charcoal in generating the technical progress that led to the steam machine of the first industrial revolution; the development of agriculture in the USA during the 1930s, which, once the extensive, prevalently mechanized phase had run its course, generated and assimilated technical progress in vegetable genetics and chemical technologies, entering into a phase of intensive development; the adjustment, presently taking place, which can be seen in the employment of oil per unit of output (Quadrio-Curzio, 1978; Quadrio-Curzio and Pellizzari, 1981).

Modern economic theory of the classical kind, then, will have to take account of this evidence deriving from economic history. It would, indeed, be very strange with respect to its origins were the problem of scarcity to appear only in marginalist and neoclassical theories (or, for that matter, in the design and construction of certain large-scale models – often catastrophic – of most recent years).

We now come to the *premisses of economic theory*, and address our attention, in the first place, to a pure post-classical theory (known by some as the neo-Ricardian theory), which originated in Piero Sraffa's publication of 1960, but which had already been formulated by the 1930s.

The frequent swings in economists' moods – brought about by reason of their 'need' for clear-cut categories, quasi-political parties to be attacked or defended – means that this theory has frequently been viewed in an unconvincing way by both its supporters and detractors. As in similar cases, the Sraffa case could give rise to what I would call, in a quasi-Schumpeterian way, the psychology of economic analysis, on which, however, we are unable to dwell here. I cite it merely as an indication that my own point of departure is that of Sraffa and his contribution, though freely examined with a Ricardian eye and with the aid of the additional texts of Leontief (1941) and von Neumann (1945/6). There is thus no literal interpretation, no intention of utilizing Sraffa as a critical yardstick by which to measure all other theories; the intent is only that of using Sraffa's theories as a way of proceeding to further free construction.

Having said this, it is as well to state that the decision to start from Sraffa has an objective explanation. I do, in fact, believe that Sraffa was the first contemporary author of pure post-classical persuasion to insert both non-produced means of production and raw materials in a circular theory of production. This variant, in comparison with the inspiration motive of circular theories, has mistakenly induced many commentators and many constructive revivals of Sraffa's theory to avoid the problem, considering chapter XI ('Land') of his volume as secondary, if not, indeed, incoherent, with respect to the dominant theme of the 'production of commodities by means of commodities'. This has occurred to such an extent that, as far as I know, it was only in 1967 that a work based on circular theories of production, with the inclusion of non-produced means of production and raw materials, appeared (Quadrio-Curzio, 1967). Subsequently, the issue has attracted the more general attention of scholars, but only in the first half of the 1970s.

Most of the contributions, however, have concentrated on the price-distribution problem, limiting to a minimum or completely avoiding excursions into the above-mentioned problems of production. It is possible that this choice, truly limiting, derives from a misguided sense of faithfulness to Sraffa's initial approach, in which variations in the quantities produced are left unconsidered. If this was legitimate when trying to construct a price-distribution theory with a minimum number of assumptions, it cannot be so when proceeding to investigate new phenomena.

What has been said already shows that the present study of the theory of production is closely linked to previous theories of post-classical hue, but that it also has its own autonomy. The initial inspiration is Ricardian; though sharing with Sraffa his interest in non-produced means of production, I distance myself in studying the dynamics and activity-level variaons in production neglected by him. Dynamics and activity-level variations are, indeed, considered by authors such as Leontief (1951), von Neumann (1945/6) and Pasinetti (1981); here, however, I differ widely in taking into account non-produced means of production, which have been neglected by the above authors. For these reasons, I believe the present study to possess a considerable degree of independence.

II DATA AND PROBLEMS OF THE ECONOMIC SYSTEM

I shall henceforth assume a knowledge of the basic notions of linear models of production. These notions can be found in the appropriate manuals. I should like, in particular, to draw attention to the volume by Pasinetti (1977) and, for a more detailed investigation of the notions of linear algebra, to those by Gantmacher (1959) and Manara and Nicola (1970).

The data, assumptions, principal definitions and symbols which provide the point of departure and to which I shall henceforth be referring are as follows.

1 *Basic commodities*. In the economic system, $m + 1$ basic commodities are produced and used as means of production. They are of two types. Commodity 1 represents raw materials and it will be henceforth referred to as (RM–C1). It is produced also by means of non-produced means of production and its quantity is indicated with $q_1(h)$. The other m commodities, whose quantities are indicated with q_j for $j = 2,\ldots,m + 1$, are produced without subordination to the direct constraint of non-produced means of production.

2 *Non-produced means of production* (NPMP) and related production processes. RM–C1 also utilizes NPMP of different qualities as means of production, up to a maximum number of K. For RM–C1, it is thus possible to represent the h-th process by the following technical coefficients:

$$[\mathbf{a}_{i1}(h);l_1(h);t_1(h)]$$

it being that

$$\mathbf{a}'_{i1}(h) = [a_{11}(h); \ldots; a_{m+1,1}\ (h)] \quad h = I, \ldots, K \tag{1}$$

where $\mathbf{a}'_{i1}(h)$ is the technical coefficient vector $\mathbf{a}_{i1}$ transposed, and represents the inputs of commodities augmented by quantities of 'necessary consumption' (see point (4) below); $l_1(h)$ are the technical labour coefficients; $t_1(h)$ are the technical coefficients for NPMP of type h. Each of the vectors $\mathbf{a}_{i1}(h)$ is such as to allow viability of the economic system (see point (6) below), and the RM–C1 produced from it is denoted by $q_1(h)$. The availability of each NPMP of particular quality is given by $T_1(h)$; this quantity will determine the relation:

$$T_1(h) \geqslant q_1(h)t_1(h) \tag{2a}$$

Since $T_1(h)$ and $t_1(h)$ are technical data from relation (2a), it also follows that the maximum producible quantity of $q_1(h)$ is:

$$\max q_1(h) = T_1(h)/t_1(h) \tag{2b}$$

3 *Production processes* for commodity of type j. Each commodity j is produced using a single process:

$$[\mathbf{a}_{ij}; l_j]$$

it being that

$$\mathbf{a}'_{ij} = [a_{1j}, \ldots, a_{m+1,j}] \tag{3}$$

are the usual input–output coefficients augmented by necessary consumptions. The viability conditions are respected (see points (4) and (6) below).

4 *Technical coefficients* and *necessary consumption quotas*. Each coefficient of the vectors $\mathbf{a}_{j1}(h)$ and $\mathbf{a}_{ij}$ is augmented in comparison with the Leontief vectors by the quotas of necessary consumption (that is, by amounts of single commodities which figure in a conventional 'shopping-basket' of necessary consumptions). This assumption will allow us to exclude, in the cases of dynamic analysis, the explicit consideration of final consumption demand.

5 *Production techniques*. It being that the $m + 1$ commodities are of the basic type, for their production it will be necessary to have techniques that always include all the processes of type (3) and a process (1). Since the (1) processes are in the total number of K, then the K production techniques can be described as follows:

$$\begin{aligned} \mathbf{A}(h) &= [\mathbf{a}_{i1}(h);\mathbf{a}_{i2};\ \ldots;\mathbf{a}_{i,m+1}] \qquad h = \mathrm{I},\ldots,K \\ \mathbf{L}'(h) &= [l_1(h);l_2;\ldots;l_{m+1}] \\ t_1(h) &\leqslant T_1(h)/q_1(h) \end{aligned} \tag{4}$$

6 *Viability of production techniques*. This is assumed for each technique and therefore each one allows a uniform rate of positive net product or, in the assumption of a zero unit wage, it allows a uniform rate of positive profit (see pp. 319–20 and 323–4 below).
7 *Scale constraints on production techniques*. Given the limited availability of each NPMP of type h, and thus the maximum quantity $q_1(h)$ (see above, equation (2b)), and that the RM–C1 is basic, each technique (4) will be unable to produce more than a certain quantity of all commodities.
8 *Production technologies*. These are composed of a set of techniques of type (4) and can be represented in two alternative ways: as 'global technologies', when techniques (4) are 'jointed' in a particular way in order to analyse uni-periodal situations; as 'composite technologies', when techniques (4) are 'disjointed', but connected with each other in the analysis of uni-periodal and dynamic situations (see pp. 322–6 and 327–34 below).

The problems to be examined can for the present be summarized in the following five categories.

1 *The order of efficiency*: to arrange in this order the NPMPs or processes (1). This order is then followed in activating them.
2 *Levels of activity* or production scale of the economic system: the determination of the number of NPMPs to be activated, the quantities produced for the $m + 1$ commodities, the levels of employment.
3 *Technologies of the economic system*: this problem is closely connected with the issue of the levels of activity. As we have said, since technology is a structure composed of simpler elements given by each technique (4), the following elements will vary in accordance with the levels of activity: the number of techniques activated, and thus the size and structure of the means of production, productions, net products and employment.
4 *Changes in technology*: these can be studied in uni-periodal and dynamic contexts. In the latter case, of course, the rules of accumulation governing growth should be indicated. In our analysis, two factors, jointly or separately, give rise to technical change: the choice of techniques and technical progress, which in turn depend upon dynamics and/or innovation.

The problem of the order of efficiency among the NPMPs

A first order of efficiency might be defined as 'uni-periodal' or 'prices-distribution'. This has been studied elsewhere (Quadrio-Curzio, 1967, 1980). On the basis of each technique (4), it is possible to construct a prices-distribution subsystem capable of measuring the efficiency of the NPMP which it includes. The complexity of production processes, in fact, does not make it possible to establish efficiency on the basis of 'corn per acre'.

Each price-distribution subsystem is given by:

$$[1+r(h)]\ \mathbf{A}'(h)\mathbf{P}(h) + \mathbf{L}(h)\ w(h) = \mathbf{P}(h) \tag{5}$$

where $r(h)$ = uniform profit rate; $w(h)$ = uniform unit wage; $\mathbf{P}(h)$ is the prices vector of $m+1$ commodities.

Since the K price-distribution subsystems which can thus be constructed differ only by virtue of the process $[\mathbf{a}_{i1}(h), l_1(h)]$ related to the production of the RM–C1, it follows that the sequence:

$$w(\mathrm{I}) > w(\mathrm{II}) > \ldots > w(K) \tag{6}$$

gives the order of efficiency of the NPMPs when r is fixed exogenously. In turn, the sequence:

$$r(\mathrm{I}) > r(\mathrm{II}) > \ldots > r(K) \tag{7}$$

gives the order of efficiency of the NPMPs when w is fixed exogenously, and when the h indexes have been suitably permuted with respect to case (6) in such a way as process I, II, . . ., K of (6) does not necessarily correspond to process I, II, . . . K of (7).

The order of efficiency is thus determined on the basis of the costs of circulating capital and labour used in each process. Given w, the lower the cost of labour and of circulating capital, the higher will be the r associated with each process using NPMP.

This order of efficiency, assuming that w and r are uniform for all the processes of the economic system, can also be expressed in terms of rent imputed to each NPMP. The process with NPMP that, at zero rent, generates negative rents for all the others is the most efficient; similarly, the process that, at zero rent, generates positive rent for all the others is the least efficient.

We shall call this order of efficiency – which is unique for each level of w or r – the 'uni-periodal order of efficiency' or 'price-distribution order of efficiency'.

A second 'order of efficiency', of 'physical' or 'dynamic' type, can be defined. In this case, the order of efficiency can be determined without recourse to the prices-distribution system. The $\mathbf{A}(h)$ techniques can, in fact, be ordered on the basis of the respective uniform net product rate $s(h)$, which is obtained by solving the following system (10) for each h (see p. 323 below).

From this:

$$s(\mathrm{I}) > s(\mathrm{II}) > \ldots > s(K) \tag{8}$$

always with suitable permutation of the h indexes. It is well known that this order of efficiency coincides, by reason of standard theorems of linear algebra, with the order of efficiency defined by the prices-distribution system, in correspondence with $w = 0$, on the basis of the maximum profit rates of the K techniques. It is also well known that the uniform net product rate is an index of growth potential in the economic system.

For this reason, we shall call the inequality quality (8) the 'dynamic order of efficiency' or 'physical order of efficiency' remembering henceforth that it has a natural relevance for the analysis of dynamic processes. Certain readers might point out that this order of efficiency has little sense, since it does not take account of labour. This observation is obvious, but not relevant, in so far as with this order of efficiency it is intended to define the maximum growth potential of the economic system in relation exclusively to the NPMPs and produced commodities.

When w is given exogenously and is positive, the order of efficiency deriving from inequality (7) can be different from that which derives from inequality (8). In the extreme case we might have:

$$\begin{aligned} r(\mathrm{I}) > r(\mathrm{II}) > \ldots > r(K) \\ s(\mathrm{I}) < s(\mathrm{II}) < \ldots < s(K) \end{aligned} \tag{9}$$

(The numbering of techniques is the same in the two previous sets of inequalities.)

This means that the processes with NPMPs are activated in a different order, depending on whether criterion (7) or criterion (8) is followed, with notable consequences for activity levels, technologies and the dynamics of the economic system. So there might be the problem of choosing between the prices-distribution order of efficiency (which is followed by operators in the market economy) and the physical order of efficiency.

III ECONOMIC SYSTEM, PRICES-DISTRIBUTION SYSTEM, PRODUCTION-INTERDEPENDENCE SYSTEM

In order to examine the other problems introduced above and related to the production-interdependence system, it will be necessary to reflect on the relationships between the economic system and its component parts: the prices-distribution system and the production-interdependence system.

With the introduction of NPMPs, the respective independence between the prices-distribution system and the physical production system is considerably reduced. This independence is typical of linear production models, where labour is the only non-produced input. Meanwhile, the distinction between the prices-distribution system and the production-interdependence system (henceforward alternatively denominated the physical system, productions system or quantities system) remains quite as clear as before. But as we shall see, relationships of sequential type come to be established between these two systems.

In our preceding design, the economic system can be seen as composed of two large interconnected 'sections': the first includes sectors, up to a maximum of *K*, which produce a single raw material using produced and non-produced means of production; the second includes *m* sectors, each of which produces a different commodity, using raw materials and produced commodities as means of production. Naturally, both the sections of the economy also utilize labour.

Of the *K* processes that independently produce the raw material, at least one must be activated, in that the raw material is, directly or indirectly, a means of production for the entire economic system. When the activity of the economic system reaches certain levels, the number of processes producing the raw material must also increase in accordance with an order of efficiency.

The determination of the level of activity of the economy presupposes therefore the choice of an order of efficiency. To adopt the prices-distribution order of efficiency is equivalent to ordering *K* prices-distribution systems, each one of which contains a process with NPMP more than the preceding one. The smallest prices-distribution system contains a single process with NPMP, which produces the RM–C1 commodity, in addition to the other *m* processes for the remaining commodities. The largest prices-distribution system includes *K* processes with NPMP, besides the usual *m* processes. But each of these prices-distribution systems is theoretical, in the sense that it is necessary to choose among them. The actual prices-distribution system will depend on the level of activity of the economy and on the number or processes with NPMP put into operation.

This gives rise to sequential relationships between the prices-distribution system and the production-interdependence system. These relationships can be represented as follows: given *r* (or *w*) ∴ K 'theoretical' prices-distribution systems are defined ∴ then is determined the order of efficiency between the K available NPMPs ∴ on the basis of the production-interdependence system the number of NPMPs to be activated is determined ∴ then it is possible to determine the actual prices-distribution system.

If, alternatively, it is decided to adopt the physical order of efficiency, the sequential relationships would be as follows: physical order of efficiency ∴ on the basis of the production-interdependence system, the number of NPMPs to be activated is determined ∴ finally, given r (or w), the actual prices-distribution system is determined. In this case, however, there arise problems of compatibility or, rather, of necessary constraints on the exogenous choice of r (or w) in order to satisfy the condition that the processes selected according to the physical order of efficiency and to the activity levels be also economical in terms of production costs. For reasons that will be explained later, I shall not consider this aspect in the present study, supposing that these conditions are fulfilled.

In previous studies (Quadrio-Curzio, 1967, 1980), I have examined the prices-distribution system, and hence the uni-periodal order of efficiency between the processes with NPMP; the order of rentability between these processes; the autonomous changes in the distribution of income between wages, profits and rent generated by exogenous variations in r or w; changes in income distribution generated by variations in the level of activity of the economy.

These latter changes have, nevertheless, been put forward by way of hypothesis in the work published in English. There the changes in the number of operative processes using NPMPs were assumed to be determined by exogenous factors. In other words, the production-interdependence system has not been studied. As mentioned at the outset, it is on this system that I shall now concentrate exclusively.

The study of the problem of the level of activity, of technology, and variations in both these, can be carried out with two different methods (*see* Quadrio-Curzio, 1967 and 1975): the 'jointed techniques or global technology' method; the 'disjointed techniques or composite technology' method being the latter more general and such to include the previous one which is nevertheless a useful and clear first and partial approach to the problem.

IV PRODUCTION-INTERDEPENDENCE REPRESENTED WITH JOINTED TECHNIQUES AND GLOBAL TECHNOLOGIES IN A UNI-PERIODAL SITUATION

First of all, I shall consider the jointed techniques method, in which technology is represented so as to make it possible to describe in a synthetic way the physical system. The essence of this method, which is suitable for uni-periodal analysis, is that of enclosing in a single technological matrix the processes with NPMPs – which are subsequently activated – together with the processes producing commodities without the use of NPMPs.

Let us consider a 'small' production system with a single technique (other definitions and symbols are now introduced in addition to those discussed on pp. 316–18 above). Given an order of efficiency, let us consider the productive structure that corresponds to the determination of a uniform net product rate. Let us, moreover, suppose that the overall objective of the economy is the full employment of a given labour force.

The first technique activated, coinciding with the technology of the economic system, is given by:

$$[(1+s(\mathrm{I}))\,\mathbf{A}(\mathrm{I}) - \mathbf{I}]\,\mathbf{Q}(\mathrm{I}) = \mathbf{0} \tag{10a}$$

$$[\mathbf{A}(\mathrm{I}) - \lambda(\mathrm{I})\mathbf{I}]\,\mathbf{Q}(\mathrm{I}) = \mathbf{0} \tag{10b}$$

with

$$\lambda(\mathrm{I}) = 1/(1+s(\mathrm{I})) \tag{11}$$

$$q_1(\mathrm{I}) \leqslant \max q_1(\mathrm{I}) = T_1(\mathrm{I})/t_1(\mathrm{I}) \tag{12}$$

$$\mathbf{L}'(\mathrm{I})\,\mathbf{Q}(\mathrm{I}) \leqslant \bar{L} \tag{13}$$

The above relations and magnitudes require some comment: $s(\mathrm{I})$ is the uniform net product rate; $\lambda(\mathrm{I})$ is the maximum eigenvalue of $\mathbf{A}(\mathrm{I})$; $\mathbf{Q}(\mathrm{I})$ is the production vector; $\bar{L}$ is the existing labour force.

When only the first technique is operated, system (10) coincides with the entire production system. But when more than one system (10) is activated, each one becomes a production subsystem. Therefore system (10) defines production subsystem of type I. Substituting into system (10) for the technical coefficients vector $\mathbf{a}_{i1}(\mathrm{I})$, the vector associated with each of the other NPMPs, that is $\mathbf{a}_{i1}(h)$, it will be then possible to define K distinct techniques or production subsystems. Each one of these is technically autonomous, but its production scale has an upper limit given by the availability of NPMP of type h.

On the basis of known theorems of linear algebra, since $\mathbf{A}(\mathrm{I})$ is non-negative, indecomposable and viable, its maximum eigenvalue $\lambda(\mathrm{I})$ will be real, positive and less than one. The associate eigenvector $\mathbf{Q}(I)$ will be positive, but defined only in structure, and the scale has to be determined. This scale factor, and thus also the solution to system (10), is dependent on conditions (12) or (13).

Let us consider the situation in which full employment of the labour force is required. In this case, leaving (12) aside, (13) is taken as an equality in order to find out the solution of system (10) and (13). If this solution is not compatible with the boundary (12), this means that the quantity of NPMP of type I is not sufficient to allow full employment of labour.

It is thus necessary to widen the economic system from a single technique to a technology. A further increase in the level of activity necessary for the full employment of labour thus requires at least the introduction of the NPMP of type II, that is, the working of a second production process which generates RM–C1. Following the order of efficiency – for the moment it is irrelevant whether this is (6), (7) or (8) – this process will be:

$$\mathbf{a}'_1(\mathrm{II}) = [a_{11}(\mathrm{II}); a_{21}(\mathrm{II}); \ldots ; a_{m+1}(\mathrm{II})] \tag{14}$$

The technology of the economic system can now be represented as with two 'jointed techniques' or with a 'global technology' $\mathbf{A}_\alpha(\mathrm{I,II})$. The compact notation $\mathbf{A}_\alpha(\mathrm{I,II})$ indicates that it is possible to include – in a way which will not be discussed, since it is too technical – in this new type of technological matrix two processes that produce RM–C1, and that this matrix varies with changes in the 'splitting coefficients' αs (these are the coefficients used to 'split', in proportions to be determined, the known technical coefficients) that connect RM–C1 as input to all other m processes of the economy.

It seems to us that these splitting coefficients represent an innovation in the field of production-theory schemes. This makes it possible, on the one hand, to construct new technological matrices that include several processes that produce the same RM–C1, and, on the other, to keep into account the technical necessity of 'substitution' of the process using NPMP of type II to that of type I, which, though remaining activated to its maximum, given by (12), as an equality, undergoes a diminution of its relative weight in the economic system.

The splitting coefficients must then be varied, within an upper limit imposed by the usual technical coefficients, in order to satisfy the conditions given by the following system:

$$[(1+s_\alpha(\mathrm{I,II}))\,\mathbf{A}_\alpha\,(\mathrm{I,II})-\mathbf{I}]\;\mathbf{Q}_\alpha(\mathrm{I,II}) = \mathbf{0} \tag{15}$$

$$\alpha_{1j}(\mathrm{I})+\alpha_{1j}(\mathrm{II}) = a_{1j} \quad j=2, \ldots, m+1 \quad \alpha > 0 \tag{16}$$

$$q_1(\mathrm{I}) = \max q_1(\mathrm{I}) = T_1(\mathrm{I})/t_1(h) \tag{17}$$

$$q_1(\mathrm{II}) \leqslant \max q_1(\mathrm{II}) = T_1(\mathrm{II})/t_1(\mathrm{II}) \tag{18}$$

$$\left[\sum_{h=\mathrm{I}}^{\mathrm{II}} l_1(h)\, q_1(h) + \sum_{j=2}^{m+1} l_j q_j\right] / \bar{L} \leqslant 1 \qquad (19)$$

A solution of system (15), (16), (17) and (18), assuming (18) as an equality, can be found taking α as parameters. In other words, the α coefficients are made to change in a continuum, so that the constraint represented by the NPMP of type I – which is and remains fully employed – does not prevent the growth of production; this means that the RM–Cl is supplied in increasing quantities, in its quality as basic means of production, by the increasing utilization of NPMP of type II.

The growth of the productions considered nevertheless finds an upper constraint in the full utilization of $T_1(\mathrm{II})$, as can be seen from (18). When this occurs, if full employment of the labour force, kept into account in (19), has not been reached, it will be necessary to operate further processes with NPMPs, following the chosen order of efficiency. The technology of the economic system will be represented by matrices of type $\mathbf{A}_\alpha(\mathrm{I,II})$, to which a new line and new column will be added for each new process with NPMP.

The global technology of the productive system can therefore assume much larger dimensions. If, in order to satisfy the objective of full employment of labour, it were necessary to activate all of the K processes with NPMP, this would give a system whose global technological matrix $\mathbf{A}_\alpha(\mathrm{I,II}, \ldots, K)$ would include K processes that produce the RM–C1 and m processes related to the other m commodities produced. $\mathbf{A}_\alpha(\mathrm{I,II}, \ldots, K)$ would thus be a matrix with $K + m$ lines and columns, though it would represent a technology that produces only $1 + m$ commodities.

In this case, the production system would be represented as follows:

$$[(1+s_\alpha[\mathrm{I}, \ldots, K))\, \mathbf{A}_\alpha(\mathrm{I}, \ldots, K) - \mathbf{I}]\, \mathbf{Q}_\alpha(\mathrm{I}, \ldots, K) = \mathbf{0} \qquad (20)$$

$$\sum_{h=\mathrm{I}}^{K} \alpha_{1j}(h) = a_{1j} \quad \alpha_{1j}(h) > 0 \qquad j=2, \ldots, m+1 \qquad (21)$$

$$q_1(h) = \max q_1(h) = T_1(h)/t_1(h) \qquad h=\mathrm{I}, \ldots, K-1 \qquad (22)$$

$$q_1(K) \leqslant \max q_1(K) = T_1(K)/t_1(K) \qquad (23)$$

$$\left[\sum_{h=\mathrm{I}}^{K} l_1(h)\, q_1(h) + \sum_{j=2}^{m+1} l_j q_j\right] / \bar{L} = 1 \qquad (24)$$

or, as alternatives to (23) and (24):

$$q_1(K) = q_1(K) = T_1(K)/t_1(K) \tag{25}$$

$$\left[\sum_{h=1}^{K} l_1(h)\, q_1(h) + \sum_{j=2}^{m+1} l_j q_j \right] / \bar{L} < 1 \tag{26}$$

The relationships given above can be examined in two possible cases. In the first case, given by (20), (21), (22), (23) and (24), full employment of labour is reached with(out) complete utilization of NPMPs. In the second case, given by (20), (21), (22), (25) and (26), the constraint imposed by the NPMPs, which are fully used, makes full employment of labour impossible.

To conclude, I want to stress that the above analysis makes it possible to see how technology changes when there are two categories of limited means of production: labour and NPMPs. In turn, the changes of the global technology can be of two types: those that affect only the relative weight in the economy of the processes with NPMPs activated, with consequences on net products (s_α), productions ($\mathbf{Q}_\alpha$) and employment; and those that imply an increase in the number of processes with NPMPs activated, an enlargement of the global technology activated, with consequences on net products, productions and employment.

V VARIATIONS IN LEVELS OF ACTIVITY AND DEGREES OF EFFICIENCY

With the above analysis, we have determined the productions vector to which is associated the maximum employment of labour allowed by the successive activation of processes with NPMP. If the number and the extension of NPMPs is large enough, full employment of labour will be reached. We must now ask ourselves what will happen to the efficiency of the economic system in the growth of productions.

A measure of the 'physical efficiency' of an economic system is given by its uniform net product rate. This is, in fact, just one of the possible measurements, but probably one of the most succinct and concise. It is well known that in the linear theories of production and growth of the type propounded by von Neumann, the net product rate is coincident with the growth rate of the economic system; for this reason, there exists no better measurement of the dynamic efficiency.

The representation that we have given above, however, differs in many respects from the von Neumann type. In the first place, it is uni-periodal analysis with uni-periodal comparisons. In the second place, the growth in the levels of activity obtained by increasing the weight of the 'last' activated process with NPMP always determines a variation in the uniform net product rate. The same happens when a further process with NPMP is put into operation. Since there exists an obvious connection – in this case, nevertheless, not an identity – between net product rate, accumulation rate and growth rate, it follows that a change in the net product rate will necessarily have a bearing on accumulation and growth.

More precisely, let us suppose that the order of efficiency followed in activating the NPMPs is of type (8), that is that given by the decreasing sequence of net product rates of the *K* techniques (or of the *K* production subsystems of type (10)). In this case, the increasing activation of the final process with NPMP placed in operation (that is, the least efficient), and after that, the activation of new processes with NPMPs, reduces the uniform net product rate of the global technology. This is an 'index' of reduction in the accumulation and growth potential of the economic system.

In order to examine these consequences, especially those on the dynamics and accumulation path, it will be necessary to represent the economic system in another way, which is based on disjointed techniques and on composite technologies. Before proceeding further along these lines, however, it is worth noting that if the order of efficiency (6) or (7), which is given by production costs, is followed in activating the NPMPs (see p. 319 above), it can happen that this will differ from (8) or actually be its opposite, as in the case of (9). In this latter case, the physical efficiency of the economic system (that is, its potential for accumulation and growth) might increase with the successive activation of NPMPs, since the first to have been set in operation were the least efficient, followed by those that have a physical increasing efficiency. The reason for this is that the labour factor, which is supposed to be non-scarce, and its cost will be left out in the analysis of dynamic efficiency, which is dependent only on the physical accumulation capacity of the economic system, as we will see in detail later.

VI PRODUCTION-INTERDEPENDENCE REPRESENTED WITH DISJOINTED TECHNIQUES AND COMPOSITE TECHNOLOGIES IN DYNAMIC SITUATIONS

Let us proceed, then, to a dynamic analysis based on many techniques $\mathbf{A}(h)$ that will be seen to be connected in time, in that they rely upon the means of production of techniques already activated. These disjointed, but temporally connected techniques, will give rise to composite technologies which, in our opinion, represent a fair approximation to reality when account is taken of the NPMPs. This approach is more general than that based on a global technology as it includes both the uniperiodal and the dynamic features of the economic system.

The beginning of the dynamic process hinges only on the technique $\mathbf{A}(\mathrm{I})$ and on the productive system (already described above, p. 323), with the difference that the magnitudes are now also dependent on time, *t*:

$$[(1+s(\mathrm{I}))\mathbf{A}(\mathrm{I}) - \mathbf{I}]\ \mathbf{Q}(\mathrm{I},t) = \mathbf{0} \quad t_0 \geqslant t \geqslant t_{\mathrm{I}} \tag{27}$$

Let us suppose that the initial supply of means of production $\mathbf{A}(\mathrm{I})\mathbf{Q}(\mathrm{I},t_0)$ is *una tantum* anticipated and that the labour does not represent a constraint on growth. The productions $\mathbf{Q}(\mathrm{I},t)$ and all the other magnitudes will expand at the rate of growth $s(\mathrm{I})$ in a succession of periods $t_1, t_2, \ldots, t_{\mathrm{I}}$, in which $\mathbf{Q}(\mathrm{I},t)$ comes up against the constraint given by max $q_1(\mathrm{I})$. The constraint max $q_1(\mathrm{I})$ can become operative at time t_{I} in two alternative ways:

1 The full accumulation of available net products at $(t_{\mathrm{I}} - 1)$ leads to full employment of $T_1(\mathrm{I})$ and thus to the production of exactly max $q_1(\mathrm{I})$ at time t_{I};
2 a share of the available net products at $(t_{\mathrm{I}} - 1)$ cannot be accumulated with techniques $\mathbf{A}(\mathrm{I})$, since this would lead to violation of the constraint $T_1(\mathrm{I})$ at time t_{I}.

Let us suppose the occurrence of the first case. At t_1 the production system (27) is no longer able to grow and enters into a stationary state. From this period onwards, the said production system generates net products, which cannot be accumulated within it. This means that the net products of technique $\mathbf{A}(\mathrm{I})$ at t_{I},

$$\mathbf{S}(\mathrm{I};t_1) = \mathbf{Q}(\mathrm{I};t_{\mathrm{I}}) - \mathbf{A}(\mathrm{I})\mathbf{Q}(\mathrm{I};t_{\mathrm{I}}) = s(\mathrm{I})\mathbf{A}(\mathrm{I})\mathbf{Q}(\mathrm{I};t_{\mathrm{I}}) \tag{28}$$

can be utilized as a means of production to set in motion another technique $\mathbf{A}(\mathrm{II})$. The production system will thus come to consist of two techniques $\mathbf{A}(\mathrm{I})$ and $\mathbf{A}(\mathrm{II})$, each of which represents a production subsystem. The two techniques are disjointed and the technology to which they give rise is composite.

The dynamics associated with these two techniques becomes rather complex, neither equiproportional between the various sectors, nor with constant growth rate, as we will see. The production subsystem II is given by:

$$[(1+s(\mathrm{II}))\ \mathbf{A}(\mathrm{II}) - \mathbf{I}]\ \mathbf{Q}(\mathrm{II},t) = 0 \quad t > t_{\mathrm{I}} \tag{29}$$

and can grow at the maximum and constant rate $s(\mathrm{II})$ – which represents its internal growth rate – unlike the entire production system. Two cases are considered in this context.

1 *Case with residuals*. If the structure of the processes $\mathbf{a}_{i1}(\mathrm{I})$ and $\mathbf{a}_{i1}(\mathrm{II})$, and thus also of $\mathbf{A}(\mathrm{I})$ and $\mathbf{A}(\mathrm{II})$, are different, this will prevent the

entire accumulation of $\mathbf{S}(\mathrm{I};t_{\mathrm{I}})$ in $\mathbf{A}(\mathrm{II})$; a residual $\mathbf{SR}(\mathrm{I};t_{\mathrm{I}})$, with quantities which will be determined later, will thus be created. The residual, which will consequently emerge in each period from $t_{\mathrm{I}} + 1$ to t_{II}, can have various destinations; that is, consumed, placed in stocks, exported. In turn, these destinations, which can be adopted only in part, have various consequences for growth. Considering the most simple case, let us assume that the residuals are consumed and thus have no effect on growth. This consumption joins that already included in the matrices **A** through the necessary consumption coefficients.

2 *Case without residuals*. This occurs when the processes $\mathbf{a}_{i1}(\mathrm{I})$ and $\mathbf{a}_{i1}(\mathrm{II})$ have the same structure. In this case, the net product generated by technique I can be fully accumulated in the production subsystem II. For now we shall leave this case aside.

The existence of residuals means that the net products $\mathbf{S}(\mathrm{I};t_{\mathrm{I}})$ cannot be accumulated in technique $\mathbf{A}(\mathrm{II})$ in a measure given by:

$$\mathbf{SR}(\mathrm{I};t_{\mathrm{I}}) = \mathbf{S}(\mathrm{I};t_{\mathrm{I}}) - \mathbf{A}(\mathrm{II})\mathbf{Q}(\mathrm{II};t_{\mathrm{I}}+1) \geqslant 0 \tag{30}$$

In order to find $\mathbf{A}(\mathrm{II})\mathbf{Q}(\mathrm{II};t_{\mathrm{I}} + 1)$ and thus $\mathbf{SR}(\mathrm{I};t_{\mathrm{I}})$, it is necessary to consider the $m+ 1$ eigenvectors associated with $\lambda(\mathrm{II})$, maximum eigenvalue of $\mathbf{A}(\mathrm{II})$. These $m+ 1$ eigenvectors are distinguished by virtue of their normalization, given by:

$$\mathbf{e}'_i\mathbf{S}(\mathrm{I};t_{\mathrm{I}}) = \mathbf{e}'_i \; \mathbf{A}(\mathrm{II})\mathbf{Q}(\mathrm{II};t_{\mathrm{I}}+1) \tag{31}$$

$$\mathbf{e}'_i\mathbf{S}(\mathrm{I},t_{\mathrm{I}})\,\frac{1}{\lambda(\mathrm{II})} = \mathbf{e}'_i\mathbf{Q}(\mathrm{II};t_{\mathrm{I}}+1)$$

where $\mathbf{e}'_i = [0, 0, \ldots, 1\,(i), \ldots, 0]$ for $i = 1, \ldots ,m + 1$, and the position of number 1 is changing with the index i. Among the $m + 1$ vectors $\mathbf{Q}(\mathrm{II},t_{\mathrm{I}} + 1)$ thus obtained, only one satisfies the non-negativity condition (30). This is the vector $\mathbf{Q}(\mathrm{II};t_{\mathrm{I}} + 1)$ that gives minimum residuals. For one of the $m + 1$ commodities of the production vector, that in which the latter is normalized, the residual of net product will be zero. We shall indicate this commodity with the index i^*.

We are now in the position of examining how the economic system – including the techniques $\mathbf{A}(\mathrm{I})$ and $\mathbf{A}(\mathrm{II})$ – grows. It can be said that in each period $t > t_{\mathrm{I}} + 1$ a new production subsystem of type (29) starts up, utilizing the net products of subsystem I, which reproduces itself in stationary conditions. In turn, the already activated subsystems II grow at their internal rate $s(\mathrm{II})$. In figure 10.1, in which the magnitudes enclosed

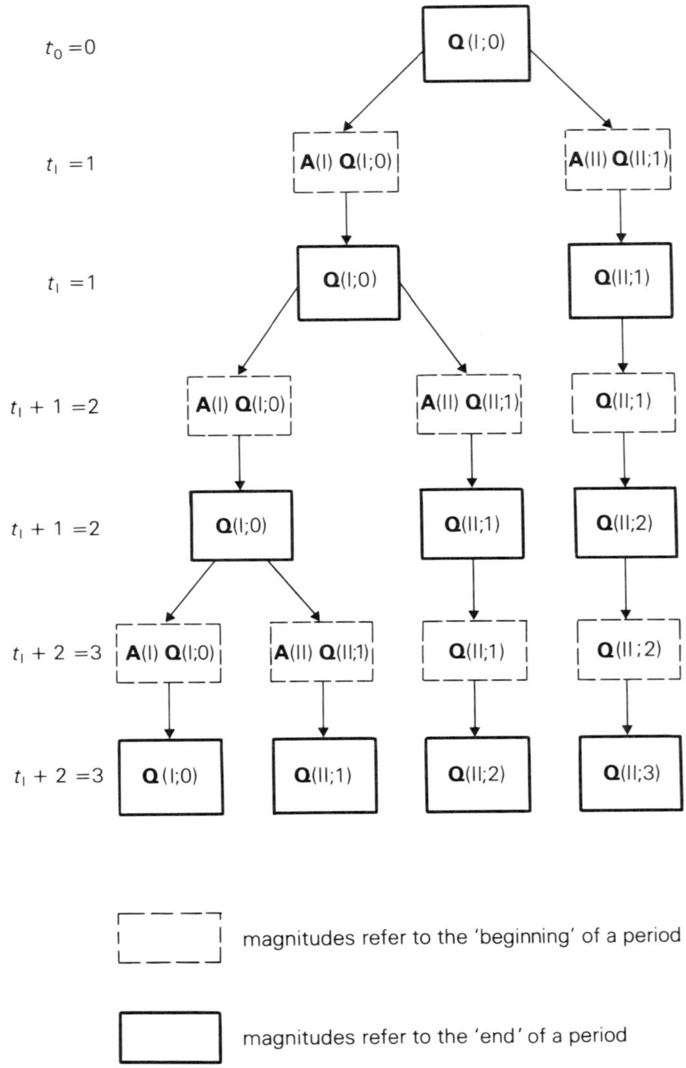

FIGURE 10.1 A simple expansion scheme of the economy

within the dotted lines refer to the 'beginning' of a period, and those within continuous lines to the 'end', the 'expansion' of the economy is described up to the period $t_I + 2$.

The production system described above exhibits many differences with respect to models of the von Neumann type. As the formal analysis of the growth process dealt with in my earlier study (1975) would require considerably more space than is available here, I shall limit myself to the results concerning the growth rates.

From this respect, the production model exhibits three principal features.

1. There is no coincidence between net product rate (s), production growth rate (g) and net product growth rate (r).
2. A multiplicity of net product rates and production and net product growth rates exists, up to a maximum number equivalent to the number of commodities of the economic system.
3. The above-mentioned rates vary with time, even if the techniques do not change.

Let us examine these differences, leaving aside the net product rates, which do not have a particularly significant role in these situations of analysis of growth processes, in that the other two growth rates give enough information on the dynamic process. In order to illustrate these phenomena, I shall henceforth refer to figures 10.2 and 10.3, constructed on the basis of numerical examples with three-commodity techniques.

In the first place, let us consider the production growth rates for the various commodities, $g_i(\text{I},\text{II};t)$. These are indicated in this way since they are dependent on techniques I and II, and also on time. They are weighted means, which are dependent on the internal growth rates of techniques **A**(I) and **A**(II), on the net products of **A**(I), which can be accumulated in **A**(II), and on non-accumulative residuals. The first property is that the equiproportional dynamics is no longer possible. In fact we shall always have:

$$g_{i*}(\text{I};\text{II};t) > g_i(\text{I};\text{II};t) \quad t > t_\text{I}+1 \atop \qquad\qquad i(\neq i^*) = 1, \ldots, m+1 \qquad (32)$$

The commodity i^* is that for which there are no residuals and the inequality is precisely due to the residuals for the other commodities. The g_i are probably different from each other, even if equalities cannot be excluded. Commodity i^* is thus given in figure 10.2 by commodity 3 and in figure 10.3 by commodity 1. In neither case is there any coincidence in the production growth rates of the three commodities.

The second property, given $s(\text{I}) > s(\text{II})$, is

$$s(\text{I}) > g_{i*}(\text{I};\text{II};t) > g_i(\text{I};\text{II};t) \qquad (33)$$

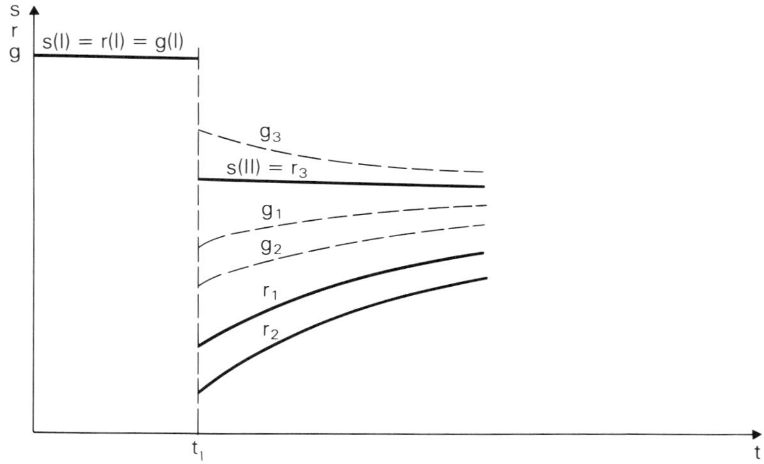

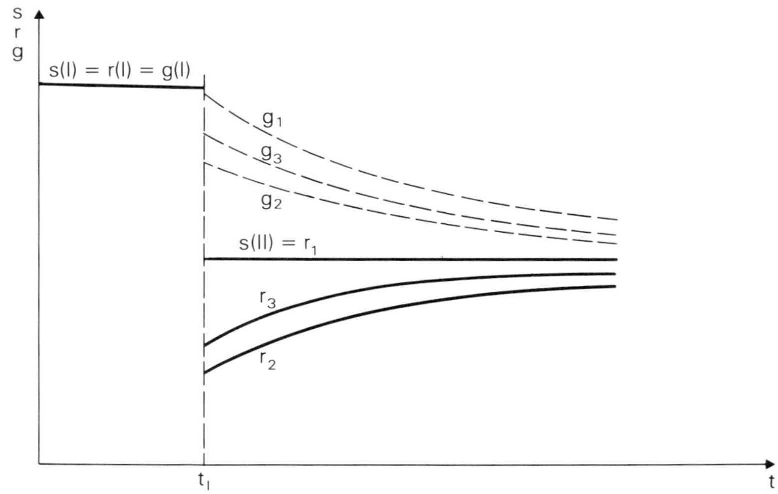

FIGURES 10.2 AND 10.3 Two alternative growth processes with three commodity techniques

The introduction of technique **A**(II) thus determines a discontinuity in the production growth rates; as can be seen from figures 10.2 and 10.3, this discontinuity increases in proportion to an increase in the residuals and a decrease in s(II) with respect to s(I).

The third property is more complex, and regards the relationships between g_i, g_i^* and s(II). Although it is easy to demonstrate that:

$$g_{i*}(\text{I};\text{II};t) > s(\text{II}) \tag{34}$$

Figure 10.2 shows a case with $g_i(\mathrm{I;II};t) < s(\mathrm{II})$, whereas figure 10.3 shows a case with $g_i(\mathrm{I;II};t) > s(\mathrm{II})$.

The fourth property is the convergence of the g_i growth rates to $s(\mathrm{II})$ with the passing of time. In the case of figure 10.2, the production growth rates of commodities 1 and 2 increase, tending asymptotically to $s(\mathrm{II})$, to which position, however, they can only draw near to a certain degree, by virtue of the constraints imposed by the NPMP of type II. The reason for the increase in these rates is that the relative weight of the residuals, which are themselves constant, diminishes with respect to the productions of techniques **A**(II), which in turn increase. In the case of figure 10.3, the convergence takes place from above, in that the residuals are less than in figure 10.2. In this case, it is the influence of the greater efficiency of technique **A**(I) that loses relative weight with time. This is always the case with commodity i^*, whose $g_i{}^*$ converges to $s(\mathrm{II})$ from above.
We now come to the net product growth rates. Given the non-coincidence of these rates with the production growth rates, it is well to remember that it is the latter that influence the entity of use of the NPMPs (and of labour), whereas it is the net product growth rate that influences the accumulation capacity. The first property of the net product growth rates is as follows:

$$r_i(\mathrm{I;II};t) < s(\mathrm{II}) \qquad r_{i*}(\mathrm{I;II};t) = s(\mathrm{II}) \tag{35}$$

This means that the growth rate of the commodity without residuals is maximum. The second property is that, for these rates too, there is not a pattern of equiproportional growth. The third property is that the growth rates inferior to $s(\mathrm{II})$ converge asymptotically to this level with the passing of time. The fourth and final property is:

$$g_i(\mathrm{I;II};t) > r_i(\mathrm{I;II};t) \qquad g_{i*}(\mathrm{I;II};t) > r_{i*}(\mathrm{I;II};t) \tag{36}$$

Having arrived at this point, the reader will have realized that the types of growth of the economic system, in the presence of NPMPs, are dependent on a wide variety of elements that do not emerge in models of the von Neumann type. In particular, the following elements are relevant:

1 the time t_{I}, at which production subsystem I ceases to grow, and hence the size $T_1(\mathrm{I})$;
2 the size of the net products generated by subsystem I and available for accumulation in techniques **A**(II); this size is also dependent on t_{I};
3 the dimension of $s(\mathrm{I})$ and $s(\mathrm{II})$;
4 the dimension of the residual of net products generated by **A**(I) and not accumulated in **A**(II);
5 the time t_{II}, which depends also on the dimension of $T(\mathrm{II})$, at which the activity of techniques **A**(II) ceases to grow.

When we consider the cases in which K techniques are activated, all these elements imply an analysis that is so articulated as to make any discussion in the present context quite impossible.

The wide variety of possible situations would suggest, moreover, that these situations should be dealt with using numerical cases, which are often clearer than formal cases. Elsewhere I have examined many situations in this way, among which is the case in which the introduction of techniques successive to II leads first to the elimination of the residuals, then to their reappearance, and so on.

VII TECHNICAL CHANGE, CHOICE OF TECHNIQUES AND TECHNOLOGIES, TECHNICAL PROGRESS

The above analysis reveals how the presence of NPMPs complicates the relationships between degrees of efficiency, the choice of techniques and technical progress. In fact, although the physical and dynamic efficiency of a single technique $\mathbf{A}(h)$ is given by its uniform net products rate $s(h)$, which is also its internal growth rate, the dynamic efficiency of a technology composed of several $\mathbf{A}(h)$ depends not only on the $s(h)$, but also on the residuals due to the different structures of the $\mathbf{A}(h)$ techniques, as well as on the other elements indicated in the preceding paragraph.

In turn, the most immediate index of technical progress for a single technical matrix is provided by a decrease in its coefficients, which generates an increase in the uniform net product rate. And yet this increase is not necessarily or immediately translated into a greater efficiency of a composite technology. I shall now summarize some of the many possible cases which show how the evaluation of technical change – which can be both choice among existing techniques and/or introduction of new techniques due to technical progress – is very complex in the case of composite technologies.

The first case is that of an increase in efficiency without technical progress. Let us consider two technologies: the first consists of two techniques $\mathbf{A}(\mathrm{I})$ and $\mathbf{A}(\mathrm{II})$, each with given degrees of dynamic efficiency $s(\mathrm{I})$ and $s(\mathrm{II})$; the second technology includes the same technique $\mathbf{A}(\mathrm{I})$ and a technique $\mathbf{A}^*(\mathrm{II})$, whose structure is different from that of $\mathbf{A}(\mathrm{II})$, but whose $s^*(\mathrm{II})$ is equal to $s(\mathrm{II})$.

First of all, let us see how to construct $\mathbf{A}^*(\mathrm{II})$. Taking as our point of departure the case examined in the preceding paragraph, and varying only the technical coefficients of the process that produces the RM–C1, it is possible to construct an $\mathbf{A}^*(\mathrm{II})$ that does not give rise to residuals with respect to the net products of technique $\mathbf{A}(\mathrm{I})$. It is logical to concentrate on the change in the process relating to the RM–C1, in so far as it is only by reason of this process and its correlated NPMP that it is necessary to pass from technique $\mathbf{A}(\mathrm{I})$ to technology $[\mathbf{A}(\mathrm{I}),\mathbf{A}(\mathrm{II})]$.

The utilization of technology [**A**(I),**A***(II)], with the elimination of residuals, determines an increase – with respect to the utilization of technology [**A**(I),**A**(II)] – in quantities produced, net products and growth rates. For the latter, in particular, we have the uniformity of the net product growth rates, their constancy with time, and their coincidence with s(II); the uniqueness of the production growth rates that change with time and coincide with that of commodity i^* of the cases examined above (p. 332).

The situation with composite technology, however, remains different from the von Neumann case, even in the absence of residuals; this is because there will no longer be coincidence between the production growth rate and the net product rate. Nevertheless, **A***(II) is the technique which, in association with **A**(I), gives greatest dynamic efficiency; this is determined by the better choice of techniques, despite the absence – be it noted – of technical progress.

A comparison between technologies composed of techniques that have the same s(I) and s(II) does not always give the preceding results. In fact, if a new technique **A****(II), with s^{**}(II) equal to s(II), has residuals that are not orderable with respect to those of **A**(II), the efficiency comparison between **A**(II) and **A****(II) is no longer possible on the basis of the comparison between **A**(II) and **A***(II).

The second case considers a technical progress without increases of efficiency. Let us consider the introduction of an additional technique **A*****(II) with a rate $s^{***}(\mathrm{II}) > s(\mathrm{II}) = s^{*}(\mathrm{II})$ and thus a case of true technical progress. Yet it is not certain that the efficiency of the composite technology [**A**(I),**A*****(II)] (**A**(I) being the first technique activated and not affected by technical progress) is immediately superior to that of the composite technology [**A**(I),**A***(II)] and to that of [**A**(I),**A**(II)].

In fact, while for t tending to infinity the technology [**A**(I),**A*****(II)] is the most efficient one – since all the growth rates converge to s^{***}(II), which is greater than s(II) and s^*(II) – it is also possible that the structure of **A*****(II) increases the residuals with respect to **A**(II) in such a way as to give rise for a certain period of time to a lower [**A**(I),**A*****(II)] efficiency in comparison to **A**(II) and **A***(II).

If T(II) is insufficiently large to allow g_i^{***} to exceed the g_i, and the r_i^{***} to exceed r_i, the greater efficiency of **A*****(II) will be 'cancelled out' by the greater residuals that result from the connection with technique **A**(I) inside the given technology. This complicates considerably the relationships between the choice of techniques and technical progress, and opens a chapter of study to which further analysis should be addressed.

One final consideration concerns another criterion for the choice of techniques, that is, that of uni-periodal efficiency or prices-distribution efficiency. If this criterion (illustrated in pp. 319–20 above) is also adopted for the dynamic choices of the techniques, it could happen that the techniques will be activated following an order of increasing net product rates.

Assuming for the present that the structure of these techniques does not generate residuals, we would thus have a phenomenon of 'technical illusion' in that, with the growth of the net product growth rate, it is possible to mistake for technical progress that which, in reality, is the consequence of having adopted a prices-distribution order of efficiency. The 'disadvantage' involved in following this order of efficiency can be seen in the case of technical progress not applicable to techniques already activated. In this case, in fact, technical progress would lead, in the short term, to the exclusion of techniques with a higher internal growth rate than that of other techniques already in operation.

VIII CONCLUDING REMARKS

The above analysis leads to a number of conclusions and provides the equipment for further developments. The first conclusion is that the production system, in the presence of non-produced means of production and raw materials, allows for a description in terms of global technologies and jointed techniques (useful in uni-periodal situations), or of composite technologies and disjointed techniques (typical of both uni-periodal and dynamic situations) that is much more complex than those represented by the standard linear and circular theories of production. The second conclusion is that the 'physical' efficiency of the production system changes, both by virtue of the greater activation of the last non-produced means of production put into operation and by reason of further non-produced means of production also put into operation. Third, technical change (a phenomenon which includes both technical progress and the choice of techniques and technologies) due to choice of techniques is dependent not only on the degree of internal efficiency of each of the single techniques available, but also on the compatibility of the structures of the various techniques, which will be put successively into operation on account of the constraints imposed by the non-produced means of production. Fourth, technical progress in the individual techniques cannot be transformed *ipso facto* into an increase in the efficiency of those technologies that use several techniques; this is due to the problems arising from the different production structures of the techniques and from the possibility that the residuals will reduce or eliminate the effects of the technical progress. Finally, the order of efficiency between non-produced means of production, established on the basis of prices-distribution criteria, might not coincide with that allowing maximum accumulation and growth. The explanatory roles of the theories of prices-distribution and production-interdependence are thus different. This leads to the necessity of integrating these theories in a more general scheme.

On these bases, at least two developments (on which I have worked elsewhere) are possible within the system of production. The first concerns the integration international trade can bring to bear on the technologies of an economic system, allowing the means of production needed to be 'reproportioned' in the most suitable way in order to take account of the structure of the technologies themselves, increasing their efficiency and means of production by reducing the residuals.

The second development concerns technical progress. The brief discussion given above reveals the complexity of this theme. If the technical progress falls on those techniques that are still inactive, the choice of techniques that follow must not only take account of the greater efficiency of the new techniques taken singly, but also of their combination with already activated techniques in order to allow better utilization of the means of production generated by previous techniques.

A similar problem arises in the event that technical progress also falls on already operative techniques. In this case, although it is clear that the internal growth rates of the various techniques will be shifted upwards, it is not in general equally possible to say that, for each t, the production and net product growth rates will also be shifted in an upward direction. This is due to the problem of the residuals associated with the structure of the various techniques.

Finally, technical progress might fall selectively on some techniques $\mathbf{A}(h)$ already in operation and not on others. If it is thought that the non-produced means of production utilized for the production of the raw material-commodity 1 can differ greatly in quality, it might also be accepted that a very specialized kind of technical progress might concern only some of the already operative production processes.

The above analysis, and what can be constructed upon it, along the lines on which I am working now, are thus very complex and allow for the determination of many cases. This is no different from reality, which is itself complex and rich in cases. And, in reality, the antagonism–coexistence between produced and non-produced means of production, between commodities and raw materials, between what is scarce and what is producible, together with the triggering effect that the various scarcities have had on technical progress, have been constants of economic history.

REFERENCES

Gantmacher, F.R. (1959) *The Theory of Matrices*, Chelsea, New York.

Leontief, W.W. (1941) *The Structure of the American Economy 1919–1929*, Harvard University Press, Cambridge, Mass.

— (1951) *The Structure of the American Economy 1919–1939*, 2nd edn, Oxford University Press, New York.

Manara, C.F. and Nicola, P.C. (1970) *Elementi di economia matematica*, 2nd edn, Viscontea, Milan.

von Neumann, J. (1945/6) 'A Model of General Equilibrium' *Review of Economic Studies*, 13, pp. 1–9. (English translation of the original published in Vienna, 1937.)

Pasinetti, L.L. (1977) *Lectures on the Theory of Production*, Macmillan, London.

— (1981) *Structural Change and Economic Growth*, Cambridge University Press, Cambridge.

Quadrio-Curzio, A. (1967) *Rendita e distribuzione in un modello economico plurisettoriale*, Giuffré, Milan.

— (1975) *Accumulazione del capitale e rendita*, Il Mulino, Bologna.

— (1978) 'Intervento', in *La tecnologia e i limiti delle risorse naturali*, Bologna Università degli Studi, Biblioteca della Facoltà di Economia e Commercio, pp. 22–8.

— (1980)'Rent, Income Distribution, Order of Efficiency and Rentability', in *Essays on the Theory of Joint Production*, ed. L.L. Pasinetti, Macmillan Press, London, pp. 218–40. (Originally published in Italian, 1977, Bologna, Il Mulino.)

— (1983) 'Primary Commodity Prices, Exhaustible Resources and International Monetary Relations: Alternative Explanations', in *Distribution, Effective Demand and International Economic Relations*, ed. J.A. Kregel, Macmillan, London, pp. 142–52.

Quadrio-Curzio, A. and Pellizzari, F. (1981) 'La teoria economica delle risorse naturali', *Energia*, 2, pp. 14–29.

Quadrio-Curzio, A. and Scazzieri, R. (1983) *Sui momenti costitutivi dell'economia politica*, Il Mulino, Bologna. Reprinted in *Giornale degli Economisti*, n.s. 43, 1984, pp. 37–76.

Sraffa, P. (1960) *Production of Commodities by Means of Commodities*, Cambridge University Press, Cambridge.

11

Production and Exchange in Theories of Price Formation and Economic Transition

KRISHNA BHARADWAJ

I INTRODUCTION

The relation between the spheres of production and exchange have been a recurrent theme in economic theory in the context of the explanation of price formation, as well as in debates among economic historians and development theorists on the role that trade plays in transforming societies. The two issues are somewhat closely related, in that the theoretical view of price formation and of the role prices play in directing economic decisions and shaping economic magnitudes also suggests the strength and efficacy that could be attributed to the influence of trade. It is attempted here to illustrate this argument by contrasting the structures of two alternative economic theories – the one proposed by classical and Marxian political economy, and the other by marginalist (neoclassical) theories. The former theory was constructed around the central concept of social surplus (whether expressed in the form of 'surplus product' or 'surplus value'), modes of its appropriation, distribution and utilization characteristic of the relevant mode of production. The marginalist economic theory, on the other hand, was constructed around the concept of market equilibrium attained by the balancing of opposite and independent, symmetrically counterposed forces of supply and demand.[1]

---

[1] It is not being suggested that there are no differences among the various contributors to either of the streams, but that a broad division may nevertheless be envisaged. It may be recalled that Marx titled his critical review of earlier classical political economy 'Theories of Surplus Value', and a broad and basic methodological and conceptual agreement among the neoclassical writers of various schools will not be challenged by its adherents, despite differences in specifications. Some neoclassical writers like Marshall would even suggest an essential continuity in theory from Adam Smith onwards, which, however, I do not share. (For a detailed exposition, see Bharadwaj, 1978a, 1978b, 1983a.)

The neoclassical theory has been criticized both by economists from the Marxist tradition and social anthropologists (for example, Polanyi, Arensberg and Pearson, 1957) for viewing, implicitly or otherwise, the price formation on competitive capitalist markets as a universal phenomenon and attributing to the notions of 'price' and 'markets' a universal and ahistorical content, generalizing thus the operation of forces of supply and demand conceptualized in the theory. It is observed in history, on the contrary, that there have been systems of exchange of the most diverse forms, displaying vastly different social formations.[2] The marginalist theory is also criticized for shifting emphasis from production to the sphere of circulation or exchange. My purpose here would be to discuss these issues in relation to the structures of the two theories.

In the following section, I attempt to bring out, historically, but only illustratively, the relation between production and exchange – that is, I view the arena of exchange and the associated notions of price as reflecting conditions under which surplus is produced, appropriated and distributed. It is, however, only the competitive capitalist mode that has been theorized most rigorously and completely in the two theories. In section III, I look comparatively at the structures of the value and distribution theory in order to interpret 'primacy of production' in the Marxian value theory and 'the shift to circulation' in the marginalist theory. The fourth and final section contains concluding observations.

II PRODUCTION AND EXCHANGE IN ECONOMIC HISTORY AND THEORY

Exchange of products and money in the form of specific commodities used as media of exchange and as units of reckoning has existed from ancient times. Speculations too about 'price' have a long history. Economists writing on the history of ideas have often been tempted to read into the common parlance ('scarcity', 'want', 'market', etc.) the primitive beginnings and initial formulations of the now-dominant supply- and demand-based explanations, the presumption being that economic theory has progressed unilinearly towards today's mainstream theory. However, another view (to be found, for example, in the works of Dobb, 1973; Sraffa, 1960), which I support here, is

[2] This is a criticism at a different level from, although related to, the forceful critique on the internal logical consistency of the marginalist theory initiated by Piero Sraffa (1926, 1960). To the extent that the ahistoricity emerges endemically, due to the structure of the theory, the two critiques complement each other.

that a significant divide occurred in economic theory when a new theory – the supply- and demand-based equilibrium theory – came to submerge and replace the earlier approach of classical political economy, whose most mature and critically advanced form was to be found in Marx (see Bharadwaj, 1978a).

Even in Marx's time it was not unusual for 'vulgar' representations[3] of theory to fail to distinguish between different kinds of exchange situations:

> We may notice two methods characteristic of the apologetic economy. The first is the identification of the circulation of commodities with direct barter of products, by simple abstraction from the point of difference; the second, is the attempt to explain away the contradictions of capitalist production by reducing the relations between the persons engaged in the mode of production to the simple relations arising out of the circulation of commodities. The production and circulation of commodities are, however, phenomena that occur to a greater or less extent in modes of production most diverse. If we are acquainted with nothing but the abstract categories of circulation which are common to all modes of production, we cannot possibly know anything of the specific points of difference of these modes, nor pronounce any judgement on them. (Marx, 1867, vol. I, p. 114, n. 1)

Social anthropologists analysing markets in history have noticed the qualitatively different characteristics of markets. Polanyi, for example, protests against treating all economies, 'as a potential supply and demand price mechanism', 'The whole of history', he writes, 'apart from the last century had different types of economies' and the *differentia specifica* lies in their not having 'price-making markets' (Polanyi, Arensberg and Pearson, 1957, p. 239). Polanyi suggests a taxonomic reconstruction based on categories of exchange organizations and institutions different from the one I intend to follow here.[4] I argue that the *extent* and the *form* of exchange, and

[3] Marx distinguished 'vulgar economy' from political economy, the former dealing 'with appearances only' (Marx, 1867, vol. I, p. 81 n.). We may note, however, that the post-1870 supply and demand theory is a complete logical construction, and no such comprehensively developed theoretical alternative was yet available in Marx's time.

[4] I do not propose to go into a detailed critique of Polanyi, whose contribution is significant. A related work of Hicks, *A Theory of Economic History* (1969) attempts to outline history in terms of gradual transformation of systems of exchange leading to the Rise of Markets, which is antecedent to Marx's Rise of Capitalism (see, for brief observations, Bharadwaj, 1978a).

hence the role that exchange can play in shaping and modifying social relations, are intimately connected with the organization of productive forces and production relations prevalent in the economy, which determine the size of social surplus, the modes of its appropriation, distribution and utilization. That the form of exchange primarily reflects the existent conditions and relations of production does not rule out the extent of market influencing the latter. Dynamically expanding markets can stimulate advances in productive forces and necessitate changes in production relations. However, trade and circulation of commodities, although a necessary condition for transforming economies, may not prove to be a sufficient one. Here I look more closely at the form that exchange-value takes. Although this account refers to historical conditions chronologically, I have chosen only some important landmarks in the analytical history of price theory, as illustrating my argument.

When property has yet to develop and techniques of harnessing nature are still primitive, exchange in the form of barter is performed directly by the producers. Use-values are exchanged for use-values, mainly to satisfy elementary needs of a primitive existence.[5] That the circulation of goods and/or of persons is the necessary component of sustaining life is reflected in the fact that primitive settlements chose river-banks or settled along trade routes, or tribal hordes moved from one region to another to exchange and more often to rob and plunder.

It is with settled agriculture that surplus arises regularly over and above subsistence. From primitive barter, commoditization grows only gradually.

> In order that the alienation [of objects] is reciprocal, it is only necessary for man, by a tacit understanding, to treat each other as private owners of these alienable objects and, by implication, as independent individuals. But such a state of reciprocal independence has no existence in a primitive society based on property in common, whether such a society takes the form of a patriarchal family, an ancient Indian community, or a Peruvian Inca state. The exchange of commodities, therefore, first begins on the boundaries of such communities, at their points of contact with other similar communities, or with members of the latter. (Marx, 1867, vol. I, p. 87)

The external commerce paves the way for internal intercourse, products becoming commodities initially in external trade and, as production expands, the surplus becomes increasingly available for internal commerce also. Although, in the barter system, it is the mutual desire to alienate products that settles the exchange as a matter of chance, the constant replication of exchange as well as establishment of regular exchanges externally to the community induces producers to produce part of the

[5] The articles that are bartered are not yet commodities, but become so only by the act of barter.

produce for exchange. The distinction between use-value and exchange-value emerges clearly. Use-values, however, continue to motivate production predominantly at this stage, when conditions of production are still primitive and private property in land and labour yet to be established.

In the slave-based production system of Graeco-Roman times, surplus was commanded primarily as a tribute by the aristocratic ruling classes, with slaves provisioned and maintained in the way that cattle were. Slaves were themselves a commodity, purchased and sold. External trade was basically confined to satisfying the needs of the ruling classes – procuring slaves and luxury goods. A gradation of commodities and wants naturally emerged, and also a recognition that the price of traded goods was dependent upon the relation between 'wants', on the one hand, and 'scarcity', on the other, reference to which occurs frequently in Graeco-Roman writings. That exchange and valuation are confined to particular kinds of commodities is evident from the fact that 'scarcity' is interpreted in terms of physical availability of specific goods, and no explicit analysis of costs is brought in. Plato writes, 'Only what is rare is valuable, and water which is the best of all things is also the cheapest' (quoted in Bowley, 1973, p. 66). The water-diamond paradox was already noted by Plato and others.[6] Aristotle noted the existence of value in use and value in exchange, pointing out that the value of anything is determined according to men's need to use it (see *Ethics*, IX), but no further discussion regarding the separate bases for the two concepts was explored, nor was the need-determined *value* identified with either.[7] Thus neither was 'scarcity' linked with 'relative costs', nor 'use' with utility. It is thus far-fetched to read into these references to 'scarcity' and need 'a realization of the obvious fact that demand and supply, usually stated in terms of use and scarcity provide an explanation of actual exchange value' (Bowley, 1973, p. 66).

Further, in the slave society, with its natural basis founded 'on the inequality of men and their labour powers', as Marx observes, labour could not be conceived yet as a 'value-forming substance' (Marx, 1867, vol. I, pp. 59–60). Aristotle, though extending the barter between two commodities to the general form of transactions in money, fails to reach the basis of exchange; he merely comments that exchanges involve equality between

---

[6] For example, Sextus Empiricus, in the second century AD (quoted in Bowley, 1973, p. 66).

[7] As Bowley observes: 'No new words were introduced to distinguish between the inherent capacity of a good for satisfying some requirement, its use value and its exchange value' (1973, p. 66). No attempt was made to relate the two concepts analytically: in writings of later classical political economy, it was recognized that although the use-value is a necessary condition for a commodity to possess exchange-value, it does not determine the level of exchange-value. The paradox was thought to be resolved in marginalist theory by differentiating between total and marginal utility.

commensurable quantities. A deeper analysis into the basis of exchange-value would have presupposed already the existence of a society with the greater bulk of its production produced for exchange and the social division of labour widened sufficiently, signifying interdependence among producers.

The first important speculations on the notion of exchange and price formation appear in the discussions of the schoolmen of the twelfth and thirteenth centuries, the writing of St Thomas Aquinas (1224–74) being one of the principal sources. After the disintegration of the Roman Empire, the early medieval economy of Europe had gradually receded into land-locked, largely self-sufficient, small communities, where production was mainly for subsistence (see Pirenne, 1936). Although surplus product was appropriated by the ruling feudal classes and the Church, there was no extended production for exchange.

> The medieval peasant produced quit-rent-corn for his feudal lord and tithe-corn for his parson. But neither the quit-rent-corn nor tithe-corn became commodities by reason of the fact that they had been produced for others. To become a commodity a product must be transferred to another, whom it will serve as a use-value, by means of exchange. (Engels's explanatory footnote in Marx, 1867, vol. I, p. 41, n. 1)

Trade in luxuries and other commodities, particularly to satisfy the needs of the ruling classes, developed around medieval towns and cities and at regularly held fairs, carried on by itinerant traders and Jews (Pirenne, 1936). However, in the early medieval period, both usury and trader's profits were frowned upon and ethically condemned, although even by Aquinas's time the need of exchange and credit as a stimulant to productive activity was gradually being acknowledged. Manufactures were produced mainly by artisans and craftsmen, who owned their own means of production and carried out their own exchange. The predominant concern of such a society, where surpluses are generated by a few producers and where internal exchange has already developed, although to a limited extent, is the needs of social reproduction. The 'just price', an ethical notion, was advanced as a price that enables social reproduction, bringing to the various producers a return that is adequate to pay for their costs and efforts.

Some aspects of the 'just price' need to be noted. First, it was based on the objective conditions and requirements of production, rather than on 'need'. Unlike in the slave society, the direct producers were also the owners of the means of production, although the surplus that remained with them, if at all, for disposal on market was what remained after the deductions due to feudal rents, tithes and such like impositions and levies by the ruling classes had been made. Secondly, the 'just price' was fixed by *Communis aestimatio*, that is, 'by the common opinions of the well-informed body of buyers or sellers' so as to cover the needs of social reproduction. 'Forestalling, regrating, engrossing' were condemned as unfair advantages extracted by particular individuals in privileged positions in production or trade. Thirdly, the components of just price reveal the nature of costs permitted to be included, reflecting, in turn, the prevalent production relations. Apart from costs of material inputs, all reckoned at their respective customary or just price, provision had to be made for the various services (concrete labour services), which had to be paid their legitimate rewards, determined by custom and tradition, and which were seen mainly as providing them for their customary levels of living. Labour services appear therefore in their concrete forms and the hierarchy within the social system determines the parameters of distribution. Fourthly, it was recognized that actual market prices deviate from the 'just price' and such deviations were frowned upon when arising, particularly when due to trader's 'profits upon alienation'. The Christian concept of justice initially disallowed such profiteering. However, already by the time of Aquinas, assuaging conditions were provided to legitimize traders' profits when 'the trader has improved the thing in some way', or 'the price has changed with a change of place and time' or when the trader undertakes risks. However, we see no systematic discussion of the relation between just price and market price. Nor do we find any attempt to theorize about distributive relations – whether to explain wage differentials or to explain the relation between wages and the trader's profits or rents, etc.

In the later medieval period, trading, earlier confined to isolated centres and occasional fairs, etc., grew, reflecting also the growing commoditization of production. As trading secured greater acceptance, particularly in England, the mercantilist system came to dominate, and traders increased the surplus at their command and extended the arena of exchange internationally as well as internally. In fact, sustenance of accelerated trade necessitated closer controls on production and surplus appropriation. A regime of regulations – strict labour management with labour tied to land, controls over wages and prices, controls over commodity movements, strict control by guilds over manufactures and skilled labour, and regulations both on internal and external commerce – prevailed.[8] We see, during this period, the return of a concern for the state of market and of the explanations of prices based on counterposing 'needs' with 'scarcity'. The seventeenth-century writings on value (by Malynes, Misselden and Mun, for example) discuss pricing, mainly prompted by policy questions in relation to monetary problems and foreign trade, the concern being the relevance of the need–scarcity view of price to the foreign exchange rate.[9]

[8] See, for an absorbing account of economic conditions and policies of the period, Wesley Mitchell (1967).

[9] See M. Bowley (1973) for a brief discussion; also, Schumpeter (1954).

The earlier mercantile concern with the acquisition of as much specie as possible or excessive obsession with export surplus to be achieved through restrictive trade policies was being moderated by arguing for the free play of market forces. Coming at the end of the seventeenth century, Barbon's *Discourse of Trade* marks the high point in the theoretical position: Barbon (1905; 1st edn 1690) stresses that 'the Value of all Wares arise from their Use' (p. 13), but depends upon the 'Difference betwixt the Occasion and the Quantity' (that is, 'the occasion or use for them' (p. 15) and 'the Quantity to serve that Occasion' (p. 15)). He also declared 'the Market is the best Judge of Value' (p. 20). Barbon's discussion of wants, with their classification into physiological and psychical needs, 'Individual Appetites' and aspirations has induced some writers to see an early Jevons in him. There was, however, not much effort made to go behind 'Quantity to serve the Occasion' and the 'Occasion' itself, apart from taxonomically classifying wants of different kinds. Thus the 'demand' and 'supply' sides of the argument are not analysed. The emphasis on the market, rather than on the conditions of production, appears to have been impelled by opposition to mercantilist restrictions and regulations on the market, which were proving counterproductive by restraining the growing forces of production, particularly in manufacture. The feudal regime in agriculture too was already disintegrating.

Very soon, however, attention was to revert to real conditions of production; Sir William Petty was one of the first to do so, and Marx associates the beginnings of scientific political economy in England with Petty.[10] Petty was to focus on the land and labour content of production, and emphasize 'objective' as opposed to 'subjective' considerations, as a part of his overall method.

> The Method is not very usual for instead of using only Comparative and Superlative Words and Intellectual Arguments, I have taken the course to express myself in terms of Number, Weight or Measure, to use only Arguments of sense and to consider only such causes as have Visible Foundations in Nature; leaving those that depend upon the mutable minds, Opinions, Appetites, Passions of particular Men to the consideration of Others. (Petty, 1899, vol. I, p. 244)

Following this view, Petty's work concentrated on detailed quantitative analysis of material conditions of production. He constructed the first national product accounts. He also defined 'natural price' in terms of the real resource content of land and labour, differentiating it from 'political'

[10] Meek (1956, p. 18) writes: 'The writers of the time, broadly speaking, were the spokesmen of the merchant manufacturers and parvenue industrial capitalists of the town whose increasing concern with production costs was indicative of far-reaching changes which were taking place in the organization of production'.

price, which was affected by temporary circumstances and interventions from political authority.

It is in Cantillon (1755), however, that we find a systematic attempt to present interrelations between production, appropriation and utilization of surplus produced in agriculture, a preview of the physiocratic depiction of commodity circulation within the economy. With the entire surplus accruing to the landed proprietors, Cantillon analysed the growth of artisan production and manufacture, leading to the formation of towns and cities, and influencing population, and the entire demand provided by the surplus-appropriating landed proprietors. Cantillon was the first to analyse social consumption on the basis of class-based patterns of consumption; he was also the first to analyse the 'subsistence' wages required to feed the worker, his wife and two children in terms of the constituents of the wage basket and thus gave a concrete meaning to historically 'given wage'.

Cantillon also introduced the concept of 'intrinsic price' of a commodity, measured by 'the quantity of land and of labour entering into its production having regard to the fertility or produce of the land and to the quality of labour', and clearly distinguished it from 'market price', which fluctuated, depending upon 'Humours and Fancies of men and their consumption'. Taking the cue from Petty, he also attempted to establish a par between land and labour by considering labour to be paid a fixed subsistence wage, which he then attempted to reduce ultimately into the land required to produce it. Two features of his analysis, which continue in that of the Physiocrats, stand out. The attempt to identify stable material conditions of production as 'normal', on which to base the definition of material costs, differentiating it from temporary fluctuations; and secondly, the identification of surplus as net product, after considering consumption of direct producers as 'productive consumption' and viewing the economy as a reproductive process, producing and circulating the surplus.

The Physiocrats gave a more rigorous form to the circulation of commodities within a reproductive cycle. They emphasized the *produit net* (net product) as a central concept. The various components of the commodity circuits were identified: 'advances' forming the capital, and the intersectoral demands (such as the consumption of the sterile sector's products by the proprietors, and consumption requirements of the productive workers). The social division into classes was based directly on production and appropriation of surplus: those who produced surplus – and, in their case, they considered agriculture alone as generating surplus – were called 'productive' class. The appropriators of surplus also were included in the productive class as proprietors. The workers in industry were considered as not contributing to surplus and called 'sterile'. However erroneous or limited their view of attributing surplus only to agriculture, they derived consistently therefrom their social-class divisions and their policy prescription of imposing a single tax on rents. Given the dominance of feudal land relations of the time, and the fact that industry mainly depended on agriculture for providing consumption to workers and raw-material inputs, as well as for demand for its product from the proprietory class, this emphasis on agriculture is not surprising. However, capitalist relations were already rising and trade too was active. One of the physiocratic concerns was how to ensure a *bon prix* (fair price) for agricultural produce at a time when contradictions in the feudal set-up were deepening, the agrarian conditions were fast deteriorating and the agricultural practices were degenerating. The fair price (as well as the flows in the *Tableau Economique*) were reckoned on the basis of average, viable, reproductive conditions, making reasonable allowance for wages, rents and other service payments. This method of taking the 'dominantly observed' or 'optimum' methods of production as the benchmark to define a price appears to have been followed in later constructions of the natural price or prices of production. The actual prices, it was recognized, carried the effects of the various regulations and restrictions imposed by the state, the Church, the feudal authorities on movements of goods and persons, and the multiple levies in terms of taxes, tithes, etc. In policy, the Physiocrats supported, on the one hand, the clarion call of the merchant Vincent de Gournay for *laissez-faire*, the uninterfered play of free markets, which it was hoped would create a free environment for productive forces in agriculture to grow, and, on the other, they argued in favour of the *impôt unique* (the single tax) on rents to replace all the vexatious impositions on labour and direct producers. At the time that the Physiocrats wrote, feudalism was already disintegrating, and the peculiar oddities and contradictions in their analysis[11] are best captured by Marx when he describes them to be:

> contradictions of capitalist production as it works its way out of feudal society, and interprets feudal society itself only in a bourgeois way, but has not yet discovered its own peculiar form. ... Hence also, in the conclusions which physiocrats themselves draw, the ostensible veneration of landed property becomes transformed into the economic negation of it and the affirmation of capitalist production. (Marx, 1862–3, p. 52)

Adam Smith's *Wealth of Nations* (1776) broke new ground. It was the first systematic and comprehensive work to lay down the analytical categories in political economy pertaining to the capitalist mode of production. It would be no exaggeration to say that the later discourses on the subject followed the elaboration, rigorous derivation and critical extensions of the questions raised in his seminal work. Adam Smith recorded the rise of capitalism in first recognizing capitalist profits as an independent revenue

---

[11] See Meek (1963) and Marx (1862–3, vol. I, pp. 44–68) for a detailed discussion.

category, and expressly distinguishing it from rents or 'superior wages' or 'profits upon alienation'. He identified the tendency towards a uniform rate of profit as an outcome of the pursuit of profit maximization by competing producers under the force of free competition; he also recognized labour, as an abstract category whose productive use, enhanced by the division of labour, formed the source of the wealth of a nation. He classified different kinds of capital, different components of the cost of production, and defined 'effectual demand' as the normal position of social demand, whose level and composition was determined by customs, tradition, etc. affecting consumptions by the various classes in the society.

A clear analytical distinction was made by Smith between the natural position of an economic variable – the one conceived in terms of the action of stable and permanent forces – and 'temporary', 'market' values attained by it when accidental and momentary forces intervened. Thus he defined the natural price as the one which 'is neither more nor less than what is sufficient to pay the rent of the land, the wages of the labour, and the profits of stock employed in raising, preparing and bringing to the market, according to their natural rates', and stated that 'the natural price . . . is, as it were, the central price, to which the prices of all commodities are continually gravitating' (Smith, 1776, p. 58). Given the effectual demand, and given the methods of production and the 'natural' distributive rates of revenue, the natural price was sufficient to cover the material costs of production and the revenues to land, labour and capital. (Smith was also the first one to formulate the tripartite division of distributive classes.)

Smith emphasized the role of labour and analysed the reinvestible surplus available for accumulation in terms of the differential between productivity of labour and its maintenance, later conceptualized and developed by Marx into surplus labour. He advanced the proposition that relative values in exchange of products are determined by the labour embodied in them, at the 'early and rude' stage of society, before capital is accumulated and land is appropriated. Thereafter, however, the relevant price was conceived as the 'natural price'. Smith included rent in natural price and held that it was resolvable ultimately into wages, profits and rents; this suggests that he adhered to the 'adding up view' of prices – the one to be criticized by Ricardo later – that the rates of profits, wages and rents were *all* determined independently of each other, and the natural price therefore was reached by adding up these separately and independently determined revenues.[12]

Ricardo began by being critical of Smith's theory of profit as determined by 'competitions of capital', and he opposed the 'additive view'. Ricardo's

[12] Smith held apparently contradictory opinions, which have given rise to conflicting claims by the marginalist- as well as the surplus-based theories on Smith as the progenitor. For a detailed critique of these issues see Bharadwaj (1979).

central concern remained the theory of profit. He built up his surplus-based explanation of profit through successive stages;[13] he first explicated it through the 'corn rate of profit' in his *Essay on Profits* (1815), where, using the Malthusian theory of rent and of population, he demonstrated the inverse relation between the share of rents and the rate of profit by using a simple corn example. The determination of profit was then generalized to the more complex multi-basics[14] economy with the help of the labour theory of value, which he enunciated rigorously for the first time. The results, which he sought to establish in the theory of profit, were mainly that, given the output level and composition, and the methods of production, the rate of profit moves inversely with the share of wages in net product. The labour theory of value, if rigorously applicable, afforded Ricardo to establish that proposition unambiguously, as the heterogeneous aggregates that entered the profit-rate determination[15] could all then be expressed in homogeneous labour magnitudes. Ricardo, however, realized that relative values tended to deviate from labour values, and sought to explain these deviations, which he saw in the context of a changing wage, in terms of the different structures of material inputs and labour use of different products. Ricardo attempted to evolve the device of an invariant standard to handle these deviations in his theory of profit, but without success. His demonstration of the rate of profit determination remained confined to the case of all capital reducible to wages, although he suggested routes by which a solution could be attempted.

The opposition to Ricardian theory, particularly to his conclusions on distribution, was already building up during the last days of his brief career. Ricardo's followers, who were not to confront the analytical intricacies of Ricardo's later efforts, resorted to a mechanical and simplistic assertion of labour theory, on the one hand, and eroded Ricardo's theory of profit and the surplus-based structure of his theory, on the other. (See Bharadwaj, 1983a, 1983b.) They introduced modifications and reformulations, which were not only analytically unconvincing, but departed from Ricardo's basic approach. A state of confusion arose in theory, which explains the seemingly paradoxical developments. Marshall, who estab-

---

[13] See, Bharadwaj (1983a, 1983b) for a detailed exposition.

[14] A basic commodity is one that enters directly or indirectly in the production of all others (see Sraffa, 1960).

[15] Ricardo worked on the basis of the following formula:

$$r = \frac{\text{Social net product} - \text{Wages}}{\text{Social Capital}}$$

All the three magnitudes on the right-hand side are aggregates with heterogeneous composition.

lished, among others, the new marginalist theory, claimed continuity with Ricardo (see Bharadwaj, 1978b), whereas Marx, forewarned by the deviant directions that Ricardianism had taken, critically restated and interpreted the labour theory of value within the surplus approach. Marx was the first to define prices of production in a capitalist economy within an interdependent, multi-sector framework. We turn to a closer examination of the structure of this theory in the following section. Ricardo's theory was developed mainly in the context of a historical juncture, when the main conflict of interest was between 'landlords' and 'the rest of the society', although the capital–labour relation was emerging into focus, as evinced in the 'machinery problem'. Marx spelt out the full implications of the capitalist mode of production, its historical emergence as well as its 'laws of motion'. The critical feature of the capitalist mode, to Marx, was the labour-power becoming a commodity as a culmination of a historical process by which labour becomes 'free' in a double sense – 'free of the means of production and of sustenance' and freed of personalized feudal bonds. Generalized commodity production under competitive conditions implies that exchange is carried out on 'equivalent' terms – no exploitation can occur on markets. Marx's purpose, then, was to explain the source of surplus (and hence of profits) under such conditions. While, in the sphere of exchange, 'Bentham, Equality and Property' rule, it is in the sphere of production, in the control that the capitalist possesses as owner of the means of production, including the labour-power purchased by him, that the surplus can be generated. It is the surplus value (that is, the difference between productivity of labour and the necessary wage) that is realized as profits in circulation. Marx thus tried to explain not only the level of profits, but also its source. Using the concepts of relative and absolute surplus value to explain the source and variations in the level of surplus value, he acknowledged that profits are actually realized only in circulation. He also was fully aware that the exchange value of commodities deviated from labour values and developed, in the context of an interdependent production system, the notion of 'prices of production'. Probably forewarned by the confusions Ricardo had created amongst his followers by trying to deal simultaneously with labour values and values (meaning prices), Marx approached the problem in a two-stage analysis. He analysed first the factors influencing the rate and mass of surplus value, the relation between wages and the rate of surplus value, etc., concentrating on the arena of the shop floor, where the capital–labour relation could be kept directly under view. However, since it was profits that were realized and the prices of production that were 'observed', he attempted to 'transform' 'surplus value into profits and values into prices', thence to show that the theoretical results and analytical relations obtained more perceptibly and easily using value analysis continue to hold after the transformation.

The early 1870s mark a turning point in economic theory. Opposition to classical political economy had already gathered strength, and a new theoretical framework of marginalist theory was constructed by Jevons, Marshall, Walras and Menger. This attempt at a new construction appeared in the form of a more cogent explanation of relative prices – the labour theory along with the surplus approach thus abandoned due to its theoretical weakness. The primary aim, however, was to alter radically the view concerning distribution – particularly the explanation of profits.[16]

These alternative theories attempt to explain relative prices as formed at the equilibrium between opposite, symmetrical forces of demand and supply. Furthermore, 'land', 'labour' and 'capital' are viewed as primary resources with their own respective factor-markets, and the rates of revenue they obtain are likewise determined by demand for and supply of the factors. Thus a perfect symmetry obtains among all the factors regarding their placement in the process of production and an identical explanation of their revenues.

The forces of demand and supply are generated by the optimizing behaviour of individual producers and consumers. A certain symmetry characterizes the behaviour of both: each individual producer, given the technological transformation possibilities, chooses the profit-maximizing set of outputs at the going prices; similarly, each consumer, given a budget constraint and a scale of preferences, maximizes his satisfaction at the going prices. Thus the data of the system are the initial endowments and their distribution among individuals, technology and preferences of individuals. All these elements have, of course, been variously specified by different schools in the neoclassical tradition.

A cardinal notion for the theory is the principle of substitution, which is expected to give the system the resilience to generate the appropriate quantity–price relations. A relative cheapening of a factor induces producers to adopt methods making intensive use of it, and consumers to buy products that are produced with greater intensity in that factor. The combined consequence of such substitution is expected to generate an inverse relation between the return to the factor and its intensity of use.[17] Given the availabilities of factors and their distribution, preferences and technology, under certain conditions imposed upon the last-mentioned, the existence of an equilibrium yielding 'market-clearing' prices for factors and commodities is sought to be established under the theory.[18] The new

---

[16] One may note that it is the theory of profits on which theories have been constructed or have floundered in the analysis of capitalism.

[17] Recent capital theory debates have established that such an inverse relation between capital intensity and rate of profit cannot be logically sustained.

[18] Although the existence of such an equilibrium has been proved for the pure exchange model, difficulties arise for the model when capitalist production is brought into consideration.

theory thus erected is not a mere modification, but a radical departure from classical theories.

III THE NATURE OF MARKETS AND THE FORM THAT 'PRICE' TAKES

Looking at the structure of the two theories, we may here attempt to interpret and clarify, in this narrower context of the theory of price formation, the notion of a shift to circulation in the neoclassical theory. At the outset, we may note that both Marx's prices of production and the neoclassical normal equilibrium prices refer to the 'long period' positions in a competitive capitalist economy, where competition ensures the active operation of tendencies towards uniform profit rate and uniform wage. The tripartite division of revenues – profits, wages and rents – are common to both, although it is the first two that usually enter into the price. Both schema presuppose generalized commodity production, with each commodity having a unique price. Both schema also conceive of an interdependent multi-commodity production structure.

As already seen, prices of production in Marx are derived under the uniformity of the rate of profits, given social demand ('effectual demand' in Smith's sense), the dominant observed methods of production and the historically determined wage. Although the single 'natural' or 'long-run' position is so defined, Marx not only acknowledges, but analyses the interaction among these elements (that is, demand, technology and distribution) outside the 'core' of his theory. (See Bharadwaj, 1978a, 1978b; Garegnani, 1984.) The interdependence is seen not merely to act through the price-forming market forces, but to have a wider social arena. Given a circular view of social reproduction, where commodities are produced by means of commodities, unlike the one-way avenue of neoclassical theory, beginning from primary factors and ending up with consumption or final goods (see Sraffa, 1960), there is a two-way relation between production and consumption. Although consumption motivates production ultimately, the form and content of consumption is influenced by production – the availability of commodities in a specific form sets the pattern and content of consumption. 'Supply' and 'demand' cannot be conceived of as mutually independent forces. As Marx observes (1857–8, pp. 88–94), production produces the 'consumer' himself, not only by furnishing the object of consumption, giving it a specific character, but shaping the composition of social consumption, which depends upon the class-based distribution of incomes, with the character of consumption of individuals significantly linked with the social class they belong to. On the other hand, 'the extent of the market', as Smith argued, stimulates technological developments through the division of labour and, given increasing returns to scale, this stimulus can bring about rapid changes in techniques and productivity.

Demand acts here not so much through price effects as via production (see Allyn Young, 1928).

Similarly, the pace of accumulation – growth of output – does affect wage, which is also dependent upon the state of organization of the working class, capitalists' strategies, the size and composition of the reserve army of labour (that is, the unemployed seeking work), etc. The level of the wage, in turn, does influence the capitalists' strategies of adopting methods of production, although again it may not be the only consideration. In analysing the rapid and significant changes that occurred in technology, the labour–capital relations and the pace of output growth during the eighteenth and nineteenth centuries, Marx brings out these interactions as they were observed to operate historically (1867, vol. I).

In the Marxian view, the relations of exchange – the extent and the specific form that exchange takes – are primarily a manifestation of the conditions of production and production relations. As we have seen, the nature of markets and the form that 'price' takes depends upon the extant property relations; the notion of wage labour can arise only under capitalist conditions. Further, the intensity of exchange and its extent also depends upon the development of productive forces. In history, although trade between communities occurred sparsely and in limited number and kind of commodities, it was only when the productive forces were accelerated within the economy that internal commerce could grow and make a larger and wider surplus produce available for external commerce as well. The availability and extensive variety and range of use-values for exchange presupposes a well-developed social division of labour, and sufficiently diversified and large effective demand. This, however, is not to rule out the mutual interaction between exchange and production: as already noted, the 'extent of market' does provide a stimulus to production. How far such a stimulus is absorbed and succeeds in bringing about changes in production, however, depends upon the organization and relations of production. Further, commerce cannot exist autonomously. How far the pace of growing commerce can be sustained is crucially dependent upon the stable and regular availability of exchangeable surplus produce and sustained demand. The medieval city economies that forged ahead on the strength of their being centres of trade could not continue their expansion, as the hinterland dried up of tradeable surpluses. To acquire dominance in trade itself, as shown in history, the trading society needed to have material backing to develop supremacy in technology of transport and, quite frequently, superiority in military capability.

There appears to be a reason, however, why exchange, although primarily supported and constrained by the real conditions of production, nevertheless 'leads an antidiluvian existence' as an economic category, particularly under capitalism. As production for exchange extends generally, circulation of commodities increasingly takes an abstract and seemingly independent form, as though diverted from conditions of production. When commodity production and social division of labour are so generalized as to draw the producers into a closely knit, interdependent network, where producers face a price generated by the seemingly autonomous market forces, the circulation of commodities appears to assume the role of the dominant character.[19] It may appear then that the key to the changes in production and distribution is to be found entirely in the 'market'.

In another way, this high degree of interdependence manifests itself in a paradoxical appearance. It is only in such a historical epoch that personalized relations in production cease and the individual 'individuates' himself. It is this 'freeing' of the individual to participate on markets as an apparently autonomous decision-making entity that gives market relations a primary significance, concealing the underlying production relations. This occurs precisely when the social interdependence is most advanced. Marx, too, acknowledges that 'labour-power' becomes a commodity. But it does so, due to the labourer acquiring, through a historical process, 'double freedom'. He is also freed of the means of production and sustenance, so that he is now in possession of a peculiar commodity (labour-power), to sustain and produce which, he has to alienate it; for the labour-power resides in the labourer, and in order to produce it, he has to maintain *himself*, in a situation where he no more possesses his own means. The sphere, 'within whose boundaries the sale and purchase of labour-power goes on, is in fact a very Eden of the innate rights of man. These alone rule Freedom, Equality, Property and Bentham' (Marx, 1867, vol. I, p. 176). It is on leaving the sphere, on the shop floor where production takes place, that the real capital–labour relations are perceived.

In focusing on market relations, the supply- and demand-based theories drew a certain inspiration from these apparent manifestations of capitalist relations. First, the sphere of exchange (circulation) is presented as the one where the community is in action, as an aggregate, in the form of price-determining collective demand and supply relations, while all production and consumption decisions are deemed to be taken by free, autonomous and isolated individuals, on the basis of their individual optimization. Further, an all-comprehensive role is given to relative prices, which determine not only the levels and composition of consumption and production, but also distribution, which is subsumed within the same process of price determination. Consequently a symmetry is introduced – and an apparent harmony of interests – among the various revenue classes. As we know, in classical political economy, rents, profits and wages are explained on

---

[19] Marx begins *Capital* with the opening sentence: 'The wealth of those societies in which the capitalist mode of production prevails, presents itself as "an immense accumulation of commodities", its unit being a single commodity. Our investigation must therefore begin with the analysis of a commodity' (1867, vol. I, p. 35).

different principles, and the laws of distribution are not sought to be found in the determination of values of individual commodities. Rather, the exchange values of individual commodities are posited to be such as to be consistent with the particular way in which surplus is being distributed among the surplus sharers within the mode of production under study. Also, in the neoclassical theory, since collective supply and demand relations, aggregated over individual supplies and demands, are supposed to determine equilibrium prices, aided by the effective operation of the principle of substitution, leading to appropriate price–quantity adjustments, no room is left for the direct intervention by social classes as such. This is a particularly strong omission in the case of distribution. 'Social relations between men assume the fantastic form of relations between things.'

In such a framework, the vehicle of change is the market, and all changes are to be explained in terms of 'well-behaved' price–quantity responses in production, consumption and in quantities of factors demanded and supplied. It is in this sense that a shift to circulation (exchange) has occurred in the neoclassical theory, from an earlier emphasis on production, appropriation and distribution of surplus in the surplus-based theories.

IV SPECIFICATIONS OF CAPITALIST EXCHANGE

In the previous section we have been concerned with the relation between exchange and production, in the context of price formation under competitive capitalist conditions. This is the arena where economic theory has largely been engaged and where rigorous results are sought. We may briefly remark here on the directions in which advances are being attempted, and where the focus on specifications of production and exchange conditions is different from the one under competitive premisses.

One of the 'internal contradictions' of the capitalist mode that Marx emphasized is the tendency towards concentration and centralization of capital, which accompanies advances of technology and the growth of credit and finance. Although the basic features of capitalism still remain, the monopoly phase sets in – a prognostication which has indeed come true. A consequence of this for the production–exchange relation in the theory of price formation is to be found in the introduction of 'market power' that the monopolist or oligopolist enjoys to varying degrees, depending upon the structure of the market, as contrasted with the premiss of 'equivalent exchange' under competition. A number of theories of price formation under alternative assumptions concerning market structures and market strategies have been proposed.[20] A serious shortcoming of these is that the micro-level models are still to be satisfactorily integrated into macro, system-level analysis; thus, macro-foundations still remain to be provided. Secondly, since the focus of discourse has been shifted to market conditions – the state and the structure of market – faced by individual producers, the theory of price formation stands severed from the theory of distribution. No explanation obtains for distribution between wages and profits, or for the intra-capitalist distribution of profits. One noteworthy exception to this is to be found in the writings of Kalecki, where an attempt at an integration is made.

Another area of theoretical research in which specifications of capitalist exchange have received a prominent role is in the context of 'developing economies' of the 'Third World' today. It has been argued that the economically laggard, poor countries who suffer from a colonial past have been drawn into the orbit of the international capitalist exchange network, which is dominated by the rich advanced capitalist countries. 'Unequal exchange' ensues between them, widening the differentials further so that 'underdevelopment' may be seen as an integral counterpart of 'development';[21] the former is an inescapable consequence of, as well as an essential condition for the latter. This view of development, propounded by Emmanuel, Gunder Frank, Samir Amin and others, and inspired mainly by the experience of the Latin American countries, emphasizes the crucial role of exchange (trade and market relation) in shaping the structure and pace of development.[22] However, such a view, focusing primarily on trade and exchange relations, tends to underestimate the role played by conditions and relations of production specific to particular economies and the historical differences among the ex-colonial countries.[23] It is easily noticed that colonial policies and forms of exploitation varied from country to country, and from one phase to another, depending upon the level and structure of development of both the ruling as well as the ruled country. Further, the repercussions which particular colonial policies entailed on the structure, pace and direction of development of the colony crucially

---

[20] For early discussions and contributions to 'imperfect competition', see American Economic Association (1953, section V). Among Marxists, a pioneering study was undertaken by Baran and Sweezy (1966). Many game theoretic models have been constructed to introduce a variety of postulates concerning objectives and various specifications of constraints and feasible alternative strategies.

[21] See, for example. Emmanuel (1972) and, for a critique, among others, Bharadwaj (1984a).

[22] The issues raised have a family resemblance to the Dobb–Sweezy debate on transition from feudalism to capitalism (see Hilton, 1978), where the major point at issue was whether trade provided a necessary and sufficient condition for the transition.

[23] It must be forewarned that neither the 'forces of production' nor 'production relation' are to be treated as purely 'economic' determinants. See Heilbroner (1980, pp. 64–7) and Engels (1890, quoted in Heilbroner, 1980, p. 66).

depended upon its extant conditions and relations of production and internal exchange. Thus, although they share many common features of 'underdevelopment' and of linkages with the advanced capitalist countries, the 'Third World' countries differ markedly in their economic and social structure and, more particularly, reveal significant differences in the dynamics of economic responses to external factors.

It is this question of identifying the peculiarities of production and exchange processes at work and their dynamic outcomes that a number of recent studies in Indian agriculture have taken up.[24] Emphasis is put on the class-differentiation of the peasantry, and the nature of extant production relations determining the nature and extent of the exchange involvement of the different classes. Any external intervention (like the induction of commercialization into the economy by the state) stimulates differential responses in the situation and generates different patterns of dynamics for different agrarian classes. It is on the basis of the concrete conditions under which surplus is produced, appropriated and distributed that the dynamic interaction between production and exchange is attempted to be worked out. It is in this sense that the surplus-based approach appears to find a resurgence here.

REFERENCES

American Economic Association (1953) *Readings in Price Theory,* Allen and Unwin, London, section V, pp. 361–466.

Baran, P.A. and Sweezy, P.M. (1966) *Monopoly Capital*, Monthly Review Press, New York and London.

Barbon, N. (1905) *A Discourse of Trade* (1st edn 1690), edited with introduction by J.H. Hollander, Lord Baltimore Press, Baltimore.

Bhaduri, A. (1983) *The Economic Structure of Backward Agriculture*, Academic Press, London.

Bharadwaj, K. (1974) *Production Conditions in Indian Agriculture: A Study based on Farm Management Surveys*, Cambridge University Press, Cambridge.

— (1978a) *Classical Political Economy and Rise to Dominance of Supply and Demand Theories*, R.C. Dutt Lectures, 1976; Longman Orient, Calcutta.

— (1978b) 'The Subversion of Classical Analysis; Alfred Marshall's Early Writing on Value', *Cambridge Journal of Economics*, 2, pp. 253–71.

— (1979) 'The Historical Conditioning of Theory – A Study of Adam Smith's Political Economy', *Studies in History*, January–June, pp. 45–73.

— (1983a) 'On a Controversy over Ricardo's Theory of Distribution', *Cambridge Journal of Economics*, 7, pp. 11–36.

[24] Although there is a voluminous literature on this subject, illustrative reference could be made to Bhaduri (1983) and Bharadwaj (1974, 1984b).

— (1983b) 'Ricardian Theory and Ricardianism', *Contributions to Political Economy*, 2, pp. 49–77.
— (1984a) 'A Note on Emmanuel's Unequal Exchange', *Economic and Political Weekly*, 28 July, pp. PE 81–7.
— (1984b) 'A View of Commercialization in Indian Agriculture and Development of Capitalism', mimeo, to appear in *Journal of Peasant Studies*.
Bowley, M. (1973) *Studies in the History of Economic Theory before 1870*, Macmillan, London.
Cantillon, R. (1755) *Essai sur La Nature du Commerce en Général*, ed. H. Higgs, 1931; reprinted Augustus M. Kelley, New York, 1964.
Dobb, M.H. (1946) *Studies in the Development of Capitalism*, Routledge and Kegan Paul, London.
— (1973) *Theories of Value and Distribution since Adam Smith*, Cambridge University Press, Cambridge.
Emmanuel, A. (1972) *Unequal Exchange: A Study in the Imperialism of Trade*, Monthly Review Press, New York.
Garegnani, P. (1984) 'Value and Distribution in the Classical Economists and Marx', *Oxford Economic Papers*, 36, pp. 291–325.
Heilbroner, R.L. (1980) *Marxism: For and Against*, W.W. Norton, London.
Hicks, J.R. (1969) *A Theory of Economic History*, Oxford University Press, Oxford.
Hilton, R. (ed.) (1978) *The Transition from Feudalism to Capitalism*, Verso, London.
Kula, W. (1962) *An Economic Theory of the Feudal System*, New Left Books, London.
Lopez, R.S. (1976) *The Commercial Revolution of the Middle Ages, 950–1350*, Cambridge University Press, Cambridge.
Marx, K. (1857–8) *Grundrisse: Introduction to the Critique of Political Economy*, Pelican, London, 1973.
— (1862–3) *Theories of Surplus Value*, pt I, Progress Publishers, Moscow, 1963.
— (1867) *Capital: A Critique of Political Economy*, vol. I, Progress Publishers, Moscow, 1965.
Meek, R.L. (1956) *Studies in the Labour Theory of Value*, Lawrence and Wishart, London.
— (1963) *The Economics of Physiocracy*, Harvard University Press, Cambridge, Mass.
Mitchell, W. (1967) *Types of Economic Theory*, ed. Joseph Dorfman, Augustus M. Kelley, New York.
Petty, W. (1662–76) *The Economic Writings*, republished in C.H. Hull (ed.) (1899) *The Economic Writings of Sir William Petty*, 2 vols, Cambridge University Press, Cambridge; also ed. C.H. Hull, Augustus M. Kelley, New York, 1963.
Pirenne, H. (1936) *Economic and Social History of Medieval Europe*, Routledge and Kegan Paul, London.
Polanyi, K. (1957) *The Great Transformation* (1st edn 1944), Beacon Press, Boston.
Polanyi, K., Arensberg, C. and Pearson, H.W. (ed.) (1957) *Trade and Markets in the Early Empires*, Free Press, Glencoe, Ill.
Ricardo, D. (1815) *An Essay on the Influence of a Low Price of Corn on the Profits of Stock*, John Murray, London.

— (1821) *On the Principles of Political Economy and Taxation*, vol. I in *The Works and Correspondence of David Ricardo*, ed. P. Sraffa, Cambridge University Press, Cambridge, 1951.

Schumpeter, J.A. (1954) *History of Economic Analysis*, George Allen and Unwin, London.

Smith, A. (1776) *An Inquiry into the Nature and Causes of the Wealth of Nations*, ed. E. Cannan, 1904 edn, Methuen, London.

Sraffa, P. (1926) 'The Laws of Returns under Competitive Conditions', *Economic Journal,* XXXVI, pp 535–50.

— (1960) *Production of Commodities by Means of Commodities: Prelude to a Critique of Economic Theory*, Cambridge University Press, Cambridge.

Young, A.A. (1928) 'Increasing Returns and Economic Progress', *Economic Journal*, XXXVIII, pp. 527–42.

Part IV
From the Ancients to the Moderns: A Reappraisal of the Dynamics of Change in Economic Theory

12

Progress and Anti-Progress in Economic Science

CHRISTOPHER BLISS

I INTRODUCTION

My use of the term 'economic science' in the title will seem to some of my readers tendentious, misleading and simplistic. It would be all of these things, if I were suggesting, in using the term science, that economics is the same as the physical or natural sciences. However, it seems to me that undue concentration on the natural sciences disguises the fact that there is a wider sense of 'science', which embodies those features that make scholarship in the modern world essentially different from most of the scholarship of pre-modern times. The natural sciences are certainly scientific in this sense, but so are other disciplines far removed from physics. These other disciplines include, for example, as I shall shortly explain, such an improbable candidate for the title of science as biblical criticism. In applying the noun science so widely, I admit to an unusual usage, although it is interesting to note that more is commonly called 'scientific' than is called 'science'. However, in the present context it is enlightening to bring out what is common to different disciplines.

Although I am going to develop the idea of a progressive science without reference to a particular science, the present aim is to apply it to the history of economics in the last two hundred years. It sharpens the discussion of the general case to examine a particular claim that economics regressed after the middle of the nineteenth century. Of course it is far from clear that, put so simply, this corresponds to anyone's actual view. The point at issue is whether the development of 'catallactics', to borrow Hicks's term (Hicks, 1976, pp. 207–18), represented such a regress. Certainly Hicks does not suggest that it did. But Pasinetti comes so close to expounding this view that it is difficult to see how he could deny the attribution (Pasinetti, 1981, introduction).

What is the essence of a science in my broad use of the term? The answer is that a science is defined by its method, and that this method must include certain features, if we are to count the case concerned as 'scientific'. These features include the following.

1 The discourse of the discipline should be conducted according to the tenets of open and rational argument. Appeals to tradition, to authority or seniority, or to considerations extraneous to the subject matter (for example, the political or moral consequences of a view about a natural phenomenon) have no place in a science.
2 The conduct of the discipline must embody the evaluation of beliefs by means of *evidence*. This will typically be the observation or examination of the world, including its historical archives. Crucial in this context is the ability to incorporate new evidence, or evidence recently come to light. The experimental method is not essential.
3 It should be the practice to maintain *records* of what the researchers are doing, what they observe, and the ideas that they propose, and to disseminate this material widely and without favour. These records, or archives, should be maintained, so that what has been done in the past is accessible to the present worker.

The justification of these criteria, and even the elucidation of some of the terms employed, would make an essay in itself. But it is hoped that my claims, though simply put, will seem convincing. Obviously the revolution in human knowledge that began in the seventeenth century, and gathered pace in the eighteenth and nineteenth centuries, involved a complex interaction between the application of the scientific method to the natural world and its application to history, for example. There is no sense in which the disciplines that became scientific in the modern period were simply aping natural science.

It should not now seem strange that the epithet 'science' could be applied to biblical criticism. Before the eighteenth century, it was generally held that the Bible and the Christian gospels contained the revealed words of God. This attitude naturally precluded any critical approach to them as historical documents. But the intervening time, and particularly the last hundred years, has changed all that. Biblical criticism today, at least as it is practised in reputable universities, satisfies all my conditions. The veracity of the sacred sources is freely questioned. Archaeological evidence, and evidence from sources unconnected with the religion of the source document, is routinely admitted. So far has this process gone, and so much has it called into question the reliability of some of the sources, that it is hard to see sometimes how the practitioners of this discipline, a majority of whom still retain some kind of belief, can continue so to do. But this intellectual difficulty in no way impunes the scientific standing of modern biblical criticism.

My argument will be that any discipline that satisfies the properties listed above as essential to a science is possessed of a natural *progressive tendency*.

To call something progressive sounds like a commendation, and it is my view that the progressive tendency of a scientific discipline is something to which positive value attaches. But the term as I use it does not necessarily carry the meaning 'going forward, towards the good'. What is meant is that the subject cannot turn back on itself and retrace its past. It is driven on by an ordered principle, something like the principle of entropy. In the light of these ideas, I shall offer an evaluation of the seemingly similar, but in fact rather different, claims concerning the role of exchange in economic theory advanced by Sir John Hicks (1976) and Luigi Pasinetti (1981).

II THE PROGRESSIVE TENDENCY OF SCIENCE

The tendency of science to progress comes from two sources, and it is worth noting what they are, and distinguishing between them. First, consider item (3) above. We can refer to this feature of a scientific discipline as *collective memory*, or *memory* for short. The mere fact of memory tends to make a discipline go forward in a directed manner, simply because it makes it difficult, indeed nearly impossible, to go backwards. One can see this even in a discipline that could not be claimed for science. Musical composition is in that category. It is no science on account of a failure to satisfy criterion (2) above, and because (1) does not mean anything in this case.

Despite not being a science, musical composition is very much subject to the principle of memory, and this gives to its development an order, of which anyone who listens to music from many periods cannot fail to be aware. On many occasions composers have rediscovered past compositions and been excited and inspired by them. They have even used material taken from these compositions and incorporated it into their own. But no composer could, or could want to, simply go back to a previous age. We have musicians who play as if they were from the age of the European Renaissance, but we have no composers who write as if they were from that age.

Yet music is not a science. It lacks an essential feature of a science: there is no *teleo* in music, no ultimate musical truth. And so there can be no evidence and no refutation. In this connection, it is worth quoting from the article on 'Composition' in the *Oxford Companion to Music*:

> Popular books upon the history of music often leave the impression that each great composer goes beyond the achievements of his predecessors, so that the art of composition undergoes a process of progressive improvement.
>
> It is common for more instructed writers to scoff at this, to represent that the music of any age represents that age and is not better nor worse than what precedes or follows it, but only different.
>
> The truth seems to lie between these two extremes. There are periods when the resources of a new style are being gradually exploited, and during such a period improvement does undoubtedly go on until at last that style attains

> completeness and is exemplified by masters whose works supersede those of their predecessors and often cast them into comparative or even complete obscurity.

This thoughtful passage perfectly illustrates the division between science, on the one hand, and various activities which resemble it, but only partially. Progress in music consists in the development of a style to its highest level of attainment. And this is the case because style is inescapable for music. It is what defines its ends. Science knows style too, because the questions which can be asked are too many to tackle at the same time, and the decision of which points to attack, and which to leave until later, in answerable only by guesswork. But because science is concerned with reality and must involve the use of evidence, reality ultimately makes itself felt.

Kuhn, who writes about the history of science as if it were the history of musical composition, plays down the realist aspect of science. But he is wrong to do so. That the scientist confronts his ideas with evidence, however incompletely and ineptly he may do so in some historical case, is what makes him a scientist. Unless there is a given and immovable reality in the universe, there can be no science.

III ECONOMICS AS SCIENCE

I have postponed the consideration of the case of economics until after I have had the opportunity to introduce some ideas. In particular, I wanted to discuss a rather general concept of science, not limited to the natural sciences or to the experimental method. How far does economics, as usually practised, satisfy the criteria that have been laid down for a science? I shall consider each of the tests in turn.

On the first test, open and rational discourse, I do not think that complete agreement about whether economics satisfies it would be forthcoming, even from economists themselves. But my own opinion is that the subject passes this test. The doubters would maintain that argument is inhibited by something which operates like tradition, it is what they call the 'neoclassical paradigm'. The idea is that arguments that are not based upon an atomistic competitive model are, as it were, shouted down by the neoclassical bully boys. I do not think that this view can be maintained. For example, more than one Nobel prize has been awarded to an economist who never employed an atomistic competitive model. And the view that everything must accord with a certain approach, though it is certainly encountered, does not predominate.

The appeal to authority sometimes finds its way into economics. The temptation to use this illegitimate kind of argument is irresistible, and it is encountered at times even in fields which are unquestionably sciences. But the important point is that it is a rather ineffective type of argument. It may occasionally get a theory a better hearing than it deserves, but no theory can subsist on it. This is what we demand of a science, and economics seems to satisfy that requirement.

So the appeal to authority is something rather peripheral to economics. It is interesting nevertheless to see which economists get selected as authorities, which economists current writers like to suggest believed what they want to show. For the Marxists, not unnaturally, the authority is Marx. For others, Ricardo and Keynes seem to be the figures whose sponsorship is most assiduously sought.

We come now to the second of our criteria for a science, the use of evidence. The reader is reminded again that the term science is being used in a particularly broad sense, and that it is certainly not our intention to confine the discussion to experimental science. But the admission of evidence, and the modification of theories according to what that evidence shows, is at the heart of the scientific method. How does economics come out of that test?

Some people would expect, or want, at this point a disquisition on the problems of statistical inference in economics, perhaps an apology for the limitations of econometrics, and a hopeful view that many problems which presently make the testing of economic models a difficult and uncertain task will be overcome in the future. That does not seem to me to be the point. It is true that the evaluation of evidence is a difficult business, and it is also true that once one begins to want to evaluate theories more questionable than those that can hardly be doubted once one hears them, then there are considerable problems to be overcome. More than that, some of these problems will always turn out to be insoluble within the limitations of real life data. But these are difficulties of evaluating evidence. They are the day-to-day problems of the working scientist. The point is not that every question in economics can be settled by examining the evidence, which it surely cannot. Rather, what matters is that economics has always made use of evidence, including informal and possibly unreliable evidence, and that everyone recognizes the legitimacy of introducing it into economic arguments.

Some economists like to accuse others of living in ivory towers, of building models which recklessly ignore the brute facts of reality. This type of criticism raises complex questions concerning the role of abstraction in science, particularly social science, which need not concern us here. What matters is that everyone agrees that empirical observation is relevant to eonomics, and arguments from observation are commonplace in all branches of the subject. On the test of the employment of evidence, economics passes.

However, we cannot leave the discussion of the use of evidence in economics without considering another point. Evidence plays an important role in giving to the typical science its directed progressive tendency. One reason for this is that it functions like an archival collection in which there are only new acquisitions, and no deletions. The size of the archives, then, operates like a principle of entropy. However, this is a patent idealization of real science. In truth, it is no surprise to discover that some old evidence tends to go stale. Sometimes it cannot all be absorbed and retained, and is simply forgotten, but this is somewhat unusual. More importantly, evidence may be assembled according to systems which theoretical progress subsequently renders obsolete.

Evidence is especially likely to become obsolete if the problem is constantly changing. This is an idea which has been vigorously canvassed in the case of economics. It has often been argued that all economics is historically relative, that theories depend upon particular historical circumstances, which pass with time. If this view is completely conceded, then a wedge is driven between economics and many other sciences. One of the things which lends a direction to some other sciences and which is not arbitrary is that each generation confronts a reality some of which is unchanging, so that one may meaningfully learn about it, if not once-for-all, then at least for a long time.

Of course there is something in the idea that economics pursues a moving target, but the argument has been overworked. It ignores the enormous carry-over of problems, ideas and insights which give continuity to economics, even while the object of its study is radically changing over the course of decades. What makes this possible is that economics is in some ways a box of tools, and old tools turn out to be useful in new applications. This is not dissimilar to the situation in other sciences, including the natural sciences.

We come again to memory, the archival aspect of science. It is not necessary to elaborate the point that economics is a subject with a high level of professional communication. Indeed, more than many 'harder' sciences, economics is practised by specialists who are in close contact with each other, and who have a comparatively lively sense of the history of the discipline. Perhaps this is because economics in the modern sense was as good as invented in one country (Scotland) only 200 years ago, and even now a relatively small number of countries still provide the majority of its high exponents.

I have proposed the idea that a science, defined rather broadly, has an inherent progressive tendency, and I have tried to show that economics satisfies the conditions required of a science in this sense. It does not follow from the argument that science in general, or economics in particular, cannot go through periods of stagnation, during which there is a slow rate of progress, or none at all. In a relative sense, this obviously does and must occur. For one only needs to say that a certain science progressed exceedingly rapidly during a certain period to imply that in some other period its progress was less.

These, then, are the ideas on which my approach will be based. The time has come to apply them, in turn, to the consideration of what Hicks and Pasinetti have to say about the development of economic theory.

IV HICKS ON CATALLACTICS

At the start it should be said that in writing about progress and anti-progress as central considerations, I am placing the emphasis rather differently from the writers whose essays I want to discuss. Thus Hicks, whose contribution is the subject of this section, is not concerned with progress explicitly, but with 'revolutions' in economics. This subject is not the same as progress, but it is not unconnected with it either. Revolutions are sharp changes of direction. If economics can go backwards, the most likely way for that to happen is for it to undergo a 'revolution' in the simple meaning of the term, a development which turns it right around. Moreover, those who have most notably wanted to identify certain periods of the history of economic thought as regressive, the Marxist economists on post-Marxian bourgeoise economics, have attributed a considerable share of the blame to the marginalist revolution.

Sir John Hicks is too good a theorist, and too good a student of the history of economic thought, to attribute more significance to marginalism than really attaches to it. Indeed he deliberately places the emphasis elsewhere. He writes:

> The 'margin' is no more than an expression of the mathematical rule for a maximum (or minimum); any sort of economics is marginalist that is concerned with maximizing. (Ricardo himself could be quite marginalist at times.) The essential novelty in the work of these economists was that instead of basing their economics on production and distribution, they based it on exchange. I therefore propose to make use of a term that was sometimes used, at the time in question, to mean the theory of exchange; it was called catallactics. (Hicks, 1976, p. 212)

Hicks discusses the idea that the rise of catallactics was due to a reaction against socialism, and he does not dismiss the idea out of hand. However, he makes clear his view that this cannot be much of the story, and in this I am sure that he is right. There are two things that the Marxist (for that is what it is) account of this piece of the history of economic thought leaves out.

First, there is the point argued by Hicks. If I may put it in my own words, economic theory is a technology, and its progress is subject to the laws that govern technical progress. To assume that technical progress occurs when it suits the prevailing class to have it occur is to assume more than is reasonable. But if we do not assume that, then we are left with the curious conclusion that by about 1870 it suited the bourgeoisie to have economists stop worrying about production and consider catallactics, and that when they obediently did so, *they at once initiated one of the largest intellectual break-throughs that economics has ever seen*. For that, make no mistake, is what the marginalist revolution was.[1]

We are trespassing here on one of the notoriously difficult problems of Marxist social dynamics, the explanation of technical progress, and particularly scientific progress. If economic theory is ideology, an apology for capitalist exploitation, why should it make new discoveries? And if these discoveries are always there, waiting to be made, what stops them being made earlier? Can a scholar, or those who pay for his dinner, always feel instinctively where every path may lead?

For Hicks, the explanation is quite different. Walras and Menger succeeded in doing what others would have been well pleased to have done earlier, but they did not pull it off. As he puts it: 'The possibility of a utility theory had been there all the time; what the catallactists showed was that something could be done with it' (Hicks, 1976, p. 215).

Two points reinforce Hicks's case. First, the neglect of production did not persist for long. The application of the maximization principle to the theory of production soon became a major concern. (Pasinetti's particular claims about that application will be considered below.) This point is fairly obvious. The second point is more subtle. There is no reason in logic why a concentration on exchange is apologetic in character. It is only because we view questions of economic apologetics through Marx-tinted spectacles (even non-Marxists find it hard not to) that it could seem to be so. But to regard writers, to many of whom, to quote Hicks, 'Marx . . . must have been practically unknown', as producing what from a Marxist perspective is particularly germane to apologetics, is to commit a rather obvious fallacy.

My point is that Marx located exploitation in the sphere of production, and provided a particular account of it, which has the property that one cannot even apply it to a pure exchange economy. If the economic agents start with given resources and then engage in exchange, one cannot define surplus value and exploitation in any way that will tally with Marx's concepts. But why should it be supposed that the invalidity of these particular concepts shows the economic system in a particularly favourable light? The theory says that, under market exchange, the individual does better:

1 the better endowed he is with goods to offer in exchange; and

[1] Pasinetti argues that marginal ideas had been around for a long time, so that significance should be attached to the rapid growth in the application of them at the time at which it took place. In fact this point merely reinforces Hicks's claim that so-called 'marginalism' was much more than the idea of the margin.

2 the scarcer relative to wants are the particular goods that he happens to hold.

It implies also, and this implication was elaborated, that trade cannot make any of the participants worse off than he would be without trade, and will typically benefit some. But the economy is depicted as providing well for those who have, but being parsimonious when it comes to allocating to those who have little. Many socialist critiques of the market are based on just these points.

Hicks's discussion of catallactics is quite at variance with Pasinetti's argument in the introduction to his book on structural change (1981). This is most obvious on the question of the ideological explanation of economic ideas, but the differences are not only apparent there. However, before comparing the ideas of the two writers, we must first examine Pasinetti's argument.

V PASINETTI ON PRODUCTION AND EXCHANGE

In his extensive introduction, Pasinetti (1981) puts forward a number of arguments, which are somewhat connected, but not inextricably so. I shall concentrate mainly on his discussion of marginalism, since this is both a central issue and one which connects with what Hicks was writing about in his examination of catallactics. This selection of topic should not be taken to imply that I am happy with the rest of the essay, which I am not. I am utterly unconvinced, for example, by the assertion that trade, even in ancient times, was a mere exchange of goods and was not associated with increases in production. It is a view which, I believe, would be impossible to reconcile with historical evidence. The truth is that production and exchange are, and always have been, intimately connected. Adam Smith saw this clearly when he enunciated his famous principle according to which the division of labour is limited by the extent of the market.

This, however, is by the way. So is Pasinetti's allusion to Ricardo's treatment of land. As is well known, Ricardo convinced himself that by confining attention to the margin, where land earns no rent, he could eliminate the consideration of land from his analysis, and with it all the problems that arise from having two scarce non-produced goods in the economy. According to Pasinetti, Ricardo's method of approaching the problem in this manner 'solved it'. Of course it did not. We get nothing from assuming production at the margin at which land earns no rent, unless we know where that margin will be. Otherwise, even the marginal product of labour, the average product on the marginal land, will be unknown. To solve Ricardo's problem properly, the natural tool is marginal economic analysis. Let us therefore turn to marginal economic analysis, which is at the centre of the concerns of Pasinetti's introduction.

Marginal theory for Pasinetti is very much tied to exchange, or to catallactics in Hicks's terminology. In the history of economic analysis, there is some justification for this idea. It was from the concept of marginal utility that economists first became conscious of the extraordinary potential of the marginal method, and marginal utility can be, and was, very well illustrated in a pure exchange economy.

However, the history of economic analysis, just as the history of any other science, is not, and could not be, the arbiter of the final status of concepts. What matters to us today is *what can be shown* – can be shown, that is, with the best and surest reasoning now available. And the last thing that can be shown with any kind of logical force is that marginalism, or maximization as Hicks reminds us it should be called, is only to do with exchange. It is a travesty for Pasinetti to say, as he does say, that 'the typical marginalist scheme of general equilibrium, as it has been called, is what has become known as a pure exchange economy'.

What does it mean to say that the typical general equilibrium scheme is a pure exchange model? In a footnote, Pasinetti states that in standard treatises the pure exchange case is 'always the first to be worked out'. But this, even if true, is surely a matter of exposition. It cannot affect the ultimate logic of equilibrium theory. One could as well say that the typical model of ballistics is concerned with motion *in vacuo*, because that is where virtually every textbook on dynamics begins its presentation of that topic.

No, given endowments are simply a degenerate case of the production set. One cannot reasonably drive a wedge between maximization models with and without production, and claim that they are fundamentally different. In some of the best expositions of general equilibrium theory, in which the pedagogic requirement is secondary, notably in Debreu (1959), equilibrium is introduced only after a discussion of both consumer and producer theory.

Professor Pasinetti knows that the principle of maximization has been widely extended since the first ideas in marginal theory saw the light of day, and I doubt that he would want to make his claim that general equilibrium is typically about pure exchange central to his case. It is not the fact that he is unaware of the progress that has occupied the last century which distinguishes his argument; it is that he disapproves of the path it has taken. His reasons are fairly familiar to those who have followed the writings of those economists, notably in Cambridge and Italy, who have tried to establish that there is some fundamental logical difficulty with the application of, as they would put it, the marginal principle to production.

This is old and over-cultivated ground, and this is not the place to plough it yet again. What concerns us here is the progress, or lack of it, in economic science, and it is to what Pasinetti has to say on this subject that I shall confine myself.

In my account, the progressive tendency of a science comes from the accumulation of knowledge and from the fact that a science, at least to some extent, is dealing with an objective reality which may be comprehended more or less effectively. Not everyone will agree with this unashamedly realist view of the scientific process, but even those inclined to agree may want to insist that the system may be side-tracked by misdirected research into avenues which turn out not to be fruitful. This is what Pasinetti asserts about the marginal revolution. He offers an interpretation of why this side-shift occurred, which is simply that it diverted attention from the dangerous questions to which Marx had drawn attention. This is a familiar argument and Pasinetti brings no subtlety to it.

> If only one could find an economic theory that made no reference to labour, no reference to means of production, possibly even to production itself . . . that would surely be the sort of thing that a frightened Establishment could not but most warmly welcome. Marginal utility theory provided precisely that. (Pasinetti, 1981, p. 13)

There are difficulties with this crude reduction of the theory of knowledge to a simple matter of conspiracy by self-serving academics, but aside from such generalities, the particular application runs into difficulties of historical fact and logic, as I have argued above. Most important of all, the view that the marginal revolution was a diversion will not stand up to serious examination. One need only compare the theoretical power of economics at the end of the nineteenth century with its state fifty years earlier to see what benefits the new methods brought.

If Hicks is right and marginalism is simply a name for maximization, how can it be claimed that the extension to production was illegitimate? The short answer is not easily. Pasinetti argues the point on the not unexpected basis that the extension required capital to be treated as if it were a scarce good on a par with non-produced land. This is not correct. Although plenty of confusion can be detected in writings on this problem, both old and contemporary, there are also clear and well-specified theoretical solutions to the general equilibrium model with produced capital goods. Pasinetti's difficulties are to a great extent of his own making, and a lot of the trouble can be attributed to the introduction of a false dichotomy between produced goods and scarce goods. If a scarce good is defined as one the supply of which cannot be increased by the application of labour and other inputs, then capital is not scarce. But if, more usefully, scarcity is defined in terms of opportunity cost, then capital goods are scarce. The quantities of capital goods available at a certain time can only be augmented by diverting to their production at some time goods which Pasinetti would agree to be scarce. This makes them scarce in the opportunity-cost sense.

Pasinetti is right to argue that there are large and important areas of economic theory that do not come wholly under the ambit of maximizing theory. He is wrong to identify these areas with legitimate production theory.

VI CONSENSUS AND SCIENTIFIC PROGRESS

My definition of science, which I argued to be inherently progressive, did not include consensus among its practitioners. In this respect, my definition is weaker than Kuhn's 'normal science' (1970, ch. 3). In fact there is a great deal of accord among the majority of economists, and there has been since the foundation of the subject. But there have also been some strong and persistent disagreements. Pasinetti's disparaging discussion of orthodoxy, for example, is not the product of an isolated point of view. But what is interesting to note is that such disagreements have in many cases not resulted in schism.

There is indeed a good deal of rhetoric and exaggeration in the anti-orthodox position, because their positive ideas, as opposed to their attacks, which often have to do with method, could very often pass unnoticed as normal contemporary economics. Therein lies a seemingly insurmountable problem for the critics of economic orthodoxy. As Kuhn has argued, what displaces science is more science, that point is but an aspect of the progressive tendency already alluded to. What is disappointing about the school with which Pasinetti is associated is the paucity of its new and completed theory. Sraffa's production model, for example, is quite consistent with Debreu's general equilibrium theory, if the appropriate assumptions are included in the latter.

A belief in progress may seem to entail complacency, but it need not be so. There is a great deal in orthodox economic theory at the present time not to be complacent about. It includes a good part of the treatment of production, the firm and technical progress. When Pasinetti writes: 'No concern has ever been shown ... about extending, by assumption, the properties of giveness and definiteness, which are characteristic of scarce natural resources, to the state of technical knowledge, namely to something which is exactly the opposite' (Pasinetti, 1981, p. 16), he gives a false impression. But it is true to say that what has been achieved in the theory of induced technical progress leaves much to be desired.

VII CONCLUSION

Kuhn's paradigm is a 'mode of scientific activity'. Although it is certainly normal for an active science to include several distinct programmes of research or modes of activity, no concept has been more abused of recent years. As used in the social sciences, it has come to mean criteria for evaluating the quality of work and whether it succeeds or not. Looked at this way, the paradigm becomes like the rules of a game: do not shout because I have picked up the ball and run with it; my paradigm is Rugby football, not soccer.

The coexistence within a science of more than one paradigm in this second sense indicates a very serious and fundamental division. The division between psychotherapy and orthodox psychiatry would serve as an example. The issue to which this volume addresses itself may be briefly summarized in two questions:

1 Is economics today divided by paradigms in the second sense above?
2 Does that division follow the lines of production-oriented versus exchange-oriented schema?

My answers to the two test questions are respectively No and No, the second No being louder and more emphatic than the first. It is true that different economists in different places are working on different problems and with different priorities, and it is true that they do not always agree about what counts as good work. There is considerable disagreement at the present time, for example, concerning the legitimacy of so-called *ad hoc* assumptions. However, these disagreements, embarrassing though they may be, span no more than the normal range of a normal science. As I have argued above, what Professor Pasinetti does, despite what he writes in his Foreword, is normal economics.

However, even if I am wrong about the absence of paradigm divisions within the economics profession, I am sure that any that there may be will not be reducible to exchange versus production. This division has no basis in the logic of contemporary economic theory, which makes the shift from exchange to production rather a slight one (from degenerate to full production sets). It played a role in history certainly, which, as Hicks explains, was due to the concentration on one aspect of reality during the development of ideas. But the creation of a grand schism within economics, on the basis of this division, carries little conviction.

REFERENCES

Debreu, G. (1959) *The Theory of Value: An Axiomatic Analysis of Economic Equilibrium*, Cowles Foundation for Research in Economics, Yale University, John Wiley, New York.

Hicks, J.R. (1976) '"Revolutions" in Economics', in *Methods and Appraisal in Economics*, ed. S.J. Latsis, Cambridge University Press, Cambridge, pp. 207–18.

Kuhn, T.S. (1970) *The Structure of Scientific Revolutions*, 2nd edn, University of Chicago Press, Chicago.

Oxford Companion to Music (1955), 9th edn, ed. P.A. Scholes, Oxford University Press, Oxford.

Pasinetti, L.L. (1981) *Structural Change and Economic Growth: A Theoretical Essay on the Dynamics of the Wealth of Nations,* Cambridge University Press, Cambridge.

13

The Exchange–Production Duality and the Dynamics of Economic Knowledge

ALBERTO QUADRIO-CURZIO
AND ROBERTO SCAZZIERI

I THE 'CLASSICS' OF POLITICAL ECONOMY: THE DISCIPLINE VIEWED AS A CONTINUITY OF THE PAST INTO THE PRESENT

A widespread, though not general conviction among modern economists is that the contributions of the great economists of the past belong exclusively to the history of economic thought. This opinion must be reconsidered, as economics is, in certain respects, more similar to art and philosophy than to the natural sciences in the use it can and must make of its own history. Thus, even if it is relatively acceptable that the astronomer neglects in his current research the Ptolemaic system, the same cannot be said for economists facing the systems of thought elaborated by the mercantilists, the Physiocrats, the English and Scottish classical economists, Marx, the marginalists, Keynes and others.

This statement is not incompatible with the fact that economists study 'continually changing' phenomena. It does not follow in the least from this fact that theories that analyse economic phenomena must change as fast as the phenomena themselves and those of the past become part of history, this being taken as an indicator of progress in political economy. Changes in studied reality have in fact had another task: that of distinguishing 'fundamental' from 'conjunctural' ideas, of generating progress and modification in fundamental ideas, and of generating new conjunctural ideas. Economics is thus founded on the work of great economists, who formulated, thanks to real revolutions in thought, fundamental ideas that are often alternative visions of the nature and functioning of economic systems, with such profound roots that time could not change them significantly.

A fundamental idea is the ideal model of economic life underlying one or more theories, and from which the theories themselves derive problems to analyse, even if they cannot derive the precise explanations that are given on every particular occasion. The dynamics of economic knowledge gives prominence to two fundamental ideas: production and exchange, making them essential in the definition of political economy. It is worth stressing that these fundamental ideas must not be confused with complete theoretical systems; for the former are instead spheres of interest, and also points of view, with which economists initially begin in the formulation of their theories.

The fundamental idea of exchange was the first to be developed systematically. It was present in the studies of money and value between the sixteenth and the seventeenth centuries, and it dominated the minds of the mercantilists, who applied it to the study of trade relations between states. The principle of the maximization of national wealth constitutes an early expression of such an idea. With the early marginalists, the fundamental idea of exchange was applied to individual behaviour for the maximization of utility; in later marginalism, it was applied to the behaviour of producers and consumers for the maximization of profit and utility. Finally, this fundamental idea was used for the determination of the 'welfare' of society as a whole. Step by step, the fundamental idea of exchange gains precision and articulation, with the concepts of 'scarcity' of resources with respect to ends, of 'efficiency' in the use of given resources, of 'one-wayness' of production from 'primitive' factors of production to products. This fundamental idea is finally crystallized in the principle that every economic problem can be reduced to the mathematical problem of maximizing an objective function subject to scarcity constraints.

The history of the fundamental idea of production is no less complex. Already with English political arithmetic (William Petty and others), with Quesnay and other Physiocrats, the central problem of political economy had been identified in the process of the production (and reproduction) of an economic system. And soon appeared the concepts of the 'circular flow' of production (that is to say, of the production of commodities by means of commodities), of 'interdependence' between sectors of the economy, of 'net product' or 'surplus' (the excess of social product over aggregate means of production). These concepts were elaborated in various ways, and not always in the same direction by later authors. Classical English and Scottish economists like Smith, Malthus and Ricardo examined the relations between net product and accumulation, the problem of the distribution of social product between different classes in society and between wages, profits and rents, and the question of effective demand. The breaking away of Marx from these economists on the problems of the functioning of a capitalist economy occurred basically because he founded these problems on conflicts between social classes and on the concept of exploitation.

After a period of relative inactivity (during which, however, important contributions to the theory of value and the theory of structural dynamics can be found), the fundamental idea of production became once again of primary significance, with Kalecki, Keynes, von Neumann, Leontief, Sraffa and others. In contrast with the fundamental idea of exchange, one can say that the core of the fundamental idea of production is that the 'wealth' of an economic system depends on its capacity to create a net product or surplus, on the distribution of the latter between the recipients of wages, profits and rents, and on the distribution of the surplus between consumption and investment (the growth of wealth through time is made to depend on this latter variable).

Even if each fundamental idea concerned initially a limited aspect of economic life, it has later shown the tendency to expand to almost all the spheres of economic theory. Thus English and Scottish classical economists, parting from the fundamental idea of production, were interested in international trade no less than the mercantilists, and in exchange no less than the marginalists. The same is true of the marginalists with respect to the problem of production. Nevertheless, the differences between the points of departure are as evident as the differences between the priorities accorded to the phenomena studied, and the interpretations of the phenomena themselves are often very different between the two approaches.

The fundamental ideas of exchange and production suggest a way of classifying economic theories according to certain thematic concepts, which they may have in common. An interesting feature of the thematic concepts that we are considering ('exchange' and 'production') is that they make it possible to connect systematically the dynamics of economic knowledge with the dynamics of economic events. Before explicitly considering how this connection can be established, it is worth noting that economic history, even if it is taken at its purely descriptive stage, presupposes some way of blending factual accounts with theoretical concepts. The economist, in particular, cannot make sense of economic history unless economic events are simplified and organized by certain abstractions developed in economic theory.

The work of theoretical economists has brought to the fore the fact that an economic system can be considered in two different ways, depending on whether the economist describes the 'circular flow' of production of commodities by means of produced commodities, or the transformation of primary resources into final consumption goods. In the former case, the network of processes delivering to each other the respective means of production forms the core of the economy (this we may call the *structural apparatus* of the economic system). In the latter case, the whole economic system is described as a set of vertically integrated sectors, and the existence of 'loops' within the productive system is not explicitly considered.[1] (The

[1] The logical properties of the vertical integration of production processes are identified and discussed in L.L. Pasinetti (1973). This work also analyses the relationship between vertical integration and the 'inter-industry' description of a productive system.

economic system is thus described as a *transformation apparatus*, 'extracting' consumption goods from primary resources.)[2]

The dynamics of industrial economies allow a distinction between two phases which, in the classical model of industrialization, were consecutive. In the first phase, which is characterized by productive transformation, productive activity is only an intermediate stage between primitive factors of production (land and labour) and final consumption. Transformation increases the productiveness of primitive factors and thus the possibilities of final consumption, but remains a stage having little autonomy.

In the second phase, the industrial and intersectoral structure acquires growing autonomy. With the development of industries that produce means of production, and the production of machinery by means of machinery, inter-industry relations gain priority, the gap between primitive factors of production and final consumer goods grows, and the relations between primitive factors and the means of production are modified profoundly.

As noted above, in the classical model of industrialization, these two phases were historically consecutive. Nevertheless, the structural phase did not remove the apparatus of transformation, which on the contrary gained priority again in certain periods of economic history. It could be said that during periods of rapid growth, the inter-industry network gains priority, whereas in the periods of decline in growth, the apparatus of transformation comes to the fore. It could also be said that the transformational feature is typical of economies where the growth potential is being exhausted, of economies perhaps characterized by a high level of welfare, but in a 'climacteric' phase of development. Conversely, the structural aspect is typical of more dynamic economies (although these latter might be under the pressure of particular scarcities).

Hypothetically, even if in an economic system all the sectors that produced the means of production were to cease their activity, the apparatus of transformation would nevertheless continue to function until the exhaustion of the supplies of produced means of production and until the physical destruction of machinery. After which, with a further regression, it could continue to function by substituting primitive factors of production for the produced means of production. To conclude, the apparatus of structure generates both the means of production and the final consumption goods, whereas the apparatus of transformation generates only the latter.

The difference between productive transformation and industrial interdependence is essential to an understanding of the distinctive features of periods of rapid growth and periods of stagnation and crisis.

In fact, often in economic history, periods of high welfare are also

---

[2] The distinction between structural apparatus and transformational apparatus is discussed in Quadrio-Curzio and Scazzieri (1982a, 1982b). Here we give a summary account of our argument there.

periods of a decline in growth and therefore, due to the greater influence of the apparatus of transformation with respect to that of interdependence, periods of considerable pressure on the resources available. In this case, there is an increase in the importance of commercial markets, in which the intermediary (the merchant) regulates the sales price according to availability before consumer's demand. Simultaneously, the importance of industrial markets where the means of production are exchanged diminishes. The result can be a temporary advantage of scarcity over producibility, with the ensuing emergence of inflationary tensions. Under such circumstances, a further decline in the rate of growth may reduce short-term inflation, but with the risk of aggravating the crisis of the apparatus of interdependence, and thus of eventually increasing the pressure on available resources.

On the other hand, the prevalence of producibility over scarcity and of industrial markets over commercial markets is typical of periods of rapid growth. In this case, there exists the possibility of pressure on the availability of particular means of production or consumption goods (with the emergence of inflationary tensions). In general, however, scarcity, which the further expansion of the structural apparatus helps to overcome in the medium and long term, is relative rather than absolute.

Economic knowledge can be considered the product of economic theory, 'stylized' descriptions of economic history and economic policy (man's deliberate intervention on economic phenomena). Theory and stylized history are interdependent, and they both compete to influence policy. But policy, even when it is not logically derived from theory, can leave a mark, through actions, on the apparatuses whose variations are registered by history and transmitted to theory. It follows that economic policy is a fundamental element in the formation of economic knowledge.

The mutual influence between theory, 'stylized' history and policy produces a characteristic feature in the dynamics of economic knowledge: the recurrency of themes and thus the continuing interest of classical economic authors (those economists to whom we owe fundamental contributions to the scientific traditions of 'exchange' or 'production').

The aim of this paper is to show that the structure–transformation duality within the productive system is a powerful element in shaping economic theory and in connecting the dynamics of economic theory with the structural dynamics of the economic system.

II EXCHANGE AND PRODUCTION AT THE BEGINNING OF SYSTEMATIC ECONOMIC THEORY

Economic thought has often been guided in the choice of problems to be tackled and of causal links to investigate by the dynamics of 'exchange–

production' relationships within the economic system. Naturally, this relationship between the evolution of economic theory and the evolution of economic reality is a long-term process, and it would be unfair to explain by the economic conjunctural trends the changes in the orientations of economists. Nevertheless, the evolution of political economy in the last two or three centuries suggests that the fundamental ideas of exchange and production are becoming stronger respectively, and they constitute alternatively the point of departure of theoretical inquiries, when the phenomena 'set alight' by theory coincide with the phenomena 'set alight' by economic reality.

The development of markets and trade precedes, in European history, the beginning of the radical transformation of the productive structure. On the other hand, in the theoretical contributions characteristic of the fifteenth, sixteenth and seventeenth centuries, the phenomenon of exchange holds a central position in economic thought, and the construction of a system of concepts founded on the fundamental idea of exchange is initiated. This can be seen by the interest of economists like Davanzati and Montanari in the problems of money and market value, and by the interest of the mercantilists in a conception of wealth as the stock of goods and services, the distribution, but not the total quantity of which may be modified by exchange.

The formation of a system of markets leads economic theory to study the relationships between the individual phenomena of production and exchange, and to the identification of a unifying framework for such relationships in the actions of supply and demand. This approach is conducive to emphasis on the fundamental idea of exchange and to the interpretation of production processes as processes for the transformation of primitive factors into consumer goods: '[the] land is the source or matter from whence all wealth is produced. The labour of man is the form which produces it; and wealth in itself is nothing but the maintenance, conveniencies, and superfluities of life' (Cantillon, 1931, p. 3).

In this way it becomes possible to explain the normal value of commodities by referring to their utility and their scarcity, and reducing the effect of the techniques of production to the special case of those natural resources, the scarcity of which depends 'only on the quantity of labour spent on them' (Galiani, 1963, p. 47).

The theory of Galiani is founded on an understanding of production processes similar to that of Cantillon, for the importance attributed to the links between non-produced factors of production (labour and natural resources) and the available quantity of each commodity. In this manner the productive system is reduced to the apparatus of transformation of primitive factors into consumer goods, and there follows immediately the dependence of the available quantity of each commodity on the available quantity of primitive factors.

Already with Galiani and Cantillon the fundamental idea of exchange reaches one of its most characteristic conclusions, especially as regards the crucial role of individual preferences and the endowment of resources in the determination of prices. This is accompanied by reflections on the production process that take exchange as their point of departure and are only interested in particular aspects of production, such as the possibility of varying the quantity of commodities offered on the markets. Other important aspects, such as the interdependence between processes and the necessity of satisfying always and independently from the quantity produced, certain conditions for the reproducibility of the whole economic system, are completely neglected.

In the following decades, economic theory based on the concept of exchange is gradually improved and expanded with the analysis of the relations between the equilibrium price and competitive actions (Beccaria, 1804), with the development of the concept of reciprocal demand (Turgot, 1769/70), and with the earliest formulation of supply and demand functions (Verri, 1771; Valeriani, 1806). Finally, we are indebted to Achille Nicolas Isnard (Isnard, 1781) for the first mathematical formulation of a general equilibrium system of exchange, in which the interdependence between equilibrium commodity prices is expressed through a system of simultaneous equations.

Nevertheless, towards the middle of the eighteenth century, the spheres of interest of some of the leading economists shifted from the phenomena of exchange to those of production. The first rigorous and complete formulation of the new way of thinking is due to the French Physiocrats, and primarily to François Quesnay, whose conception of national wealth is posed in clear antithesis to the theories founded on the fundamental idea of exchange:

> A nation's wealth is not regulated by the amount of monetary wealth. Monetary wealth can increase or diminish without anyone noticing it, for it is always available in a state, by reason of its quantity or its velocity of circulation, in proportion to the abundance and the value of raw produce. Spain, which owns the treasure of Peru, is always impoverished by its needs. England maintains its opulence by means of its real wealth. (Quesnay, 1962, p. 77)

The physiocratic point of view, which had partly been anticipated by English political arithmetic (William Petty, for instance), reveals the depth of the difference between the fundamental ideas of exchange and production. In fact, whereas the fundamental idea of exchange leads economists to the identification of the wealth of a nation with the endowment or *fund* of economic resources available (mercantilists, Cantillon), the fundamental idea of production leads to the identification of the wealth of a nation with the capacity of this nation to produce a yearly *flow* of goods and services.

The physiocratic conception of wealth is shared by a number of subsequent authors. For example, Pietro Verri, in his *Meditazioni sull'economia politica*, writes:

> Primarily two objects should be observed and those are *annual reproduction* and *annual consumption*. In every state production is made through agriculture and manufactures and in every state there is consumption. . . . When the total value of reproduction is equalled by the annual value of consumption, that nation remains in the situation it is, given that all circumstances are the same. The nation where the annual consumption exceeds annual reproduction declines, and instead there is an improvement in the state where annual reproduction exceeds annual consumption. (Verri, 1771, pp. 18–19)

III FROM SMITH'S *WEALTH OF NATIONS* TO RICARDO'S *PRINCIPLES*

The resemblance between the previous assertions by Verri and some famous passages of the *Wealth of Nations* is remarkable:

> [the] annual labour of every nation is the fund which originally supplies it with all the necessaries and conveniences of life which it annually consumes, and which consist always, either in the immediate produce of that labour, or in what is purchased with that produce from other nations. According therefore, as this produce, or what is purchased with it, bears a greater or smaller proportion to the number of those who are to consume it, the nation will be better or worse supplied with all the necessaries and conveniences for which it has occasion. (Smith, 1976, p. 10)

Further on, Smith observes:

> There is one sort of labour which adds to the value of the subject upon which it is bestowed: there is another which has no such effect. The former, as it produces a value, may be called productive; the latter unproductive labour. . . . Both productive and unproductive labourers, and those who do not labour at all, are all equally maintained by the annual produce of the land and labour of the country. This produce, how great so ever, can never be infinite, but must have certain limits. According, therefore, as a smaller or greater proportion of it is in any one year employed in maintaining unproductive hands, the more in the one case and the less in the other will remain for the productive, and the next year's produce will be greater or smaller accordingly; the whole annual produce, if we except the spontaneous productions of the earth, being the effect of productive labour. (Smith, 1976, pp. 330–2)

Nevertheless, the central position of productive phenomena in his thought leads Smith to delve much deeper than Verri into the study of the circumstances on which the variations in the net product of an economic system depend (there is particular emphasis on the division of labour and on its effects on labour productivity in the first three chapters of the *Wealth of Nations*). From a theoretical point of view, it is even more important to note the connection, established by Smith, between the conception of wealth as a flow of net product and the concept of exchange-value: 'It was not by gold or by silver, but by labour, that all the wealth of the world was originally purchased; and its value, to those who possess it, and who want to exchange it for some new productions, is precisely equal to the quantity of labour which it can enable them to purchase or command' (Smith, 1976, p. 48).

The centrality of the fundamental idea of production in Smith induced him to avoid an explanation of the exchange-value of commodities that was becoming quite popular among economists in the latter half of the eighteenth century.

In fact the problem of value is no longer approached starting from the relations between the supply and demand of commodities (as is the case, for instance, in Galiani, Cantillon, Turgot and Verri). Rather, Smith starts from the idea that in a system of production based on the division of labour, the problem of value consists in the first place, in the determination of the relations of exchange between commodities and labour (that is to say, in the determination of a systematic link between productive activities exercised separately by isolated producers, by associating with each commodity product its equivalent in terms of 'socially acknowledged' labour).

This approach to the problem of value is accompanied in the *Wealth of Nations* by the use of vertical integration in the description of production processes. (The economic system is seen as a group of sectors that link 'primitive' factors to the final consumption goods, neglecting the production of commodities by means of commodities that are themselves produced.)

The method of vertical integration permits the elimination of intermediate commodities from the analysis of the nature and causes of wealth, through a series of logical steps only implicit in Adam Smith. Here, every commodity produced is first connected to the quantity of labour directly and indirectly used to obtain it in the economic system, and then to a group of commodities required, directly and indirectly, for the same ends in the whole economic system. The same logical procedure can be repeated for the means of production, by reducing them as well to a quantity of labour and to a new residual of the means of production. Vertical integration can be repeated a third, a fourth time and so on, and at each step the residual, made up of produced means of production, will be reduced.

The emphasis on the producibility of commodities leads Smith to neglect the detailed examination of the role of non-reproduced means of production in the formation of wealth. This particular point of view, together with the consideration of the economic system through vertically integrated sectors, thus provides a logical justification of the special role attributed by Smith to the 'stock of labour' as the origin of the material prosperity of an economic system.

The attention paid to the processes of the production of wealth (itself a consequence of the conception of wealth as a flow of net products) leads to two important results. On the one hand, the problem of value presents itself as the search for a rate of exchange between commodities and labour (labour as 'commanded labour'); on the other hand, the conditions of production of each commodity are connected to its value (and therefore also to the corresponding 'commanded labour') independently of the conditions of production of other commodities (in fact every commodity is obtained by a vertically integrated sector, where intermediate products do not appear explicitly).

Vertical integration leads Smith to maintain that the natural price of a commodity is determined by the *sum* of the costs of production necessary to obtain it, notwithstanding the indirect effects induced by the use of intermediate products. From this perspective, Smith maintains that wages, profits and rents determine the natural prices of commodities, and that the latter resolve into 'some one or other, or all of those three parts; and in every improved society, all the three enter more or less, as component parts, into the prices of the far greater part of commodities' (Smith, 1976, p. 50). For this reason, the natural prices of commodities (and therefore, also, the corresponding quantities of 'commanded labour') depend on the natural level of wages, profits and rents, while the latter are connected to corresponding long-term relations between demand and supply. Only in a special case do the relations between supply and demand seem irrelevant in the determination of natural prices. This is the 'early and rude state of society which precedes both the accumulation of stock and the appropriation of land' (Smith, 1976, p. 65), where 'the proportion between the quantities of labour necessary for acquiring different objects seems to be the only circumstance which can afford any rule for exchanging them for one another' (Smith, 1976, p. 65). In this state of nature, in fact, 'the whole produce of labour belongs to the labourer; and the quantity of labour commonly employed in acquiring or producing any commodity, is the only circumstance which can regulate the quantity of labour which it ought commonly to purchase, command, or exchange for' (Smith, 1976, p. 65).

In Smith's theory, the vertical integration of production processes 'sets alight' the activity of the transformation of primitive resources into final consumption goods and allows the concentration of attention on the productive function of labour as the origin of wealth. This course, on the one hand, allows Smith to study the problem of value from the point of view of 'commanded labour' (a point of view which by itself constitutes a characteristic result of the fundamental idea of production) and, on the other hand, requires the establishment of a link between the endowment of primitive resources and 'commanded labour', thus returning to a characteristic theme of the fundamental idea of exchange.

Ricardo's *Principles of Political Economy* (1951; 1st edn 1817), by expanding Smith's work, signals the first attempt to provide a *general* interpretation of the economic system based on the fundamental idea of production and concentrating on producible commodities.

In fact, Ricardo's work is founded on the idea that, in a modern industrial economy, the most important feature of the productive sphere is that it is made up of the production of commodities by means of commodities. This conception leads to an emphasis on the commodities, which are themselves means of production, rather than on the final consumption goods. In particular, the consumption goods necessary for workers' subsistence are considered a special case of produced means of production.

This approach implies a vision of the production process quite different from that of the *Wealth of Nations*. In fact, Ricardo's interest is directed towards a 'horizontal' definition of production processes, where the identity of each physical process of production is not lost in the succession of reductions to the quantities of labour and other primary inputs that are, directly or indirectly, embodied in the commodities under consideration.

In particular, instead of being understood as a stock from which, *in the last analysis*, derives the wealth of a nation (Smith), here labour has the function of a necessary element for the carrying out of productive operations, in the same way as machinery and land.

An important consequence of the inter-industrial approach followed by Ricardo is to be found in the field of the theory of natural prices. In fact, natural prices are studied without taking into account the relations between supply and demand in single markets, and by considering the quantities of labour needed to obtain the commodities between which exchange takes place: 'The value of a commodity, or the quantity of any other commodity for which it will exchange, depends on the relative quantity of labour which is necessary for its production' (Ricardo, 1951, p. 11).[3]

[3] This rule is considered by Ricardo to be the 'foundation of the exchangeable value of all things, excepting those which cannot be increased by human industry' (Ricardo, 1951, p. 13). The principle of embodied labour allows the formulation of a theory of natural prices completely internal to the fundamental idea of production. The exceptions to this principle confirm the links between relative prices of products and relative conditions of production. In fact, according to Ricardo, an increase or decrease in the unit wage can lead to a change in relative prices, if there are differences between the proportions of fixed and circulating capital in the various industries (*Principles*, ch. I, s. IV), or differences in the duration of capital

The problem of value presents itself to Smith and to Ricardo in two very different ways. For Smith, as we have seen, it is essential to determine the rate of exchange between commodities and labour (the 'commanded labour' corresponding to each commodity, or group of commodities). For Ricardo, it is essential to determine the proportions in which commodities exchange with one another, and such proportions are associated with the proportions between the corresponding quantities of 'embodied labour'. Smith's approach thus places at the centre of the theory the productive activity of men, showing that, in an economic system founded on the division of labour, single producers are linked to each other through a particular system of values (the quantities of 'commanded labour' corresponding to each commodity or group of commodities).

Instead, Ricardo's approach places the relations between techniques of production at the centre of the analysis, thus showing that in an economic system consisting of different production processes, the production of each commodity is generally linked to the production of other commodities (the commodities necessary as its means of production or those of which it is a means of production). In the latter case, the link is provided by a different system of values (the ratios between the quantities of 'embodied labour' corresponding to every commodity).

IV EVOLUTION OF CLASSICAL POLITICAL ECONOMY: FROM RICARDO TO KEYNES

The subsequent evolution of classical political economy is characterized by the distinct development of concepts present in the writings of Smith and Ricardo. The idea that the main function of the theory of value is to study the formation of 'labour equivalents', so as to permit the functioning of an economic system based on the activity of producers independent of each other, remains dominant in the thought of 'Ricardian socialists', and later on constitutes the basis of the theory expounded in Marx's *Capital* (the labour theory of value and surplus value). In this sense, the theoretical contribution of Marx begins with the attempt to integrate the 'commanded labour' theory of Smith (in a society based on the division of labour, the value of products is 'measured' by the quantity of labour that society itself recognizes as equivalent to the commodity produced) with the Ricardian theory of technical relations between production processes (the value of products is the result of the relative conditions of production of commodities, which depend on technological interdependence between

and in its period of circulation (*Principles*, ch. I, s. V). In any case, variations in supply and demand can lead to temporary changes in the rates of exchange between any two commodities, but they cannot alter the natural prices of those commodities (*Principles*, ch. XXX).

processes and express the exchange relations compatible with the reproducibility of the system).

The application of the Ricardian method, and of the 'inter-industry' aspect characteristic of it, permits Marx to consider labour power as a commodity produced within the economic system. Nevertheless, taken to its extreme conclusion, this approach might not lead to the labour theory of value. On the contrary, it might lead one to consider exchange-values as being independent from the proportions between quantities of 'embodied labour', as each quantity of labour can be reduced to the quantity of physical commodities necessary for the subsistence consumption of workers. However, the emphasis on the 'natural' properties of an economic system, understood as the organization of human activity for the production of material wealth, is characteristic of Marx. This last point of view allows Marx to integrate the circular view of the productive system, derived from Ricardo (and from Quesnay), with the conception of vertically integrated sectors, derived from Smith. Thus the idea that labour is the stock from which, *in the last analysis*, material wealth is derived, acquires primary importance. So does the idea that, precisely for the reason above, the system of 'labour equivalents', used in a particular exchange economy in order to compare the productive activities taking place in different places and under different conditions, is of central importance. We can say that the originality of Marx's theoretical contribution, and some of the problems internal to his logical scheme are due, in part, to the fact that in *Capital* the conception of production for vertically integrated sectors, characteristic of Smith, is combined with the circular conception of production, characteristic of Ricardo.

The Marxian attempt to found, on the existence of 'labour equivalents', a general theory of value for an exchange economy is taken up and developed by Nikolay Ivanovič Ziber in his *Teoria tsennosti i Kapitala D. Rikardo* (The Theory of Value and Capital in David Ricardo), published in Kiev in 1871.

Ziber criticizes the method followed by Ricardo and Marx in examining the effects of a change in the unit wage (or in the rate of profit) on the relative prices of commodities. The two authors began with the hypothesis of a uniform rate of profit and allowed that, in economic systems where different industries are characterized by different proportions between labour and the means of production, a change in the distribution of social product leads to variations in the relations of exchange between commodities. Under such conditions, therefore, it will no longer be correct to maintain that the relative values of commodities depend exclusively on the relative quantities of labour necessary for their production. Instead, according to Ziber, the modifications and exceptions to the pure labour theory of value considered by Ricardo and Marx should be attributed to an inadequate analysis of the effects that the variations in one component of value (wages) exercise on the profit component. The Russian economist proposes taking account of the differences in the composition of capital (and therefore of intersectoral differences in the proportions between labour and the means of production), before determining which variation in the rate of profit corresponds to a given variation of the unit wage. According to Ziber, it will thus be possible to maintain the proportionality between values and the quantities of 'embodied labour' (some of the passages of Ziber on this problem are quoted in Quadrio-Curzio and Scazzieri, 1982b, pp. 44–6).

We have already seen that the circular and 'inter-industry' conception of the productive system, characteristic of Ricardo, leads economic theory to concentrate on technical relations between production processes, and on the production of commodities by means of commodities, rather than on labour understood as the 'fund which originally supplies [every nation] with all the necessaries and conveniences of life which it annually consumes' (Smith).

As a matter of principle, the 'inter-industry' approach is independent of the explanation of relative prices in terms of the relations between quantities of 'embodied labour'. This explains the position adopted by Robert Torrens in his *Essay on the Production of Wealth* (1821), where the Ricardian labour theory of value is rejected, in order to maintain that 'when the capitals employed are of equal value, and of equal degrees of durability, the goods produced by them will bear equal prices in the market', and that 'when capitals equal in amount, but of different degrees of durability, are employed, the articles produced, together with the residue of capital, in one occupation, will be equal in exchangeable value to the things produced, and the residue of capital, in another occupation' (Torrens, 1821, p. 29).

In the following decades, the 'inter-industry' approach was developed mostly by economists in continental Europe. Foremost was Marx, who used it to study the formation of relative prices and the dynamic of the economic system (schemes of simple and extended reproduction). Other important works, sometimes directed to the study of specific problems, but always linked to the circular vision of production processes, should also be mentioned.

Contributions to price theory and the development of the Ricardian position are due to Emilio Nazzani (*Saggi di economia politica*, 1881; *Sulle prime cinque sezioni del capitolo 'On Value' di Ricardo*, 1883); Vladimir Karpovič Dmitriev (*Ekonomičeskie Očerki*, 1904); Ladislaus Von Bortkiewicz (*Wertrechnung und Preisrechnung in Marxschen System*, 1906/7; *Zur Berichtigung der grundlegenden theoretischen Konstruktion von Marx in III. Band des Kapitals*, 1907).

Beginning with the work of Tugan-Baranovsky on the industrial crises in Britain (*Promyshlennye Krizisy v sovremennoi Anglii*, 1894), the 'inter-industry' description of productive phenomena is at the basis of some of the most important contributions to the theory of economic fluctuations. The explicit use of a scheme of industrial interdependence allows Tugan-Baranovsky to argue that the existence of economic fluctuations is not so much due to the possibility of a general glut (a general overproduction of commodities), as to the difficulty of maintaining the correct proportions between fixed capital and circulating capital on the expansion path of a market economy.

The connection between economic fluctuations and overproduction of the means of production is also at the centre of the contributions by Arthur Spiethoff (*Die Krisentheorien von Tugan Baranovsky und Pohle*, 1903), Albert Aftalion (*Les crises périodiques de surproduction*, 1913), Dennis Holme Robertson (*A Study of Industrial Fluctuation*, 1915; *Banking Policy and the Price Level*, 1926).

The influence of the Ricardian tradition based on the 'inter-industry' conception of the productive system, and on the consideration of the proportions of fixed and circulating capital, is also to be found in other studies of fluctuations, which in other respects are far from a circular vision of the economic system, such as those by Costantino Bresciani Turroni (*Le vicende del marco tedesco*, 1931) and by Friedrich August von Hayek (*Prices and Production*, 1931).

Finally, the interest in problems of the structural apparatuses is central to the studies of Michal Kalecki, on the conjunctural oscillations in an economic system, beginning with *Próba teorii Koniunktury* (1933). In fact, for Kalecki, who in part derives his conception of the trade cycle from the studies of Aftalion, oscillations can be explained by concentrating upon investment processes and by paying special attention to the construction time of fixed capital.

More recently, the approach based on the 'inter-industry' conception of the productive system has provided fundamental contributions on economic dynamics (Jan von Neumann, *Ueber ein ökonomisches Gleichungssystem und eine Verallgemeinerung des Brouwerschen Fixpunktsatzes*, 1937), on the relations between final consumption and the structural apparatus (Wassily Leontief, *The Structure of American Economy, 1919–1929*, 1941), and on the relations between the interdependence of production processes, prices and the distribution of the social product (Piero Sraffa, *Production of Commodities by Means of Commodities*, 1960).

However, the main line of evolution of classical political economy shows a progressive weakening of interest in the production of commodities by means of commodities, and more particularly in the role of produced means of production. This tendency is manifest in John Stuart Mill, who returns to a description of the productive system according to vertically integrated sectors, with the result that the structural apparatus loses all autonomy and ends up being reduced to a simple appendix of the apparatus of transformation: 'the things used as materials in some process or other of manufacture are of a most miscellaneous character, drawn from almost every quarter of the animal, vegetable, and mineral kingdoms. And besides this, the finished products of many branches of industry are the materials of others' (Mill, 1965, p. 36).

Mill's vision leads to an emphasis on the unidirectional, rather than the 'circular' aspects of production. The process of production thus ends up looking like a 'one-way' course that leads from primitive productive factors to consumption goods. This approach has important consequences for the theory of value. In fact, the interdependence between productive processes becomes of secondary importance, as does the idea that relative prices of commodities are explained by the relative conditions of production of the same commodities.

On the other hand, the direct link between primitive factors of production and final consumption goods ends up emphasizing even more the phenomena of exchange (reallocation of given resources). The relation between supply and demand thus acquires primary importance, even if only through the mediation of the cost of production in the case of producible commodities.

This position, already manifest in Mill, is accentuated in John Elliott Cairnes (*Some Leading Principles of Political Economy*, 1874). On the one hand, Cairnes replaces the concept of 'natural price' with the concept of 'normal value' (the 'gravitational centre' of current values) and, on the other hand, he shows the possibility of determining in some cases the normal value notwithstanding the cost of production ('international values . . . are not governed by cost of production, and we have thus normal values which are not connected with cost, but come under the influence of some other principle' (Cairnes, 1874, pp. 46–7).

This evolution is completed by Marshall (*Principles of Economics*, 1961; 1st edn 1890), who extends 'the general idea, underlying the proposition that Value is determined at the equilibrium point of Demand and Supply, . . . so as to discover a whole Copernican system, by which all the elements of the economic universe are kept in their places by mutual counterpoise and interaction' (Keynes, 1924, p. 350).

This result is made possible by 'completing' the classical theory with a systematic analysis of the relations between final demand and individual utility, with the distinction between short and long term, and with the consideration of the equilibria relative to particular industries.

In this context it would be suitable to recall that before Marshall, John Elliott Cairnes had recognized in the relations between supply and demand the main cause of international and domestic prices in 'all cases in which groups of producers, excluded from reciprocal industrial competition, exchange their products' (Cairnes, 1874, p. 99). Nevertheless, the conviction that the relations between supply and demand allow the determination of 'normal' exchange relations only in the case of given productive resources, had led Cairnes to exclude the determining influence of supply and demand in the case of the normal value of single produced commodities:

> while the prices of particular commodities may fluctuate indefinitely in international as in other trade, the same possibility does not exist for the prices of aggregates of commodities exchanged by definite groups of producers, such as independent nations, or the non-competing sections in domestic industry. The limits to such fluctuations are set in the limited purchasing power, incident to the limited productive power, at any given time possessed by such trading groups. It is in this way that a normal relation arises in the terms of the transactions carried on, and that a central point is furnished towards which the fluctuations of the market gravitate, performing in such trade the same function discharged under a *régime* of competition by the principle of cost. (Cairnes, 1874, pp. 104–5)

Variations in the endowment of productive resources modify the normal value of commodities or of groups of commodities. Such resources, nevertheless, can be considered as given for each 'non-competing group':

> In the absence of any great changes in the condition of productive industry, and of legislation specially contrived for this purpose, neither the aggregate production of a community nor the proportion of its means employed in interchanges with other communities can easily undergo a sudden serious variation. The total production will depend on the nature and extent of its resources; and the proportion employed in external trading on the comparative character of those resources as they stand related to those of the communities with which it trades. (Cairnes, 1874, pp. 103–4)

On the other hand, the transfer of resources can easily occur between productive units internal to each 'non-competing group'. Consequently, supply and demand do not appear to Cairnes as a safe basis on which to found the 'normal' value of single commodities produced within each group. In this last case, the determining influence on 'normal' value is attributed to the cost of production (Cairnes, 1874, p. 94).

The laws of decreasing marginal utility and of non-proportional cost allow Marshall to establish a systematic link between the price and quantity of single commodities. On the other hand, the distinction between short and long term allows him to include in his theoretical scheme different criteria for the determination of price, without contradicting the general principle based on the relations between supply and demand.

Thus, in the short term, when the fund of productive resources 'is practically fixed', utility and demand constitute the predominant influence on exchange-value, whereas in the long run, when the production of productive instruments responds to the demand for final consumption goods, the cost of production eventually represents the prevailing influence over exchange-value (see Marshall, 1961, vol. I, pp. 348–50).

The Mill–Cairnes–Marshall line constitutes one of the most significant examples of integration between the fundamental ideas of production and exchange. The relative eclecticism of this scientific tradition is due to the attempt to give primary importance to the aspects connected with the producibility of consumption goods, neglecting, however, the producibility of the means of production. Such an attempt leads to an almost exclusive emphasis on the apparatus of transformation of primitive resources into final consumption goods, neglecting the inter-industry relationships and referring to a description of the productive system for vertically integrated sectors.

In the contributions referred to so far, the most important implication of such an approach is the explanation of prices of goods through a mechanism (supply and demand) that has its origins in the sphere of exchange, rather than in that of production. On the other hand, other contributions call attention to the origins of national wealth, its distribution and its dynamics, following a line of inquiry which starts with Smith and Malthus. In this context, the work of Arthur Cecil Pigou on welfare economics (*Wealth and Welfare*, 1912; *The Economics of Welfare*, 1929; 1st edn 1920) and that of Keynes on the connections between production of wealth, levels of activity and levels of employment (*The General Theory of Employment, Interest and Money*, 1973; 1st edn 1936) should be especially mentioned.

Besides the sometimes radically different approaches, in both of these authors, it is possible to single out a vision of the productive system for vertically integrated sectors, together with a definite interest in the aspects of economic life linked to the producibility of commodities, rather than to their scarcity. This last feature is obvious in the links established by Pigou between welfare and the 'national dividend':

> generally speaking, economic causes act upon the economic welfare of any country, not directly, but through the making and using of that objective counterpart of economic welfare which economists call the national dividend or national income. . . . The two concepts, economic welfare and the national dividend, are thus co-ordinate, in such wise that any description of the content of one of them implies a corresponding description of the content of the other. (Pigou, 1929, p. 31)

In a different manner, Keynes also pays special attention to producible commodities, remarking that the major defect of the theoretical apparatus of his *Treatise on Money* is the fact that it is based on an 'instantaneous picture taken on the assumption of a given output' (Keynes, 1973, p. xxii). On the other hand, the *General Theory* is considered by Keynes to be 'primarily a study of the forces which determine changes in the scale of output and employment as a whole' (Keynes, 1973, p. xxii).

In Pigou, the study of the causes on which changes in the 'national dividend' depend is based on a description of the productive system for vertically integrated sectors, so much so that the link between primitive factors of production and consumption goods gains primary importance: 'We are concerned with causes that increase or diminish the size of the national dividend by acting on the way in which the productive resources of no matter what kind belonging to the country are distributed among different uses or occupations' (Pigou, 1929, p. 129).

In Keynes also, the emphasis on the apparatus of transformation leads to a neglect of the problems posed by the production of commodities by means of commodities. The link between Keynesian theory and the definition of the productive system for vertically integrated sectors is manifest in the chapter on the choice of units in the *General Theory* (ch. IV): 'In the case of an individual firm or industry producing a homogeneous product we can speak legitimately, if we wish, of increases or decreases of output. But when we are aggregating the activities of all firms, we cannot speak accurately except in terms of quantities of employment applied to a given equipment' (Keynes, 1973, p. 40). The direct link between primitive factors of production and final consumption goods (a consequence of the vertical integration of productive activities) is shown in the basic structure of the *General Theory*:

> We take as given the existing skill and quantity of labour, the existing technique, the degree of competition, the tastes and habits of the consumer, the disutility of different intensities of labour and of the activities of supervision and organisation, as well as the social structure including the forces, other than our variables set forth below, which determine the distribution of the national income. ... The given factors allow us to infer what level of national income measured in terms of the wage-unit will correspond to any given level of employment; so that within the economic framework which we take as given the national income depends on the volume of employment ... in the sense that there is a unique correlation between the two. (Keynes, 1973, pp. 245–6)

Seen in this perspective, Keynes's contribution to the theory of employment belongs to the classical line of inquiry concerning the amount of national wealth (an inquiry started by economists such as Smith and Malthus). Nevertheless there do exist important differences between these authors and Keynes, as to the attention the latter pays to 'the pure theory of what determines the *actual employment* of available resources' (Keynes, 1973, p. 4), instead of to the factors on which *maximum* wealth depends. This feature of Keynesian theory is also an essential distinction from the inquiries on the formation of national revenue conducted in the previous years by Pigou.

V THE SPREADING OF THE FUNDAMENTAL IDEA OF EXCHANGE: FROM THÜNEN TO PARETO

Problems concerning the producibility of commodities and wealth dominate the evolution of political economy from the end of the eighteenth to the beginning of the nineteenth century. This is especially true for countries where, as a result of the industrial revolution, the transformation of the productive structure was faster. Nevertheless, during the same years, contributions to the theoretical line that embraces the fundamental idea of exchange can also be found.

We have seen that, in the eighteenth century, important developments had already taken place, concerning the relations between individual preferences and demand for consumption goods (Galiani), and the determination of price under conditions of competition and on the basis of supply and demand (Beccaria, Turgot, Verri and Valeriani). The concept of general equilibrium in exchange had found its first expression in the contribution of Isnard.

In the first decades of the nineteenth century, the fundamental idea of exchange was extended, so as to cover productive phenomena (these phenomena are analysed on the assumption of given resources) and the distribution of the social product obtained through the employment of resources.

In this sphere, most of all, the contributions of Johann-Heinrich von Thünen (*Der Isolierte Staat*, 1826; *Der naturgemässe Arbeitslohn*, 1850) and of Mountifort Longfield (*Lectures on Political Economy*, 1834) should be remembered. In these works, the vertical integration of productive activities permits the 'displacement' of capital at the beginning of each production process (considered as a vertically integrated sector). The description of the production process thus obtained is later on used to give priority to the relations between 'primitive' factors of production (labour, capital, land). Thus it becomes possible to conceive of a direct link between the quantity produced of each commodity and the 'productive contribution' provided by each factor.

The theory of production, transformed in the study of combinations between non-produced factors of production, becomes compatible with the allocative logic of exchange models and constitutes the premiss for explaining the distribution of the social product through the principle of marginal productivity (every 'primitive' factor of production receives, under conditions of equilibrium, a remuneration equal to the increase in product corresponding to the 'last' unit dose of the factor that has been used).

In this period, the principle of diminishing marginal utility, conjectured by Galiani (see above), is expressed in a definite formulation by Etienne-Juvénal Dupuit, to whom we owe the idea that each product delivers a particular type of utility, not only for each consumer, but also for every need in the satisfaction of which it is used (Etienne-Juvénal Dupuit, *De la mesure de l'utilité des travaux publiques*, 1844). To Dupuit we are also indebted for the anticipation of the concept of 'consumer's surplus' (the difference between what a consumer would be willing to pay and what he actually pays), a concept which was later developed in complete form by Marshall in his *Principles*.

In the first decades of the nineteenth century, the theoretical apparatus based on the fundamental idea of exchange finally underwent important developments in the determination of the equilibrium price in different market forms. In particular, Antoine-Augustin Cournot 'appears to have been the first to represent by means of an equation, or curve, the relation between the price of a commodity and the quantity saleable at that price in a market consisting of purchasers competing with each other' (Edgeworth, 1894/5, p. 445). On these premisses, Cournot formulates the equations to determine the equilibrium prices of commodities produced under conditions of monopoly, duopoly and perfect competition (Antoine-Augustin Cournot, *Récherches sur les principes mathématiques de la théorie des richesses*, 1838).

With the above contributions, the premisses of a general systematization of economic thought, based on the principle of the allocation of given resources, are advanced. In the ensuing decades, the works of Francesco Ferrara and of Hermann-Heinrich Gossen represent one of the peaks of the tradition of thought based on the concept of exchange. The first explicit attempts to formulate a general theory of economic phenomena, beginning with this concept, are due to them.

The theoretical system of Ferrara (Introductions to the first and second series of *Biblioteca dell'Economista*, 1850–68) is based on the idea that every economic action is determined by a judgement of convenience (see, in particular, Ferrara, 1854, 1859). On the other hand, according to Ferrara it would be a 'capital error' to conceive of 'the subject of our science' as consisting 'of things rather than of actions' (Ferrara, 1859, p. LXXXI). The result is that the sphere of political economy is reduced to the area of phenomena regulated by the judgement of convenience. Thus production and consumption appear as particular cases of exchange, regulated by the principle of substitution (the special form that the judgement of convenience takes when 'from the necessity of comparing heterogeneous materials, is born the need to invoke utility as the common element' (Ferrara, 1863, p. LXIX).

In the study of value, the approach adopted by Ferrara leads to a closely individualistic conception: 'value, even in its most elaborate form as *exchange value* has all of its elements in a state of achieved development in the individual, independently of all relations of exchange with others of his kind' (Ferrara, 1854, p. XLIX). Nevertheless, this does not mean that Ferrara attributes exclusive importance to utility in the determination of value: for him, value is a judgement formulated on two elements, utility and cost, and it cannot be attributed to only one of the two (see Montemartini, 1982, pp. 100–15).

Finally, the laws of production and distribution appear to Ferrara as particular cases of the law of substitution, by which all phenomena of exchange are regulated. Consequently, every process of production is seen as a combination of 'primitive' factors of production, established on the basis of a judgement of convenience. Thus a sort of 'law of variable proportions' is constructed, and the principle of decreasing productivity in the use of any given factor of production is extended from agriculture to include all productive activity.

In the study of distribution, Ferrara's approach naturally leads him to criticize the residual character assumed by certain forms of revenue in some theories, such as is the case with profits in the theory of Ricardo (see Ferrara, 1863, pp. XCIV–C).

Gossen substitutes for Ferrara's 'judgement of convenience' a system of deduction derived in a rigorous way from the principle of diminishing marginal utility (see his work, *Entwickelung der Gesetze des menschlichen Verkehrs*, 1854). This approach permits a symmetric study of consumption and production (to which the criterion of the increasing disutility of labour is applied), and a determination of the position of equilibrium of the economic system on the basis of a single psychological law.

Around the 1860s, studies based on the fundamental idea of exchange gained vigour once more, and acquired a progressively growing influence among economists. Within the space of a few years, and in various countries, fundamental works affirming political economy as the science of scarcity and of the allocation of given resources were published. The consideration of individual utility and disutility is at the core of the price theories formulated almost simultaneously by William Stanley Jevons (*Theory of Political Economy*, 1871), Carl Menger (*Grundsätze der Volkswirtschaftslehre*, 1871) and Léon Walras (*Eléments d'économie politique pure*, 1874).

Despite considerable differences in method, these three authors share a conception of political economy as the science of exchange, the importance attributed to final consumption goods, and the reconstruction of production processes as processes for the transformation of non-produced resources into consumption goods. Therefore, from their theoretical system, the producibility of commodities recedes into the background, and is replaced by the basic concept of scarcity, common to all commodities exchanged, whether or not they are produced within the economic system.

An important consequence of this point of view is the reduction of the means of production to 'primitive' factors of production, which are more or less distant in time from the final product. Or, they are reduced to consumption goods more or less close to the phase of the 'distribution of utility'. The most important contributions to this theme are to be found in Jevons and Menger. When writing to Edgeworth, the former comments: 'I fear you have not yet approached to a comprehension of my theory of capital as involving solely the element of time. . . . Indeed, as long as you speak of "capital" instead of "capitalisation", I think you are pretty sure to go wrong' (Jevons, 1886, p. 439). On the other hand, Menger suggests a distinction between goods of the first, second, third and higher order, where the produced means of production lose their identity, as the 'circularity' of production processes has been eliminated.

The following years are characterized by developments of great importance in this line of research. Francis Ysidro Edgeworth proposes in *Mathematical Psychics* (1881) a refined analysis of the links between the calculation of sensations (pain and pleasure), exchange and economic equilibrium. The result is a rigorous reconstruction of the situations of economic exchange as particular cases of contract, where it is concluded that the contract is indeterminate in all cases of market imperfection (important examples are provided by cases where the number of competitors are limited, contracted articles are not perfectly divisible, and pre-established forms of agreement exist between labourers or between producers).

The importance of cases of market imperfection leads Edgeworth to conclude that 'the reverence paid to *competition*; in whose results – as if worked out by a play of physical forces, impersonal, impartial – economists have complacently acquiesced' (Edgeworth, 1881, p. 50) should be questioned. In fact: 'almost every species of social and political contract is affected with an indeterminateness like that which has been described; an evil which is likely to be much more felt when, with the growth of intelligence and liberty, the principle of *contract* shall have replaced both the appeal to force and the acquiescence in custom' (Edgeworth, 1881, p. 51). In these cases, recourse has to be made to a 'principle of arbitration' (Edgeworth, 1881, pp. 51–6).

Another important direction for research is provided by the attempt to extend the theory of resource allocation to the systematic study of production and income distribution. In this context, the development of the theory of marginal productivity, which concerns both the study of production in the strict sense and the study of distribution, is fundamental.

The description of production processes is a central concern of Eugen von Böhm-Bawerk and of Friedrich von Wieser, and it constitutes the premiss of their results on income distribution. The idea that the valuation of produced commodities should be made by explicitly considering certain aspects of the interdependence between production processes is characteristic of Wieser (see Wieser, 1893, pp. 184–5).

The position of Böhm-Bawerk is different (*Positive Theorie des Kapitales*, 1889), for this author avoids the explicit consideration of the interdependence between production processes, by reducing the produced means of production to dated quantities of labour. The complete vertical integration of production processes achieved by such an operation permits Böhm-Bawerk to establish a systematic link between the choice of the technique of production (reduced to a choice of *duration* of the production process) and the rate of interest of which Böhm-Bawerk exposes the psychological foundations (the higher rate for existing and immediately enjoyable goods, and the lower rate for the goods to be enjoyed in the future). The approach of Böhm-Bawerk to the study of production and distribution is therefore characterized at the same time by the vertical integration of production processes and by the 'temporal' integration of such processes (any process that leads to a final consumption good is reconstructed as a sequence of successive operations over time). This approach is developed in the studies of distribution by Knut Wicksell (*Über Wert, Kapital und Rente*, 1893; *Föreläsningar i Nationalekonomi*, 1901–6), where the treatment of capital in terms of a given quantity of labour reaches its most elaborate form.

In the same years, other economists studied the distribution of income within the 'allocative' line of thought, limiting themselves to the vertical integration of production processes in a timeless context. This is the case with Philip Henry Wicksteed (*An Essay on the Coordination of the Laws of Distribution*, 1894; *The Common Sense of Political Economy*, 1910), John Bates Clark (*The Distribution of Wealth*, 1899), Walras (beginning with the second edition of *Eléments d'économie politique pure*, 1899), Vilfredo Pareto (*Cours d'économie politique*, 1896/7; *Manuale di economia politica*, 1906) and Enrico Barone (*Studi sulla distribuzione*, 1896).

The distance of these authors from the solutions proposed by Böhm-Bawerk and Wicksell is precisely described by Wicksell in his comments on the approach followed by Walras and Pareto:

> the idea of a *period* of production or of capital-investment does not, as we have said, exist in the Walras–Pareto theory; in it capital and interest rank equally with land and rent; in other words, it remains a theory of production under essentially non-capitalistic conditions, even though the existence of durable, but apparently indestructible instruments, is taken into account. (Wicksell, 1934, vol. I, p. 171)

In spite of the common use of 'static' vertical integration, there exist important differences between the economists of the latter group. In the case of Clark,

> Labor is a fund of interchangeable units of equal productive power; and capital is a somewhat similar fund of productive goods, normally maintained

> by reproducing particular instruments and materials as they wear out or are used up. It can move, by investing the replacement fund in different industries, without requiring particular 'capital goods' to be moved. Any considerable change in the amount of capital per worker (or per unit of labor) in an industry requires the capital to be put in different forms – for example, substituting power shovels for picks and spades. (J. M. Clark, 1952, p. 609)

The vertical integration of productive activities leads Clark to consider each production process (vertically integrated) as a combination of a limited number of 'primitive' factors, each one composed of interchangeable units ('capital', 'labour', 'land'). On this premiss, a theory of the functional distribution of income is formulated. It covers the same ground of Ricardian theory, but it is based on the criterion of marginal productivity.

A different approach is followed by Wicksteed, according to whom: 'there seems to be no possible scientific division of the factors of industry into great groups, and still less any possibility of an exhaustive enumeration of them. . . . In proceeding, therefore, to a closer examination of the laws of distribution and the function of the undertaker we shall entirely ignore all attempts to enumerate and classify the factors of production' (Wicksteed, 1933, pp. 366–7).

In Wicksteed, the vertical integration of production processes is not carried to the point of requiring the introduction of 'malleable' factors of production as in Clark; each factor of production maintains, in appearance, its own identity (its physical characteristics). Nevertheless, the entire process of production is considered by Wicksteed to be a 'one-way' flow that leads from the scarce resources available to employers, to the finished goods that the employer himself presents for sale: 'by hypothesis he [the entrepreneur] is dealing with limited resources, and in applying these resources he must draw commodities, services, and privileges out of the circle of exchange, and so combine and direct them as to produce a result, that can itself be returned into the circle of exchange with value higher than that of the factors or ingredients that were drawn out' (Wicksteed, 1933, p. 367).

In this way, also, Wicksteed employs vertical integration in production processes, in the sense that the category of intermediate products disappears from the description of productive activity, and each produced commodity seems to be the result of the employment of 'limited' and 'primitive' resources.

The method of vertical integration is taken to its extremes by Vilfredo Pareto. In fact, this author, tracing a line of inquiry started by Senior and Ferrara, ends up by eliminating completely the category of 'capital' from the complex of the factors of production, by considering capital as a particular consumption good. To this purpose, Pareto observes that it is possible 'to identify two big classes of elements of production, the first containing what is not consumed, or is consumed slowly: the second containing what is consumed rapidly' (Pareto, 1906, p. 281).

To this observation, Pareto adds: 'such classification is arbitrary and not rigorous, just like the terms *slowly* and *rapidly*; however, experience shows that it is of use in treating economic matters. . . . For the things that are not consumed, or are consumed slowly in the act of production, a name was required, and they were called "capital"' (Pareto, 1906, p. 281).

Therefore, not only is the circularity of the processes of production eliminated in Pareto, but there is also a shift in the treatment of capital from the theory of production to the theory of consumption. In this way, the premisses for a theory of distribution centred exclusively on the phenomena of exchange are set. In fact the link between profit and produced means of production disappears, and it becomes possible to reduce profit to interest, that is to say to a form of compensation for the purchase of goods 'which are not consumed, or are consumed slowly'.

This approach opens the way for the replacement of capital with *savings* in the list of factors of production (see Enrico Barone, *Principi di economia politica* (1908), Rome, Athenæum, 1929, pp. 33–49), and for an explanation of interest within a theory of choice between alternative flows of revenue (see Irving Fisher, *The Rate of Interest*, 1907; *The Theory of Interest*, 1930).

VI CONCLUDING REMARKS

The above analysis now permits some general conclusions, both on the pattern of scientific change within political economy and on the time sequence in which the thought of great economists influenced successive developments in theory.

First of all, it is worth noting that the differences within the two main strands of thought (constructed by beginning from the fundamental ideas of exchange and production, respectively), as well as the continuity in time of those strands, render impossible the reconstruction of the evolution of political economy according to the 'model' of a succession of phases, where each stage replaces and renders the preceding phase obsolete. It is more appropriate to consider the two fundamental ideas as lines of interpolation, useful in linking contributions which are sometimes distant in time, but close to each other in some fundamental characteristics. This criterion helps us to avoid simplistic unilineal visions as to the 'progress' of economic theory, and allows us to place some economists on more than one line of interpolation, thus providing the possibility of comparison between fundamental ideas based on the process of their formation.

With this perspective in mind, it is possible to place, on the line of interpolation provided by the fundamental idea of exchange, contributions where almost total concentration on the apparatus of transformation and on final demand brings to the fore the direct relationships between 'primitive' factors of production, and where exchange activity replaces productive activity as the fundamental determinant of economic relations. On the other hand, the line of interpolation supplied by the fundamental idea of production provides the link between contributions sharing a vision of the economic system, to which the activity of production and the interdependence of processes are fundamental.

The course of economic theory can thus be seen as a case of multilineal evolution, with many points in common between the two major trends (consider Smith, John Stuart Mill, Marshall, and to a lesser extent Dmitriev and Schumpeter). In this context, the dynamics of political economy can be considered to be the result of an interaction between a dichotomy internal to the manner of thinking of economists (due mainly to a different understanding of productive phenomena), and an external dichotomy, based on the antagonism–coexistence between the fundamental apparatuses of transformation and structure.

Economists interested in the inter-industry structure generally adopt a 'horizontal' integration of productive activities, considering the activities producing similar goods to be part of the same 'industry' or 'sector'. They then examine transactions between sectors. On the other hand, the economists focusing on the transformation of primary resources into final products generally consider a limited number of vertically integrated sectors (each one corresponding to a final consumption good), and avoid explicit study of inter-industry transactions. In this latter case, the direct relationship between primary resources and producers' preferences is brought to the fore.

The internal dichotomy forces economists to consider the structural or the transformation apparatus, depending on whether they adopt a view of the productive system based on inter-industry transactions or on vertically integrated sectors, respectively. The external dichotomy gives prominence to the transformation apparatus with respect to the structural apparatus, when the slowdown of growth brings to the fore the scarcity aspect of goods. On the other hand, the structural apparatus is more clearly in view than the transformation apparatus, when scarcity bottlenecks are overcome and the acceleration of growth brings to the fore the producibility aspect of goods.

Before applying this general criterion, scarcity itself ought to be carefully considered. For, when the slowdown of growth is due to a bottleneck in the supply of certain primary inputs, the network of inter-industry transactions is often affected, and the structural apparatus may become the object of careful consideration (think of the corn-law debates in nineteenth-century Britain, in which attention to the inter-industry structure was brought about by consideration of limited land availability). On the other hand, when the slowdown of growth is due to the 'climacteric' of the structural apparatus, the transformation of primary resources into final consumption goods comes to the fore. This might explain why the circular view of the economic system gained wide acceptance in Britain during the first decades of the nineteenth century. For a number of reasons (such as the relative closedness of the economy during the Napoleonic wars, or the rise of productive sectors specializing in the production of means of production), inter-industry transactions came to the fore. The same principles might also explain the dominance of the 'one-way' view of economic activity (from primary resources to final consumption goods) during the 'climacteric' period of British economic history at the end of the nineteenth century.

Further cases in which our general principles can be easily applied are provided by the strength of British classical political economy in Germany and Russia around the close of the nineteenth century (this was, for these countries, a time of accelerating growth and deep structural changes), and by the relative weakness of classical political economy in Italy for a great part of the nineteenth century (this was, for Italy, a time of economic stagnation, in which the 'transformation aspect' of the economic system was more clearly in view).

But we should not forget that historical phases of the 'dominance' of the structural apparatus over the transformation apparatus have not prevented, in other cases, the formulation of theories based on the description of the economic system for vertically integrated sectors (consider Malthus in Britain, Cournot in France and Mangoldt in Germany).

Similarly, but less frequently, the dominance of the transformation aspect in economic life has not prevented certain economists from accepting the circular view of the economic system (a case in point is given by the work of Nazzani in Italy).

Thus, in each historical phase, economic theory remains open to a variety of developments. However, the effective dynamic of economic systems provides an important criterion for distinguishing developments that widen the explanatory and intervening capacity of theory, from purely academic developments, which in some cases seem to be just entangled theoretical schemes.

It seems to be clear that in economics, judgement on the 'progressive' or 'degenerate' features of any given research programme cannot exclude a value judgement on the relative importance of the problems tackled. The general question of the basic characteristics of human activity within economic systems therefore arises. To this problem we will devote a few remarks, which, concluding this study, pose the new (and ancient) question of the role of value judgements in economic thought.

In this context, it is helpful to begin with the distinction between 'acquisitive' behaviour and 'creative' behaviour. Consumption and production represent characteristic examples of the first and the second categories, respectively. From our point of view, 'acquisitive' behaviour, although deep-rooted in man, is not his distinctive characteristic. The situation is different with 'creative' behaviour, and particularly with the production of wealth through the strengthening of the resources nature has provided. Behaviour belonging to this second category is in fact a distinctive characteristic of the human being. Nevertheless, the same capacity to produce wealth can be expressed both in the apparatus of transformation and in the apparatus of structure.

In the apparatus of transformation, the given availability of non-produced resources determines an absolute upper limit on the capacity to produce final consumption goods. In this situation, the creative capacity of man is strongly limited. Instead, in the apparatus of structure, the capacity to produce is only relatively restricted in terms of the availability of resources. Within this apparatus, the capacity of human beings to produce is in fact opposed to scarcity, since the apparatus of structure tends to remove scarcity by increasing the distance between final products and primitive resources, thus rendering possible an increase in the quantity of final products, without necessarily increasing the resources employed.

The apparatus of transformation brings to the fore the capacity of human beings to 'extract' goods from resources that are limited in amount. Instead, the apparatus of structure stresses the aspects of producibility of goods, thereby emphasizing the opposition between the capacity to produce and the scarcity of primitive resources. The fundamental idea of production should therefore be carefully specified, in order to identify the distinctive features of what we may call 'creative producibility' and 'transformational producibility', respectively. (The former finds its expression in the apparatus of structure, the latter in the transformation of primitive resources into final consumption goods.) In fact, only creative producibility allows man to 'strengthen' the endowment of primary resources, by increasing the distance between primary resources and final products, and by widening the set of production possibilities.

The capacity to produce is bounded in each historical phase by the existence of a 'correct' proportion between the apparatus of transformation and that of structure. An economic system where the capacity to produce is realized exclusively or mainly through the apparatus of transformation will in fact be dominated by 'acquisitive' behaviour, will favour the seeming 'freedom from needs' linked to direct consumption of primary resources, and, due to the absolute scarcity that acquisitive behaviour tends to generate, will end up in declining conditions.

The antagonism–coexistence between producibility and scarcity is therefore at the basis of the actual dynamics of economic systems, just as it is at the basis of attempts to understand their functioning and intervene in them. The interpretation of such antagonism–coexistence requires a further fundamental specification: producibility appears in fact effectively to be opposed to scarcity, provided that the 'creative' aspects of producibility prevail over its 'acquisitive' aspects (on the condition, therefore, that the apparatus of structure does not end up diminished with respect to the apparatus of transformation).

This point of view provides us with a hypothesis of development both for economic theory and for economic action, since it suggests to the former to set alight mechanisms through which the capacity of men to produce is strengthened, even in the presence of non-producible primitive resources, and to the latter to engage in progressively widening the distance between primitive resources and final products.

REFERENCES

Beccaria, C. (1804) *Elementi di economia pubblica* (ms 1771–2), in *Scrittori classici italiani di economia politica,* modern part, vols XI and XII. Custodi, Milan.

Cairnes, J.E. (1874) *Some Leading Principles of Political Economy*, Macmillan, London.

Cantillon, R. (1931) *Essai sur la nature du commerce en général* (1st edn 1755); English translation, by H. Higgs (1931), same title, Macmillan, London.

Clark, J.M. (1952) 'John Bates Clark', in Spiegel, H.W. (ed.), *The Development of Economic Thought*, ed. H.W. Spiegel, John Wiley, New York, pp. 592–612.

Edgeworth, F.Y. (1881) *Mathematical Psychics*, Kegan Paul, London.

— (1894/5) 'Antoine-Augustin Cournot', in *Palgrave's Dictionary of Political Economy*, Macmillan, London, vol. I, pp. 445–6.

Ferrara, F. (1854) *Introduzione* to vol. V, series I, *Biblioteca dell'Economista*, UTET, Turin, pp. [V]–LXIV.

— (1859) *Introduzione* to vol. VII, series II, *Biblioteca dell'Economista*, UTET, Turin, pp. [V]–CXXV.

— (1863) *Introduzione* to vol. III, series II, *Biblioteca dell'Economista*, UTET, Turin, pp. [V]–CXXXV.

Galiani, F. (1963) *Della Moneta* (1st edn 1750), Feltrinelli, Milan.

Isnard, A.N. (1781) *Traité des richesses*, F. Grasset, London.

Jevons, W.S. (1886) *Letters and Journal*, Macmillan, London.

Keynes, J.M. (1924) 'Alfred Marshall, 1842–1924', *Economic Journal*, 34, pp. 311–72.

— (1973) *The General Theory of Employment, Interest and Money* (1st edn 1936), Cambridge University Press, Cambridge.

Marshall, A. (1961) *Principles of Economics* (1st edn 1890) 9th (variorum) edn, Macmillan, London.

Mill, J.S. (1965) *Principles of Political Economy with some of their Applications to Social Philosophy* (1st edn 1848), edited by J.M. Robson, with an introduction by R.F. McRae, University of Toronto Press, Toronto; Routledge and Kegan Paul, London.

Montemartini, G. (1982) 'In memoria di Francesco Ferrara' (1900), in *Protagonisti del pensiero economico. Struttura produttiva, scambio e mercati (1848–1872)*, ed. A. Quadrio-Curzio and R. Scazzieri, Il Mulino, Bologna, pp. 100–15.
Pareto, V. (1906) *Manuale di economia politica*, Società Editrice Libraria, Milan.
Pasinetti, L.L. (1973) 'The Notion of Vertical Integration in Economic Analysis', *Metroeconomica*, 25, pp. 1–29.
Pigou, A.C. (1929) *The Economics of Welfare* (1st edn 1920), Macmillan, London.
Quadrio-Curzio, A. and Scazzieri, R. (1982a) 'La formazione delle idee cardine: rivoluzione industriale e economia politica', in *Protagonisti del pensiero economico. Rivoluzione industriale e economia politica (1817–1848)*, Il Mulino, Bologna, pp. 11–38.
— (1982b) 'La formazione delle idee cardine: struttura produttiva, scambio e mercati', in *Protagonisti del pensiero economico. Struttura produttiva, scambio e mercati (1848–1872)*, Il Mulino, Bologna, pp. 11–48.
Quesnay, F. (1962) 'Grains' (1757): English translation in R.L. Meek, *The Economics of Physiocracy. Essays and Translations*, Allen and Unwin, London.
Ricardo, D. (1951) *On the Principles of Political Economy and Taxation* (1st edn 1817), in *Works and Correspondence of David Ricardo*, vol. 1, Cambridge University Press, Cambridge.
Smith, A. (1976) *An Inquiry into the Nature and Causes of the Wealth of Nations*, (1st edn 1776), ed. R.H. Campbell, A.S. Skinner and W.B. Todd, Clarendon Press, Oxford.
Torrens, R. (1821) *An Essay on the Production of Wealth*, Hurst, London.
Turgot, A.R.J. (1769–70) 'Réflexions sur la formation des richesses', *Ephémérides du citoyen*, 1769, 11, 12; 1770, 1.
Valeriani, L. (1806) *Del prezzo delle cose tutte mercatabili*, Ramponi, Bologna.
Verri, P. (1771) *Meditazioni sull'economia politica*, nella Stamperia dell 'Enciclopedia, Livorno.
Wicksell, K. (1934) *Lectures on Political Economy* (1st edn 1901–6), J. Routledge, London.
Wicksteed, P.H. (1933) *The Common Sense of Political Economy* (1st edn 1910), J. Routledge, London.
Wieser, F. von (1893) *Natural Value* (1st edn 1889), Macmillan, London.

14

Theory of Value – a Source of Alternative Paradigms in Economic Analysis

LUIGI L. PASINETTI

There is a dichotomy, in economic analysis, between production-oriented theories and exchange-oriented theories, as is portrayed and investigated from many different angles in the present book. In the following pages, I want to argue that the source of this dichotomy can be traced back to a deeper dichotomy, which can be found in the theory of value.

I *JUSTUM PRETIUM*: THE PRE-THEORETICAL STAGE

Value and, more specifically, prices represent an old subject for discussion and disquisitions among scholars. However, the formulation of *theories* of value is a modern concern, which began to emerge only towards the end of the eighteenth century. In earlier times, we find, for many centuries, a series of disquisitions about the *ethics* of prices and, more specifically, about the concept of 'just price' (*justum pretium*). These disquisitions originated as a result of the preoccupation of moral philosophers with specifying what is justified and what is not justified in the fixation of prices.

The historians of economic thought have by now distilled the sentences of the ancient and medieval moral philosophers from many angles. Without going into details, or trying to give exhaustive lists, let me recall schematically a few representative points.[1]

[1] I may mention, for the interested reader, at least a few references. The development of the concept of 'just price' from the Romans to the Scholastics may be seen in Baldwin (1959). In Selma Hagenauer's article (1931) the just price is seen as an anticipation of the labour theory of value; see also Sapori (1955). An interesting article in which both 'objective' and 'subjective' hints are singled out is that by de Roover (1958). See also Schumpeter (1951, pt II, chs 1–2), Hollander (1965) and Spicciani (1977).

1 *Justum pretium* (or *verum pretium*) has its origin in Roman law. It is, however, from the ancient Greek philosophers that we have received the most notable arguments on the subject. Aristotle (384–322 BC) is credited with condemning the price of the single seller (or monopolist, in the etymological sense of the word, μόνοσ πωλεῖν) as contrary to justice, as it arises from artificial scarcity. He is also credited – from sentences such as 'There will be reciprocity, . . . as farmer is to shoemaker, so the amount of the shoemaker's work is to that of the farmer's work for which it exchanges' (*Nichomachean Ethics*, 1133[a] 17; Ross, 1925) – with trying to find a sort of cost principle and, more specifically, a sort of labour principle underlying the notion of a *just price*. What is certain is that Aristotle explicitly faced the problem of what he called 'commutative justice' in the pricing process; and in trying to single out a common standard on which to gauge the 'equivalence' of what is given and what is received, he used various arguments, among which freedom from artificial scarcities and labour costs appear to be the most prominent.

2 Among the scholastic philosophers, St Thomas Aquinas (1225–74) and many others – notably Albertus Magnus (1206–80) and John Duns Scotus (1266–1308) – have all resumed the Aristotelian arguments and have developed them further. St Thomas's main references are his *Commentaries* on Aristotle's *Nichomachean Ethics*, and his famous 'Quaestio LXXVII' (*Summa Theologiae*, pt II, 2), where the ethics behind *justum pretium* is spelt out. The Aristotelian flavour of the disquisitions is unmistakable. The historians have seen in the references to *aestimatio* an implicit admission of subjective elements, and in the reference to expenditures, and particularly to *expensae et labores* (in the search for a standard of 'equivalence' in 'commutative justice'), an explicit reference to the cost and, more particularly, to the labour principle in price determination.

3 The moral philosophers who, in the following centuries, dealt with the pricing problem did perfect the disquisitions of the Scholastic philosophers in many directions, and added further details; notable to this effect are the works of St Antoninus of Florence (1389–1458) and of Luis de Molina (1535–1600). But the basic approach, in spite of increasing sophistication, remained the same.

My conclusion is that it would be wrong to try – as so many modern scholars are continually trying – to look meticulously at the works of the moral philosophers for hints that anticipate either one or the other of the modern theories of value. When one takes this attitude, one inevitably ends up either straining the meaning of words and seeing in the works of the moral philosophers whatever one would like to see in them, or concluding with words of surprise at the 'contradictions' between the various principles that those moral philosophers were 'unable' to distinguish. This is not only unfair, but also – it seems to me – incorrect.

We can trace, in the arguments of the ancient and medieval philosophers, hints at subjective elements (coming from the concept of estimation), hints at objective elements (referring to costs and labour), hints at the working of a possibly efficient mechanism (competitive markets) and other hints too. But clearly, they were *not* aiming at proposing theories. They were trying to state standards of ethical behaviour and – given this purpose – it was not contradictory for them to try to set out, not one, but many separate arguments, provided that they all helped, in various cases and occasions, to achieve the final effect. Far from considering these various arguments as being in contradiction with one another, they regarded them as enriching their discussions.

II FERDINANDO GALIANI – A REMARKABLE SYMBOL OF PRE-THEORETICAL WRITING

Perhaps the most symbolic of all pre-theoretical writers on 'value' is Ferdinando Galiani, who has bequeathed to us that delightful chapter II from book I of *Della Moneta*, first published in 1751. Galiani was writing only 25 years before Adam Smith's *Wealth of Nations* was published. Galiani wrote as an economist, in the modern sense of the word, rather than as a moral philosopher, yet as an economist still at a pre-theoretical stage. Anyone looking, from today's standpoint, at his rather sophisticated arguments can choose the hints to the theory of value he likes. Consider, as examples, the following excerpts:[2]

> Il valore delle cose ... è da molti definito la stima che di esse hanno gli uomini (Galiani, 1751, p. 27)

> Il valore adunque è una ragione; e questa composta da due ragioni, che con questi nomi esprimo: d'*utilità* e *rarità* (ibid., p. 28, author's italics)

---

[2] Galiani's remarkable book (which the author published at the age of 23!) has never been translated into English. Here is my translation of the passages quoted in this section:

> The value of things ... is by many people defined as the estimation men have of them (p. 27)

> Value therefore is a relationship ('ragione') and this is composed of two relationships, which I call: *utility* and *rarity* (p. 28)

Utilità io chiamo l'attitudine che ha una cosa a procurarci la felicità (ibid., p. 28, author's italics)

Ma la più gran parte degli uomini, insieme con Bernardo Davanzati, ragiona così: 'Un vitello naturale è più nobile di un vitello d'oro, ma quanto è pregiato meno?' Rispondo. Se un vitello naturale fosse così raro come uno d'oro, avrebbe tanto maggior prezzo del vitello d'oro, quanto l'utilità e il bisogno di quello è maggiore di questo. Costoro immaginansi che il valore derivi da un principio solo, e non da molti che si congiungono insieme a formare una ragione composta. Altri sento che dicono: 'Una libbra di pane è più utile d'una libbra d'oro'. Rispondo. Questo è un vergognoso paralogismo, derivante dal non sapere che *più utile* e *meno utile* sono voci relative e che secondo il vario stato delle persone si misurano . . . ma a chi è sazio, vi è cosa più inutile del pane? Bene è dunque, se egli allora altre passioni soddisfa . . . Perciò, se il Davanzati dice che 'un uovo, il quale un mezzo grano d'oro si pregia, valeva a tener vivo dalla fame il conte Ugolino nella torre ancora il decimo giorno, che tutto l'oro del mondo non valeva', egli equivoca bruttamente fra il prezzo che dà all'uovo chi non teme morir di fame se non lo ha, e i bisogni del conte Ugolino. Chi gli ha detto che il conte non avria pagato l'uovo anche mille grani d'oro? . . . Ecco che pur una volta, grazie al cielo, ha confessato che *caro e buon mercato* sono voci relative (ibid., pp. 34–5, author's italics)

I call *utility* the attitude of things to generate happiness (p. 28)

But most people, like Bernardo Davanzati, argue as follows: 'An actual calf is nobler than a golden calf yet how less is valued? I answer. If an actual calf were as rare as a golden one, it would have a higher price than a golden calf, as the utility and need of the former is higher than the latter. These people think that value derives from one single principle, and not from many which combine to form a composite relationship. I hear others saying: 'a pound of bread is more useful than a pound of gold'. I answer. This is a shameful paralogism, deriving from not knowing that *more* or *less* useful are relative terms which are measured according to the subjective conditions of people . . . but for he who is satiated, is there a thing more useless than bread? He is therefore doing well if he satisfies other inclinations. . . . Hence, when Davanzati says that 'an egg, which is worth less than half a grain of gold, was enough to keep conte Ugolino alive in the tower, even on his tenth day [a famous scene from Dante's *Inferno*], which all the gold in the world could not have done', he fails to make a distinction between the price someone might pay for an egg, when that person does not fear starvation without it, and the needs of conte Ugolino. Who has said that conte Ugolino would not have paid even a thousand grains of gold for an egg? . . . Here he has actually admitted that *dear* and *cheap* are relative terms (pp. 34–5)

> Io chiamo *rarità* la proporzione che è fra la quantità d'una cosa e l'uso che ne è fatto (ibid., p. 38, author's italics)
>
> Passando ora a dire sulla quantità della cosa, dico che senovi due classi di corpi. In alcuni ella dipende dalla diversa abbondanza, con cui la natura gli produce: in altri solo dalla varia fatica ed opera che vi s'impiega (ibid., pp. 38–9)
>
> Entro ora a dire della fatica, la quale non solo in tutte le opere che sono intieramente dell'arte, come le pitture, sculture, intagli, ecc., ma anche in molti corpi, come sono i minerali, i sassi, i frutti silvestri ecc., è l'unica che dà valore alla cosa. La quantità della materia non per altro coopera in questi corpi al valore se non perchè aumenta o scema la fatica (ibid., pp. 39–40).

What a splendid collection of arguments and hints! The modern economist can see very clearly in these excerpts the concept of utility, the concept of decreasing marginal utilities, and the relativity of all these concepts; one can also see the concept of cost of production and, more particularly, the principle of labour cost ('fatica', an expression corresponding to Adam Smith's 'toil and trouble'), which is defined as nothing less than 'the only one that gives value to things' ('l'unica che dà valore alla cosa'). One may go much further, however. Consider these other excerpts:

> se, per esempio, in un paese si consumassero cinquantamila botti di vino ed altrettante se ne raccogliessero, sopravvenendo in questo paese un esercito improvvisamente, incarisce il prezzo del vino, perchè più se ne bee ... (Galiani, 1751, pp. 48–9)

I call *rarity* the proportion between the existing quantity of a thing and the use made of it (p. 38)

Going on now to tell of the quantity of things, I say there are two classes of bodies. For some of them, it depends on the different abundance with which nature produces them; in others only on the different toil and trouble, and work, that is bestowed on them (pp. 38–9)

I now begin to speak of toil and trouble (*'fatica'*), which, not only in all creative works or art, such as pictures and sculptures, etc., but in many objects such as minerals, stones and wild fruits ... etc., is the only thing that gives value to things. The quantity of matter for nothing else contributes to the value of these things, but because the toil and trouble increase or diminish ... (pp. 39–40).

if, for example, in a village, fifty thousand casks of wine are harvested and consumed; if suddenly an army were to come, the price of wine will increase because more of it will be drunk (pp. 48–9)

> siccome gli uomini posseggono ineguali ricchezze, così a un certo grado di ricchezze corrisponde sempre la compra di certe comodità. Se queste avviliscono, anche chi è nell'ordine inferiore della ricchezza le compra: se incariscono, coloro, che prima usavanle, cominciano ad astenersene (ibid., p. 49)

> la moda è malattia dell'animo ... Si vuol trovare qualche ragionevolezza, bisogna dire che nasce in gran parte questa varietà di gusto dall'imitazione dei costumi delle nazioni predominanti. (Ibid., p. 46)

Who cannot see in all this the interplay of demand and supply, the concept of *elasticity* of demand with respect to both prices and income, and in fact also a clear enunciation of the hierarchy among goods (which was later to be known as 'Engel's law')? Who cannot see even a clear indication of the 'demonstration' and 'imitation' effects, and thus of the interdependence among individual preferences?

I have quoted at length to show the many principles referred to. Ironically, it has become difficult for us today to give Galiani all the credit he deserves, precisely because – carried away by our modern theories – we tend to see contradictions among the various principles he has so remarkably anticipated.[3]

III THE EMERGENCE OF THEORIES

The approach to discussions on value changed dramatically towards the end of the eighteenth century. From the ethical pronouncements on value, writers began to move on to *theories* of value.

Theory means abstraction. It means making a choice from among the maze of interconnections that a superficial glance can capture, and then trying to get down to the fundamentals. In social sciences, this also means simplifying, sometimes very crudely, by minimizing what appears as secondary, and singling out and magnifying what the theorist (in his intuition)

> Since men own unequal wealth, so to each degree of wealth there always corresponds the purchase of certain goods and services. If the prices of the latter fall, those people who are at the lower level of wealth will also buy them; if their prices increase, those who used to buy them will begin to give them up (p. 49)

> fashion is the illness of the soul. ... If a reason for it is to be found, we must say that this variety of tastes springs from the imitation of usage of the predominant nations (p. 46)

[3]Schumpeter himself (1951, pp. 300–2), though a great admirer of Galiani, cannot refrain from pointing out how abruptly Galiani jumps from one theoretical principle to another.

identifies as the major or basic element that is capable of providing the explanation that is sought.

Since the end of the eighteenth century, economic theorists have concentrated on fewer and fewer basic elements. On the concept of value, they have narrowed themselves down to a choice between two quite different and alternative routes: the 'objective' route of a cost-of-production and, more particularly, of a labour theory of value; and the 'subjective' route of a 'marginal utility' theory of value.

I think the source of each of these two alternative theories may well be symbolized by the following two quotations, taken from Adam Smith and William Stanley Jevons respectively:

> In that early and rude state of society which precedes both the accumulation of stock and the appropriation of land, the proportion between the quantities of labour necessary for acquiring different objects seems *the only circumstance* which can afford any rule for exchanging them for one another. If among a nation of hunters, for example, it usually costs twice the labour to kill a beaver which it does to kill a deer, one beaver should naturally exchange for or be worth two deer. It is natural that what is usually the produce of two days or two hours labour, should be worth double of what is usually the produce of one day's or one hour's labour. (Adam Smith, 1904, p. 49; 1st edn 1776; my italics)

> The science of Political Economy rests upon a few notions of an apparently simple character ... it is in treating the simple elements that we require the most care and precision, since the least error of conception must vitiate all our deductions ...
>
> Repeated reflection and inquiry have led me to the somewhat novel opinion, that *value depends entirely upon utility*. (Jevons, 1871, p. 1; author's italics)

Both Smith and Jevons have taken precisely the same step, but in opposite directions. In striking contrast with Galiani, for example, who chided those who 'thought value derives from one single principle' ('Costoro immaginansi che il valore derivi da un principio solo'), both Smith and Jevons concentrate precisely on *one single principle*, to be put at the foundation of their elaborations. This does not, of course, mean closing their eyes to everything else. But it does mean putting everything else on a secondary, or subordinate, position. It means that everything else must be excluded from the first skeleton of the theory, and only be introduced later on, at a second, third or fourth, ... stage. This is not merely a sort of successive approximation process; it is something much more basic to the theorizing process, because whatever does not fit properly into the core of the theory must impiously be omitted, or left to play a subordinate role.

It should be added that individual writers may not always be themselves clear about which features are secondary and subordinate to the basic propositions. But the unmistakable sign of a basic principle is that it can never be left out. Conversely, the unmistakable sign of subordination is that when, or if, in successive developments and re-elaborations, any logical difficulty arises, the subordinate elements are the ones to be sacrificed, in the sense that, by one assumption or another, they are further minimized, or modified, or even eliminated, through a process of logical abstraction, in order not to invalidate the major, or basic, elements characterizing the theory.

It will be useful to consider succinctly, but with the aid of some formalization, the essentials of the two major theories of value proposed so far.

IV A PURE EXCHANGE, OR PURE PREFERENCE MODEL

It may be useful to start with the subjective theory of value, which – although proposed, chronologically, after the objective theory of value – is the one about which most efforts of formalization have been carried out so far.

To single out the essentials of the theory, one must look for those bare elements, and only for those bare elements, that the theory cannot do without. The elements a subjective theory of value cannot do without are all contained in that simple formalization that has become known as the model of *a pure exchange economy*, but which I would rather call a model of *a pure utility*, or *pure preference* economy; for it is the utility, or preferences, of the individuals that play the crucial role in it. Such a model can be found on the first pages of almost all standard treatments of traditional economics. I shall follow here, very synthetically, a formalization given by Mosak (1944), which has the advantage of being complete for all general purposes, and at the same time more accessible to the general reader than the more sophisticated, recent formalizations by Arrow and Debreu (1954; Debreu, 1959).

Suppose there is a society of individuals, each of whom owns, or – as is also said – has been 'endowed' (we do not enquire by whom) with a certain set of 'resources':

$$\bar{x}_1, \bar{x}_2, \ldots, \bar{x}_n \tag{1}$$

which in general are different from one individual to another. Each individual can freely exchange his/her resources with those of the other individuals, at the prices:

$$p_1, p_2, \ldots, p_n \tag{2}$$

which are accepted from a competitive market. The only constraint each individual faces is a budget constraint:

$$p_1\bar{x}_1 + p_2\bar{x}_2 + \ldots p_n\bar{x}_n = p_1x_1 + p_2x_2 + \ldots p_nx_n \tag{3}$$

where $\bar{x}_1, \bar{x}_2, \ldots, \bar{x}_n$ are the physical quantities he/she starts with and $x_1, x_2, \ldots, x_n$ are the physical quantities he/she ends up with.

Each individual is supposed to have a complete and well-defined set of preferences, in the sense of being able to rank any combination of goods in order of preference. More specifically, he/she can specify all possible combinations of goods among which he/she is indifferent:

$$u(x_1, x_2, \ldots, x_n) = \bar{u} \text{ (a constant)} \tag{4}$$

and can also specify all combinations of goods that are preferred to (4) (that is, give rise to a higher constant – a higher utility), and those that are not preferred to (4) (that is, give rise to a lower constant – a lower utility). Hence, there exists, for each single individual, a utility function:

$$u = u(x_1, x_2, \ldots, x_n) \tag{5}$$

This is supposed to be only ordinally (not necessarily cardinally) measurable. In other words, if u is an index of utility for the combination $x_1, x_2, \ldots, x_n$, then any arbitrary function $F(u)$ of u is also a suitable index of utility, provided only that $F' > 0$. It is also assumed that relation (5) is continuous and has partial derivatives of the first and second order:

$$u_s = \frac{\partial u}{\partial x_s} \qquad u_{st} = \frac{\partial^2 u}{\partial x_t \partial x_s} \qquad s,t = 1,2, \ldots, n \tag{6}$$

and moreover that:

$$u_{st} = u_{ts} \tag{7}$$

which means that utility does not depend on the *order* in which the goods are arranged.

Suppose now that each individual behaves rationally and maximizes his/her utility function, subject to his/her budget constraint, that is:

$$u - \lambda[\Sigma p_s \bar{x}_s - \Sigma p_s x] = \text{a maximum} \tag{8}$$

where λ is the usual Lagrange multiplier. The solution to this problem is well known. To find a maximum, we must take all the first partial derivatives with respect to x and equate them to zero:

$$u_s - \lambda p_s = 0 \qquad s = 1, 2, \ldots, n \tag{9}$$

And to ensure that equation (9) defines a maximum (and not a minimum), we must impose the second-order condition:

$$\mathrm{d}^2 u = \Sigma\Sigma\, u_{st}\, \mathrm{d}x_s\, \mathrm{d}x_t < 0 \tag{10}$$

the meaning of which is that the multidimensional hyper-indifference curves (4) taken for all $\bar{u}$, must be convex towards the origin. When the necessary condition (10) is satisfied, then (9) and (3) form $n + 1$ equations, which determine λ and the n physical quantities $x_1, x_2, \ldots, x_n$. This is the solution that defines the *equilibrium of the single individual.*

It may be noticed that the solutions to equation (9) are characterized by:

$$\frac{u_s}{p_s} = \frac{u_t}{p_t} \qquad s,t = 1,2, \ldots, n \qquad (11)$$

In other words, each single individual's equilibrium is characterized by the equality of *all* the partial derivatives (that is, the *marginal utilities*) divided by the corresponding prices. Of course, the equilibrium of each single individual is *relative* to his/her set of preferences, initial endowments *and* market prices, which the individual takes as given, but which are determined on the market. Now, if any price were to change, each individual's equilibrium would also change. This means that, for each physical resource x_s ($s = 1,2, \ldots, n$) and for each single individual i ($i = 1,2, \ldots, m$), we can formulate a *demand function*:

$$x_{si} = f_{si}(p_1, p_2, \ldots, p_n; \bar{x}_1, \bar{x}_2, \ldots, \bar{x}_n)$$

It can be shown that, under the assumptions taken, this demand function is homogeneous of the zero degree in all prices (that is, for any given amount of physical resources, the multiplication of all prices by the same multiplicative factor leaves each single individual's demand unchanged).

At this point, we may sum up the demands of all individuals for the same 'resource' to obtain the *aggregate* demand function for that 'resource'. Then, by equating this aggregate demand function to the corresponding aggregate amount that is available, we obtain the n equations:

$$\sum_{i=1}^{m} \bar{x}_{si} = \sum_{i}^{m} f_{si}(p_1, p_2, \ldots, p_n; \bar{x}_1, \bar{x}_2, \ldots, \bar{x}_n) \quad s = 1,2, \ldots, n \qquad (12)$$

which, with the budget constraint extended to the whole market:

$$\sum_{s}^{n} \sum_{i}^{m} p_s x_{si} = \sum_{s}^{n} \sum_{i}^{m} p_s \bar{x}_{si} \qquad (13)$$

define the general equilibrium of the market.

Equations (12) make up n equations, which are, however, constrained by (13), so that they form in fact only $(n - 1)$ independent equations. These yield $(n - 1)$ solutions for $(n - 1)$ prices. Hence, the general equilibrium of the market determines *relative* prices, whereas the general level of prices remains indeterminate. To determine also the absolute level of prices, one should at this point go on to introduce money, but we do not need to go into this field for the present purposes. We may well remain at the stage of the determination of the $(n - 1)$ *relative* prices, which define the *general equilibrium* of the market as a whole.

V THE MEANING OF PRICES IN A PURE PREFERENCE ECONOMY

As may be seen, the pure preference model is a beautiful theoretical construction. It proposes a clear and well-defined problem: the problem of allocation, through exchange, of given resources, and it provides a well-defined and elegant solution. If individuals behave rationally, a set of relative prices emerge which lead both to the equilibrium of each single individual and to the equilibrium of the market as a whole. The resource allocation thereby reached can be shown to have optimal properties. At the equilibrium point, no individual can be made better off without making some other individual worse off (a situation which has been called of 'Pareto optimality' – optimality relative to given endowments and given individual preferences). The set of prices associated with the equilibrium (optimum) solution has a very evident economic meaning – it provides an index of relative scarcities.

It is sometimes said that this is a static model. But it would be more appropriate to say that time is not a relevant element in the model. The problem which is posited is a once-for-all problem (how to allocate given resources); and the solution which is provided is a once-for-all solution (optimum allocation). Once the solution has been given, there is nothing more to be done, except to investigate the mathematical conditions that make it meaningful (existence, uniqueness and stability) or to illustrate the elegant properties it possesses (optimality). It might also be observed that the theoretical choice that is implied in the formulation of the pure preference model, and with it the subjective theory of value, spring from a particular way of looking at society; it springs, so to speak, from a particular 'social philosophy'. This is a social philosophy that relies on the individual's rational behaviour; on the idea of the consumer's sovereignty over the whole economy; on a great faith in the market as an institutional mechanism that brings about the utilization of all resources; and on the private property of all goods, as an institution that must in fact be taken as a basic postulate of the theory.

It is interesting to note how all these features are inherent in the pure preference model. They are all there, without the need to consider anything else, or to introduce any other phenomenon. In fact, from this point onwards, the introduction of any complication becomes possible *only if* it does not affect any of these basic features.

VI EXTENSIONS OF THE PURE PREFERENCE MODEL

The model of a pure preference economy, if taken at face value, would refer to a very limited problem. But the theoretical construction has proved flexible enough to afford extensions and generalization in many directions.

I have had the opportunity elsewhere of pointing out how the first phenomenon to be introduced into the model was of course the phenomenon of production.[4] This was done by replicating all the functions and concepts of a pure preference economy – a convex, continuous, differentiable 'production function', in all analogous to a utility function; 'marginal productivities', in all analogous to marginal utilities; a postulate of profit maximization, in all analogous to the postulate of utility maximization; and so on and so forth. Labour, which does not explicitly appear at the basic stage, has been introduced by considering it as one of the many 'endowments' that each individual possesses and can market, etc.

But, most of all, the 'generalizations' have taken place by way of 'shaping', by a series of assumptions, the phenomena to be investigated in such a way as to make them suitable for the applications of the ready-made analytical tool. In other words, the 'generalizations' basically consist in *looking at* all economic problems *as if* they were problems of optimum allocation of given resources. When the analytical tool and the phenomenon to be investigated do not match, it is not the tool, but the phenomenon that has to be changed (by assumption), so that it can be made to be 'well-behaved' (that is, suitable for the application of the analytical tool). In this way, the very basic analytical tool of the model – maximization under constraints – has become 'the foundation of economic analysis'.[5]

Without going into further details here, I may simply mention a very significant and symbolic case, in this respect; namely, the way in which the theory has recently responded to the discovery that an aggregate production function does not exist in general, and that an inverse monotonic relation between rate of profit and the 'quantity' of capital was an 'intuition' (deriving from a too naive extension of the pure preference model) that has turned out to be without foundation. Capital goods had always created trouble in this model. But the new criticisms have elicited the most logical response. The solution has been found by adopting an interpretation that had not been taken very seriously, when originally proposed, but that has revealed itself as the only logical one. It consists of an intertemporal reinterpretation of the transactions that are represented by the model. The capital goods, as all goods, that exist at the beginning are taken as given resources, and all the goods (capital goods or consumption goods), that become available or may become available in the future are taken as themselves transacted on present markets for future deliveries, or on

---

[4]This can be seen very clearly on the historical scene. The theory of marginal productivity was developed twenty years after the theory of marginal utility, as an immediate and direct extension of it. See Pasinetti, (1981, ch. 1).

[5]This is precisely the basis of Samuelson (1947).

contingency markets, which are supposed to be held at the very same point in time. This maintains the basic once-for-all character of the problem. At a unique point in time, a gigantic higgle-haggle is supposed to take place, which allocates all resources from now to eternity. Thereby, nothing is changed in the model; only its symbols are *reinterpreted* at a higher level of abstraction. All the properties of the solution, as well as the meaning of prices, are preserved.

This is perhaps the extreme stage reached by the generalization of the pure preference model, but it is a most logical one. A theory can admit of no exception to logical consistency. If 'anomalous' cases arise, they must be excluded or modified by assumption so as to be reabsorbed at a higher level of abstraction.

VII A PURE LABOUR MODEL

The objective theory of value, on which the earlier classical economists took the first steps, has undergone considerably less analytical work, especially by way of formalization, than the subjective theory of value. It is, however, also possible for the objective theory of value to present a bare skeleton of a theory that includes those essential elements, and only those essential elements, that the theory cannot do without.

I think that the essentials of the objective theory of value can be found in what may be called a model of a *pure labour economy*.[6] One must go back for this to the very initial intuition of Adam Smith. However, it is not necessary to refer such a model to a primitive society, as Adam Smith did. In our theorizing, we may well refer it to a technologically advanced society, which has, however, the characteristic of using only labour. On this subject I shall follow a formalization I have given myself in earlier works (Pasinetti, 1962, ch. 2; 1980/1; 1981, ch. 2).

Suppose there is an economic system in which a society of individuals carry out an activity of production and an activity of consumption. All consumption goods are made by labour alone; labour is therefore the only 'factor of production'. The activity of production is carried out with extensive division of labour, and thus with a marked specialization. Each individual produces only one type of good, or even a *fraction* of one type of good, thereby being able to achieve very high productivity. This means that each individual will then need to obtain all the consumption goods he/

[6] This term (after calling the model presented in section IV a 'pure preference' model) now seems to me more appropriate to characterize the initial stage of the present model, than the term 'pure production' model, used (in symmetry to the term 'pure exchange model') in Pasinetti (1981).

she needs through exchange. This is the way in which a series of rates of exchange, or prices, come into being.

Suppose technology is represented by a series of labour coefficients $l_1, l_2, \ldots, l_m$, for the production of m consumption goods, and suppose that per-capita demand is represented by a series of consumption coefficients $c_1, c_2, \ldots, c_m$. Let us denote the physical quantities produced by $X_1, X_2, \ldots, X_m$, the prices of the m consumption goods by $p_1, p_2, \ldots, p_m$, the total quantity of labour by L, and the wage rate by w. Then we can represent the economic system, in a closed Leontief model fashion, by two linear and homogeneous systems of equations:

$$\begin{bmatrix} 1 & & & & -c_1 \\ & 1 & & & -c_2 \\ & & \ddots & & \vdots \\ & & & & 1-c_m \\ -\ell_1 & -\ell_2 & \ldots & -\ell_m & 1 \end{bmatrix} \begin{bmatrix} X_1 \\ X_2 \\ \vdots \\ X_m \\ L \end{bmatrix} = \begin{bmatrix} 0 \\ 0 \\ \vdots \\ \\ 0 \end{bmatrix} \tag{14}$$

$$[p_1, p_2, \ldots, p_m, w] \begin{bmatrix} 1 & & & & -c_1 \\ & 1 & & & -c_2 \\ & & & & \vdots \\ & & & & 1-c_m \\ -\ell_1 & -\ell_2 & \ldots & -\ell_m & 1 \end{bmatrix} = [0, 0, \ldots, 0] \tag{15}$$

The necessary condition for non-trivial solutions is

$$\sum_{i=1}^{m} c_i l_i = 1 \tag{16}$$

and the solutions for relative quantities and for relative prices, respectively, are:

$$X_i = c_i L \tag{17}$$

$$p_i = l_i w \qquad i = 1, 2, \ldots, m \tag{18}$$

Necessary condition (16) turns out to be the Keynesian effective demand condition for full employment, and comes to link together the economic system as a whole (see Pasinetti, 1981, pp. 33ff.). Solutions (17) evince a demand-determined theory of production, and solutions (18) *a pure labour theory of value*.

In perfect analogy with the previous case (see the end of section IV), the solutions determine *relative* prices, whereas the absolute level of prices remains indeterminate. Here, again, one should go on to introduce money (and other things) in order to deal with the determination of the absolute level of prices. But, for our purposes, we do not need to go any further, and may remain at the stage of relative prices. Relative prices turn out to be proportional to physical quantities of labour. If the wage rate were to be used as *numéraire*, prices would actually turn out to be *equal* to physical quantities of labour. The beauty of the model is that it can give rise to no ambiguity or complication. Value is labour; and it makes no difference whether it is referred to as 'labour embodied' or as 'labour commanded'. Any good or service can 'command' an amount of labour that is always equal to the amount of labour it embodies. This is the really basic and original feature of a pure labour theory of value.

VIII THE MEANING OF PRICES IN A PURE LABOUR ECONOMY

As may be seen quite clearly, the explanation of value that emerges from the theoretical scheme of a pure labour economy, and indeed the whole conception of an economic system are strikingly different from those emerging from the pure preference model presented in the previous sections.

The economic phenomenon at the very basis of the model is the technological process of production, with division and specialization of labour. And the explanation of prices that emerges follows as a consequence. Prices, that is the rates of exchange among commodities, arise from the fact that each individual specializes in producing only one (or even a fraction of one) consumption good, but at the same time needs *all* consumption goods, which must therefore be obtained through exchange. Production and exchange are inherently linked by labour specialization. In this context, prices express the 'toil and trouble' of production. Hence the physical quantity of labour emerges as the clearest objective standard with which to compare all goods and services. The most elementary notion of cost of production ('labour embodied') coincides with the most elementary notion of purchasing power ('labour commanded') to give a concrete expression to that old Aristotelian intuitive idea of a homogeneous common constituent of all goods.

In synthesis, prices simply emerge from the necessity of an extensive division of labour – this is their *raison d'être*. And their meaning is consequential: they represent indexes of costs, in terms of the ultimate constituent of all commodities – physical labour.

As far as time is concerned, it may be noted that, already at its essential and simple stage, the theoretical scheme is inherently sequential. Production and labour services are flows, that is, they have a time dimension. The solution to the problem which is proposed refers to a particular period of time. But this period of time will be followed by another period of time, and therefore by another solution, which in its turn will be followed by yet another period of time, and yet another solution, and so on. One may well start by assuming a production process that repeats itself unchanged in time (a stationary economy), but this is clearly an artificial case. Different periods of time will be characterized by different technical coefficients, and therefore by *different* solutions. The model naturally leads to the investigation of *changes*, and movements, through time (that is, to *dynamic* analysis).

It may here be added too that the theoretical choice implied in the formulation of a pure labour model – and with it the objective theory of value – springs from a particular way of looking at society; from a particular 'social philosophy' so to speak, which is indeed different from the one pointed out with reference to a pure preference model. It is a social philosophy that, through division of labour, stresses the necessarily *co-operative aspects* of an organized society; that looks for responsibility of society as a whole in bringing about situations that are considered as socially desirable. Of this, the fulfilment of the necessary condition (16), which expresses Keynes's requirement of an effective demand sufficient to ensure full employment, is the clearest indication. And it is important to realize that it is there, right at the initial and essential stage. Postulates concerning private ownership, or for that matter public ownership, are not made, and the problem of how the net product is distributed, both at a given point in time and through time, is thrown wide open for investigation.

These are clear and sharp features, which are to be maintained from this point on, in any elaboration of this theoretical scheme beyond the simplest and essential stage of a hypothetical economy of pure labour.

IX EXTENSIONS OF THE PURE LABOUR MODEL

The theoretical process of *extending* and generalizing the model of a pure labour economy has been more laborious and roundabout than the analogous process for the pure preference model. There can be little doubt that such a process of generalization is still far from having reached a satisfactory stage. This may be partly due to the fact that the *type of economy* the model envisages is more complex than the one envisaged by the pure preference model. The model of a pure exchange economy could, in principle, have been developed centuries ago. For the concept of individual preferences and the process of exchange that are at its basis are centuries old. By contrast, the process of production with division of labour, which is at the basis of the pure labour model, has become crucially relevant only with the development of industrial societies, and the conceptual magnitudes that are considered make up more numerous categories (labour, in addition to commodities; physical quantities; and rates of wage and profit, in addition to commodity prices).

Adam Smith was himself unable to extend the pure labour theory of value beyond the simplest stage of a pure labour economy (which he associated with a primitive society, see section IV above). When he came to deal with an advanced society, in which there is accumulation of capital and appropriation of land, he could do no better than adopt an 'eclectic' approach, consisting of considering cost of production, and thus value, as made up of three components: wages, profits and rent, without, however, being clear about how they are determined.

It looked as if the central problem to be faced was that of income distribution. And it was Ricardo (1821) who took the really remarkable theoretical step forward. At one stroke, Ricardo was able to 'eliminate' rent from the determination of value (by his differential theory of rent) and to extend the pure labour theory to production with capital (circulating or fixed), by relying on the assumption of uniform capital intensity in all production processes, or rather by relying on the 'hope' that deviations from pure labour proportionality might be empirically negligible, when uniformity of capital intensity is not realized. It was precisely the difficulties in answering the objections to this assumption that got Ricardo into an *impasse*, from which his followers have been unable to take him out.

After Ricardo, Marx (1894) made a bold attempt at a complete solution of the problem of value, but on alternative lines. By overturning the whole approach of the classical economists, he *defined* value as labour embodied, and then threw on the intrinsic characteristics of the capitalist economies the fault of making producton prices deviate from values (owing to their institutional necessity of uniformity of the rates of profit and labour exploitation). This led him to an indictment of the whole capitalist institutional set-up.

The emotions and passionate discussions that followed Marx's controversial works, and his revolutionary calls, came to complicate enormously the analytical work of the theoretical economists. On pure analytical ground, this may well have contributed to discouraging a dispassionate pursuit of the generalization of the pure labour theory of value on genuine classical lines.

It is only with Sraffa (1960) that the discussion has recently been resumed, by going right back to the point where Ricardo had left it. Sraffa's analysis has clarified the meaning of Ricardo's 'elimination' of rent from the determination of value. Land and natural resources are shown to play a role which, in reverse, is analogous to that of the non-basic commodities: they do not affect the determination of prices of basic commodities, nor the relation between profits and wages. Secondly, the enrichment of the production model into a full-fledged inter-industry scheme, and the analysis of its mathematical properties have clarified enormously the complex relations between prices and quantities of labour, between prices and distribution of income, both in the simple case of single production and in the more intricate cases of joint production. Thirdly, through the analytical construction of Sraffa's 'standard commodity', expressing what, from Ricardo's works, could only appear the *chimera* of an 'invariable standard' of value, it has been shown that income distribution is indeed a phenomenon that can be dealt with independently of value.

The field has thereby been cleared of the many conceptual difficulties into which Ricardo's analysis had stumbled. Indeed the whole field of classical analysis has been shown to be quite open to the application of the modern rigorous tools of formal logic and mathematics. But the major analytical work on the way to a complete generalization is still waiting to be carried out. Sraffa has only provided a 'prelude', as he has said, to further work.

I myself am convinced that, for a fruitful use, even of the analytical work done so far, the logical process of generalization will have to proceed. I have argued elsewhere (Pasinetti, 1981) that this can be done precisely through a very logical and indeed complete generalization of the pure labour theory of value. Through the development of a labour theory of the rate of profit, and of a (separate) labour theory of the rate of interest, which together imply a theory of income distribution based on physical quantities of labour, both at a given point of time and inter-temporally, a complete generalization of the labour theory of value is possible, for which the original equality of 'labour embodied' and 'labour commanded' is realized in general (that is, in a complete, full-fledged production model, even with joint production) and not only in the hypothetical case of a pure labour economy.

If this theoretical construction stands, the consequences are far-reaching in economic theory. For, it would imply a revolutionary change even in economic methodology, in terms of a separation of those economic relations that are to be investigated at a *normative* level (giving a complete content to the classical notions of natural features of an economic system) from those relations that are to be investigated at a *behavioural* level, on rules and criteria that are no longer constrained by the limitations of the individualistic and competitive scheme of traditional economic theory, though being capable of absorbing it.[7]

I think we may therefore conclude on a note of expectation, but also of clear sense of direction. It is quite logical to expect that the process of

---

[7]This very brief sketch of the lines toward a complete generalization of the pure labour theory of value should not be taken as a simple and vague indication of direction. The generalization can be carried out in full; see Pasinetti (1981).

generalization of the model of a pure labour economy will proceed (to the extent that it has not yet done so) to the extreme stage of a complete coverage of *all* economic phenomena, including those (though to be faced in a different way) that have been so far investigated only through the pure preference model.

X THEORIES AND SOCIETY

A few 'methodological' remarks may not be out of place, as a way of conclusion. An examination of the development of the theories of value would seem to evince, within the theorizing process, an internal logic that imposes on the modern theorist a strict discipline, on the use and development of concepts and on the relation of assumptions to deductions, that was unknown in older discussions. This is not merely due to requirements of conciseness and elegance, but to more profound requirements of rigour and logical consistency, with few and simple principles at the basis of any theory that deserves this name.

The 'eclectic' treatment of value used by the old moral philosophers may appear to have taken advantage of wider degrees of freedom. But there obviously is no question of going back to that stage. Those degrees of freedom, if they are to be recovered, will have to be recovered at another level.

A theoretical approach in itself, once taken, becomes quite demanding. It can allow of no compromise, and yet it has to cover the whole hypothetical world it is supposed to represent. So a theory *must* be general, or must be generalized to cover, in principle, the whole reality it is supposed to refer to.

Not surprisingly, Debreu does not call his theory *a* theory of value; he calls it *Theory of value* (1959), without any qualification. The alternative, and competing, labour theory of value, to the extent that it has not yet done so, will have to aim at doing the same. It will have to aim at being general, or at being generalized, so as to cover the whole of economic reality (including the scarce natural resources).

The advantage of this generalizing impetus is enormous; for it allows us to extricate ourselves, on the guidance of a few simple principles, in the middle of a very complex economic reality, by never losing the sense of direction.

At the same time, one should not lose sight of the fact that economic phenomena, and all social relations in general, are extremely complex – much more than physical phenomena. So that, in order to reduce this complexity to simple rules, very drastic simplifications may sometimes become necessary. Sir John Hicks has talked of economic theories as 'a sort of blinkers' (Hicks, 1976, pp. 208–9), which do not allow one to see outside a certain angle. The foregoing analysis would rather suggest the image of the theorizing process as a sort of telescope, which is used in both directions: to magnify, in one direction, those aspects on which the theorist has chosen to concentrate; and to shrink, in the opposite direction, or reduce to irrelevance, those aspects that are to play a secondary role.

But who is going to choose those aspects that are to be magnified and those aspects that are to be reduced? This is a worrying question. The obvious answer – 'the intuition of the theorist' – begins to sound less satisfactory at this point. It has been pointed out already, with specific reference to the theory of value, that one may identify, at a pre-theoretical stage, so to speak, the choice of a particular conception, or 'vision', of the world. This, in the social sciences, may well be a device to achieve consistency among the type of simplifications that are made.

But it would be wrong to derive from this any conclusion about any necessary dependence of the theorizing process on pre-theoretical conceptions. It would also be wrong to derive any conclusion on any supposed lower standard of the theorizing process in the social sciences, with respect to what happens in the more traditional sciences. Once the postulates have been stated, an economic theory acquires complete autonomy; as a theory it is entirely independent of the motivations that may have affected the choice of the postulates. And the standards of rigour and logical consistency of the analysis must obviously be the same as in any other field of investigation (including that of the physical sciences).

Yet it is undeniable that, quite apart from the logical consistency and rigour of any economic theory, the particular features of the simplifying process pose a problem at the stage of applicability and utilization. This problem arises – it must be stressed – not at the level of the theorizing process, but at the level of utilization, and hence it arises for society as a whole. How is society going to take heed of the recommendations emanating from the prevailing theories, when alternative theories exist and are being proposed? And again, to what extent should the development of alternative theories be encouraged or discouraged?

These questions are not simply academic ones. A neutral attitude on this respect may not suffice, because, in a world like our own, the costs of so much research fall on the community as a whole. It is in fact here – that is, at the stage of the application of theories to actual policies – that the recovery of a certain 'eclecticism' might find some justification.[8] But the

[8]The attitude of the major economists of our time, in this respect, shows wide variety. Milton Friedman and Nicholas Kaldor, for example, are always as uncompromising in their practical recommendations as they (rightly) are in their theories. On the other hand, Paul Samuelson, for example, though strictly rigorous in his theories, always becomes rather eclectic when coming down to evaluations, and recommendations, of actual economic policies.

criteria to follow are not at all clear; a lot of searching on this aspect seems to be needed.

In the discussions on the nature of scientific progress, which have followed the publication of Kuhn's classic book (Kuhn, 1962), it has been taken for granted (but with a view to physical sciences!) that the 'scientific revolutions' through which science is seen to proceed leave space for only one 'paradigm' at a time, and – in particular – that each paradigm, once discarded, is irretrievably obsolete.

A crucial question is whether this is also the case in the social sciences. It seems to me that there are too many reasons to be doubtful. In economics, we do certainly identify quite distinct paradigms. (The previous pages themselves provide plenty of evidence.) But it is by no means clear that they should always succeed one another in a one-way direction. Or at least, a distinction should be made between the evolution of the analytical tools and the evolution of the ideas at the basis of any paradigm.

Very often, in the physical sciences, the development of a new paradigm is indissolubly linked with the development of new analytical or technological tools. This is not so in the social sciences. The development of new analytical tools may well lead to resuming and giving new vitality to an older paradigm, which had been discarded in the past and had fallen into oblivion, because of unsolved difficulties which the new analytical tools permit to overcome.

Therefore if a certain one-way direction can be seen in the evolution and application of analytical tools, one cannot say the same of the succession of paradigms.[9] This seems to indicate the importance and necessity, in economics (and in the social sciences in general), of a certain protection so to speak of the potentialities of the minority theories. Discussions on lines alternative to the prevailing ones should be promoted, and encouraged, not suppressed (as the supporters of the prevailing theories have an inevitable tendency to do).

Some rules of behaviour among economic theorists would also be very helpful. Given the crude simplifications that economists are compelled to make, some considerable dose of humility about the merits and applicability of one's theories, and at the same time the avoidance of quite unwarranted attitudes of intolerance against other theorists' theories, would seem a code of behaviour much more appropriate to the state and nature of knowledge in economics.

We might well need some new rules of the theoretical game, precisely in order to enhance the development of economic analysis. Meanwhile, the

---

[9]It is important, of course, to investigate the aspects of similarity of the physical sciences and the social sciences, but it is even more important to investigate the aspects in which they are dissimilar. On this, see my own Comment on Edmond Malinvaud's paper (in Hägerstrand, 1985, pp. 183–6).

coexistence of competing paradigms, even for long periods of time, far from being regarded as a sign of anomaly, might well come to be recognized as the normal way of proceeding in the development of economic theory.

REFERENCES

Arrow, K. and Debreu, G. (1954) 'Existence of Equilibrium for a Competitive Economy', *Econometrica*, 22, pp. 265–90.

Baldwin, J.W. (1959) 'The Medieval Theories of the Just Price: Romanists, Canonists and Theologians in the Twelfth and Thirteenth Centuries', *Transactions of the American Philosophical Society*, 49, pt IV.

Debreu, G. (1959) *Theory of Value*, Cowles Commission Monograph no 17, John Wiley, New York.

de Roover, R. (1958) 'The Concept of the Just Price: Theory and Economic Policy', *Journal of Economic History*, XVIII, pp. 418–34.

Galiani, F. (1751) *Della Moneta, Libri Cinque*, Giuseppe Raimondi, Naples; reprinted in *Della Moneta e scritti inediti*, introduced by Alberto Caracciolo and edited by Alberto Merola, Feltrinelli, Milan, 1963.

Hagenauer, S. (1931) 'Das "justum pretium" bei Thomas von Aquino. Ein Beitrag zur Geschichte der objectiven Werttheorie', *Vierterljahrschrift für Sozial und Wirtschaftsgeschichte*, 24, von W. Kohlhammer, Stuttgart.

Hägerstrand, T. (1985) *The Identification of Progress in Learning, Proceedings of a Conference promoted by the European Science Foundation*, Cambridge University Press, Cambridge.

Hicks, Sir J. (1976) '"Revolutions" in Economics', in *Method and Appraisal in Economics*, ed. S.J. Latsis, Cambridge University Press, Cambridge, pp. 207–18.

Hollander, S. (1965) 'On the Interpretation of the Just Price', in *Kyklos*, XVIII, pp. 615–34

Jevons, W.S. (1871) *The Theory of Political Economy*, Macmillan, London.

Kuhn, T.S. (1962) *The Structure of Scientific Revolutions*, University of Chicago Press, Chicago.

Marx, K. (1894) *Das Kapital*, vol. 3 ed. F. Engels, Otto Meissner, Hamburg.

Mosak, J. (1944) *General Equilibrium Theory in International Trade*, Cowles Commission Monograph no. 7, Principia Press, Bloomington, Indiana.

Pasinetti, L.L. (1962) '*A Multi-Sector Model of Economic Growth*', unpublished PhD dissertation, University of Cambridge.

— (1977) *Lectures on the Theory of Production*, Macmillan, London.

— (1980/1) 'The Rate of Interest and the Distribution of Income in a Pure Labour Economy', *Journal of Post-Keynesian Economics*, III, pp. 170–82.

— (1981) *Structural Change and Economic Growth – A Theoretical Essay on the Dynamics of the Wealth of Nations*, Cambridge University Press, Cambridge.

Ricardo, D. (1821) *Principles of Political Economy and Taxation*, 3rd edn, John Murray, London.

Ross, W.D. (ed.) (1925) 'The Works of Aristotle', vol. IX (Nichomachean Ethics), Oxford University Press, Oxford.
Samuelson, P.A. (1947) *Foundations of Economic Analysis*, Harvard University Press, Cambridge, Mass.
Sapori, A. (1955) 'Il giusto prezzo nella dottrina di San Tommaso e nella pratica del suo tempo', *Studi di Storia economica*, I, pp. 265–303, Florence.
Schumpeter, J.A. (1951) *History of Economic Analysis*, Oxford University Press, New York.
Smith, A. (1904) *An Inquiry into the Nature and Causes of the Wealth of Nations* (1st edn 1776), ed. Edwin Cannan, vol. I, Methuen, London.
Spicciani, A. (1977) 'La mercatura e la formazione del prezzo nella riflessione teologica medievale', in *Atti della Accademia Nazionale dei Lincei, Classe Scienze morali storiche e filologiche*, serie VIII, vol. XX, pp. 127–293.
Sraffa, P. (1960) *Production of Commodities by Means of Commodities – Prelude to a Critique of Economic Theory*, Cambridge University Press, Cambridge.

Name Index

Subject Index